RESEARCH IN ORGANIZATIONAL BEHAVIOR

RESEARCH IN ORGANIZATIONAL BEHAVIOR

Series Editors: Barry Staw and L. L. Cummings

Volumes 1–20:   Research in Organizational Behavior – An
                Annual Series of Analytical Essays and Critical
                Reviews

Series Editors: Barry Staw and Robert I. Sutton

Volumes 21–22: Research in Organizational Behavior – An
                Annual Series of Analytical Essays and Critical
                Reviews

RESEARCH IN ORGANIZATIONAL BEHAVIOR
VOLUME 22

RESEARCH IN ORGANIZATIONAL BEHAVIOR

AN ANNUAL SERIES OF ANALYTICAL ESSAYS AND CRITICAL REVIEWS

EDITED BY

BARRY M. STAW

Haas School of Business, University of California, USA

ROBERT I. SUTTON

*Department of Management Science and Engineering,
Stanford University, USA*

2000

JAI
An Imprint of Elsevier Science

Amsterdam – London – New York – Oxford – Paris – Shannon – Tokyo

ELSEVIER SCIENCE Inc.
655 Avenue of the Americas
New York, NY 10010, USA

First edition 2000

Library of Congress Cataloging in Publication Data
A catalog record from the Library of Congress has been applied for.

ISBN: 0-7623-0641-6
ISSN: 0191-3085 (Series)

∞ The paper used in this publication meets the requirements of ANSI/NISO Z39.48-1992 (Permanence of Paper).
Printed in The Netherlands.

CONTENTS

LIST OF CONTRIBUTORS

Ronald S. Burt	Graduate School of Business, University of Chicago
Gerald Davis	Graduate School of Business, University of Michigan
Peter Degoey	Haas School of Business, University of California, Berkeley
Robin Ely	School of International and Public Affairs, Columbia University
Chip Heath	Fuqua School of Management, Duke University
Paul Ingram	Graduate School of Business, Columbia University
Dacher Keltner	Department of Psychology, University of California, Berkeley
Doug McAdam	Department of Sociology, Stanford University
Debra E. Meyerson	Department of Management Science and Engineering, Stanford University
Calvin Morrill	Department of Sociology, University of Arizona
Michael W. Morris	Graduate School of Business, Stanford University
Hayagreeva Rao	Goizueta Business School, Emory University

Tal Simons   Graduate School of Business, Columbia
                                University

Nancy Staudenmayer   Fuqua School of Management, Duke
                                University

Mayer N. Zald   University of Sociology, University of
                                Michigan

PREFACE

More than twenty years ago, one of our trusted friends and colleagues warned that a series like *Research in Organizational Behavior* was a good idea . . . but only for a limited period of time. He worried that the field of organizational behavior was incapable of generating enough quality material (especially papers of a theoretical nature) to sustain a series such as ROB. After more than two decades of publication we feel the series has safely put these fears to rest.

This volume provides several exciting theoretical developments as well as some important unification of prior research. To begin, Michael Morris and Dacher Keltner present an analysis of emotional expression in negotiations. Although the public has long been attracted to conflict and negotiation, at least in part because of the intense emotions aroused in these situations, most recent research has treated these contexts as simple arenas (or extensions) of cognitive decision making. Morris and Keltner bring emotions back into negotiations by presenting a social-functional analysis of emotions in organizational relationships. Their analysis goes well beyond the common treatment of emotion as a source of decision error; instead, providing a model for studying the role of discrete emotions in a range of interpersonal relationships.

In the second chapter, Peter Degoey pushes the justice literature forward by taking seriously the social construction of beliefs and emotions about fairness. Whereas most justice research considers the notion of 'fairness' either as a product of objective organizational conditions or impression management, seldom have scholars considered the contagion of beliefs and emotions about justice. Degoey shows that thoughts and feelings about justice are communicated among individuals and that they spread across networks or groups in organizations, ultimately working to institutionalize a dominant justice view.

The third chapter in this volume furthers our understanding of gender in organizations. Robin Ely and Debra Meyerson summarize the limitations of traditional treatments of gender, proposing a new approach which treats gender as a complex set of social relations enacted across a range of social practices in organizations. They argue that many prejudicial practices become so deeply embedded in organizations as to appear gender-neutral, or simply the norm. Ely and Meyerson then propose an emergent, localized approach to change whereby organization members continuously identify, disrupt, and revise these gendered practices.

In the fourth chapter, Chip Heath and Nancy Staudenmayer maintain that two principal and long-standing problems of organization theory are those of aligning goals (the agency problem) and aligning actions (the coordination problem). They argue that, due to systematic tendencies (or biases), most of the research and theory on organizations has been devoted to the problem of goals rather than coordination – that we tend to solve problems by partitioning and focusing on component parts. Heath and Staudenmayer then propose solutions to repair the damage caused by tendencies to over- differentiate, emphasizing ways to integrate individuals and work units within organizations.

The next two chapters in the volume advocate some radical changes in the way we currently theorize about organizations. Gerald Davis and Doug McAdam start by describing changes that have occurred in the industrial economy – changes that often provoke the label, 'New Economy'. They then argue that the way corporations organize production and how they are financed have undergone substantial transition toward decentralization, yet our conception of organizations has largely remained that of durable and coherent entities. Davis and McAdam describe how prevailing theories of organization (e.g. resource dependence and population ecology) have become less useful as these fundamental economic transformations have taken place, and they propose social movement theory as the model best able to inform contemporary forms of economic action.

In the following chapter, Hayagreeva Rao, Calvin Morrill and Mayer Zald take the social movement approach to organizations several steps forward. They conceptualize the construction of new organizational forms as a political process led by institutional entrepreneurs who identify political opportunities, frame issues, and mobilize constituencies. They outline four types of organizational and market failures from which social movements can arise and illustrate (through case examples) how new organizational forms are produced.

In the seventh chapter, Tal Simons and Paul Ingram provide a descriptive analysis of one of the products of an important social movement, that of the Israeli kibbutz. This rather unique organizational form has received much popular and research attention, but has not been systematically examined for its lessons on organizational behavior. This chapter shows how ideology shaped specific practices of kibbutzim (such as job rotation and equal pay) and provided a source of both influence and conflict within its larger social environment. From the experience of kibbutzim we learn a great deal about social equality, participation, and commitment in organizations, as well as the interaction of a utopian organization within its broader political context.

For the final chapter of this volume, Ronald Burt reviews the evidence on the connection between social networks and social capital. He argues that certain people and groups do better because they are better connected. Their exchange relationships, sources of trust and obligations bring them social capital which can be utilized in economic and social organizations. He also argues that location in a social network, especially the ability to span structural holes, provide some people with special capabilities to broker the flow of information between people. Using the metaphor of social capital, new ideas are suggested for the understanding of careers, innovation, and the success of corporate ventures.

From this brief overview, one can see that the essays in this volume of *Research in Organizational Behavior* represent a diverse set of issues, ranging from individual emotion and cognition to social movements and networks. Yet, cutting across this diversity is a rather consistent quality of argumentation. Being both thorough and thoughtful, many of the papers in this volume provide substantial contributions to research on organizations. In fact, we have little doubt that present and future scholars of organizational behavior will find a host of new ideas in the pages that follow.

Barry M. Staw
Berkeley, California

Robert I. Sutton
Stanford, California

HOW EMOTIONS WORK: THE SOCIAL FUNCTIONS OF EMOTIONAL EXPRESSION IN NEGOTIATIONS

Michael W. Morris and Dacher Keltner

ABSTRACT

Behavioral research on negotiation in recent years has been dominated by the decision-making research paradigm, which accords a relatively narrow role to emotions. Decision-making researchers have considered emotions primarily in terms of how an individual's positive or negative affect impacts, and usually impedes, his or her information processing. Drawing on recent advances in psychology and other fields, we propose an alternative perspective that highlights more social and more functional aspects of emotion in negotiation. We conceptualize emotions as interpersonal communication systems that help individuals navigate the basic problems that arise in dyad and group relations. Emotions are evoked by these specific relational problems and one person's emotional expression impacts other persons, often with the consequence of resolving the relational problem. From this social functional perspective, we draw insights concerning: (a) the influence of specific emotions upon negotiation-related cognition and behavior; (b) the transitions between qualitatively different phases within negotiations; and (c) the ways in which negotiations are shaped by contextual variables such as culture and communication media.

Research in Organizational Behaviour, Volume 22, pages 1–50.
2000 by Elsevier Science Inc.
ISBN: 0–7623–0641–6

1

INTRODUCTION

Mid 20th century scholarship on conflict and negotiation described contentious labor conflicts, fierce legal battles, and tense international disputes (e.g. Douglas, 1962; Schelling, 1960). These portrayals of negotiation were much like those in Hollywood films of the era such as *Casablanca* or *Twelve Angry Men* – as interactions propelled by powerful and shifting emotions. Social science and cinema converged on the subject of conflict because negotiation reveals the range of human emotion. That is, negotiatiors use emotions in order to initiate relationships, make demands, seek cooperation, and seal commitments. Also, the dramatic emotional displays in high-stakes negotiations are but more extreme versions of the expressive performances required by the more mundane conflicts that people face in everyday interactions. A focus on emotions remains in contemporary cinematic portrayals of negotiations, yet emotions have nearly disappeared in recent scholarship on negotiation. The dominant picture of negotiations has been of a cognitive puzzle, a sequence of informationally complex decisions.

An initial goal of this chapter is to trace the ascent of the decision-making approach to research on negotiations and then delineate how this approach shaped subsequent approaches to emotion and negotiation. At the heart of this approach is an emphasis on the cognitive heuristics used to make decisions about what to give and take in negotiation. Tendencies in negotiation that had been traditionally ascribed to emotional dynamics have been reinterpreted in as emanating from the limitations of cognitive heuristics. When emotions have been incorporated into the decision-making approach to negotiation, researchers have focused on how individual's general affective state impacts that individual's information processing tendencies. We argue that this affect-and-cognition approach misses the central way that emotions function in negotiation – that is, one's emotional expression affects others who observe it. Consider the ability of some individuals (e.g. Bill Clinton) to use emotions to negotiate their way out of seemingly any predicament. The key is not how Clinton's emotions impact Clinton's cognition; it is how Clinton's emotional expressions impact his audience's cognitions and emotions.

In this chapter, we advocate a different approach to incorporating emotions into negotiation research. Drawing on recent advances in psychology and other fields, we suggest that many insights can be gleaned by attending to the *social functions* of emotion. By *social*, we emphasize the consequences of emotion that occur between people who are observing and responding to each other's emotions, rather than consequences within one individual. By *functions*, we emphasize that emotions occur in response to particular problems in social relations, and often help resolve or change the relational problem. The point is not that the consequences of emotional expression are always adaptive but merely that emotions do 'work' in negotiations. As we shall see in many specific examples, the expression of emotion provides information to a negotiation counterpart, evokes complementary emotions in that person, and can create incentives or deterrents affecting that person's future behavior. Our approach therefore differs from the affect-and-cognition approach by shifting the focus from the intrapersonal dynamics of how private feelings bias decisions to the interpersonal dynamics of how overt expressions of emotion guide interactions between individuals.

Before detailing our approach, we first review the paradigm shifts in negotiation research in recent decades, associated with the decline in emphasis on emotions. We then turn to the field of emotion, laying out some conceptual distinctions between the affect-and-cognition approach and our social functional approach. We next develop a framework, drawing on findings from social psychology, organizational studies, anthropology, and ethology, that specifies how emotions are triggered by relational problems in negotiations and often work to resolve these problems. As we shall see, the social functional perspective has the advantage of elucidating several problems that negotiation researchers have struggled over, such as why negotiators transition between qualitatively different phases in bargaining, why some aspects of emotion in conflict differ across cultures whereas some do not, and, finally, why communication media impact negotiations.

PARADIGMS IN NEGOTIATION RESEARCH

A brief review of the paradigms that have structured negotiation research sets the stage for understanding the vicissitudes in research on emotion. Guided by principles of the sociological field study, early descriptions of negotiations in collective bargaining contexts and other settings devoted considerable attention to emotionally expressive behavior. Such studies on the emotional fireworks between opposing negotiators (Douglas, 1962). For many scholars, emotional displays were best understood in terms of the dramaturgical metaphor of role theory, which highlighted the performative, script-based nature of emotional expression (Goffman, 1959). Emotional expressions, from this perspective, are strategic, informative, and essential for the joint navigation of an interaction – themes we will return to in this chapter.

Early social psychological theorists likewise viewed emotions and conflict resolution as inextricably linked. Lewin (1951) suggested that resolving conflicts depends greatly on opposing partisans' specific emotions. Deutsch and colleagues followed these theoretical insights by identifying the role of emotions in crucial moments of negotiation, such as the formation of trust (Deutsch, 1960) and responses to threat (Deutsch & Krauss, 1962). For example, research suggested that threats succeed when they induce fear yet backfire when they induce anger (for a review, see Rubin & Brown, 1975). These scattered observations, however, never amounted to a systematic study of the roles of different emotions in negotiations. Researchers were constrained by the lack of tools for reliably measuring distinct emotions, particularly for measuring emotions in the stream of ongoing social interaction. Also, such research existed under the shadow of proclamations by behaviorists that emotions were not amenable to scientific investigation.

Another longstanding paradigm in the study of negotiation is the game-theoretic analysis of rational strategy in interdependent relationships. This tradition of formal economic analysis describes what perfectly rational agents do in abstract conflict situations. A key idea is that one's best move depends on the other person's best move. In a labor negotiation, for example, if management can see that a union has no better decision alternative than to concede and accept the current offer level, then management will simply wait for this level of concession rather than making a better offer. Several ideas from game-theoretic analysis have been successfully adapted into theories of actual behavior in negotiations (Walton & McKersie, 1965). Although game theory itself offers little analysis of emotion in negotiations, conflict theorists drew on game-theoretic ideas when speculating about roles that emotions might play in negotiation. Schelling (1960), for example, argued that bargaining behaviors send signals to the counterpart. He described emotional outbursts as signals of one's willingness to act in an irrational manner – signals that would reduce one's predictability to the opponent. In this way, a negotiator in a weak bargaining position, such as a union leader facing a strong management, might use emotional displays to break down management's confidence in their ability to leverage their bargaining position through intransigence. We will return to this idea that emotions convey negotiation-relevant information later.

In sum, several early theorists of conflict and negotiation recognized social consequences of emotion. Relying upon field study methods, social psychology experiments, and game theoretic analysis, early theorists recognized that emotions – whether genuine expressions or strategic displays – move negotiations forward. And, importantly, in all these traditions, researchers drew attention to emotions that arise in response to one's counterpart, emotions that are part of the interpersonal communication between the two negotiators. These early research programs on negotiation, however, would eventually give way to the emergence of a new and influential perspective in the social sciences, one that shifted the focus away from emotions and the interpersonal level of analysis.

With the spread of the 'cognitive revolution' through psychology and related disciplines in the 1960s, interest in emotions and social communication waned. Researchers acquired more precise tools for modeling thought processes, and consequently attention shifted to the individual level of analysis and, more specifically, to what happens inside the individual's head. Whereas previous models of organizational decision making described limitations in rationality as arising from limited consideration of decision options (March & Simon, 1958), cognitive psychologists identified deeper departures from rationality. Research suggests that individuals do not make decisions through computations of expected outcomes but rather through simple heuristics that produce systematic errors (Tversky & Kahneman, 1974). These information-processing errors were advanced as mechanisms to explain phenomena traditionally seen as emotion-driven (Kahneman, Slovic & Tversky, 1982; Nisbett & Ross, 1980).

Ultimately the cognitive analysis of decision making tradition spread to negotiation theory. A catalyst was Raiffa's (1982) theoretical synthesis of descriptive findings about fallibilities of cognition within the pre-existing tradition of prescriptive, game-theoretic decision analysis. Raiffa's (1982) 'asymmetrically prescriptive' analysis demonstrated that prescriptions for rational negotiation decisions could be conditioned on an accurate description of a counterpart's (often irrational) tendencies. Bazerman, Neale, Thompson and others drew upon behavioral decision research to identify systematic departures from rationality in negotiators' decision making (for reviews, see Bazerman & Carroll, 1987; Neale & Bazerman, 1991; Thompson, 1990). For example, the anchoring heuristic leads negotiators to be irrationally influenced by an opponent's extreme opening offer (Northcraft & Neale, 1987). The availability heuristic leads negotiators to overestimate the extent to which the arguments favor their side (Bazerman & Neale, 1982). Modeling negotiator behavior in terms of heuristics and biases, researchers reinterpreted tendencies in negotiation that had been formerly interpreted in terms of emotional dynamics. The tendency of parties to enter costly strikes and lawsuits that they have no chance of winning, for example, had been tied to pride and face-saving motives. The decision-making paradigm suggested an alternative interpretation in terms of the availability heuristic and its tendency to make negotiators overconfident in their chances of prevailing (Bazerman & Neale 1982).

The cognitive approach to negotiation quickly dominated earlier, more-emotion-centered paradigms for several reasons: (a) specific cognitive processes were easier to measure and manipulate than specific emotions; and (b) cognitive explanations dovetailed with decision-analytic approaches to generate prescriptions about how to capitalize on an opponent's biases. Soon the decision-making perspective on negotiation had become so influential that the study of negotiation had come to resemble a branch of behavioral decision research. Critiques of this state of affairs began to mount. In reviewing negotiation research, Neale & Northcraft (1991) concluded that emotion was one of the least studied areas. Sociologically oriented critics raised the general issue of whether negotiation behavior can be modeled as decision tendencies abstracted from the contexts in which negotiators meet (Barley, 1991). That is, evidence that cognitive heuristics are important determinants of outcome variance in hypothetical role-play negotiations does not entail that heuristics are crucial determinants in real negotiations embedded within real relationships. From the perspective of role theory, scholars argued that negotiation tactics and outcomes are highly shaped by institutionalized norms (Friedman, 1994) as well as social roles, such as gender (Kolb, 1993). Taken together, these critiques challenged the external validity of purely cognitive analyses of negotiation dynamics.

With mounting critiques of the cognitive approach to negotiation, researchers in some subfields of organizational behavior have turned their attention to emotional expression and its consequences. Whereas many organizational researchers had long emphasized internal emotional experience such as stress and job satisfaction, a new wave of researchers examined expressed emotion (Rafaeli & Sutton, 1989). Field studies of service and sales occupations noted the use of expressed emotions to influence other persons in an interaction. Salespersons, store clerks, and bill collectors (Cialdini, 1984; Rafaeli & Sutton, 1989; 1991) learn patterns of emotional display that help them structure and control transactions. These transactions are not always negotiations of a formal contract, but nevertheless they are negotiations over the give and take of resources. Other studies focused on the consequences of expressed emotion in the workplace for the person who expresses the emotion. The potential strain of role-appropriate emotional displays or 'emotional labor' has become a topic of its own (Hochschild, 1983; Rafaeli & Sutton, 1989). Studies of how individuals respond to managerial efforts to control organizational culture have similarly focused on emotional expression and its consequences for self and others (Van Maanen & Kunda, 1989).

In sum, at the same time negotiation research moved away from emotions, other organizational researchers were identifying important roles of emotions in workplace interactions. The combination of theory-based demands for attention to emotions and empirical evidence about the work done by emotions in many interactions has spurred a recent renaissance in research on emotions in negotiation, to which we now turn.

PERSPECTIVES ON THE CONSEQUENCES OF EMOTIONS

In the last decade a number of theorists have attempted to incorporate (or re-incorporate) emotions into models of negotiator behavior. We will analyze the dominant conception of emotions underlying these arguments and then suggest reasons why it fails to capture the full role played by emotions in negotiations, and social life more generally. We then propose a different, and potentially complementary, conceptualization of emotion. The contrast between these approaches is best appreciated in light of a few basic distinctions between ways that researchers conceptualize emotion.

Background: Some Key Conceptual Distinctions
Emotions are evanescent and multifaceted phenomena. To capture them in scientific models, researchers make simplifying assumptions. Several such assumptions differentiate models of emotion. A first distinction is between focus on *general* affective states, such as positive or negative moods, and focus on *specific* emotions, such as anger or embarrassment. On the one hand, models of affect give explanatory emphasis to general variables such as the valence (i.e. positive or negative) or intensity of the feeling state. Affective valence is a variable that can describe stable temperamental dispositions (Watson, Clark & Tellegen, 1988) as well as moods and acute emotions. (Moods differ from acute emotions in being less intense and less centered around a specific object). On the other hand, models of specific, discrete emotions, such as anger, embarrassment, or love, emphasize short-term reactions to particular stimuli in the environment and within the individual (Ekman, 1992; Plutchik, 1980).

A second distinction is between *intrapersonal* vs. *interpersonal* character-istics and consequences of emotions. Most emotion researchers have been interested in the intrapersonal characteristics of emotion, examining the physiology of emotion, internal emotional experience, and the consequences of moods and emotions that play out within the mind of the person feeling the emotion (Isen, 1991). In contrast, another strand of emotion theory has seen emotions as interpersonal interactions. This perspective directs attention to shared emotion (McDougal, 1920) and to the role of external, observable expressions of emotion in communication (Ekman, 1993; Rafaeli & Sutton, 1987, 1989).

Finally, theorists diverge in their assumptions about whether emotions serve *functions* in guiding behavior. In psychology and other disciplines, emotion theory has alternated between two contrasting positions. At one pole, theorists assume (often implicitly) that emotions are primarily impediments to adaptive action. According to this view, emotions disorganize or interrupt current thought and disrupt ongoing social interactions. Emotion-related thought processes are seen as lacking the direction and principled orderliness of reason (e.g. Dewey, 1895; Hebb, 1946; Mandler, 1984). Emotional expressions, from eruptions of anger to proclamations of love, are seen as reflecting the more primitive, uncontrollable side of human nature that threatens the social order.

At the other pole, theorists assume that emotions function in organized, useful ways. Emotions are reliable guides to action and help sustain the harmony and continuity of social interactions. Emotions prioritize and organize ongoing behaviors in ways that optimize the individual's adjustment to the demands of the physical and social environment (Darwin, 1872; Ekman, 1992; Keltner & Haidt, 1999; Lazarus, 1991; Plutchik, 1980; Rosaldo, 1984; Trivers, 1971). According to this view, emotions help people respond to the basic problems presented by social living and thus help sustain the social order.

We have drawn three distinctions about emotion. The varying positions vis-à-vis these distinctions allow for many possible theoretical stances, yet the common approaches to emotions relevant to negotiation fall more-or-less into two clusters. The approach that has emerged within the cognitive paradigm takes the first position on all three issues. This approach, which we will refer to as the affect and cognition (AC) perspective, has focused on general affect and on the intrapersonal level of analysis. It has discovered for the most part dysfunctional consequences of emotions. By contrast, the social functional (SF) perspective on emotions that we advocate in this essay involves the opposite position on each dimension; that is, we focus on specific, acute emotions, an interpersonal level of analysis, and functional consequences.

These two approaches to the role of emotions in negotiation involve asking very different questions. It is quite possible, of course, that emotions are involved in different dynamics at different levels of analysis. Hence, the two appraoches are potentially complementary rather than mutually exclusive. It is worth reviewing the accomplishments and limitations of the established AC approach before developing insights from the more novel SF approach.

The AC Perspective – Affect as a Determinant of Negotiator Cognition

The prevailing approach to emotion in negotiation research has been to study how a negotiators' affect impacts his or her cognitive tendencies (e.g. Isen, 1991). Working within this tradition, researchers examine the intrapersonal consequences of emotion, attempting to model how emotions shape, direct, or guide internal thought processes. Some even view emotions as a special class of cognitive processes (e.g. 'hot cognitions') that shape attention, thought, memory, and judgment in systematic ways. To understand this research program, let us review its theoretical and empirical contributions.

Hypothesized Mechanisms

Researchers working within the AC tradition have identified at least three mechanisms through which an individual's affect impacts his or her subsequent cognition. According to some, emotions are 'nodes' in semantic networks that spread activation to nodes involved in memory and judgments (Bower, 1991). Thus, when a negotiator is in a negative mood in the context of a negotiation, he or she will be disposed to recall issues associated with negative moods. Another view is that emotions are units of information that contribute directly to judgment (Schwarz, 1990). A negotiator might rely on his or her momentary surges of negative feeling, both relevant and irrelevant to the negotiation, to evaluate the fairness of the counterpart's actions and plan responses.

A more recently explored view moves away from a general conception of affect to argue that different negative emotions involve different levels of arousal and therefore different information processing modes. For instance, relative to sadness, anger prompts less controlled, more automatic social judgment (e.g. Bodenhausen, Sheppard & Kramer, 1994). Hence, an angry negotiator might be more likely to process negotiation-relevant information (e.g. proposals, concessions, promises) in relatively unsystematic, superficial ways and, for this reason, might be prone to certain kinds of cognitive biases resulting from heuristic processing.

Empirical Record

Research in the affect and cognition (AC) tradition has succeeded in identifying striking consequences of affective states upon cognitive processes. The primary research method involves manipulating affect in experiments. Sometimes researchers manipulate mood prior to the negotiation with such techniques as gifts (Isen & Levin, 1972; Carnevale & Isen, 1986), exposure to emotionally evocative films (e.g. Kramer et al., 1991), or exposure to pleasant scents (Baron, 1990). Even such subtle levels of affect have been observed to influence diverse cognitive processes (for review, see Forgas, 1995). Studies of autobiographical recall indicate that the positive or negative content of memory is shaped by current mood (Bower, 1991). Studies of satisfaction with work, personal life, marriage, political leaders, and consumer goods find these evaluations are influenced by current mood (Baron, 1990; Brief, Butcher & Roberson, 1995; Keltner, Locke & Audrain, 1993; Oliver, 1993; Schwarz & Clore, 1993; Schwarz, 1990). Studies of social judgment have found that the tendency to stereotype rather than individuate others is determined in part by the social perceiver's current mood (Bodenhausen et al., 1994; Forgas, 1995). Moreover, AC research with decision making tasks has found that the willingness to take risks or avoid them is influenced by whether one is feeling happy or not (Isen, 1991; Johnson & Tversky, 1983). Many such findings from experiments have been corroborated in research with individual difference methods, in which cognitive tendencies are correlated with dispositional measures of affect (Watson, Clark & Tellegen, 1988). In findings that parallel those with manipulations of affect, organizational researchers have linked dispositional affectivity to job satisfaction (Brief et al., 1995; Staw, Bell & Clausen, 1986) and to certain job skills (Staw, Sutton & Pelled, 1994).

Negotiation researchers have extended AC research in a number of ways to document how affective influences on cognitive tendencies matter in negotiation (Barry & Oliver, 1996). For example, given the effects of mood upon memory, one can easily imagine that a negotiator's state of negative affect would color the way he or she recalled the history of interactions with the counterpart, thus justifying an enduring sense of pessimism and a defensive strategy. This would reduce the likelihood of building trust, learning about the counterpart's interests, and ultimately generating an integrative agreement. Indeed, research has found that negotiators put in a negative mood attained less accurate impressions of their counterparts' interests (Allred, Mallozzi, Matsui & Raia, 1996). Consistent with findings that negative affect leads to "seeing the glass as half empty," one can imagine how negative affect would make negotiators more likely to reject offers. Indeed, participants were more likely to reject ultimatum offers (that economically dominated their alternative option) when they were in a negative mood (Pillutla & Murnighan, 1996). These sorts of findings are consistent with prior conclusions from basic psychological research that states of negative or positive affect distort good judgment and impede adaptive action.

The pattern of findings from inductions of positive affect in negotiation experiments is a bit more complex. Positive affect should lead to "seeing the glass as half full" or, in the context of negotiations, seeing the counterpart as trustworthy and his or her offers as acceptable, if not desirable. Consistent with these assertions, negotiators in positive moods engage in fewer competitive behaviors and are more willing to make concessions (Baron, 1990). Although in some issue structures this would lead to lower individual outcomes, in other issue structures it leads to value creation and the attainment of high outcomes for both counterparts (e.g. Carnevale & Isen, 1986). Other researchers have reached conclusions that are less ambiguous with regard to the negative consequences of positive mood in negotiation. For example, negotiators in positive moods have an illusory sense of having performed very well in the negotiation (Kramer, Newton & Pommerenke, 1993), which suggests that they will not learn from their mistakes. Overall, some studies have linked positive mood with cooperation and high joint outcomes, yet most empirical studies have focused on how positive moods distort negotiators' perceptions in ways that make them vulnerable to several negotiation-related problems.

In summary, the extension of AC research to the context of negotiation has been successful and influential. These studies have illuminated how, even those exogenously produced and unrelated to the affective states content of the negotiation at hand, shape negotiators' thoughts and actions. Notwithstanding these important advances, there are several limitations to this work, which highlight the need for alternative conceptions of emotion.

A first limitation of the AC approach stems from the reduction of emotions to positive vs. negative affective valence. Valence-based analyses fail to specify whether different emotions of the same valence, such as anger and fear, differentially influence cognition and behavior. In fact, given the centrality of valence to affect, the AC approach strongly suggests the generalization that emotions of similar valence, such as anger, fear, sadness, and guilt, would influence negotiator cognition in the same ways. Yet this generalization can be challenged by counterexamples. For example, one would certainly expect to negotiate differently if one were angry as opposed to afraid, or if one were facing an angry counterpart as opposed to a guilty counterpart. Furthermore this limitation of the AC approach has been exposed by research on the consequences of specific emotions. Recent research has highlighted how emotions of the same valence, such as fear and anger, have opposite effects upon cognitive processes, such as risk perception and preference (Lerner & Keltner, 2000) and attributions of causality (Keltner, Ellsworth & Edwards, 1993). Approaches that solely focus upon general positive or negative valence thus sacrifice precision in the name of parsimony.

A second limitation stems from the lack of attention to how emotions operate in real social interactions, and in terms of our present interests, the process of negotiating. With few exceptions, AC researchers have focused on the effects of incidental moods, that is, they measure the effects of moods that are elicited by events unrelated to the negotiation (e.g. by watching a film clip or receiving a gift prior to the negotiation). In many studies, the negotiators may not have even been aware of the actual cause of their moods. To a large extent, this focus on incidental rather than integral affect was required by methodological and conceptual considerations. Indeed, some AC theorists hold that affect is most likely to influence judgments when the cause of the affect is distinct from the object of judgment (e.g. Schwarz, 1990). On this view, it is important that the source of affect not be semantically related to the negotiation. Yet these studies do not speak to the question of how emotions originating within negotiations influence negotiators' cognition, behavior, and outcomes, a key question given that so many emotions do arise within negotiations. Nor do AC studies illuminate how moods and emotions exert different effects upon negotiations at different stages of the bargaining process, a limitation which spurred a recent call for reformulation of affect and negotiation research (Barry & Oliver, 1996).

A third limitation of the AC approach is the methodological individualism it inherits from the cognitivist tradition (see Sampson, 1977). The search for the consequences of affect has focused on what happens within one individual's mind, because the individual mind is the unit at which systems are conceptualized. To the extent that the functions served by emotions extend beyond the individual mind, they will not be discovered by studying one individual at a time but only by studying interpersonal interactions. The choice to conceptualize at the level of the individual affects not only descriptive research but also prescriptive and normative evaluations, as well. When cast in terms of individual interests, expected return is maximized in games such as the Prisoner's Dilemma by a strategy of not cooperating. Yet when cast in terms of the collective interests (i.e. interest of the pair of prisoners), the expected return is maximized through the cooperative strategy. Considerations such as these have led to the suggestion that tendencies that appear irrational from the individual perspective may be rational from the perspective of the dyad or group (Bazerman, Gibbons, Thompson & Valley, 1998). In this light, the consequences of some emotions may be adaptive in ways that past research has not elucidated.

In sum, the prevailing AC approach to emotion in negotiation has looked at the effects of exogenously produced positive or negative mood states upon the individual negotiator's cognition, behavior, and outcomes. In the section that follows we present a different approach to emotion in negotiation that complements the AC tradition. This approach highlights how specific expressions of emotions that are endogenous to the course of negotiation directly guide the dyadic interactions of negotiators.

Social Functions of Emotion in Negotiation

Our proposal is that emotions can be fruitfully seen as serving functions (as 'doing work') to enable coordinated interactions. This perspective has roots in early studies of the instrumental uses of specific emotional displays, such as ingratiation (Jones & Pittman, 1982), as well as in recent studies of the social consequences of spontaneous displays of emotion (Clark, Pataki & Carver, 1996; Keltner & Kring, 1998). Several developments suggest the promise of a functional perspective that emotions are means of solving relational problems in negotiations. Emotion researchers have begun to document how interpersonal problems provoke specific emotions (e.g. Averill, 1980; Keltner & Buswell, 1997; Miller & Leary, 1992) and how the behavioral manifestations of these emotions trigger interpersonal interactions that can resolve the originating problem (Hazan & Shaver, 1987; Lutz & White, 1986; Nesse, 1990; Johnson-Laird & Oatley, 1992). Emotional expression, for example, plays an important role in the resolution of problems in relationships between parents and children (e.g. Bowlby, 1969), siblings (Dunn & Munn, 1985), and romantic partners (Levenson & Gottman, 1983). Naturalistic observations of people around the world have further illuminated how emotional expressions guide social interactions such as courtship and appeasement rituals (Eibl-Eibesfeldt, 1989).

Interestingly, other scholars investigating the socio-cultural construction of emotions have hit upon a similar level of analysis, being interested in how different relational problems yield different emotional patterns (e.g. Frijda & Mesquita, 1994; Keltner & Haidt, 1999). Research in this vein indicates that emotional expressions are more than simple readouts of internal experience; rather, expressions are other-directed, intentional (although not always consciously controlled) communicative acts that organize social interactions (Bavelas et al., 1986; Fernandez-Dols & Ruiz-Belda, 1995; Kraut & Johnston, 1979). Within these interactions, emotional expression communicates social intentions, desired courses of actions, and role-related expectations and behaviors. Theorists have captured the simultaneously visceral and social nature of emotions by describing them as embodied relationships (de Rivera, 1984; Lutz & White, 1986).

We have seen that research traditions have converged on the view that emotions serve social functions. That is, the consequences of emotions are best examined in light of the recurrent problems in interpersonal and group relations, such as allocating resources fairly, honoring personal contracts, or maintaining friendships (e.g. Averill, 1980; Eibl-Eibesfeldt, 1989; Ekman, 1992; Lutz & White, 1986). This involves a teleological stance that assumes that emotions can be seen as serving specific functions – not because they were designed but because they have been selected for on the basis of their adaptiveness, both at the biological level for their contribution to individual fitness, and at the cultural level for their contribution to individual and group functioning (see Keltner & Haidt, in press). This does not mean that emotions serve an actor well all or most of the time that they occur. Nor does it entail a prescriptive or normative argument in favor of emotional negotiating. Rather, this social functional approach is a theoretical stance that directs one's attention to exploring particular kinds of consequences when making observations for a descriptive model of emotion in negotiation.

Another way of introducing the social functional (SF) approach is to describe the steps researchers take in analyzing the social functions of emotions. First, researchers identify the diverse contexts that elicit a particular emotion and look for a problem common to these diverse contexts. Motivated by this aim, researchers have found that emotions are elicited by identifiable problems in relationships (e.g. Lazarus, 1991; Shaver, Schwartz, Kirson & O'Connor, 1987). That is, the contexts triggering a particular emotion tend to involve a common relational problem, to which the emotion may provide a solution. For example, anger can be produced by myriad events, including: a biased performance appraisal, inconsiderate interruptions in a meeting, a counterpart's extremely ambitious opening offer in negotiation, to name just a few. Uniting these diverse contexts is perceived injustice, a problem when scarce resources are allocated in a relationship (e.g. Smith & Ellsworth, 1985).

Researchers interested in providing evidence for the functions of an emotion then consider how emotion-related behavior helps the individual or the dyad respond to the problem in the interaction. Research has documented that emotions involve several kinds of behavior, including action tendencies (Frijda, 1986), communicative behavior (Keltner & Ekman, 2000), and physiological responses (Levenson, Ekman & Friesen, 1990). Thus, anger involves: facial cues (furrowed brow, narrowed eyes, tightened and pressed lips); postural cues changes (e.g. head shaking sideways, expansive chest); gestural cues (e.g. clenched fists, finger pointing); and speech cues (a deep, forceful tone of voice; hostile comments). In addition to these cues, there are expressive courses of action, such as storming out of the room. Importantly, an SF approach to emotion looks to how these expressive behaviors influence the other person, the receiver of cues. In the case of anger, SF research would explore whether it works to reduce injustice by spurring redistribution of resources.

Obviously, not all behaviors expressing anger have the impact of reducing injustice (e.g., anger might prompt a bout of house cleaning or drinking binge). As Fig. 1 illustrates, an SF analysis does not assume a tight chain of necessity or sufficiency linking triggering contexts, relational problems, emotional expressions, and their functional consequences. Many contexts share the same relational problems; this problem may trigger one of several emotions; each emotion involves several expressive behaviors or cues; these behaviors have a variety of social consequences; some of these consequences ameliorate the triggering problem, but others do not. As this diagram makes explicit, there is no claim that emotional expressions solve problems always or even most of the time. A functionalist view of social emotions is a just a general heuristic guiding our hypothesis generation and post-hoc interpretation of past findings.

A task for future research is to test more specific, descriptive models concerning the benefits of particular forms of emotional expression. Such models will have to take into account that potentially functional expressive acts may be dysfunctional in practice, depending on whether they are performed in ways that are appropriate to the current context. To illustrate, expressions of anger by an authority figure after a subordinate's mistake may potentially spur motivation to perform better in the future. Yet this may go awry in practice for various reasons. Somewhat obviously, a manager who angrily charges the wrong subordinate with a mistake will inspire feelings of injustice and outrage. Or, even if the manager directs anger at the right target, an emotional signal

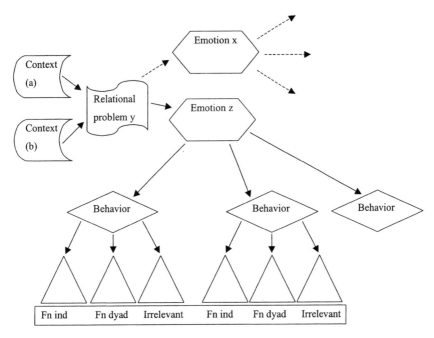

Fig. 1. Diagram illustrating the SF assumption that emotions are triggered by relational problems common to many specific contexts. These emotions involve many expressive behaviors, each of which has a variety of consequences. Some of these may solve the problem from the standpoint of the individual's interest (Fn ind), some may solve the problem from the standpoint of the dyad's interest (Fn dyad), and some may have effects irrelevant to the relational problem.

more extreme than that condoned by local norms may evoke reactance against rather than compliance with the manager's authority.

Another important concern in making functionalist arguments is the difference between past adaptiveness and current adaptiveness. Some displays, for example anger-related threats of aggression directed at subordinates, that may have been generally adaptive for humans in hunter-gatherer hands during the Pleistocene-era conditions that shaped human evolution would not be adaptive in many settings today (Symons, 1990). More generally, the behavioral consequences of emotions that have been shaped by biological evolution were adaptive once in a different ecology but they are not necessarily adaptive today (Buss, 2000). In sum, 'evolved' does not entail 'functional' and 'functional' does not entail 'evolved'.

Hypothesized Mechanisms

We have asserted that emotional expressions can function or 'do work' to guide an interaction, yet we have not yet delineated the mechanisms underlying this process. Several distinct mechanisms have been identified in research on personal interactions, where the SF approach has been pursued more than in research in workplace interactions. SF accounts involve interpersonal mechanisms through which one person's emotional expression impacts other persons. Several interpersonal processes have been identified as mechanisms (see Keltner & Kring, 1998).

First, emotional expressions *provide information* to help individuals know others' emotions, beliefs, and intentions. Emotional expressions convey information to receivers about senders' current emotions (Ekman, 1993; Haidt & Keltner, 1999; Scherer, 1986), their social intentions (Fridlund, 1992), and their orientations towards the relationship, for example as trustworthy or antagonistic (Knutson, 1996). Emotional expressions also convey information about objects in the environment, for example whether an object is dangerous and to be avoided or safe and to be trusted (Klinnert et al., 1983; Mineka & Cook, 1993). Even though emotionally expressive behavior only briefly appears in the stream of interaction, recent studies indicate that people are quite able to detect the meaning of emotional expressions (e.g. Keltner & Ekman, 2000). Thus, emotional expression helps individuals solve one of the basic problems of social interaction: reliably knowing the thoughts and feelings of others. A negotiator's brief expression of anger signals the individual's feelings about the issue at hand, whether it be a proposal or counterproposal, it conveys likely courses of action, and it conveys a sense of dominance and power vis-à-vis the other negotiator or negotiators.

Second, emotional expressions *evoke complementary emotions* in others. People respond emotionally to others' emotional expressions, even when those displays are presented subliminally and the perceiver cannot describe what he or she has seen (Dimberg & Ohman, 1996). For example, if someone flashes a brief expression of anger to another who fails to consciously recognize the anger, he or she will still respond with elevated arousal. In turn, emotions evoked in others are associated with behaviors such as avoidance, helping, affiliation, and soothing, which help individuals respond together to significant social events. To cite two examples, displays of embarrassment evoke forgiveness in others, which helps individuals restore social relations following norm violations (Keltner, Young & Buswell, 1997). Anger displays elicit fear-related responses in observers (Dimberg & Ohman, 1996), which may deter one's audience from a course of action that would damage the relationship, as when parents flash anger to their children to dissuade the child from undesirable behavior. By evoking emotional responses and the concomitant behavior in others, emotional expression is often the starting point for complex interactions. When a high-status negotiator expresses anger towards a lower-status counterpart, this is likely to lead the counterpart to respond with certain emotions, such as fear, and to pursue actions based on those emotions. The counterpart's deferential behaviors, in turn, have the effect of tempering the anger, and the crisis is more likely to be resolved.

Third, emotional expressions *operate as incentives*, reinforcing other individuals' behavior (Klinnert et al., 1983). Expressions of gratitude and positivity serve to reward certain courses of action or states of affairs; expressions of negativity serve to punish undesired behavior. Laughter and smiling, for example, encourage a wide variety of behaviors in others, including shifts in attention and conversation and more specific goal-directed behaviors that are specific to the interaction at hand (Provine, 1993; Tronick, 1989). Parents smile to keep their children on the right course. A flirtatious smile encourages the efforts of a potential suitor.

Empirical Record
In making our case that the SF approach is a useful research strategy for the study of negotiation, we note that, in addition to plausible hypotheses about mechanisms, the SF approach has a track record of identifying consequences of emotions in the domain of family relationships. In the case of some emotions, a SF analysis has been applied successfully to document relatively intuitive outcomes of emotional expression. For example, research has found that romantic love is associated with a variety of behaviors, from gift giving to intimate prose, that promote closeness and long term interactions with a

potential mate. And in general, these behaviors will help romantic partners form and maintain romantic relationships (e.g. Frank, 1988).

In other instances, a SF analysis has led researchers to document regularities and benefits associated with emotions that were previously believed to be disruptive or even destructive. For example, embarrassment was long viewed as a chaotic, disorganized state of little benefit to the individual, and often disruptive to the dyad. A SF take on embarrassment documented, instead, that the display of embarrassment serves as an apology for preceding social transgressions and helps individuals restore relationships disrupted by the transgression (Keltner & Buswell, 1997).

The insights gained by a SF analysis are perhaps even more apparent in its application to jealousy, which is conventionally regarded as a debilitating emotion, one that healthy individuals transcend. When considering a single individual, it is hard to see what benefits jealousy might bring about, or what problems it might solve. If anything, jealousy seems to bring about more problems than it solves. Yet when considering the dyad as the unit of analysis in SF analyses, one sees that jealousy serves to reduce interest in potential rivals and to display commitment and devotion. In this way jealousy promotes stable intimate relationships (Buss, 1999; Daly, Wilson & Weghorst, 1989). Table 1 summarizes the insights from SF research in this domain.

Just as a SF analysis has helped organize findings concerning consequences of emotions in family relationships, we suggest that it can similarly elucidate the consequences of emotions in organizational relationships, and in particular negotiations. Negotiations present a number of qualitatively different relational problems to negotiators, including the problems of initiating an exchange with a stranger, protecting oneself from exploitation, claiming value, creating value through efficient trades, locking in a commitment to a settlement, and so forth. Although there are some obvious strategies for each of these problems, these

Table 1. Example: A Social Functional Analysis of Emotions in Family Relationships

Problem	Emotions	Specific function
Ensuring procreation	Sexual desire	Increases likelihood of sexual contact
	Jealousy	Fosters vigilant guarding against rival suitors
Protection of children	Filial love	Ensures parental care for offspring
	Sympathy	Leads others to help vulnerable young

strategies often interfere with solving other problems. For this reason, theorists (Kelley & Thibaut, 1969; Lax & Sebenius, 1986; Pruitt & Rubin, 1986) have described 'dilemmas' that negotiators face in choosing their tactics – an explicit vow to be cooperative impedes ones ability to claim value, a warning to the other about commitment may interfere with building a relationship, etc. We will suggest that these relational predicaments trigger distinct emotions in negotiators and that these emotions may often have consequences that ameliorate the originating relational problems.

Scholars working in different theoretical traditions have speculated about how emotions might solve problems like those that negotiations pose. For example, in his discussion of reciprocal altruism, the biologist Trivers highlighted the role of anger and gratitude in promoting cooperative alliances, a critical element of stable, long-term relationships (Trivers, 1971). The economist Frank has argued that any transaction, be it a business partnership or marriage, requires that individuals remain committed to the relationship and its agreements when self-interest would lead to other courses of action (e.g. embezzling from a business partner, cheating on a spouse) (Frank, 1988). The solution to the 'commitment problem', Frank contends, lies in how certain emotions, such as love or guilt, convey commitment to others and motivate the self to transcend self-interest when necessary to preserve the relationship. Also the psychiatrist Nesse has speculated about how emotions help individuals cooperate in interpersonal relations that have the reward structure of the prisoner's dilemma game (Nesse, 1990). These observations converge on the theme of this chapter: that specific emotions shape the negotiation of organizational relations. In Table 2 we list a number of emotions that may

Table 2. Proposal: A Social Functional Analysis Of Emotions In Organizational Relationships

Problem	Emotions	Specific function
Maintaining Reciprocal Cooperation	Gratitude	Rewards other for cooperating
	Anger	Punishes other for defecting, motivating restitution
	Guilt	Spurs own efforts to repair the harm one has done
Maintaining Hierarchies	Contempt	Reduces the status of the other, usually a subordinate
Maintaining Group Norms	Shame	Signals to group a transgressor's awareness and regret, reducing the likelihood of needless sanctioning

function to resolve general types of problems involved in organizational relationships. This list is illustrative rather than comprehensive. The emotions listed may play important and under-appreciated roles in negotiation and other organizational relationships. Yet these are not the only emotions with important implications for negotiations; we will see that other emotions are important as well (e.g. interest, empathy). The specific problems that arise in negotiations, which we detail below, are examples of these general problems and give rise to predictable kinds of emotions.

The arguments represented in Table 2 derive from a now familiar functionalist hypothesis-generation heuristic: we first consider the emotions elicited in a variety of organizational interactions. We then analyze the relational problem to the contexts where a given emotion recurs. Finally, we consider ways that the emotions may function to help resolve the problems.

The first general class of problems individuals face in organizational relationships is maintaining reciprocal cooperation (Kramer, 1991). Organizational relationships at their core are cooperative alliances that are dependent upon mutual trust and reciprocity (Kramer & Tyler, 1996). Certain emotions are important to the formation and maintenance of cooperative alliances (see Nesse, 1990). For example, liking motivates the initiation of cooperative bonds. Gratitude rewards others for engaging in cooperative behavior. Cooperative alliances are obviously vulnerable to competition, greed, and defection. Certain emotions act as safeguards against those threats to cooperative alliances. For example, anger occurs in response to others' actions that undermine the cooperative alliance, such as openly competitive behavior or the inappropriate use of resources (e.g. Averill, 1982). Expressions of pain and distress upon being cheated likewise motivate others to engage in cooperative behavior (e.g. Eisenberg et al., 1989). And guilt motivates individuals to restore cooperative bonds when they themselves have violated the terms of a cooperative relationship (e.g. Keltner & Buswell, 1996). In the section that follows we will elaborate upon how many of these emotions shape the course of negotiations.

A second general problem in organizational relationships is maintaining status hierarchies. In all human groups, status hierarchies structure the distribution of resources, such as mates, food, and social attention (Fiske, 1990; de Waal, 1986, 1988). Certain emotions justify individuals' claims to specific resources (e.g. Clark, 1990; Kemper, 1993). Emotions related to dominance, such as contempt and variants of anger, convey strength vis-à-vis others, and certain rights to resources. We shall see in the ensuing section that the displays of dominance are an important part of the process by which negotiators communicate the specific nature and importance of their preferences and positions.

Another general class of problems in organizational relationships arises in maintaining group norms. Norms are crucial in regulating the extent to which individuals volunteer labor required for collective endeavors. Individuals who intentionally violate norms are punished, and so it is important that individuals who have accidentally violated norms can signal this to the group in order to avoid punishment. Embarrassment and shame convey submissiveness, and in the context of human interactions often serve as apologies or appeasement gestures, prompting reconciliation following actions that disrupt social relationships (Keltner & Buswell, 1996; Miller & Leary, 1992). The broad array of displays of submissiveness, we shall see, may play a critical role in negotiations when negotiators have encountered difficulties and seek to shift the tone toward a less aggressive, more cooperative interaction.

In sum, we have argued that emotions help people solve many important problems of family and organizational relationships. Many of these same problems, theorists have long argued, are central to negotiations. By implication, emotions may function to solve these problems in negotiations by coordinating the behavior of negotiators in the ways that we have described. We now present arguments about how the SF approach elucidates particular phenomena identified in negotiation research.

INSIGHTS ABOUT NEGOTIATION FROM A SOCIAL FUNCTIONALIST PERSPECTIVE

A social functionalist analysis has illuminated the importance of emotions in a variety of interpersonal contexts. We believe this approach applies just as fruitfully to the study of negotiations, and in this application, sheds light on three longstanding topics in negotiation research. First, descriptions of negotiation in many different arenas have identified transitions between phases of qualitatively different styles of interaction. For example, the opening moments of negotiations tend to involve a constellation of sentiments, gestures, and actions that are unlike those that occur at other points in a negotiation. Although researchers have converged in their observations, the reasons for these patterns have remained unclear. We will argue that the different behaviors negotiators engage in at different phases of the negotiation – as well as the temporal sequence of phases – reflect the specific relational problems that arise at different points and the accompanying emotions. Negotiators should display different expressive behaviors at different stages, and these specific behaviors should be associated with fairly specific interpersonal consequences.

Second, negotiation research has sought ways of understanding the impact of culture. Our framework suggests hypotheses about cultural variations and similarities in that it elucidates different emotion-based solutions to the same relational problems.

Finally, studies of negotiation have long found that communication media can impact negotiation outcomes. Many studies have found, for example, that face-to-face conversations result in higher joint outcomes than do exchanges with more impoverished communication (e.g. written notes). Yet these effects do not appear across all kinds of negotiation tasks, and an explanation of these nuances has not emerged from analyses focusing purely on the information-carrying potential of the respective media. We will argue that the impact of communication media on negotiation outcomes can be understood in terms of the extent to which communication media enable or impede certain emotional dynamics and the extent to which these dynamics are required to solve the problems that a conflict presents.

Temporal Phases of Negotiation

A recurrent finding in negotiation research – both laboratory experiments and field studies – is that the way negotiators interact changes over the course of their meeting or meetings. Influential models of the phase-structure of project group interactions and the dynamics underlying this structure have been developed recently (Gersick, 1988). However, studies have found that such models of group interaction phase structure do not extend to negotiations (Lim, 1994). Yet the possibility for a model of negotiation phase-structure is suggested by striking parallels in the observations of different conflict researchers.

Several qualitatively distinct phases have been distinguished in a number of literatures. First, the *opening moves* of an interaction have been highlighted by experimental psychologists modeling conflict with repeated-play games, who suggest that negotiation success depends on cooperation in opening rounds (Rubin & Brown, 1975). Similar observations have been made in ethnographic studies of dispute resolution practices, who have noted ritualized ways of initiating the negotiation conversation (Gulliver, 1979). Once the "ice has been broken," negotiators enter a phase of contentious moves or *positioning*. A key transition later in a negotiation is from this aggressive interaction to a more collaborative interaction of *problem solving*. This transition has been observed in ethnographic observation of labor vs. management conflict in organizations (Douglas, 1962) as well as students vs. administration conflict on campuses (Pruitt & Rubin, 1986). Negotiation researchers have also pointed out the unique aspects of the closing moments or the *endgame*. An aggressive tone returns to the conversation as ultimatums and threats are delivered. Kochan (1980) suggests that the final phase of collective bargaining occurs as negotiators attempt to signal that they cannot make more concessions. A similar emphasis in the endgame has been described in works on individual bargaining (Lewicki, Hiam & Olander, 1996).

Although negotiation scholars have long referred to negotiation phases and transitions, no one has yet offered a cogent account of the order, forms, and functions of these phases. Contemporary negotiation theorists have increasingly emphasized that 'value claiming' and 'value creating' tactics inevitably occur within the same negotiation (Lax & Sebenius, 1986; Bazerman & Neale, 1992). Yet these scholars have devoted less attention to why these sets of tactics tend to predominate in separate phases of the negotiation. In the collective bargaining literature, the phases of negotiation were interpreted in terms of political needs of representatives to impress constituencies with tough, aggressive grandstanding in order to earn license to later work collaboratively with the counterpart (Stevens, 1963). For instance, union representatives display toughness in early rounds of negotiations to protect against the impression that their later concessions to management reflect weakness or selling out. Yet a political account of phases does not explain why the same patterns are seen in laboratory experiments where these political pressures do not exist (Morley & Stephenson, 1977). Still other scholars have explained the phase transitions in negotiations in terms of ritualized roles rather than rational calculations (Goffman, 1959). For instance, Friedman (1994) claims that "when negotiators do improvise, they still maintain their roles – their comments display anger and distrust toward the opponent, as well as solidarity with their teammates" (p. 5). Perhaps the scripted roles calling for transitions in negotiating style are so culturally pervasive that they guide participants in experiments as well as professional negotiators. Yet script explanations beg the question of why the phase structure appears similar across different cultures (Gulliver, 1979; Pye, 1982). Why have cultures independently produced scripts with the same phase transitions, unless this pattern results from functional responses to the inherent relational problems that negotiation presents?

We will argue that the phase structure of negotiations arises because negotiations involve a series of linked relational problems and these problems trigger distinct emotions. Our analysis, summarized in Table 3, distinguishes the following phases: Opening moves, Positioning, Problem solving, and Endgame. While the precise division of phases is somewhat arbitrary, we will propose a framework delineating the relational problems and emotional solutions that arise in these four phases of a negotiation encounter. For each phase, we will review the observations of previous researchers, examine the problem that this phase presents, and then speculate about how these problems may trigger particular emotions. In short, we propose in a given phase, emotions that underlie negotiators' behaviors. In considering how the consequences of such emotions serve individual or dyadic interests, we will pay particular attention to how emotional expression enables emotions to work between negotiators, through information, evocation, and incentives.

Opening Moves
A key finding in psychology experiments simulating negotiations is the crucial importance of the first impressions that negotiatiors make on each other. In the early literature, negotiation was operationalized as a multiple-round Prisoner's Dilemma game. Rubin and Brown (1975) reviewed a number of findings that suggested that mutually beneficial cooperative patterns emerge only when some signs of cooperativeness are conveyed in the 'opening moves'. Studies using varying methods found that if a negotiator is competitive at the start, this is reciprocated, and a 'lock-in' effect ensues (Pilisuck & Rapoport, 1964).

Table 3.   A Phase Model of Relational Problems, Emotions, and Behavioral Signs in Negotiations

Negotiation phase:	Opening moves	Positioning	Problem solving	Endgame
Relational problem:	Initiation	Influence	Trust	Binding
Emotion:	*Liking*	*Anger*	*Embarrassment*	*Pain*
Signs:	Eye contact, Smiles, Close interpersonal distance, Open palmed gestures	Hostile criticism of other's point, Furrowed brow, Postural expansion, Chopping gestures	Apologies, Blushing, Submissive posture, Bowed face, Self-touching	Wincing during final concessions, Cringing posture
Emotion:	*Interest*	*Contempt*	*Empathy*	*Exasperation*
Signs:	Personal questions, Raised eyebrows, Cocked head, Forward lean	Dismissive vocal tone, Looking away from other when other is speaking, Sneering expression	Synchronous positivity, e.g. simultaneous smiling, nodding, laughter	Surprise and anger at other's reluctance to reach final settlement

From a purely rational standpoint it is puzzling why negotiators insist that cooperativeness be displayed in the opening rounds when they are more forgiving of competitiveness in later phases of the negotiation. Rubin & Brown (1975) suggested that the opening moves in a negotiation have the primary role of conveying a party's general intentions and character, which in turn establishes a climate for the negotiation.

Insight about the puzzle of why opening moves matter so much may be found in ethnographic studies of conflict resolution in different cultures (Gulliver, 1979). Anthropologists have suggested that cultures vary in the greeting rituals with which strangers initiate a conversation. Of course, North Americans shake hands, Europeans kiss cheeks, East Asians exchange bows, and the subtleties of these gestures vary in more fine-grained and at times ineffable ways. Yet these rituals occur reliably at the outset of attempts at conflict resolution. Implicit in comparing these gestures is a notion that they serve some common role or function. What is that function?

In considering which emotions may be involved in the opening moments of negotiation encounters, we begin by asking what relational problems confront a pair of negotiators at this moment? Embarking on a negotiation with any new counterpart may bring a settlement of high value, but it is also potentially quite costly. Negotiation takes time and energy, so initiating talks with one counterpart often means lost opportunities to settle with others. Moreover any earnest negotiation requires revealing information about one's goals, interests, and alternatives, and these revelations can undermine one's bargaining position for the future. Hence, the dilemma of whether to "give it a shot" with a counterpart can be called the *initiation* problem. A negotiator asks: Is it worth the gamble of trying to negotiate with this person? Is this person entering the process in an insincere way, negotiating 'in bad faith'? If one knew the answers to this question, one would know whether to walk away or to launch into the negotiation. But just as one cannot learn to swim without getting wet, one cannot figure this out without beginning to negotiate. The problem can be seen in terms of individual and dyadic interests. From the standpoint of the individual negotiator, there are two problems: deciding whether the other is worth talking to and (so long as this decision has not been answered in the negative) conveying to the other that one is worth talking to. From the standpoint of the dyad, the problem is of how to 'break the ice' and establish forward momentum in a conversation.[2] In Table 3 we posit that two specific emotional states are triggered by the relationship initiation problem. The first is *liking*, by which we refer to the attraction and affiliative intent one feels towards potential companions (Hatfield & Rapson, 1993). Ethological studies of both humans and non-humans have shown that liking, broadly defined, is associated with a variety of expressive behaviors, some of which are listed in Table 3. Behavioral signs of liking are distinct from those of love (Hatfield & Rapson, 1993). These behaviors include certain facial displays, such as pleasurable smiles, head nods and mutual gaze, postural asymmetry and relaxation, increased physical proximity, and affiliative hand gestures, such as open palms. Sociologists (e.g. Goffman, 1967) have observed that these markers of liking play essential roles in interactions as individuals initially enter into cooperative relations. Ethologists have identified the same behaviors in the opening moments of interactions between primates who do not have a previous history of extensive interaction (Eibl-Eibesfeldt, 1989). Studies of the contagion of smiling and laughter (e.g. Provine, 1993) suggest that these behaviors call forth matching behavior from the other person. Cialdini (1984) reviews extensive experimental evidence that liking induces compliance. This dovetails with field study evidence that smiles and good cheer are used by service employees to control customers, a tactic noted in studies of waiters (Whyte, 1946), milkmen (Bigus, 1972) and cocktail waitresses (Tidd & Lockard, 1978). From the standpoint of the individual, these expressions of liking induce in the other a willingness to talk. From the standpoint of the dyad, liking displays are strong triggers of reciprocity. At both levels of analysis, an adaptive function of liking expressions can be seen.

Secondly the emotional expression of *interest* may also help negotiators solve the initiation problem. Interest can be expressed by simple behaviors such as a forward lean or a cocked head, which are seen across cultures and in non-human primates (e.g. Izard, 1977). Interest can also be displayed through more subtle facial expressions, such as the widening of the eyes and the raising of the eyebrows (see Fig. 2). Interest can be conveyed verbally through personal questions. Expressing interest in the other sends a message to the other that one is a promising candidate as a negotiation counterpart. Yet expressing interest not only functions by providing information, it also functions by evoking emotions in the other person. Interest is flattering and hence begets a positive and compliant state. Experiments have found that pedestrians who were gazed at were more likely to accept a pamphlet from a researcher than those not gazed at (Kleinke & Singer, 1979). In these ways, interest displays benefit the displayer. Interest displays in early conversations also benefit the dyad by steering the two negotiators toward issues that the two parties care most about.

In sum, we have argued that the initiation problem faced by negotiators upon first meeting is worked through by emotional interactions generated by the behavior related to liking and interest. In our observations of negotiations between business executives (Morris & Keltner, 1998), negotiators often begin

STAGE:	OPENING MOVES	POSITIONING	PROBLEM SOLVING	ENDGAME
PROBLEM:	*INITIATION*	*INFLUENCE*	*TRUST*	*BINDING*

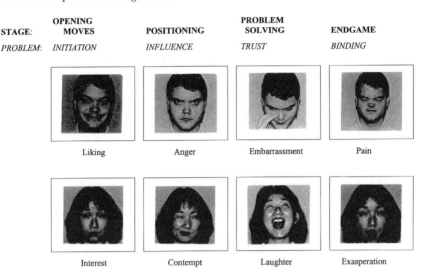

Liking	Anger	Embarrassment	Pain
Interest	Contempt	Laughter	Exasperation

Fig. 2.

with a host of liking and interest expressions. These include greeting rituals, gift giving, and casual yet vital talk about family, friends, shared acquaintances and common experiences. These interactions are not incidental to the negotiation; rather, through their evocation of liking and interest and the coordinated interactions that ensue, they lubricate and set in motion the process of negotiation. These emotional displays are strongly evocative of responses and hence create momentum for a dyad that carries into the harder work of exchanging concessions on issues. Having solved this first problem of initiating the interaction, negotiators make the transition to a new phase of the negotiation, where they must stake out their position. In the next phase, expressions of liking and interest recede as the conversation becomes more confrontational and other emotions guide negotiators' behavior.

Positioning
In descriptions of how negotiations change after the somewhat ritualized opening moves, many scholars have referred to a period of contention and positioning. One literature where this has been observed is the study of collective bargaining over labor contracts. Early in the process, negotiators often display toughness and intransigence. It is generally understood that most

negotiations involve both a dimension of claiming value and creating value and that there is a tension between these two strategies (Lax & Sebenius, 1986). It is hard for negotiators to pursue both ends simultaneously. Research suggests that after the opening moves negotiators typically pursue value claiming for a period of time before moving on to value creation. In thinking about why this might be the case, we will analyze the context in terms of the social emotions involved. Consider the predicament of individuals who have initiated a negotiation with a counterpart. They are embarking on a process that will require some concessions so it is imperative that each start by requesting they get their way on their most crucial issues. The phase is one of straight haggling or distributive bargaining. The relational problem inherent in this phase is that of asserting one's preferences in a contest of dominance with the counterpart. The problem of dominance exemplifies a point made earlier: that there are many solutions to the same relational problem. This problem can trigger one of several distinct emotions, each of which involves behaviors that potentially play a role in redressing the problem.

A first example of an emotion that functions in the problem of asserting dominance or positioning oneself early in negotiations is *anger*. Studies of people's espoused reasons for displaying anger have found that people express anger to change others' behavior or extract a favor (Averill, 1982) and in negotiations to induce a concession (Adler, Rosen & Silverstein, 1998). Although the negotiation of most routine business contracts does not occasion vivid subjective feelings of anger (as in contentious divorce or strike), negotiators often do evince the behavioral signs of anger. Indeed, expert negotiators are often surprised when watching videotapes of themselves negotiating at the facial expressions of anger (see Fig. 2) that they manifest.[3]

What are the signs of anger in a negotiation? The empirical literature has identified many markers of anger, some of which we summarize in Table 3. The role of aggressive glaring stares in intimidating an opponent has been documented in bargaining studies (Lewis & Fry, 1977) as well as in field studies of professions, such as police interrogators, who engage in contentious bargaining (Arther & Caputo, 1959). Anger is also expressed in speech. For example, the president of a firm undergoing bankruptcy reports meetings with an angry creditor's representative who endured glaring, sneering, and verbal jabs, such as responding to explanations by saying "quit making excuses for your incompetence" (Sutton & Callahan, 1987, p. 13). In more tempered settings, negotiators reveal anger through more indirect verbal aggression. Hostility to a person is often expressed by critiquing their ideas or affiliations (Freud, 1913/1959). Tone and volume of voice express anger. Gestures come into play as well. Negotiators punctuate their positioning statements with thrusting back-handed gestures, rather than the fluid, palm-exposing gestures used in opening moves (Keating, 1985). Moreover, negotiators adopt postures expressing anger and dominance, which involve expansive positions with shoulders thrown back, hands on hips, or arms akimbo (Dovidio & Ellyson, 1985). The most celebrated chapter of Wolfe's (1999a) novel *A Man in Full* provides elaborate descriptions of such non-verbal dominance tactics used in the 'workout room' of an overextended bank to extract concessions from debtors. Wolfe (1999b) reports that this chapter is based closely on real examples studied in his field research in banks.

Displays of anger have an impact on one's counterpart. Anger displays convey information that one cares deeply and that one may be prone to rash action, such as abandoning the negotiation and taking alternative measures (e.g. Schelling, 1960). Studies have found that anger-expressing people are seen as dominant (Clark, 1993) and worthy of status (Tiedens, 1999). Anger also evokes complementary emotions in the counterpart such as fear and guilt (e.g. Dimberg & Ohman, 1996). Fear can lead a negotiator to cave in, to avoid courses of actions that could offend or upset the other. Ethnographic studies of poker players indicate that anger-related expressions cripple some opponents. Hayano (1982) describes players who express hostility by talking "in the idioms of power and dominance" and non-verbally by "splashing chips and money around" and can succeed by "frightening and intimidating opponents who are too confused to defend themselves" (p. 57). Sometimes the reaction is not fear but guilt, and this most likely depends on the power differential. Yet the counterpart's guilt that his or her actions have caused offense may motivate restitution in the form of concessions. Even if they do not induce fear or guilt, anger displays can influence through incentives by punishing the counterpart. Over a longer time span, the influence of anger displays may have a deterrent effect on the counterpart's demands about an issue. Hence, from the standpoint of the individual negotiator, anger displays function by asserting one's dominance on one's critical issues. From the standpoint of the dyad, anger displays can function by signalling issues that are sensitive and require special attention; that is, eruptions of anger indicate potential 'deal breakers', strong preferences on issues that need to be accommodated in order for the dyad to find an agreement.

Contexts of dominance may also trigger *contempt*, which involves different behaviors than those involved in anger. If anger signals a latent aggressive challenge toward the counterpart, contempt conveys obliquely that the counterpart is not worthy as a rival. Contempt is rarely expressed in an overt statement but rather through ignoring one's counterpart or responding in dismissive tone. Or, a sneering expression can convey the essential point that the other has become unworthy (see Fig. 2). Also, contempt is powerfully expressed through gaze patterns. Targets of contempt are unlikely to be looked at, especially when they are speaking and would like attention (Ellyson & Dovidio, 1985). The use of contempt cues to communicate messages about another person's status are seen even at the highest levels of executive ranks. A description of the recent struggle for control between Citibank co-CEOs John Reed and Sandy Weill describes exchanges of subtle contempt expression toward the other.

> At another meeting, Mr. Weill asked Mr. Reed to explain how the effort generated profits. "Can you quantify the bottom line?" Mr. Weill asked. When Mr. Reed began, Mr. Weill rolled his eyes, said one person who witnessed the exchange. When it was Mr. Weill's turn to speak, Mr. Reed started reading, the person said. ("How Reed," 2000, p. A8).

In ordinary language, contempt has the connotation of a very strong, intense feeling, so it is worth emphasizing that we use the term in its scientific sense, not intending these connotations. When negotiators (in executive education classes) are queried about their emotions after a negotiation, few report feelings of contempt. This is not simply the tendency to describe one's behavior in socially desirable ways; these negotiators are surprised when later shown videotapes of themselves negotiating that reveal behavioral signs of contempt when positioning or reacting to that of their opponents (Morris & Keltner, 1998). Contempt tends to occur as a fleeting reaction to statements of the other side rather than as a premeditated, planned display. For this reason, negotiators may not be consciously aware of the contempt that they evince. Or, they may be aware of reacting to the other side, but they may believe their expressions to be transmitting only puzzlement or skepticism rather than the stronger condescension inherent in displays of contempt.

Displays of contempt in the positioning phase, although sometimes destructive to progress, often serve to advance the negotiation. First, contempt conveys information about status vis-à-vis others. Tiedens (in press) found that higher status individuals are more likely to experience and express emotions such as anger and contempt. And, accordingly, actors who display emotions related to contempt are judged by observers to be of high status (Tiedens, Ellsworth & Mesquita, 2000).

Furthermore, contempt displays in the context of negotiations are likely to evoke complementary emotions. That is, to the extent that the counterpart internalizes the message of low regard, he or she will feel somewhat demoralized. The counterpart may lose self-confidence and become easier to persuade. Or, the counterpart may become motivated to make to concessions to win back the contemptuous one's approval. Either way, contempt expressions have consequences that can resolve the relational problem of dominance. From the individual's standpoint, contempt can resolve the dominance contest by cowing the counterpart into submission. From the dyad's standpoint, contempt can resolve the problem of intransigence associated with the positioning efforts by inducing from each side the concessions needed in order to reach agreement.

In summary, negative emotions such as anger and contempt can serve important functions in negotiations. Granted, the consequences of anger and contempt are not always beneficial. Nor do we contend that these emotions are beneficial most of the time. After all, research on romantic partners discussing conflicts finds that anger and contempt often lead to conflict spirals and in the long run, marital dissolution (e.g. Levenson & Gottman, 1983). No doubt similar dynamics occur in business relationships. Nevertheless, when expressed in timely fashion displays of anger and contempt often provide important information about negotiators' preferences, positions, and concerns. Further, anger displays sometimes warn counterparts to steer away from particular arguments and courses of action that offend certain sensitivities and hence might rupture the relationship. Importantly our analysis suggests that anger and contempt are most likely to have these functional benefits when they occur during the positioning phase of the negotiation. Displays of anger and contempt in the opening moves are likely to abort the negotiation before progress begins. Displays of anger or contempt in the problem solving stage, as we shall see, are likely to interfere with the crucial development of trust and information exchange.

Problem Solving
Researchers who describe a transition to a collaborative or problem solving phase of negotiation refer to a period in the conversation characterized by free discussion, exchange of information about priorities, mutual generation of options and mutual evaluation of these options (Pruitt & Rubin, 1986; Lewicki et al, 1996). The opposing negotiators who had been competitive in the positioning phase let down their guards and become cooperative. Many classic accounts of negotiation have described this transition, yet they have lacked a language to explain the mechanisms through which it is achieved. Consider this account by Peters (1952) in a labor-management negotiation that had been stuck on a contentious wage issue:

> Frazier and Turner looked each other in the eye. Somewhere a communication established itself without a word between them. The question in each other's eye was, "If I move to 9 cents will you move to 9 cents?" . . . Frazer said "Well we are willing to give it some consideration . . ." Turner nodded his acquiescence. The tension was gone. (p. 18).

Our SF perspective suggests that non-verbal communication of emotions may be critical in transforming the contentious interaction into a cooperative, problem-solving interaction. But which emotions are involved? In answering this question, we start by asking what relational problem is presented by the context. What kind of relationship do negotiators need in order to advance into the problem solving stage of the negotiation? Let us assume for the sake of simplicity that a negotiation has marched through the ideal-typical phases. First with displays of interest and openness, the negotiators have initiated a relationship. Then negotiators have commenced the positioning phase, seeking dominance on particular issues through aggressive arguments and flashes of anger or contempt. After a while negotiators often discover that pushing alone will not bring an acceptable solution; unless they find an integrative agreement neither will be able to obtain the desired outcome. To do so they have to exchange accurate information about their preferences and this requires a relationship of trust. Yet one or both may have pushed too far and strained their initial trust.

Which social emotions are evoked by the recognition of having pushed too far? How might displays of this emotion repair the damage to the relationship caused by the positioning phase? Some clues come from recent research on *embarrassment*. Embarrassment involves a distinct set of expressive behaviors, including: averted gaze, slight shrugging, subtle bowing, self-conscious smiling, and blushing (e.g. Keltner, 1995). These behaviors, interestingly enough, resemble many of the appeasement displays seen in other species, suggesting that embarrassment displays may serve an appeasement function (Keltner & Buswell, 1997). That is, displays of embarrassment, or related behaviors like those associated with politeness and modesty (Keltner, Young, & Buswell, 1997), lead observers to forgive and trust the embarrassed person. Embarrassment provides a credible signal of the wrongdoer's regret – more credible than an apology in that certain components of the display, such as blushing, cannot be feigned (Keltner & Buswell, 1997). Hence, the pivotal moment that enables many negotiations to transition away from escalating aggressive positioning toward problem-solving discussion may be a brief expression of embarrassment.[4]

Although embarrassment helps repair the damage to allow a transition from a competitive tone, it does not bring a relationship all the way forward to trust. Another social emotional process that may be triggered as negotiators seek to establish trust is *rapport*. Although rapport has long figured prominently in the popular literature on negotiation (Brooks, 1991; Ury, 1993), there has existed little scientific evidence for rapport or its consequences until recently (DePaulo & Bell, 1990). Initial research on the rapport between physicians and clients found that certain qualities of the interaction corresponding to rapport predicted whether clients cooperate with the treatment plan (see Harrigan & Rosenthal, 1986). For these researchers, rapport is a state of mutual positivity and interest that arises through convergence and resonance of emotional expression (Argyle, 1990; Tickle-Degnen & Rosenthal, 1990). The link between rapport in negotiation and mutual cooperation has been established in a number of studies by Morris and colleagues (Drolet & Morris, 1999; Moore et al., 1999; Morris & Drolet, 1999; Morris et al., 2000).

The non-verbal cues of rapport exhibited during negotiations can be reliably judged by observers watching a videotape of the interaction without a sound track; a particularly strong cue to rapport is synchrony of expressive movements, such as nodding, leaning, and gesturing (Bernieri, 1988, 1991; Bernieri et al., 1994). Quite literally, observers can judge whether the two members of the conversation are 'in synch' or 'on the same wavelength'.

In sum, the moment in negotiation when positioning can go no further presents a problem to negotiators: They need to move to a higher level of trust in order to make progress. Two social emotional processes may be triggered by this predicament: embarrassment on the part of a negotiator who has been overly demanding; and rapport between the negotiators as they discuss their common fate. The work done by these emotions may go a long way towards explaining the transitions of tone that have been observed by conflict researchers.

Endgame

The final phase noted in the negotiation literature, referred to as the end game, involves a shift away from the fully cooperative tone of the problem-solving phase. In the end game, the value creation possibilities have been reaped and negotiators turn again toward more contentious tactics aimed at bringing the opponent to commit to a given settlement. The problem is to lock in or bind the opponent to a deal. Reviewing evidence from labor-management negotiations, Kochan (1980) noted that one often faces counterparts who delay in accepting a final settlement until convinced that one will not make further concessions. Hence, to solve the binding problem in the end game phase, negotiators have to shift the opponent's attention away from the goal of one more concession.

Encountering new demands for concessions after having engaged in problem solving with an opponent is a predicament likely to evoke several kinds of expressive behavior. Among these, two kinds – displays of pain and displays of exasperation – are relevant to our thesis in that they can work to resolve the problem. These emotions, in their own respective ways, can have the consequence of binding the opponent to a contract. When one is asked for more concessions after having already been pushed to one's limit, a natural response is pain. Negotiators display pain through a variety of behaviors, such as wincing or holding one's head in hand (see Fig. 2). Others verbally protest in the language of assault victims (e.g. "Enough, I'm bleeding all over the floor here!"). Such expressions of pain can function to signal to counterpart that one has made all possible concessions – signal that one is not merely pretending to be at one's limit when in fact one has a tremendous surplus of value. In addition to the informational consequence of lending credence to one's claims, displays of pain may also have an effect through the mechanism of evoking a complementary emotion. A compelling display of pain evokes sympathy and may lead the counterpart not only to abandon a final demand but also to help ease the other's pain by making a concession.

Another reaction is to express *exasperation* or indignation at the opponent's indecision or eleventh-hour demands. These reactions hinge on the fact that a close working relationship was formed during the problem-solving phase and this relationship raises expectations of cooperative behavior. Expressions of exasperation or indignation obliquely convey an accusation of 'bad faith' or betrayal. Opponents are highly motivated to redress perceived socials sins of this sort, because reputations could be at stake. Indeed, an expression of indignation conveys not only a veiled accusation but a veiled threat – a threat that one will label the opponent as negotiating in bad faith, as pretending to seek a mutually beneficial agreement and then reversing course. This label differs from that of a tough negotiator in that it implies a degree of dishonesty or insincerity. Many opponents will quickly make a concession to avoid this possible reputational damage. Further, a complement to the power of exasperation is the power of subsequent gratitude once an opponent has dropped his or her demands, while avoiding outright happiness about one's final outcome (Thompson, Valley & Kramer, 1995).

Summary

In sum, the transitions of tone between different phases of bargaining may be greatly elucidated by a SF analysis of emotion. Different temporal points in negotiation present distinct relational problems; these problems tend to trigger particular emotions and expressive behaviors; these in turn shape the interaction, sometimes resolving the problem so that negotiators can advance to the next phase. Thus far we have shown that past findings about bargaining can be understood in part as arising from relational problems and emotional solutions. Now we will demonstrate that our proposal also yields novel, straightforward, empirically testable predictions. The simplest predictions specify when specific negative and positive emotions are likely to occur during the course of the negotiation. Specifically, our framework yields predictions about the emotions that will become more likely as negotiators confront a given problem and less likely it has been resolved.

Moreover there are SF predictions which complement insights from AC research, concerning the cognitions that follow from emotions. For example, anger potentiates placing blame upon others (Keltner et al., 1993) and increased risk seeking (Lerner & Keltner, 2000). Hence, we predict increases in these specific patterns of cognition as negotiators are in the positioning phase of the negotiation, where anger is evoked. Thus, our model not only provides a basis for predicting when particular emotions are likely but also when particular cognitive tendencies are most likely.

In addition to predicting likely patterns of emotions and cognitions, the SF approach also yields predictions about predictors of progress in conflict resolution. In deriving such predictions, it is important to recognize that commencing a negotiation is an important step in itself. Too often, research on conflict is based on experiments that, in essence, 'assume' a negotiation will occur between two parties. In reality, of course, one important dependent variable is whether one chooses to seek a negotiation at all. And, if there is a choice of counterparts, with whom? Our analysis allows predictions about these dependent variables. For instance, liking and interest upon meeting a person should predict whether one chooses to negotiate at all. Given that negotiation begins, displays of anger should predict success in claiming value on the issues where one cares the most. Rapport displays should predict a dyad having a high joint outcome through collaborative seeking of optimal settlements.

Now let us examine how the phase framework helps us understand two other important and perplexing factors affecting negotiations: culture and communication media.

Understanding Cultural Influences on Negotiation

There is a great deal of interest among negotiation researchers in the role of culture. However, negotiation theory, like other areas of social science, has struggled to model how culture influences emotion and expression (e.g., Babad & Wallbott, 1986). One common argument is that some cultures negotiate more logically and others, more emotionally. For instance, ethnographers of Japan have argued that appeals to the other's feelings are common and appeals to logic rare (Goldman, 1994; March, 1988). That is, the value of dispassionate reason in separating "the person from the problem" described in Western popular treatments of negotiation (Fisher & Ury 1981) may not apply in non-

Western cultures that are less saturated by the post-enlightenment valorization of logic (Markus, Kitayama & Heiman, 1997). Although this contrast between rational and emotional cultures has some appeal, the current analysis suggests reasons to question the presumption that negotiation is dispassionate and rational in Western culture. It may be that our own cultural forms of emotional expression are not as salient to us as those of other cultures.

A different analysis is that cultures differ in the content rather than the amount of emotion in negotiation. From fields such as ethnography come descriptions of concrete behavioral routines in conflict resolution that differ dramatically according to historical and cultural contingencies. Cultural differences in the forms of expressive behavior during conflict are not confined to exotic rituals; they can be seen in even the most mundane workplace interactions. Rafaeli & Sutton (1989) describe differences in the displays rules for expressing a socioemotional message as a function of national culture as well as of occupational and organizational cultures. For example, in American society a smile is obligated in a service encounter; in Israel it is not; and in some Muslim countries, it is avoided because it would constitute a sexual advance. Many of the expressive behaviors described in our phase framework differ in this way across cultures. For instance, in opening moves, Americans shake hands and make eye contact, whereas Japanese bow and avert their eyes. Although these behaviors differ in concrete details, at a more abstract level, the cultures are alike in having greeting rituals. One can understand that handshaking and bowing play parallel roles in serving this greeting function. Cultural differences look less incommensurable as the behavior is described more abstractly (for a review, see Morris, Leung, Ames & Lickel, 1999).

The functional analysis of emotions that we have developed provides a means to abstract beyond the concrete particulars of emotional expression and ask whether cultures differ at functional level. In many cases, cultural differences may take the form of different norms about how to appropriately express the same sentiment. Consider for example the non-verbal signs used in establishing rapport in Latin versus East Asian cultures. Latin societies are characterized by overt, harmonious displays of warm emotion, a tendency referred to as *simpatia* in Latin America (Burton, 1994; Diaz-Guerrero, 1967; Lindsley & Braithwaite, 1996; Sanchez-Burks, Nisbett & Ybarra, 1998; Triandis, Marin, Lisansky & Betancourt, 1984). This energetic, active display differs from the restrained, subdued displays through which rapport is established in East Asian cultures, as captured in the Chinese virtue of *jen* (Hsu, 1985) or the Japanese tradition of *amae* (Doi, 1962). Hence, although rapport involves mutual displays of positive affect and interest, the way these are behaviorally enacted differs across cultures.

Alternatively, in other cases, cultures may differ in which of two functionally interchangeable emotions are triggered by a relational problem. For example, we have suggested that anger and contempt are two alternative emotions that are triggered by the problem of positioning. It is hard to simultaneously express anger and contempt toward a counterpart in a conflict because, to some extent, anger indicates an involvement with the other person whereas contempt conveys that the other is not worthy of one's attention or involvement. In a culture that discourages overt emotion, contempt will be preferred. For example, it may be that the occupational cultures of management negotiators encourage contempt whereas their union counterparts are free to express anger. Jackall (1988) argues that managers "need to exercise iron self-control and to have the ability to mask all emotion and intention behind bland, smiling, and agreeable public faces . . . [outbursts are] seen as irrational, unbenefitting men or women whose principle claim to social legitimacy is dispassionate rational calculation" (p. 47–49).

Similarly, whether anger or contempt will be deployed in positioning attempts most likely varies across organizational cultures. Morrill (1995) conducted one of the few ethnographic studies of conflict among high-level executives. Morrill compares the handling of conflicts at two firms that differed sharply in communication patterns and culture, one more bureaucratic and the other more organic and communicative. In the bureaucratic organization, a consulting firm, norms prohibited overt acts of aggression and dominance, so positioning in meetings over contested issues was largely conducted through behaviors expressing contempt. As one aging manager complains:

> It's not like some of the scenes I've watched at some of my clients: people raising their voices to one another, threatening each other. It's not at all like that here. No sir. It's deadly silent. You notice at meetings that when you speak, people look out the window, light their pipes, get called away to another meeting *all the time* [emphasis by the informant]. After a while, no amount of money can keep your sanity in a place like that (p. 163).

By contrast, in the communicative organization, a toy company, norms encouraged positioning through direct confrontations at meetings. Morrill reports a meeting concerning a decision on which the preferences of two managers M. and P. conflict. Here positioning occurs not through ignoring each other's statements but, instead, clashing directly with words and gestures suggesting violence and dominance.

> M. waited several minutes until P. had finished her complaints about his reactions to the plan. He then stood up and, in his words, "threw her a couple of hand grenades by looking her in the eye and saying that [he] would not allow her to kill every idea he brought up in public." P. then stood up and said, "If you want a war, we'll give you a war."

In this organizational culture, it is not as though status was without impact. Contempt was the preferred emotion in positioning efforts by managers of relatively higher status. In contrast, anger would erupt between lower level managers, as in the following event:

> At another team meeting, Ingle interrupted Pound loudly again and Pound responded by raking his hand across the burgundy teak meeting table, pushing his and two other colleagues' materials to the carpet. Pound and Ingle then had a meltdown, pushing each other and swinging their fists. The meltdown lasted several minutes, spilling out into the hallway, where a security guard watched for two or three minutes before breaking it up . . . Pound commented in the aftermath that he "couldn't let that dick get away with pretending not to listen to me again." (p. 207).

Interestingly, the incendiary behavior was contempt from a peer – (i.e. pretending not to listen). Higher ranking executives did not intervene in these flare-ups of anger "because of the same trepidation one would have, an executive noted, in intervening in a fight between rabid dogs." (p. 212). In any case, the contrast between organizational cultures exhibits that some cultural differences can be understood as norms about which of two functionally similar emotions is allowed in conflicts.

In sum, the framework for linking sets of emotions to phases of negotiation offers an abstract functional level at which to recognize cultural similarities and differences in uses of emotions. That is, cultural differences in display rules can be seen as different means toward the same end.

On a practical level, cultural differences can pose challenges in negotiation. Emotions as communication systems can break down just as verbal language as a communication system breaks down when the sender and receiver are working in a different code. In a study of Chinese negotiating styles, Pye (1982) describes a number of ways in which American negotiators might send the wrong signal to a Chinese host. However, to the extent that our phase model description holds across cultures, it might serve as an abstract interpretive frame that negotiators can use to interpret the other parties likely meaning. It may be that cultural differences, rather than pointing to limitations of the usefulness of a functional analysis, provide a reason to seek more abstract descriptions that ultimately facilitate mutual understanding.

Understanding Effects of Communication Media on Negotiation

Studies of negotiation have long found that communication media can impact negotiation outcomes. Thus, one way negotiators can potentially influence their outcomes is through their choice of communication media (for reviews, see Poole, Shannon & DeSanctis, 1992; Bazerman, Curhan, Moore & Valley, 2000). Different communication media, such as face-to-face, video conference, telephone, and electronic mail, differently impact negotiators' interpretation of negotiation and its rules (e.g. Valley & Keros, 1999). Researchers suggest that the effects of communication media on negotiation reflects inherent differences in their so-called 'richness', the sheer amount of information that they can convey (Poole et al., 1992). Many studies have found, for example, that face-to-face conversations result in higher joint outcomes than do exchanges of written notes. Yet these effects do not appear across all kinds of negotiation tasks. Research focusing on attributes of the media per se have not uncovered the crucial mechanisms and boundary conditions. We will argue that the impact of communication media on negotiation outcomes can be understood in terms of how communication media enable or impede certain emotional dynamics and the extent to which these dynamics are required to solve the problems that a conflict presents.

Let us review the literature on communication media and negotiation outcome. On the one hand, research has shown that face-to-face communication improves negotiated outcomes. For example, Valley, Moag & Bazerman (1998) found that face-to-face negotiation was associated with less deceit and higher joint gain. And, Drolet & Morris (1999) revealed that participants who communicated face-to-face vs. on the telephone were more likely to cooperate in a mixed-motive conflict. In both the Valley et al. and Drolet and Morris studies, the positive effects of face-to-face communication may be linked to the non-verbal (e.g. facial and postural) rather than the verbal cues transmitted through the medium. Drolet and Morris suggest that exposure to these nonverbal emotional cues leads to a shared feeling of rapport between negotiators. Although this implies that rapport is less likely to be established in media lacking visual access, such as e-mail, an understanding of the limitations of such media can also show the way toward using them effectively. Research suggests that successful email negotiators make frequent explicit references to the relationship in order to do the emotional work that would be otherwise accomplished by nonverbal cues (Morris et al., 2000). Also, experiments show that the liabilities of e-mail negotiation are reduced when a basis of trust is established by a foregoing phone call (Morris et al., 2000) or by the exchange of personal information (Moore et al., 1999) or by shared group membership (Moore et al., 1999).

On the other hand, research has also shown that under certain conditions face-to-face communication leads to adverse joint outcomes. For example, Lewis & Fry (1977) show that face-to-face contact enables dominance tactics. In their study, individualistically-oriented negotiators used more pressure tactics, were more likely to impasse, and obtained lower joint profit when they negotiated face-to-face vs. when they could not see each other. Findings from studies that have oriented participants to define their task competitively have found that negotiators in a face-to-face condition obtain lower collective outcomes than negotiators in a condition where visual access was blocked by a barrier (Carnevale, Pruitt & Seilheimer, 1981; Lewis & Fry, 1977). Process measures in these studies suggest that negotiators in the barrier condition visually attended to their issue information and this enabled a problem-solving dynamic. By contrast, negotiators in the face-to-face condition were more likely to engage in nonverbal dominance tactics, such as staring at their opponent, and this accentuated a competitive dynamic. Likewise, Carnevale, Pruitt & Seilheimer (1981) found that face-to-face communication magnifies tensions by allowing dominance expressions. As with the positive effects, the negative effects of face-to-face communication on negotiation have been linked to the medium's conveyance of non-verbal behaviors. In the Carnevale et al. study, face-to-face negotiators engaged in aggressive staring that, for some, led to an escalation of competitive motives. In contrast, communication media that prevent exposure to nonverbal cues may impede dominance tactics.

To summarize, an analysis of how emotions work in negotiations is valuable not only for understanding emotions and their direct consequences but also because these emotional dynamics are important mechanisms through which more remote variables – such as culture or communication media – have influences on negotiation processes and outcomes. Studies (Morris, Nadler, Thompson & Kurtzberg, 2000) have also identified strategies that skilled e-mail negotiators use to inject cues that prevent misreading of their emotion and intent. Based on these observations, other studies have identified how e-mail communication can be bolstered so as to mitigate the tendency toward misunderstanding and impasse (Moore, Kurtzberg, Thompson & Morris, 1998; Morris et al., 2000). Overall, results suggest that the liability of e-mail can be reduced by the cushion of trust created by conditions such as: (a) a pre-negotiation non-task-oriented phone-call, (b) a pre-negotiation exchange of pictures and personal information, and (c) the existence of shared group affiliations between the two negotiators. In short, an understanding of the emotional dynamics that underlie effects of communication media enables an understanding of how to exploit the advantages of a given medium with reduced vulnerability to its liabilities.

Conclusion

Negotiations are inherently emotional. In this essay we have sketched the history of research on emotion in negotiations. Early negotiation researchers portrayed emotions as prominent factors in determining the course of negotiations, an emphasis that dwindled with the rise of cognitivist accounts of social behavior. More recently, with improvements in the conceptualization of emotion, negotiation research has seen a renaissance of interest in emotion. A first wave studied emotion intra-personally, and documented ways that positive and negative affective states influence negotiator cognition. In this chapter we develop a complementary approach that emphasizes how the expression of specific emotions shapes inter-personal interaction during negotiation.

More specifically, drawing upon the insights of diverse fields, we argue that emotional expression can resolve relational problems, such as initiating and maintaining reciprocity, hierarchy, trust and fitness. Many of these relational problems arise in negotiations. Thus, this broad conceptual analysis engenders hypotheses about the different phases of negotiations, the problems negotiators face within those phases, and how emotional expression moves negotiators from one phase to the next. This approach generates precise predictions concerning the prevalence and effects of specific emotions at different stages of negotiation. This approach also may illuminate cultural differences and similarities in negotiation and communication media effects on negotiation process and outcomes. More generally, we hope our essay spurs a shift in views of emotions: they are not dysfunctional forces that disrupt thought and disorganize social interactions such as negotiations; rather, they are functional processes that coordinate social interactions in often very adaptive ways.

NOTES

1. In the ever-swelling popular literature on negotiation, the classic emphasis on emotions can still be found in the form of dictums about emotional intelligence and body language (Rosci, 1981). Yet the popular treatments which are close to the academic literature and most influential take a predictably rationalistic stance that negotiation always proceeds best through dispassionate discussion of principles (Fisher & Ury, 1981). On this view, emotions should be 'checked at the door' when entering a negotiation.

2. In a negotiation between two individuals who already know each other well, this first problem may be minimized. However, we would contend that the problem exists most of the time. First, negotiations are generally required when conflicts arise outside of a close relationship. Second, even if counterparts know each other from one domain of life, they may not know each other's intent and capabilities in the negotiator role. Hence, they still face an initial dilemma concerning whether or not to embark on a negotiation.

3. The authors conduct such an exercise as part of the Advanced Negotiation Program in the Stanford GSB Executive Education Curriculum.

4. The transition we have described from positioning to problem-solving phases corresponds to what early bargaining studies called the 'tough-then-soft' pattern whereas the opposite transition would correspond to the 'soft-then-tough' pattern. Studies in this tradition found that negotiators respond more positively to the tough-then-soft or 'reformed sinner' pattern than to the soft-then-tough or 'lapsed saint'

pattern (Harford & Solomon, 1967). As these labels suggest, to the extent that negotiators implicitly read the reformed sinner pattern as an expression of repentance, the psychology of appeasement may be involved in negotiators acceptance of the reformed sinner transition. This interpretation in terms of social emotions may help explain the finding that clinically paranoid participants depart form normal populations and even other clinical populations; paranoid patients do not respond positively to the reformed sinner pattern (Harford & Solomon, 1969).

REFERENCES

Adler, R. S., Rosen, B., & Silverstein, E. M. (1998). Emotions in negotiation: How to manage fear and anger. *Negotiation Journal*, 161–177.

Allred, K. G., Mallozzi, J. S., Matsui, F., & Raia, C.P (1997). The influence of anger and compassion on negotiation performance. *Organ. Behav. Human Decis. Process.*, *70*, 175–187.

Argyle, M. (1990). The nature of rapport. *Psychological Inquiry*, *1*(4), 297–300.

Arther, R. O. & Caputo, R. R. (1959). *Interrogation for investigators*. New York, NY: William C. Copp and Associates.

Averill, J. R. (1980). A constructivist view of emotion. In: R. Plutchik & H. Kellerman (Eds), *Emotion: Theory, Research, and Experience* (pp. 305–339). Orlando, Florida: Academic Press.

Averill, J. R. (1992). The structural bases of emotional behavior. In: M. S. Clark (Ed.), *Emotion* (pp. 1–24). Newbury Park, CA: Sage.

Babad, E. Y., & Wallbott, H. G. (1986). The effects of social factors on emotional reactions. In: K. R. Scherer, H. G. Wallbott & A. B. Summerfield (Eds), *Experiencing Emotion: A Cross-Cultural Study*. Cambridge: Cambridge University Press.

Barley, S. (1991). Contextualizing conflict: Notes on the anthropology of dispute and negotiation. In: M. H. Bazerman, R. J. Lewicki, and B. H. Sheppard (Eds), *Handbook of Research Negotiation*, vol. 3, (pp.165–199). Greenwich, CT: JAI Press.

Baron, R. A. (1990). Environmentally induced positive affect: Its impact on self-efficacy, task performance, negotiation, and conflict. *Journal of Applied Social Psychology*, *20*, 368–384.

Barry, B., & Oliver, R. L. (1996). Affect in Dyadic Negotiation: A Model and Propositions. *Organizational Behavior and Human Decision Processes*, *67*(2), August, 127–143.

Bavelas, J., Black, A., Lemery C., & Mullet, J. (1986). 'I show how you feel': Motor mimicry as a communicative act. *Journal of Personality and Social Psychology*, *50*, 322–329.

Bazerman, M. H., & Carroll, J. S. (1987). Negotiator cognition. *Research in Organizational Behavior*, *9*, 247–288.

Bazerman, M. H., Curhan, J. R., Moore, D. A., & Valley, K. L. (2000). Negotiations. *Annual Review of Psychology*, *51*, 279–314.

Bazerman, M. H., Gibbons, R., Thompson, L., & Valley, K. L. (1998). Can negotiations outperform game theory? In: J. J. Halpern, & R. N. Stern (Eds), *Debating Rationally: Nonrational Aspects in Organizational Decision Making*. Ithaca, NY: ILR.

Bazerman, M. H., & Neale, M. (1982). Improving negotiator effectiveness under final offer arbitration: The role of selection and training. *Journal of Applied Psychology*, *67*, 543–548.

Bazerman, M. H., & Neale, M. (1992). *Negotiating Rationally*. New York, NY: Free Press.

Bernieri, F. J. (1988). Coordinated movement and rapport in teacher-student interactions. *Journal of Nonverbal Behavior, 12*(2), 120–138.

Bernieri, F. J. (1991). Interpersonal sensitivity in teacher-student interactions. *Personality and Social Psychology Bulletin, 17*(1), 98–103.

Bernieri, F. J., Davis, J. M., Rosenthal, R., & Knee, R. C. (1994). Interactional synchrony and rapport: Measuring synchrony in displays devoid of sound and facial affect. *Personality and Social Psychology Bulletin, 20*(3), 303–311.

Bigus, O. E. (1972). The milkman and his customer: a cultivated relationship. *Urban Life and Culture, 1*, pp. 131–165.

Bodenhausen, G. V., Sheppard, L. A., & Kramer, G. P. (1994). Negative affect and social judgment: The differential impact of anger and sadness. Special issue: Affect in social judgments and cognition. *European Journal of Social Psychology, 24*, 45–62.

Bower, G. H. (1991). Mood congruity of social judgments. In: J. P. Forgas (Ed.), *Emotion and Social Judgments.* Oxford: Pergamon Press.

Bowlby, J. (1969). *Attachment.* New York: Basic Books.

Brief, A. P., Butcher, A. H., & Roberson, L. (1995). Cookies, disposition, and job attitudes: The effects of positive mood-inducing events and negative affectivity on job satisfaction in a field experiment. *Organizational Behavior & Human Decision Processes, 62*, 55–62.

Brooks, M. (1991). *The Power of Business Rapport.* New York: HarperCollins, Inc.

Burton, K. (1994). *The Business Culture in Spain.* Boston, MA: Butterworth-Heineman.

Buss. D. (1992). Male preference mechanisms: Consequences for partner choice and intrasexual competition. In: J. H. Barkow, L. Cosmides & J. Tooby (Eds), *The Adapted Mind* (pp. 267–288). New York: Oxford University Press.

Buss, D. (1999). *Evolutionary Psychology: The New Science of the Mind.* Boston, MA: Allyn & Bacon.

Buss, D. (2000). The Evolution of Happiness. *American Psychologist, 55*(1), 15–23.

Carnevale, P. J., & Isen, A. M. (1986). The influence of positive affect and visual access on the discovery of integrative solutions in bilateral negotiating. *Organizational Behavior and Human Decision Processes, 37*, 1–13.

Carnevale, P. J., Pruitt, D., & Seilheimer, S. (1981). Looking and competing: Accountability and visual access in integrative bargaining. *Journal of Personality and Social Psychology, 40*, 111–120.

Cialdini, R. B. (1984). *Influence: The Psychology of Persuasion.* New York, NY: William Morrow.

Clark, C. (1990). Emotions and the micropolitics in everyday life: Some patterns and paradoxes of 'Place'. In: T. D. Kemper (Ed.), *Research Agendas in the Sociology of Emotions* (pp. 305–334). State University of New York Press: Albany, NY.

Clark, M. S. (1993). Reactions to and strategic self-presentation of happiness, sadness, and anger. Paper presented at an invited symposium at the meeting of the American Psychological Society, Chicago, IL.

Clark, M. S., Pataki, S. P., & Carver, V. (1996). Some thoughts and findings on the self-presentation of emotions in relationships. In: G. J. O. Fletcher & J. Fitness (Eds), *Knowledge Structures In Close Relationships: A Social Psychological Approach* (pp. 247–274). Mahwah, NJ: Lawrence Erlbaum Associates.

Daly, M., Wilson, M., & Weghorst, S. J. (1982). Male sexual jealousy. *Ethology and Sociobiology, 3*, 11–27.

Darwin, C. (1872). *The Expression of the Emotions in Man and Animals.* London: Murray de Rivera, J. (1984). The structure of emotional relationships. In: P. Shaver (Ed.), *Review of Personality and Social Psychology: Emotions, Relationships, and Health* (pp. 116–145). Beverly Hills, CA: Sage.

de Waal, F. B. M. (1986). The integration of dominance and social bonding in primates. *The Quarterly Review of Biology, 61*, 459–479.

de Waal, F. B. M. (1988). The reconciled hierarchy. In: M. R. A. Chance (Ed.), *Social Fabrics of the Mind* (pp. 105–136). Hillsdale, NJ: Erlbaum.

DePaulo, B. M., & Bell, K. L. (1990). Rapport is not so soft anymore. *Psychological Inquiry, 1*(4), 305–307.

Deutsch, M. (1960). The effect of motivational orientation upon trust and suspicion. *Human Relations, 13*, 123–169.

Deutsch, M., & Krauss, R. M. (1962). The effect of threat upon interpersonal bargaining. *Journal of Abnormal & Social Psychology, 61*, 181–189.

Dewey, J. (1895). The theory of emotions II: The significance of emotions. *Psychological Review, 2*, 13–32.

Diaz-Guerrero, R. (1967). *Psychology of the Mexican.* Austin, TX: University of Texas Press.

Dimberg, U., & Ohman A. (1996). Behold the wrath: Psychophysiological responses to facial stimuli. *Motivation and Emotion, 20*, 149–182.

Doi, L. T. (1962). Amae. A key concept for understanding Japanese personality structure. In: R. J. Smith & R. K. Beardsley (Eds), *Japanese Culture: Its Development and Characteristics.* Chicago, IL: Aldine.

Douglas, A. (1962). *Industrial Peacemaking.* New York, NY: Columbia University Press.

Dovidio, J. F., & Ellyson, S. L. (1985). Patterns of visual dominance behavior in humans. In: S. L. Ellyson & J. F. Dovidio (Eds), *Power, dominance, and non-verbal behavior* (pp. 129–149). New York: Springer-Verlag.

Drolet, A., & Morris, M. W. (2000). Rapport in conflict resolution: Accounting for how face-to-face contact fosters mutual cooperation in mixed motive conflicts. *Journal of Experimental and Social Psychology, 36*, 26–50.

Dunn, J. & Munn, P. (1985). Becoming a family member: Family conflict and the development of social understanding in the second year. *Child Development, 56*, 480–492.

Eibl-Eibesfeldt, I. (1989). *Human Ethology.* New York: Aldine de Gruyter Press.

Eisenberg, N., Fabes, R. A., Miller, P. A., Fultz, J., Shell, R., Mathy, R. M., & Reno, R. R. (1989). Relation of sympathy and distress to prosocial behavior: A multimethod study. *Journal of Personality and Social Psychology, 57*, 55–66.

Ekman, P. (1992). An argument for basic emotions. *Cognition and Emotion, 6*, 169–200.

Ekman, P., (1993). Facial expression and emotion. *American Psychologist, 48*, 384–392.

Esteves, F., Dimberg, U., & Ohman, A. (1994). Automatically elicited fear: Conditioned skin conductance responses to masked facial expressions. *Cognition and Emotion, 8*, 393–413.

Fernandez-Dols, J., & Ruiz-Belda, M. (1995). Are smiles signs of happiness? Gold medal winners at the Olympic games. *Journal of Personality and Social Psychology, 69*, 1113–1119.

Fisher, R., & Ury, W. (1991). *Getting to Yes* (2nd Edition). New York, NY: Penguin Books.

Fiske, A. P. (1990). Relativity within Moose culture: Four incommensurable models for social relationships. *Ethos, 18*, 180–204.

Forgas, J. P. (1992). Affect in social judgments and decisions: A multi-process model. In: M. P. Zanna (Ed.), *Advances in Experimental Social Psychology* (Vol. 25, pp. 227–275). San Diego: Academic Press.

Forgas, J. P. (1995). Mood and judgment: The affect infusion model (AIM). *Psychological Bulletin, 117*, 39–66.

Frank, R. H. (1988). *Passions Within Reason.* New York: Norton.

Freud, S. (1959). On beginning the treatment. In: E. Jones (Ed.) & J. Riviere (Trans.). Collected Papers, (Vol. 2, p. 360). New York: Basic. (Original work published 1913).

Fridlund, A. J. (1992). The behavioral ecology and sociality of human faces. In: M. S. Clark (Ed.), *Emotion.* Newbury Park, CA: Sage.

Friedman, R. A. (1994). *Front Stage, backstage.* Cambridge, MA: The MIT Press.

Frijda, N. (1986). *The Emotions.* Cambridge: Cambridge University Press.

Frijda, N. H., & Mesquita, B. (1994). The social roles and functions of emotions. In: S. Kitayama & H. Marcus (Ed.), *Emotion and Culture: Empirical Studies of Mutual Influenced.* (pp. 51–87). Washington, DC: American Psychological Association.

Gersick, C. (1988). Time and transition in work teams: Toward a new model of group development. *Academy of Management Journal, 31,* 9–41.

Goffman, E. (1959). *The Presentation of Self in Everyday Life.* Garden City, NY: Doubleday.

Goffman, E. (1967). *Interaction Ritual: Essays on Face-to-face Behavior.* Garden City, NY: Anchor.

Goldman (1994). The centrality of 'ningensei' to Japanese negotiations and interpersonal relationships: Implications for U.S.-Japanese communication. *International Journal of Intercultural Relations, 18,* 29–54.

Gulliver, P. H. (1979). *Disputes and Negotiations: A Cross-cultural Perspective.* New York, NY: Academic Press.

Haidt, J., & Keltner, D. (1999). Culture and facial expression: Open-ended methods find more expressions and a gradient of recognition. *Cognition and Emotion, 13,* 225–266.

Harford, T., & Solomon, L. (1967). 'Reformed sinner' and 'lapsed saint' strategies in the prisoner's dilemma game. *Journal of Conflict Resolution, 11,* 104–109.

Harford, T., & Solomon, L. (1969). Effects of a 'reformed sinner' and lapsed saint' strategy upon trust formation in paranoid and nonparanoid schizophrenic patients. *Journal of Abnormal Psychology, 74,* 498–504.

Harrigan, J. A., & Rosenthal, R. (1986). Empathy and rapport between physicians and patients. In: P. D. Blanck, R. Buck & R. Rosenthal (Eds), *Non-verbal Communication in the Clinical Context.* The Pennsylvania State University Press.

Hatfield & Rapson (1993). Love and the attachment process. In: J. Haviland & M. Lewis (Eds), *Handbook of Emotions.* (pp. 595–604). New York: Guilford Press.

Hayano, D. M. (1982). *Poker Faces.* Berkeley: University of California Press.

Hazan, C., & Shaver, P. (1987). Romantic love conceptualized as an attachment process. *Journal of Personality and Social Psychology, 52,* 511–524.

Hebb, D. O. (1949). *The Organization of Behavior: A Neuropsychological Theory.* New York: Wiley.

Hochschild, A. (1983). *The Managed Heart: Commercialization of Human Feelings.* Berkeley, CA: University of California Press.

Horney, K. (1945). *Our Inner Conflicts: A Constructive Theory of Neurosis.* New York, NY: Norton.

How Reed Lost the Reins of Citigroup to Sandy Weill (2000, April 14). *The Wall Street Journal,* p. A1, A8.

Hsu, F. L. K. (1985). The self in cross-cultural perspective. In: A. J. Marsella, G. De Vos & F. L. K. Hsu, *Culture and Self,* (pp. 24–55).

Isen, A. M. (1991). Positive affect as a factor in organizational behavior. In: B. M. Staw & L. L. Cummings (Eds), *Research in Organizational Behavior, 13.* Greenwich, CT: JAI Press.

Isen, A. M., & Levin, P. F. (1972). Effect of feeling good on helping: Cookies and kindness. *Journal of Personality and Social Psychology, 21*, 384–388.

Izard, C. E. (1977). *Human Emotions.* New York: Plenum Press.

Jackall, R. (1988). *Moral Mazes: The World of Corporate Managers.* Oxford: Oxford University Press.

Johnson, E. J., & Tversky, A. (1983). Affect, generalization, and the perception of risk. *Journal of Personality and Social Psychology, 45*, 20–31.

Johnson-Laird, P. N., & Oatley, K. (1992). Basic emotions, rationality, and folk theory. *Cognition and Emotion, 6*, 201–223.

Jones, E. E., & Pittman, T. S. (1982). Toward a general theory of strategic self-presentation. In: J. Suls (Ed.), *Psychological Perspective on the Self.* Hillsdale, NJ: Lawrence Erlbaum Associates.

Kahneman, D., Slovic, P., & Tversky, A. (1982). *Judgment under Uncertainty: Heuristics and Biases.* New York, NY: Cambridge University Press.

Keating, C. F. (1985). Human dominance signals: The primate in us. In: S. L. Ellyson & J. F. Dovidio (Eds), *Power, Dominance, and Nonverbal Behavior* (pp. 89–108). New York, NY: Springer-Verlag.

Kelley, H. H., & Thibaut, J. W. (1969). Group problem solving. In: G. Lindzey & E. Aronson (Eds), *Handbook of Social Psychology* (2nd Edition), Vol. IV. Reading, MA: Addison-Wesley.

Keltner, D. (1995). The signs of appeasement: Evidence for the distinct displays of embarrassment, amusement, and shame. *Journal of Personality and Social Psychology, 68*, 441–454.

Keltner, D. & Buswell, B. (1996). Evidence for the distinctness of embarrassment, shame, and guilt: A study of recalled antecedents and facial expressions of emotion. *Cognition and Emotion, 10*(2), 155–172.

Keltner, D., & Buswell, B. N. (1997). Embarrassment: Its distinct form and appeasement functions. *Psychological Bulletin, 122*, 250–270.

Keltner, D., & Ekman, P. (2000). Facial Expression of Emotion. In: M. Lewis & J. Haviland-Jones (Eds), *Handbook of Emotion* (pp. 236–249). New York, NY: Guilford Press.

Keltner, D., Ellsworth, P. C., & Edwards, K. (1993). Beyond simple pessimism: Effects of sadness and anger on social perception. *Journal of Personality and Social Psychology, 64*(5), 740–752.

Keltner, D., & Gross, J. J. (1999). Functional accounts of emotion. *Cognition and Emotion, 13*, 467–480.

Keltner, D., & Haidt, J. (1999). Social functions of emotions at multiple levels of analysis. *Cognition and Emotion, 13*, 505–522.

Keltner, D., & Kring, A. (1998). Emotion, social function, and psychopathology. *Review of General Psychology, 2*, 320–342.

Keltner, D., Locke, K. D., & Audrain, P. C. (1993). The influence of attributions on the relevance of negative emotions to personal satisfaction. *Personality and Social Psychology Bulletin, 19*, 21–29.

Keltner, D., Young, R., & Buswell, B. N. (1997). Appeasement in human emotion, social practice, and personality. *Aggressive Behavior, 23*, 359–374.

Kemper, T. D.(1993). Sociological models in the explanation of emotions. In: M. Lewis & J. M. Haviland (Eds), *The Handbook of Emotions* (pp. 41–51). New York: Guilford.

Kleinke, C. L., & Singer, D. A. (1979). Influence of gaze on compliance with demanding and conciliatory requests in a field setting. *Personality and Social Psychology Bulletin, 5,* 386–390.

Klinnert, M., Campos, J., Sorce, J., Emde, R., & Svejda, M. (1983). Emotions as behavior regulators: Social referencing in infants. In: R. Plutchik & H. Kellerman (Eds), *Emotion Theory, Research, and Experience: Vol. 2. Emotions in early development* (pp. 57–68). New York: Academic Press.

Knutson, B. (1996). Facial expressions of emotion influence interpersonal trait inferences. *Journal of Nonverbal Behavior, 20,* 165–182.

Kochan, T. A. (1980). *Collective Bargaining and Industrial Relations.* Homewood, Ill: Irwin.

Kolb, D. M. (1993). Her place at the table: Gender and negotiation. In: L. Hall (Ed.), *Negotiation: Strategies for Mutual Gain.* Sage Publications: Newbury Park.

Kramer, R. (1991). Intergroup relations and organizational dilemmas: The role of categorization processes. *Research in Organizational Behavior, 13,* 191–228.

Kramer, R. M., Newton, E., & Pommerenke, P. L. (1993). Self-enhancement biases and negotiator judgment: Effects of self-esteem and mood. *Organ. Behav. Human Decis. Process, 56,* 110–133.

Kramer, R. M., & Tyler T. R. (1996). *Trust in Organizations: Frontiers of Theory and Research.* Thousand Oaks, CA: Sage.

Kraut, R., & Johnston, R., (1979). Social and emotional messages of smiling: An ethological approach. *Journal of Personality and Social Psychology, 37,* 1539–1533.

Lax, D. A., & Sebenius, J. K, (1986). *The Manager as Negotiator.* New York, NY: The Free Press, a division of MacMillan, Inc.

Lazarus, R. S. (1991). *Emotion and Adaptation.* New York: Oxford University Press.

Lerner, J. S., & Keltner, D. (2000). Beyond valence: Toward a model of emotion specific influences on judgment and choice. *Cognition and Emotion, 14,* 473–493.

Levenson, R. W., & Gottman, J. M. (1983). Marital Interaction: Physiological linkage and affective exchange. *Journal of Personality and Social Psychology, 45,* 587–597.

Levenson, R. W., Ekman, P., & Friesen, W. V. (1990). Voluntary facial action generates emotion-specific autonomic nervous system activity. *Psychophysiology, 27,* 363–384.

Lewicki, R. J., Hiam, A., & Olander, K. W. (1996). *Think before you speak: The complete guide to strategic negotiation.* New York, NY: John Wiley & Sons Inc.

Lewicki, R. J., & Stark, N. (1996). What is ethically appropriate in negotiations: An empirical examination of bargaining tactics. *Soc. Just. Res., 9,* 69–95.

Lewin, K. (1951). *Field theory in social science.* New York, NY: Harper and Row.

Lewis, S., & Fry, W. (1977). Effects of visual access and orientation on the discovery of integrative bargaining alternatives. *Organizational Behavior and Human Decision Processes, 20,* 75–92.

Lim, S. G.-S., & Murningham, J. K. (1994). Phases, deadliness, and the bargaining process. *Organizational Behavior and Human Decision Processes, 58,* 53–171.

Lindsley, S. L., & Braithwaite, C. A. (1996). You should 'wear a mask': Facework norms in cultural and intercultural conflict in Maquiladoras. *International Journal of Intercultural Relations, 20*(2), 199–225.

Lutz, C., & White, G. (1986). The anthropology of emotions. *Annual Review of Anthropology, 15,* 405–436.

Mandler, G. (1984). *Mind and Body: Psychology of Emotion and Stress.* New York: W. W. Norton.

March, J. G., & Simon, H. A. (1958). *Organizations.* New York, NY: John Wiley.

March, R. M. (1988). *The Japanese Negotiator: Subtlety and Strategy beyond Western Logic*. New York, NY: Kodansha International.

Markus, H. R., Kitayama, S., & Heiman, R. J. (1997). Culture and 'basic' psychological principles. In: E. T. Higgins & A. W. Kruglanski (Eds), *Social Psychology: Handbook of Basic Principles* (pp. 857–913). New York, NY: Guilford Press.

McDougal, W. (1920). *An Introduction to Social Psychology* (14th ed.). Barnes and Noble: New York.

Miller, R. S., & Leary, M. R. (1992). Social sources and interactive functions of emotion: The case of embarrassment. In: M. Clark (Ed.), *Emotion and social Behavior* (pp. 202–221). Beverly Hills, CA: Sage.

Mineka, S., & Cook, M. (1993). Mechanisms involved in the observational conditioning of fear. *Journal of Experimental Psychology: General, 122,* 23–38.

Moore, D. A., Kurtzberg, T. R., Thompson, L. L., & Morris, M. W. (1999). Long and short routes to success in electronically-mediated negotiations: Group affiliations and good vibrations. *Organizational Behavior and Human Decision Processes, 77,* 22–43.

Morley, I. E., & Stephenson, G. (1977), *The Social Psychology of Bargaining*. London: George Allen & Unwin.

Morrill, C. (1995). *The Executive Way: Conflict Management in Corporations*. Chicago, IL: The University of Chicago Press.

Morris, M. W., & Drolet, A. L. (1999). Rapport and dominance dynamics in the resolution of multiple-issue conflicts by expert and novice negotiators. Unpublished manuscript, Stanford Graduate School of Business.

Morris, M. W., & Keltner, D. (1998). Unpublished data.

Morris, M. W., Leung, K., Ames, D., & Lickel, B. (1999). Views from Inside and Outside: Integrating Emic and Etic Insights about Culture and Justice Judgments. *The Academy of Management Review, 24,* 781–796.

Morris, M. W., Nadler, J., Kurtzberg, T., & Thompson, L. (2000). Schmooze or lose: Social friction and lubrication in e-mail negotiations. Stanford University, GSB Research Paper no. 1639.

Neale, R. E., & Northcraft, G. B. (1991). Behavioral negotiation theory: A framework for conceptualizing dyadic bargaining. In: L. Cummings & B. Staw (Eds), *Research in Organizational Behavior, 13* (pp. 147–190). Greenwich, CT: JAI Press.

Neale, M. A., & Bazerman, M. H. (1991). The role of perspective taking ability in negotiating under different forms of arbitration. *Industrial and Labor Relations Review, 36,* 378–388.

Nesse, R. (1990). Evolutionary explanations of emotions. *Human Nature, 1,* 261–289.

Nisbett, R. E., & Ross, L. (1980). *Human inference: Strategies and shortcomings of social judgment*. Englewood Cliffs, NJ: Prentice-Hall.

Northcraft G. G., & Neale, M. A. (1987). Expert, amateurs, and real estate: An anchoring-and-adjustment perspective on property pricing decisions. *Organ. Behav. Human Decis. Process., 39,* 228–241.

Oliver, R. L. (1993). Cognitive, affective, and attribute bases of the satisfaction response. *Journal of Consumer Research, 20,* 418–430.

Peters, E. (1952). *Conciliation in Action*. New London, CT: National Foremen's Institute.

Pilisuck, M., & Rapoport, A. (1964). A non-zero-sum game model of some disarmament problems. In: W. Isard, & J. Walpert (Eds), *Peace Research Society (International) Papers,* 1, pp. 57–78.

Pillutla, M. M., & Murnighan, J. K. (1996). Unfairness, anger and spite: Emotional rejections of ultimatum offers. *Organizational Behavior & Human Decision Processes, 68,* 208–224.

Plutchik, R. (1980). *Emotion: A Psychobioevolutionary Synthesis*. New York: Harper & Row.

Poole, M. S., Shannon, D. L. & DeSanctis, G. (1992), Communication media and negotiation processes. In: L. L. Putnam & M. E. Rolloff (Eds), *Communication and Negotiation, Sage Annual Reviews of Communication Research* (pp. 46–66). Sage Publications.

Provine, R. R. (1993). Laughter punctuates speech: Linguistic, social, and gender contexts of laughter. *Ethology, 95*, 291–298.

Pruitt, D. G., & Rubin, J. Z. (1986). *Social Conflict: Escalation, Stalemate, and Settlement*. New York: Random House.

Pye, L. (1982). *Chinese Commercial Negotiating Style*. Cambridge, MA: Oelgeschlager Gunn, & Hain.

Rafaeli, A., & Sutton, R. I. (1989). The expression of emotion in organizational life. In: L. L. Cummings & B. M. Staw (Eds), *Research in Organizational Behavior, 11* (pp. 1–42). Greenwich, CT: JAI Press.

Rafaeli, A., & Sutton, R. I. (1991). Emotional contrast strategies as means of social influence: Lessons from criminal interrogators and bill collectors. *Academy of Management Journal, 34*, 749–775.

Raiffa, H. (1982). *The Art and Science of Negotiation*. Cambridge, MA: Belknap Press.

Rosaldo, M. (1984). Toward an anthropology of self and feeling. In: R. Shweder & R. LeVine (Ed.), *Culture Theory*. Cambridge: Cambridge University Press.

Rosci, F. (1981). Grin and sell it. *Successful Meetings*, June, 106–107.

Rubin, J. Z. & Brown, B. R. (1975). *The Social Psychology of Bargaining and Negotiation*. London: Academic Press.

Sampson, E. E. (1977). Psychology and the American ideal. *Journal of Personality and Social Psychology, 35*, 767–782.

Sanchez-Burks, J. Nisbett, R. E., & Ybarra, O. (1998). Relational schemas, cultural styles, and prejudice against outgroups. Unpublished manuscript. Universoty of Michigan, Pyschology Department.

Schelling, (1960), *The Strategy of Conflict*, Oxford University Press.

Scherer, K. R. (1986). Vocal affect expression: A review and a model for future research. *Psychological Bulletin, 99*, 143–165.

Schwarz, N. (1990). Feelings as information: Informational and motivational functions of affective states. In: E. T. Higgins & R. M. Sorrentino (Eds), *Handbook of motivation and cognition*, Vol. 2 (pp. 527–561). New York: Guilford Press.

Schwarz, N. N., & Clore, G. L. (1993). The use of mood as information. In: P. Ekman & R. J. Davidson (Eds), *The Nature of Emotion: Fundamental Questions*. New York: Oxford Press.

Shaver, P., Schwartz, J., Kirson, D., & O'Connor, C. (1987). Emotion knowledge: Further exploration of a prototype approach. *Journal of Personality and Social Psychology, 52*, 1061–1086.

Skinner, B. F. (1948). *Walden Two*. Englewood Cliffs, NJ: Prentice Hall.

Smith, C., & Ellsworth, P (1985). Patterns of cognitive appraisal in emotion. *Journal of Personality and Social Psychology, 48*, 48, 813–838.

Staw, B., Bell, N., & Clausen, J. (1986). The dispositional approach to job attitudes: A lifetime longitudinal test. *Administrative Science Quarterly, 31*, 56–77.

Staw, B. M., Sutton, R. I., & Pelled, L. H. (1994). Employee positive emotion and favorable outcomes at the workplace. *Organziation Science, 5*(1), 51–71.

Stevens, C. M. (1963). *Strategy and Collective Bargaining*. New York: McGraw-Hill.

Sutton, R. I., & Callahan, A. L. (1987). The stigma of bankruptcy: Spoiled organizational image and its management. *Academy of Management Journal, 30,* 405–436.

Symons, D. (1990). Adaptiveness and adaptation. *Ethology and Sociobiology, 11,* 427–444.

Thompson, L. (1990). Negotiation: Empirical evidence and theoretical issues. *Psychological Bulletin, 108,* 515–532.

Thompson, L., Valley, K. L., & Kramer, R. M. (1995). The bittersweet feeling of success: An examination of social perception in negotiation. *Journal of Experimental Social Psychology, 31,* 467–492.

Tickle-Degnen, L. & Rosenthal, R. (1990). The nature of rapport and Its non-verbal correlates. *Psychological Inquiry, 1*(4), 285–293.

Tidd, K. L., & Lockard, J. S. (1978). Monetary significance of the affiliative smile: A case for reciprocal altruism. *Bulletin of the Psychonomic Society, 11,* 344–346.

Tiedens, L. Z. (in press). Anger and advancement versus sadness and subjugation: The effects of negative emotion expressions on social status conferral. *Journal of Personality and Social Psychology.*

Tiedens, L. Z., Ellsworth, P. C., & Mesquita, B. (2000). Stereotypes about sentiments and status: Emotional expectations for high and low status group members. *Personality and Social Psychology Bulletin, 26,* 560–575.

Tooby, J., & Cosmides, L. (1990). The past explains the present: Emotional adaptations and the structure of ancestral environments. *Ethology and Sociobiology, 11,* 375–424.

Triandis, H. C., Marin, G., Lisansky, J., & Betancourt, H. (1984). Simpatia as a cultural script of Hispanics. *Journal of Personality and Social Psychology, 47*(6), 1363–1375.

Trivers, R. L. (1971). The evolution of reciprocal altruism. *Quarterly Review of Biology, 46,* 35–57.

Tronick, E. Z. (1989). Emotions and emotional communication in infants. *American Psychologist, 44,* 112–119.

Tversky, A., & Kahneman, D. (1974). Judgment under uncertainty: Heuristics and biases. *Science, 185,* 1124–1131.

Ury, W. M. (1993). *Getting Past No.* New York: Bantam Books.

Van Maanen, J., & Kunda, G. (1989). 'Real Feelings': Emotional Expression and Organizational Culture. In: L. Cummings & B. Staw (Eds), *Research in Organizational Behavior* (vol. 11, pp. 43–103). Greenwich, CT: JAI Press.

Valley K. L., & Keros, A. T. (1999). It takes two: interactively determined bargaining scripts. Unpublished research paper, Harvard Business School, Boston, MA.

Valley, K. L., Moag, J., & Bazerman, M. H. (1998). A matter of trust: Effects of communication on the efficiency and distribution of outcomes. *J. Econ. Behav. Organ., 34,* 211–238.

Walton, R. E., & McKersie, R. B. (1965). *A Behavioral Theory of Labor Negotiations: An Analysis of a Social Interaction System.* New York, NY: McGraw-Hill.

Watson, D., Clark, L. A., & Tellegen, A. (1988). Development and validation of brief measures of positive and negative affect: The PANAS Scales. *Journal of Personality and Social Psychology, 54*(6), 1063–1070.

Whyte, W. F. (1946). *Human Relations in the Restaurant Industry.* New York, NY: McGraw-Hill Book.

Wolfe, T. (1999a). *A Man in Full.* New York: Bantam Books.

Wolfe, T. (1999b). Personal communication, Stanford University, March.

CONTAGIOUS JUSTICE: EXPLORING THE SOCIAL CONSTRUCTION OF JUSTICE IN ORGANIZATIONS

Peter Degoey

ABSTRACT

This chapter addresses one of the most enduring questions underlying the justice literature: How do organizational actors know what is just or fair? *It notes that despite increasingly frequent theoretical and empirical efforts to explore the 'social side' of justice in organizations, the literature continues to be dominated by a highly individualistic perspective on the justice judgment process. In contrast, the chapter develops the premise that the often ambiguous and emotionally charged nature of justice-related events compels organizational actors to engage in social 'talk' and arrive at a shared, socially constructed interpretation of justice. Using the concept of social contagion as a guide, I trace the developments of these shared justice beliefs at several levels of analysis and suggest that they can instigate a qualitative change in how organizational actors think and feel about justice. I further present arguments showing that storytelling and talk about reputations can enable organizational populations to maintain and strengthen their shared justice interpretations over time, and examine how these shared interpretations may become expressed at a broader organizational level in justice-related actions such as collective protests, group-based impression management efforts, and group-based antisocial behaviors. Finally, I outline implications of a contagion approach to justice for future research and organizational development efforts.*

Research in Organizational Behaviour, Volume 22, pages 51–102.

INTRODUCTION

During the past three or four decades, justice theorists and researchers have made many significant contributions to our understanding of organizational behavior. An expansive track record of research detailing that people care about fair treatment in the workplace and that justice perceptions influence a wide variety of attitudes and behaviors facilitated this development (for summaries, see Folger & Cropanzano, 1998; Sheppard, Lewicki & Minton, 1992). In a relatively recent monograph however, Greenberg (1993) characterized most of the extant research as merely "celebrating the existence of the procedural [and distributive] justice concept and joyously discovering its involvement in various aspects of organizational life" (p. 136). Greenberg warned that the justice field has entered a critical era of 'intellectual adolescence', in which a number of enduring questions need to be resolved. One of the most enduring of these questions is the focus of this chapter: *How do organizational actors know what is just or fair?*

Although many studies and theoretical frameworks have addressed this topic over the years, the literature to date has reflected a tension between two fundamental ideas. On the one hand, the bulk of the literature has viewed the processes by which people develop perceptions and judgments about justice from a highly individualistic perspective. Most existing frameworks have simply been built on the assumption that organizational actors conceive of justice by personally matching their perceptions of an organizational event with some standard of what is just or fair to arrive at a personal judgment. Such an individualistic perspective was often grounded in the belief that people's justice opinions are based on a set of universally recognized justice criteria or standards, and hence that the study of individuals could reveal which criteria or standards might exist. On the other hand, justice scholars have long expressed dissatisfaction with this individualistic perspective, and instead have stressed that the field should reflect a more socially oriented paradigm. In the early 1980s, for instance, Deutsch (1983) commented on the state of the literature at the time as:

> The approach to 'justice' has been too psychological and not enough social psychological; that is, it focused on the individual rather than upon the social interaction in which 'justice' emerges (p. 312).

Deutsch's remarks were primarily directed at equity theory (Adams, 1965), the dominant justice paradigm of the 1960s and 1970s. Though equity theory gave tribute to the role of interpersonal comparisons in people's fairness evaluations, its emphasis on intrapsychic calculations of work-related inputs and rewards made the theory indeed focused on the individual. Since the 1970s, justice researchers have developed more social context sensitive approaches. Deutsch's own work demonstrated that group goals and norms can lead people to consider other distributive justice standards than equity, such as equality and need (Deutsch, 1975, 1985). Procedural justice researchers further illustrated that, among other factors, dignified treatment by organizational authorities can be weighted in judgments about fairness (Lind & Tyler, 1988; Tyler & Lind, 1992). Researchers also examined justice from an impression management angle, suggesting that managers can influence employee assessments of justice by providing explanations and justifications for a situation (Bies, 1987; Greenberg, 1990).

Despite an increased emphasis on the social context in which judgments of justice arise, the individualistic tenure of the literature has largely persisted. While it is now perhaps more commonplace to examine the direct influences of social context cues on perceptions of a situation, it is still assumed that individuals personally weigh the relevance of these cues for their personal judgments. One aspect of the 'social side' of justice that has yet to be fully recognized is the fact that the development of a justice judgment can also be a form of action in which organizational actors collectively engage. Many organizational events about which such judgments are formed – such as layoffs, wage negotiations, and performance appraisals – are highly complex and ambiguous occurrences, and it is probable that employees exchange opinions and perceptions of the events with their peers in search of finding some consensus on whether a justice or injustice has occurred (e.g. Festinger, 1954). Such shared interpretative processes are made especially likely because people's experiences with these situations tend to be emotionally charged and rife with feelings of potential threat or harm. One can expect that these conditions trigger an effort in which people seek social support for their emotional reactions and worries about fairness (e.g. Schachter, 1959). And perhaps most importantly, justice concerns often emerge in situations that involve conflicting views of management and employees about what constitutes appropriate or 'deserved' organizational treatment. The development of shared interpretations regarding fair or unfair organizational practices may well serve as one of the bases for how various groups of employees cope and react to these conflicts.

Taken together, these observations emphasize that people's judgments about justice are best viewed as 'socially constructed realities'. Although it is increasingly common to find statements in the literature suggesting that justice is such a social phenomenon (e.g. Bies, 1987; Greenberg, 1990; Lind, Kray & Thompson, 1998; Lind & Tyler, 1988; Tyler & Smith, 1998; see also Weick, 1969), no framework currently exists that outlines the social processes by which shared opinions about justice emerge in organizational populations. Towards developing such a framework in this chapter, I break with the individualistic perspective of the extant literature and adopt an alternative metaphor – that of *social contagion* – as a guide. The contagion concept suggests that thoughts and feelings about justice can be communicated from one individual to another, and ultimately spread and be maintained across entire networks or groups. Just as epidemiologists study the social transaction patterns that may lead to the spread of a virus, I am drawing attention to the importance of examining the mechanisms by which ongoing social discourse, conducted for instance in the hallways and lunchrooms of organizations, serves as a critical source of people's justice opinions. How these contagious processes alter people's responses to justice-related events, and how such responses can become manifested at the individual, group, and organizational levels of analysis, is central to the exploration of the concept.

The chapter is divided into four sections. In the first section, I briefly provide some background on the contagion concept and then examine various social mechanisms by which cognitions and emotions about a justice-related event can become shared among organizational actors. I also discuss several conditions that may determine whether these cognitions and emotions fall on deaf ears or cascade throughout a group or network. In the second section, I examine how social opinions about justice can be maintained within groups across situations, focusing in particular on the role of organizational stories and reputations in the contagion process. The third section takes a more macro-oriented view and explores the organizational consequences of contagious justice. In this section, I discuss how the development of a group consensus on justice may give rise to such collective actions as striving to establish a dominant justice view in an organization, attempting to institutionalize a group's justice claims in organizational rules and procedures, or engaging in group-sanctioned antisocial behaviors. I conclude by stating some of the implications of a contagion approach for future research and organizational practice.

JUSTICE AS A CONTAGIOUS PROCESS

This chapter arises from the observation that 'talk' about justice is a ubiquitous social phenomenon, and that such talk often may affect how people think and feel about an event or situation. The observation is not an entirely new one. The recognition, for instance, that people frequently express claims about justice to strategically advance their goals and beliefs has been part of the literature for a long time (e.g. Walster, Walster & Berscheid, 1978; Greenberg & Cohen,

1982). In part, this recognition has recently been applied to understand how managers can attempt to convey impressions of fairness in organizations. But at a more fundamental level, talk about justice may also serve as a shared sense-making mechanism. In societal settings for instance, public discourse about the fairness of policies on such issues as abortion or affirmative action not only occurs to convince others of one's point of view, but also to collectively define the meaning of these complex and emotionally charged issues. Quite similarly, most of us are still familiar with the heated discussions that took place in response to the O. J. Simpson and Rodney King trials. Although personal perceptions or strategic intentions may have colored people's views, these discussions undoubtedly helped shape their fairness judgments of the trials. Such shared interpretative processes about justice are also likely to occur in day-to-day organizational contexts, yet existing research has given little attention to examining them.

The concept of social contagion serves as a useful metaphor (Morgan, 1980) or 'guiding idea' (McGuire, 1983) for broadening our understanding of these processes in several ways. First, by suggesting a loose parallel to the spread of a virus through a population, the concept highlights that people's perspectives on justice can, in part, be based on social interaction and exposure to others' thoughts and feelings. By drawing attention to the largely unintended ways in which organizational actors may influence each other when interpreting a situation, the concept also provides the basis for a framework that is distinct from models which address more goal-driven social influence processes (e.g. models of impression management, persuasion, etc.). As I have already indicated, a number of situational characteristics exist that may compel individuals to engage in social discourse about justice. Thus, developing an understanding of these characteristics, and of the patterns by which justice-related thoughts and feelings are communicated in organizational populations, becomes an important topic for investigation.

Second, the core imagery of the contagion concept suggests that the simple act of conversing about justice can instigate a significant shift in people's attitudes and behaviors. Akin to how the spread of a virus can manifest itself in a qualitatively different disease, publicly expressing one's thoughts and feelings about a potential justice or injustice (and especially, hearing others express similar thoughts and feelings) may have pervasive consequences. Such acts may, for example, increase people's confidence in and commitment to a particular point of view on a situation. As will be explored in the pages that follow, these acts may also enable groups of individuals to maintain their justice views across multiple situations, or even provide the basis for strategic collective responses to situations. None of this, of course, is to imply that a perfect match exists between the imagery of the contagion concept and the social construction of justice. But the metaphor does express the fundamental idea underlying the approach developed here; that understanding the social dynamics of the justice evaluation process can provide a substantially different perspective on justice-related outcomes in organizations than that provided by most of the extant research and theory.

Though the contagion concept has not been used before in justice research, it has been successfully applied to many other social phenomena. Historically for example, contagion has been used to explain such exceptional occurrences as the sudden spread of panics, psychogenic illnesses, and rioting behaviors (e.g. Le Bon, 1895/1903; Kerckhoff & Back, 1968; Wheeler, 1966; see Levy & Nail, 1993 for a review). In these cases, it was often postulated that an extreme loss of self-awareness and inhibition in social settings was a necessary condition for contagion to occur (see Turner, 1964). More recent applications have not invoked such strong postulates. Organizational network researchers, for instance, have referred to contagion (see Burt, 1982, 1987) when examining people's tendencies to develop similar moods (Barsade, 1994), feelings of job satisfaction (Krackhardt & Porter, 1985), levels of organizational commitment (Hartman & Johnson, 1989), attributions of leadership (Meindl, 1990, 1993), claims about job stress (Barley & Knight, 1992), and perceptions of work conditions (Ibarra & Andrews, 1993) in interpersonal networks.[1] Although the contagion approach I develop here focuses primarily on the role of social discourse in shaping people's perceptions and attitudes, rather than on the role of network characteristics in allowing these perceptions and attitudes to become similar, it shares with these recent applications the view that the contagion concept is useful for understanding naturally occurring organizational phenomena.

To start developing the approach, I begin with an examination of the microprocesses by which individuals may choose to converse about justice, noting how these conversations can shape their thoughts and feelings into a shared perspective on their situation. In this section of the chapter, I follow the practice common in the justice literature of examining people's reactions to a single organizational event (e.g. a layoff or performance appraisal). That is, for the time being, I ignore the historical context in which shared judgments of justice may become maintained across situations, and instead focus on uncovering the social mechanisms by which people exchange their cognitions and emotions about a particular event.

To distinguish among several dimensions of the contagion process, I discuss the spread of justice-related cognitions and emotions separately. *Cognitive contagion of justice* refers to processes by which the communication of information or opinions about an event influences the development of similar justice judgments among organizational members. *Emotional contagion of justice* refers to processes by which a person's or group's emotional reactions to a justice-related event influence, and are influenced by, the emotions or opinions of others. I conclude this section with a discussion of several conditions that may promote or impede justice contagion in organizations.

Cognitive Contagion of Justice

Some of the most obvious starting points for examining the contagion of justice are the cognitive processes by which organizational actors judge the fairness of an event. Cognitive processes have by far been the dominant focus of the justice literature to date, and research efforts have particularly focused on identifying the various distributive and procedural standards or criteria on which people's justice assessments can be based. As the literature has progressed over the years however, it has become increasingly evident that individually evaluating whether a justice or injustice has occurred is, under many circumstances, a difficult endeavor. Not only are the types of organizational events that are commonly subject to justice considerations highly complex in nature, but organizational actors also tend to have many justice criteria at their disposal by which the events can be evaluated.

For instance, since Adams' (1965) first investigations of the role of the criterion of equity in judging the fairness of resource distributions over 35 years ago, criticisms of equity research have led to the discovery of other distributive criteria, such as equality and need (Deutsch, 1975, 1985). Gradually, the list of criteria that people potentially could use to assess distributive justice has proliferated to seventeen (Reis, 1984, 1987). Research on procedural justice has reflected similar developments. Most initial studies in this stream of work have focused on Thibaut & Walker's (1975) criterion of 'process control' or 'voice', the opportunity to express one's opinions to a decision-maker. But Leventhal (1976, 1980) identified at least seven structural components of procedures (e.g. selection of decision-making agents) and six justice rules (e.g. consistency, ethicality) that in various combinations can impact people's evaluations of justice. Recent research has also shown that several factors reflecting the interpersonal manner in which managers treat employees (e.g. treatment with dignity and respect) play a significant role (Bies & Moag, 1986; see Lind & Tyler, 1988; Tyler & Lind, 1992 for reviews).

As the literature steadily documented this proliferation of potential determinants of people's justice opinions, theorists proposed several psychological mechanisms that can guide individuals in the justice judgment process.

For instance, I have already referred to some of the more 'social context-sensitive' approaches to justice, according to which group goals and norms (Deutsch, 1975, 1985) and social identities (Lind & Tyler, 1988; Tyler & Degoey, 1995) can determine which justice criteria are most salient or relevant to individuals. Some theorists have also argued that individuals use fairness as a heuristic, applying some pre-conceived 'script' of what constitutes a fair process or outcome when a situation is too complex to evaluate (e.g. Van den Bos, Lind, Vermunt & Wilke, 1997; Lind, Kulik, Ambrose & de Vera Park, 1993; Messick, 1993). A third approach has been to examine how explanations and justifications provided by an organizational authority can guide people's justice judgments (Bies, 1987; Greenberg, 1990). A contagion approach to justice is compatible with all these propositions, but emphasizes that organizational actors engage in social discourse with their peers to make sense of an event.

The notion that people rely on others to help define 'reality' in ambiguous circumstances has long been a core tenet in social psychology (Ash, 1956; Deutsch & Gerard, 1955, Festinger, 1954; Sherif, 1935; Weick, 1969), a notion that was given renewed attention in organizational research by Salancik & Pfeffer (1977, 1978) under the label of social information processing. Festinger's (1954) social comparison theory still provides some of the most eloquent insights into these processes. Festinger argued that people prefer to base their judgments about a situation on objective, non-social standards, but when such standards are unavailable or ambiguous, seek out social information from others that can help them arrive at the most 'appropriate' or 'accurate' interpretation of the situation. Although Festinger's propositions have often been operationalized as processes by which individuals desire to obtain comparative information *about* the perceptions and opinions of others, he originally developed the theory as a social one, proposing that they solicit information *from* others; that is, people are motivated to converse about the meaning of a situation. Thus, a contagion perspective on justice suggests that organizational actors talk to their peers and rely on each other to, for example, point out which justice criteria are most appropriate for evaluating an event at hand; make salient which dimensions or characteristics of the event are more critical than others for an evaluation of justice; or furnish information about each other's interpretations of these characteristics.

Of course, as Festinger (1954) has pointed out, not all people are considered equally important in providing information about an event, nor does unanimity in viewpoints about a situation always develop. Certain reference groups (Merton & Kitt, 1950) may serve as more important sources of information, and their opinions may be considered to be more relevant or trustworthy than those of other groups (Cook, 1975). At times, individuals may also disagree with the opinions of others, or prefer to rely on their personal assessments of an event. At a later point in this chapter, I will discuss some of the factors that may lead people to seek out social information from one individual or group over another, and consider some of the conditions that strengthen the likelihood that a consensus on justice develop between them. But at this point it is important to note that, in the process of conversing about justice, common social psychological dynamics (see Hackman, 1992) can affect the final form that people's consensual justice judgments might take. For instance, due to pressures towards uniformity within groups, certain viewpoints may acquire dominance and one or a few aspects of an organizational event may become the primary target of people's justice evaluations. Conversations with others may also result in increased confidence in the validity of and commitment to a particular point of view; and people's perspectives may become polarized as a result of public discussion, so that each person becomes more extreme in his or her fairness opinions of an event. As contagious processes instigate these changes in people's perspectives on justice, such changes can also become reflected in their attitudes and behaviors.

Although justice researchers have generally paid little attention to the social dynamics of the justice judgment process, there have been several studies that provide some support for a contagion perspective. A recent experiment by Brockner et al. (1997; see also Brockner & Wiesenfeld, 1993) examined how subjects reacted to the 'layoff' of another subject when the layoff survivors allegedly could communicate their thoughts about the layoff to one another. In reality, subjects were provided with a message prepared by the experimenters. Subjects who received a message that indicated a negative reaction to the layoff (including statements that the layoff was unfair) were subsequently less committed to their tasks and performed worse on those tasks than subjects who were led to believe that their co-workers reacted positively. Brockner and colleagues did not assess how their subjects' fairness judgments were influenced by the co-workers' messages, but their study does suggest that justice-related information provided by others can alter people's attitudes and behaviors in a given situation.

A set of experiments conducted by Folger, Rosenfield, Grove & Corkran in the late 1970s (1979; see also Greenberg & Folger, 1983) approximates the contagion perspective more closely. Folger et al. noted that although numerous studies since Thibaut & Walker's initial research have shown that opportunities for expressing voice have a strong positive effect on people's procedural justice evaluations, at least one study (Thibaut, Friedland & Walker, 1974) has found the opposite effect; expressing voice led to lower satisfaction with a procedure.

Folger suggested that the effect occurred because, in this particular study, the experimental subjects were both given the opportunity to express their opinions and were made aware of the disapproving opinions of others. Thus, Folger designed a set of experiments in which he manipulated these factors independently. In these studies, the voice effect was not evident when subjects were told that a note, allegedly written by a fellow subject, suggested that the outcome of a resource allocation was inequitable. When no information about the fellow subject's opinions was provided, or when the information indicated that the fellow subject felt the outcome was equitable, the voice effect was again found.

Two experimental studies have also examined group polarization effects in regards to justice. Greenberg (1979) examined whether subjects differed in their allocations of pay in hypothetical scenarios and their distributive justice judgments following group discussion. Greenberg found that subjects made more extreme allocation decisions and had greater confidence in the fairness of their decisions following group discussion than individual allocators did. More recently, Lind, Kray & Thompson (1998) found roughly similar effects in regards to procedural justice. In this study, a confederate supervisor denied voice to either one or all three subjects in a team. Subjects rated the procedural fairness of the supervisor lower when they were made aware that one of their team members had been denied voice, even though they themselves had been given consideration of voice. Not surprisingly, subjects rated the supervisor's procedural fairness even lower when all three team members had been denied voice. Group discussion led to more extreme ratings of unfairness, and this polarization effect was retained to some extent in post-discussion individual ratings.

Unfortunately, the studies described above were all conducted in highly controlled experimental conditions, and they therefore provide little insight into the contagion of justice in real-world organizational settings. The most convincing, yet indirect support in this regard can be drawn from research stimulated by Salancik & Pfeffer's (1977, 1978) social information processing model of job attitudes. Partially based on Festinger's contributions, Salancik and Pfeffer proposed that job attitudes are shaped as much by the social context in which work is performed as by objective job characteristics. Many studies have indeed found that social cues such as the opinions of co-workers have an equal or greater influence on people's job attitudes than work conditions (see Zalesny & Ford, 1990, for a review). Although this research literature has often operationalized social cues by assessing or providing information about group norms, a few studies have also examined how job attitudes converge through communication within interpersonal networks (e.g. Ibarra & Andrews, 1993;

Krackhardt & Porter, 1985). These studies provide important insights into the likelihood that justice is contagious. Simply put, if job attitudes are susceptible to social cues, then so might be judgments about justice. It can be argued that issues which are subject to justice considerations – such as organizational policies, resource allocations, and managerial conduct – are in many cases more ambiguous and less frequently encountered than people's daily experiences with their jobs. Hence, organizational justice judgments may well be more susceptible to social influence effects than are job attitudes.

Emotional Contagion of Justice

So far, I have primarily addressed how the communication of knowledge or opinions between organizational members can influence their judgments about justice. Another, potentially potent source of such judgments is the spread of people's emotional reactions to justice-related events. Although emotions are an inherent part of many conceptualizations of justice, to date they have mostly been treated as a by-product of cognitive evaluations (e.g. feelings of resentment or dissatisfaction derived from evaluations of an outcome or procedure). In recent years however, a considerable amount of evidence has been generated showing that emotions directly influence people's perceptions and behaviors (see Isen & Baron, 1991). Moreover, a number of studies have demonstrated that emotions are subject to contagion effects (Barsade, 1994; see Hatfield, Cacioppo & Rapson, 1992, 1994; Sullins, 1991). Therefore, before discussing the role of emotional contagion in the formation of people's justice judgments, I briefly review some arguments on the relationship between emotions and cognitions about justice.

Justice and emotion
Justice theorists have long posited that perceptions of justice – and particularly, injustice – are intimately linked to emotions. According to Adams (1965), for instance, experiencing underpayment inequity leads to anger, whereas experiencing overpayment inequity results in guilt. Relative deprivation theorists (e.g. Crosby, 1976; Folger, 1986, 1987) have also associated people's sense of injustice regarding disparities in treatment they receive with such emotional experiences as feelings of resentment, outrage, and indignation. Cahn (1949) has described this proposed association in rather colorful language:

> [The sense of injustice is] the sympathetic reaction of outrage, horror, shock, resentment, and anger, those affections of the viscera and abnormal secretions of the adrenals that prepare the human animal to resist attack. Nature has thus equipped all men to regard injustice to another as personal aggression (cited in Bies, 1987, p. 24).

While direct empirical evidence of the emotional qualities of justice has historically been scarce recent studies have somewhat reversed this tendency. Bies & Trip (1996), for instance, have examined people's feelings of outrage that accompanied suspicions of unfair treatment in organizations and found that such feelings were associated with intentions to take revengeful actions against the perpetrator of the treatment. Recent studies on relative deprivation have also demonstrated that affective measures of relative deprivation are more closely related to people's willingness to engage in collective protests than are cognitive measures (Dube & Guimond, 1986; Olson & Hafer, 1994). Support for the suggestion that emotions and injustice are closely linked was furthermore found in a study of people's prototypical emotional experiences: over 95% of respondents' descriptions of situations involving anger included judgments about illegitimate and unjust treatment (Shaver, Schwartz, Kirson & O'Conner, 1989). A similar study (Mikula, Scherer & Athensteadt, 1998) found that, in addition to anger, events perceived as unjust are accompanied by disgust, sadness, and fear. Conversely, a number of studies reported by Tyler (e.g. Tyler, 1994) have shown that fair treatment is consistently linked to feeling pleased and satisfied.

Despite the re-emerging recognition that emotions play a significant role in people's fairness experiences, the literature has yet to address one important issue: namely, the causal direction of the justice-emotion link. To date, researchers have generally depicted the causal sequence as flowing from cognitions to emotional experiences – that is, from judgments that a situation is unfair to feelings of anger or resentment. However, in line with a growing body of research on the effects of emotional states on cognitive processes (see Isen & Baron, 1991; Sinclair & Mark, 1992 for reviews), some emotion researchers (e.g. Scher & Heise, 1993) have argued that emotional reactions to events are most likely to *precipitate* judgments about justice. According to this line of reasoning, an event first triggers an emotion, which in turn sets off a cognitive search for its meaning in which people construct a justice interpretation that is consistent with their initial feelings.

There is now considerable evidence that affective reactions to situations (including events that are not justice-related) can occur quickly and then rapidly trigger associated cognitions and attitudes (Bargh, 1988; Tesser & Martin, 1996). Unfortunately, emotion theorists have remained rather vague about what triggers people's initial emotional reactions to an event. Some theorists (e.g. Lazarus, 1991; Frijda, 1986) have proposed, for example, that people's perceptions of whether an event is 'beneficial' or 'harmful' lead them to react along either positive or negative affect dimensions (see Plutchik, 1994, for alternative perspectives). But most emotion theorists working in this area appear to agree that the type and intensity of the initial emotion determine both the intensity and outcome of people's sense-making activities.

Whether emotions precede or follow cognitions is still a matter of debate in various domains of psychological research (Lazarus, 1982; Zajonc, 1980; see Forgas, 1991, for a review), and a detailed review of the rapidly growing literature on this topic is beyond the scope of this chapter. What can be concluded at this point, however, is that the arousal of emotions *may* occur before cognitive awareness, and that under many circumstances emotions arise *at least* hand-in-hand with cognitive processes. Below, I develop two sets of arguments that illustrate why justice-related events may arouse people's feelings before (or in conjunction with) their cognitive assessments. Linked to these arguments, I review several literatures that lend support to the premise that organizational justice judgments are susceptible to emotional contagion.

Emotional contagion of justice and coping with threat or distress
One way of illustrating the emotional contagion of justice is by considering the potentially distressing or threatening nature of justice-related events. Many such events are a serious matter for employees because the events can have significant consequences. The consequences can be practical – as a result of potentially unfair treatment, for example, a person's job may be on the line or a promotion denied. The events may also have psychological consequences – for example, Tyler and others have shown that unfair treatment can negatively impact a person's sense of self-esteem (Koper et al., 1993; Tyler, Degoey & Smith, 1996). And the consequences may be more normative or social – as equity and relative deprivation research has illustrated, people are concerned that resource allocations may be biased in favor of some other person or group. Particularly because these consequences may differ from what people expect or feel they deserve (cf., Lerner, 1980), being confronted with a potentially unfair event may arouse distressing emotions (e.g. elicit worry, sadness, or anger). A contagion approach proposes that organizational actors cope with these stressors by seeking social support, and in the process, arriving at a shared interpretation about the fairness of their situation.

The proposition builds on Schachter's (1959) pioneering experiments in which he examined people's preferences to affiliate with others during anxiety-inducing situations (in this case, when subjects anticipated undergoing electric shocks). Partially based on his work, an extensive set of literatures has developed showing that the emotional impact of stressful life events such as divorce, illness, and even job-related strain can lead individuals to seek out social support (see Buunk, 1990; Kessler, Price & Wortman, 1985 for reviews).[2] These literatures have demonstrated that seeking social support is only one of many possible responses to real-world stressors. Attempts at changing a situation or suppressing the emotions it engendered are other tactics. But when these alternatives are unavailable or difficult to accomplish, people tend to rely on others in order to come to terms with the situation. Because individual attempts at changing the outcome of a *justice*-related event in organizations are often difficult due to existing power differences between managers and subordinates, employees may respond emotionally to this context as well by seeking social support.[3]

According to Schachter's (1959) affiliation model, soliciting social support under stressful circumstances serves two interrelated functions. Like Festinger (1954), Schachter suggested that uncertainty motivates individuals to seek out social information from others. Schachter, however, gave prominence to the role of emotional uncertainty, in addition to uncertainty about the environment, in people's search for information. Thus, he suggested that people want to learn how others have emotionally reacted to a stressful event in order to validate their own emotions and help them comprehend the meaning of the event. In regards to coping with the emotional reactions that can be triggered by a justice-related event, then, Schachter's social validation hypothesis would suggest that organizational actors seek out others who may experience similar emotions or who may share their doubts about the fairness of the event. If such persons can be found, it is likely that the parties will conclude that the event must have been either just or unjust. Moreover, we can expect that social validation operates in mutually reinforcing cycles between the parties, so that eventually a consensus emerges about both the 'appropriate' emotional reaction to and the 'appropriate' justice interpretation of the event. Social comparisons of emotional states have been extensively researched in the literature on stressful life events (see Taylor, Buunk & Spinal, 1990 for a review), and findings have generally provided support for the occurrence of these activities under stress or threat.

A secondary function that Schachter suggested underlies people's affiliative tendencies is that companionship during stressful episodes can reduce anxiety levels. Schachter's suggestion was based on his belief that companionship could provide opportunities for mutual comfort and thus could buffer emotional arousal. However, research on the buffering effects of social interaction has provided inconsistent results. Some studies conducted in organizational settings, for example, have found that as social interaction increases, job stress also increases (Buunk, 1990). Research on the dynamics of 'self-help' groups has demonstrated similar effects: people generally join such groups to find psychological relief from their troubles, but often end up more distressed than before because others share and reinforce similar perspectives on their problems (e.g. Gottlieb, 1988).

At least three complementary explanations can account for these findings; they also provide additional insights into the contagious nature of the justice. The studies on self-help groups already suggest one explanation – namely, that discussions with others who share a similar perspective on a situation can lead to a polarization of emotions and cognitions. Polarization effects in group discussions are well documented (see Isenberg, 1986), and I have previously reviewed evidence which suggests that similar effects are likely to occur in people's conversations about justice.

The other two explanations can be found in the contagion literature itself. Underlying most historical studies of contagion has been the assumption that social situations lead people to experience decreased levels of self-conscious-ness and to express (and adopt) exaggerated emotions under stressful circumstances (Blumer, 1946; Kerckhoff & Back, 1968; Turner, 1964). Although this classical interpretation of emotional contagion has mainly been used to explain the occurrence of extreme social phenomena (e.g. the rapid spread of mass hysteria or psychogenic illness), the essence of the interpretation is quite similar to the concept of social facilitation, the idea that the mere presence of others facilitates the expression of people's dominant responses when placed in a threat situation (Zajonc, 1965). Extended to justice, social interactions in response to a justice-related event may indeed lead individuals to express (and experience) their emotions and opinions about the event more strongly than they would otherwise.

More recent work on emotional contagion has taken a less extreme stance, demonstrating that even in everyday interactions people 'tune in' to the emotional states of others and take on their joy, fear, sadness, anger, and so on. (Barsade, 1994; Hatfield et al., 1992, 1994). Tuning effects are suggested to occur because attending to the emotional states of others provides individuals with crucial information about their environment, including inferences about the likely causes of the emotional states (Hatfield et al., 1992; Shaver et al., 1987). Tuning in to other people's emotions, then, may provide a 'heuristic' for understanding the emotions' antecedents – for example, fair or unfair treatment. Although not directly addressed by this work, tuning effects may 'boomerang' under distressing circumstances because individuals tune in to increasingly negative emotions over time and develop increasingly polarized interpretations of their causes.

The insights provided by these literatures can thus be summarized as follows: (1) people tend to be motivated to affiliate with others when faced with a distressing or threatening event; (2) they do so in order to receive social validation for their emotional reactions to and interpretations of the event; (3) affiliation may alleviate feelings of emotional distress (and potentially, soften people's interpretations of the sources of distress), but it can also exacerbate these feelings and interpretations due to polarization, social facilitation, and/or emotional tuning effects. To date, none of these insights has been considered in relation to justice, but the affiliation and justice literatures' similar focus on the effects of potentially distressing or threatening events on people's inter-pretations and behaviors suggests that emotional contagion may be a viable explanation for the development of judgments about justice.

Emotional contagion of justice and feelings of entitlement
Another way of illustrating the emotional contagion process is by considering how judgments about justice can be influenced by people's feelings of entitlement in organizations. Feelings of entitlement – expectations that one 'ought' or 'deserves' to receive something – are central constructs in many theories of justice, and perceived entitlement violations have frequently been equated with the perception that an injustice has occurred (e.g. Crosby, 1984; Major, 1994). As a matter of fact, much of what organizational actors view as an injustice can be cast in terms of grievances about violated entitlement beliefs: violations of the 'appropriate' moral standard by which employees feel they should be treated, for instance, or violations of what they consider to be 'deserved' rewards or organizational policies. The extant justice literature, however, has provided only limited insight into the psychological processes that may lead people to believe a violation has occurred. To date, researchers have mainly focused on the cognitive processes by which individuals may compare, for instance, their own outcomes to those of others or to outcomes they received in the past (see Major, 1994). These comparison processes have also been linked to such emotional outcomes as moral outrage and resentment (Crosby, 1984; Folger, 1986). In contrast, the primary role that emotions, and emotional contagion in particular, can play in influencing these interpretative processes has not been the focus of attention.

Writings by legal anthropologists and sociologists on the emergence of disputes can provide such a focus (e.g. Nader & Todd, 1978; Miller & Sarat, 1980; Felstiner, Abel & Sarat, 1980). Whereas these scholars have primarily been concerned with identifying when individuals will seek redress for a dispute (e.g. by filing a legal claim), their insights into the psychological processes that lead up to these actions are relevant for our purposes. Most useful in this regard is Felstiner, Abel & Sarat's (1980) well-known 'naming, blaming, claiming' framework of how people come to define a negative life experience as a dispute. Felstiner et al. suggested that, for a dispute to occur, individuals must first interpret or 'name' a negative emotional experience in their lives as injurious; that is, they must designate an event that was unpleasant to them as intentionally harmful. A perceived injury does not necessarily lead to a full-blown dispute, however, unless 'blame' for the injury is attributed to a particular person or institution. Finally, if blame is laid, individuals must choose to lodge a complaint against the offender in order to 'claim' restitution for the injury incurred.

Two aspects of Felstiner et al.'s framework make it particularly relevant to an emotional contagion perspective on justice. First, their framework suggests that during the interpretative activities described above (and especially the 'naming' and 'blaming' stages), a person's emotional reactions to an experience can become translated into a grievance that the perpetrator of the experience denied them treatment to which they felt entitled (Miller & Sarat, 1980). That is, the victim believes that the perpetrator engaged in an act that was unjust or undeserved (Nader & Todd, 1978). But perhaps most importantly, Felstiner et al. recognized that these interpretative processes are frequently social in nature. Because it is often unclear to what extent an unpleasant experience is truly injurious or whether blame can be assigned to a particular agent, individuals in a person's social environment – such as family, friends, neighbors, or colleagues – often play a key role in defining the experience. These so-called 'sponsors' may, for instance, reinforce negative images of the potential offender or activate and support the idea that the treatment received was indeed unjust and undeserved. They may also act as 'reality testers' against whom people voice their grievances about the potentially unfair treatment, and who may encourage or discourage the expression of these grievances in a dispute resolution setting.

I am not the first to draw attention to the theorizing of Felstiner et al. (1980) as an important framework for understanding perceptions of justice. Sheppard, Lewicki & Minton (1992), for instance, have used the framework to explain how justice judgments arise in organizations, but they viewed these processes from a highly cognitive and individualistic perspective. In contrast, some recent studies have underscored the role of emotional contagion. Bies & Tripp (1996), for example, examined people's feelings of outrage that accompanied suspicions of unfair treatment in organizations and found that their subjects engaged in frequent rumination about the treatment. Striking about the rumination process was that it often took place in the company of co-workers and friends. As Bies & Tripp reported: "Rumination occurred publicly, in which the victim received social support and reinforcement of the suspicion and outrage" (p. 254). Bies and Tripp further reported that it was in these social interactions that attributions of responsibility on the part of the perpetrator or the organization emerged (and hence, I would infer, that judgments of injustice were formed or strengthened).

Studies by researchers working in the domain of organizational conflict and dispute resolution provide further support for an emotional contagion perspective on justice. Van Maanen (1992), for example, conducted a study of drinking bouts among London police detectives and found that, among the usual gossip and cajoling, detectives used these bouts as occasions to vent their frustrations about organizational policies and discuss the perceived injustices inflicted upon them by other officers. Drinking bouts also enabled detectives to adjust their feelings to those of their friends and reassess their perspectives on events. Barley (1991) has also reviewed a number of ethnographic studies of disputes from which he concluded that people's interactions within their friendship networks influence how they come to perceive an emotional grievance as an injustice:

> Other people play a significant role in helping disputants frame or formulate the meaning of their experience. Potentially aggrieved individuals may not even think of labeling some experience as an injury until they have discussed the matter with friends. Friends may convince the party that what at first appeared to be a bit of bad luck was, in fact, a *violation of his or her rights* (p. 188, italics added).

In summary, then, the literature on the psychological dynamics of disputes, in addition to the literatures on coping with threat or distress, suggest that people's emotional reactions to an event can awaken their cognitive search for its meaning. Furthermore, both literatures suggest that others play an important role in validating an individual's emotional reactions to events and developing a shared point of view on their causes. Although neither literatures have directly focused on issues of justice, they both can be interpreted to support the view that justice judgments are susceptible to emotional contagion. The fact that two distinct literatures, which derive from vastly different backgrounds, provide this kind of theoretical convergence strengthens this alternative interpretation of the justice judgment process. Taken together with my earlier discussion of cognitive contagion, it may thus be fruitful to direct justice theory and research away from the individualistic perspective that has so dominated prior work.

Conditions which Promote or Impede the Contagion of Justice

To provide insight into the viability of a research program based on a contagion approach to justice, it may be helpful to outline some of the conditions under which justice contagion is more or less likely to occur. I first discuss several structural and psychological characteristics of the types of social environments that can facilitate contagion effects. I then follow with a discussion of several individual differences, characteristics of justice-related events, and organizational/societal characteristics that may influence the speed and extent to which justice cues may spread within these environments. The discussions are meant to be suggestive rather than comprehensive.

Social environment characteristics
Central to both Festinger's social comparison theory (1954) and Schachter's affiliation model (1959) is the premise that people seek out social information from similar others when coping with uncertainty. Most recent studies have investigated this premise in terms of similarities within friendship networks and have found that friendship ties are powerful conduits for contagion effects. Such ties may be the primary conduit through which people seek social support and information about justice as well, especially for their emotional reactions to a potential injustice. Because friends are often selected on the basis of shared values and attitudes (Byrne, 1971), organizational actors can expect to find the greatest support among friends for any negative emotional reactions they may experience, and they may share these reactions with less fear of social disapproval or rejection (see Buunk, 1990). Because empathy is more easily to be evoked when distress is suffered by those one cares about, friends may also be more prone to take on each other's emotional reactions and interpretations of events (Roloff, 1987). In contrast, non-friends may frequently deny a person the acknowledgment or shared emotion that an injustice might have taken place, and instead 'blame the victim' for his or her own plight (Lerner, 1980).

Friendship ties, however, are not the only source of social support or information about a potential injustice. Especially in regards to cognitive contagion, peers who have been confronted with a similar justice-related event or who have experienced a 'similar fate' may be best suited to provide insight into relevant aspects of the event. The suggestion that shared experiences may be a source of social validation about justice is supported by research findings in the group decision-making literature on the 'common knowledge effect' (Gigone & Hastie, 1993; see Lind, Kray & Thompson, 1998). Distinguishing between sources of emotional and cognitive contagion of justice is also supported by research on social support seeking. Studies have shown that people turn to different individuals for emotional versus informational support (e.g. Dakof & Taylor, 1990), and that information on how to handle a stressful event is most successfully provided by individuals who have faced similar situations.

Proposing that both network and non-network characteristics can play a role points to various conditions that may promote or impede the contagion of justice. In terms of network structure, the number of network ties within a group (i.e. network 'density') and the number of interpersonal contacts a person has to other individuals (i.e. network 'centrality') could predict both the speed and extent to which one person's perceptions and emotions about justice influence those of others. The degree to which subgroupings of individuals interact more frequently with each other than with members of other subgroupings (i.e. form network 'cliques') may also predict the relative homogeneity of justice judgments within and such groupings (see Monge & Eisenberg, 1987 for other relevant network characteristics). Beyond structural characteristics, psychological factors such as social identification – people's awareness of their group membership and sense of psychological closeness to other group members (Tajfel, 1982) – can act to speed the transmission of social cues about justice. Related social psychological constructs such as group cohesion and social integration may also play a role. Higher levels of cohesiveness and integration are characterized by more frequent communication and increased pressures for conformity among group members (see Hackman, 1992).

Individual differences

Personality differences in both sensitivity to social cues and tendencies to seek out such cues can moderate the contagion process. Several dispositional traits already examined in the justice literature may be relevant. For example, research on the well-known "belief in a just world" construct (Lerner, 1980) has shown that some individuals are more disposed than others to view events they personally experience as unfair. A related dispositional measure of "sensitivity to befallen injustice" (Schmitt, 1996) has demonstrated that justice-sensitive individuals are also more prone to ruminate about events. These individuals may be more likely to ruminate in public and to seek social support for their feelings and perceptions.

Similar effects can occur for individuals who have low self-esteem. Previous justice studies have found that perceptions of unfair treatment can negatively impact a person's sense of self-esteem (e.g. Tyler, Degoey & Smith, 1996). Because low self-esteem individuals tend to feel more threatened by negative self-relevant information (Brockner, 1988), they may also be more inclined to seek out social support that helps avoid blaming themselves for potentially unfair treatment, and instead place blame on the injustice of the treatment itself. A significant body of literature also suggests that individuals with low self-esteem are more susceptible to social influence (see Brockner, 1988). Weiss & Shaw (1979), for instance, have shown that social cues about work conditions shaped job perceptions to a greater degree among low self-esteem subjects than among high self-esteem subjects.

Several personality constructs not previously considered in the justice literature may also be relevant. Research on self-monitoring (Snyder, 1974) suggests that people differ in terms of their sensitivity to social cues about the appropriateness of their feelings and actions. High self-monitors, those most sensitive to social cues, have been found to take on the moods of those around them to a greater extent than low self-monitors (Barsade, 1994). Individuals with more expressive communication styles (Friedman & Riggio, 1981) have also been found to influence the moods of others to a greater degree than less expressive individuals (Sullins, 1991). Conversely, people who generally hold strong opinions on issues may be less inclined to seek out social support for their positions and less influenced by the opinions of others.

Event characteristics
As Festinger (1954) has argued, people are most likely to use social information when events are ambiguous. Thus, it is reasonable to expect for instance that justice judgments of broad organizational policies will be socially construed, since they are often ambiguously defined and most employees have little direct experience with them. Especially because these policies (e.g. concerning affirmative action) are geared towards structuring the organizational life of entire groups of employees, such groups may be highly inclined to develop a collective understanding of their fairness.

Novel and unexpected events (such as those concerning wage settlements or layoffs) may also be susceptible to social contagion. There is widespread evidence that discrepancies between expected and actual experiences elicit a need for explanation (Wong & Weiner, 1981) and activate more thoughtful information processing (Langer, 1989). In this regard, Brockner, DeWitt, Grover & Reed (1990) have found that managerial explanations for a layoff influenced employees' work-related attitudes to a greater degree when employees felt the layoff was unusual for their organization. Peer explanations could likewise have a larger effect on employee interpretations of justice when events are unexpected or unusual.

Research on the link between emotions and justice also indicates that interpretations of injustice, more than justice, may be particularly susceptible to contagion. Both the affiliation and conflict literatures suggest that distressing life events elicit more social coping responses in individuals. Shelly Taylor (1991) reviewed several other literatures and concluded that negative events generally evoke stronger cognitive and emotional responses than do neutral or positive events. Furthermore, she concluded that negative events evoke more attempts at minimizing the emotional impact of these events. As I have noted, seeking social support for one's emotional reactions to a potentially unjust event, and arriving at a socially sanctioned interpretation that the event was indeed unjust, may serve such a purpose.

Organizational/societal characteristics

Not only can individuals or groups be characterized as more or less prone to contagious justice effects but organizational can as well. Those that have a history of antagonistic labor-management relations, for instance, may provide grounds for frequent employee discussions about fairness. In contrast, organizations with a more participative work climate, along with those that have instituted procedures which enable employees to voice their grievances about unfair treatment, may be able to minimize the spread of justice-related opinions and emotions (Sheppard, Lewicki & Minton, 1992). As several studies have pointed out however, many grievance procedures are ineffective because employees often expect negative consequences for those who use them (see Kolb, 1987). Hence, organizational avenues for addressing an injustice may seldom be the major channels through which grievances are worked out.

Other organizational characteristics may also determine the degree of justice contagion. Many researchers for instance have noted the increasingly demographically diverse nature of the workforce. To the degree that people prefer to interact with others who are similar to them, such diversity can become reflected in stronger contagion rates within than across demographically similar organizational groups. When organizational work involves collaboration within close-knit interpersonal networks and team-based systems, it will also be more likely to promote contagion effects. Though team-based work is often pursued in the belief that it will improve productivity and coordination, increased use of work teams may provide employees with more opportunities to talk about justice. Whether the resulting effects are negative or positive will, of course, depend on the content as well as the process of these discussions.

Finally, larger societal and legal environment characteristics may also play a potent role in the contagion process. The concept of power distance, for instance – the degree to which unequal distributions of power are accepted or rejected within a given society (Hofstede, 1980) – may determine whether people even consider raising issues of justice or injustice. When inequalities are powerfully justified (e.g. by political leaders), viewing an organizational event or experience in justice terms may simply remain suppressed. In contrast, when a particular issue has become codified into law – such as sexual harassment – such codification may greatly contribute to people's recognition of it in the work place. Sexual harassment was not legally recognized as an injustice in the U.S. until recently (and still is not in many cultures). This recognition has likely increased the frequency with which people feel grieved about harassment issues. Despite the fact that legal recourse may be possible, it is probably still far more common for them to air their grievances among co-workers or friends in order to seek support for the injustices inflicted upon them than to seek legal remedies.

CONTAGION OF JUSTICE ACROSS SITUATIONS: THE ROLE OF JUSTICE STORIES AND REPUTATIONS

Up to this point, I have concentrated on examining the emergence of socially shared opinions about justice in response to a single, situation or organizational event, and have outlined some of the conditions that may promote or impede justice contagion. My focus on reactions to a single situation paralleled the bulk of the justice research conducted to date. A contagion approach, however, also implies that social opinions about justice can arise and be maintained across situations. Once organizational actors within a group or network develop a shared perspective on justice, such a perspective may be elaborated upon in social settings and applied when new situations present themselves. This accumulated perspective can help individuals or groups interpret the often ambiguous and emotionally charged stimuli comprising a justice-related event.

Below, I explore two social mechanisms that seem particularly relevant for understanding how historical perspectives on justice can develop and be maintained across situations: I focus on organizational storytelling and talk about reputations. I first place these mechanisms within the context of existing theory and research, showing that their relevance to justice has frequently been implied but never fully acknowledged or explored. Then I discuss various ways in which a more explicit focus on these social mechanisms can inform future theory and research on organizational justice.

Contagion and Storytelling about Justice

Although the existing literature has primarily examined people's justice assessments of single situations, few researchers would deny that such assessments can carry over across situations. When people have experienced a blatant injustice, for example, residual thought and feeling about the event can influence their perceptions of subsequent events. Conversely, relative deprivation theorists have suggested that individual comparisons between current and past outcomes can affect people's sense of justice (Crosby, 1984; Major, 1994). But to the extent that justice is a socially constructed phenomenon, there may often be more than a simple carry-over effect of personal experiences or individual comparisons. Since most justice-related events are ambiguous emotional occurrences, relying on how others viewed and experienced previous events can be useful. Moreover, many of the events have implications for entire groups of individuals, and group members may want to learn about past critical events that they did not experience themselves but that nevertheless have a bearing on their own or their group's current situation.

Storytelling may be one social mechanism by which people collectively make sense of past justices or injustices. By providing an interpretative account of an event's sequences, stories can be powerful communication vehicles because they can convey complex information in a highly concentrated and concrete manner (Martin, 1982; Taylor & Thompson, 1982). Stories also allow people to infuse thought and feeling into their recollections of past events in ways that go beyond the mere "facts" enabling them to infer meaning from history (e.g. see Schank & Abelson, 1995; Middleton & Edwards, 1990). Thus, at a societal level for example, stories about the popular uprising and subsequent massacre at China's Tiananmen Square, the internment of Japanese-Americans during World War II, or even the treatment of a Karen Silkwood or Rodney King, serve as poignant reminders of alleged injustices perpetrated in the past. Few individuals may actually have experienced the events, but the vivid imagery provided by these stories (especially when accompanied by graphic media coverage) makes the injustices salient and memorable. Such stories often do not capture all that has transpired, nor do all groups necessarily share the same interpretation of events (e.g. note how Black's and White's divided on interpreting the O. J. Simpson saga). But, by publicly commemorating the events in a narrative fashion and selectively reconstructing what has transpired, various groups can highlight those justice concerns that are most important to them. Such narrative sense-making activities about the past can affect group members' perceptions and attitudes towards current events, and may even highlight what they envision an alternative 'just world' should look like.

Storytelling in organizational contexts can reflect quite similar dynamics. Researchers have long noticed that stories about critical events in an organization's history can convey the organization's cultural values and guide people's perceptions and behaviors (e.g. Martin, 1992; Mitroff & Killmann, 1976). Studies have also shown that varying interpretations of history can be maintained in the storytelling repertoires of organizational subcultures or subgroupings (Martin, 1992). Although the literature in this area has not explicitly focused on issues of justice, it is striking how many organizational stories appear to concern a past justice or injustice. In examining the central themes of a large number of these stories, Martin, Feldman, Hatch & Sitkin (1983), for example, described managerial conduct that one might note occurs in many of the same situations as have been studied in the justice literature – layoffs, conflict resolutions, and so on. Moreover, the conduct often reflected either particularly fair behavior (e.g. consideration of an employee's view-points; unbiased enforcement of organizational rules) or a blatant lack thereof. This by no means suggests that all organizational stories are about justice. But when it comes to stories that signify people's beliefs about an organization's core values, a prevalent theme may well be how fairly or unfairly the organization has dealt with its employees in the past.

The types of justice stories I have emphasized so far reflect broad cultural interpretations of justice and its implementation by authorities. In contrast, recent justice research has emphasized how perceptions of justice can be influenced by managerial explanations and justifications for specific events (e.g. Bies & Shapiro, 1988; Sitkin & Bies, 1993; see Bies, 1987; Greenberg, 1990). The underlying rationale of these studies is that potentially unfair situations create a 'predicament of injustice' in which employees suspect intentional harmful conduct by an organizational authority, yet look to the authority to provide some exonerating account of the circumstances in which their actions occurred (Bies, 1987). What is commonly not recognized in this research is the fact that employees are likely to jointly develop their own 'story-like' accounts about these actions, especially since suspicions about the authority's intentions have already been raised. Because these kinds of accounts are generated among relative equals, they may more readily be regarded as truthful or accurate by fellow employees. Shared recollections of past encounters with the authority in which an injustice was suspected may have equally significant effects.

To date, the link between storytelling and perceptions of justice has perhaps been brought most to the forefront in Folger's referent cognitions theory of relative deprivation (see Folger, 1986, 1987; Folger & Cropanzano, 1998). Folger developed his theory in reaction to research findings which showed that feelings of deprivation not only arise from people's comparisons of their own outcomes to those of others or to outcomes they received in the past, but also from their thoughts and feelings about imagined alternative outcomes (e.g. Bernstein & Crosby, 1980). Thus, Folger suggested that people's justice evaluations are shaped by several types of mental simulations (or "referent cognitions") they construct about a situation. Through various iterations of the theory, he showed that people's sense of injustice can be influenced by thoughts about alternative outcomes to what they actually received (what *could* have been); outcomes they would have received if different procedures had been used (what *would* have been); and their moral beliefs about what ought to have occurred (what *should* have been).

Referent cognitions theory has not received as much attention in the organizational justice literature as it perhaps deserves, but the points it makes are quite valuable for the study of contagious justice. First, the construct of mental simulations proposed by Folger can easily be seen as a set of stories that individuals tell themselves in a justice situation (see Folger, 1987). Although the theory was primarily formulated to explain how individuals arrive at a justice judgment, it is not difficult to imagine how groups can generate and maintain these story-like constructions through ongoing communication among their members. Second, Folger's theory suggests that people's mental simulations about justice may not solely be based on direct experiences with past or current events, but may also contain alternative or idealized scenarios of what people would like to see happen in a given context. Such idealized stories, especially when they are collectively generated and elaborated upon in social settings, may serve as critical guideposts for a person's justice evaluations across many situations. Although Folger has primarily tested his theory in controlled experiments (e.g. by encouraging his subjects to expect a desired reward and then withholding it), examining how these story-like constructions are developed and maintained within organizational populations will be helpful for extending a theory of contagious justice.

Contagion and Reputations about Justice

A second social mechanism by which perspectives on justice may arise and be maintained across situations is talk about the fairness reputation of an organizational entity. Much like storytelling, talk about an entity's reputation (whether it concerns a specific manager or co-worker, an organizational division, or even the organization at large) can provide a perspective on the past. Rather than representing an account of a particular incident, however, reputations tend to reflect the recognition of a relatively enduring characteristic of the entity that has been inferred from accumulated patterns of behaviors across situations (Emler, 1990). Such a recognition or judgment can then serve as a proxy for evaluating and predicting its behaviors in the present and future. The existence of a social consensus, for instance, that a manager has generally behaved as a 'fair person' (or conversely, could not be trusted to behave fairly) may override any doubts that people have about the fairness of his or her current actions.

Reputations have not been the subject of any justice research, but they have been found to be of importance in studies of economic exchange situations (Kollock, 1994; Wilson, 1985) and in the social dilemma literature (Axelrod, 1984). Scholars in various domains of organizational theory have also recognized that acquiring a reputation for fairness is a highly sought-after quality. In the justice literature itself, Greenberg (1990) has pointed to comments from managers indicating that they believe that 'looking fair' in the eyes of subordinates is one of their most valuable assets for getting things done. Greenberg suggested that 'reputation building' – managing the appearance of fairness across repeated encounters – can be a powerful tool for accomplishing this in the long run. Writers on negotiation and mediation, too, have stressed that developing a reputation for integrity and fairness is essential if negotiators/ mediators are to be effective (e.g. Friedman, 1994). And even at the firm level, the importance of fairness reputations has been implied. Kahneman, Knetsch & Thaler (1987) and others have argued that one of the reasons many firms may not cut wages during periods in which market conditions indicate they could (e.g. when unemployment is high) is for fear that they will acquire a reputation for unfair conduct.

Although the importance of acquiring or maintaining a reputation for fairness has been widely recognized, writings on this topic have generally failed to acknowledge that reputations are, ultimately, a social judgment that is accorded by others. Economic and social psychological treatises on reputation stress that reputations only matter if they are entertained in a broader social context (e.g. Bromley, 1993; Emler, 1990; Wilson, 1985). Because it is often impossible to personally observe all relevant behaviors of an entity across several situations, individuals frequently lack sufficient information to arrive at a reliable judgment of its enduring characteristics. Thus, the knowledge provided by others about its reputation is often critical. Indeed, as social psychologists point out, people tend to "assiduously research the reputations of others" (Emler, 1990, p. 171) when they cannot directly infer the qualities of a person from their own observations. Particularly when these qualities are in doubt, reputational talk may have a powerful influence on people's judgments of the individual.

Considering that reputations are a socially constructed phenomenon can be helpful in understanding how people react to efforts by organizational authorities who attempt to portray themselves as 'fair'. At times, these attempts may be accepted as valid and truthful, or even be augmented by relevant knowledge about an authority's background characteristics that group or network members share and discuss (e.g. knowledge about a recent divorce or lack of promotion that could explain a seemingly unfair action). But at other times, organizational groups can also create their own perspectives on the fairness image of the authority. Akin to how groups of employees may develop their own story-like accounts of an event, they may through gossip and rumor provide each other with data or stories about a manager's fairness character-istics that were intentionally omitted in the manager's representations of his or her own behaviors. When managers are perceived as being too manipulative or heavy-handed in their efforts to appear fair (i.e. when managers 'protest too much'; Ashforth & Gibbs, 1988), these efforts may also provoke a judgmental response in which organizational actors generate 'counter-reputations' and vent their feelings and thoughts about the manager by discussing these with peers. Such counter-reputations can then become reinforced through continuous talk within groups or networks – the more they are told and the more people hear about them, the more reliable they will appear to be.

To my knowledge, the only research that provides some empirical evidence of the role of social interaction in disseminating a reputation for fairness is a recent study conducted by Burt & Knez (1996), who examined the transmission of reputations for trustworthiness through interpersonal networks in an organization. Measures of their subjects' perceptions of trustworthiness, however, closely reflected commonly used measures of the perceived fairness of a person. For example, in describing their measure of distrust, Burt and Knez cited comments from subjects that a target person "did not follow through on commitments" and "had great power but withheld help" (p. 77). Roughly similar descriptions have been used by Tyler (1994) in his research on the perceived fairness of group authorities. Burt and Knez (1996) found that when their subjects were unsure of a target person's trustworthiness (or fairness), interpersonal linkages to third parties within a network strengthened existing doubts about that person. Moreover, the amplification effect of the target person's reputation being broadcast across network linkages was much more pronounced when the person was considered somewhat untrustworthy than when he or she was considered somewhat trustworthy. Burt and Knez's work does not directly address the process of reputational talk about justice, but it provides some indication of the importance of studying this process.

The Significance of Justice Stories and Reputations

The discussions above illustrate that a focus on organizational storytelling and talk about reputations presents a conceptually appealing way of broadening a contagious justice framework. By facilitating the communication of thoughts and feelings about past justice events, these mechanisms can provide organizational actors with a shared, historical perspective on their situation. I have especially emphasized the socially constructed nature of these mechanisms, suggesting that it is not mere 'facts' or personal views, but rather, ongoing interpretation and reinterpretation within groups or networks that may determine people's opinions about justice.

Incorporating increased attention to storytelling and reputational talk into research on justice in organizations has several significant implications. At a basic level, it suggests a more social process-sensitive approach for studying people's reactions to the kinds of organizational events commonly examined in the justice literature (such as layoffs and conflict resolutions). For example, future studies could explore the contents of specific justice stories and reputations that are communicated within a group or network setting and how such localized interpretative schemes influence people's evaluations of an event. One might expect that the types of prior justice issues made most salient or memorable in these mechanisms (e.g. past arbitrary enforcement of organizational rules, rude managerial conduct) are also the types of issues to which group or network members are most acutely sensitive when confronted with a new event. Since many justice events are ambiguously defined and emotionally charged, one could also expect that organizational actors will, at least to some extent, rely on storytelling and reputational talk to fill in missing gaps in their fairness assessments of an event in ways that are biased by the story or talk.

An increased focus on storytelling and reputational talk, however, may also encourage justice theorists and researchers to direct some of their attention away from the usual analysis of people's reactions to specific events. As opinions about justice spread by contagious means and become contained in organizational stories and reputations, these opinions can, over time, become self-reinforcing and depend little or not at all on how a specific event has actually occurred. Rather than examining people's reactions to events, then, research should focus on examining, for example, how storytelling and reputational talk affect the unanimity with which group or network members define the overall fairness of their situation; the intensity with which they maintain their shared justice beliefs over time; and the forcefulness with which they pass their shared beliefs on to others who are unfamiliar with them. Ultimately, developing an understanding of these ongoing social processes may invite attempts at building conceptual linkages between justice theory and other areas of organizational research, such as those on norm emergence and maintenance in groups (e.g. Bettenhausen & Murnighan, 1985; Feldman, 1984), workgroup culture (e.g. Martin, 1992), and newcomer socialization (e.g. Louis, 1980). Fully exploring these linkages is beyond the scope of this chapter, but here I suggest that research on stories and reputations may provide but a starting point for developing broader and more integrated conceptualizations about justice than has been done to date.

FROM COLLECTIVE PERCEPTIONS TO COLLECTIVE ACTION: SOME NOTES ON THE ORGANIZATIONAL CONSEQUENCES OF CONTAGIOUS JUSTICE

In the preceding sections, I have laid out a set of arguments showing that contagion processes can shape individual thoughts and feelings about organizational events into collectively shared opinions about justice. I have argued that this shared awareness about justice can come about in regards to a single event as well as be maintained in groups across multiple events and over time. To illustrate the relevance of a contagion framework at a broader organizational level, I will now explore how such a shared awareness may become translated into action, and particularly group-based actions, suggesting that the contagion of justice makes group-based actions more likely. Below, I discuss three forms that these collective actions might take in organizations: (a) collective protests, (b) group-based impression management efforts; and (c) group-based antisocial behaviors. The discussions also serve to illustrate the dynamic nature of justice contagion across multiple organizational groups.

Justice Contagion as a Pre-Condition for Collective Protests

One of the most significant behavioral consequences of perceptions of injustice that has long held interest among justice researchers is the occurrence of collective protests aimed at improving or rectifying an unjust situation. Thus, in societal settings, researchers have examined the link between people's feelings of injustice and their willingness to participate in social movements, political rebellion, and even riots (see Taylor & Moghaddam, 1994; Tyler & Smith, 1998 for reviews). Little of this research has permeated the current literature on organizational justice, however. Instead, most of the research conducted in organizations has examined the effects of justice perceptions on such individual attitudes and behaviors as commitment and good citizenship (and, occasionally, individual protests; see Greenberg, 1987). As I have previously noted, justice contagion can affect these types of behaviors as well. On the positive side of the perceived justice-injustice spectrum, for instance, the development of a shared perspective on justice may lead to a climate of commitment and loyalty in workgroups. On the negative side of the spectrum however, contagion may not only lead to a lack of commitment or citizenship behavior, but it may also provide the basis for collective protests.

For an understanding of the link between justice contagion and the propensity to engage in collective protests, the relative deprivation literature is particularly instructive. Based on original work by Runciman (1966), deprivation researchers have distinguished between feelings of personal (or 'egoistical') and group-based (or 'fraternal') deprivation, and have shown that, at least in societal settings, those who feel that their group is deprived of fair treatment are more likely to be involved in social efforts to seek structural changes (e.g. Dube & Guimond, 1986; Walker & Mann, 1987). Although deprivation researchers have primarily focused on inter-group comparisons as a source of feelings of group-based deprivation, they have also suggested that such factors as frequent communication between group members (Rhodebeck, 1981), shared feelings of a 'common fate' and identity (Gurin & Townsend, 1986), and a group consensus on the illegitimacy of the treatment (Martin, 1993) can be important contributors to people's willingness to engage in collective protests. These suggestions accord well with the contagion approach proposed here. As group or network members arrive at a shared perspective on justice, such a perspective can create a sense of solidarity and cohesion that makes collective action more likely. Particularly when this perspective results from emotional contagion, shared grievances that a group's well-being is threatened and its (perceived) entitlements are not met may contribute to an emotional climate that galvanizes and legitimizes such behavior.

It should be noted that considerable controversy has surrounded relative deprivation theory and its ability to predict collective protests. Much of the controversy derives from the observation that many societal groups who seem, from an objective point of view, unfairly treated (e.g. women, minorities) rarely press for systematic changes (see Major, 1994). These observations have led researchers to explore a number of mediating factors that may play a role in people's choices to support or participate in collective behavior. Social psychologists have focused, for instance, on the importance of people's beliefs about the feasibility of attaining a desired goal and the stability of existing arrangements (Tyler & Smith, 1998). Conversely, sociologists working from a resource mobilization perspective have argued that the pragmatic 'costs' of collective action (e.g. need for leadership or difficulties in organizing for action) are important determinants (e.g. McCarthy & Zald, 1977). Certainly, some of these enabling mechanisms can also mediate between contagiously derived opinions about injustice and collective protest. Nevertheless, the fact remains that justice contagion may be a potent pre-condition for such protests that has not been explicitly examined. Especially in organizational settings, where opportunities for frequent contact between group or network members are present, and where a variety of actions are possible (ranging, for instance, from collectively lobbying one's supervisor to voting as a block in labor negotiations or participating in work slowdowns and strikes), studying collective protest behaviors from a contagion perspective can be fruitful.

The occurrence of collective protests also has potentially significant implications for the dynamics of justice contagion at an organizational level. For instance when disadvantaged groups succeed in their efforts at seeking systematic changes, these changes may create a ripple effect throughout the organization, so that advantaged groups who previously felt fairly treated (or to whom justice was not even a salient concern) consider the changes 'unfair'. Any deviations from existing arrangements can thus spark public discussions about the fairness of the entire distribution of relevant organizational resources/ procedural arrangements. Such issues of 'macro justice'; (Brickman, Folger, Goode & Schul, 1981) can lead various groups to reassess their shared perspectives on justice. Moreover, members of advantaged groups who feel threatened by systematic changes may try to thwart or minimize the efforts of disadvantaged groups by promoting the status quo and making public claims about the fairness of existing arrangements. This has been observed, for instance, in opposition to affirmative action policies (Veilleux & Tougas, 1989). Collective protests and systemic organizational changes, then, especially those that are highly visible or controversial, may provide an excellent opportunity for examining the contagion of justice across multiple groups.

Contagion and Group-Based Impression Management of Justice

As some of the examples above already indicate, related forms of collective action that can arise from justice contagion are efforts by group or network members to manage justice impressions. Throughout this chapter, I have often referred to existing impression management (or 'social accounts') approaches to justice (Bies, 1987; Greenberg, 1990), suggesting that they provide an important, but incomplete, perspective on the social construction of justice in organizations. Rather than treating the generation of interpretations for justice-related events as the sole prerogative of management, I have argued that groups or networks are likely to generate their own interpretations, which on occasion may differ greatly from those provided by managers. Taking the argument further, one can also posit that group or network members may choose to express their shared justice views to others outside their primary reference group.

There are at least two potential targets for group-based impression management efforts: managers and other organizational groups. For instance, when group or network members perceive that they have experienced a collective injustice they may express their views to an organizational authority in order to gain sympathy for their plight and press for change, or even to impress upon the authority that its accounts of events are inadequate, unacceptable, or believed to be outright false. A sense of solidarity and shared grievances concerning the injustice received makes such group-based efforts more likely than individual efforts. Publicly claiming a group-based injustice – and especially, making group-based claims about the inadequacy of managerial accounts – is also less risky than individual claims, making one less vulnerable to reprisals from management.

Considering that organizational groups and managers can present competing justice interpretations of events suggests that the impression management of justice is often a much more interactive process than previously indicated in the literature. In an article critical of research on organizational impression management efforts in general, Ginzel, Kramer & Sutton (1993) made precisely this argument, suggesting that impression management often resembles a process of 'reciprocal sensemaking' in which both managers and their audiences present initial accounts for an event and then try to resolve any 'interpretative conflicts' that may arise through ongoing adjustment and negotiation. As the authors noted, once interpretative conflicts arise and managerial accounts have been called into question, it can be extremely difficult to find a mutually acceptable solution. In regards to justice, the occurrence of interpretative conflict between managers and organizational groups raises such questions as how group members can actively shape managerial interpretations of justice, and how they may respond when a manager changes his or her "story" once group members have challenged it. Informed by a contagion approach, these kinds of questions are important new topics for investigation that can augment existing work on impression management in the justice arena.

The kinds of interpretative conflicts that are of most interest from a contagion perspective are those that may arise *between* various organizational groups. As members of a group or network arrive at a shared opinion on justice, they are likely to discover that other groups judge and comprehend the same apparent situation in different ways. Such differences can arise because some groups are, in effect, treated differently than others (e.g. high-level versus low-level employees). But various groups or networks may also focus on different aspects of the same treatment, or simply assign their own interpretations to similar aspects. Particularly when significant organizational outcomes are at stake (e.g. resource allocations to one organizational division over another; promotional opportunities based on behaviors that co-vary with justice judgments, such as citizenship), members of these respective groups or networks may engage in considerable argumentation in order to impress upon one another what is the 'appropriate' justice interpretation of a specific situation. Presumably, those who prevail in establishing a dominant justice view also increase the likelihood that their views will be taken into consideration by management and that these prevailing views, at least in the long run, will be maintained or become institutionalized in organizational resource allocations and/or procedures.

Although it is common in order to find references in the justice literature to people using claims about group-based justices or injustices to advance their goals and beliefs (see Taylor, Wright & Porter, 1994; Tyler & Smith, 1998), virtually no research has examined how these processes actually occur in organizations. As a starting point, future studies could focus on the manner in which group or network members choose to convey some of the same types of social accounts as have been examined in existing work on managerial impression management of justice (see Bies, 1987; Greenberg, 1990). Thus, researchers could explore how people make use of accounts that communicate group explanations and justifications of events, group opinions about perceived entitlements, and so on, in order to bring their own justice views across to others. One can expect that those accounts that are most effective are not necessarily the most accurate representations of the 'facts', but rather are those that are presented with the greatest unanimity among group/network members and with the most consistent arguments. Alternatively, the resolution of group-based interpretative conflicts could be studied through a 'negotiation' lens, examining how group or network members rely on such negotiation tactics as strategic positioning, co-optation of managerial views, and coalition formation (for a review, see Kramer, 1991). These types of tactics have been extensively examined in organizational settings, but not explicitly within the context of group-based claims about justice.

A critical point to stress, however, is that the ways in which interpretative conflicts about justice are addressed between groups may not solely be a matter of tactical or self-interested choices. Surely, at times, people may make claims about a collective justice or injustice simply because it advances their interests, while there is little basis in fact for making such claims (either in terms of actual group treatment or a group concensus on its fairness). The self-interested, tactical uses of justice claims have been widely recognized in the literature (e.g. Leventhal, 1976; Greenberg & Cohen, 1982; Walster et al., 1978). But one has to assume that group or network members must develop at least some collective rationale for their situation before they can make any believable or sustainable claims about their collective treatment. Moreover, because of the inherent ambiguity regarding what constitutes fair treatment, people's views about justice are never resolved completely. Hence, as ideas about justice spread, these ideas may instigate both *proactive* processes by which group or network members attempt to convince others outside their group of their point of view, and *reactive* processes by which they make internal adjustments to their shared justice perceptions based on the views expressed by others. These proactive and reactive processes are likely to be dynamically linked, so that inter-group impression management efforts affect intra-group interpretative processes about justice, and vice versa. How these dual processes interact and unfold over time is clearly more complicated and intricate than presented here, but they are another set of relatively unexplored areas of organizational justice research that can be fruitfully examined from a contagion perspective.

Justice Contagion and Group-Based Antisocial Behaviors

The types of behaviors considered thus far reflect efforts by group or network members to change or maintain organizational arrangements based on their shared justice beliefs. A final form of behavior to consider is how feelings of injustice may become expressed in more indirect efforts, in attempts to 'even the score' with the organization or individual who perpetrated the unfair treatment. Such behaviors have been the focus of several recent justice studies. For example, researchers have examined the relationship between employee perceptions of injustice and organizational petty theft (Greenberg & Scott, 1996), spreading rumors and damaging equipment (Skarlicki & Folger, 1997), doing sloppy work and engaging in excessive absenteeism (Lewicki, Poland, Minton & Sheppard, 1997), and revenge (Bies & Tripp, 1996). Under such labels as "deviance" (Robinson & Bennett, 1997), "misbehavior" (Vardi &Weiner, 1996), and "antisocial behavior" (Giacalone & Greenberg, 1996), these kinds of behaviors have also recently attracted attention in the broader organizational literature (I adopt the general term 'antisocial' behavior here). As with many other constructs related to justice, however, antisocial behavior in organizations has mostly been examined as an individual-level phenomenon. When researchers have viewed the behaviors from a group perspective, they have referred to concepts such as norms and social learning to explain their occurrence (e.g. Greenberg & Scott, 1996; Robinson & O'Leary-Kelly, 1998).

There is substantial empirical evidence showing that antisocial behaviors often occur in group contexts (e.g. Altheide, Adler, Adler & Altheide, 1978; Mars, 1982; Scott, 1985), and a contagion approach to justice can further our understanding of their etiology. A distinction made by researchers in this area between 'instrumental' and 'expressive' motivations underlying antisocial acts is particularly helpful (Robinson & Bennett, 1997; see also Greenberg & Scott, 1996). Instrumental motives for these acts are those that lead people to seek restitution for an unfair situation (e.g. by engaging in theft to compensate for a perceived inequity). Although it may be preferable to seek amelioration for a perceived injustice by directly confronting an organizational authority, such actions are not always a viable option for members of groups that are at a distinct power disadvantage vis-à-vis an authority or other groups (Tyler & Smith, 1998). Worse, members of these respective groups have often learned that confrontation only leads to further injustices (Hogan & Emler, 1981). Collectively engaging in antisocial acts, then, can be a 'rational' way of attempting to avoid trouble and restore justice. In what Scott (1985) has called "the weapons of the weak," group or network members who collectively feel unfairly treated may, for instance, share information about which types of restitutory acts are available to them or provide cover for each other's actions (for further examples of such acts, see Greenberg, 1997).

From a justice contagion perspective, expressive motivations underlying antisocial acts are perhaps more significant. Expressive motives reflect a need to release or vent one's emotions about unjust treatment by retaliating against the perpetrator of the treatment (e.g. by vandalizing equipment, sabotaging work processes, or spreading damaging gossip), regardless of the material benefits of these actions (Robinson & Bennett, 1997). As I have noted, emotions such as anger and frustration are frequently triggered by unjust events, and emotional contagion can be a particularly potent source of people's justice judgments. Just as the emotional climate resulting from these social processes may bolster people's resolve to engage in collective protests, such a climate may also boost their inclination to retaliate against the perpetrator of the unjust treatment, either individually or in some collaborative fashion. Such retaliatory acts are not necessarily only committed by members of relatively powerless groups. Depending, for instance, on the level of blame attributed to the organization or management and the strength of emotional contagion triggered by the events, various groups can engage in these behaviors. Moreover, expressive motives for retaliation may be particularly strong for members of those groups who, based on their shared justice beliefs, have made legitimate attempts at seeking redress for a perceived injustice, but feel that managerial responsiveness has been lacking or inadequate.

Finally, a contagion approach may also be able to provide insight into one of the more intriguing questions raised in antisocial behavior research, namely how people justify or rationalize their 'deviant' conduct. As several researchers have noted, engaging in antisocial acts can pose a moral dilemma for the actors because most people prefer to see themselves as honest and good (Greenberg

& Scott, 1996; Robinson & Bennett, 1997). Building on work by Sykes & Matza (1957), they have proposed that so-called 'techniques of neutralization' – that is rationalizations and justifications that somehow define antisocial acts as situationally appropriate – make the behaviors possible. To date, however, there has been little systematic understanding of the processes by which these neutralizations actually arise in organizational settings. Some qualitative evidence suggests that neutralizations for antisocial conduct (e.g. revenge), at least at an individual level, evolve around viewing one's actions as 'morally right' and 'in service of justice' (Bies & Tripp, 1996). Other qualitative evidence suggests that neutralizations are particularly effective when they are contained in informal group norms and supported through ongoing communication among group members (e.g. Mars, 1982; Hollinger, 1989). Mars (1982), for instance, has referred to rationalizations for antisocial conduct as 'vocabularies of adjustment' that are widely shared and maintained within groups. Combining these findings and building on a contagion approach would suggest that just as social 'talk' can lead people to develop shared opinions about the injustice or justice of organizational actions, such talk may also enable them to develop shared beliefs about the justice of their *own* actions.

IMPLICATIONS FOR FUTURE RESEARCH AND ORGANIZATIONAL PRACTICE

This chapter has sought to provide an outline of a social contagion perspective on justice. I have drawn on various research streams and theoretical paradigms to develop an understanding of how and when organizational actors may rely on their peers to learn what is just or fair, how they may maintain their shared justice beliefs over time, and how they may choose to express their shared beliefs in collective actions. Although I cited several studies whose findings provide some support for the perspective, most of its components and their potential consequences for organizational behavior have yet to be fully addressed in the literature. In light of this, it might be appropriate to follow with some guidelines for future research and some recommendations for organizational practice.

Implications for Future Research

A contagion perspective suggests a substantial research agenda that significantly differs from existing approaches to justice research. The bulk of the research conducted to date has relied on experimental and anonymous survey methods. Although these methodologies have often been quite useful for studying individual-level interpretations and responses to justice, they are much less amenable to the analysis of a broad range of contagion effects. For example, the significance of long-term social bonds is generally ignored in experimental settings, while the aggregation of anonymous survey responses glosses over the potential clustering of justice judgments and their consequences within organizational subgroupings. At least three alternative methodologies – network designs, more qualitatively oriented ethnographic studies, and longitudinal designs – are better suited for gaining insight into the paths by which justice is socially construed.

As many of the issues raised throughout this chapter already indicate, network methods are an obvious starting point for studying contagion effects. Such methods have been used to explore the association between personal interaction patterns and such varying constructs as turnover, job satisfaction, and moods, and there is strong reason to believe that perceptions of justice are similarly affected. Simply put, knowing who talks to whom, and knowing some characteristics of a network itself (e.g. the density of network ties), can provide important information about how a person might react to justice-related events. Examining justice from a network perspective also offers the potential to contribute an understanding of something that most network studies have ignored, namely how interaction patterns between organizational actors may develop and change over time. As I have noted, not only can social discourse about justice occur between organizational actors who have existing relationships (e.g. friends), but also between those who previously had little contact but who feel they are similarly affected by a justice-related event. Thus, the event-driven nature of justice may provide for significant changes in the patterns by which organizational actors communicate with one another, and such changes themselves are an important topic of investigation.

To acquire a more in-depth understanding of the dynamics of justice contagion, researchers may also have to rely more on qualitatively oriented ethnographic approaches. Greater reliance on such methods can be particularly helpful for studying the emotional qualities of justice contagion. Because it is often difficult to ask people to accurately reflect on their emotional reactions to a justice-related event, real-time observations of how they express their feelings and receive peer support during organizational 'time-outs' (Van Maanen, 1992) such as coffee breaks or hallway gatherings, for instance, can provide an improved understanding of the interpretative processes by which people's emotions are translated into shared justice judgments. Ethnographic studies could also fruitfully examine the resolution of group-based interpretative conflicts about justice. These kinds of activities can have a significant influence on people's perceptions and behaviors, yet they have largely remained hidden from view in existing justice research. Studies could focus, for instance, on the ways in which members of groups that base their shared justice opinions on different dimensions of an event (e.g. distributive versus procedural justice) 'negotiate' a common understanding of the event or escalate their views in an effort to establish a dominant perspective on justice. Ultimately, a better ethnographic understanding of the dynamics of justice contagion could provide a framework for studying these dynamics under more controlled conditions.

Finally, implied in many of the issues raised here is the need for more longitudinal research. While most existing justice studies have assumed that people judge the fairness of each organizational event anew, a contagion model suggests that social processes can be a potent force in the carryover of justice interpretations across events. Thus, a critical research issue is the temporal stability of contagious justice: under which conditions do group or network members impose shared interpretations of past events on a new event, and conversely, when do they perceive little relationship between the past and present? Studies could focus on such determinants as situational characteristics (e.g. the novelty or surprise of an event), as well as the salience and content of justice stories and reputations that are perpetuated within interpersonal networks. Longitudinal research clearly presents more of a challenge than the usual one-shot justice studies do, but such research may ultimately prove useful for guiding organizational change and development efforts.

Implications for Organizational Practice

Perhaps one of the most significant consequences of shifting our attention from individualistic models of justice towards a contagion framework lies in its potential implications for organizational practice. To date, justice researchers have been content to provide practitioners with prescriptive advice suggesting that employee perceptions of fairness can be managed by designing organizational processes on the basis of the many distributive and procedural justice criteria identified by the literature. Thus, managers have been told to create 'equitable' pay systems, allow for 'voice' in decision-making proce-dures, treat employees with 'dignity and respect', and so forth. Managers have also been told they should provide adequate explanations for events. A contagion approach certainly suggests that some of this advice can be warranted. As employees talk about justice and develop a shared perspective on their situation, their perceptions of organizational efforts at managing fairness can become amplified due to contagion. But the approach also points towards several limitations of these kinds of efforts. For one, precisely due to the potential amplification effects of contagion, it would appear that managers have only a small margin of error in the ways they can conduct themselves. For another, if social processes rather than objective characteristics of organizational events are predominantly at the core of people's justice judgments, then designing these characteristics based on some general criterion of justice may actually have little effect. Finally, it may be very hard to restore perceptions of justice simply by manipulating these characteristics when opinions about injustice have already become widely shared and persistent within organizational groups or networks.

This is not to say that a contagion framework suggests that attempts at managing perceptions of fairness in organizations are impossible or futile. Rather, it points to several alternative avenues by which practitioners can influence these perceptions. For instance, by paying closer attention to the kinds of shared justice beliefs that may be held within particular organizational groups or networks, managers could target specific justice-based interventions towards these respective sources. Such specific interventions might facilitate any restorative work required by managers, since having only one or a few aspects of justice to address can be far easier than implementing a dozen or more universal justice criteria. Moreover, managerial attempts at keeping up appearances of fairness by basing interventions on a broad set of criteria may actually drive injustice perceptions and contagion processes underground if these attempts ignore the specific views of group or network members. Of course, managers must also be cautious about directly asking employees about their shared justice beliefs. As Salancik & Pfeffer (1978) have cogently argued, organizational inquiries about employee attitudes and beliefs may actually increase the salience of these beliefs and create expectations for improvement. Instead, tapping into the 'grapevine' and, for instance, getting a sense of the kinds of justice stories and reputations that are shared within a group or network may be more useful.

Ultimately, managing fairness perceptions may not only require attempts at creating fair organizational practices but also at influencing the interpretative activities by which justice opinions are socially construed. A potential starting point might be the socialization of newcomers to an organization. Newcomers bring with them preconceived notions about fairness that derive from their previous work and life experiences. They also tend to remain on the periphery of social networks within their new work setting for some time (Van Maanen & Schein, 1979), yet feel a strong need to learn what is expected of them, including acquiring information about situational or culture-specific interpretative schemes that can help them make sense of events (Louis, 1980;

Morrison, 1993). Both formal and informal managerial socialization efforts regarding what constitutes 'appropriate' interpretations of fairness in the new organizational context may help inoculate these newcomers against future contagion effects.

Changing the fairness perceptions of veteran employees may require more than simple socialization efforts. As I have noted, as group or network members develop shared perspectives on justice, these perspectives can become highly resistant to change. Although managers may attempt to influence these perspectives by, for instance, making changes in organizational arrangements highly salient or noticeable to employees (or, as noted above, targeting their shared beliefs with specific, group or network-based interventions), changing interaction networks and rotating employees into different areas of the company may ultimately be required. Alternatively, employees who serve as opinion leaders within a given network or group might be targeted for special consideration. Providing them with detailed explanations and justifications of specific organizational actions (and potentially seeking their involvement in those actions) may serve to guide their personal justice opinions, thereby indirectly shaping the opinions of their co-workers. Finally, sensitizing employees to the possibility that they are subject to contagion forces may also help them gain greater control over their personal views and resist those who currently influence their justice beliefs in more covert ways.

A final note is in order about the kinds of 'people processing' techniques (Van Maanen & Schein, 1979) suggested here. Some of these techniques may appear aversive or manipulative to some justice researchers and theorists. A potential explanation for these reactions might be that justice theory has tended to be applied in a normative fashion; that is, justice theory has been used to promote a preferred view of how organizations should be run for the benefit of employee well-being, happiness and so on. Implicit in this view is the assumption that people's needs for fairness or justice an inherent part of human nature and hence cannot (or should not) be manipulated or changed. Implicit is also the assumption that, ultimately, the responsibility for fairness lies squarely with an organization's management. Folger & Bies (1989), for example, have argued that managers need to be taught to accept their 'fairness responsibilities' by being to be courteous, truthful, unbiased, timely, and considerate in their interactions with employees. Thus, in a sense, people processing techniques have already been applied in regards to justice in organizations, but predominantly with managers. Applying these techniques to *all* levels of an organization may not only be useful, but also a more even handed usage of justice theory than previously practiced.

CONCLUSION

This chapter started with the observation that although the justice literature over the past several decades has increasingly turned towards the 'social side' of justice in organizations, it continues to be dominated by a highly individualistic perspective on the justice judgment process. Therefore, the aim of this chapter has been to provide an alternative perspective, using the concept of social contagion as a guide to how organizational actors arrive at a shared, socially constructed interpretation of justice. The chapter explored how such social processes may be driven by both cognitive uncertainty and people's emotional reactions to justice-related events, and how the resulting inter-pretations may manifest themselves at various levels of analysis. It was also shown how a contagion approach can further our understanding of some long-standing problems in justice research such as the emotional bases of justice, impression management, collective protests, antisocial behavior, and justice reputations. Finally, suggestions were provided that could help practicing managers guide and influence some of the contagious processes that underlie employees' opinions about fairness. As always, the viability of these insights and suggestions depends largely on future empirical efforts that may validate, refine, or even refute the many speculations outlined in this essay.

ACKNOWLEDGMENTS

I thank Barry Staw for his encouragements and feedback while I wrote this chapter, and Tom Tyler for initiating me into the justice literature. Many thanks are also due to Jenny Chatman and Larry Cummings for their thoughtful comments on earlier drafts of this study. To Sigal Barsade, Jennifer Berdahl, Joel Brockner, Rob Folger, Rod Kramer, Mel Lerner, Allan Lind, and Leigh Thompson. I am sincerely grateful for their help.

NOTES

1. It is important to note that network researchers have examined the spread of various concepts in interpersonal networks through two separate mechanisms: (1) communications between individuals who are in direct contact with each other, and (2) comparisons between individuals who occupy similar positions within a network. Burt (1982, 1987) has used the term *contagion* to describe both types of processes, labeling the first 'contagion by cohesion', and the second 'contagion by structural equivalence'. Contagion by structural equivalence is not the focus of this chapter and could better be described as 'imitation' or 'social learning' based on social comparisons among similar actors.

2. One can argue that feelings of distress and threat are distinct psychological constructs. However, because the research literatures that address these constructs show a strong overlap in both theoretical propositions and empirical findings, and because I am primarily concerned with illustrating the relevance of these literatures for understanding the social dynamics underlying the justice judgment process, the constructs are treated jointly.

3. Such arguments are further supported by Lazarus and Folkman's (1987) model of coping activity in which they distinguish between problem-focused coping – altering a situation – and emotion-focused coping – managing emotional distress. Their research has shown that both coping strategies are used in almost any stressful circumstance, but that emotion-focused coping (of which seeking social support can be one facet) is more prevalent when people believe a situation is difficult to change.

4. In more recent years, similar processes have been proposed in the psychological contract literature (e.g. see Rousseau & McLean Parks, 1993). In this literature, psychological contracts have been defined as employee beliefs about the obligations or promises an organization has made to them, and contract violations as employee perceptions about discrepancies between what they actually received relative to what they were promised. The latter have also been linked to emotional reactions on the part of employees. Morrison & Robinson (1997) write, for example: "We reserve the term *violation* for the *emotional* and *affective* state that may, under certain conditions, follow from the belief that one's organization has failed to adequately maintain the psychological contract" (p. 230, italics in original). Although this literature has suggested similar causal sequences from cognitions to emotions as has been done by justice researchers, much of the discussion that follows could equally well apply to this literature. That is, people's emotional reactions to organizational events may lead them to discuss these reactions with coworkers or friends before reaching any conclusion that a contract violation has occurred.

REFERENCES

Adams, J. S. (1965). Inequity in social exchange. In: L. Berkowitz (Ed.), *Advances in Experimental Social Psychology*, vol. 2, (pp. 267–299). New York: Academic Press.

Altheide, D. L., Adler, P. A., Adler, P., & Altheide, D. A. (1978). The social meanings of employee theft. In: J. M. Johnson & J. D. Douglas (Eds), *Crime at the Top: Deviance in Business and the Professions* (pp. 90–124). New York: Lippincott.

Arvey, R. D., & Ivancevich, J. M. (1980). Punishment in organizations: A review, propositions, and research questions. *Academy of Management Review, 5*, 123–132.

Ash, S. E. (1956). Studies of independence and conformity: A minority of one against a unanimous majority. *Psychological Monographs, 70*, 177–190.

Ashforth, B. E., & Gibbs, B. W. (1990). The double-edge of organizational legitimation. *Organization Science, 1*, 177–194.

Axelrod, R. (1984). *The evolution of cooperation*. New York: Basic.

Bargh, J. A. (1988). Automatic information processing: Implications for communication and affect. In: L. Donohew & H. E. Sypher (Eds), *Communication, Social Cognition, and Affect* (pp. 9–32). Hillsdale, NJ: Lawrence Erlbaum.

Barley, S. R. (1991). Contextualizing conflict: Notes on the anthropology of disputes and negotiations. In: M. H. Bazerman, R. J. Lewicki, & B. H. Sheppard (Eds), *Research on Negotiation in Organizations*, vol. 3 (pp. 165–202). Greenwich, CT: JAI Press.

Barley, S. R., & Knight, D. B. (1992). Toward a cultural theory of stress complaints. In: B. M. Staw & L. L. Cummings (Eds), *Research in Organizational Behavior*, vol. 14 (pp. 1–48). Greenwich, CT: JAI Press.

Barsade, S. G. (1994). Emotional contagion in groups. Unpublished doctoral dissertation, University of California at Berkeley.

Bernstein, M., & Crosby, F. (1980). An empirical examination of relative deprivation theory. *Journal of Experimental Social Psychology, 16*, 442–456.

Bettenhausen, K., & Murnighan, J. K. (1985). The emergence of norms in competitive decision-making groups. *Administrative Science Quarterly, 30*, 350–372.

Bies, R. J. (1987). The predicament of injustice: The management of moral outrage. In: L. L. Cummings & B. M. Staw (Eds), *Research in Organizational Behavior*, vol. 9 (pp. 289–319). Greenwich, CT: JAI Press.

Bies, R. J., & Moag, J. S. (1986). Interactional justice: Communications criteria of fairness. In: R. J. Lewicki, B. H. Sheppard & M. H. Bazerman (Eds), *Research on Negotiation in Organizations*, vol. 1 (pp. 43–55). Greenwich, CT: JAI Press.

Bies, R. J., & Shapiro, D. L. (1988). Voice and justification: Their influence on procedural fairness judgments. *Academy of Management Journal, 31*, 676–685.

Bies, R. J., & Tripp, T. M. (1996). Beyond distrust: 'Getting even' and the need for revenge. In: R. M. Kramer & T. R. Tyler (Eds), *Trust in Organizations: Frontiers of Theory and Research* (pp. 246–260). Thousand Oaks, CA: Sage.

Blumer, H. 1946. Collective behavior. In: A. M. Lee (Ed.), *New Outline of the Principles of Sociology* (pp. 165–220). New York: Barnes & Noble.

Brickman, P., Folger, R., Goode, E., & Schul, Y. (1981). Microjustice and macrojustice. In: M. J. Lerner & S. C. Lerner (Eds), *The Justice Motive in Social Behavior* (pp. 173–204). New York: Plenum.

Brockner, J. (1988). *Self-esteem at work: Research, theory and practice*. Lexington, MA: Lexington Books.

Brockner, J., DeWitt, R. L., Grover, S., & Reed, T. (1990). When it is especially important to explain why: Factors affecting the relationship between managers' explanations of a layoff and survivors' reactions to the layoff. *Journal of Experimental Social Psychology, 26*, 389–407.

Brockner, J., & Wiesenfeld, B. (1993). Living on the edge (of social and organizational psychology): The effects of job layoffs on those who remain. In: J. K. Murnighan (Ed.), *Social Psychology in Organizations* (pp. 119–140). Englewood Cliffs, NJ: Prentice-Hall.

Brockner, J., Wiesenfeld, B., Stephan, J., Hurley, R., Grover, S., Reed, T., DeWitt, R. L., & Martin, C. (1997). The effects on layoff survivors of their fellow survivors' reactions. *Journal of Applied Social Psychology, 27*, 835–863.

Bromley, D. B. (1993). *Reputation, image and impression management*. Chichester, UK: John Wiley & Sons.

Burt, R. S. (1982). *Toward a structural theory of action*. New York: Academic Press.

Burt, R. S. (1987). Social contagion and innovation: Cohesion versus structural equivalence. *American Journal of Sociology, 92*, 1287–1335.

Burt, R. S., & Knez, M. (1996). Trust and third-party gossip. In: R. M. Kramer & T. R. Tyler (Eds), *Trust in Organizations: Frontiers of Theory and Research* (pp. 68–89). Thousand Oaks, CA: Sage.

Buunk, B. P. (1990). Affiliation and helping interactions within organizations: A critical analysis of the role of social support with regard to occupational stress. In: W. Stroebe & M. Hewstone (Eds), *European Review of Social Psychology*, vol. 1 (pp. 293–322). Chichester, UK: John Wiley & Sons.

Byrne, D. (1971). *The attraction paradigm*. New York: Academic Press.

Cahn, E. (1949). *The sense of injustice*. New York: New York University Press.

Cook, K. S. (1975). Expectations, evaluations and equity. *American Sociological Review, 40*, 372–388.

Crosby, F. (1976). A model of egoistical relative deprivation. *Psychological Review, 83*, 85–113.

Crosby, F. (1984). Relative deprivation in organizational settings. In: B. M. Staw & L. L. Cummings (Eds), *Research in Organizational Behavior*, vol. 6 (pp. 51–93). Greenwich, CT: JAI Press.

Dakof, G. A., & Taylor, S. E. (1990). Victim's perceptions of social support: What is helpful to whom? *Journal of Personality and Social Psychology, 58*, 80–89.

Deutsch, M. (1975). Equity, equality and need: What determines which value will be used as the basis for distributive justice? *Journal of Social Issues, 31*, 137–149.

Deutsch, M. (1983). Current social psychological perspectives on justice. *European Journal of Social Psychology, 13*, 305–319.

Deutsch, M. (1985). *Distributive justice*. New Haven, CT: Yale University Press.

Deutsch, M., & Gerard, H. B. (1955). A study of normative and informational social influences upon individual judgment. *Journal of Abnormal and Social Psychology, 51*, 629–636.

Dube, L., & Guimond, S. (1986). Relative deprivation and social protest: The personal/group issue. In: J. M. Olson, C. P Herman & M. P. Zanna (Eds), *The Ontario Symposium: Relative Deprivation and Social Comparison*, vol. 4 (pp. 201–216). Hillsdale, NJ: Erlbaum.

Emler, N. (1990). A social psychology of reputation. In: W. Stroebe & M. Hewstone (Eds), *European Review of Social Psychology*, vol. 1 (pp. 171–193). Chichester, UK: John Wiley & Sons.

Feldman, D. C. (1984). The development and enforcement of group norms. *Academy of Management Review, 9*, 47–53.

Felstiner, W. L. F., Abel, R. L., & Sarat, A. (1980–1981). The emergence and transformation of disputes: Naming, blaming, claiming . . . *Law and Society Review, 15*, 631–654.

Festinger, L. (1954). A theory of social comparison processes. *Human Relations, 7*, 117–140.

Folger, R. (1986). A referent cognitions theory of relative deprivation. In: J. M. Olson, C. P. Herman & M. P. Zanna (Eds), *The Ontario Symposium: Relative Deprivation and Social Comparison*, vol. 4 (pp. 33–55). Hillsdale, NJ: Lawrence Erlbaum.

Folger, R. (1987). Reformulating the preconditions of resentment: A referent cognitions model. In: J. C. Masters & W. P. Smith (Eds), *Social Comparison, Social Justice, and Relative Deprivation: Theoretical, Empirical, and Policy Perspectives* (pp. 183–215). Hillsdale, NJ: Lawrence Erlbaum.

Folger, R., & Bies, R. J. (1989). Managerial responsibilities and procedural justice. *Employee Responsibilities and Rights Journal, 2*, 79–90.

Folger, R., & Cropanzano, R. (1998). *Organizational justice and human resource management*. Thousand Oaks, CA: Sage.

Folger, R., Rosenfield, D., Grove, J., & Corkran, L. (1979). Effects of 'voice' and peer opinions on responses to inequity. *Journal of Personality and Social Psychology, 37*, 2253–2261.

Forgas, J. P. (1991). *Emotion and social judgments*. Oxford, England UK: Pergamon Press.

Friedman, H. S., & Riggio, R. E. (1981). Effect of individual differences in nonverbal expressiveness on transmission of emotion. *Journal of Nonverbal Behavior, 6,* 96–107.

Friedman, R. A. (1992). The culture of mediation: Private understandings in the context of public conflict. In: D. M. Kolb & J. M. Bartunek (Eds), *Hidden Conflict in Organizations: Uncovering behind-the-Scenes Disputes* (pp. 143–164). Newbury Park, CA: Sage.

Frijda, N. H. (1986). *The emotions.* Cambridge: Cambridge University Press.

Giacalone, R. A., & Greenberg, J. (1997). *Antisocial Behavior in Organizations.* Thousand Oaks, CA: Sage.

Gigone, D., & Hastie, R. (1993). The common knowledge effect: Information sharing and group judgment. *Journal of Personality and Social Psychology, 63,* 959–973.

Ginzel, L., Kramer, R., & Sutton, R. (1993). Organizational impression management as a reciprocal influence process. In: L. L. Cummings & B. M. Staw (Eds), *Research in Organizational Behavior,* vol. 15 (pp. 227–266). Greenwich, CT: JAI Press.

Gottlieb, B. H. (1988). *Marshaling social support: Formats, processes, and effects.* Newbury Park, CA: Sage.

Greenberg, J. (1979). Group vs individual equity judgments: Is there a polarization effect? *Journal of Experimental Social Psychology, 15,* 504–512.

Greenberg, J. (1987). Reactions to procedural injustice in payment distributions: Do the means justify the ends? *Journal of Applied Psychology, 72,* 55–61.

Greenberg, J. (1990). Looking fair versus being fair: Managing impressions of organizational justice . In: B. M. Staw & L. L. Cummings (Eds), *Research in Organizational Behavior,* vol. 12 (pp. 111–157). Greenwich, CT: JAI Press.

Greenberg, J. (1993). The intellectual adolescence of organizational justice: You've come a long way, maybe. *Social Justice Research, 6*(1), 135–148.

Greenberg, J. (1997). The STEAL motive: Managing the social determinants of employee theft. In: R. A. Giacalone & J. Greenberg (Eds), *Antisocial behavior in organizations* (pp. 85–108). Thousand Oaks, CA: Sage.

Greenberg, J., & Cohen, R. L. (1982). Why justice: Normative and instrumental interpretations. In: J. Greenberg & R. L. Cohen (Eds), *Equity and Justice in Social Behavior* (pp. 437–469). New York: Academic Press.

Greenberg, J., & Folger, R. (1983). Procedural justice, participation, and the fair process effect in groups and organizations. In: P. B. Paulus (Ed.), *Basic Group Processes* (pp. 235–256). New York: Springer-Verlag.

Greenberg, J., & Scott, K. S. (1996). Why do workers bite the hands that feed them? Employee theft as a social exchange process. In: B. M. Staw & L. L. Cummings (Eds), *Research in Organizational Behavior,* vol. 18 (pp. 111–156). Greenwich, CT: Jai Press.

Gurin, P., & Townsend, A. (1986). Properties of gender identity and their implications for gender consciousness. *American Political Science Review, 67,* 514–539.

Hackman, J. R. (1992). Group influences on individuals in organizations. In: M. D. Dunnette & L. M. Hough (Eds), *Handbook of Industrial and Organizational Psychology* (2nd ed.), vol. 3 (pp. 199–267). Palo Alto, CA: Consulting Psychologists Press.

Hartman, R. L., & Johnson, J. D. (1989). Social contagion and multiplexity: Communication networks as predictors of commitment and role ambiguity. *Human Communication Research, 15,* 523–548.

Hatfield, E., Cacioppo, J. T., & Rapson, R. L. (1992). Primitive emotional contagion. In: M. S. Clark (Ed.), *Emotion and Social Behavior* (pp. 151–177). Newbury Park, CA: Sage.

Hatfield, E., Cacioppo, J. T., & Rapson, R. L. (1994). *Emotional contagion.* New York: Cambridge University Press.

Hofstede, G. (1980). *Culture's consequences: International differences in work related values.* Beverly Hills, CA: Sage.

Hogan, R., & Emler, N. P. (1981). Retributive justice. In: M. J. Lerner & S. C. Lerner (Eds), *The Justice Motive in Social Behavior* (pp. 125–144). New York: Plenum.

Hollinger, R. C. (1989). *Dishonesty in the workplace: A manager's guide to preventing employee theft.* Park Ridge, IL: London House.

Ibarra, H., & Andrews, S. B. (1993). Power, social influence, and sense making: Effects of network centrality and proximity on employee perceptions. *Administrative Science Quarterly, 38,* 277–303.

Isen A., & Baron, R. (1991). Positive affect as a factor in organizational behavior. In: L. L. Cummings & B. M. Staw (Eds), *Research in Organizational Behavior,* vol. 13 (pp. 1–53). Greenwich, CT: JAI Press.

Isenberg, D. J. (1986). Group polarization: A critical review and meta-analysis. *Journal of Personality and Social Psychology, 50,* 1141–1151.

Kahneman, D., Knetsch, J. L., & Thaler, R. H. (1986). Fairness as a constraint on profit seeking. *The American Economic Review, 76,* 728–741.

Kerckhoff, A. C., & Back, K. W. (1968). *The June Bug: A study of hysterical contagion.* New York: Appleton-Century Crofts.

Kessler, R. C., Price, R. H., & Wortman, C. B. (1985). Social factors in psychopathology: Stress, social support, and coping processes. *Annual Review of Psychology, 36,* 531–572.

Kolb, D. (1987). Corporate ombudsman and organizational conflict resolution. *Journal of Conflict Resolution, 31,* 673–691.

Kollock, P. (1994). The emergence of exchange structures: An experimental study of uncertainty, commitment, and trust. *American Journal of Sociology, 100,* 313–345.

Koper, G., Van Knippenberg, D., Bouhuijs, F., Vermunt, R. et al. (1993). Procedural fairness and self-esteem. *European Journal of Social Psychology, 23,* 313–325.

Krackhardt, D., & Porter, L. W. (1985). When friends leave: A structural analysis of the relationship between turnover and stayers' attitudes. *Administrative Science Quarterly, 30,* 242–261.

Kramer, R. M. (1991). The more the merrier? Social psychological aspects of multiparty negotiations in organizations. In: M. H. Bazerman, R. J. Lewicki, & B. H. Sheppard (Eds), *Research on Negotiation in Organizations,* vol. 3 (pp. 307–332). Greenwich, CT: JAI Press.

Langer, E. J. (1989). *Mindfulness.* Reading, MA: Addison-Wesley.

Lazarus, R. S. (1982). Thoughts on the relations between emotion and cognition. *American Psychologist, 37,* 1019–1024.

Lazarus, R. S. (1991). *Emotion and adaptation.* New York: Oxford University Press.

Lazarus, R. S., & Folkman, S. (1987). Transactional theory and research on emotions and coping. *European Journal of Personality, 1,* 141–169.

Le Bon, G. (1903). The crowd: A study of the popular mind (4th ed.). London: T. Fisher Unwin. (originally published: *Psychologie des foules,* 1895)

Lerner, M. J. (1980). *The belief in a just world.* New York: Plenum Press.

Leventhal, G. S. (1976). The distribution of rewards and resources in groups and organizations. In: L. Berkowitz & E. Walster (Eds), *Advances in Experimental Social Psychology,* vol. 9 (pp. 91–131). New York: Academic Press.

Leventhal, G. S. (1980). What should be done with equity theory? In: K. J. Gergen, M. S. Greenberg, & R. H. Willis (Eds), *Social Exchange: Advances in Theory and Research* (pp. 27–55). New York: Plenum.

Levy, D. A., & Nail, P. R. (1993). Contagion: A theoretical and empirical review and reconceptualization. *Genetic, Social, and General Psychology Monographs, 119,* 233–284.

Lewicki, R. J., Poland, T., Minton, J. W., & Sheppard, B. H. (1997). Dishonesty as deviance: A typology of workplace dishonesty and contributing factors. In: R. J. Lewicki, R. J. Bies & B. H. Sheppard (Eds), *Research on Negotiations in Organizations,* vol. 6 (pp. 53–86). Greenwich, CT: JAI Press.

Lind, E. A., Kulik, C. T., Ambrose, M., & De Vera Park, M. V. (1993). Individual and corporate dispute resolution: using procedural fairness as a decision heuristic. *Administrative Science Quarterly, 38,* 224–251.

Lind, E. A., & Tyler, T. R. (1988). *The social psychology of procedural justice.* New York: Plenum Press.

Lind, E. A., Kray, L., & Thompson, L. (1998). The social construction of injustice: Fairness judgments in response to own and others' unfair treatment by authorities. *Organizational Behavior and Human Decision Processes, 75,* 1–22.

Louis, M. R. (1980). Surprise and sense making: What newcomers experience in entering unfamiliar organizational settings. *Administrative Science Quarterly, 25,* 226–251.

Major, B. (1994). From social inequality to personal entitlement: The role of social comparisons, legitimacy appraisals, and group membership. In: M. P. Zanna (Ed.), *Advances in Experimental Social Psychology,* vol. 26, (pp. 293–355). New York: Academic Press.

Mars, G. (1982). *Cheats at work: An anthropology of workplace crime.* London: George Allen & Unwin.

Martin, J. (1982). Stories and scripts on organizational settings. In: A. Hastorf & A. Isen (Eds), *Cognitive Social Psychology* (pp. 225–305). New York: Elsevier-North Holland.

Martin, J. (1992). *Cultures in organizations: Three perspectives.* New York: Oxford University Press.

Martin, J. (1993). Inequality, distributive justice, and organizational illegitimacy. In: J. K. Murnighan (Ed.), *Social Psychology in Organizations* (pp. 296–321). Englewood Cliffs, NJ: Prentice-Hall.

Martin, J., Feldman, M. S., Hatch, M. J., & Sitkin, S. B. (1983). The uniqueness paradox in organizational stories. *Administrative Science Quarterly, 28,* 438–453.

McCarthy, J. D., & Zald, M. N. (1977). Resource mobilization and social movements: A partial theory. *American Journal of Sociology, 82,* 1212–1241.

McGuire, W. J. (1983). A contextualist theory of knowledge: Its implications for innovation and reform in psychological research. In: L. Berkowitz (Ed.), *Advances in Experimental Social Psychology,* vol. 16 (pp. 1–47). New York: Academic Press.

Meindl, J. R. (1990). On leadership: An alternative to the conventional wisdom. In: B. M. Staw & L. L. Cummings (Eds), *Research in Organizational Behavior,* vol. 12 (pp. 159–203). Greenwich, CT: JAI Press.

Meindl, J. R. (1993). Reinventing leadership: A radical, social psychological approach. In: J. K. Murnighan (Ed.), *Social Psychology in Organizations* (pp. 89–118). Englewood Cliffs, NJ: Prentice-Hall.

Merton, R. K., & Kitt, A. (1950). Contributions to the theory of reference group behavior. In: R. K. Merton & P. F. Lazarsfeld (Eds), *Continuities in Social Research: Studies on the Scope and Method of 'The American Soldier'* (pp. 35–54). Glencoe, IL: Free Press.

Messick, D. M. (1993). Equality as a decision heuristic. In: B. A. Mellers & J. Baron (Eds), *Psychological Perspectives on Justice: Theory and Applications* (pp. 11–31). New York: Cambridge University Press.

Middleton, D., & Edwards, D. (1990). *Collective remembering*. London: Sage.

Mikula, G., Scherer, K. R., & Athenstaedt, U. (1998). The role of injustice in the elicitation of differential emotional reactions. *Personality and Social Psychology Bulletin, 24*, 769–783.

Miller, R., & Sarat, A. (1980–1981). Grievances, claims and disputes: Assessing the adversary culture. *Law and Society Review, 15*, 525–566.

Mitroff, I. I., & Kilmann, R. H. (1976). On organizational stories: An approach to the design and analysis of organizations through myths and stories. In: R. H. Kilmann, L. R. Pondy & D. P. Slevin (Eds), *The Management of Organization Design* (pp. 189–207). New York: North Holland.

Monge, P. R., & Eisenberg, E. M. (1987). Emergent communication networks. In: F. M. Jablin, L. L. Putnam, K. H. Roberts, & L. W. Porter (Eds), *Handbook of Organizational Communication* (pp. 304–342). Newbury Park, CA: Sage.

Morgan, G. (1980). Paradigms, metaphors, and puzzle solving in organization theory. *Administrative Science Quarterly, 25*, 605–622.

Morrison, E. W. (1993). Newcomer information seeking: Exploring types, modes, sources, and outcomes. *Academy of Management Journal, 36*, 557–589.

Morrison, E. W., & Robinson, S. L. (1997). When employees feel betrayed: A model of how psychological contract violation develops. *Academy of Management Review, 22*, 226–256.

Nader, L., & Todd, H. (1978). *The disputing process – Law in ten societies*. New York: Columbia University Press.

Olson, J. M., & Hafer, C. L. (1996). Affect, motivation, and cognition in relative deprivation research. In: R. M. Sorrentino & E. T. Higgins (Eds), *Handbook of Motivation and Cognition*, vol. 3 (pp. 85–117). New York: Guilford Press.

Plutchik, R. (1994). *The psychology and biology of emotion*. New York: Harpercollins.

Reis, H. T. (1984). The multidimensionality of justice. In: R. Folger (Ed.), *The Sense of Injustice: Social Psychological Perspectives* (pp. 25–61). New York: Plenum Press.

Reis, H. T. (1987). The nature of the justice motive: Some thoughts on operation, internalization, and justification. In: J. C. Masters & W. P. Smith (Eds), *Social Comparison, Social Justice, and Relative Deprivation: Theoretical, Empirical, and Policy Perspectives* (pp. 131–150). Hillsdale, NJ: Lawrence Erlbaum.

Rhodebeck, L. (1981). Group deprivation: An alternative model for explaining collective political action. *Micropolitics, 1*, 239–267.

Robinson, S. L., & Bennett, R. J. (1997). Workplace deviance: Its definition, its manifestions, and its causes. In: R. J. Lewicki, R. J. Bies & B. H. Sheppard (Eds), *Research on Negotiations in Organizations*, vol. 6 (pp. 3–27). Greenwich, CT: JAI Press.

Robinson, S. L., & O'Leary-Kelly, A. M. (1998). Monkey see, monkey do: The influence of work groups on the antisocial behavior of employees. *Academy of Management Journal, 41*, 658–672.

Roloff, M. E. (1987). Communication and reciprocity within intimate relationships. In: M. E. Roloff & G. R. Miller (Eds), *Interpersonal Processes : New Directions in Communication Research* (pp. 11–38). Newbury Park, CA: Sage.

Rousseau, D. M., & McLean Parks, J. (1993). The contracts of individuals and organizations. In: L. L. Cummings & B. M. Staw (Eds), *Research in Organizational Behavior*, vol. 15 (pp. 1–43). Greenwich, CT: JAI Press.

Runciman, W. G. (1966). *Relative deprivation and social justice*. Berkeley, CA: University of California Press.

Salancik, G. R., & Pfeffer, J. (1977). An examination of need-satisfaction models of job attitudes. *Administrative Science Quarterly, 22*, 427–456.

Salancik, G. R., & Pfeffer, J. (1978). A social information processing approach to job attitudes and task design. *Administrative Science Quarterly, 23*, 224–253.

Schachter, S. (1959). *The psychology of affiliation*. Stanford, CA: Stanford University Press.

Schank, R. C., & Abelson, R. P. (1995). Knowledge and memory: The real story. In: R. S. Wyer Jr. (Ed.), *Advances in Social Cognition*, vol. 8 (pp. 1–85). Hillsdale, NJ: Lawrence Erlbaum.

Scher, S. J., & Heise, D. R. (1993). Affect and the perception of injustice. In: B. Markovsky & K. Heimer (Eds), *Advances in Group Processes*, vol. 10 (pp. 223–252). Greenwich, CT: JAI Press.

Schmitt, M. (1996). Individual differences in sensitivity to befallen injustice (SBI). *Personality and Individual Differences, 21*, 3–20.

Scott, J. C. (1985). *Weapons of the weak*. New Haven: Yale Unversity Press.

Shaver, P., Schwartz, J., Kirson, D., & O'Connor, C. (1987). Emotion knowledge: Further exploration of a prototype approach. *Journal of Personality and Social Psychology, 52*, 1061–1086.

Sheppard, B. H., Lewicki, R. J., & Minton, J. W. (1992). *Organizational justice: The search for fairness in the workplace*. New York: Lexington Books/Macmillan.

Sherif, M. (1935). A study of some social factors in perception. *Archives of Psychology, 27*, 1–60.

Sinclair, R. C., & Mark, M. M. (1992). The influence of mood state on judgment and action: Effects on persuasion, categorization, social justice, person perception, and judgmental accuracy. In: L. L. Martin & A. Tesser (Eds), *The Construction of Social Judgments* (pp. 165–193). Hillsdale, NJ: Lawrence Erlbaum.

Sitkin, S. B., & Bies, R. J. (1993). Social accounts in conflict situations: Using explanations to manage conflict. Human Relations, 46, 349–370.

Skarlicki, D. P., & Folger, R. (1997). Retaliation in the workplace: The roles of distributive, procedural, and interactional justice. *Journal of Applied Psychology, 82*, 434–443.

Snyder, M. (1974). The self-monitoring of expressive behavior. *Journal of Personality and Social Psychology, 30*, 526–537.

Sullins, E. S. (1991). Emotional contagion revisited: Effects of social comparison and expressive style on mood convergence. *Personality and Social Psychology Bulletin, 17*, 166–174.

Sykes, G., & Matza, D. (1957). Techniques of neutralization. *American Journal of Sociology, 22*, 664–670.

Tajfel, H. (1982). *Human groups and social categories*. New York: Cambridge University Press.

Taylor, D. M., & Moghaddam, F. M. (1994). *Theories of intergroup relations: International social psychological perspectives* (2nd ed.). Westport, CT: Praeger.

Taylor, D. M., Wright, S. C., & Porter, L. E. (1994). Dimensions of perceived discrimination: The personal/group discrimination discrepancy. In: M. P. Zanna & J. M. Olson (Eds), *The Ontario Symposium: The Psychology of Prejudice*, Vol. 7 (pp. 233–255). Hillsdale, NJ: Lawrence Erlbaum.

Taylor, S. E. (1991). Asymmetrical effects of positive and negative events: The mobilization-minimization hypothesis. *Psychological Bulletin, 110*, 67–85.

Taylor, S. E., Buunk, B. P., & Aspinwall, L. G. (1990). Social comparison, stress, and coping. *Personality and Social Psychology Bulletin, 16*, 74–89.

Taylor, S. E., & Thompson, S. C. (1982). Stalking the elusive 'vividness' effect. *Psychological Review, 89*, 155–181.

Tesser, A., & Martin, I. (1996). The psychology of evaluation. In: E. T. Higgins & A. W. Kruglanski (Eds), *Social Psychology: Handbook of Basic Principles* (pp. 400–432). New York: Guilford Press.

Thibaut, J., Friedland, N., & Walker, L. (1974). Compliance with rules: Some social determinants. *Journal of Personality and Social Psychology, 30,* 792–801.

Thibaut, J. W., & Walker, L. (1975). *Procedural justice: A psychological analysis.* Hillsdale, NJ: Erlbaum Associates.

Turner, R. H. (1964). Collective behavior. In: R. E. L. Faris (Ed.), *Handbook of Modern Sociology* (pp. 382–425). Englewood Cliffs, NJ: Prentice-Hall.

Tyler, T. R. (1994). Psychological models of the justice motive: Antecedents of distributive and procedural justice. *Journal of Personality and Social Psychology, 67,* 850–863.

Tyler, T. R., & Degoey, P. (1995). Collective restraint in social dilemmas: Procedural justice and social identification effects on support for authorities. *Journal of Personality and Social Psychology, 69,* 482–497.

Tyler, T. R., Degoey, P., & Smith, H. (1996). Understanding why the justice of group procedures matters: A test of the psychological dynamics of the group-value model. *Journal of Personality and Social Psychology, 70,* 913–930.

Tyler, T. R., & Lind, E. A. (1992). A relational model of authority in groups. In: M. P. Zanna (Ed.), *Advances in Experimental Social Psychology,* vol. 25 (pp. 115–192). New York: Academic Press.

Tyler, T. R., & Smith, H. J. (1998). Social justice and social movements. In: D. T. Gilbert & S. T. Fiske (Eds.), *Handbook of Social Psychology* (4th ed.), vol. 2 (pp. 595–629). Boston, MA: Mcgraw-Hill.

Van den Bos, K., Lind, E. A., Vermunt, R., & Wilke, H. A. M. (1997). How do I judge my outcome when I do not know the outcome of others? The psychology of the fair process effect. *Journal of Personality and Social Psychology, 72,* 1034–1046.

Van Maanen, J. (1992). Drinking our troubles away: Managing conflict in a British police agency. In: D. M. Kolb & J. M. Bartunek (Eds.), *Hidden Conflict in Organizations: Uncovering Behind-the-Scenes Disputes* (pp. 32–62). Newbury Park, CA: Sage.

Van Maanen, J., & Schein, E. H. (1979). Toward a theory of organizational socialization. In: B. M. Staw (Ed.), *Research in Organizational behavior,* vol. 1 (pp. 209–264). Greenwich, CT: JAI Press.

Vardi, Y., & Weiner, Y. (1996). Misbehavior in organizations: A motivational framework. *Organization Science, 7,* 151–165.

Veilleux, F., & Tougas, F. (1989). Male acceptance of affirmative action programs for women: The results of altruistic or egoistical motives? *International Journal of Psychology, 24,* 485–496.

Walker, I., & Mann, L. (1987). Unemployment, relative deprivation, and social protest. *Personality and Social Psychology Bulletin, 13,* 275–283.

Walster, E., Walster, G. W., & Berscheid, E. (1978). *Equity: Theory and research.* Boston: Allyn & Bacon.

Weick, K. E. (1969). *The social psychology of organizing.* Reading, MA: Addison-Wesley.

Weiss, H. M., & Shaw, J. B. (1979). Social influences on judgments about tasks. *Organizational Behavior and Human Performance, 24,* 126–140.

Wheeler, L. (1966). Toward a theory of behavioral contagion. *Psychological Review, 73,* 179–192.

Wilson, R. (1985). Reputations in games and markets. In: A. Roth (Ed.), *Game-theoretic Models of Bargaining* (pp. 27–62). Cambridge: Cambridge Press.

Wong, P. T. P., & Weiner, B. (1981). When people ask 'why' questions, and the heuristics of attributional search. *Journal of Personality and Social Psychology, 40,* 650–663.

Zajonc, R. B. (1965). Social facilitation. *Science, 149,* 269–274.

Zajonc, R. B. (1980). Feeling and thinking: Preferences need no inferences. *American Psychologist, 35,* 151–175.

Zalesny, M. D., & Ford, J. K. (1990). Extending the social information processing perspective: New links to attitudes, behaviors, and perceptions. *Organizational Behavior and Human Decision Processes, 47,* 205–246.

THEORIES OF GENDER IN ORGANIZATIONS: A NEW APPROACH TO ORGANIZATIONAL ANALYSIS AND CHANGE[1]

Robin J. Ely and Debra E. Meyerson*

ABSTRACT

This chapter presents a framework for understanding gender and organizational change. We consider three traditional treatments of gender and discuss the limitations of each as a basis for organizational analysis and change. We then propose a fourth approach, which treats gender as a complex set of social relations enacted across a range of social practices in organizations. Having been created largely by and for men, these social practices tend to reflect and support men's experiences and life situations and, therefore, maintain a gendered social order in which men and particular forms of masculinity dominate (Acker, 1990). We provide numerous examples of how social practices, ranging from formal policies and procedures to informal patterns of everyday social interaction, produce inequities while appearing to be gender-neutral. Drawing on previous research and our own three-year action research project, we develop an intervention strategy for changing gender relations in organizations accordingly.

* Order of authorship is alphabetical; we produced this chapter in full collaboration.

Research in Organizational Behaviour, Volume 22, pages 103–151.
2000 by Elsevier Science Inc.
ISBN: 0–7623–0641–6

INTRODUCTION

There can be little doubt that women have made progress in raising the height of the glass ceiling – that invisible barrier that prevents some groups from ascending to the highest-level positions in organizations. Recent statistics show that the number of Fortune 500 companies that have at least one woman among their top five earners has doubled since 1995, and, for the first time, over half of these companies have more than one woman corporate officer (Catalyst, 1999a). The data also suggest, however, that the progress toward equity has been slow, partial, and superficial. In Fortune 500 companies, women hold only 11% of board seats and just 5.1% of the seven top titles – Chairman, Vice Chairman, Chief Executive Officer, President, Chief Operating Officer, Senior Executive Vice President, and Executive Vice President. In addition, only 7% of corporate officers holding line jobs, which are those most likely to lead to leadership positions, are women. Top earning women earn only 68 cents in salary and bonus to every dollar their male counterparts earn (Catalyst, 1999a). The data also indicate that it is almost exclusively white women who have made these advances. Although 12.1% of women in the U.S. workforce are African American, they constitute only 6.6% of women managers. Women of color hold far fewer corporate officer positions in Fortune 500 companies than do white women. Women managers of color earn 58 cents to every dollar white men managers earn, which is also less than men managers of color earn (Catalyst, 1999b).

Not only has women's progress been slow and restricted primarily to white women, those who have progressed have often done so by assimilating, however uncomfortably, into predominantly male organizations (Ely, 1995a). The organizations themselves have changed little, and women who ascend to top positions tend to be relatively disempowered (Martin & Meyerson, 1998). Moreover, there is ample evidence that neither sex roles nor relations between men and women within the home have changed appreciably (Hochschild, 1989), which limits the level and kinds of changes that can take place at work.

What explains the tenacity of these disparities? Why has the large number of organizational efforts to recruit and advance women failed to result in substantial gains for women? Why do women remain relatively powerless at work? We propose that the answers to these questions lie in organizations' failure to question – and change – prevailing notions about what constitutes the most appropriate and effective ways to define and accomplish work, recognize and reward competence, understand and interpret behavior. These unquestioned work practices support deeply entrenched divisions and disparities between men and women, often in subtle and insidious ways. We argue further that the failure of organizations to change prevailing work practices is due in part to the limited conception of gender traditionally used to define and address problems of gender inequity. This limited conception of gender also results in solutions that do little to broaden men's opportunities to participate at home or to relieve men of the burdens they face in the traditional masculine role.

In this chapter, we review three traditional approaches to gender and organizational change, outline the shortcomings of each, and propose an alternative approach. (See Table 1 for a summary.) We based our approach on a broad range of theoretical and empirical work, and illustrate it with examples from our own and others' research.[2] Despite the considerable insights we have gained from our analysis, our proposed alternative remains at the level of theory, supported by empirical observations but as yet largely untested.

THREE TRADITIONAL APPROACHES TO GENDER AND ORGANIZATIONAL CHANGE

The burgeoning literature on feminist theory and feminist treatments of organizations suggests a variety of ways to classify different approaches to gender and the 'gender problem' in organizations (e.g. Calas & Smircich, 1996; Ely, 1999; Harding, 1986; Tong, 1989). In our typology, we identify three traditional approaches as well as a fourth, non-traditional approach (Kolb, Fletcher, Meyerson, Merrill-Sands & Ely, 1998). This typology is rooted in the distinctions we see among different conceptions of gender and the resultant courses of action organizations have taken to address the problem of gender inequity. We conceptualize each approach as a 'frame' for understanding what gender is and why inequities exist between men and women at work. Implied within each frame is a vision of gender equity and an approach for achieving that vision.

Frame 1: Fix the Women

The first and perhaps most common approach to gender equity stems from a liberal strain of political theory, which posits that individuals rise and fall on their own merits. From this perspective, gender is an individual characteristic marked by one's biological category as male or female. Sex-role socialization produces individual differences in attitudes and behaviors between men and women, which have rendered women less skilled than men to compete in the world of business. These socialized differences account for inequalities between men and women in the workplace. Accordingly, if women developed appropriate traits and skills, they would be better equipped to compete with men. They would advance at rates comparable to men and would assume a proportionate share of leadership positions. Within this frame, organizational interventions designed to eliminate sex inequality eradicate socialized differences by strengthening women's skills to give them the wherewithal, as individuals, to perform on a par with men. Women are the sole targets of such efforts.

Table 1.   Approaches to Gender Equity and Change

	Definition of Gender	Problem Definition	Vision of Gender Equity	Approach To Change	Benefits	Limitations
Frame 1 Fix the Women	Socialized sex differences	Women lack skills, know-how to 'play the game'	No differences between men and women; women are just like men	Develop women's skills through training, mentoring, etc.	Helps individual women succeed; creates role models when they succeed	Leaves system and male standards intact; blames women as source of problem
Frame 2 Value the Feminine	Socialized sex differences; separate spheres of activity	Women's skills not valued or recognized	Differences recognized, valued, preserved	Diversity training; reward and celebrate differences, 'women's ways'	Legitimates differences; 'feminine' approach valued; tied to broader diversity initiatives	Reinforces stereotypes; leaves processes in place that produce differences
Frame 3 Create Equal Opportunities	Sex differences in treatment, access, opportunity	Differential structures of power and opportunity yield less access, fewer resources for women	Create level playing field by reducing structural barriers, biases	Policies to compensate for structural barriers, e.g. affirmative action, work family benefits	Helps with recruiting, retaining, advancing women; eases work-family stress	Has minimal impact on organizational culture; backlash; work-family remains 'woman's problem'

Table 1. Continued.

	Definition of Gender	Problem Definition	Vision of Gender Equity	Approach To Change	Benefits	Limitations
Frame 4 Assess and Revise Work Culture	System of oppressive relations reproduced in and by social practices	Social practices designed by and for white, heterosexual, class-privileged men appear neutral but uphold gender as fixed, ranked oppositions	Process of identifying and revising oppressive social practices; gender no longer an axis of power	Emergent, localized process of incremental change involving critique, narrative revision, experimentation	Exposes apparent neutrality of practices as oppressive; more likely to change organization culture; continuous process of learning	Resistance to deep change; difficult to sustain

According to this approach, educating and training more women for business and professional careers is key to easing the difficulties organizations have had recruiting them into positions traditionally held by men. These efforts produce an enhanced applicant pool and create a pipeline of qualified women to fill these positions. Executive training programs, leadership development courses, networking workshops, and assertiveness training programs that focus on helping women develop the skills and styles considered requisite for success are representative of this approach (Hennig & Jardim, 1977; Powell, 1987). These interventions, which are aimed at 'fixing' women, are the ameliorative strategies organizational researchers commonly recommend to create greater equality in the workplace (for review, see Ely, 1999). Typically organizations use these strategies as their first response to difficulties they experience promoting and retaining women at the same rates as men.

Extensive organizational and psychological research on sex differences, in which sex is a predictor of such attributes as leadership style (for reviews, see Eagly & Johnson, 1990) and negotiation skills (e.g. Stevens, Bavetta & Gist, 1993; Kolb & Coolidge, 1992) is rooted in this general perspective. Yet those who have conducted meta-analyses of sex difference research typically conclude that such differences are minimal at best (e.g. Eagly & Johnson,

1990). Consequently a number of scholars have urged social scientists to abandon this line of inquiry (e.g. Epstein, 1988; Mednick, 1989). Moreover, women have not made significant inroads into their respective fields despite the fact that they currently constitute nearly 50% of graduating law and medical school classes and hold nearly 38% of MBA degrees granted annually in the U.S. (AACSB, 1999; Epstein, 1993). While better education has unquestionably increased the number of eligible women in 'the pipeline', and training programs have helped women develop valuable skills and play the game as well as – or better than – many men (Heim, 1992), the glass ceiling persists (Benokratis, 1998; Valian, 1998). In addition these interventions are typically predicated solely on an understanding of the needs of white women in the managerial and professional ranks, as if those needs coincided with the needs of all women in the organization. This bias is likely reinforced by an over-emphasis on sex differences, which have been more fully developed and explored between white, middle-class men and women, as the primary means to understanding the role of gender in organizations (Nkomo, 1992). This has left other women to fend for themselves and places additional stresses on race and class relations in organizations, especially among women (Blake, 1999). Finally, these interventions can also have a negative impact on gender relations by generating backlash among men who see these programs, at best, as providing unfair advantages to women and, at worst, as causing an erosion of the organization's talent pool (e.g. Tsui, Egan & O'Reilly, 1992).

Interventions recommended in this frame purposely leave existing organizational policies and structures intact and are meant to assimilate (some) women with minimal disruption to the status quo. We argue that the limited and sometimes negative impact these interventions have had is due largely to this fact. As others have noted, unless change efforts challenge existing power arrangements in organizations, people from traditionally under-represented groups will remain marginalized in tenuous and often untenable positions (Cox, 1993; Thomas, 1991; Thomas & Ely, 1996).

Frame 2: Value the Feminine

The second approach to gender we have identified exists in nearly perfect opposition to the first. Although its conception of gender remains socialized differences between men and women, its proponents argue that these differences should not be eliminated, but rather, celebrated. According to this perspective, 'women's difference' from men, in particular, their 'relationship-orientation' (Belenky, Clinchy, Goldberger & Tarule, 1986; Gilligan, 1982), which has traditionally marked them as ill-suited for the hard-driving, task orientation of the workplace, in fact, constitutes an effective and much-needed management style (Calvert & Ramsey, 1992; Fondas, 1997). Women have been disadvantaged because organizations place a higher value on behaviors, styles, and forms of work traditionally associated with men, masculinity, and the public sphere of work, while devaluing, suppressing, or otherwise ignoring those traditionally associated with women, femininity, and the private sphere of home and family (e.g. Collinson & Hearn, 1994; Fletcher, 1999; Kilbourne, Farkus, Beron & Weir, 1994). The goal of interventions developed from within this frame, therefore, is to give voice to a women's perspective, to articulate and exonerate women's ways of being. It envisions a revised social order in organizations, one that would celebrate women in their feminized difference rather than devalue them as "imperfect copies of the Everyman" (Di Stefano, 1990: 67).

Interventions suggested by this approach include consciousness-raising and training to make people aware of the differences between women's and men's styles, skills, and perspectives; to point out the ways in which feminine activities, such as listening, collaborating, nurturing, and behind-the-scenes peacemaking, have been devalued in the public sphere of work; and to demonstrate the benefits of these activities. Rosener (1995) has been a strong and vocal proponent of this view, arguing further that capitalizing on 'women's advantage' can strengthen a company's competitive advantage in its global markets.

Although many corporations have undertaken the kinds of gender-awareness programs this approach recommends, usually under the rubric of 'valuing diversity', there is no evidence that simply recognizing something as valuable will make it so (Fletcher & Jacques, 1999). Rather, feminine attributes are valued only in the most marginal sense, since they stand in contrast to the organization's norms, which continue to reflect some version of masculine experience. Moreover, critics of this approach have suggested that it can actually reinforce sex stereotypes and the power imbalance between men and women (e.g. Ridgeway, 1997). Calas & Smircich (1993), for example, have argued that the case for the 'feminization' of management fails to alter the relative status and value of these traditionally female activities. Rather, it does little more than reinforce women's appropriateness for performing what are essentially the 'housekeeping' duties of management, tending the corporate fires on the home front, while men are out conquering the global frontiers and exercising the real power in today's multinational corporations. Thus, this approach may simply create and justify an ever more sophisticated form of sex segregation at work. Others (e.g. Epstein, 1988; Mednick, 1989) have urged social scientists to abandon notions about women's unique qualities and contributions, based on the lack of quantitative empirical support for sex differences.

In addition, feminist theorists of gender have pointed out that the attempt within this approach to preserve 'women's difference' is also problematic because it does so at the expense of women's transformation and liberation from the oppressive conventions of femininity (Di Stephano, 1990: 77). Indeed, some have argued that a fundamental flaw of this approach is its failure to recognize that the feminine itself has been partly constituted by its existence within the male-dominated social structure it ostensibly seeks to oppose (Fletcher, 1994). Its proponents have mistakenly taken the meanings that have come to be associated with women under certain oppressive conditions of history to inhere in the real nature of women themselves. This refusal to criticize the feminine assumes that women are not in some ways damaged by their social experience. Ironically, if proponents of this view were to examine too critically the oppressive structures that give rise to this highly exalted, woman's point of view, they would invite a question that subverts their central premise: What would happen to woman's point of view if these oppressive structures were destroyed? Hence, the wish to celebrate woman's goodness would seem to require the perpetuation of her subordination (Ely, 1999; Hare-Mustin & Marecek, 1988).

Finally, like the preceding frame, this one fails to incorporate other aspects of people's identity. Organizational interventions based on a Frame 2 understanding are predicated on particular, dominant images of feminine and masculine, those that are heterosexual, white, and class-privileged. They not only fail to challenge the hierarchical valuing of these categories, they are erroneously based on particular versions of masculine and feminine as if these were universal, enacted in the same way with the same meaning across all groups of men and women. As a result, this approach also targets a limited group of women.

Frame 3: Create Equal Opportunity

The third approach to gender equity focuses on structural barriers to women's recruitment and advancement. From this perspective, gender is still framed as differences between men and women; however, these differences result, not from socialization processes, but from differential structures of opportunity and power that block women's access and advancement. These include hiring, evaluation, and promotion processes that not only reflect sexist attitudes toward and expectations of women, but also reward men's structural position over women's (Kanter, 1977; Reskin, 1988; Ridgeway, 1993; Strober, 1984). For example, differences in the composition of men's and women's social and professional networks gives men greater access to information and support (Podolny & Baron, 1997; Burt 1992; Ibarra, 1992; Kram, 1986; Morrison, White & Velsor, 1987). Professional and managerial women, who are more likely to be in token positions, are subject to increased performance pressures, isolation from informal social and professional networks, and stereotyped role encapsulation (for reviews, see Konrad & Gutek, 1987; Konrad, Winter & Gutek, 1992; Martin, 1985). Similarly, women's under-representation in the upper echelons of organizations has had a negative effect on women both at those levels and lower down in the organization (Ely, 1994; 1995a). These problems contribute to the sex segregation of occupations and workplaces, which, in turn, both accounts for and justifies pay and status inequalities between men and women (England, 1984; Kanter, 1977; Pfeffer & Davis-Blake, 1987; Reskin & Padavic, 1994; Reskin & Roos, 1990; Ridgeway, 1997; Strober, 1984). The goal of interventions in this frame is to create equal opportunities for men and women in the organization by dismantling these structural barriers to equality.

Interventions designed within this frame are largely policy-based. They include a number of familiar remedies, such as: instituting affirmative action programs that revise recruiting procedures with the aim of increasing the proportion of women in positions traditionally held by men; establishing more transparent promotion policies to ensure fairness (Acker & Van Houten, 1974); instituting formal mentoring programs to compensate for men's greater access to informal networks (e.g. Kram, 1986; McCambley, 1999); constructing a range of possible career paths to provide alternatives to 'up or out' internal labor market practices (Schwartz, 1989); and introducing flexible work requirements and other work-family programs to accommodate the dispropor-tionate responsibility for dependent care, which typically falls to women (Hochschild, 1989; Kossek & Block, 1999; Lewis & Lewis, 1996; Raabe, 1996). All of these policy-based programs are designed to eliminate or compensate for structural barriers that make it more difficult for women to compete with men.

These interventions have undoubtedly helped improve the material condi-tions of women's lives. In particular, they have helped organizations recruit, retain, and promote more women in entry and middle levels and, to a lesser extent, senior levels as well. This, in turn, has increased the number of role models and same-sex mentors for women and decreased the constraints and stresses of tokenism, creating an environment that is more hospitable to women (Crosby, 1999). Nevertheless, they have provided no panacea. Some of these efforts have facilitated little progress and, in some cases, have even caused regress (Bailyn, 1993). For example, formal mentoring programs have generally not proved successful in giving women useful connections to influential colleagues (Chao, Walz & Gardner, 1992). In addition, while flexible work benefits might be on the books, many resist using them for fear that doing so will hurt their careers or create backlash (Rapoport et al., 1996). These programs are typically implemented as accommodations to women, and sometimes only as a device to placate and retain individual women who have proved their worthiness (Hochschild, 1989). Using these programs in this way can reinforce sex stereotypes, or generate backlash among men who feel excluded from such benefits and resentful of the extra work they feel they must do to compensate for labor losses these programs incur. Backlash against affirmative action has gained momentum as well, and even its proponents warn of the negative impact affirmative action can have if perceived as an excuse for lowering standards (Heilman, Block & Lucas, 1992; Heilman, Simon & Repper, 1987). All of these interventions attempt to change structures that produce inequality without corresponding interventions into beliefs that legitimate the inequality. Without the latter form of intervention, gender inequality will play out in alternative structural forms (Ridgeway, 1997). Finally, as with those efforts undertaken within Frames 1 and 2, many of these efforts – especially those aimed at promotion and retention – have tended to assist only certain women: those who are white and relatively class-privileged. In a recent survey of women managers of color in Fortune 1000 companies, for example, the vast majority of respondents reported that while their organizations were increasingly gearing their recruitment efforts toward women of color, parallel efforts to promote and retain them have lagged (Catalyst, 1999b). Thus, as in the first two frames, race, class, and other aspects of identity, when considered, are rarely more than add-on concerns, despite many scholars' conclusions that these aspects of identity shape women's experiences differently from the way they shape men's (Cox & Nkomo, 1990; Nkomo, 1992).

We conclude that, although interventions recommended by this approach, unlike the previous two, target organizational policies and structures, their impact on gender inequities is limited. Implementing policies that accommodate existing systems does not fundamentally challenge the sources of power or the social interactions that reinforce and maintain the status quo.

A number of scholars has traced the shortcomings of these three approaches to their roots in different strands of liberal feminist theory, pointing to these theories' limited conceptions of gender as at least partially responsible for organizations' inability to achieve fully their gender equity goals (e.g. Meyerson & Kolb, forthcoming; Calas & Smircich, 1996). In particular, the interventions derived from liberal feminist theories, though responsible for important changes in organizations, are not sufficient to disrupt the pervasive and deeply entrenched imbalance of power in the social relations between men and women. To augment these efforts, we depart from these more traditional approaches and introduce a fourth frame for understanding and addressing the problem.

Frame 4: A Non-traditional Approach to Gender

Frame 4 is distinguished by its conception of gender and its grounding in a different set of theoretical and epistemological positions.[3] From this perspective, gender is neither an individual characteristic nor simply a basis for discrimination. Rather, it is a complex set of social relations enacted across a range of social practices that exist both within and outside of formal organizations. Here we focus our attention on the social practices, ranging from formal policies and procedures to informal patterns of everyday social interaction, within formal organizations. These social practices tend to reflect and support men's experiences and life situations, because they have been created largely by and for men (Acker, 1990; Bailyn, 1993; Martin, 1996; West & Zimmerman, 1987). Now taken as the *sine qua non* of organizational life, they appear to be gender neutral. These social practices, however, maintain a gendered social order in which men and particular forms of masculinity predominate, because they grow out of the conditions that characterize men's lives. The intervention strategy implicated in this conception of gender is one that continuously identifies and disrupts that social order and revises the structural, interactive, and interpretive practices in organizations accordingly (Meyerson & Fletcher, 2000). There is no identifiable endpoint of this approach; rather, the process of change it advocates is both means and ends.

Below, we explicate further this conception of gender, the formulation of the problem of gender inequity that grows from it, the vision we developed as an alternative, and the approach to change we propose to achieve that vision. Throughout, we draw on existing literature as well as our own and others' research (Rapoport et al., 1996; Coleman & Rippin, forthcoming; Kolb & Merrill-Sands, 1999; Merrill-Sands, Fletcher & Acosta, 1999; Meyerson & Kolb, forthcoming) to illustrate how gender operates from a Frame 4 perspective.

Conception of Gender

Within Frame 4, gender is the set of social relations through which the categories male and female, masculine and feminine, derive meaning and shape experience. These categories are situated within and grow from specific social, political, and historical conditions, and are influenced in part by all other social relations, including class, race, ethnicity, nationality, religion, age, and sexual identity. Thus, gender is neither static nor universal; its meaning and consequences are socially constructed (e.g. Acker & Van Houten, 1974; Wharton, 1992). Nevertheless, it appears from what we know currently that gender has been constituted more or less by relations of power: "Gender relations have been (more) defined and (imperfectly) controlled by one of their interrelated aspects – the man" (Flax, 1990: 45). The particular form this imbalance of power takes among actors is shaped by other social relations, such as race, class, ethnicity, and so on, as well as the social, political, and historical circumstances within which actors are situated.

The social relations that constitute gender are manifest in concrete social practices that act to preserve – or challenge – male ascendancy. We refer to these social practices as 'gendered'. In organizations, they include at least four categories of social phenomena that either uphold or contest the value of (some) men above women, masculine above feminine, thereby either reinforcing or challenging traditional interpretations of what it means to be male or female. These social practices build the mechanisms that produce and justify the allocation of resources, information, and opportunities into the culture of organizations. The four categories include: (1) formal policies and procedures; (2) informal work practices, norms, and patterns of work; (3) narratives, rhetoric, language, and other symbolic expressions; and (4) informal patterns of everyday social interaction. We derived these categories from other classifications of gendering processes (Acker, 1990), as well as our own fieldwork in organizations. Because they contain both oppressive and resistive possibilities, these social practices constitute the analytical categories we use to assess gender relations in organizations, and are the avenues for organizational intervention and change.

This approach represents a radical reframing of both gender and the role organizations play in shaping it. Within this frame, it is not sex difference per se that is focal, but rather, the often subtle, seemingly neutral organizational processes that lead to differentiation. We turn now to the problem of gender inequity this conception of gender implies.

FORMULATION OF THE PROBLEM OF GENDER INEQUITY

The problem of gender inequity from the fourth frame perspective is rooted in traditional notions of male and female, masculine and feminine, as fixed categories distinguished by a series of putatively natural, hierarchically-ranked oppositions. In Western organizations, these oppositions are defined by the prototypical white, Western, heterosexual male experience in contrast with the prototypical white, Western, heterosexual female experience. They include: public-private, individualism-collectivism, reason-emotion, mind-body, competition-cooperation. In Western cultures, the first term in each pair is deemed a universal feature of maleness and, in alleged accordance with the dictates of nature and reason, is more highly valued and generously rewarded than its opposite term, a universal feature – by default if nothing else – of femaleness. Although the particular content of the pairs appears to be culture- and history-specific, their oppositional, hierarchical structure appears to remain universal, with men and masculinity, however defined, in the privileged position (e.g. Levi-Strauss, 1962). This conception of gender as *difference* undergirds the approaches advocated in the first three frames; in the fourth frame, it lies at the root of the problem.

According to Frame 4, the representation of gender as oppositions both originates in and preserves male privilege. Its status as fixed in universal truth obfuscates the interests it serves and perpetuates the myth that organizational and social arrangements are gender-neutral (Flax, 1990). Central to this conception of gender is the notion of work as part of the public domain in which particular men – those who are white, heterosexual, Western, and class-privileged – and the particular forms of masculinity associated with them 'naturally' reign. Many workplace social practices thus tend to favor these men without question and often in subtle and insidious ways. The first three frames miss this, leaving these more subtle and insidious sources of inequity intact.

These workplace social practices include *formal policies and procedures*, such as work rules, labor contracts, managerial directives, job descriptions, and performance appraisal systems. They also include *informal practices, norms, and patterns of work*, such as the organization's or work group's norms about how work is to be done and what kinds of relationships are required to do it, the distribution of roles and responsibilities, the information people receive about how to advance in the organization, and the organization's tacit criteria for competence, commitment, and 'fit'. Many of these practices implicitly or explicitly place a higher value on the prototypical male, masculine identity, or masculine experience (Bailyn, 1993). Job descriptions for positions of authority that call for masculine-gendered traits, such as aggressiveness, independence, and competitiveness, without consideration of other traits that may be equally or more relevant to the job requirements, are one example of a formal procedure in organizations that is oppressively gendered. Tenure clocks in academia, which coincide with women's 'biological clocks', are another. An example of an informal practice that is oppressively gendered is using unrestricted availability to work as evidence of one's commitment to the organization, which disadvantages women, who, as the traditional caretakers of home and family, typically have more demands on their time outside of work. The informal practice of using geographical mobility as a prerequisite to upward mobility is also gendered because, although applied equally to men and women, it is more limiting for women, who are more likely to be in dual career situations than men. These social practices, which recognize and reward committed, hard-working employees, who seek aggressively to advance their own and the company's goals, seem gender-neutral, even honorable, on the surface. As these examples suggest, however, a closer look at the gendered nature of these practices reveals an implicit gender bias that reflects and maintains women's relative disadvantage.

Narratives, and the *social interactions* within which people construct and convey them, can also take oppressive forms and play a crucial role in the gendering process in organizations. This notion is based in our understanding of reality as socially constructed, maintained, and modified, in large measure through the stories organization members tell about particular persons or events, and the sense they make more generally of what goes on around them (Barry, 1997; Ewick & Silbey, 1995; Ford & Ford, 1995; Weick, 1995). This sense-making occurs interactively, often in conversation with others in both formal settings, as in hiring and evaluation, and informal settings, as in everyday social interactions (Ridgeway, 1997). It produces narratives that represent and construct what people 'know' about organizations, themselves, and each other. These narratives embody general understandings of the world that by their repetition come to constitute that which is true, right, and good. Yet because narratives often depict specific persons existing in particular circumstances or address concrete matters of immediate concern, the general understandings become the 'ground' in the narrative against which the particular and concrete are 'figure'. Hence, these general understandings typically remain unacknowledged and unquestioned.

Other unacknowledged social norms specify the rules for interacting and participating in these constructions. These include who speaks and who listens, whose questions and contestations are legitimate, and whose interruptions are allowed. To the extent that these social and political aspects of narrative production remain concealed, narratives enact and draw on unexamined knowledge claims, without displaying them or opening them to challenge or testing.

Narratives, therefore, are not just stories or statements related *within* social contexts nor are social interactions simply the vehicle for relating them; they are social practices that are *constitutive of* social contexts. They reproduce, without exposing, the connections of the specific story, persons, or 'facts' to the structure of relations within the organization. In this way, the unarticulated and unexamined plausibility of the narrative that fails to make explicit the gendered aspects of its content and construction sustains dominant cultural images of organizational life, images that come to be seen as "the natural and received shape of the world" (Camaroff & Comaroff, 1991: 23).

Narratives thereby construct and sustain all aspects of organizational 'reality'. For example, many organizations rely on oral histories about who succeeds, who fails, and why as their primary resource for selecting, assessing, and developing people for leadership roles (Martin, Feldman, Hatch & Sitkin, 1983). These narratives and the images they construct are gendered in unacknowledged ways, such as narratives of successful leaders that evoke images of an entrepreneurial, visionary, risk-taker. Such narratives typically fail to mention the support provided by an array of staff whose diligent attention to detail gives these 'leaders' the wherewithal to perform in those roles. As organization members construct and convey such narratives, norms for interaction and propriety keep the voices of these staff either silent or marginalized. Like other oppressively gendered social practices in organiza-tions, this narrative tacitly appeals to a binary and oppositional logic that perpetuates the dominance and apparent neutrality of masculine traits and masculine experience – being entrepreneurial, visionary, and risk-taking – while devaluing the traits and experiences more typically associated with women – being attentive to detail, supportive, and behind-the-scenes.

These kinds of workplace social practices thus operate collectively and in clandestine ways to preserve male dominance by coding activity and assigning meaning as either superior (male, masculine) or inferior (female, feminine), while at the same time maintaining the plausibility of gender neutrality. Implicit in these social practices as well is the differential valuation associated with other identity-based distinctions, for example, race, class, and sexual identity, which anoint particular men and shape the particular forms of masculinity that dominate. These social practices create systematic distinctions between and among men and women, depending in part on their ability and willingness to conform to the dominant cultural images these practices uphold, distinctions that serve to justify disparities in the material conditions of their lives (Reskin & Padavic, 1994). Hence, these social practices constrain and limit opportunities not only for women, but for many men as well. Identifying these social practices and documenting their effects on women's and men's experiences forms the basis of an analysis of gender inequity from within Frame 4.

Origins and Consequences of Social Practices that Produce Gender-based Inequities

Table 2 depicts oppositional representations of gender, which we call 'gendered themes', manifest in organizations' social practices to produce gender-based inequities. These themes are imported into organizations from the larger culture in the form of masculine-feminine dichotomies. For purposes of illustration, we identify three of the most pervasive themes in Western culture and describe how each is implicated across a range of social practices, often with consequences for both gender equity and organizational effectiveness. We then explore organizational narratives, a particular type of social practice that pervades these themes. These narratives disguise the gendered nature of other practices by legitimating them as simply 'the way things are'.

Theme 1: Public-private
Perhaps the single most pervasive gendered theme in modern organizations today is the split between public and private domains of activity and knowledge (Bailyn, 1993). This split is predicated on and upholds the notion of a sexual division of labor in which men's capacity for instrumental work in the public sphere is naturally complemented by women's ability to manage the expressive aspects of family life in the private sphere (Conway, Bourque & Scott, 1989; Elshtain, 1997). In accordance with this opposition, idealized images of workers and parents rest on idealized images of manhood, achieved through one's status as provider, and idealized images of womanhood, achieved through one's status as mother, respectively. Thus, as many have observed, the concepts of 'worker' and 'man' are inextricably bound, as are the concepts of 'parent' and 'woman', a condition that is both reflected in and sustained by the structure and culture of most workplaces (Acker, 1990; Holcomb, 1998). In many organizations, this theme is manifest prominently in narratives and images that portray the ideal worker as someone who is willing and able to put work first, above all other commitments and activities in life (Rapoport et al., 1996). A variety of ostensibly gender-neutral social practices helps to uphold this image of the ideal worker. These include crisis-oriented work patterns and chaotic work routines, which are disruptive, make it difficult to plan or bound time commitments, and demand that people be constantly present at work and available to deal with unanticipated events and their consequences as they arise. Using time spent at work to measure one's contribution and commitment to the organization, either formally, as in performance appraisals, or informally, as in managers' assessments of employees' promise, reinforces this image of the ideal worker, as do public actions and declarations that uphold 'committed'

Table 2. The Fourth Frame: Gendered Themes, Social Practices, and Outcomes

Gendered Theme	Examples of Social Practices	Gendered Outcomes	Unintended Organizational Consequences
Theme 1: Public–Private Dichotomy	Narratives of ideal worker as one able to put work first; crisis-oriented work patterns; norms intended to maintain illusion of workplace as asexual.	Women, who carry disproportionate responsibility for dependent care, perceived as less committed; obfuscates sexuality as dimension of heterosexual male power	Perpetuates inefficient use of time; encourages crises; little time for planning and reflection; rewards behavior that may not be associated with competence or task
Theme 2: Individualism–Collectivism Dichotomy	Narratives, images that portray competence as heroic individualism; rewards for producing immediate, visible results; lack of recognition and rewards for collaborative, developmental (i.e. 'relational') work	Heroic individualism associated with men/masculinity; 'relational' activities associated with women/femininity; differential rewards for men and women performing heroic and 'relational' activities	Allows heroes to create roles for themselves that may be unnecessary or irrelevant to business demands; discourages developing others, planning, building systems and infrastructure
Theme 3: Male Identity–Female Identity Dichotomy	Narratives that portray men and women as fixed, stereotyped opposites; evaluations, perceptions that invoke sex stereotypes, penalize people when they fail to uphold them	Women do not fit masculine image, so do not fit model of success; women ignored or devalued when behave stereotypically feminine; denigrated when behave stereotypically masculine	Relies on narrow set of criteria for model of success and who fits it; suppresses broader range of styles and approaches that could inform and enhance work; increases dissatisfaction and turnover among those who do not 'fit'

workers as those who are willing to put family obligations second to work obligations. We are reminded here of Martin's (1990) report of a senior woman in one corporation who scheduled a C-section for the delivery of her baby so that she could attend an important meeting. Her action and, more importantly, the public praise she received within the company for her action, are examples of social practices of this sort.

Although these social practices are ostensibly gender-neutral in that everyone is similarly subjected to them, they penalize people who cannot be available for work all the time and thus have a differential impact on women and men. Because they tend to bear disproportionate responsibility for home and family, women, on average, have less flexibility to work the long hours many companies require without feeling they are abdicating responsibility on the home front. Thus, women appear to be less committed and are more likely to be unavailable when 'needed'. In addition, when the need to respond to crises diverts women from their primary tasks, they fulfill the negative stereotype that they are less task-oriented than men. They are, therefore, more quickly judged in negative terms than their male counterparts behaving in the same manner (Jamieson, 1995).

These social practices are especially advantageous to relatively high-income, married men, whose spouses are less likely to be employed outside the home, relative to single women or to married/partnered women and gay men of all income levels, whose spouses/partners are more likely to be employed. At the same time, low-income women, who are often women of color, and who, if single parents, are likely to be the sole supporters of their family, suffer disproportionately from such practices. Their higher-income, typically white woman counterparts, who have the economic wherewithal, can choose to hire people to help with their child-care and household responsibilities (see Coleman and Rippin, forthcoming, for further discussion of the impact of these kinds of social practices on low-income women).

As the foregoing analysis suggests, the problems that the public-private split presents for women are typically understood as problems concerning time and the allocation of time between work and family. This is because this is how white, middle- and upper-middle-class women experience the problem most obviously and acutely. As we have just done, we can describe how race and class oppression increase, in an additive fashion, the burdens women of color experience in this regard. It is also important to recognize how race and class oppression interact with gender to produce qualitatively different experiences of the public-private split in organizations. When examined through the lives and circumstances of women of other racial, ethnic, or social class backgrounds, the manifestations of the traditional separation of public and private spheres become more complex and multifaceted. Hurtado (1989) has suggested that for low-income women of color, the notion of 'the personal as political' is old news and does not galvanize their political consciousness in the same way it has for many middle- and upper-middle-class white women. This is due to their experiences of the government constantly intervening in their private lives and domestic arrangements through, for example, welfare programs and policies. Hence, she argues, the relationship between public and private, though still clearly gendered, is qualitatively different for these women. Others have noted that because the private sphere of family and community often provides a refuge for men and women of color from the racism they experience in the public sphere of work, gender relations in communities of color are structured differently from gender relations in white, middle- and upper-middle class communities. Bell (1992: 371) notes, for example, that the "experience of racial oppression serves as a powerful bond between black men and women. Black women understand the devastating effects of racism on black men" and "feel compelled to protect, or at least not add to, [their] already fragile status." Black women are subject to a 'code of silence' that discourages them from speaking out against sexism or sexual harassment at work when the victimizer is a black man. Referring to the ambivalence felt within the black community during the Clarence Thomas–Anita Hill controversy, Bell (1992: 372) explains, "Women who speak out are perceived [within large segments of the black community] as co-conspirators of white men. They provide the white power structure with ammunition that can be used against black men." Thus, to speak out is to wield a double-edged sword. This makes the public–private split even more complicated for women of color, who must navigate much more carefully than their white woman counterparts between the two spheres.

Sexuality at work is another aspect of gender relations that is shaped by the notion of public and private as distinct spheres, again with different consequences for organization members depending on their sex, race, class, and sexual identity. The supposed separation of public and private spheres fosters the myth that people can control their experiences and feelings by compartmentalizing them: sexual feelings and expressions belong in the private sphere. Although statistics on dating and 'sexual talk' among co-workers attest to the reality that sexuality is far from absent in the workplace (Gutek, 1985), taboos against these behaviors have made it difficult to develop policies and norms that might govern a more realistic and constructive role for sexuality at work (Thomas, 1989). In the absence of such policies and norms, sexuality remains a largely unacknowledged, yet pervasive, aspect of social processes in organizations that appeal to and uphold the masculinity of those in power – white heterosexual men. Thus to treat the personal, sexual dimension as an anomalous incursion of the private sphere into the public is to overlook strategies of power and control in which sexuality is an important dimension (Pringle, 1989).

These strategies of power and control are evident in a number of asymmetries that characterize different groups' experiences of sexuality at work. First, because women are typically in subordinate positions, dependent on men for their continued employment, it is up to women to market their sexual attractiveness to men and not vice-versa. Thus, women are often perceived as inappropriately using sex to their advantage. In fact, however, women are much less likely than men to initiate sexual encounters and are more likely to be hurt by sex at work (Gutek, 1985; Gutek & Dunwoody, 1987). Second, although some women do use sex as an advancement strategy, however dubious or ill advised, it is not an option that is equally available to all women. Those who conform to conventional images of beauty and who share private sphere relations with those in power – young, conventionally attractive, white, heterosexual, middle- and upper-class women – are more likely both to reap its benefits and to incur its costs. Third, even when an individual woman does benefit from using this strategy, her conformity to traditional gender roles reinforces oppressive gender arrangements and can have detrimental effects on women's credibility more generally. Finally, the norm that organizations must appear to be sexless is problematic for those suspected or known to be other than heterosexual (Hall, 1989). The sexuality of gay, lesbian, bisexual and transgendered people, for whom simply *to be* is to be in violation of this norm, must "remain within the darkest penumbra, sealed away from any illuminating awareness" (Hall, 1989: 125). These asymmetries suggest that social practices that uphold the prevailing ideology of sex and work as separate make more sense from the perspective of heterosexual men than they do from anyone else's (Pringle, 1989).

Feminists' attempts to remove sexual forms of oppression from the workplace have also had some unintended ill effects attributable to Western culture's investment in the notion of a public-private split. In the interest of banishing sexuality from the public sphere, courts and companies have responded to feminists' concerns by singling out sexual advances as the essence of workplace harassment directed toward women. While clearly an advance over a time when courts insisted on the traditional view of sexual relations as a private phenomenon, not amenable to public scrutiny, the emphasis on sexual advances as the quintessential form of harassment not only ignores non-sexual forms of gender-based hostility at work, it encourages the protection of women for the wrong reasons (Schultz, 1998). "Rather than emphasizing the use of harassment law to promote women's empowerment and equality as workers, it subtly appeals to [men in positions of decision-making authority] to protect women's sexual virtue or sensibilities" (Schultz, 1998: 1729). As Schultz has noted, the 'benefits' of this sexual paternalism are "limited to women imagined to possess the sexual purity that renders them deserving of protection. Such protection historically has been reserved for white, middle-class women, who did not upset the gender order by abandoning the domestic sphere for wage work or politics . . . . [E]ven being an older, married woman who aspires to a male-dominated occupation is sufficient to remove a woman from the court's protection" (1998: 1729). These efforts to protect (some) women thus stem from and affirm notions of the private sphere as women's right and proper place.

Finally, some feminist organizational scholars have argued that the separation of public and private is, in itself, disempowering because it removes sexuality as a potentially positive resource for women and others at the margins of organizations (Cockburn, 1991; Pringle, 1989; Vance, 1984). The priority given to the dangerous and coercive aspects of sexuality has led to an anti-sexual stance, potentially precluding women's exploration of what it means to be a sexual subject rather than object (Pringle, 1989). Although admittedly hard to know what a 'free' choice in the context of male power would be, these scholars urge women to reintroduce to organizational life their bodies, sexuality, and emotions on their own terms (Cockburn, 1991). They argue that attempts merely to drive sexuality from the workplace leave the ideology of separate spheres and the myth of male rationality effectively intact and unchallenged (Pringle, 1989).

In addition to their consequences for gender equity, social practices that arise from the split between public and private domains may also produce less than optimal consequences for organizations (Bailyn et al., 1997; Kolb & Merrill-Sands, 1999; Merrill-Sands et al., 1999). For example, unbounded time demands on employees, especially when coupled with crisis-oriented work patterns, can lead to the inefficient use of time, which, in turn, reinforces a chaotic, unpredictable work environment. Thus, the unbounded demands on people's time ironically both reflect and can reproduce a situation in which employees are still unable to fulfill their responsibilities effectively. In addition, despite the long hours, this kind of work environment leaves little time for planning and reflection, and people, therefore, have little opportunity to learn from their mistakes (Coleman & Rippin, forthcoming).

Theme 2: Individualism-collectivism
A second gendered theme in Western organizations is the tension between an individualistic and collectivistic orientation in which the individualistic invariably prevails (Gergen, 1994). This split is a clearly gendered one in that the former is associated with men and masculinity, and the latter with women and femininity (Connell, 1987; Meyerson, 1998). It is deeply rooted in Western

culture and, many have noted, woven into the fabric of most Western organizations (Hofstede, 1984). It is predicated on beliefs in individual achievement and a meritocratic system of reward and stratification. In many organizations, this theme is manifest most prominently in narratives and images that portray competence as heroic independence, and collaborative and developmental activities as tangential – nice, but not necessary – to the effective functioning of the organization. A range of formal policies, informal practices and work patterns reinforces these images. These include social practices that support and sustain individual heroism as the most effective strategy for getting ahead, such as informal recognition and formal rewards for self-promoting 'stars', but not for behind-the-scenes builders and planners. Similarly, demands for immediately visible results can encourage heroics, as can ambiguous roles, responsibilities, and lines of authority, which allow people to define problems that fit solutions they can heroically provide (March & Olsen, 1976). In organizations with these social practices, collaboration, team-work, capacity-building, smoothing difficulties, and developing others is often invisible work (Fletcher, 1999; Jacques, 1996). Narratives about success and failure that celebrate heroic individuals for resolving crises and solving pressing organizational problems are popular, reinforcing people's belief that they will rise or fall on their own merits.

Practices that differentially value individual heroics and collaborative building activities can lead to gender inequities because these domains are gendered. In Western cultures, heroic behaviors are consistent with the traits people tend to associate with masculinity: strong, assertive, independent, self-sufficient, risk-taking. By contrast, building behaviors are consistent with the traits many associate with femininity: collaborative, consultative, inclusive, non-hierarchical, supportive, and concerned with relationships. Despite the increasing recognition of the importance of these more feminine characteristics in Western management circles (Fondas, 1997; Rosener, 1995) and the espoused valuing of these attributes in some organizations, building activities are ignored or implicitly discouraged in organizations that promote heroic behavior, especially, as some have observed, when women are doing them (Fletcher, 1999; Jamieson, 1995). This may be because the actions and interactions involved in developing a team, developing people's skills, and working behind the scenes for a group's success are considered 'natural' behaviors for women and are therefore not considered a developed competency when women do them (Fletcher, 1998; 1999). Calas & Smircich (1993) have speculated further that efforts to 'feminize' management simply reinforce traditional sex roles at work, since they justify a division of labor in which women managers tend to the companies' more mundane domestic affairs while the men explore the higher pay-off, more exciting global frontiers.

The devaluation of support activities relative to more visible, individual acts of heroism further disadvantages members of racial and ethnic minority groups, who tend to engage – even more often than their less scarce white woman counterparts – in a range of behind-the-scenes support activities as token representatives of their groups. These include recruiting, mentoring, and serving as role models for other members of their group; providing resources and opportunities for them that the organization would not otherwise provide; and serving as group representatives on committees, task forces, and panels, often at the organization's request. This work is rarely recognized as part of the formal responsibilities of one's job; it is extra work that these people perform over and above their regular responsibilities, which leaves them with less time to do work that 'counts' in the formal evaluation and reward system (Martin & Meyerson, 1998). Again, when sexism becomes entangled in racism, the consequences of the individualist-collectivist split can be qualitatively different, and disproportionately negative, for women of color. For example, relative to men of color and white women, women of color are especially burdened by obligations they feel to mentor the more junior members of their identity group (Murrell & Tangri, 1999). This is because their junior counterparts – women of color—are uniquely vulnerable to problems that can arise in cross-race or cross-sex career-enhancing relationships, whether with white women (Blake, 1999), men of color (Bell, 1992), or white men (Thomas, 1989). As a result, the relatively few women of color who occupy senior positions experience inordinate pressures to serve as role models and as mentors for these women and, therefore, pay an especially high price for the organization's failure to recognize and reward this kind of work (Murrell & Tangri, 1999).

These social practices may also have implications for the organization's effectiveness (Bailyn et al., 1997; Kolb & Merrill-Sands, 1999; Merrill-Sands et al., 1999). The emphasis on heroics, for example, independent of any rigorous assessment of the organization's needs, allows heroes to create roles for themselves that may well be irrelevant or unnecessary to the real demands of the business, thereby wasting both individual and organizational resources (Coleman & Rippin, forthcoming). In addition, an emphasis in the organization's culture on immediate results discourages people from spending time developing others or building the systems and infrastructure required to sustain and carry forward the organization's work. A self-perpetuating process thus occurs whereby the lack of adequate systems fosters a chaotic work environment, which reinforces the felt need for immediate solutions, and in turn, encourages would-be heroes to provide them.

Theme 3: Male identity-female identity

A third, gendered theme is the opposition of male identity to female identity as mutually exclusive categories rooted and fixed in the presumably determinate categories of biological sex. In accordance with this opposition, woman is defined by what her opposite, man, is not; each person has only one gender and is never the other or both (Flax, 1990; Ridgeway, 1997). The binary and oppositional logic that underlies this conception of gender identity stems from and reinforces the idea of a true essence of femaleness, embodied within all women, and likewise, a true essence of maleness, embodied within all men. This theme often emerges in narratives about sex differences, which evoke narrow, idealized images of men and women as monolithic categories distinguished by a series of mutually exclusive, stereotyped traits. In Western organizations, these idealized images are the ones associated with white, Western, heterosexual men and women (Ely, 1995a). Whether the object of such narratives is to reduce sex differences, ignore them, deny them, or celebrate them, the presumption of fixed differences between men and women characterizes most talk of gender in organizations (Epstein, 1988). A range of social practices in organizations is imbued with these images. These include evaluations of performance, attributions of success and failure, and inter-pretations of behavior shaped by fixed, stereotyped expectations concerning men's and women's skills and deficits. They also include practices that penalize or criticize people for failing to uphold gender stereotypes, such as negative images associated with women who are seen as overly aggressive and men who are seen as overly sensitive.

These social practices implicitly or explicitly reinforce adherence to stereotypical sex roles and behaviors. In particular, they reflect expectations and criteria for success that are conflated with stereotypical images of white, Western, heterosexual masculinity and construed as antithetical to stereotypical images of white, Western, heterosexual femininity. Thus, if for no other reason than women are in bodies that do not fit this masculine image, they do not fit the operative model of success in many companies (Brenner, Tomkiewicz & Schein, 1989). As a result, when women fail to meet performance expectations that are based on masculine images of competence, their failures are construed as stereotype-confirming; they are less likely than their male counterparts to receive the benefit of the doubt and therefore have less slack within which they can maneuver to accomplish their goals. At the same time, when women confirm the more positive feminine stereotypes, as they do when they engage in building work, they receive no kudos since feminine competencies tend to be ignored or devalued (Fletcher, 1999). Finally, reactions to people who do not fit these gender expectations are often asymmetric: for example, aggressively task-oriented women may be denigrated (Faludi, 1991; Martin, 1996), whereas relationship-oriented men are not (Van Vianen & Willemsen, 1992). In these ways, social practices that provide differential rewards and penalties to men and women for displays of stereotypical masculinity and femininity can place women in a series of double-binds and contribute to the greater difficulty they have in assessing and achieving their potential. As a result, many organizations remain stubbornly male-dominated.

As with social practices arising from the public-private and individualistic-collectivistic splits, the nature and consequences of these practices are also shaped by other aspects of identity. To the extent that social practices reinforce conformity to white, Western, heterosexual images of masculinity, it is not only women who suffer, but some men as well. For example, men's forays into traditionally feminine work are often celebrated, but only for those who have already established their masculinity (Faludi, 1999; Baker-Miller, 1999). This suggests that men who fail to conform to the conventional image of heterosexual masculinity may have less latitude to deviate from that image.

In addition, all women do not necessarily suffer from these practices in the same ways or to the same degrees. Women of color and working class or poor women, who by definition deviate from the idealized—white, middle- and upper-middle class – image of femininity, will likely suffer different consequences, depending in part on the ways in which their race, ethnicity, religion, class, etc., shape stereotypes, including sex stereotypes, about them. Stereotypic expectations about women of Asian descent as ultra-feminine, for example, put them in an even further polarized position than white women from masculine images of success. In addition, men may acknowledge a woman for her ability to act like men with such compliments as, "she kicks ass with the best of them" or "she's hard as nails," but these compliments cut two ways (Martin, 1996: 191), and they cut differently for different women. While they provide some positive recognition for a woman's ability to mobilize competitive masculinity, they also serve as strong reminders to white women that they have violated societal norms associated with femininity and thereby raise questions about their status as women (Ely, 1995a; Martin, 1996). By contrast, Hurtado (1989) suggests that women of color are sometimes granted a measure of leniency in their violations of feminine stereotypes. Since white men are less likely to see women of color as potential mates, they are less invested in their conformity to traditional gender roles. At best, she argues, women of color are simply invisible. At worst, when women of color violate gender-stereotypes, perceptions of them may be distorted in ways that can be personally damaging and severely limiting to their careers. According to Bell (1992), black women, accused historically of being difficult, castrating, and overbearing, may be especially vulnerable in this regard. "Due to the legacy of slavery," she argues, "black women have never had the privilege of being submissive, docile, or fragile. Rarely, if ever, have black women been afforded the feminine characteristics attributed to white women" (Bell, 1992: 369). Institutionalized racism, which restricts opportunities for work among black men, as well high rates of black male incarceration, have forced disproportionate numbers of black women to assume the roles of family provider as well as family caretaker, and they are often the ones to whom other members of their communities look for leadership (Brown-Collins & Sussewell, 1986; Gilkes, 1980). Given these prospects, black women are taught from a young age to be self-reliant. Those who become professionals typically "know how to speak out for themselves, and they possess an inner confidence, because they know how to survive against the odds" (Bell, 1992: 370). Whites, however, have a tendency to distort these strengths, often interpreting black women who show competence, assertiveness, and self-confidence – the behaviors most organizations claim to value – as overly controlling, manipulative, and aggressive (Bell, 1992). Thus, the very characteristics that help black women to survive in work settings where they must contend with both racism and sexism – and that would bring kudos for white men – may limit their success in these same settings.

In addition to gender inequities, social practices that support gender identity as a mutually exclusive proposition may produce a number of negative consequences for the organization as well. These are due largely to the narrow set of criteria for determining who 'fits' the model of success and the often-circumscribed set of strategies that constitute the available ways for doing work. These practices suppress a broader range of styles and approaches that might be useful for operating, not only in diverse markets worldwide, but in organizations' core activities as well (Bailyn, 1993; Thomas & Ely, 1996). To the extent that employees find it difficult to conform to the image of the successful employee, or find it difficult to bring all of their relevant skills and insights to their jobs, important human resources are lost. Finally, turnover is often high among women who find these aspects of their organization's culture especially inhospitable. In a study of women lawyers in large law firms, for example, women associates in male-dominated firms were particularly vitriolic about the company's masculine definitions of success, expressed disappointment at the absence of feminine or female role models, and, as a result, felt demoralized (Ely, 1994, 1995a). In short, we suspect that this situation discourages and disempowers many committed, dynamic, and creative employees, and instead reinforces models of success that may well compromise the company's effectiveness in the long-run.

Maintenance of the gender status quo
Finally, there are social practices that disguise the gendered nature of other social practices. These are primarily narratives – those symbolic representations, most often communicated through language – that people rely on to make sense of what goes on around them. They include narratives about gender, as well as competence and incompetence, commitment and lack of commitment, success and failure, that draw on gender distinctions or reinforce gendered themes explicitly or implicitly. Through the process of retelling, these narratives and the particular set of assumptions, preferences, and interests upon which they are based, become taken for granted by members of the organization, reified, "perceived as 'objective' and independent from those who created them" (Mumby, 1987: 119). Hence, they function to naturalize 'the way things are' in organizations and serve as powerful, but usually invisible, legitimating devices. Some organizational theorists have referred to these narratives as institutionalized myths, which construct as legitimate, neutral, and natural particular versions of reality that might otherwise be open to question (DiMaggio & Powell, 1991; Meyer & Rowen, 1977).

For example, in a study we conducted to identify the causes of senior women's high rates of turnover, senior managers in the company continually attributed women's failures to personal and idiosyncratic factors, without attention to the possible systemic factors at play (Ely & Meyerson, forthcoming). In doing so, however, they failed to state explicitly the set of assumptions that undergirded their understanding of the problem: that women and men are simply people, without gender identities, occupying the same cultural, historical, material, and political positions, subject to and participating in the same *neutral* organizational processes and *impartial* interpersonal interactions. These assumptions were therefore uncontestable. In this way, the narrative helped to sustain existing gender arrangements, and only the women themselves were implicated in their failures.

Although narratives are the predominant form of social practices that function this way, other kinds of institutionalized social practices can also serve as legitimating devices by precluding consideration of alternatives to generally accepted understandings of the way things are. For example, training programs for women that implicitly and narrowly define the company's gender problems as attributable to women's skill deficits can preclude consideration of alternative explanations, such as the gendered nature of the company's practices.

As with other oppressively gendered social practices, narratives and one's analysis of them are shaped in important ways by other salient aspects of identity, such as race and class. For example, one's understanding of how narratives neutralize and legitimate gender-oppressive social practices is limited to those narratives that conceal inequitable gender relations within the particular group of men and women in question. If an all-white research team analyzes gender relations by focusing on managers who are also all white, their analysis of gender relations in that company will likely take white, middle- or upper-middle-class experience for granted, as if it were the standard experience, in much the same way that organizations implicitly take male experience for granted, as if it were the standard. When the focal group in the organization or the research team is more diverse, it can become clearer how narratives neutralize and legitimate gender-oppressive practices in multiple and complex ways, for example, how they might be implicitly predicated on racial as well as gender distinctions. A study of race relations in a racially diverse law firm, whose mission was to advance the rights and interests of low-income women, is illustrative (see Ely, 1995b). In the course of data collection, the multiracial-multiethnic research team discovered a common narrative, repeated by firm members from various racial and ethnic backgrounds, about the unique contributions of women lawyers of color to the firm's success. According to the narrative, Latina and Asian-American women, who made up the majority of lawyers in the firm, "practiced law from their gut"; they knew "out of instinct" what the important issues were, and, based in their "experiential background as women of color," knew how to deal effectively with the firm's clients, many of whom were women of color. When analyzing the data, the African-Native-American member of the research team recognized this narrative as one that carried a dual message. On the one hand, it explicitly lauded and reinforced the value of women of color in advancing the mission of the firm. On the other hand, it had a way of implicitly undermining their value by suggesting that their ability to practice law rested more on their 'softer' intuitive skills of connection and empathy than on their 'harder' technical skills as trained, experienced lawyers, as if they had not all graduated from top law schools and passed the state's bar exam. The explicit, laudatory message in this narrative, together with the fact that all of the lawyers in question were women, served to obfuscate the gendered split between the lawyers of color and the white lawyers, a split the implicit message in the narrative tacitly reinforced. During the feedback session when the research team advanced this hypothesis, a woman lawyer of color in the firm confirmed and extended the analysis by explaining how she, as a woman of color, felt disadvantaged relative to her white counterparts, when it came time to assess people's candidacy for management roles in the firm. She explained that she had internalized the narrative's implicit devaluation of women of color – partly in order to claim the competencies it explicitly conveyed about her group – and, as a result, felt less confident about her technical skills, especially in the areas of 'management' and 'finances'. As members of the all-white management team acknowledged, however, she was no less technically capable in management and finance than they had been when they took up the management roles of the firm. Thus, it was only by recognizing the racial overtones of the narrative about women of color practicing law 'from their gut' that the oppressively gendered aspects of it, which systematically disadvantaged the women of color, also became visible. As this example suggests, more diversity in a company can reveal more complexity and more nuance in its gender relations. Lack of diversity seems a particularly acute limitation in the identification of gendered narratives, however, since the neutralizing and legitimating functions narratives serve seem to remain more stubbornly opaque.

Once again, as with other social practices we discuss here, those that disguise the gendered nature of other practices may also compromise the organization's effectiveness and limit its potential for learning. By constraining the interpretation of events, these social practices legitimate and institutionalize particular courses of action as logical and rational, while obscuring others or causing them to appear "strange or lacking in sense" (Mumby, 1987: 114), courses of action that might, in fact, prove fruitful. As a result, organization members have a relatively narrow range of possibilities before them for organizing and accomplishing work, solving problems, and strategic planning. For example, organizations that suppress discussion of relevant aspects of people's cultural identities at work foster hostility and unproductive conflict between cultural identity groups and are less likely to realize the potential benefits of a multicultural workforce (Donnellon & Kolb, 1994; Thomas & Ely, 1996). Narratives are particularly insidious culprits in this regard, again, because their neutralizing and legitimating functions remain opaque, thereby protecting as 'truth' beliefs that might otherwise be open to question. Thus, to the extent that narratives obscure the gendered nature of organizations, they also obscure the ways in which gendered practices undermine both equity and effectiveness goals.

Vision of Gender Equity

The vision of gender equity that grows from this understanding of gender and its role in organizational life is a process whereby organization members continuously identify and disrupt oppressively gendered social practices in organizations and revise them accordingly. Because we are limited in our vision of a gender equitable state by the gender relations of which we are currently a part (Flax, 1990), we cannot anticipate what precisely a transformed, end-state looks like, and suggest instead that the process of transformation – of resistance and learning – continues indefinitely and itself constitutes the gender equity goal. The intent of this process is to locate and enact a vision of work and social interaction that is less constrained by gendered and other oppressive roles, images, and relations. It begins as organization members learn to question their own and others' deeply held assumptions about roles, work, and effectiveness, including what constitutes individual and organizational success. This leads to change in the way work is defined, assigned, executed, and evaluated. We anticipate that this process of reflection, learning, and change will eventually transform the organization, its members, and their relations with one another by challenging and redefining their sense of what it means to be male or female, masculine or feminine. By breaking down the hard oppositions traditionally associated with gender, this process will begin to reveal other, more fluid conceptions of identity and social organization. In this way, our goal with this approach is to resist and ultimately eliminate gender as an axis of power.

Our vision goes beyond gender equity, however. We propose that advancing gender equity objectives can often serve the organization's instrumental goals (Bailyn et al., 1997; Kolb & Merrill-Sands, 1999; Merrill-Sands et al., 1999; Thomas & Ely, 1996). This is because very often the same processes that create gender inequities also undermine an organization's effectiveness. Intervening in these processes can therefore have dual effects. Many of an organization's social practices are so deeply entrenched in beliefs and values long taken for granted as simply 'the way things are' that organization members assume them to be not only gender-neutral, but wise business practices. As our examples above suggest, neither assumption is necessarily the case, and we believe that the kind of questioning and examination we are advocating can reveal otherwise. Therefore, an analysis of gender from this perspective can also suggest ways for improving the organization's effectiveness.

Frame 4: A Non-traditional Approach to Organizational Change

Our analysis of gender and our vision of gender equity suggest the need for organizational change that is no less than revolutionary. Indeed, others whose analyses of the gendered nature of organizations parallel our own have called for a wholesale, radical restructuring of organizations as a way to advance feminist principles at work (e.g. Acker, 1990; Calas & Smirch, 1996). We too call for a radical restructuring of organizations. The approach to change we advocate, however, is not a wholesale revolution but, rather, an emergent, localized process of incremental change (Meyerson & Fletcher, 2000). With this approach, any one intervention is an act of resistance, not intended by itself to transform the gender relations of the organization; instead, it is through a series of interventions, each designed to subvert traditional gender arrangements, that the possibility of organizational transformation exists (Meyerson & Scully, 1995).

We advocate a process of incremental change over the more broad-based, all-encompassing change some of our colleagues have urged for at least three reasons. First, as Weick (forthcoming) has noted, large-scale, organization-wide change efforts typically fail: diffusion tends to be uneven; significant short-term losses are difficult to recover; and organizations often relapse to their original state. Second, the kinds of changes we are advocating involve challenges to existing power relations and the dismantling of practices that have long been institutionalized as rational approaches to the organization's work. We believe, therefore, that change would be both politically and pragmatically difficult, if not impossible, to initiate – let alone sustain – if undertaken as part of a single, all-encompassing change effort. Finally, our analysis points to the deeply embedded nature of traditional gender arrangements and to the particular, concrete, and often idiosyncratic ways these arrangements manifest in different parts of the organization. Change therefore must be highly context-sensitive; emergent; in tune with local politics, constraints, and opportunities; and pervious to experimentation, reflection, and learning (Weick, forthcoming).

In developing our approach to change, we found direction from several traditions, including different varieties of participatory action-research (e.g. Agyris, 1970; Brown, 1985; Brown & Tandon, 1983; Rapoport, Bailyn, Fletcher & Pruitt forthcoming; Reason, 1988; Reason & Rowan, 1981) and feminist research methods (Reinharz, 1992). We found this work appealing for both political and epistemological reasons. With it, we share the goal of producing knowledge through a research process that increases participants' capacity for autonomous action and self-reflection (Coleman & Rippin, forthcoming). We also share its premise that research should be done *with* people, rather than *on* people, based on the notion that "the process of research and meaning-making is itself an intervention that changes the situation for those involved, and that should, as far as possible, be under their control" (Coleman & Rippin, forthcoming). A collaborative approach is justified on pragmatic grounds as well. Since the kind of change we envision requires in-depth understanding of the organization's culture, members inside the organization must help identify and decipher the organization's cultural codes. The researcher, who attempts to take nothing for granted, can ask naive questions, such as why certain social practices exist, who gets ahead and why, and what various symbols mean. In the course of this questioning, internal members can learn to see their organization in a new light and to question their practices accordingly. Finally, we know that whatever we discover about the organization or about change cannot be useful to the organization unless there is an internal capacity to build on and make continued use of this knowledge after the researchers leave. The agenda for change that we envision is, after all, a process that requires ongoing efforts within the organization in order to sustain it. For these reasons, a central methodological requirement of our approach to change is collaboration between external researchers and internal organization members, such that the internal members not only support but also commit to participating actively in each phase of the project.

With our sense of the appropriateness of incremental change and the importance of collaboration firmly in place, we, together with four other colleagues, undertook a three-year, participative action research project in a large, multinational manufacturing and retail company to test these ideas and further develop our approach to change.[4] This project was one in a series of projects designed to develop participative action research methods for this purpose (Rapoport et al., 1996; Kolb & Merrill-Sands, 1999; Merrill-Sands et al., 1999). We jointly initiated this project with the CEO of the company, who had asked us to investigate the reasons for their high rates of turnover among senior women and for the dramatically lower representation of women in senior management positions relative to men and relative to women in middle management. (See Meyerson and Kolb, forthcoming; Coleman and Rippin, forthcoming; and Ely and Meyerson, forthcoming, for more detailed descriptions of this project.) Over the course of our work there, our team interviewed over 160 employees, many repeatedly, who represented virtually all functions located in headquarters; observed numerous team and organization-wide meetings; and examined much written material, including formal organizational policies and plans as well as less formal works in progress. We experimented with and tracked numerous change tactics and types of interventions in the various local projects that emerged over the course of our collaboration with this company. These took place in a range of functions across the organization, from top management at corporate headquarters to the shop floor of one of their manufacturing plants.

In sum, beginning with the notion that an incremental approach to change was most appropriate to our project and drawing on models of participative action research, previous, related change projects, and our own 3-year action research venture, our research team refined a method for organizational change that would advance our vision of gender equity. That method involves an iterative process of critique, narrative revision, and experimentation. In the critique, the project team, composed of external researchers and internal organization members, surfaces social practices that appear to compromise both gender equity and organizational effectiveness. Narrative revision begins with feeding back the critique to other organization members and engaging them in new dialogues about gender, the organization, and its effectiveness. Finally, organization members experiment with new ways of doing work, explicitly articulating both the gender and business rationales for – and consequences of – these changes as they are taking place. The insights people gain from these experiences then provide occasions for altering or extending their critique and further revising their narratives, which, in turn, make it possible for them to consider and experiment with new, previously inconceivable courses of action. Our emphasis on revising narratives as a central feature of the change process is a unique contribution of our research team's work to the foundational work of our predecessors. Drawing examples from our project, we describe each of these phases in more detail below.

Phase 1: Critique

The first phase of the change project is the critique of the organization. It begins after the researchers have negotiated the terms and scope of the work and secured the commitment of the appropriate internal, organizational partners, who will join them to form the project team.[5] The purpose of the critique is to identify oppressively gendered social practices in the organization, especially those that appear to compromise organizational effectiveness. The critique entails data collection and analysis. The project team moves back and forth between these two activities, as is common in traditional qualitative methods (Glaser & Strauss, 1967; Miles & Huberman, 1984). A full range of data collection methods, however, both qualitative and quantitative, are appropriate to assist the team in constructing a detailed portrait of daily life in the organization, including one-on-one interviews, observations, review of documents, focus groups, and surveys. From these data, the team can learn the answers to such questions as: How do people accomplish their work? Who does and who does not succeed in the organization? What are the norms that govern social interaction? What kinds of work and work styles are valued and what kinds are not? What impedes and what propels the work process? As the portrait begins to take shape, the team also begins to explore whether and how the organization's social practices might be systematically gendered in oppressive ways. The portrait and analysis should be sufficiently grounded in detailed accounts of organization members' daily work experiences to yield a comprehensive understanding of how the organization's social practices influence the work and non-work lives of its employees. This portrait is unlikely to depict a single version of reality; rather, it will more likely represent the multiple, often seemingly contradictory perspectives and experiences that coexist among different groups within the organization (Alderfer & Smith, 1982; Martin, 1992; Martin & Meyerson, 1988).

A brief description of some of the gendered social practices our team surfaced in the company in which we conducted our action research project is illustrative of the work a team undertakes during the critique phase of a change project. Working with our internal partners and using the data we jointly collected, we traced the roots of many gender inequities in corporate headquarters to a cultural pattern we referred to as the organization's 'underboundedness': their use of time was undisciplined, roles were unclear, and authority was ambiguous and easily eroded. People tended to respond to the underbounded culture in one of three ways. First were the 'reactors'. These were people who spent most of their time reacting to the endless crises that the organization's lack of structure inevitably created by putting out fires, trying to recover quickly, and scrambling to clarify misunderstandings and mis-communications. Because they were always in reactive mode, these people rarely took initiative in their work. As a result, their careers tended to stagnate. Second were the 'builders'. These people tried to build systems, structures, and teams to create the clarity they lacked and to develop deeper and more lasting competence in the organization. Much of this work was seen, at best, as uninspiring and, at worst, as a waste of time. Finally, there were people who became 'heroes'. Of the three strategies, only this one led to any measure of recognition or success in the company. Heroes applied quick solutions to problems to gain visibility. Because of the lack of clarity in the company, people were often able to achieve hero status by creating problems for which only they had solutions. Not surprisingly, this system of rewards perpetuated the underbounded culture of the organization. As we suggest above, this strategy – a quintessential expression of individualism – overwhelmingly favored men. Behaviors regarded as heroic were consistent with traits that are associated with masculinity and contrary to those associated with femininity. Men, therefore, could more easily and legitimately enact the hero role. In contrast, women were more likely to enact the less valued building strategy. Consistent with our analysis of gender identity, those women who attempted the hero strategy by asserting high profile solutions or otherwise assuming a high degree of visibility were scorned as 'self-promoting' and 'control freaks'.

Men who behaved in comparable ways were praised as 'passionate' and 'creative'. Finally, the public-private split also surfaced here, to the detriment of women, since the underbounded culture rewarded those with unbounded schedules, and those with unbounded schedules tended, more often than not, to be men.

We propose three criteria for assessing the gendered nature of an organization's social practices during the critique phase. First, it is important to assess the extent to which social practices may *have a differential impact* on: (a) men and women, (b) different groups of women, and (c) different groups of men. In our case above, rewards for those with unbounded schedules meets this criterion, since, although applied equally to men and women, it affected them differently as a result of the differences in constraints they experienced outside of work. Second, the team should consider whether there are social practices that *are differentially applied* to: (a) men and women, (b) different groups of women, and (c) different groups of men. A social practice that meets this criterion from our case above is the high value the company placed on heroic behaviors, but only when men behaved this way. Third, the team must identify which social practices, particularly narratives, *conceal the oppressive nature of other social practices* in the legitimating guise of neutrality. An example of this from our case is the labels people used to describe the behaviors of (men) heroes, 'creative' and 'passionate'. These labels seem gender-neutral until they are compared to the more negative labels people used to describe women enacting the very same behaviors. Thus, the narrative about heroes disguised the macho form this strategy took in this company and the way it systematically disadvantaged women.

Phase 2: Narrative Revision

The second phase of the method our team used involves revising the organization's narratives (e.g. Barry, 1997). Narrative revision actually begins during the critique when, analyzing the data through the lens of Frame 4, internal partners on the project team begin to see a different reality and develop a different story about their own and others' experiences in the organization. Telling this story, relating their analysis, and inviting dialogue in formal feedback sessions with others in the organization then moves narrative revision beyond the project team. Internal partners are essential in helping to orient the feedback appropriately to targeted groups within the organization, generally beginning with senior managers, but convening a variety of groups across multiple sessions, including extended retreat formats when possible.

In these sessions, the team works with other members of the organization to learn new ways of understanding and naming their experience in light of the data presented and to begin to invent alternative images of work and social relations at work. This feedback process gives organization members their first opportunity to question previous understandings and consider new alternatives in public. Ideally, it enables marginalized groups to "name themselves, speak for themselves, and participate in defining the terms of interaction ..." (Hartsock, 1981: 158), thus bringing to the fore voices that have been silenced and conflicts that have been suppressed. This process is not intended to generate a single, coherent alternative narrative, but rather to disrupt existing narratives that suppress, by failing to acknowledge, the range of experiences that exist in the organization (Kilduff & Mehra, 1997). Thus, revised narratives can appear fragmented and ambiguous (Bakhtin, 1981; Martin, 1992; Martin & Meyerson, 1998).

A primary purpose of feedback, therefore, is to interrupt existing narratives with new narratives that attempt to subvert prevailing notions of the organization's gender-neutrality. Leaving gender out of narratives about how people work and how the organization operates both reflects and contributes to the dominant cultural view that gender is irrelevant. According to Ewick & Silbey (1995), these are hegemonic narratives. The unarticulated and unexamined plausibility of the story that leaves gender out is its contribution to hegemony. For example, in our own case, the team offered alternatives to the standard explanations provided for women's relative lack of success, by systematically linking individual women's seemingly idiosyncratic experiences to the cultural, political, and social patterns of life within the organization. This alternative narrative made connections across individual women's experiences, locating the problem in the gendering processes of the organization, rather than in the characteristics of individual women. Thus, the construction and diffusion of this alternative narrative was itself an act of resistance to the status quo.

Because feedback challenges many deeply held beliefs about the neutrality of institutionalized social practices and the wisdom of the organization's current modus operandi, it often feels threatening, and many people will likely resist it. Indeed, the process of feeding back the critique to organization members is designed to surface and name suppressed conflicts that many would prefer to keep suppressed. It is important, therefore, to emphasize that the process of feedback does not *create* these conflicts; it only *surfaces* what was already there, so that the organization might learn and change (Gadlin, 1994). In addition, just as surfacing suppressed conflicts can take a toll on members of the majority, failing to surface them may be costly to those who have borne the brunt of them, and may also be costly to the organization as a whole. The feedback sessions therefore should provide an appropriately contained environment, so that people can air their feelings and reactions, and the project team should be available afterward to discuss the analysis further. In feedback sessions and in these discussions, the analysis is often altered or extended as people offer their own experiences as either validating or invalidating evidence. Narrative revision is thus an ongoing activity over the course of change and is, in fact, a crucial aspect of the next phase.

Phase 3: Experimentation

The third phase of the method involves experimenting with changes in the way work is defined, executed, and evaluated.[6] This can include changes in any of the social practices we identified above, from formal policies and procedures to informal patterns of everyday social interaction. The project team, which already includes members of the organizational groups targeted for change, together with any other key members of those groups, makes the decision about which social practices would be good candidates for change. They make these decisions based on two considerations. First, of those social practices identified in the critique as oppressively gendered, which appear to have the strongest link to gender inequities in the organization? Second, of these, which seem linked most closely to compromises in people's ability to be maximally effective? Clearly, not every social practice linked to inequities also compromises effectiveness, and, of those that do, some may be more clearly or more immediately compromising than others. For example, in our project, candidates for change were chaotic work patterns and rewards for heroic problem-solvers. These had negative implications for women, but also created disincentives for people to develop other people, build systems, prevent crises, and plan. Attending to business considerations in the decision about which of the many possible practices to target, and giving priority to those that have the greatest, clearest potential to enhance people's effectiveness, helps the team strategically to make choices about how to intervene. It also helps pragmatically by recognizing that organization members will be more interested in and find it easier to justify interventions that they can link not only to gender equity outcomes but to instrumental outcomes as well.

Calling these interventions 'experiments' is important for several reasons. First, people are typically less resistant to the notion of an 'experiment', which they can think of as a temporary trial rather than a necessarily permanent change. Second, it calls attention to these efforts as disruptions to the status quo, as deviations from institutionalized notions of what is 'normal'. Experiments are wedges that open opportunities for critical reflection, dialogue, and learning. They provoke questions about alternatives, spark debate, and have the potential to surface previously suppressed conflicts (Kolb & Bartunek, 1992). Finally, an 'experiment' evokes the image of a test, and, in the spirit of action research, the interventions we envision serve as tests of the validity of the analysis that suggested them. Much like medicine, in which the reaction to a treatment confirms or disconfirms a diagnosis, the validity of these experiments lies ultimately in whether and to what extent people's experiences change in anticipated ways after they have undertaken the experiment. Thus, it is important that the project team identify concrete outcomes – changes they expect to see both in gender relations and in people's effectiveness – and to monitor these accordingly.

We do not envision any single experiment as providing the solution to the organization's problems. Instead, the possibility of transformation exists in a series of experiments, each designed to change a set of social practices that express and hold in place asymmetric gender relations. It therefore matters less that any given experiment be the 'perfect' intervention and more that the experiment be positioned and interpreted appropriately as part of a process of change meant to interrupt and transform existing gender relations. Understood this way, the experiment is but one intervention into the larger cultural dynamics that create inequities, and opens the way for additional experiments to serve as interventions into the same cultural dynamics. This is consistent with Weick's 'small wins' approach to change (Weick, 1984) and his recent theory of emergent change (Weick, forthcoming). According to Weick, the basic idea of emergent change is that as accommodations and experiments are "repeated, shared, amplified, and sustained, they can, over time, produce perceptible and striking organizational changes" (Orlikowski, 1996: 89: quoted in Weick, forthcoming). For example, one of the first experiments our team undertook as part of our action research project was to create penalties for being late and for running meetings over the allotted time. This in itself was only moderately successful. Yet, this experiment had a snowball effect on the practice of scheduling meetings because it was linked to the larger problem of the organization's unreasonable and unnecessary demands on people's time, which routinely put working parents in an untenable position. A norm evolved whereby meetings were scheduled only during regular work hours to avoid penalizing parents. (For other examples of this incremental approach to change, see Bailyn et al., 1997; Kolb& Merrill-Sands, 1999; Meyerson & Fletcher, 2000; and Merrill-Sands et al., 1999.)

In the course of this research, our team came to see that whether experiments hold, diffuse, and result in meaningful change depends largely on the sense-making processes that accompany them. Thus, we invoke the previous phase of our approach, narrative revision, as a crucial and continuing part of this third phase. This is consistent with Weick's (forthcoming) perspective on change. He claims that in the course of a change effort "the role of the change agent becomes one of managing language, dialogue, and identity" (Weick & Quinn, 1999: 381). Similarly, our team learned that to approach the vision of gender equity we outlined above, members of the organization need consciously to construct alternative narratives about their change efforts. These narratives must make explicit how social practices that seem neutral contribute to the existing gendered order. Narratives need also to reveal how alternative ways of working will interrupt and revise that order and how they will open new possibilities for men and women. The change effort provides the occasion for conversations in which people reflect critically on the organization's practices and on their own behavior as they consider the ways in which these reinforce or resist oppressive gender relations. The experiments generated from and legitimated by this critique are interventions that change the material conditions of work. These changes provide further occasions for building narratives about what is possible for men and women and what is possible as meanings for masculinity and femininity, which, in turn, suggest and legitimate further experimentation and change (Weick, 1995). In this way, shifts in the material conditions of work are accompanied by shifts in the conversations around which organization members interact and behave. These shifts create new realities and new possibilities for effective action in the organization (Ford & Ford, 1995; Gergen, 1991).

This approach to change is consistent with theories of power and resistance. As Foucault (1977) and others (e.g. Wilmott & Knights, 1994) have suggested, power relations change at the margins through dispersed forms of resistance as alternative possibilities for action, meaning, and identity become possible. Although Foucault would argue that such resistance is always countered – and sometimes annexed – by those in power, we are more sanguine. Following others (Hartsock, 1987; hooks, 1984), we see the transformational potential of this kind of change process. We have learned, however, from both our own and others' efforts to change organizations, that to achieve that transformational potential and to resist the cooptation of change efforts, narratives are crucial. Without a sustained narrative that links the experiment to gender-related objectives, the potential for resistance and change will likely be subordinated, even lost, to the instrumental objectives of the experiment. (See Ely and Meyerson, forthcoming, for an extended discussion of the challenge of 'holding onto gender' in this work.)

CONCLUSION

In contrast to other perspectives on gender, our understanding of gender in organizations begins with the notion that organizations are inherently gendered as a result of having been created by and for men. Their gendered nature has been sustained through social practices that organize and explain the structuring of daily life inside, as well as outside, the organization. These social practices reflect gendered themes, in the form of masculine-feminine dichotomies, which have become deeply embedded in organizations, so deeply embedded as to appear to be gender-neutral, simply the norm. Yet, because they are rooted in men's lives and experiences, these social practices tend, in often subtle and insidious ways, to privilege men and disadvantage women, frequently compromising their ability to be maximally effective at work. We propose an emergent, localized approach to systemic, organizational change whereby organization members continuously identify and disrupt oppressively gendered social practices and revise them accordingly.

As we have suggested throughout, how gendering occurs and which particular men and women are most likely to be affected varies systematically as a function of other aspects of identity, such as race, ethnicity, social class, and sexual identity. Thus, for each theme, we have considered how social practices shape experiences differently for different groups of men and women, depending on other identity group memberships. Nevertheless, a critique that has gender as its orientation will likely surface a different set of themes than one that is focused on, for example, race or class. No single critique, no matter how complex or how attentive to multiple bases of privilege and oppression, is likely to reveal all forms or sources of inequities that people experience at work. Different starting points will likely lead the team to focus on different processes and outcomes in their change efforts. Holvino (1999) suggests that to be comprehensive in this regard requires multiple critical lenses applied simultaneously. Acker (1999) argues similarly that this would create a more inclusive portrait of the 'regimes of inequality' in organizations.

Our own experience suggests that the most appropriate orientation of a critique will depend on the particular groups in question, the kind of work they do, their organizational context, and the presenting problems or issues with which they are most explicitly grappling (Ely, Meyerson & Thomas, 1999). For example, to understand the experience of oppression among working class white women, it may be necessary to lead with class relations as the focal point, and then examine how gender operates within and between the different social classes in question. This approach allows the organization's concerns and the particular way those concerns have manifested in the organization, rather than the researcher's interests, to define at least the initial, orienting framework for the analysis. Once begun, the framework would then presumably become increasingly complex as the project team strives to consider the various intergroup relations at play. This requires that researchers engaged in this kind of work have the capacity to move with relative ease in their analyses across the various group memberships that are represented in the organization, a capacity that we believe is enhanced to the extent that the cultural composition of the project team mirrors the cultural composition of the organization (Alderfer et al., 1983). An exploration of how substantively an analysis that begins with a set of relations other than gender would take shape is beyond the scope of this chapter. We nevertheless believe that the general framework we propose here provides a useful template for any such analysis.

NOTES

1. We are grateful to Lotte Bailyn and our colleagues affiliated with the Center for Gender in Organizations, Simmons Graduate School of Management – Gill Coleman, Joyce Fletcher, Deborah Kolb, Deborah Merrill-Sands, Rhona Rapoport, and Bridgette Sheridan – for their contributions to these ideas and for their foundational research, on which this paper builds. We also appreciate the feedback we received on an earlier draft from members of the FSC Research Group, Elaine Backman, Herminia Ibarra, Maureen Scully, and Kathleen Valley. We thank Joanne Martin and Barbara Reskin for their comments, which helped in our conceptual framing of the paper. Finally, we thank Bob Sutton and Barry Staw for their helpful suggestions. This research was funded in part by the Ford Foundation.

2. The research on which we draw was primarily action research to develop theory and methods for advancing gender equity while at the same time improving organizational effectiveness. Our own efforts in this regard (Coleman & Rippon, Ely & Meyerson, and Meyerson & Kolb, all forthcoming) build on and are among a series of related projects, which others have conducted over the past ten years (Rapoport et al., 1996; Kolb & Merrill-Sands, 1999; Merrill-Sands, Fletcher & Acosta, 1999).

3. See Diamond & Quinby (1988), Nicholson (1990), and Holvino (1994) for the kinds of feminist post-structuralist perspectives on which we draw here; see Calas & Smircich (1996) for a typology of feminist positions.

4. Members of the project team were Gill Coleman, Robin Ely, Deborah Kolb, Debra Meyerson, Ann Rippin, and Rhona Rapoport.

5. The internal members of the project team should include both those people who have sufficient authority and reach within the organization to be able to influence the change process, as well as those who represent a hierarchical, functional, and demographic cross-section of the organizational groups of interest. In addition, research suggests that the data collected will be more valid to the extent that external researchers also reflect the demographic composition of employee groups of interest (Alderfer, Tucker, Morgan & Drasgow, 1983).

6. See Meyerson & Fletcher (2000) for a description of experiments as 'small wins'. Through a number of examples, this articles demonstrates how small wins act as local interventions into systemic phenomena.

REFERENCES

AACSB (The International Association for Management Education) Web site, http://www. acsb.edu.

Acker, J. (1990). Hierarchies, jobs, bodies: A theory of gendered organizations. *Gender & Society, 4*, 139–158.

Acker, J. (1999). Revisiting class: Lessons from theorizing race and gender: Relevance for the study of gender and organizations. Working paper, Center for Gender in Organizations, Simmons Graduate School of Management, Boston, MA.

Acker, J., & Van Houten, D. (1974). Differential recruitment and control: The sex structuring of organizations, *Administrative Science Quarterly*, 152–163.

Alderfer, C. P., & Smith, K. K. (1982). Studying intergroup relations embedded in organizations. *Administrative Science Quarterly, 27*, 35–65.

Alderfer, C. P., Tucker, R. C., Morgan, D. R., & Drasgow, F. (1983). Black and white cognitions of changing race relations in management. *Journal of Occupational Behavior, 4*, 105–136.

Argyris, C. (1970). *Intervention theory and method.* Reading, Mass: Addison Wesley.

Bailyn, L., Fletcher, J., & Kolb, D. (1997). Unexpected connections: Considering employees' personal lives can revitalize your business, *Sloan Management Review*, Summer: 11–19.

Bailyn, L. (1993). *Breaking the mold: Women, men and time in the new corporate world.* New York: Free Press.

Baker-Miller, J. (1999). Relationship practice. Paper presented at the Conference on Relational Practice, University of Michigan, October.

Bakhtin, M. (1981). Discourse in the novel. In: M. Holquist (Ed.), *The Dialogial Imagination* (pp. 259–442). Austin, TX: University of Texas Press.

Barry, D. (1997). Telling changes: From narrative family therapy to organizational change and development. *Journal of Organizational Change Management, 10*, 32–48.

Belenky, M. F., Clinchy, B. M., Goldberger, N. R., & Tarule, J. M. (1986). *Women's ways of knowing: The development of self, voice, and mind.* New York: Basic Books.

Bell, E. L. (1992). Myths, stereotypes, and realities of Black women: A personal reflection. *Journal of Applied Behavioral Science, 28*, 363–376.

Benokratis, N. (1998). Subtle sexism: Current practices and prospects for change. Newbury Park, CA: Sage Publications.

Blake, S. (1999). At the crossroads of race and gender: Lessons from the mentoring experiences of professional Black women. In: A. J. Murrell, F. J. Crosby, & R. J. Ely (Eds), *Mentoring Dilemmas: Developmental Relationships Within Multicultural Organizations* (pp. 83–104). Mahwah, N. J.: Laurence Earlbaum Assoicates, Publishers.

Brenner, O. C., Tomkiewicz, J., & Schein, V. E. (1989). The relationship between sex role stereotypes and requisite management characteristics revisited. *Academy of Management Journal, 32*, 662–669.

Brown, D. L. (1985). People-centered development and participatory research. *Harvard Educational Review, 55*, 6–75.

Brown, D. L., & Tandon, R. (1983). Ideology and political economy in inquiry: Action research and participatory research. *Journal of Applied Behavioral Science, 19*, 277–294.

Brown-Collins, A. R., & Sussewell, D. R. (1986). The Afro-American woman's emerging selves. *The Journal of Black Psychology, 13*, 1–11.

Burt, R. (1992). *Structural Holes.* Cambridge, MA: Harvard University Press.

Calas, M., & Smircich, L. (1993). Dangerous liaisons: The 'feminine-in-management' meets globalization. *Business Horizons*, March/April.

Calas, M., & Smircich, L. (1996). From the woman's point of view: Feminist approaches to organization studies. In: S. Clegg, C. Hardy, & W. Nord (Eds), *Handbook of Organization Studies*, London: Sage.

Calvert, L. and Ramsey, V. J. (1992). Bringing women's voice to research on women in management: A feminist perspective. *Journal of Management Inquiry, 1* (1), 79–88.

Camaroff, J., & Camaroff, J. (1991). *Of revelation and revolution.* Chicago: University of Chicago Press.

Catalyst. (1999a). *1999 Catalyst Census of women corporate officers and top earners of the Fortune 500.* New York: Catalyst.

Catalyst, (1999b). *Women of color in corporate management: A statistical picture.* New York: Catalyst.

Chao, G. T., Walz, P. M., & Gardner, P. D. (1992). Formal and informal mentorships: A comparison on network functions and contrast with nonmentored counterparts. *Personnel Psychology, 45*, 619–636.

Cockburn, C. (1991). *In the way of women: Men's resistance to sex equality within organizations.* Ithaca, NY: ILR Press.

Coleman, G., & Rippin, A. Putting feminist theory to work: Collaboration as a means towards organizational change. *Organization*, forthcoming.

Collinson, D., & Hearn, J. (1994). Naming men as men: Implications for work, organizations, and management. *Gender, Work and Organization, 1*, 2–22.

Connell, R. W. (1987). *Gender and power: Society, the person, and sexual politics.* Stanford, CA: Stanford University Press.

Conway, J. K., Bourque, S. C., & Scott, J. W. (1989). *Learning about women: Gender, politics, and power.* Ann Arbor, MI: The University of Michigan Press.

Cox, T. (1993). *Cultural diversity in organizations: Theory, research, and practice.* San Francisco: Berrett-Koehler Publishers.

Cox, T., & Nkomo, S. M. (1990). Invisible men and women: A status report on race as a variable in organizational behavior and research. *Journal of Organizational Behavior, 11*, 419–431.

Crosby, F. J. (1999). The developing literature on developmental relationships. In: A. J. Murrell, F. J. Crosby, and R. J. Ely (Eds), *Mentoring Dilemmas: Developmental Relationships Within Multicultural Organizations*: 3–20. Mahwah, N. J.: Laurence Earlbaum Assoicates, Publishers.

Di Stefano, C. (1990). Dilemmas of difference: Feminism, modernity, and postmodernism. In: L. J. Nicholson (Ed.), *Feminism/postmodernism*: 63–82. New York: Routledge.

Diamond, I., & Quinby, L. (1988). *Feminism and Foucault: Reflections on resistance.* Boston: Northeastern University Press.

DiMaggio, P., & Powell, W. (1991). *The new institutionalism in organizational analysis.* Chicago: University of Chicago Press.

Donnellon, A., & Kolb, D. (1994). Constructive conflict for all: Dispute resolution and diversity in organizations. *Journal of Social Issues, 50* (1), 139–155.

Eagly, A. H., & Johnson, B. T. (1990). Gender and leadership style: A meta-analysis. *Psychological Bulletin, 108*, 233–256.

Elshtain, J. (1997). *Real politics: At the center of everyday life.* Baltimore: Johns Hopkins Press.

Ely, R. J. (1999). Feminist critiques of research on gender in organizations. Working paper, no. 6, Center for Gender in Organizations, Simmons Graduate School of Management, Boston, MA.

Ely, R. J. (1994). The effects of organizational demographics and social identity on relationships among professional women. *Administrative Science Quarterly, 39*, 203–238.

Ely, R. J. (1995a). The power in demography: Women's social constructions of gender identity at work. *Academy of Management Journal, 38*, 589–634.

Ely, R. J. (1995b). The role of dominant identity and experience in organizational work on diversity. In: S. E. Jackson, & M. N. Ruderman (eds.), *Diversity in Work Teams: Research Paradigms for a Changing Workplace:* 161–186. Washington, D. C.: American Psychological Association 161–186.

Ely, R. J., & Meyerson, D. E. Advancing gender equity in organizations: The challenge and importance of maintaining a gender narrative. *Organization*, forthcoming.

Ely, R. J., Meyerson, D. E., & Thomas, D. A. (1999). Integrating gender into a broader diversity lens in organizational diagnosis and intervention. *CGO Insights*, No. 4. Boston, MA: Center for Gender in Organizations, Simmons Graduate School of Management.

England, P. (1984). Wage appreciation and depreciation: a test of neoclassical economic explanations of occupational sex segregation. *Social Forces, 62*, 726–749.

Epstein, C. F. (1988). *Deceptive distinctions: Sex, gender, and the social order.* New Haven: Yale University Press.

Epstein, C. F. (1993). *Women in law,* second edition. New Haven: Yale University Press.

Ewick, P., & Silbey, S. S. (1995). Subversive stories and hegemonic tales: Toward a sociology of narrative, *Law and Society Review, 29*, (2), 197–226.

Faludi, S. (1991). *Backlash: The undeclared war against American women.* New York: Doubleday.

Faludi, S. (1999). *Stiffed.* New York: Doubleday.

Flax, J. (1990). Postmodernism and gender relations in feminist theory. In: L. J. Nicholson (Ed.), *Feminism/Postmodernism*: 39–62. New York: Routledge.

Fletcher, J. K. (1994). Castrating the female advantage: Feminist standpoint research and management science. *Journal of Management Inquiry, 3* (1), 74–82.

Fletcher, J. K. (1998). Relational practice: A feminist reconstruction of work', *Journal of Management Inquiry 7*, 163–186.

Fletcher, J. K. (1999). *Disappearing acts: Gender, power, and relational practice at work.* Cambridge, MA: MIT Press.

Fletcher, J. K., & Jacques, R. (1999). Relational practice: An emerging stream of theorizing and its significance. Working Paper no. 2, Center for Gender in Organizations, Simmons Graduate School of Management, Boston, MA.

Fondas, N. (1997). *Feminization unveiled: Management qualities in contemporary writings.* The Academy of Management Review, *22*, 257–282.

Ford, J. D., & Ford, L. W. (1995). The role of conversations in producing intentional change in organizations, *The Academy of Management Review 20*, 541–570.

Foucault, M. (1977). *Discipline and punish.* London: Allen Lane.

Gadlin, H. (1994). Conflict resolution, cultural differences, and the culture of racism. *Negotiation Journal, 10*, 33–47.

Gergen, K. J. (1991). *The saturated self.* New York: Basic Books.

Gergen, K. J. (1994). *Realities and Relationships.* Cambridge: Harvard University Press.

Gilligan, C. (1982). *In a different voice.* Cambridge, MA: Harvard University Press.

Gilkes, C. T. (1980). Hold back the ocean with a broom: Black women and community work. In: L. Rodgers-Rose (ed.), *The Black Woman.* Beverly Hills, CA: Sage Publications.

Glaser, B. G., & Strauss, A. (1967). *The discovery of grounded theory: Strategies for qualitative research.* Chicago: Aldine.

Gutek, B. A. (1985). *Sex and the workplace: Impact of sexual behavior and harassment on women, men and organizations.* San Francisco, CA: Jossey-Bass.

Gutek, B. A., & Dunwoody, V. (1987). Understanding sex in the workplace. In: A. Stromberg, L. Larwood, & B. A. Gutek (eds.), *Women and Work: An Annual Review.* Vol. 2: 249–269. Newbury Park: Sage.

Hall, M. (1989). Private experiences in the public domain: Lesbians in organizations. In: J. Hearn, D. L. Sheppard, P. Tancred-Sheriff, & G. Burrell (eds.), *The Sexuality of Organization*: 125–138. London: Sage Publications.

Harding, S. (1986). *The science question in feminism.* Ithaca, NY: Cornell University Press.

Hare-Mustin, R. T., & Marecek, J. (1988). The meaning of difference: Gender theory, postmodernism, and psychology. *American Psychologist, 43,* 455–464.

Hartsock, N. (1981). Political change: Two perspectives on power. *Building feminist theory: Essays from Quest,* (pp. 3–19). New York: Longman.

Hartsock, N. (1987). The gender of power. Paper presented at University of Leiden, September.

Hennig, M., & Jardim, A. (1977). *The managerial woman.* New York: Pocket Books.

Heilman, M. E., Block, C. J., & Lucas, J. A. (1992). Presumed incompetent? Stigmatization and affirmative action efforts. *Journal of Applied Psychology, 77,* 536–544.

Heilman, M. E., Simon, M. C., & Repper, D. P. (1987). Intentionally favored, unintentionally harmed? Impact of sex-based preferential selection on self-perceptions and self-evaluations. *Journal of Applied Psychology, 72,* 62–68.

Heim, P. (1992). *Hardball for women.* New York: Plume.

Hochschild, A. (1989). *The second shift.* New York, NY: Viking Penguin.

Hofstede, G. (1984). *Culture's consequences, international differences in work-related values.* Beverly Hills, CA: Sage.

Holcomb, B. (1998). *Not guilty: The good news about working mothers.* New York, NY: Scribner.

Holvino, E. (1994). Women of color in organizations: Revising our models of gender at work. In: E. Cross, J. Katz, F. Miller, & E. W. Seashore (eds.), *The Promise of Diversity* (pp. 52–59). New York: Irwin.

Holvino, E. (1999). Intersections of gender, race, and class in organizations. Working Paper, Center for Gender in Organizations, Simmons Graduate School of Management, Boston, MA.

Hooks, B. (1984). *Feminist theory: From margin to center.* Boston: South End Press.

Hurtado, A. (1989). Relating to privilege: Seduction and rejection in the subordination of white women and women of color. *Signs, 14,* 833–855.

Ibarra, H. (1992). Homophily and differential returns: Sex differences in network structure and access in an advertising firm. *Administrative Science Quarterly, 37,* 422–447.

Jacques, R. (1996). *Manufacturing the employee.* London: Sage Publications.

Jamieson, K. H. (1995). *Beyond the double bind: Women and leadership.* New York: Oxford University Press.

Kanter, R. M. (1977). *Men and women of the corporation.* New York: Basic Books.

Kilbourne, B. England, P., Farkus, G., Beron, K., & Weir, D. (1994). Returns to skill, compensating differentials, and gender bias: Effects of occupational characteristics on the wages of white women and men. *American Journal of Sociology, 100*, 689–719.

Kilduff, M., & Mehra, J. (1997). Postmodernism and organizational research. *Academy of Management Review, 22*, 453–481.

Kolb, D., & Bartunek, J. (1992). *Hidden conflict in organizations: Uncovering behind the scenes disputes.* Newbury Park, CA: Sage Publications.

Kolb, D., & Coolidge, G. (1992). Her place at the table. In: J. Z. Rubin and J. W. Breslin (eds.), *Negotiation Theory and Practice.* Cambridge: Harvard Program on Negotiation Books.

Kolb, D, Fletcher, J., Meyerson, D., Merrill-Sands, D., & Ely, R. (1998). Making change: A framework for promoting gender equity in organizations. *CGO Insights*, No. 1. Boston, MA: Center for Gender in Organizations, Simmons Graduate School of Management.

Konrad, A., & Gutek, B. A. (1987). Theory and research on group composition: Applications to the status of women and ethnic minorities. In: S. Oskamp, & S. Spacapan (eds.), *Interpersonal Processes* (pp. 85–121). Newbury Park, CA: Sage Publications.

Konrad, A. M., Winter, S., & Gutek, B. A. (1992). Diversity in work group sex composition: Implications for majority and minority members. *Research in the Sociology of Organizations, 10*, 115–140.

Kossek, E. E., & R. Block. (1999). *Management human resources in the 21st century: From core concepts to strategic choice.* Cincinnati, OH: Southwest Publishing.

Kram, K. E. (1986). *Mentoring at work: Developmental relationships in organizational life.* Glenview, IL: Scott, Foresman.

Lewis, S., & Lewis, J. (1996). *The work-family challenge: Rethinking employment.* Newbury Park: Sage Publications.

Levi-Strauss, C. (1962). *The savage mind.* Chicago: University of Chicago Press.

March, J., & Olsen, J. (1976). *Ambiguity and choice in organizations.* Bergen, Norway: Universitesforlaget.

Martin, J. (1990). Deconstructing organizational taboos: The suppression of gender conflict in organizations. *Organization Science, 1*, 339–359.

Martin, J. (1992). *Cultures in organizations.* New York: Oxford University Press.

Martin, J., Feldman, M., Hatch, M., & Sitkin, S. (1983). The uniqueness paradox in organizational stories. *Administrative Science Quarterly, 28*, 438–453.

Martin, J., & Meyerson, D. E. (1988). Organizational cultures and the denial, channeling, and acknowledgement of ambiguity. In: L Pondy, L. Boland, & H. Thomas (eds.), *Managing Ambiguity and Change:* 93–125. New York: Wiley.

Martin, J., & Meyerson, D. E. (1998). Women and power: Conformity, resistance, and disorganized coaction. In: R. Kramer and M.. Neale (eds.), *Power and Influence in Organizations*: 311–348. Thousand Oaks, CA: Sage Publications.

Martin, P. Y. (1996). Gendering and evaluating dynamics: Men masculinities, and managements. In: D. Collinson & J. Hearn (Eds.), *Men as Managers, Managers as Men: Critical Perspectives on Men, Masculinities, and Managements* (pp. 186–209). London & Newbury Park, CA: Sage Publications.

Martin, P. Y. (1985). Group sex composition in work organizations: A structural-normative model. *Research in the Sociology of Organizations, 4*, 311–349.

McCambley, E. (1999). Testing theory by practice. In: A. J. Murrell, F. J. Crosby, and R. J. Ely (Eds), *Mentoring dilemmas: Developmental Relationships Within Multicultural Organizations* (pp. 173–188). Mahwah, N. J.: Laurence Earlbaum Assoicates, Publishers.

Mednick, M. T. (1989). On the politics of psychological constructs: Stop the bandwagon, I want to get off. *American Psychologist, 44*, 1118–1123.

Merrill-Sands, D., Fletcher, J. K., & Acosta, N. (1999). Engendering organizational change: A case study of strengthening gender-equity and organizational effectiveness in an international agricultural institute. In: A. Rao, R. Stuart, and D. Kelleher (eds.), *Gender at Work: Organizational Change for Equality* (pp. 77–128). West Hartford, CT: Kumarian Press.

Meyer, J., & Rowan, B. (1977). Institutionalized organizations: Formal structure as myth and ceremony. *American Journal of Sociology, 83*, 340–363.

Meyerson, D. E. (1998). Feeling stressed and burned out: A feminist reading and re-vision of stress in medicine and organization science, *Organization Science, 9*, 103–118.

Meyerson, D. E., & Fletcher, J. K. (2000). A modest manifesto for shattering the glass ceiling. *Harvard Business Review,* Jan.-Feb.: 126–136.

Meyerson, D. E., & Kolb, D. Moving out of the armchair: Developing a framework to bridge the gap between feminist theory and practice. *Organization*, forthcoming.

Meyerson, D. E., & Martin, J. (1987). Culture change: An integration of three different views. *Journal of Management Studies, 24*, 623–648.

Meyerson, D. E. and Scully, M. A. (1995). *Tempered radicalism and the politics of ambivalence and change. Organization Science, 6* (5), 585–600.

Miles, M., & Huberman, M. (1984). *Qualitative data analysis.* Beverly Hills: Sage Publications.

Morrison, A. M., White, R. P., & Velsor, E. (1987). *Breaking the glass ceiling: Can women reach the top?*

Mumby, D. (1987). The political function of narrative in organizations. *Communication Monographs, 54*, June: 113–127.

Murrell, A. J., & Tangri, S. S. (1999). Mentoring at the margin. In: A. J. Murrell, F. J. Crosby, & R. J. Ely (Eds), *Mentoring Dilemmas: Developmental Relationships Within Multicultural Organizations*: 211–224.

Nicholson, L. J. (1990). *Feminism/Postmodernism.* New York: Routledge.

Nkomo, S. M. (1992). The Emperor has no clothes: Rewriting 'race in organizations'. *Academy of Management Review, 17*, 487–513.

Pfeffer, J., & Davis-Blake, A. (1987). The effect of the proportion of women on salaries: The case of college administrators. *Administrative Science Quarterly, 32*, 1–24.

Podolny, J., & Baron, J. (1997). Resources and relationships: Social networks, mobility and satisfaction in the workplace. *American Sociological Review.*

Powell, G. (1987). The effects of sex and gender on recruitment, *Academy of Management Review, 12*, 731–743.

Pringle, R. (1989). Bureaucracy, rationality and sexuality: The case of secretaries. In: J. Hearn, D. L. Sheppard, P. Tancred-Sheriff, & G. Burrell (eds.), *The Sexuality of Organization* (pp. 158–177). London: Sage Publications.

Raabe, P. H. (1996). Constructing pluralistic work and career arrangements. In: S. Lewis and J. Lewis (eds.), *The Work-Family Challenge: Rethinking Employment.* Newbury Park, CA: Sage Publications.

Rapoport, R., Bailyn, L. Fletcher, J., & Pruitt, B. Collaborative interactive participatory action research, forthcoming.

Rapoport, R., Bailyn, L., Kolb, D., Fletcher, J., Friedman, D., Eaton, S., Harvey, M., & Miller, B. (1996). *Relinking life and work: Toward a better future.* Report to the Ford Foundation based on a collaborative research project with three corporations. New York: Ford Foundation.

Reinharz, S. (1992). *Feminist methods in social research.* New York: Oxford University Press.

Reason, P. (1988). *Human inquiry in action: Developments in new paradigm research.* London: Sage Publications.

Reason, P., & Rowan, J. (1981). *Human inquiry.* Chichester, England: John Wiley.

Reskin, B. F. (1988). Bringing the men back in: Sex differentiation and the devaluation of women's work. *Gender and Society, 2,* 58–81.

Reskin, B. F., & Padavic, I. (1994). *Women and men at work.* Thousand Oaks, CA: Pine Forge Press.

Reskin, B. F., & Roos, P. (1990). *Job Queues, Gender Queues.* Philadelphia: Temple University Press.

Ridgeway, C. L. (1993). Gender, status, and the social psychology of expectations. In: P. England (ed.), *Theory on Gender/Feminism on Theory* (pp. 175–198). New York: Aldine.

Ridgeway, C. L. (1997). Interaction and the conservation of gender inequality: Considering employment. *American Sociological Review, 62,* 218–235.

Rosener, J. (1995). *America's competitive secret: Utilizing women as management strategy.* New York: Oxford University Press.

Rosener, J. (1990). Ways women lead. *Harvard Business Review,* Nov-Dec: 119–125.

Schultz, V. (1998). Reconceptualizing sexual harassment. *The Yale Law Journal, 107,* 1683–1805.

Schwartz, F. (1989). Management women and the new facts of life. *Harvard Business Review,* Jan/ Feb: 65–76.

Stevens, C. K., Bavetta, A. G., & Gist, M. E. (1993). Gender differences in acquisition of salary negotiation skills: The role of goals, self-efficacy, and perceived control. *Journal of Applied Psychology, 78,* 723–735.

Strober, M. (1984). Toward a general theory of occupational sex segregation: The case of public school teaching. In: B. Reskin (Ed.) *Sex Segregation in the Workplace* (pp. 144–156). Washington, D. C.: National Academy Press.

Thomas, D. A. (1989). Mentoring and irrationality: The role of racial taboos. *Human Resource Management, 28* (2), 279–290.

Thomas, D. A., & Ely, R. J. (1996). Making differences matter: A new paradigm for managing diversity, *Harvard Business Review* September-October.

Thomas, R. R. (1991). *Beyond race and gender: Unleashing the power of your total work force by managing diversity.* New York: AMACOM.

Tong, R. (1989). *Feminist thought: A comprehensive introduction.* Boulder, CO: Westview Press.

Tsui, A. Egan, T., & O'Reilly, C. A. (1992). Being different: Relational demography and organizational attachment. Administrative Science Quarterly, *37,* 549–579.

Valian, V. (1998). *Why so slow? The advancement of women.* Boston: MIT Press.

Van Vianen, A. E. M., & Willemsen, T. M. (1992). The employment interview: The role of sex stereotypes in the evaluation of male and female job applicants in the Netherlands. *Journal of Applied Social Psychology, 22,* 471–491.

Vance, C. (1984). *Pleasure and danger: Exploring female sexuality.* Boston, MA. London: Routledge and Kegan Paul.

Wharton, A S. (1992). The social construction of gender and race in organizations: A social identity and group mobilization perspective. *Research in the Sociology of Organizations, 10,* 55–84.

Weick, K. E. (1995). *Sensemaking in organizations.* Thousand Oaks: Sage.

Weick, K. E. (1984). Small wins: Redefining the scale of social problems. *American Psychologist:* 40–49.

Weick, K. E. and R. E. Quinn. (1999). Organizational change and development. *Annual Review of Psychology, 50*, 361–386.
Weick, K. E. Emergent change as a universal in organizations. In: M. Beer and N. Nohria (eds.), *Breaking the Code of Change*. Boston: Harvard Business School Press, forthcoming.
West, C., & Zimmerman, D. H. (1987). Doing gender. *Gender and Society, 1*, 125–151.
Wilmott, H., & Knights, D. (1995). Culture and control in a life insurance company. *Studies in Culture, Organizations, and Societies, 1*, 1–18.

COORDINATION NEGLECT: HOW LAY THEORIES OF ORGANIZING COMPLICATE COORDINATION IN ORGANIZATIONS

Chip Heath and Nancy Staudenmayer

ABSTRACT

We argue that organizations often fail to organize effectively because individuals have lay theories about organizing that lead to coordination neglect. *We unpack the notion of coordination neglect and describe specific cognitive phenomena that underlie it. To solve the coordination problem, organizations must divide a task and then integrate the components. Individuals display shortcomings that may create problems at both stages. First, lay theories often focus more on division of labor than on integration. We discuss evidence that individuals display* partition focus *(i.e. they focus on partitioning the task more than on integration) and* component focus *(i.e. they tend to focus on single components of a tightly interrelated set of capabilities, particularly by investing to create highly specialized components). Second, when individuals attempt to integrate components of a task, they often fail to use a key mechanism for integration: ongoing communication. Individuals exhibit* inadequate communication *because the 'curse of knowledge' makes it difficult to take the perspective of another and communicate effectively. More importantly, because specialists find it especially difficult to communicate with specialists in other areas, the general problem of communication will often be compounded by insufficient translation.*

Research in Organizational Behaviour, Volume 22, pages 153–191.
2000 by Elsevier Science Inc.
ISBN: 0–7623–0641–6

THE IMPORTANCE OF COORDINATION

Highly motivated individuals often fail in their attempts at organizing. At Xerox during the 1970s, top managers feared that Xerox might falter when business transactions shifted from paper to electronic forms. They were savvy enough to create the group of researchers that invented the first desktop PCs (complete with mouse graphical interface) and easy means of networking them (complete with networked laser printers and e-mail). Then top managers failed continually to organize a structure that could bring the new technologies to the marketplace (Smith & Alexander, 1988). Why? Software developers who are urgently trying to finish a major piece of software frequently organize themselves in ways that actually slow themselves down (Brooks, 1979; DeMarco, 1995). Top managers at the best firms of the era systematically complicated their own jobs by diversifying into other lines of businesses, then floundered when they tried to design organizational structures to repair the complications they created (Chandler, 1962). Front-line workers who are earnestly trying to communicate with each other choose methods of communication that make it even more difficult to organize their efforts (Dougherty, 1992; Bechky, 1999). Even when motivations far exceed the typical range of motivations available in a business setting, highly motivated individuals still fail to organize effectively. During World War II the American Navy was suffering devastating attacks on its convoys by German submarines. It spent months trying to copy the more successful British Navy, willingly borrowing every possible aspect of the British system except for the method of organizing that eventually, much later, allowed them to succeed (Cohen & Gooch, 1990). Why?

The examples above share a common characteristic: Actors were highly motivated to succeed in their task, yet they chose bad ways of organizing their actions. We belabor this point with many examples to raise a puzzling issue; although the social sciences today have much to say about the problem of motivation (which is less of a problem in the examples above), they have less to say about the problem of improper organizing (which is a much more serious problem). In order to accomplish their work, organizations must solve two problems: motivating individuals so that their goals are aligned (the agency problem) and organizing individuals so that their actions are aligned (the coordination problem). Almost all of the founding texts in organization studies emphasize the importance of both problems: agency and coordination (Barnard, 1938; Simon, 1947; March & Simon, 1958; Burns & Stalker, 1961; Galbraith, 1973). Yet although agency and coordination are both central problems for organizations, in recent years, the agency problem has received far more attention from researchers. Agency theory, a popular topic in both economics and organizational studies, examines how principals can design optimal incentives to align the goals of their employees or agents (Eisenhardt, 1989; Jensen & Meckling, 1976). Although the agency problem has become increasingly popular, the coordination problem has not seen an equivalent rise in popularity, despite the fact that it is equally central for organizations. In fact, in economics, the coordination problem predates the interest in agency (e.g. Marschak & Radner, 1972), yet it has fallen out of favor while the agency problem has become increasingly popular (Milgrom & Roberts, 1992).

In many situations, the agency problem is not the main barrier to organizing. Even when organization members are motivated to work hard, they may find it difficult to coordinate their actions. In organizational research, early research-ers recognized this fact and developed studies and theories of organizational design (Thompson, 1967; Woodward, 1965; Perrow, 1967). Now commonly thought of as an 'old' theory, organizational design research has gradually fallen out of favor (Staudenmayer, 1997) albeit with some important exceptions (e.g. Tushman, 1979; Wageman, 1995; Gresov & Drazin, 1997; Crowston, 1997). The little research that is being conducted today typically draws upon the frameworks and concepts put forth by Thompson and others in the 1960s. In fact, Thompson's 1967 book is still the most cited source in organizational design, and its citation count is falling over time (Staudenmayer, 1997).

In this chapter we try to return attention to the coordination problem as a central problem in organizational studies. However, in contrast to the research on organizational design, we explore the coordination problem by exploring the cognitive problems that individuals face when they attempt to coordinate with others. We argue that people have inadequate lay theories of organizing, and that their lay theories hinder them when they attack the problem of coordination. Our level of analysis is the individual and the cognitive processes that individuals use to approach the coordination problem. We argue that when individuals design organizational processes or when they participate in them, they frequently fail to understand that coordination is important and they fail to take steps to minimize the difficulty of coordination. To summarize this hypothesis, we say that individuals exhibit *coordination neglect*.

We do not claim that coordination neglect among individuals will *always* produce coordination failures in organizations. Industries and organizations may provide pre-packaged processes and procedures that can repair the cognitive shortcomings of individuals (Heath, Larrick & Klayman, 1998). However, if organizations exist in a dynamic environment where they must continually adapt, then individuals within organizations will continually face novel coordination problems that they cannot easily address with pre-packaged solutions. Below, we will present numerous case studies (including those above) that document how coordination neglect produced coordination failures in organizations that were confronting novel situations.

The goal of this chapter is to unpack the notion of coordination neglect and to describe more specific cognitive phenomena that underlie it. However, before we attribute specific problems to coordination neglect, we first need to explain the approach we are taking. The process of organizing is indeed difficult, and we don't want to take credit for any problem that arises when people try to organize. In the next section, we sharpen the concept of coordination neglect by stipulating what it is and what it is not.

WHAT COORDINATION NEGLECT IS AND IS NOT

In this chapter, we analyze coordination neglect as a cognitive problem that is rooted in the lay theories people use to think about organizing and coordinating with others. People have intuitive, lay theories about many things – social interactions, statistical causality, economic markets (Kahneman, Slovic & Tversky, 1982; Furnham, 1988) – and we suggest they also have lay theories about organization. All theories are incomplete, particularly lay theories, and we are interested in understanding the psychological blind spots in these lay theories that may cause people to neglect to coordinate their actions with others.

In this chapter, we will focus on several facets of coordination neglect, all of which can be located on Fig. 1. In the simplest version of the coordination problem, an organization divides an overall problem into subtasks and assigns the parts to individuals. We could imagine, for example, an organization that divides the modules of a computer program among programmers with similar

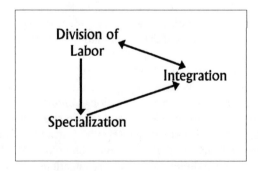

Fig. 1. The Coordination Problem.

skill. Organizations undertake this division of labor because individuals have limited information-processing abilities (Simon, 1962; March & Simon, 1958). Eventually, however, the organization must re-integrate the tasks that it originally divided. In the end, the modules of a computer program must work together as a single program, so the programmers who develop individual modules must integrate their efforts. Thus, the flip-side of division of labor is integration.

The coordination problem becomes especially complicated when organizations divide a task among specialists. Specialization reduces the problem of bounded rationality because individuals can concentrate on a component of the task that meets their unique skills, training, and abilities. Here, we move away from the computer programming example and toward, say, an automobile firm that hires a variety of people with special skills – good transmission engineers to design the transmission, knowledgeable production people to manufacture the car, and effective marketers to sell it. Now, however, the task of integration is even more complicated because the organization must integrate the efforts of specialists who speak different languages and perceive the world in different ways.

Throughout this chapter, we will explore different parts of Fig. 1 that highlight particular problems in the lay theories of individual organizers. However, first it is important for us to distinguish our approach, which depends on flaws in the lay theories of individuals, from other potential approaches. The coordination problem is difficult to solve, so we do not want to accuse people of coordination neglect any time they have difficulty solving this difficult problem.

For example, in order to argue that coordination neglect is a *cognitive* problem, we must distinguish it from motivational problems such as agency problems. Thus, it is important for us to provide examples where people really would *prefer* to coordinate so that agency problems are not an issue. Engineers and marketers may not talk to each other to coordinate their efforts because they: (1) have more fun interacting with others in their own department or (2) because they don't anticipate how much they need to interact to create a successful product. The first is not coordination neglect, it is an agency problem; an organization could presumably solve it by introducing an incentive scheme that encourages the marketers and engineers to interact. The second is more interesting because it suggests a cognitive limitation. This kind of cognitive limitation is unlikely to be solved by any of the standard incentive solutions to problems of control or agency.

Furthermore, to document that people are *neglecting* coordination, it is also important that we consider situations where people are *thinking* about how to align action. We are not concerned with situations where systems evolve organically over time in a way that produces hidden interdependencies (Staudenmayer & Desanctis, 1999). In organizations that evolve complicated processes over time (e.g. consider the process of acquiring parts at a large manufacturing firm), a procedure may span multiple people and departments and it may grow and change over time in spontaneous ways. In organizations, such processes may be completely revealed only when teams attempt to 'reengineer' them (Hammer & Champy, 1993). Although this kind of hidden interdependency is important, we want to focus on interdependencies that are more obvious. Coordination neglect is clearest when people consciously try to design or alter a process, yet they neglect to consider obvious issues of coordination, e.g. Chandler's (1962) managers who explicitly grappled with how to design their organizational structure.

In order to document coordination neglect, we not only require that people be thinking consciously about coordination, we also require that the act of thinking does not exceed their computational abilities. When we claim that people exhibit coordination neglect, we don't want to reiterate that people have difficulty performing difficult tasks. Herb Simon explained such difficulties many years ago as a product of 'bounded rationality' (Simon, 1947). In order to make the case that people exhibit coordination neglect, we should point out situations where people neglect alternative ways of coordinating that are equally or less cognitively demanding.

In sum, to provide examples of coordination neglect, we should point to situations where people do not coordinate even though they prefer to coordinate, where they are consciously considering how to coordinate, and where there is a means of coordination that does not exceed their computational abilities.

PARTITION FOCUS AND COMPONENT FOCUS

In order to accomplish a complex task, organizations typically divide up the task and assign components of the task to different people. However, whenever the organization divides a complete task into components, the people who perform the component tasks are interdependent and they must integrate their efforts (Thompson, 1967, ch. 5). As Fig. 1 indicates, division of labor compels integration.

In this section, we introduce two related aspects of coordination neglect: partition focus and component focus. *Partition focus* refers to people's tendency to neglect coordination because they focus more on dividing and partitioning the task than on integrating the components they create. People not only focus on partitioning the task into components, they also, when they are trying to diagnose or improve a process, tend to focus on individual components rather than the system as a whole. *Component focus* refers to this tendency for people to focus on components, particularly by investing in components so that specialists can become even stronger. The next two sections explore these aspects of coordination neglect.

Partition Focus

It is completely reasonable for people to divide or partition tasks carefully; this is one half of the equation for success in organizations (Simon, 1962; Lawrence & Lorsch, 1967). However, the other half of the equation for success is integration, and partition focus may cause people to neglect integration. When people partition the world, they may tend to treat small interactions between components as zero when they actually need to invoke a range of mechanisms to integrate the components (March & Simon, 1958).

The most direct evidence of partition focus is provided by situations where people consciously design a process from scratch, for example in the software industry. Coordination is a central issue in software design because software programs, which are constructed in segments or modules by individual programmers, must work seamlessly as a whole. One prominent consultant for the software industry has described the typical process that happens when software designers are given a new project (DeMarco, 1995; DeMarco & Lister, 1998). In a passage directed at team managers, DeMarco describes the typical process of design: "You make a crude division of the whole into five or ten pieces so you can put five or ten design teams to work. That crude division

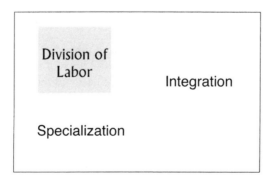

Fig. 2. Partition Focus

is a design step, but you don't approach it as such . . . That initial crude division is the heart of the design, and since there is no one directly responsible for revisiting its logic, it remains the heart of the design. The result is no design" (p. 251). In software engineering, the division of labor is less successful when there are more interfaces between modules and when the interfaces are more complex. By partitioning the work immediately, rather than thinking through the interfaces and patterns of interdependence among modules, design teams "guarantee the interfaces among people are more complex than they need to be . . . People are forced to interact with more of their teammates in order to get anything done and the interactions are more complex. The result is less possibility of independent work, more telephone tag, more meetings and more frustration" (DeMarco & Lister, 1998, p. 255; Perry, Votta & Staudenmayer, 1994; 1996).

In this example, software engineers partition the project crudely and then proceed immediately into implementation. Unfortunately, this inevitably results in greater integration problems later on because they must continuously loop back and make unanticipated changes to the original inadequate design, a phenomenon that has been documented repeatedly by researchers in software engineering (Kemerer, 1997; Boehm, 1984; Boehm & Papaccio, 1988). To combat this habitual tendency to partition the task prematurely, DeMarco (1995) argues that in a project designed to last a year, no coding should be done until the last two months. According to his recommendation, designers should spend 10 months selecting the right modules by minimizing the coordination that must take place among modules. Coding and testing will then proceed much more smoothly, requiring two months as opposed to 10 or more. Other researchers have pointed out that not all firms can afford the luxury of 10 months of design (Cusumano & Selby, 1995; Yoffie & Cusumano, 1999; Iansiti & Clark, 1994), and have suggested ways of integrating continuously. We argue that all these solutions are essentially cognitive repairs for partition focus in the lay theories of software design teams.

Partition focus runs sufficiently deep that, at times, it has become embodied in the institutional language and planning procedures of the software industry. In one of the most famous books on software design, Frederick Brooks (1979) discusses common flaws that cause large software projects to fail. Brooks is a credible observer of large software projects – he was the 'father' of the very successful System/360 project at IBM; at its time, it was the largest software project in the computer industry, comparable in size and expenditure to the NASA space program. The first flaw listed by Brooks is institutionalized in the very unit of effort that software managers used to estimate effort in the 50s and 60s: the *man-month*. Brooks notes that "men and months are interchangeable commodities only when a task can be partitioned among many workers with no communication among them." While this may be true of reaping wheat or picking cotton, "it is not even approximately true of systems programming" (p. 16). Brooks regarded this problem as so fundamental he chose it as the title of his book: *The Mythical Man-Month.* Brooks argued that it is counter-productive to focus only on partitioning the task into 'man months' because the different partitions are not interchangeable. Among software programmers, Brooks' warning against partition focus has been generalized in the well-known aphorism: "Bearing a child takes nine months, no matter how many women are assigned".

One general explanation for partition focus is that it simplifies computational costs and saves time. This does not mean that boundedly rational individuals could not calculate a more elaborate set of interactions than they do (indeed DeMarco, 1995, recommends that software managers spend the time to consider such interactions), however 'cognitive misers' might try to shortcut the process. In order to reduce computation costs, people may prefer to categorize ambiguous information into relatively crisp, well-bounded cate-gories (March & Simon, 1958). People may think that it will be easier to plan when they foreclose on a particular way of partitioning the task. Partition focus may be related to a tendency to do what is most well-learned (Staw, Sandelands & Dutton, 1981), particularly in situations where partition focus is enhanced by specialization. Typically, specialists are highly trained in their own specialty but know less about the specialties of others. Furthermore, this specialized training is often exacerbated in organizations by reward systems that inappropriately emphasize individual performance.

However, there is evidence that partition focus is not produced by environmental rewards, or even by training, but by lay theories. For example, in one experiment, groups of MBA students were given a bag of Lego blocks and were asked to assemble their blocks to match a model (a man with arms, legs, head and torso). They were given a long time to plan the exercise, but their goal was to assemble the model in the least amount of time possible. Teams could do a number of things to speed assembly both by partitioning the task and by integrating it. In terms of partitioning, groups could appoint 'experts' for the different body parts (arms, legs, torso); the individual body part experts could draw a diagram to show how their body part was constructed, and they could develop a specific plan for how to assemble it. In terms of integration, groups could develop a master diagram of how all the body parts fit together, they could talk about how to integrate the different body parts (e.g. how the arms would attach to the torso), and they could appoint an 'overseer' to guide the assembly process. Regressions showed that each partition and each integration behavior reduced assembly time by approximately the same amount. On the other hand, the partition and integration behaviors were not performed equally often; groups performed about 75% of the possible partitioning behaviors, but only about 50% of a parallel set of integration behaviors (Heath, Jost & Morris, 2000).

The Lego exercise suggests that partition focus is a problem of lay theories because the experimental procedure effectively rules out other potential explanations of coordination problems. The procedure contains no external incentives to create agency problems. There is no a priori specialization that would complicate the task of integration. There are no strong cognitive constraints that would prevent people from thinking through the problems of integration. Finally, in contrast with most coordination situations, the coordination required by this task was obvious and visible; people could see that the arms needed to join the torso, so it was obvious that the person assembling the arms should coordinate with the person assembling the torso. Yet teams often experienced problems at the 'joints' of the model; and such problems occurred simply because team members did not coordinate about how to integrate their subassemblies.

In this section we have considered the simplest version of the coordination problem where people must divide a task among individuals and then integrate the components. The examples from both organizational settings and laboratory work provide evidence that people focus more on partitioning the task than they do on integrating it, and this evidence suggests that partition focus may contribute to coordination neglect.

Component Focus

People focus not only on the process of partitioning a task, but also on the individual partitions or components they create. We will label this tendency as 'component focus' to signal that it is related to partition focus. People exhibit component focus when they try to intervene in an interrelated process by focusing only on one part of the process. When people exhibit component focus, they neglect the interrelationships and interactions among components. In lay theories that exhibit component focus, wholes are not 'the sum of their parts', they are a function of one part.

The division of labor is useful because it allows people to specialize, however specialists often ignore the task of integrating with others. One chief engineer at Ford looked back on his early years and ruefully recalled his narrow view of automobiles during the time he specialized in designing chassis: "When I saw a car driving down the road, all the rest [other than the chassis]

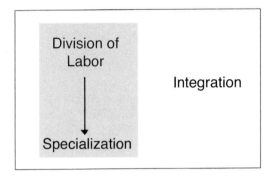

Fig. 3. Component Focus

disappeared. All I could see were the suspension arms going up and down" (Walton, 1997, p. 73). It is very easy for component focus to become embodied in the structure of the firm. Traditionally, Ford, like other automotive companies, organized around *very narrow* functional specialties, not just 'engineering' but subdivisions of engineering like "chassis, powertrain, electronics, climate control, plastics, and glass" (p. 74). These narrow units did not interact with each other except through the planners who were in charge of a given vehicle. According to one senior engineer, "In the old days, Ford had this attitude, 'You want a car, we'll give you these pieces'." (p. 73).

Component focus is often exacerbated because people focus on enhancing the quality of an individual component by making it more specialized. If people assume that components are the source of competitive advantage (and not the interrelationships among components), then a simple strategy is to get the best 'part' you can. Although specialization is useful, at some point organizations may face tradeoffs between enhancing specialization and promoting integration. Component focus may cause people to neglect coordination through overspecialization.

One example of component focus is found in Xerox's experience with its Xerox PARC unit of computer scientists. In a series of decisions that ranks among the worst business blunders of the 20th century, Xerox created the personal computer in the form we know it today, then failed to commercialize it. Xerox began well by creating an appropriate group of specialists. It assembled at its Palo Alto Research Center (PARC) the most creative group of computer scientists the computer industry has ever seen. In the 70s, it was well-known in the computer industry that "58 of the top 100 computer scientists in the world" worked at PARC. The common wisdom was somewhat exaggerated since PARC's employment roster never exceeded 50, but the general idea was approximately right because these computer scientists created a working set of networked personal computers that were far ahead of their time (Cringley, 1996). In the late 1970s, an in-house video at Xerox depicted a working computer system that was more than a decade ahead of the industry. A man enters his office, sits at his personal computer, checks his e-mail on a graphical computer interface using a mouse, and prints out a document on a laser printer. The in-house video appeared at least a decade before anyone had considered e-mail, mouses, laser printers or the graphical computer interface (which Steve Jobs later borrowed to make the Macintosh the most successful product at Apple). By 1978, over 1500 of these computers were in active use within Xerox (Smith & Alexander, 1988, p. 202).

In creating PARC, top managers at Xerox recognized the benefits of specialization: they recruited the right cadre of computer scientists, selected the right management team to lead them, and provided an effective campus-style working environment (complete with bean bag chairs). Yet according to Steve Jobs, Xerox "grabbed defeat from the greatest victory in the computer industry. [They] could have owned the entire computer industry today" (Cringley, 1996). Xerox had an extremely advanced personal computer and a sales force with direct access to every major corporation. How could it have failed to become the greatest company of the personal computer revolution?

A book titled *Fumbling the Future* documents a series of mistakes Xerox made in capitalizing on the success of PARC (Smith & Alexander, 1988). Although Xerox successfully created an effective group of specialists, top managers failed to create coordination mechanisms that would integrate the innovations of the specialists into the mainstream business of the company.

For example, because top managers at Xerox consistently focused on specialization, they made disastrous decisions about physical locations, not once, but twice in PARC's history. Throughout Xerox's experience with PARC, coordination suffered because PARC's location on the west coast was so far from Xerox's headquarters on the east coast. When Xerox was first deciding where to locate PARC, some managers argued that coordination would be enhanced if PARC were closer to the rest of Xerox. Jack Goldman, head of research for Xerox and an inside board member, noted in a memo to the CEO that "If the new research center is too isolated from a Xerox environment, the chances of relevant coupling to Xerox's needs and practices will be severely diminished." In a prescient sentence he said, "one area normally considered as an ideal research environment, Palo Alto, is eliminated because of the absence of any nearby major Xerox facility." But the head of the research lab argued strongly for the Palo Alto location because it was close to the emerging Silicon

Valley area and he won the location battle with this argument in favor of specialization (p. 56).

In the second poor location decision later in PARC's career, top management at Xerox had realized that they had failed to commercialize PARC technology, so they created a new group to do so. An outside firm recommended two sites for this new group: the San Francisco Bay area (close to PARC and the rest of Silicon Valley) and Dallas. Xerox chose Dallas. Instead of placing the new group in Silicon Valley next to the PARC researchers with whom it was supposed to coordinate, top managers at Xerox considered it as a unique, specialized component. "An elaborate financial model of a factory in Texas versus one in California conclusively proved, on the basis of labor, transportation, taxes, and other cost indicators, that Dallas would save Xerox money" (p. 162). By considering this group as a 'specialist' in manufacturing, managers chose a location that almost ensured that it would fail in its role to commercialize PARC's technology. The results were predictable: According to the manager of corporate R&D, "Dallas turned out to grow a culture that was completely orthogonal to, and independent of, the digital world in general and PARC in particular" (p. 163).

Xerox emphasized specialization in personnel choices as well. It selected an academic 'specialist' to head the research lab – George Pake, a former provost of Washington University in St. Louis. Although Pake had been an effective university provost, he was ill-equipped to be the chief integrator between PARC and the rest of Xerox. He consistently bungled opportunities to create excitement about PARC's technology within the rest of Xerox because he was too accustomed to an academic style of interaction. When he was appointed to a Xerox-wide strategy committee, Pake was given an ideal forum to proselytize for PARC technology. "Yet from the outset, others noticed that Pake had no commercial instincts . . . [He] spoke awkwardly about business, insisting that the strategy committee reach its conclusions by the 'scientific method' . . . When discussions turned to PARC's technologies, Pake emphasized the work to be accomplished in the laboratory instead of the commercial opportunities that might already exist" (p. 150).

In sum, Xerox focused on one component of a successful new product introduction: research and development. It created a group of specialists who did, in fact, live up to their billing as the greatest assemblage of computer talent ever. However, by focusing every feature of PARC around creating a specialized component, top managers at Xerox failed to integrate this specialized component with the other activities like marketing, manufacturing, and finance that were necessary to successfully commercialize the new technology. Although Xerox provides a vivid example of component focus, researchers have documented a similar emphasis on creating groups of specialists in many firms that are trying to commercialize technology (cf., Iansiti, 1995).

Component focus can be found, not only when top managers are trying to create new markets from scratch, but even when they are trying to learn from a successful past model. There is evidence that component focus may blind managers from understanding the sources of their previous success. One such example comes from a brilliant book by David Hounshell & John Smith (1988) that chronicles the history of research and development at Du Pont from 1902 to 1980. During the 1930s, Du Pont had a blockbuster decade, "Quite unexpectedly, [fundamental research] produced neoprene and nylon. Du Pont was successful in commercializing these important discoveries because it already had extensive commercial and technical capabilities in rubber chemicals, organic synthesis, high-pressure reactions, and fibers" (Hounshell & Smith, 1988, p. 596). Du Pont's managers had an opportunity to learn from their successes in nylon and neoprene. What should they have learned, and what, in fact, did they learn?

According to Hounshell & Smith (1988), Du Pont should have learned that success requires a set of integrated capabilities. In the case of nylon, Du Pont's capability in fundamental research was matched by a number of other capabilities that allowed it to develop the product and market it successfully. Du Pont had previously produced rayon, which gave it specific expertise in chemical engineering for artificial fabrics – the ability to scale up a clean, precise laboratory process to an industrial-scale plant (p. 259–73). In its work on rayon, Du Pont found that 25 variables had to be precisely controlled to produce a uniform final product (p. 165). Du Pont also had an unusual capability to manage high-pressure catalytic reactions because of its ammonia business. Although Du Pont's ammonia business was a money-loser if it was considered separately, it produced strong returns when Du Pont made nylon because nylon production required similar high-pressure catalytic reactions (p. 258), an unexpected example of economies of scope. Du Pont also had expertise marketing fabrics to industrial customers; for example, it marketed rayon as a substitute for silk in light fabrics during the fashion boom years after World War I (p. 164–67) and as a basis of tire cords that improved the life of heavy-duty tires (p. 169). In sum, Du Pont's success with nylon was produced by a range of complementary capabilities and assets spread across the firm (Teece, 1986).

Not surprisingly, Du Pont was pleased with its success in nylon, and dedicated itself to discovering "new nylons" – proprietary products that would produce the same high rates of return as nylon. Although nylon succeeded because of a wide range of complementary capabilities, when company executives talked about 'new nylons', they did not acknowledge these complex interrelationships. Instead, they primarily focused on one component of their success: fundamental research.

Over the next 30 years, Du Pont, in searching for new nylons, placed greater and greater emphasis on fundamental research. As a consequence, research programs were "pushed away from the company's commercial interests and the nylon model became skewed" (p. 597). While the company's executives believed that fundamental research would produce new nylons, the research department instead produced fundamental research in areas where Du Pont lacked complementary capabilities. The fundamental research group "lost contact with many of the industrial departments and took on the trappings of a high-quality scientific research establishment" (p. 597). During the three decades from 1940 through 1960, Du Pont continued to search for "new nylons" by investing only in its capability in fundamental research, despite the fact that the company's only two real successes during this period, Orlon and Dacron, took advantage of the same interrelated set of capabilities as nylon: not only fundamental research, but also engineering, manufacturing, and marketing of artificial fabrics. According to the historians, "In developing a mentality of 'new nylons', executives and research managers alike had forgotten why the company had so easily and swiftly developed nylon. The pioneering work on polymers had fitted neatly into the company's existing businesses, technologies, and expertise" (p. 597).

Teece (1986) notes that in order for firms to commercialize an innovation successfully, they must combine fundamental research with other capabilities or assets. Research alone is not enough, firms must integrate it with other capabilities like marketing, competitive manufacturing, and support. According to Teece, firms succeed when they have not one single competency, but when they own a set of assets that are complementary. We interpret Teece's observations as a useful corrective for approaches that primarily emphasize a single core competency (e.g. Hamel & Prahalad, 1990). Such approaches, in their extreme could enhance the kind of component focus exhibited by top managers at Du Pont.

Component focus may be exacerbated because, if people are focusing on only one component at a time, they may preserve the illusion that resources are being used efficiently. Redundancy conflicts with people's desires to avoid 'waste' (Arkes & Blumer, 1985). One consistent factor in examples of component focus is that people seem to be trying to use resources to their fullest capacity, whether personnel (DeMarco, 1995; 1997) or other resources (Chandler 1963). In large software projects, "early overstaffing tends to force people into shortcutting the key design activity (to give all those people something to do)" (DeMarco, 1995, p. 260).

This variety of component focus fooled many of the top management teams chronicled by Chandler (1962) in his famous account of the development and diffusion of the multidivisional form. In a number of Chandler's case studies, top managers diversified their product lines in an attempt to create economies of scale in some component of their business: at General Foods, it was an attempt to effectively use their central sales organization (p. 347); at the major oil companies, it was an attempt to use residual petrochemicals from oil refining (p. 361); at meat packing firms, it was an attempt to use their refrigerated distribution network to carry, not only meat, but eggs, milk, and poultry (p. 391). Although these firms sought to create economies by more efficiently using one component of their business, they almost inevitably failed to predict the administrative and coordination costs that they would incur by using the excess resources in this component. The new strategy did not typically increase the total output or size of operations, "but it quickly enlarged the number and complexity of both tactical and strategic administrative decisions" (p. 362). Chandler notes that even "a small amount of diversification in relation to total production" sufficed to create enough complexity to warrant a different structure (p. 362). We argue that many of their problems were produced by component focus. By trying to create economies of scale in one component of their organization, top managers dramatically complicated their job because they failed to anticipate how much they would have to increase coordination to use 'spare' capacity in that component.

Chandler's firms eventually solved their coordination problems by adopting the multidivisional form, but they adopted this solution slowly and only after much internal struggle. It would be fair to argue that such problems might be less likely in today's environment where the multidivisional form is a common solution to the kinds of integration problems that these managers faced. However, the historical example is useful because it points out the problems that may be caused by component focus in other situations where managers confront a novel problem of coordination but do not have automatic access to a prepackaged integration mechanism like the multidivisional form.

In many examples of component focus, managers seem to focus on technology rather than on broader issues of organization. One example of this occurred in the battle of the Atlantic during World War II. During WWII, the Atlantic Ocean was the site of a protracted struggle between the American and British ships that were trying to keep supplies flowing between the United States and Great Britain and the German submarines that were trying to sink them (Cohen & Gooch, 1990, p. 59–94). During the early stages of this struggle, the Americans were much less effective than the British in combating German subs. According to military historians Cohen and Gooch, the U.S. Navy made "a serious and protracted effort to learn from British experience" (p. 87), but it borrowed only components of the British process, particularly those involving technology (e.g. British ship designs for destroyer escorts or British sonar). On the other hand, it neglected the organizational structure that the British used to integrate the components. The British had a central Intelligence Center with a small staff who collected all incoming information (e.g. decrypted radio intercepts, photographs, prisoner interviews) and communicated this information directly with field commanders (p. 76). Field commanders could then divert their convoys away from German U-boat packs, and could concentrate their scarce escort vehicles on protecting convoys that were most endangered. This centralized operation also allowed the British to test and deploy new tactics to combat subs. Because any combat unit on the ocean might have only one or two chances to engage an enemy submarine, it was important that the combat units use the right tactics the first time (p. 83).

Only after the Navy borrowed many components of British tactics without success did they finally get around to borrowing the organizational mechanisms the British used to integrate their efforts. The U.S. Navy created an unusual military organization, the Tenth Fleet, to command all anti-submarine warfare. It could even override the positions of naval commanders who were not under its direct control. Interestingly, in the initial stages of the war, the Germans had noted the absence of coordination among American forces at sea: "enemy air patrols heavy but not dangerous because of inexperience," "the American airmen see nothing; the destroyers and patrol vessels proceed at too great a speed to intercept U-boats; likewise having caught one they do not follow up with a tough enough depth charge attack" (p. 75). This changed after the Tenth Fleet was created: "In the eighteen months before the creation of the Tenth Fleet, the U.S. Navy sank 36 U-boats. In the six months after, it sank 75" (p. 91).

Gooch and Cohen argue that many military historians who have tried to explain the early failure of American submarine warfare, have suffered from the same kind of component focus as the U.S. Navy. According to Gooch and Cohen, many historians have blamed either a single individual (the commander in chief of the U.S. Fleet) or a single cause like the absence of a coastal blackout or of convoy support, or a "single problem" such as a missing piece of technology that may have turned the tide (radar, more destroyers, etc.). However, Gooch and Cohen argue that none of these components is sufficient to explain American failures. For example, American success did not increase even after the coastal blackout was imposed in 1942; and before the reorganization disseminated effective tactics, the Americans failed even when destroyers were available and they actually spotted a U-boat (p. 79). In this case, sophisticated historians joined the sophisticated military personnel in WWII in their vulnerability to component focus.

Component focus on technology can also be seen in other organizations. For example, General Motors engaged in the famous NUMMI joint venture with Toyota, hoping they would be able to borrow some applications of technology for their other factories. Instead they were confronted by relatively low-tech machinery, but a new system for how workers interacted with each other and integrated their actions. GM failed to understand or capitalize on this different style of coordinating on the factory floor (Keller, 1989, pp. 124–144).

In the product development literature, Marco Iansiti and others (1993; 1995; Iansiti & Clark, 1994) have argued that ineffective development teams are 'element focused' while effective ones are 'system focused'. Iansiti notes that most development processes in traditional companies are sequential and element-focused. Basic researchers explore a new concept and hand it off to other scientists; these scientists elaborate the concept until they discover a new application, then they hand it off to engineers and manufacturing people; the engineers and manufacturing people prototype and produce the new product . . . This linear approach by element focused firms "tends to compartmentalize specific knowledge" (Iansiti, 1993, p. 138). In contrast, system-focused companies form a core group of managers, scientists, and engineers early in the process, and this integration team modifies and adapts the new concepts from fundamental research so that they mesh with the current capabilities of the company. Iansiti shows that systems focus is much more effective than element focus: system-focused companies solved 77% of major problems early on, while element-focused companies, which were not as attuned to integration, solved only 40% (Iansiti, 1993, see also Henderson & Clark, 1990).

Some modern organizational theorists have likewise criticized earlier scholars for component focus on technology. For example, Perrow (1984) conducted a famous analysis where he argued that some technologies are so complex that they inevitably lead to 'normal accidents'. Weick & Roberts (1993) argue that Perrow focused too much on technology rather than on the dynamics of social coordination: "We suspect that normal accidents represent a breakdown of social processes and comprehension rather than a failure of technology. Inadequate comprehension can be traced to flawed [shared] mind rather than flawed equipment" (p. 378).

In part, component focus may represent overgeneralizations of theories of organizing that are plausible in a more sophisticated form. As people learn rules, they frequently generalize rules too much before they learn the appropriate exceptions (Anderson, 1995). When lay theorists of organizing are confronted with an unfamiliar situation, they may take basic principles of organizing, like the value of specialization, and overextrapolate them. Because an organization must eventually coordinate the actions of specialists, it should not encourage specialization past a certain point, yet when managers focus only on a component of the broader organization (such as auto engineers on the chassis, Xerox managers with PARC, or Du Pont managers with 'fundamental' R&D), they may enhance specialization in a way that detracts from coordination.

Summary: Partition Focus and Component Focus

In this section, we have argued that people exhibit coordination neglect, in part, because of partition focus and component focus. People focus on the division of labor rather than on the equally important process of integration, and when they try to intervene in an ongoing process of coordination, they tend to focus on specialized components of the process rather than attending to the interrelationships as a whole.

In a clever paper, Weick & Roberts (1993) argue that in order to coordinate effectively, people must do so with heed: "carefully, critically, consistently, purposefully, attentively, studiously, vigilantly, conscientiously" (p. 361). "Heedless performance . . . is a failure to see, to take note of, to be attentive to" (p. 362). Weick and Roberts are quite correct to emphasize that it is important to understand and manage attention, but the examples above seem to indicate, not that people are inattentive, but that they neglect to pay attention to the right things. People's lay theories lead them to heed some things (division of labor, components, specialization) while simultaneously remaining heedless of others (integration, the importance of complementary capabilities).

INADEQUATE COMMUNICATION AND INSUFFICIENT TRANSLATION

Organizations can integrate their efforts in many ways (March & Simon, 1958; Thompson, 1967); they may establish routines or rules that standardize the action of different units or they may establish plans or schedules that govern the actions of independent units. But the most important means for units to integrate, particularly in complex or uncertain environments, is for them to communicate with each other on an ongoing basis. According to March & Simon (1958), 'the greater the efficiency of communication within the organization, the greater the tolerance for interdependence' (p. 183).

In this section, we examine how coordination neglect may be enhanced because individuals fail to take advantage of this key mechanism for integration. Although good communication is fundamental to integration, we argue that people often exhibit coordination neglect because of inadequate communication and insufficient translation. *Inadequate communication* is likely because a number of psychological processes make it difficult for individuals to take the perspective of another when they are trying to communicate. However, these standard problems of communication are compounded in organizations because specialists must communicate with other specialists who speak different languages. If organization members don't anticipate the need to translate across specialists, then *insufficient translation* will compound the basic problems of inadequate communication. Together, both processes may cause people to fail to integrate their efforts and may result in coordination neglect.

Inadequate Communication

Because organizations are filled with constrained information processors, communication will always be incomplete. Organizations develop filters that allow them to identify the most crucial information in the complex stream of information that enters from the outside world and flows through the organization (March & Simon, 1958; Arrow, 1974; Daft & Weick, 1984). However, communication, although incomplete, need not be inadequate. Recall that the British Navy during World War II created a successful submarine warfare unit, but it did so only after it failed in a similar task during World War I. In the successful WWII unit, analysts collected information and communicated it directly with field commanders at sea; they could not only

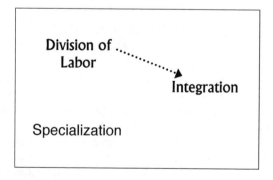

Fig. 4. Inadequate Communication

communicate "hard intelligence" about the location and activity of enemy units, they could also use their judgment to communicate "working fictions" about possible movements and tactics (Cohen & Gooch, 1990, p. 77). Interestingly, this successful Intelligence Center structure was developed only after Britain failed to capitalize on their "brilliant cryptanalysts" during WWI because of inadequate communication. In WWI, the cryptanalysts were "cut off from non-cryptologic sources of intelligence, allowed to communicate only with the Admiralty in London rather than operational commanders at sea, and discouraged by admirals from offering educated hypotheses about likely enemy behavior" (p. 77). In one spectacular failure, the British Navy failed to cripple the exposed German Fleet at the Battle of Jutland precisely because these organizational barriers prevented the Navy from adequately integrating and communicating information. By WWII, the British Navy arranged an organizational structure and procedures that allowed it to communicate more adequately.

Evidence indicates that managers systematically underestimate the importance of communication when they are planning important tasks. Recall Brook's (1979) famous book on software design, *The Mythical Man-Month*. In his list of the common flaws in large software projects, one major flaw relates to situations where managers underestimate the importance and difficulty of communication. Brooks observes that when a project falls behind, managers tend to add people to the project in hopes of delivering it more quickly. Unfortunately, this tactic compounds the difficulty of communication. When engineers are added to a project, two kinds of communication automatically increase. First, the existing engineers must communicate with new engineers to train them. Every new engineer must understand something about the technology, the project's goals, the overall strategy, and the work plan. This slows down the project because the existing engineers, who should be producing code, instead spend their time training new ones. Second, the pattern of communication becomes more complicated because the new engineers must be integrated into existing communication flows. Brooks argues that because software involves complex interrelationships, the project quickly loses more time by increasing communication costs than it reduces time by partitioning tasks among more people. This argument has been enshrined in the software industry as 'Brook's Law': "Adding people to a late software project makes it later."

In the American automobile industry, it took half a century for managers to realize that design times are cut in half when you make communication easier by putting functional representatives on a single cross-functional team in the same location. In the 1980s, research found that Japanese manufacturers routinely beat American firms in terms of both cycle time and quality; this prompted a large scale study of the world-wide auto industry that attempted to understand the reasons behind this difference (Womack & Jones, 1996; Wheelwright & Clark, 1992). Numerous studies contributed to this research effort, and, in general, they attributed a large part of the Japanese success to relatively simple structures and communications practices (e.g. forming a cross-functional team and locating them in a single site). The results have since been replicated in other industries and settings (Ancona & Caldwell, 1992; Brown & Eisenhardt, 1995; Eisenhardt & Tabrizi, 1995).

Although the experience of the American auto industry suggests that practicing managers may sometimes neglect the importance of adequate communication, perhaps academic researchers sometimes do so as well. Hinds & Kiesler (1995) note that although hierarchy and informal networks have always existed side by side, researchers and managers have historically emphasized the structural and operational significance of hierarchy, while downplaying informal networks as "ad hoc" linkages that are created through accidents of physical proximity, personal history, or demographic similarity. "When informal networks were seen as 'the grapevine'—unplanned, personal, and casual – neither managers nor researchers viewed them as integral to formal organization or crucial to accomplishing work" (p. 388).

Why is communication inadequate? One barrier to adequate communication is that we must be able to take the perspective of others and understand what we need to communicate to them. In psychology, there is a great deal of evidence that people find this kind of perspective-taking to be difficult. For example, children who are asked to direct another person around a landscape, will assume that the listener sees the landscape exactly like they do, even if their listener is in a different place (Piaget & Inhelder, 1967). Yet this phenomenon is not limited to children. When adults in an experimental market were given private information about the value of an experimental object in other markets, they found it impossible to ignore this information even though the value of the object in the experiment was determined by the people who were interacting in their own market (Camerer, Loewenstein & Weber, 1989). Here, adults lost money because they found it impossible to ignore their private information. In this study the researchers labeled their phenomenon the 'curse of knowledge' – people could not abandon their own perspective even though they should have been highly motivated to do so.

Because people suffer from the curse of knowledge and have difficulty taking another's perspective, they also overestimate how easy it would be to communicate their knowledge to the other party (Keysar, 1994; Hinds, 1999).

In a striking demonstration of this, Newton (1990) asked people to participate in an experiment in one of two roles: 'tappers' and 'listeners'. 'Tappers' received a list of 25 well-known songs and they were asked to tap out the rhythm of one of the songs; listeners tried to identify the song based solely on the taps. Note that this design induces dramatic differences in the perspective and information of the two participants. Although listeners heard only a series of disconnected taps, the tappers, according to their own reports, 'heard' the lyrics and complete musical accompaniment as they banged out the rhythm of their song. This inside information made it hard for the tappers to anticipate the states of their listeners. Although the tappers tapped out 120 songs during the experiments, listeners only identified 3 (a rate of 2.5%). Tappers, however, incorrectly predicted that listeners would identify 50%.

In the experiment above, the curse of knowledge makes communication inadequate because people have a complete picture of what they intend to convey, and this complete picture blinds them to gaps in the information they actually convey to others. An engineer on a disk drive project described this kind of communication problem on a new product team: "There were a lot of specs, but these were only detailed conceptually. They wanted 'something like this'. As a result the specs get interpreted widely. You end up delivering something they didn't ask for . . . I was working with one or two people at the customer organization, then they showed our design to fourteen others who said: 'Oh My God! We didn't want that'!!" (Dougherty, 1992, p. 189). In general, this kind of problem is exacerbated by experience and expertise (Hinds, 1999).

Allen (1977) followed multiple R&D teams who were working to develop new high-technology products for sophisticated customers using a matched-pair design. The teams that performed better were more consistent about communicating. Lower performers were more "irregular" about consulting internal colleagues and in the middle of the project they "virtually cut off contact with colleagues outside their project team." Allen notes that the high performers stayed in closer touch with organizational colleagues throughout the project, and thus "obtained the necessary information to prevent problems from getting too far out of control" (p. 103–104). Recent research in network theory by Burt (1997), Krackhardt (1996), and others re-emphasizes the value of entrepreneurial networks for individuals and groups.

The problem of communication in organizations is much more formidable than the normal problem of communication between two people. When two individuals are communicating face to face, they can use a number of strategies to repair breakdowns in communication as they occur (Clark, 1996). Communication in organizations is a more formidable problem because it requires individuals to communicate through formats (e.g. specifications, blueprints, memos or budgets) that are relatively impoverished and that separate the people who are communicating by time and space. Top managers are particularly likely to fall prey to inadequate communication because their inside information and their expertise in business may make them particularly prone to the curse of knowledge; furthermore, they are isolated by structural and social distance from feedback that might prompt them to repair inadequate communication (Heath & Walston, 2000).

The problem of inadequate communication will be particularly difficult to overcome when knowledge is tacit. Von Hippel (1990) notes that information is often 'sticky'; hard to understand and interpret away from the specific, applied context where it arose. For example, one production manager may have difficulty telling another production manager at a different plant why their new production line is successful because success may depend on a number of subtle aspects of layout, staffing, and process flow that are hard to notice and verbalize. Interestingly however, von Hippel implies that people can overcome the problem of sticky information if they become aware of how much their knowledge depends on a specific context. We interpret this to mean that information is sticky and communication inadequate, in part, because of the kinds of cognitive problems we have considered in this section.

Agency misattributions. Communication is often inadequate in organizations because people attribute coordination problems, not to inadequate communication, but to inadequate motivation on the part of their communication partner. This may lead people to stop communicating prematurely because they think their partner is not motivated to coordinate with them.

Recall the distinction earlier in this chapter between the two tasks of organizations: aligning goals and aligning actions. The first is the agency problem, the second is the coordination problem. We suggest that while both problems are important in organizations, people are likely to interpret coordination problems as agency problems, what we label an *agency misattribution*. It is harder to imagine someone having different knowledge than different motivations (Klayman, Loewenstein, Heath & Hsee, 2000). If the curse of knowledge leads people to believe that they are communicating something obvious to the other person (recall the tapping game), then when a listener fails to understand the 'obvious' message, the communicator may be less likely to assume the other person has different information (a communication problem) than different motivations (an agency problem). Indeed, even in situations where differences in knowledge are obvious, like the tapping game described above, people often attribute coordination failure to agency problems. In one variant of the tapping game, when listeners failed to understand the song tapped by the tapper, over 40% of tappers accused their listeners of "not working very hard" to understand the song. When tappers confronted a coordination failure, they failed to recognize the difficulty of the task (because of the curse of knowledge) and instead accused their listeners of lack of effort; a classic agency misattribution (Morris, Heath & Jost, 2000).

Interestingly, one could argue not only organizational participants, but also organizational theorists are subject to agency misattributions. Indeed, examples of potential agency misattributions can be found on both sides of the political/ theoretical spectrum. On the side of the spectrum that assumes individuals rationally pursue their own self-interest, economists have spent much more time pursuing the agency problem than considering the equally important problem of coordination (Milgrom & Roberts, 1992). On the opposite side of the spectrum, the human relations school has made a career arguing that non-monetary factors are important sources of motivations, yet it was famously embarrassed to find that job satisfaction didn't predict job performance (Iaffaldono & Murchinsky, 1985; Staw, 1986). Instead, performance is more determined by coordination mechanisms like organizational routines and procedures (Herman, 1973; Bhagat, 1982; Staw, 1986). Here, the human relations school engaged in a kind of agency misattribution because it assumed that performance problems were driven by dissatisfaction (an agency problem) rather than organizational routines and procedures (a coordination problem). These examples suggest that agency misattributions do not depend on a particular theory of human motivation – whether intrinsic or extrinsic. However, they do require people to emphasize motivational issues over the knowledge-based issues associated with coordination.

If agency misattributions play an important role in preventing effective communication, it may be particularly important that organizations use techniques like physical location to bring different departments together. By locating people together, people not only gain more opportunities to communicate, they may also become more willing to communicate because they may be less likely to engage in agency misattributions and assume that coordination failures signal a lack of motivation by their partner. Rich, face-to-face communication may be particularly important in establishing trust (Daft & Lengel, 1984; 1986). If we are communicating with another person who has very different knowledge than we do, then we may need to see the puzzled expressions on their face to understand their questions are motivated by ignorance rather than spite, ill feelings, or petty resistance.

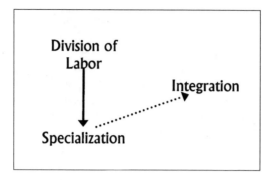

Fig. 5. Insufficient Translation

Insufficient Translation

Consider the earliest account of the dilemmas of specialization and integration in large organizations:

> And the whole earth was of one language, and of one speech. [... And the people] said, let us build a city and a tower, whose top may reach unto heaven; and let us make us a name for ourselves. And the LORD came down to see the city and the tower, which the children of men builded. And the LORD said, ... let us go down and confound their language that they may not understand one another's speech. So the LORD scattered them abroad upon the face of all the earth: and they did not build the city. Therefore the name of that place is called Babel; because the LORD did there confound the language of all the earth, and from thence did the LORD scatter them abroad upon the face of all the earth.
>
> Genesis 11: 1–9

In the traditional theological interpretation, the story of Babel is about the perils of hubris. However, it can also be read as a parable about the communication difficulties introduced by division of labor and specialization. Whenever organizations undertake a sufficiently large task (e.g. building a large tower), they must partition it into components. However, when a task is partitioned to form groups of specialists, each group of specialists tends to develop a different language. As organizations become sufficiently specialized, the specialists do "not understand one another's speech." Partitioning a task leads to Babelization, and if the Babbelings are not translated sufficiently, integration fails. In this section, we suggest that people will exhibit coordination neglect, not only because of inadequate communication, but also because of insufficient translation.

The organizational literature has long recognized the potential problems of specialization. In the classic study by Dearborne & Simon (1958), a group of business executives were given a complex case study about a failing company. It was easy to predict how executives would assess the 'core problem' in the case based on their functional background: the finance executives saw a financial problem, the marketing executives saw a marketing problem, and the production executives saw a production problem. Thus specialists see the world in different ways and stress different content. Although the potential problems of coordinating specialists are well-described in the organizational literature, our question is whether lay theories acknowledge these problems and allow people to overcome them through sufficient translation.

Some authors have been skeptical about whether people will always recognize the problems of translation. Translation was a central feature of Allen's (1977) study of gatekeepers in engineering firms. He notes that translation problems are especially difficult to identify in organizations, "Anyone who does not speak French knows his deficiency, but very often we think we know what someone from another organization is saying when in fact our understanding is very different" (p. 139). According to Allen, the "principal contribution" of gatekeepers is translation, they convert information "into terms that are relevant and understandable for the members of their organization" (p. 166). In his book, Allen devotes separate chapters to the basic communication problem (Chapter 5, The Importance of Communication Within the Laboratory) and to the translation problem (Chapter 6, Communications Among [Sub-] Organizations), yet in Chapter 7, he puzzles over the fact that both of these problems are rarely solved, "Given the obvious benefits of internal consulting, it is puzzling that it is so infrequently used" (p. 183).

Specialization would not create such serious problems if people only realized they need to work differently to translate across specialist boundaries. However, there is evidence that specialists, rather than understanding the translation problem, respond to integration issues by reasserting the same strategies that made them specialists in the first place. For example, specialists often develop symbols that can convey large amounts of information in a compact way (e.g. abbreviations, technical language, blueprints, the numerical summaries of accounting systems; March & Simon, 1958). Unfortunately, when specialists adopt these abstract symbols they often assume that they are equally meaningful for other parts of the organization. Bechky (1999) studied a manufacturing firm that designed and built the complicated pieces of machinery that are used to produce silicon chips; this firm's competitive advantage in the market depended on its capabilities in clever engineering and precision manufacturing. Not surprisingly, the engineers and the manufacturing people spoke very different languages. When engineers tried to communicate with the assemblers, they communicated in ways that reinforced the translation problem. For example, in an attempt to communicate better with the assemblers, the engineers endeavored to make their engineering drawings as comprehensible as possible: to "add intelligence to the drawing" (p. 83). However, the assemblers in the production area did not share the specialized training that allowed the engineers to read the drawings. Assemblers "mistrusted" the drawings (p. 68). Bechky implies that this was a problem of inadequate translation. "The drawing was clear to the [engineers] who created it, because they worked in the context of engineering drawings all the time . . . However, assemblers lacked this knowledge" (p. 68).

Indeed, because engineers could not abandon their perspectives, they often compounded the problem of translation. Engineers made their drawings "increasingly elaborate" in the hope that this would "clarify" the production process for the assemblers. "This drove them to greater abstraction in the documentation, which caused further communication problems . . ." (p. 94). Here, the engineers behaved a little like the American tourist who tries to translate his or her ideas in a foreign country by repeating the same English phrase at a louder volume. The interesting part of the process was that the engineers often neglected to use other means of translation that would have been simpler. Bechky (1999) notes that the physical machine was the most effective translation device. It was "the lowest common denominator" so it worked "most effectively and quickly to resolve misunderstandings" when individuals from different departments were trying to communicate. One assembler noted that, "If we do it from the engineering drawing we can get confused and make mistakes. Looking at [a physical machine] is easier and better" (p. 83). Yet even though the physical machine improved translation, the firm anointed the abstract engineering drawing as the "privileged" form of communication (p. 93). Bechky's careful study as well as other studies in the literature (e.g. Henderson, 1991) suggest that people may sometimes neglect appropriate boundary objects because they fail to recognize the importance of translation.

If people neglect the importance of translation, they may also undervalue people who act as translators by spanning boundaries among groups within an organization or outside. Anecdotes suggest that organizations often sack the wrong people during mergers (Economist, January 9, 1999) – perhaps because the first people who are fired during downsizings are those who are not clear members of one department or another (i.e. the very people who are probably bridging gaps between departments). For example, Dougherty & Bowman (1995) found that downsizing hindered strategic problem solving because it broke the networks of informal relationships that innovators use to work out strategic problems – to acquire support and resources for new initiatives and to translate the innovation into terms that will be accepted by senior managers.

Although the examples above indicate that the translation problem is important, there is evidence that even sophisticated observers of organizations may underestimate the difficulty of translation. Lawrence & Lorsch (1967), who devoted much of their book to the problems of integration, critiqued earlier organizational theorists for not realizing the inevitability of translation problems. According to Lawrence & Lorsch (1967), the "major failing" of the classical writers on organizations was that they did not recognize that partitioning the organization into departments would lead each department to "develop specialized working styles and mental processes," a process they called 'differentiation' (i.e. "not just the simple fact of partition and specialized knowledge," but fundamental "differences in attitude and behavior," p. 9). They argued that differentiation would make it impossible for an organization to coordinate itself using the simple coordination mechanisms recommended by classical writers (primarily hierarchy). If Lawrence and Lorsch are correct, then the problems of translation are not obvious even to many experts who are thinking carefully about organizations.

Emotional barriers to translation across specialists. To this point, the idea of translation has been considered at a fairly rational level. If people have trouble communicating, it is because they don't think to give all the information to another person, or because they translate insufficiently from one specialist's language to another. However, this rational approach is insufficient to understand the complete dynamics of communication and translation because it ignores an important *emotional* component of the communication process. Communication requires trust because both parties must assume that the other is making good-faith efforts to coordinate (Grice, 1975; Clark, 1996). Here it is useful to recall our earlier discussion of agency misattributions, because if people are subject to agency misattributions, then they are likely to assume that translation problems are a sign that the other person, with whom they are trying to coordinate, is operating in 'bad faith'.

Agency misattributions are quite likely when specialists communicate. Specialists may be somewhat suspicious of others' motives to begin with because they come from different groups with distinctive backgrounds, preferences, and language. Research in social psychology on 'minimal groups' has shown that dividing a group based on even trivial distinctions (e.g. liking abstract art by Klee vs. Kandinsky) has surprisingly quick effects on group dynamics; people allocate more resources to their own group, talk up the qualities of their own group, and denigrate those of the other group (Tajfel,

1970; Brewer, 1979). The minimal group experiments provide empirical parables about how easy it is to produce ethnocentrism and emotional conflict, but in organizations, differences among groups are anything but minimal. When specialists try to coordinate with each other, their suspicions about others may enhance agency misattributions; causing them to attribute integration problems to bad motives by the other party. True, group dynamics may produce real agency problems, but we predict that specialization may make groups suspicious of one another's motives even in situations where the different groups are actually quite motivated to work toward the same goal.

Consistent with the idea that agency misattributions are common among specialists, Lawrence & Lorsch (1967) noted that people "personalize the conflicts that arise with representatives of other organizational units. Of course they know logically that an organization needs different kinds of specialists, but they forget the full meaning of this when they run into a particular person who is "impossible to work with." Then they all too readily turn to an explanation based on personality traits that writes off the individual as an oddball and justifies them in withdrawing from the conflict or forcing it" (p. 217).

One researcher who has studied new product introductions argues that although outsiders may believe agency problems contribute to new product failures, they are not, in fact, very common: "From the outside looking in, one can see the conventional stereotypes for each department: technical people never settle on a design, field people are short term, manufacturing people always say no, and planning people are conceptual. But from the inside looking out, each thought world is truly concerned with the successful development of the product, and each has an important insight into the product or market that is essential to a new product's development" (Dougherty, 1992, p. 191). However, although each department is motivated to develop the product, the departments may fail to coordinate because they translate their goals and expectations insufficiently. "Technical people, for example, expect field people to tell them exactly what customers want in the design. Field people, however, cannot identify these 'specs' because [they think] product innovation involves meeting shifts in customer needs, so they expect technical people to produce alternative designs quickly" (p. 189). Agency misattributions may lead team members to ignore the translation problem because they assume the other party has the wrong incentives. According to Dougherty, differences in specialization can preclude optimal integration "by producing severe frustrations and withdrawals into separate thought worlds." If people suffer from agency misattributions they are unlikely to take the time to address such translation problems because they assume the other person is not truly motivated to cooperate.

Summary: Inadequate Communication and Insufficient Translation

Although organizations can integrate their efforts in many ways, the most important mechanism of integration, particularly in complex or uncertain environments, is for units to communicate with each other on an ongoing basis (March & Simon, 1958; Thompson, 1967). In this section we have discussed two problems that may hinder individuals from taking advantage of this integration mechanism: inadequate communication and insufficient translation.

Communication is difficult in general. People are prone to the curse of knowledge which makes it difficult for them to take another person's perspective well enough to communicate adequately. In face-to-face conversations, people have a variety of means of repairing instances of inadequate communication, but in organizations, where much communication takes place across time between individuals who do not interact face-to-face, the problems of inadequate communication become more significant (DeSanctis, Staudenmayer & Wong, 1999).

Organizations complicate the basic problem of communication, because they require people to communicate across differentiated groups of specialists. Thus, if people translate insufficiently across specialized languages or 'thought worlds', coordination will be further hindered. The problems of communication and translation are magnified because differentiation and specialization may leave people suspicious of one another so that they are more likely to make agency misattributions when they encounter coordination problems; attributing problems not, as they should, to lack of communication, but instead to misaligned motivations.

UNDERSTANDING COORDINATION NEGLECT

In this chapter, we have argued that people in organizations often exhibit coordination neglect. Even when they desire to coordinate with others, when they are thinking actively about the problem, and when coordination does not exceed their computational abilities, people may have blind spots that make them likely to fail in their coordination attempts. In the paper, we have focused on two different aspects of coordination neglect:

(1) *Partition focus and component focus.* People focus on the process of partitioning a task more than the process of integration and they tend to focus on individual components when they try to diagnose problems or intervene to provide a solution.

(2) *Inadequate communication and insufficient translation.* People do not communicate adequately in general and they fail to realize the additional problems of translating across differentiated specialists.

Although the figures in this paper indicate how both sets of problems arise from the basic process of division of labor in organizations, it is possible to think of these two sets of problems operating in a two-stage temporal sequence. In the first stage, an organization must plan the division of labor along with any integration mechanisms it deems necessary. In the second stage, the organization must integrate its efforts in an ongoing basis. Presumably, if people make errors in one stage they can offset them with superior performance in the other; effective planning may reduce some of the demands of implementation, and skilled implementation may overcome some of the problems of inadequate planning. Yet the evidence above suggests that organizations will experience predictable problems in both stages.

　　The examples in this chapter suggest that coordination neglect plays a role in many important decisions. Individuals indeed have gaps in their lay theories of organizing. Note, however, that these gaps are seen even in managers and scholars who are quite sophisticated about the problems of organizing. This observation is consistent with research in individual decision making that has suggested that any bias that can be documented in naive individuals can also be documented, in a more subtle form, in experts (Kahneman, Slovic & Tversky, 1982). It is interesting that many examples of partition focus or inadequate communication are found with sophisticated managers in otherwise successful companies. Even sophisticated organizational theorists have neglected these problems at times (e.g. see critiques of the organizational literature by Lawrence & Lorsch, 1967; Cohen & Gooch, 1990; Weick & Roberts, 1993; Hinds & Kiesler, 1995). Such examples suggest that the problem of coordination neglect is not trivial, particularly whenever people encounter problems that are, to them at least, novel (Chandler, 1962; Brooks, 1979; DeMarco, 1997).

Bad (and Good) Ways of Repairing Coordination Neglect

While we have emphasized the problem of coordination neglect, we also want to highlight that organizations may create other problems if they adopt overly simple cognitive repairs for coordination neglect. For example, if organizations attempted to repair partition focus or component focus by decreasing the division of labor, they could easily create other problems such as lack of requisite variety or expertise (Weick, 1983; Nemeth & Staw, 1989). Similarly, people may overemphasize the ability of hierarchy to coordinate complex processes. In group situations, students typically want to simplify coordination by 'appointing a leader'. Hierarchy appeals to our fascination with people as the source of action (Weber, Rottenstreich, Camerer & Knez, 1999; Meindl, Erlich & Dukerich, 1985), but it is likely to be ineffective in complex, uncertain environments (Lawrence & Lorsch, 1967; Hinds & Kiesler, 1995).

It's clear that organizations can over-apply the lessons they learn about individual shortcomings. For example, thanks to the research attention on the benefits of cross-functional teams, many organizations have tried to repair inadequate communication by using team meetings as a generic repair for every coordination problem. However, more communication is not always better. Many managers in firms today complain of the length and frequency of meetings (which interfere with their ability to get their own functional work done) (Perlow, 1995; Staudenmayer, 1997).

In fact, thoughtful organizations solve problems of coordination by integrating the efforts of their members in ways other than direct communication. For example, software teams sometimes enforce integration by using special processes that force integration among separate workers. In some firms, software teams do a nightly 'build' to put together the modules for the entire program (Staudenmayer, 1997; Cusumano & Selby, 1995). Individual developers can decide whether or not to submit an updated version of their module to the nightly build, but if they do so, they must take care that their module doesn't 'break the build', i.e. produce problems for a module other than their own, causing the overall program to crash. In this procedure, individual programmers are not forced to communicate with others to ensure that their module doesn't break the build, yet they are prompted to test their code and to anticipate what problems they may create for other modules when they change their own.

As another source of repairs for coordination neglect, Tom Malone of MIT and a group of colleagues have developed a process to suggest alternative ways of solving coordination problems (Malone et al, 1999). They collect examples of how different organizations perform similar processes of coordination, and organize these examples in an on-line 'process handbook'. They analyze processes at various levels of abstraction, so they capture both the details of the specific processes as well as the 'deep structure' of their similarities. As a result, managers can explicitly represent the similarities and differences among related processes and they can more easily generate alternatives to solve a particular coordination problem.

Although there is ample evidence of coordination neglect, organizations that attempt to repair coordination problems in an ad hoc way may find that their would-be repairs create additional difficulties. There are solutions to these problems, but they will require careful attention to the underlying requirements of integration and to overcoming the cognitive barriers we have identified.

Extensions

On a lighter note, perhaps the most extreme evidence for coordination neglect is provided by conspiracy theories. In the typical conspiracy theory, a diverse set of military, industrial, and government agencies coordinate seamlessly over long periods of time despite organizational and geographic barriers. Extreme versions of conspiracy theories feature coordination across planets and species (a serious neglect of translation problems). If individuals fully understood the difficulty of coordination, it seems unlikely that they would be quite so facile in assuming the level of coordination present in the typical conspiracy theory.

Conspiracy theories also play a role in the day-to-day analysis of sophisticated experts. In Robert Jervis' (1976) brilliant book on the psychology of international relations, he devotes a set of chapters to 'Common Misperceptions' in international relations. The first of these chapters is entitled 'Perceptions of Centralization' (pp. 319–342). According to Jervis, a common misperception is to see the behavior of others as "more centralized, planned, and coordinated than it is" (p. 319). For example, during World War II, "many observers believed the German fifth column [espionage force] was largely responsible for the Allies' difficulty in mobilizing and the swift German victories . . . Later investigation showed that the fifth columnists had done very little and that the incidents attributed to them were caused by Allied disorganization" (Jervis, 1976, p. 322–323).

Such examples suggest that coordination neglect, even in its most extreme forms, may play an active role in how we approach and interpret the coordination problem in organizations.

ACKNOWLEDGMENTS

For comments, we thank: Tony Atkinson, Beth Bechky, Efrim Boritz, Colin Camerer, Andrew Hargadon, Derek Koehler, Barry Staw, Robert Weber, and seminar participants at Cornell, Stanford, and University of Waterloo. For advice on labeling we thank Dick Thaler.

REFERENCES

Allen, T. J. (1977). *Managing the flow of technology: Technology transfer and the dissemination of technical information within the R&D organization*. Cambridge, MA: The MIT Press.

Ancona, D. G., & Caldwell, D. F. (1992). Demography and design: Predictors of new product team performance. *Organization Science, 3*, 321–341.

Anderson, J. R. (1995). *Cognitive psychology and its implications*. New York: W. H. Freeman & Co.

Arkes, H., & Blumer, C. (1985). The psychology of sunk cost. *Organizational Behavior and Human Decision Processes, 35*, 124–140.

Arrow, K. (1974). *The limits of organization*. New York: Norton.

Barnard, C. (1938). *The functions of the executive*. Cambridge, MA: Harvard University Press.

Bechky, B. A. (1999). Crossing occupational boundaries: Communication and learning on a production floor. Ph. D.Dissertation, Stanford University.

Bhagat, R. S. (1982). Conditions under which stronger job performance-job satisfaction relationships may be observed: A closer look at two situational contingencies. *Academy of Management Journal, 25*, 772–789.

Boehm, V. W. (January 1984). Software Engineering Economics. *IEEE Transactions on Software Engineering*, SE–10, No. 1, 4–21.

Boehm, V. W., & Papaccio, P. N. (1988). Understanding and Controlling Software Costs. *IEEE Transactions on Software Engineering, 14*(10), 146 2–1477.

Brewer, M. B. (1979). In group bias in the minimal inter-group situation: A cognitive-motivational analysis. *Psychological Bulletin, 86*, 307–324.

Brooks, F. P. (1979). *The mythical man-month: Essays on software engineering*. Reading, Massachusetts: Addison-Wesley Publishing.

Brown, S., & Eisenhardt, K. M. (1995). Product development: Past research, present findings, and future directions. *Academy of Management Review, 20*, 343–378.

Burns, T., & Stalker, G. M. (1961). *The management of innovation*. London: Tavistock Publications.

Burt, R. (1997). The contingent value of social capital. *Administration Science Quarterly, 42*(2), 339–365.

Camerer, C. F., Loewenstein, G., & Weber, M. (1989). The curse of knowledge in economic settings: An experimental analysis. *Journal of Political Economy, 97*, 1232–1254.

Chandler, A. D.(1962). *Strategy and structure: Chapters in the history of the American industrial enterprise*. Cambridge, MA: The MIT Press.

Clark, H. H. (1996). *Using language*. Cambridge, UK: Cambridge University Press.

Cohen, E. A., & Gooch, J. (1990). *Military misfortunes: The anatomy of failure in war*. New York: Free Press.

Cringley, R. (1996). Triumph of the nerds: An irreverent history of the PC industry. Part II. PBS documentary.

Crowston, K. (March-April 1997). A coordination theory approach to organizational process design. *Organization Science, 8*(2), 157–175.

Cusumano, M. A., & R. Selby (1995). *Microsoft Secrets*. New York: Free Press.

Daft, R. L., & Lengel, R. H. (1984). Information richness: A new approach to managerial behavior and organization design. In: B. Staw & L. Cummings (Eds), *Research in Organizational Behavior*, vol. 6 (pp. 191–233). Greenwich, CT: JAI Press.

Daft, R. L., & Lengel, R. H. (1986). Organization information requirements, media richness, and structural design. *Management Science, 32*, 554–571.

Daft, R. L., & Weick, K. E. (1984). Towards a model of organizations as interpretation systems. *Academy of Management Review, 9*, 284–295.

Dearborn, D. C., & Simon, H. A. (1958). Selective perception: A note on the departmental identification of executives. *Sociometry, 21*, 140–44.

DeMarco, T. & Lister, T. (1987). *Peopleware: Productive projects and teams.* New York: Dorset House Publishing.

DeMarco, T. (1995). *Why does software cost so much? And other puzzles of the information age.* New York: Dorset House Publishing.

DeMarco, T. (1997). *The deadline: A novel about project management.* New York: Dorset House Publishing.

DeSanctis, G., Staudenmayer, N., & Wong, S. S. (1999). Interdependence in virtual organizations. In: C. L. Cooper & D. M. Rousseau (Eds), *The Virtual Organization.* NY: John Wiley.

Dougherty, D. (1992). Interpretive barriers to successful product innovation in large firms. *Organization Science, 3*, 179–202.

Dougherty, D. & Bowman, E. H. (1995). The effects of organizational downsizing on product innovation. *California Management Review, 37*, 28–44.

The Economist (January 9, 1999). After the deal. 21–23.

Eisenhardt, K. M. (1989). Agency theory: An assessment and review. *Academy of Management Review. 14*, 54–74.

Eisenhardt, K. M., & Tabrizi, B. N. (1995). Accelerating adaptive processes: Product innovation in the global computer industry. *Administrative Science Quarterly, 40*, 84–110.

Furnham, A. (1988). *Lay theories: Everyday understanding of problems in the social sciences.* Oxford, England: Pergamon.

Galbraith, J. (1973). *Designing complex organizations.* Reading, Massachusetts: Addison-Wesley Publishing.

Gresov, C., & Drazin, R. (1997). Equifinality: Functional equivalence in organization design. *Academy of Management Review, 22*(2), 403–428.

Grice, H. P. (1975). Logic and conversation. In: P. Cole (Ed.) *Syntax and Semantics*, vol. 9, Pragmatics (pp. 225–242). New York, Academic Press.

Hamel, G. & Prahalad, C. K. (1990). The core competence of the organization. *Harvard Business Review*, 79–91.

Hammer, M., & Champy, J. (1993). *Reengineering the corporation: A manifesto for business revolution.* New York: HarperBusiness.

Heath, C., Jost, J., & Morris, M. (2000). Partition focus: Teams focus more on dividing tasks than coordinating them. Research in Progress, Stanford University.

Heath, C., Larrick, R. P., & Klayman, J. (1998). Cognitive repairs: How organizational practices can compensate for individual shortcomings. *Research in Organization Behavior, 20*, 1–37.

Heath, C., & Walston, S. L. (2000). Inadequate communication by top managers and the curse of knowledge. Working paper, Stanford University.

Henderson, K. (Autumn 1991). Flexible sketches and inflexible databases: visual communication, conscription devices and boundary objects in design engineering. *Science, Technology, and Human Values, 16*(4), 448–473.

Henderson, R. M., & Clark, K. B. (1990). Architectural innovation: The reconfiguration of existing product technologies and the failure of established firms. *Administrative Science Quarterly, 35*, 9–30.

Herman, J. B. (1973). Are situational contingencies limiting job attitude-job performance relationships? *Organizational Behavior and Human Performance*, *10*, 208–224.

Hinds, P. J. (1999). The curse of expertise: The effects of expertise and debiasing methods on predictions of novice performance. *Journal of Experimental Psychology: Applied*, *5*, 205–221.

Hinds, P. J., & Kiesler, S. (1995). Communication across boundaries: Work, structure, and use of communication technologies in a large organization. *Organization Science*, *6*, 373–393.

Hounshel, D. A., & Smith, J. K. (1988). *Science and corporate strategy: Du Pont R&D, 1902–1980*. Cambridge, UK: Cambridge University Press.

Iaffaldono, M. T., & Murchinsky, P. M. (1985). Job satisfaction and job performance: A meta-analysis. *Psychological Bulletin*, *97*, 251–273.

Iansiti, M. (1993). Real world R&D: Jumping the product generation gap. *Harvard Business Review*, May-June, 138–147.

Iansiti, M. (1995). Technology development and integration: An empirical study of the interaction between applied science and product development. *IEEE Transactions on Engineering Management*, *42*, 259–269.

Iansiti, M., & Clark, K. B. (1994). Integration and dynamic capability: Evidence from product development in automobiles and mainframe computers. *Industrial and Corporate Change*, *3*(3), 557–605.

Jensen, M. C., & Meckling, W. (1976). The Theory of the firm: Managerial behavior, agency costs, and capital structure. *Journal of Financial Economics*, *3*, 305–360.

Jervis, R. (1976). *Perception and misperception in international politics*. Princeton, NJ: Princeton University Press.

Kahneman, D., Slovic, P., & Tversky, A. (1982). *Judgment under uncertainty: Heuristics and biases*. Cambridge, UK: Cambridge University Press.

Keller, M. (1989). *Rude awakening: The rise, fall, and struggle for recovery of General Motors*. New York: Harper Perennial.

Kemerer, C. F. (1997). *Software project management: Readings and cases*. Chicago: Irwin Publishing.

Keysar, B. (1994). The illusory transparency of intention: Perspective taking in text. *Cognitive Psychology*, *26*, 165–208.

Klayman, J., Loewenstein, G., Heath, C., & Hsee, C. (2000). *If I were you: Trading places as a process for predicting the appraisals of others*. Working paper, University of Chicago.

Krackhardt, D. (1996). Groups, roles, and simmelian ties. Carnegie Mellon Working Paper.

Lawrence, P. R., & Lorsch, J. W. (1967). *Organization and environment: Managing differentiation and integration*. Boston, MA: Harvard Business School Press.

Malone, T. W., Crowston, K., Lee, X., Pentland, B., et al (March 1999). Tools for inventing organizations: Toward a handbook of organizational processes. *Management Science*, *45*(3), 425–443.

March, J. G., & Simon, H. A. (1958). *Organizations*. New York: Wiley.

Marschak, J., & Radner, R. (1972). *Economic theory of teams*. New Haven: Yale University Press.

Meindl, J. R., Erlich, S. E., & Dukerich, J. M. (1985). The romance of leadership. *Administrative Science Quarterly*, *30*, 78–102.

Milgrom, P., & Roberta, J. (1992). *Economics, organizations, and management*. Englewood Cliffs, NJ: Prentice Hall.

Morris, M., Heath, C., & Jost, J. (2000). Agency misattributions and the curse of knowledge. Research in Progress, Stanford University.

Nemeth, C. J., & Staw, B. M. (1989). The tradeoffs of social control and innovation in groups and organizations. *Advances in Experimental Social Psychology, 22*, 175–209.

Newton, L. (1990). Overconfidence in the communication of intent: Heard and unheard melodies. Unpublished doctoral dissertation, Stanford University, Stanford, CA.

Perlow, L. (1995). The Time Famine: An Unintended Consequence of the Way Time is Used at Work. Unpublished Ph.D. disssertation. Sloan School of Management, Massachusetts Institute of Technology.

Perrow, C. (1967). A Framework for the Comparative Analysis of Organizations. *American Sociological Review, 32*(2), 194–208.

Perrow, C. (1984). Normal accidents. New York: Basic Books.

Perry, D. E., Staudenmayer, N. A., & Votta, L. G. (1994). People, organizations, and process improvement. *IEEE Software*, 38–45.

Perry, D. E., Staudenmayer, N. A., & Votta, L. G. (1996). Understanding and improving time usage in software development. *Understanding Software Processses*. New York: Wiley.

Piaget, J., & Inhelder, B. (1967). *The child's conception of space*. New York: Norton.

Simon, H. A. (1947). *Administrative behavior*. New York: Macmillan.

Simon, H. A. (1962). The architecture of complexity. *Proceedings of the American Philosophical Society, 106*, 467–482.

Smith, D. K., & Alexander, R. C. (1988). *Fumbling the future: How Xerox invented, then ignored, the first personal computer*. New York: William Morrow and Company, Inc.

Staudenmayer, N. (1997). *Managing Multiple Interdependencies in Large Scale Software Development Projects*. Unpublished Ph.D dissertation. The Sloan School of Management, Massachusetts Institute of Technology.

Staudenmayer, N., & Desanctis, G. (1999) *Hidden interdependencies*. Presented at the Academy of Management Conference, August 1999, Chicago, IL.

Staw, B. M. (1986). Organizational psychology and the pursuit of the happy/productive worker. *California Management Review, 28*.

Staw, B. M., Sandelands, L., & Dutton, J. (1981). Threat-rigidity effects in organizational behavior: A multi-level analysis. *Administrative Science Quarterly, 26*, 501–524.

Tajfel, H. (1970). Experiments in intergroup discrimination. *Scientific American, 223*, 96–102.

Teece, D. J. (1986). Profiting from technological innovation: Implications for integration, collaboration, licensing and public policy. *Research Policy, 15*, 285–305.

Thompson, J. D. (1967). *Organizations in action*. New York: McGraw-Hill.

Tushman, M. L. (1979). Work characteristics and subunit communication structure: A contingency analysis. *Administrative Science Quarterly, 24*, 82–98.

Von Hippel, E. (1990). Task Partitioning: An Innovation Process Variable. *Research Policy, 19*, 407–418.

Wageman, R. (1995). Interdependence and group effectiveness. *Administrative Science Quarterly, 40*, 145–180.

Walton, M. (1997). *Car: A drama of the American workplace*. New York: Norton & Co.

Weber, R., Rottenstreich, Y., Camerer, C., & Knez, M. (1999). The illusion of leadership: Misattribution of cause in coordination games. *Organizational Science*, forthcoming.

Weick, K. E. (1983). Contradictions in a community of scholars: The cohesion-accuracy tradeoff. *The Review of Higher Education, 6*, 253–267.

Weick, K. E., & Roberts, K. H. (1993). Collective mind in organizations: Heedful interrelating on flight decks. *Administrative Science Quarterly, 38*, 357–381.

Wheelwright, S. C., & Clark, K. B. (1992). Revolutionizing Product Development. NY: Free Press.

Womack, J. P., & Jones, D. T. (1996). Beyond toyota: How to route out waste and pursue perfection. *Harvard Business Review, 74*(5), 140–149.

Woodward, J. (1965). *Industrial Organizations: Theory and Practice*. London: Oxford University Press.

Yoffie, D., & Cusumano, M. A. (1999). *Competing on Internet Time*. Boston: Harvard University Press.

CORPORATIONS, CLASSES, AND SOCIAL MOVEMENTS AFTER MANAGERIALISM

Gerald F. Davis and Doug McAdam

ABSTRACT

The traditional focus in organization theory on corporations as bounded, countable units of social structure is a poor fit with the emerging nature of the new economy. Increasingly 'boundaryless' production processes, and the predominance of evaluative standards based in financial markets, undermine the explanatory usefulness of theories such as resource dependence and population ecology. Yet economic theories of the firm are ill-equipped to make sense of the social and political processes that shape the structure and evolution of the corporation. This chapter argues that social movement theory provides an explanatory approach well-suited to forms of coordinated collective action in a post-industrial economy. We illustrate the argument by comparing the emerging media industry to the emergence of a national social movement, and everyday workings of the network economy of Silicon Valley to the routine mobilization of local movement activity. We close by describing four areas for future research.

Research in Organizational Behaviour, Volume 22, pages 193–236.
ISBN: 0–7623–0641–6

INTRODUCTION

There is widespread agreement among social scientists that the United States is witnessing the emergence of a new economy borne through a 'third industrial revolution'. Aspects of this have been described in terms of a breakdown of the mass-production paradigm, the dissolution of traditional labor market institutions, and the emergence of globally expansive and hyper-vigilant capital markets led by institutional investors. High velocity labor markets coupled with protean production structures create a sense of ongoing flux in the arrangements disciplining economic life. The American system of corporate governance in which these other institutions are embedded has come to be a model for the world, at least in the eyes of some commentators (Useem, 1998). There is also general recognition that the transition to a new economy is accompanied by enormous social dislocation, and policy recommendations range from meliorative (e.g. Reich, 1991) to Malthusian (e.g. Jensen, 1993). The stakes are high, as evidenced by events following the East Asian financial crisis of the late 1990s.

How these changes are implemented – how the new economy comes to have a particular institutional structure – is by rights a central topic on the agenda of economic sociologists, and particularly for theorists of organization. But the broad contours of the new economy undermine efforts to theorize the world in terms of social entities such as 'organizations'. Organization theory imagines society as an urn filled with balls called organizations: a 'high modernist' conception of boundary-maintaining bodies with relatively centralized control (cf. Scott, 1998). Yet economic production increasingly implicates shifting networks of actors and identities that appears more to resemble a vat of polymer goo, in Harrison White's (1992: 4) memorable terminology. In this chapter, we argue that the core problem facing organizational theory is that it uses a vocabulary and ontology rooted in an image of a mass production, managerialist economy that was roughly apt for the 30 years following World War II in the U.S. but has become inapplicable to the current institutional structure of the economy. Based on a series of recent empirical studies, we critique extant theory for its weaknesses in providing useful insights into the changing economy. Finally, we outline how contemporary theory about social movements can inform organizational research on the contemporary organization of the economy.

WHAT IS NEW ABOUT 'THE NEW ECONOMY'?

Proclamations of epochal shifts deserve skepticism. But there is substantial agreement among social scientists of various stripes that the 'post-industrial' economy in the U.S. is something different from its predecessor, and that this is realized in different ways of organizing production and different ways of organizing ownership. We first discuss these elements for the post-War U.S. economy and then describe recent changes.

The transition from competitive to monopoly capitalism has been amply documented, accomplished over the course of the twentieth century through mergers that consolidated oligopolistic producers with national scope and tall managerial hierarchies. In broad strokes, the post-War U.S. economy was populated by large, vertically integrated mass producers. Employment and economic power were disproportionately concentrated in a few hundred major corporations. By the early 1980s, 55.3% of non-governmental employees worked for the 750 largest U.S. firms, and the 200 largest non-financial corporations accounted for 35% of the assets of all non-financial corporations (Davis, 1994). Large corporations such as these were said to reflect a separation of ownership and control; that is, they were owned by thousands of dispersed and disorganized investors, but controlled by professional managers who attained their positions through bureaucratic processes and owned little of the firm themselves. This situation of 'managerialism' was argued to change the nature of class relations, from a Marxian society-wide conflict of workers vs. owners to a Weberian conflict of workers vs. managers within the enterprise (see Dahrendorf, 1959). Moreover, unshackling professional managers from the demands of organized investors was believed to free them from the strict dictates of profit maximization, enabling a 'soulful corporation' that balanced the interests of various 'stakeholders'.[1] The aptness of this description was challenged (Zeitlin, 1974), but empirical ownership patterns supported it, as few large firms had a single family owning as much as 10% of their stock.

In a society where employment and economic resources are concentrated within a relatively small number of large corporations, making sense of the corporate sector is a central – perhaps the paramount – task for social theory. Charles Perrow writes:

> [T]he appearance of large organizations in the United States makes organizations the key phenomenon of our time, and thus politics, social class, economics, technology, religion, the family, and even social psychology take on the character of dependent variables . . . organizations are the key to society because *large organizations have absorbed society*. They have vacuumed up a good part of what we have always thought of as society, and made organizations, once a part of society, into a surrogate of society (Perrow, 1991: 725–726).

By this account, to explain the structure of society entails explaining the configuration of organizations we have, as the U.S. has become a society of organizations. This synoptic view of social structure made organization theory (the branch of sociology concerned with formal organizations) the queen of the social sciences. The attainments of individuals are shaped by the reward structures and career ladders (Baron, 1984) and birth and death rates (Hannan & Freeman, 1989) of the organizations in which they work; thus, stratification should be a sub-field of organizational sociology. Creating formal organizations becomes the cover charge for participation in politics (Laumann & Knoke, 1987), and those running large organizations become distinctively influential over state policy, particularly when acting in concert with their colleagues (Useem, 1984); thus, political sociology (for the U.S.) can also be subsumed. In *The Sociological Imagination*, C. Wright Mills cast the role of social science as making sense of the intersection of biography and history in social structure. In a society of organizations, organization theory holds the master key to social structure.

But the corporate structures associated with the post-War U.S. economy have been substantially transformed in the past two decades, and with them the prospects for theories of social structure. For the sake of brevity, we emphasize two broad trends. The first is a shift in the social structures of production away from bounded organizations and toward unbounded network forms (what Sabel [1991] calls 'Moebius-strip organizations'). The second is the hyper-development of capital markets and the marginalization of financial intermediaries such as commercial banks.

Early inklings about the changing shape of production structures came from the surprising resurgence of industrial districts in Italy and elsewhere, which – coupled with the superior performance of vertically dis-integrated manufacturers in autos compared to American-style firms – came to be characterized as the breakdown of the mass production paradigm (Piore & Sabel, 1984). Organizations oriented to long production runs that made sense in a world of mass markets were disadvantaged when markets were segmented and tastes changed rapidly. Housing all or most steps of production within a single organizational boundary was not an end-state of industrial development. Alternative ways to divide labor among specialist firms, households, and individuals came to prominence.

As Sabel & Zeitlin (1996) put it, "It is as though the prehistoric and imaginary creatures in the industrial bestiary had suddenly come to life," coexisting as a strange pastiche of economic forms. Some (e.g. industrial districts; home working; project work, as in construction or film production; short-run production networks linking small specialist firms, as in the garment industry) had existed for some time or were newly revived. Others were decidedly new. Nike represents one approach: the firm designs and markets sneakers from a base in Oregon but contracts out for virtually all production with East Asian manufacturers. Ingram Micro uses the same production line to assemble computers for archrivals Compaq, IBM, Hewlett-Packard, Apple, and Acer, which it also distributes. A vice president at Hewlett-Packard explained "We own all of the intellectual property; we farm out all of the direct labor. We don't need to screw the motherboard into the metal box and attach the ribbon cable" for the computer to be a Hewlett Packard product. And Volkswagen's facility in Resende, Brazil represents perhaps a first: an assembly plant run almost entirely by multinational subcontractors, referred to as a 'modular consortium'. Units of Rockwell and Cummins from the U.S., Eisenmann from Germany, and Delga from Brazil each have shops along the assembly line, along with suppliers headquartered in Japan and elsewhere; Volkswagen employees perform R&D, marketing, and quality control. The large majority of workers on site work not for VW but for the other multinational participants. Assembly workers are paid one-third what autoworkers in Sao Paulo make; union leaders are reportedly perplexed by the web of employers at Resende. (The perplexity around the relevant bargaining unit was almost certainly part of VW's plan.) Shortly after the Resende plant opened, GM announced plans for a similar mini-car factory in Brazil, to house 20 multinational suppliers in what is seen as a prototype for future manufacturing facilities for appliances, VCRs, and other consumer goods.

If these were mere anomalies, they would hold little interest. But there is systematic evidence of a global proliferation of various network forms, described by Bennett Harrison as "the signal economic experience of our era" (1994: 127). Due in large part to advances in information technology, the basic calculus of the make-or-buy decision has been altered for tasks from payroll to manufacturing to product design, and even down to naming the organization. In effect, almost everything that a firm might do has a ready market comparison in the form of a specialist contractor. The result is that it is difficult to identify what is 'core' to an organization, and thus what needs protection from uncertainty (cf. Thompson, 1967). We have instead global production chains (McMichael, 1996) in which the boundaries around individual firms are provisional and highly permeable. Even basic facts about an organization's identity, such as whether it is a manufacturing or service business, are labile. Sara Lee Corporation, a large and diversified producer of food and clothing, announced plans in September 1997 to effectively abandon being a manufacturer in favor of being a marketer of its various brands, which range from Ball Park Franks to Hanes underwear to Coach leather goods. Its CEO, with the prodding of Wall Street analysts, came to realize that the firm's 'core competence' was not in making things but in managing their promotion and distribution, and thus the firm planned to shed most of its production capacity ('de-verticalize'). The increasing ambiguity around terms like 'manufacturing' and 'service' was reflected in 1995, when Fortune Magazine changed the definition of the Fortune 500 list from the 500 largest manufacturers to the 500 largest businesses overall.

Changes in the social organization of production have profound implications for theory about organizations, understood as boundary-maintaining systems. Network production systems no longer map onto discrete, bounded entities such as organizations, and social structures of production increasingly elude description using the traditional theoretical vocabulary of organizational sociology. But another change is perhaps even more consequential for the nature of social structure. It is the enormous global expansion of capital markets and the changing nature of the intermediaries that operate in them. The renowned 'triumph of markets' is in important ways the triumph of *capital* markets, both as a mechanism to finance (and discipline) corporations and as an outlet for the savings of households. In the United States during the 1990s, the number of public corporations doubled (to over 11,000), the number of mutual funds tripled (to roughly 9,000), and the proportion of households reporting stock ownership reached a historic high of 42% (double the figure of 30 years earlier). With the encouragement of a well-developed venture capital industry, organizations are increasingly founded with an expectation that they will eventually go public, by floating shares on a stock exchange (Black & Gilson, 1997). What has happened, in short, is that financial markets have largely supplanted alternative mechanisms (such as private ownership and bank lending) for channeling savings from households to firms in the U.S. (Davis & Mizruchi, 1999).

The shift from embedded ties to market-based transactions changes the basic nature of corporate decision making. By hypothesis, markets assign prices to financial instruments (stocks and bonds) according to the expected future income associated with their ownership, adjusted for risk. Thus, managers of firms that care about share price will seek to demonstrate their fitness to the capital markets by adhering to the standards of the most substantial market participants (Useem, 1996; cf. Meyer & Rowan, 1977). Demonstrating fitness to a dispersed financial market is rather different from managing interdependencies with exchange partners, as it requires discerning and acting on intersubjectively-held mental models of appropriate practice that are 'out there' in the market (Shiller, 1990). Indicators of fitness range from appointing CEOs of well-regarded firms to the board of directors (Davis & Robbins, 1998) to adopting particular kinds of incentive compensation systems and rationalizing them in appropriate ways (Westphal & Zajac, 1998) to streamlining the mix of industries in which the firm operates (Zuckerman, 1999). The most substantial market participants also prize liquidity, that is, the ability to sell a financial asset at any moment on a market for a known prevailing price. The marketability of a security is aided by the transparency of what it represents, which helps reduce intersubjective uncertainty about its value. Markets favor the overt over the tacit, and accounting rules and corporate strategies are designed to increase this transparency (Useem, 1996).

Who owns the U.S. corporation has changed substantially in the last decades of the 20th century, thus altering the audience for corporate decisions from individual owners to institutions. Financial assets in the U.S. are owned primarily by financial institutions rather than households. Upwards of 60% of the shares of the largest 1000 corporations is owned by institutions (pension funds, mutual funds, banks, insurance companies, and others), and this proportion has been increasing over time. Individuals are the ultimate beneficiaries of this ownership, of course, but decisions about what financial assets to buy and sell are made by professionals trained in financial analytic techniques and rewarded based on tangible measures of the performance of the assets under their management.[2] In other words, the process by which capital is allocated and accumulated in the U.S. is largely in the hands of employees of institutions, not wealthy individuals acting on their own behalf. The last vestige of the human touch in corporate finance – loans made by commercial banks, which must be approved by individuals who are willing to put a price on a loan based on their judgment – has been all but abandoned by large corporations, which can raise money more cheaply through money markets (Davis & Mizruchi, 1999). The implication, again, is that corporate decision making is oriented toward market-based evaluations.

In markets, disparate producers are compelled to make themselves comparable and thereby susceptible to ranking and valuation by buyers (White, 1992). The range of instruments traded on financial markets, and thus the set of competitors for favorable evaluation, has expanded dramatically during the past two decades through the practice of 'securitization' (that is, turning income-producing entities into tradeable securities such as bonds). Since Fannie Mae entered the mortgage-backed securities business in 1981, for instance, this market has expanded from $25 billion to over $4 trillion outstanding. In principle, almost anything that has future income associated with it can be securitized: a financial institution could bundle together a set of home mortgages, student loans, credit card receivables, or other loans it has made, divide them into shares, and sell them. The price of a share would reflect various factors likely to change the flow of income (e.g. changes in interest rates that influence whether individuals pay off mortgages early or default). Cheap computing power and new financial analytic techniques make it possible to place a value on such securities quickly in ways that would have been prohibitively expensive 25 years ago. Variations on this basic theme have become extravagant. In 1997, pop star David Bowie received $55 million for selling 10-year bonds to be paid from the anticipated royalties generated through future album sales. The entire issue was purchased by Prudential Insurance, and a unit of Nomura Securities subsequently established a division to specialize in creating securities backed by future revenues generated by music, publishing, film, and television products. Insurance companies sell 'disaster bonds' that pay attractive returns to their investors unless rare natural disasters (hurricanes; earthquakes) require the insurers to make large payouts to those they insure, in which case bondholders lose some or all of their investment. The large fees associated with underwriting these securities propel frantic innovation on the part of investment banks seeking to securitize anything with a potential income (or loss) associated with it. Again, these securities are generally purchased by institutions, not individuals. Institutions, moreover, have no inherent reason to prefer owning shares in a corporation to owning David Bowie bonds or bundles of Citibank credit card receivables sold as securities: what they own is a financial asset for which the only relevant evaluations concern risk and return. As the range of entities traded as securities expands from home mortgages to insurance claims of the terminally ill to municipal settlements with tobacco companies, corporations (understood as financial entities) face increasingly exacting standards of evaluation by financial markets.

How American corporations organize production and how they are financed have undergone a substantial transition toward decentralization. Social structures of production do not readily map onto the boundaries of formal organizations, and corporations operate in a world of disembedded, universal-istic financial markets that discipline how they look and what they do. Further, the financial intermediaries that dominate these markets have little reason to prefer investing in the securities of American corporations to investing in other flavors of securities. To paraphrase Perrow (1991), financial markets are the key to society because financial markets have absorbed society. It is organizational strategies and structures that have become the dependent variables.

PROSPECTS AND PROBLEMS FOR THEORIES OF ORGANIZATION IN THE NEW ECONOMY

Organization theory is the branch of sociology concerned with formal organizations, typically construed as entities constructed to pursue specific goals. The classic text defines organizations as "assemblages of interacting human beings [that are] the largest assemblages in our society that have anything resembling a central coordinative system . . . [This] marks off the individual organization as a sociological unit comparable in significance to the individual organism in biology" (March & Simon, 1958: 4). In this approach, "it is durable, coherent entities that constitute the legitimate starting points of . . . sociological inquiry" (Emirbayer, 1997: 285). If organizations are taken as basic units of analysis analogous to actors or organisms, the domain of the discipline follows readily. Organization theory studies the origin, structure, persistence, change, and disappearance of organizations, as well as the relations constructed among them and the impacts they have on individuals and the broader society. The basic imagery is of organizations as meaningfully bounded units responding to various pressures prompting adaptation or, failing that, selection.

The difficulty of applying this approach to the new economy will be evident from the previous discussion. What might have made perfect sense in discussions of vertically integrated managerialist firms in the 1960s has come to be nearly irrelevant to the current structure of the corporate sector, as several studies document. We illustrate this with two theories that are considered to be among the crown jewels of the field: resource dependence theory and population ecology. In each case, two problems arise: they can't account for empirical patterns in the nature of American corporations since 1980, and they show little prospect of being able to do so into the future.

Resource Dependence Theory

Resource dependence theory (RDT) builds a general framework for organizations from the base of a very parsimonious theory of exchange and power (Pfeffer & Salancik, 1978; Burt, 1983; see Davis & Powell, 1992 for a review of the empirical research). Emerson's well-known approach sees actor A's power over actor B flowing from A's control over resources valued by B. To the extent that B values what A has and can't get it elsewhere, A has power over B and B is dependent on A. The greater B's dependence, the greater its vulnerability to A's whims and the greater the incentive to take steps to reduce the dependence by changing its structural position. RDT applies this approach to making sense of organizations as actors that seek autonomy and avoid uncertainty but are embedded in webs of exchange that create power and dependence relations. The prototype is a firm that relies on a supplier of a specialized input that it can't easily get elsewhere (such as the relation of General Motors to Fisher Body before GM acquired it). The supplier can hold up the buyer by seeking to change the terms of the contract during a crunch period when the buyer is vulnerable. Organizations can respond to this condition either by maintaining alternatives (using more than one supplier of the specialized input), co-opting the supplier (e.g. by placing one of the supplier's executives on the board of directors to cultivate empathy, which GM did with Fisher), or buying the supplier (which GM also eventually did with Fisher). If none of these are possible or sufficient to reduce vulnerability, perhaps because of unavoidable conditions in the industry, organizations seeking to evade dependence will diversify, operating across a number of industries. Diversification across industries reduces the dependence and uncertainty associated with operating in any one.

Organizations thus deploy a repertoire of actions to respond to dependence that form in essence a Guttman scale: the greater the dependence, the more intense the response (from evasion to interlocking to outright merger). Evidence at the industry level appeared to support this account: the greater the uncertainty one industry posed for another, the more likely industry participants were to share directors, and the more likely were mergers between firms in the two industries (Pfeffer & Salancik, 1978). Firm-level analyses purported to show similar effects (Burt, 1983). The problem is that from about 1980 onwards, this approach fails to account for virtually anything that large corporations did. Essentially, there was little variance left to explain. First, mergers and acquisitions by large firms did not map onto 'problematic dependencies'. Between 1986 and 1990, the 500 largest manufacturers in the U.S. (the 'Fortune 500') collectively make roughly 450 acquisitions. Among these firms, only about 5% bought a firm in an industry with significant vertical relations (that is, a potentially substantial buyer or supplier). In other words, vertical integration had largely disappeared in favor of alternatives like contracting out, at least in the manufacturing sector. Unrelated diversification has also all but disappeared as a tactic: only 3% of these firms did more than one unrelated acquisition during the late 1980s, and diversifiers tended not to be the most dependent organizations, but the *least* dependent, like GE and AT&T (Davis, Diekmann & Tinsley, 1994). Conversely, about one-third of these firms sold off some businesses, usually shedding units outside their primary industries in order to focus on a 'core competence' (Galvin, 1994). In other words, very few large corporations engaged in acquisitions to manage their exchange-based dependence.

The same holds true for board interlocks (that is, cases where an executive of one firm serves on the board of directors of another firm). At one point, interlocks were feared as a device for collusion, with competing firms sharing directors in order to maintain a cartel. But since the Clayton Act of 1914 prohibiting such ties, few have appeared, and in 1994 there were no observed cases of competing major manufacturers appointing the same individual to their board. There were also few potentially co-optive interlocks: no more than 5% of large industrial firms had an executive of a firm in a major buyer or supplier industry on the board in 1994 (Davis, 1996). Ties to financial institutions followed the same pattern: among the Fortune 1000 firms in 1999 that were not commercial banks, only about one out of twenty had an interlock created via an executive of a major bank. Moreover, while 25% of firms had an executive serving on a major bank board in 1982, this number had dropped to 16% in 1994 and to under 11% in 1999, as money markets had replaced banks as sources of short-term debt for major corporations (Davis & Mizruchi, 1999).

It is possible that global markets enabled by information technology have reduced the general level of dependence of any one business on any other, thus mooting the need for the repertoire described by RDT. But it is not the case that organizations don't merge or interlock; it is that they do not do so in the way described by resource dependence theory or for the reasons it hypothesizes. The top executives of major corporations make sense of their actions almost entirely in terms of 'creating shareholder value', and actions that contradict the prevailing theories of how to create shareholder value (such as vertically integrating, or operating in several industries rather than focusing on one) are sanctioned. Strategies once construed as serving the organization's interest in stability are now seen as serving only the interests of the executives who run it. Pfeffer & Salancik (1978: 114) described their organizational rationale for acquisitions: "We will present data which suggest that merger is undertaken to accomplish a restructuring of the organization's interdependence and to achieve stability in the organization's environment, rather than for reasons of profitability or efficiency as has sometimes been suggested." Compare *The Economist's* account for the conglomerate merger wave of the 1960s: "Synergies from diversification did not exist . . . This was a colossal mistake, made by the managers, for the managers" (*The Economist*, 1991: 44). What RDT describes as an empirical regularity driven by the organization's drive to reduce uncertainty is subsequently recognized as a pathology driven by poorly-aligned managerial incentive structures.

Notions of power and exchange are certainly still useful, but they get played out in a historical context that conditions how applicable they are. RDT's greatest strength – its topicality – is also its greatest weakness, because the phenomena it meant to explain are by and large absent today. One might argue that an empirical critique focusing on the Fortune 500 is simply sampling an unrepresentative tail of the distribution. But the largest firms historically accounted for such a disproportionate amount of the assets and employment of the manufacturing sector that it matters little whether the findings generalize to the remaining smaller firms. One might also argue that the problematic dependency that firms seek to manage now comes not from buyers and suppliers but from shareholders. Thus, corporate action is now oriented toward pleasing shareholders. But to the extent that the main motivation of organizational action becomes equivalent to making profits for shareholders, rather than organizational stability and survival, then the need for a theory that is not simply the economic theory of the firm is not obvious.

Population Ecology

Much of the weakness of resource dependence theory comes from the fact that it focused on topical actions that were prevalent at the time the approach was being constructed but that subsequently disappeared. Problems with being overly topical are far less of a concern for population ecology, which seeks a general and trans-historical theory of organizations ranging from Finnish newspapers to American labor unions to German breweries to European universities. Ecology follows Perrow's 'society of organizations' thinking to its logical conclusion: if organizations are the basic units of society, then we should be able to explain the structure of society by explaining the demography of organizational forms, much as one would explain the composition of an urn full of balls by counting the number of balls of each size and color that came into or out of the urn. If we are in fact a society of organizations, what explains the proportions we have? Why are there only three U.S. automakers but dozens of hotels in Manhattan? The answer turns on the relative birth and death rates of organizations having these forms – presumably, over time selection processes insure that we end up with the number and proportions of organizations we have now (see Hannan & Freeman, 1989 for a comprehensive account). A crucial assumption of this approach is that organizations don't change in important ways over time: if balls changed colors and sizes after they were dropped into the urn, then counting which ones went in and came out couldn't tell us the composition of the urn. Thus, ecological research focuses primarily on birth and death rates of organizations sharing a form (where 'form' is generally defined by industry rather than detailed information about organizational structure).

Early studies documented that there were liabilities of newness (younger organizations are more likely to fail than older ones) and smallness (small firms fail more often than big ones; see Davis & Powell, 1992 for a review). Subsequent research has explored a pair of empirical regularities called 'density dependence'. The basic finding is that across a wide spectrum of

'populations', there is a curvilinear relation between the number of organizations in existence at any given time and the rates of birth and death of
organizations of that type. That is, when there are few organizations in an
industry (say, labor unions), the chances that any given one will fail are fairly
high, but as more organizations enter the industry, the probability of failure for
each of them goes down. After a certain point, however, the effect reverses such
that with each new entrant, the probability of failure goes up. Graphically,
plotting probability of failure on number of organizations in the population
yields a U-curve. The explanation is that there are two competing effects:
legitimacy (the more organizations sharing a form there are, the greater their
legitimacy), which dominates first, and *competition* (the more organizations
there are, the less resources available for any one), which dominates later. The
effects are reversed for births: greater density increases birth rates up to a point,
after which it decreases them (see Hannan & Carroll, 1992 for a full
elaboration).

At first blush, it appears that density dependence conflates causes and
consequences: the thing to be explained (the number of organizations of a given
type) is explained by the number of organizations of a given type. Of course,
when this quantity is on the right-hand side of the equation, it is an indicator
(simultaneously) of the constructs of legitimacy and competition, whereas
when it is (figuratively) on the left-hand side, it is the construct itself. But the
deeper problem is an ontological one: across much of the manufacturing and
service economy in the U.S., it simply no longer makes sense to count
organizations as meaningful entities that are born and die in a fashion
analogous to organisms. In a social world that looks less like an urn filled with
balls than a vat of polymer goo, explanation through counting misses the major
dynamics of the new economy. Locating boundaries around firms and even
industries becomes an increasingly fruitless task.

Biotech and the culture industries provide shopworn examples, but even the
large bureaucratic organizations that motivated the initial ecological arguments
about structural inertia (see Hannan & Freeman, 1984 on the inertial effects of
age and size) prove to be protean when it pleases financial markets. The recent
history of the entity formerly known as Westinghouse shows how: a century-
old industrial conglomerate that dabbled in media and employed well over
100,000 people, its CEO was forced out by investor pressure in 1993 and
replaced with an executive from Pepsi. Within five years, the former Pepsi
executive sold off dozens of businesses, bought CBS and other properties, and
after initially proposing to split the company in two chose instead to liquidate
its remaining industrial operations. On December 1, 1997, Westinghouse
ceased to exist, and CBS became the new identity of the remaining corporation,

which abandoned its traditional home in Pittsburgh for New York City. Its 1997 revenues and employment were less than half those of 1990, while its profits were more than doubled.

One example that strains the biological metaphor of ecology may not be proof, but the systematic evidence points in the same direction. Between 1980 and 1990, 28% of the Fortune 500 largest American manufacturers were subjected to takeover bids, which were usually 'hostile' (that is, outsiders sought to buy the company against the wishes of its current management) and usually ended up in the sale of the company. A large proportion of these takeovers were motivated by the fact that diversified companies operating across several industries could be bought for far less than one could get for dismembering them and selling off the component parts, which was what usually happened following the sale (Davis et al., 1994). In light of this, those running large corporations began dismembering their own organizations, although not usually as dramatically as Westinghouse. Within a decade, one-third of the largest corporations ceased to exist as independent organizations (almost none through business failure), and those that remained operated in half as many industries on average as they had at the start (Davis et al., 1994). The manufacturing economy of the U.S. was driven to a radical restructuring by financial concerns, through processes bearing no relation to 'birth' and 'death'. This trajectory continued without letup through the first seven years of the 1990s and showed every sign of continuing into the future, as 'creating shareholder value' had become the only acceptable rhetoric for those that run corporate America. The end state of manufacturing organization when capital markets are dominant appears to be hyper-specialization coupled with production through networks (Davis & Robbins, 1999).

There are of course contexts where organizations do seem to be born and die, and the biological imagery still seems apt. When competitors are dividing a fixed pie of demands (e.g. geographically bounded areas with a stable base of consumers, such as day care centers or hotels in a metropolitan area), ecological models apply fairly well (e.g. Baum & Mezias, 1992). But finding those (increasingly rare) contexts where the model applies is like looking for one's lost keys under the streetlight. Organizations that are elements of small-firm production networks may have readily-defined birth and death dates (e.g. the buttonhole sewing specialists that sub-contract work in the New York garment industry), but their life chances are utterly bound up in the production networks of which they are a part (Uzzi, 1997). One could bump up the unit of analysis such that the network itself is the thing that is born and dies. But new networks are born and die with utter predictability as the fashion 'seasons' change. The Procrustean bed of ecological theorizing would thus obscure rather than clarify the dynamics of the industry.

Summary

Organization theory traditionally treats corporations as meaningfully bounded, actorly entities analogous to organisms. This was a reasonable imagery for some purposes in analyzing the organization of the post-War American economy, but the metaphors of 'sovereignty' and birth and death no longer make sense of the corporate sector. In contrast to the world described by Dahrendorf, there is no ambiguity on the part of contemporary corporate executives about the purposes of corporations: they exist exclusively to maximize shareholder value, which renders any attachment to industry, employees, and place outdated sentimentality, and any efforts at managing interdependence suspect.

We do not argue that it was never appropriate to study organizations as units, and there is no denying the appeal of the biological analogy. If not the master key to explaining society envisioned by Perrow, organization theory was at least broadly descriptive of the American manufacturing economy for much of the post-War era. But even the barest description of the contours of the new economy eludes description using the traditional vocabulary of organization theory, as exemplified by resource dependence theory and population ecology. Our objection is not a philosophical concern that sociologists 'should' study relations rather than things (cf. Emirbayer, 1997) or organizing rather than organizations (Weick, 1979); it is simply that the theories don't work on their own terms any more.

PROBLEMS FOR CONVENTIONAL THEORIES OF CLASS

Although we cannot develop the theme at length here, it is worth noting that problems for theories that take organizations as basic units of analysis have analogues in theories of class. Critiques of Marxian class categories appeared in fairly short order after the discovery of a 'managerial revolution' separating ownership and control, and Ralf Dahrendorf stated the case most boldly. The post-war economy was dominated by vast mass production organizations owned by dispersed and powerless shareholders and controlled by professional managers who attained their positions through higher education and demonstrated merit. These high-level bureaucrats may clash with the production workers over the exercise of authority, and they may earn stratospheric salaries, but they do not constitute a capitalist class rooted in control of property. "A theory of class based on the division of society into owners and non-owners of means of production loses its analytical value as soon as legal ownership and factual control are separated" (Dahrendorf, 1959: 136). The managerial revolution replaced the fixed boundaries of old classes rooted in property ownership with the mobility of a meritocracy; thus, ". . . the participants, issues, and patterns of conflict have changed, and the pleasing simplicity of Marx's view of society has become a nonsensical construction" (57). There were surely strata based on income, but there were no longer politically meaningful classes whose interactions provided a trajectory to history.

Not everyone was convinced. Even if one conceded the separation of ownership and control, a variety of devices compelled managers to act in the interests of owners (who were often well-hidden wealthy families; Zeitlin, 1974). More importantly, owners and managers were mutually socialized through elite institutions that allowed them to develop and act on common class interests. Research on these institutions sought to document how members of the 'corporate elite' came to form a self-recognized class capable of exercising unique power over government policy. Various mechanisms were argued to make class cohesion more likely, including board interlocks, living in Greenwich, Connecticut, going to Bohemian Grove to network, or forming associations like the Business Roundtable (Useem, 1984).

But the danger of lumping together owners and managers as a common interest group became evident during the 1980s. The advent of the hostile takeover highlighted the fundamentally conflicting interests of those who ran corporations and those who owned them: corporate executives typically ended up stigmatized and unemployed following a successful takeover, while shareholders commonly got 30–50% premiums for selling their shares to those doing the takeover. To defend their turf against errant owners, managers and boards adopted an array of devices to make it difficult to take their firms over, such as 'poison pills', and 'golden parachutes' to ensure that they were well-compensated if they lost their jobs after a takeover (Davis & Greve, 1997).

Owners protested vigorously the encroachment on their property rights and the potential losses from unconsummated takeovers. Notably, the most vocal owners were not wealthy families but pension funds such as the College Retirement Equities Fund (CREF) and the California Public Employees Retirement System (CalPERS). The ambiguity of the class interests at play in takeovers was highlighted by the rhetoric of the contending parties when managers and owners disagreed on issues of corporate control. When adopting poison pills or lobbying state legislatures for legal protection, corporate managers routinely cited the devastation wrought by hostile takeovers and their obligations to protect employees, communities, and other 'stakeholders' in the corporation. Pension funds were not swayed by such sentimentality and argued – with some success in the policy arena – that their property rights came first (Davis & Thompson, 1994). The period of owner irrelevance described by Dahrendorf had been replaced by owner hegemony. Yet the hegemons are largely pension fund administrators and other fund managers, not elites with inherited wealth. Because the performance of the funds they manage is fairly objective, almost anyone in their positions would articulate the same interests. It takes no special enlightenment for them to recognize the interests associated with their role, or to construct devices for pursuing them. But most importantly, they can in no sense be identified with the corporate executives to whom their funds are entrusted, nor can they be identified with the wealthy individuals who live off the fruits of their own investments. Their class location may be contradictory, but their influence on the course of business is substantial.

WHY THE ECONOMIC THEORY OF THE FIRM IS NOT MUCH HELP

We have argued thus far that economic activities are not meaningfully bounded within corporations, and pressures from financial markets – both from institutional investors and more disembodied sources – drive the decisions of those who run corporations. Both shifts create problems of relevance for organization theory.

There exists a theoretical approach with a surprising amount of surface relevance for approaching these problems. It is the agency theory or contractarian approach to the corporation, which developed primarily within the school known as law and economics. The approach begins with the assertion that the "separation of ownership and control" described by Berle & Means (1932) cannot have the consequences they attributed to it, that is, managers with substantial discretion to run corporations in ways harmful to investors. Rational investors (principals) would shun corporations without safeguards against self-dealing managers, and thus such corporations would be selected out. Managers (agents) know this and thus create organizational structures that demonstrate their corporations' fitness as an investment vehicle (Easterbrook & Fischel, 1991). Indeed, the structure of the corporation and the institutions in which it is embedded (corporate and securities law; financial markets; the 'market' for takeovers) embody attempts to resolve the divergence of interests between shareholders and managers. Some practices are voluntary adaptations to demonstrate fitness (e.g. appointing a hard-headed former Secretary of State to the board of directors to be a credible watchdog), while others are devices evolved to institutionalize the resolution of conflicts (e.g. corporate law; the takeover market). But understanding institutional resolutions of the inherent conflict between owners and managers is the central agenda of the approach.

The contractarian approach also has an ontological appeal, as it questions the meaningfulness of the boundaries of organizations rather than assuming firms to be bounded units. Initially, this was stated as a critique rooted in methodological individualism (that is, the view that theoretical explanations must ultimately be reducible to the actions of individuals):

> ... most organizations are simply *legal fictions which serve as a nexus for a set of contracting relationships between individuals* . . . . Viewed in this way, it makes little or no sense to try to distinguish those things which are 'inside' the firm (or any other organization) from those that are 'outside' of it. There is in a very real sense only a multitude of complex relationships (i.e. contracts) between the legal fiction (the firm) and the owners of labor, material and capital inputs and the consumers of output . . . . We seldom fall into the trap of characterizing the wheat or stock market as an individual, but we often make this error by thinking about organizations as if they were persons with motivations and intentions (Jensen & Meckling 1976: 310–11, emphasis in original).

This view of the organization as nothing but a set of contracting relations matches well with the types of network organizational structures we described previously. In the contemporary economy, "The question is not when is a nexus-of-contracts *a firm*, but when is it *more firm-like*" (Demsetz, 1991). Rather than "assuming an organization," this approach assumes a set of markets instead.

Strong selection pressures from both product and capital markets insure that corporate structures are reasonably efficient, if not optimally so. Thus, the most prevalent institutional features of the corporate economy can be assumed to serve some discernible economic function (Easterbrook & Fischel, 1991). The separation of ownership and control, long regarded as an unavoidable cost of large size, was re-interpreted as an efficient division of labor between those who were good at managing but had little capital and those who didn't know how to manage but were good at owning. Moreover, the fact that the corporate equivalents of elections are run by management and the board and typically yield nearly unanimous support for the policies of the incumbent board is not a problem but a virtue. The costs to shareholders of gathering the information to vote intelligently are not outweighed by the benefits, and thus "investors in public firms often are ignorant and passive" for good reason (Easterbrook & Fischel, 1991: 11). If the prospective benefit of gathering more information outweighed the cost, someone would do it. Moreover, passive shareholders are protected by a phalanx of mechanisms that protect their investment without their active intervention. Managers compete among themselves to 'add value', and are rewarded appropriately. This competition in the managerial labor market redounds to the benefit of shareholders (Fama, 1980). Managerial labor markets are complemented by director labor markets, where those most vigilant and talented at finding worthy managers to promote are rewarded (Fama & Jensen, 1983). If all else fails, poorly run firms will be punished with low share prices, inviting takeover by more talented managers (a process known as the 'market for corporate control'; Manne, 1965). The end result is that we dwell in the best of all possible worlds, where only fit firms survive a Darwinian competition for capital (see Easterbrook & Fischel, 1991: Chapter 1 for a compact summary).

Recognizing that considerations of corporate finance (how corporations get the money to fund what they do) provide the motor of institutional development is a useful first step in making sense of the governance of American corporations. But it is crucial to recognize that politics and social structures hold the steering wheel. An extensive critique has appeared elsewhere (Davis & Thompson, 1994), but we want to highlight the centrality of 'contentious politics' (McAdam, Tarrow & Tilly, 1996) to the evolution of the corporation.

Even the most basic structural feature of the American corporation – the separation of ownership and control – is best explained by political struggles that resulted in the fragmentation of financial intermediaries. In contrast to banks in other industrialized nations, American banks have been relatively small, weak, and prohibited from intervening in the affairs of corporations. Allowing banks to expand nationally (rather than only within states) and to own shares in corporations would most likely have created institutions with the wherewithal to hold influential stakes in even the largest corporations. But small town bankers (who didn't want the competition), populists (who didn't trust concentrated economic power), and professional managers (who appreciated the autonomy afforded by dispersed shareholders) repeatedly induced legislators to prevent such developments (Roe, 1994).

Political events of the late 1980s caused even the most devoted contractarians to re-evaluate their faith in the efficacy of American corporate governance and in the causal primacy of markets in shaping corporate structures (see Jensen, 1993). The agency approach requires a selection mechanism to ensure that the strong survive and the weak perish, and the favored institution is the so-called market for corporate control. By hypothesis, firms that don't live up to their promise suffer low share prices, giving incentives to more talented managers to buy and rehabilitate these undervalued assets. The existence of predators (corporate raiders) is argued to keep the prey on their toes, while the consequences of allowing firms to avoid deserved takeovers (e.g. by enabling boards to adopt poison pills) are dire. Thus,

"Protected by impenetrable takeover defenses, managers and boards are likely to behave in ways detrimental to shareholders . . . The end result, if the process continues unchecked, is likely to be the destruction of the corporation as we know it" (Jensen, 1988: 347). It would be as if gazelles learned how to erect electric fences to keep out the lions. Yet this electric fence scenario happened on a vast scale, as more than 40 states passed laws making it difficult to take over local corporations; in virtually every instance, at the behest of groups of the managers of local corporations, typically making common cause with labor organizations through an impromptu social movement (Davis & Thompson, 1994).

The most contentious case, and also most informative, was the Pennsylvania statute of 1990. In late 1989 the Belzberg brothers, notorious corporate raiders from Canada, threatened Armstrong World Industries with a takeover. Pennsylvania had been hard-hit by takeovers in the 1980s, most notably when Chevron acquired Gulf in 1984, closing Gulf's Pittsburgh headquarters and eliminating thousands of jobs. Thus, there was considerable sympathy when Armstrong's management sought restrictive anti-takeover legislation that would have made it essentially impossible to take over a Pennsylvania firm without seeking its board's approval. As happened in other states, Armstrong was joined by the Pennsylvania Chamber of Commerce and Industry as well as by labor representatives and local public officials in supporting the bill. Faced with such support, the bill sailed through the state Senate with little debate and a final vote of 45–4. However, hearings in the state House mobilized substantial opposition from investors, academic lawyers and economists, newspaper editorialists, and the Chairman of the Securities and Exchange Commission. *Wall Street Journal* editorialists accused the state of 'expropriation'; the *New York Times* stated the law "intimidates legitimate challengers by penalizing them if their buyout offers fail"; and a local attorney stated "The law undermines and erodes free markets and property rights. From this perspective, this is an anti-capitalist law."

Recognizing that they were sure to lose a clash perceived as 'communities vs. markets', the Belzbergs hired The Analysis Group, a consulting organization with academic affiliates, to research and explain the potential impact of the law using economic science. Legislators received a letter denouncing the bill signed by a group of law and economics scholars organized by an Analysis Group affiliate. The Belzbergs successfully ran Michael Jensen (a noted agency theorist at Harvard Business School and Analysis Group affiliate) as a dissident for the Armstrong board. But the most interesting opposition to the law came from institutional investors. Officials of the two major Pennsylvania public pension funds strongly opposed the bill, with the chairman of the Public School

Employees' Retirement System labeling it a 'disaster' that would "lower the stock values of Pennsylvania corporations," and other pension funds voicing similar concerns. And in what was perhaps a first, institutional investors threatened a 'capital strike' – that is, to systematically divest ownership in Pennsylvania corporations if the law were to pass.

Legislators, however, were more swayed by local business and labor leaders than by non-local academics and investors, and the bill passed the House 181–11. Researchers attributed a roughly \$4 billion loss in the stock market value of Pennsylvania corporations to the bill. And in part as a result of such laws, the prevalence of hostile takeovers declined substantially during the 1990s: whereas there were 83 takeover bids for Fortune 500 firms from 1981–1986 (most hostile), there were 17 from 1991–1996, and only five could be considered hostile (Davis & Robbins, 1999). In short, the gazelles had erected their fence.

The implications of organized contention among management, labor, and capital are many. For the contractarian approach, it is evident that selection regimes are themselves political choices, and that those running corporations can be well-organized and effective in influencing these choices. We can't understand why we have the corporations we do without unpacking the politics. But politics is embedded in social structures that shape whether, when, and how collective action occurs, and how effective it is (Tilly, 1978). It is here that the relevance of social movement theory becomes apparent for the study of the new economy.

USING SOCIAL MOVEMENT THEORY TO UNDERSTAND THE NEW ECONOMY

We have argued that changes in the organization of production and the expanding scale and scope of financial markets create fundamental problems for organization theory as it applies to the contemporary American economy. Approaches such as resource dependence theory and population ecology take organizations to be basic units of analysis. As units, organizations are born, they manage interdependence with other organizations, and eventually they die. Their inner workings and vital rates structure the careers and life chances of their members. Building on this notion, Perrow (1991) envisions a 'society of organizations' in which economy and society consist of (large) organizations. Of course, organization theorists have recognized that treating organizations as bounded units was a form of reification, as organizations rarely encompass their members fully (see Pfeffer & Salancik, 1978: 29–32). Such reification was simply a justifiable cost of doing business as an organization theorist. But we have argued that the imagery of organizations-as-units has finally become more misleading than enlightening, leading one to ask the wrong kinds of questions and use the wrong kinds of mechanisms to make sense of the social structure of the economy. The contractarian approach to the corporation, widely embraced in law and economics, has some appeal but misses essential processes of social change. This is particularly the case when one considers times of economic upheaval, when institutional structures themselves (such as 'selection regimes') are in flux.

The challenge, then, is to find an appropriate theoretical vocabulary to describe and explain the types of economic structures that the new economy has brought us. Making sense of the constitution of new social structures during times of economic and social upheaval is familiar turf for students of social movements. Much of the work has been on the first two industrial revolutions, but there is no obvious reason why the so-called third industrial revolution currently underway cannot be understood using the same tools. The dynamics of episodic collective action, for instance, seem to us to be precisely parallel to those of episodic economic production. Participants are not 'members' bound by inclusion and subject to the authority of a leader, but 'citizens' who may be persuaded to act in concert voluntarily. Thus, the conceptual kit bag of social movement scholars (e.g. mobilizing structures, framing processes, perceived opportunities and threats, repertoires of contention) is equally relevant to an analysis of the emerging forms of economic action. Moreover, the assumptions characteristic of much social movement theory are consistent with the previous critique: boundaries around social units are problematized; interests and grievances are to some degree socially constructed rather than transparent; and the kinds of mobilizing structures are emergent and path dependent. And the questions that arise in understanding social movements are analogous to those concerning new forms of organization: how is collective action coordinated when participation by 'members' is impromptu and impermanent; what are the characteristic routines of collective action likely to be shared by potential participants; and how do pre-existing social structures (such as networks) influence when and where collective action will occur.

We see, in short, a strong analogy between the processes of mobilization for collective action in social movements and in contemporary business organizations. Mayer Zald & Michael Berger (1978) drew a similar parallel over 20 years ago in their pathbreaking analysis of social movements *in* organizations. Our focus is somewhat different: we see much contemporary economic activity as akin to social movements, that is, more-or-less episodic forms of more-or-less coordinated collective action. We argue that contemporary theory about social movements provides constructs and a vocabulary attuned to the types of actions and actors that we have described:

> Actors, in this view, are not neatly-bounded, self-propelling entities with fixed attributes, but concentrations of energy that interact incessantly with surrounding sources of energy, and undergo modifications of their boundaries and attributes as they interact. Actions consist not of self-deliberated emissions of energy but of interactions among sites. Identities do not inhere in fixed attributes of such sites, much less in states of consciousness at those sites, but in representations of interactions and of connections between those sites and the interactions in which they are involved. Contentious politics does not simply activate pre-existing actors and their fixed attributes, but engages a series of interactive performances that proceed through incessant improvisation within broadly-defined scripts and organizational constraints (Tilly, 1998: 3).

Theories about organizations and social movements share a common agenda of making sense of more-or-less routinized collective action: its sources, structures, and outcomes. Thus, there has been some interchange among these two traditions (see Zald & Berger, 1978; Clemens, 1993; Minkoff, 1997; and particularly Koput, Powell & Smith-Doerr, 1997). To the extent that economic action comes to look like contentious politics, we expect that theory about social movements will be applicable to the traditional domain of organization theory. We make our case by comparing the emergence of a national movement to its analogue with industry emergence, and by examining parallels between the periodic mobilization of routine contention and project-based production. In both cases, we illustrate the applicability of social movement theory to contemporary economic structures. Both strike us as relevant to the search for causal analogies between social movements and formal economic organizations.

The Origins of Social Movements

A fairly strong consensus has emerged among scholars of social movements around the question of how social movements arise. Increasingly, one finds scholars emphasizing the importance of the same broad sets of factors in analyzing the origins of collective action. These three factors are: (1) an expansion in the political opportunities or threats confronting a given challenger; (2) the forms of organization (informal as well as formal) available to insurgents as sites for initial mobilization, and (3) the collective processes of interpretation, attribution and social construction that mediate between opportunity/threat and action. We will refer to these three factors by their conventional shorthand designations: political opportunities/threats, mobilizing structures, and framing processes.

Expanding Political Opportunities or Threats

Movement scholars have come to believe that under conditions of relative political stability, excluded groups, or challengers, rarely mobilize. Instead movements arise when broader change processes serve to either significantly threaten the interests of challengers or render the existing regime newly vulnerable or receptive to challenger demands. Expansions in political opportunity or threat accompany any broad change process that serves to significantly undermine the calculations and assumptions on which the political status quo rests. Among the events and processes especially likely to destabilize the status quo are wars, rapid industrialization, international political realignments, economic crises of various sorts, and mass migrations or other disruptive demographic processes.

Extant Mobilizing Structures

If destabilizing changes to the structure of institutionalized politics shapes the likelihood of collective action, the influence of such changes is not independent of the various kinds of mobilizing structures through which groups seek to organize and press their claims. The term mobilizing structures refers to those collective vehicles, informal as well as formal, through which people mobilize and engage in collective action. These include groups, formal organizations, and informal networks that comprise the collective building blocks of social movements. The shared assumption among movement scholars is that changes in the system of institutionalized politics only afford challengers the *stimulus* to engage in collective action. It is the organizational vehicles available to the group at the time the opportunity or threat presents itself that conditions its ability to respond to this environmental stimulus. In the absence of such vehicles, the challenger is apt to lack the capacity to act even when motivated to do so.

Framing or other Interpretive Processes

If a combination of opportunity/threat and mobilizing structures affords a potential challenger a certain structural potential for action, they remain, in the absence of one final factor, insufficient to account for emergent collective action. Mediating between opportunity/threat and action are the shared meanings and cultural understandings that people bring to an episode of incipient contention. At a minimum people need to feel aggrieved and/or threatened by some aspect of their life and at least minimally optimistic that, acting collectively, they can redress the problem. Conditioning the presence or absence of these perceptions is that complex of social psychological dynamics – collective attribution, social construction – which David Snow and various of his colleagues (Snow et al., 1986; Snow & Benford, 1988) have referred to as *framing processes*. When the cognitive and affective byproducts of these processes are combined with opportunity/threat and sufficient organization, chances are very good that collective action will develop.

Though there is consensus among movement scholars regarding the basic factors that condition the initial mobilization of a social movement, such a framework does not by itself constitute a dynamic model of movement origins. How these factors combine to trigger initial mobilization and by what intervening mechanisms is less clearly specified in contemporary movement theory. To redress this deficiency, the second author has recently proposed a modified version of this basic framework in which this somewhat static list of factors has been replaced by a set of dynamic relationships which are thought to predict the onset of 'episodes of contention' (McAdam, 1999). This modified framework is sketched in Fig. 1.

Figure 1 depicts movement emergence as a highly contingent outcome of an ongoing process of interaction involving at least one set of state actors and one challenger. But while McAdam focuses on state-oriented social movements, we think the perspective can be usefully adapted to analyzing emergent innovation within any relatively coherent system of institutionalized power (e.g. an industry, a single firm, etc.). In Fig. 2 we have adapted the model to fit the case of innovative economic action within an industry.

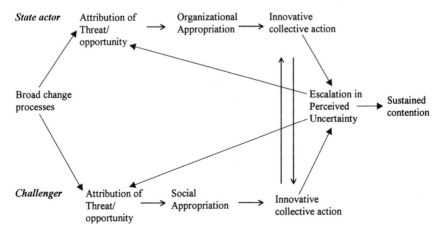

Fig. 1.

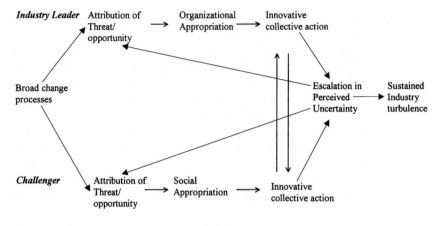

Fig. 2.

APPLYING SOCIAL MOVEMENT THEORY: INDUSTRY EMERGENCE

Figure 2 attributes innovative economic action – such as industry emergence – to a highly contingent process in which destabilizing changes (typically exogenous to the field in question) set in motion a sequence of linked mobilization dynamics. The remainder of this section is given over to a discussion of this general sequence. To make the discussion less abstract, we will use a single case – the emergence of the contemporary media industry – to illustrate the more general analytic claims being advanced.

Referring to the media as an industry is something of an act of reification, as some analysts count at least seven separate industries as constituents of the 'communications' industry: television broadcasting, film studios, cable TV, telecommunications, computers, consumer electronics, and publishing (Auletta, 1998). The identities of the core players are remarkably labile, and their web of affiliations is dense and tangled. We mentioned Westinghouse's transformation from old-line industrial conglomerate to broadcaster. GE entered the broadcasting industry via its purchase of NBC, and Disney through its purchase of Capital Cities/ABC. Seagram, the venerable purveyor of alcoholic beverages, became a filmmaker and amusement park operator through its purchase of Universal, and expanded its presence in the music industry through its acquisition of Polygram. Sony expanded from consumer electronics to music and movies. Formerly clear distinctions between industries and media have collapsed as television shows spawn movies (and vice versa), newspapers publish on the World Wide Web, and characters created for movies are merchandised through toys, software, books, fast food, theatrical productions, and other forms of branded merchandise. (Disney's film *The Lion King*, for instance, was merchandised through 186 different products and turned into a Broadway show.)

What is occurring is the emergence of a global meta-industry out of the confluence of new communication and computing technologies, deregulation in the United States, and privatization elsewhere. The identities and dominance ordering of the core players in the sector are subject to dramatic variations as long-established participants from constituent industries are overshadowed by new challengers, often from previously adjacent industries. To take a shopworn example, the World Wide Web did not exist in 1990 yet has helped spawn a vast outpouring of new businesses and new mini-industries. The market capitalization of Amazon.com, an on-line bookstore that began operations in 1994, exceeded those of Barnes & Noble and Borders combined four years later. The list of new billion-dollar communications companies is long. Conversely, older players (such as the three broadcast networks) fall further behind as the new economic order takes shape.

Currently there is an inherent and irreducible unpredictability that undermines the calculations of participants tenured under the old regime in the media industry. Figuring out what to do and how to structure oneself in order to succeed appear to hinge more on blind luck than high-level strategizing. Technological advances undermine traditional sources of monopoly power and erode industry boundaries. Television programming can be delivered over phone lines; phone calls can be sent over the Internet; Internet connections can be achieved through television cables; 'cable' programming can be delivered via satellite. Even such basic matters as morphology elude description: an initially helpful parsing of the communications industry into 'channels' (or 'distribution') and 'content' (or 'software') began to lose its analytical value as content providers (such as Disney) integrated into channels and channels (such as Microsoft) integrated into content. There is no settled model of what a 'communications' corporation should look like due to the pervasive uncertainty around the industry, and thus the shifting portfolios of the major participants (chosen from among film studios, newspapers, amusement parks, satellite delivery systems, sports teams, broadcast networks, and so on) represent diverse models of appropriate corporate practice.

Television broadcasting had perhaps the most stable dominance ordering among the constituent industries going into the 1980s. Three incumbents formed an oligopoly capturing upwards of 90% of the total viewing audience, and challengers were peripheral. For these broadcasters, a fundamental exogenous change came with the spread of cable television, which offered alternative means of distribution for 'content', and thus an opportunity for challengers. The rhetoric of challengers seeking to take advantage of this opening at times took on a populist tone: in appearing before Congress in 1976 to seek support for launching a national 'superstation', Ted Turner said:

> You have to remember there are three supernetworks . . . that are controlling the way this nation thinks and raking off exorbitant profits . . . They have an absolute, a virtual stranglehold, on what Americans see and think, and I think a lot of times they do not operate in the public good. I came into the independent television station business because I believe there should be more voices heard than the network voices out of New York . . . (quoted in Guthey, 1997: 191).

The threat from cable initially roused little concern from the established broadcasters. The offerings seemed laughable: a 24-hour news channel with no-name anchors and bargain-basement production values; a station that showed promotional videos for rock bands around the clock; an outlet where hawkers sold merchandise via a toll-free number. Within a few years, of course, CNN, MTV, and QVC grew enormously, largely at the expense of the broadcast networks. By 1997, the parents of these three (Time Warner, Viacom, and TCI) each far outstripped the venerable CBS in revenue and influence. Thus, what challengers recognized as opportunities went unrecognized as threats by incumbents until well into the process. By June 1998, more people tuned in to cable programming than the offerings of the four largest broadcast networks combined (CBS, NBC, ABC, and Fox).

How was this upheaval accomplished? The empirical literature documenting the emergence of social movements suggests that movements most commonly arise through the appropriation of existing organizations for new purposes rather than through the founding of entirely new organizations. The most famous instance of this was the transformation of the black church in the South from a generally conservative institution into a key mobilizing structure in the civil rights movement. This required a shift in the churches' missions, from an orientation to the afterlife to a focus on social justice. Similar processes occur in the media, as porous boundaries among communications industries allowed organizations in one industry to launch entries into other industries. Biographies of some of the most successful communications companies demonstrate this organizational 'appropriation'. Rupert Murdoch parlayed a small Australian newspaper that he inherited from his father into the $11 billion News Corporation, which owns 20th Century Fox, the Fox Network, numerous newspaper, magazine, and book publishers, several sports teams, satellite broadcasting systems covering much of the globe, and interests in over 90 television channels. Ted Turner used his father's billboard business as a vehicle to buy a UHF station that begat the 'superstation', CNN, and other successful cable ventures (see Guthey, 1997 for a critical recounting of the Turner legend). Edgar Bronfman Jr. turned his family business, Seagram, from a purveyor of beverages to a media behemoth through acquisitions and divestitures.

The result of the ongoing re-configuration of the largest media firms has been that organizational boundaries are resolutely tentative, essentially fictions. Where conglomerates have all but disappeared in American manufacturing, deregulation in the U.S. has allowed the construction of global media 'conglomerates' stretching across conventional industry and geographic boundaries. Moreover, because each of the largest participants in the media industry maintain eclectic portfolios of 'channels', 'software', and 'hardware', it is quite common to see corporations that are fierce competitors in one domain creating alliances in another. For example, the film *Titanic* was co-produced by Fox and Viacom's Paramount and spawned a soundtrack by Sony, a behind-the-scenes book by News Corporation's HarperCollins, and was broadcast on Time Warner's HBO (Rose, 1998). The television series *Buffy, the Vampire Slayer* was produced by News Corporation's Twentieth Century Fox, broadcast on Time Warner's WB, and spawned a soundtrack CD released by Sony and a series of 'novelizations' published by Viacom's Simon and Schuster. An analyst at PaineWebber noted that "These companies no longer make films or books. They make brands," lumps of content that can be exploited through a set of their own and other's distribution channels (*The Economist*, May 23 1998). Ken Auletta describes the resulting skein of interconnected communications firms as a 'global keiretsu' of mutual backscratching (1998: 286). Just as shifting coalitions of movement organizations routinely mobilize to bring off protest actions, the relevant unit of analysis for the media industry is the *project*: a one-time production (broadly defined) created by temporary alliances that may or may not be followed by similar productions, according to circumstance.

Thus, the emergence of the late twentieth century media industry parallels the emergence of a social movement in several important respects. It evolved from a relatively stable configuration of powerful incumbents through a period of turbulence in which challengers took advantage of exogenous shifts in the industry's opportunity structure to launch their alternatives. Challengers, often using organizational vehicles in adjacent industries (billboards, newspaper publishing, film production, and others) ultimately brought about the re-shaping of the media industry and the constitution of new rules of engagement rooted in innovation through collaboration. In this way, the media industry came to share important similarities with industrial districts, in which the 'project' rather than the organization is often the more relevant unit of analysis when making sense of episodic production structures.

ROUTINE MOVEMENT ACTIVITY

In their preoccupation with explaining the rise of broad national movements (Costain, 1992; McAdam, 1999), 'protest cycles' (Tarrow, 1989), or revolutions (Goldstone, 1991; Skocpol, 1979), theorists of social movements could well be accused of focusing on the exceptional, rather than typical, in the study of collective action. Thus, one might argue that technological revolutions of the sort that have transformed the entertainment industry are rare events that are hardly typical of 'normal' economic life. What, critics may ask, about more 'routine' economic activity?

In the contemporary democratic West, the modal form of movement activity looks very different from the broad, highly dramatic, often consequential episodes of national contention that scholars of social movements and revolutions have tended to study. In fact, against the backdrop of these exceptional episodes, one can discern a steady stream of more routine local movement activity. Drawing on recent literature, we briefly sketch an analytic framework for describing this general class of efforts. In our view, such a framework should include a concern with: (a) the nature of local mobilizing structures; (b) the importance of culturally available collective action repertoires; and (c) the typical spurs to local movement activity. We take up each of these topics in turn and then seek to apply them to the study of more routine forms of economic activity.

Local Mobilizing Structures

One of the keys to the emergence of national social movements or revolutions is what we have termed 'social appropriation'. By social appropriation we mean the processes through which previously organized, but non-political groups come to be defined as appropriate sites for mobilization. For example, in the case of the U.S. civil rights movement, it was the mobilization of black churches (and later black colleges) that keyed the movement's rise. But routine local mobilization does not depend upon or generally feature this kind of social appropriation. More often, local movement activity turns on the periodic activation of loose personal networks of 'career activists'. These networks are very likely to have arisen during a peak period of national mobilization of the sort we described in the previous section. But long after that 'protest cycle' has run its course, these loose networks survive, providing the mobilizing structure within which most local activism gets generated. At times the nominal vehicle through which action gets generated will be a formal social movement organization (SMO), but more often than not these SMOs are little more than 'paper' organizations with few members outside the network of 'career activists' mentioned previously.

This loose activist network is typically well known to city officials and other institutionalized segments of the community. So, for example, left activist networks in the U.S. will generally have fairly strong ties to liberal churches, social service agencies, local unions, and whatever institutions of higher education may exist in a community. Right-wing activist networks are also hooked in to local institutional spheres, but of a very different mix than those of their liberal/left counterparts. Right-wing networks can be expected to have fairly strong ties to conservative churches, veterans groups, and certain kinds of service organizations.

We mention these overlapping network/organizational spheres because they constitute the fields within which most local mobilization takes place. The initial stimulus to action generally arises within the activist networks themselves, with the related organizational spheres providing available pools within which the activists can seek to assemble the 'transitory team' (McCarthy & Zald, 1973) needed to stage whatever march, protest, vigil, petition campaign, or other collective action they have in mind. The contrast with the broad national movements or 'protest cycles' discussed above is stark indeed. Whereas the latter constitute a clear departure from normalcy, the kind of periodic local mobilization we are discussing here is very much 'business as usual', embedded as it is in fairly stable interpersonal/organizational networks and well understood cultural/behavioral routines.

Culturally Available Collective Action Repertoires

A second key element in social movements is what Tilly has (1995a: 41) called the 'repertoire of contention', that is, "the ways that people act together in pursuit of shared interests." Although straightforward sounding, there is an interesting cultural problematic inherent in the selection and application of forms of contention. As Tilly put it back in 1978 (p. 151): "[a]t any point in time, the repertoire of collective actions available to a population is surprisingly limited. Surprisingly, given the innumerable ways in which people could, in principle, deploy their resources in pursuit of common ends. Surprisingly, given the many ways real groups have pursued their own common ends at one time or another." When it comes to real world collective action, the seeming vast variety of action forms turns out to be quite limited. In the final analysis, all groups are constrained in their choice of tactics by the forms of contention culturally available to them. By culturally available we mean two things: (1) that the group has some working knowledge of the form, and (2) that the form enjoys a certain cultural legitimacy within the group. The first of these constraints – what might be termed the informational constraint – has been noted by any number of analysts (Tarrow, 1998; Tilly, 1978, 1995), but the second has been largely absent from writings on the concept of repertoire. But, in our view, illegitimacy constrains as surely as a lack of knowledge (cf. Meyer & Rowan, 1977). Thus, even if a group knows of a tactic and perceives it to be effective, it will avoid using it if it sees it as culturally beyond the pale.

ROUTINE MOBILIZATION OF ORGANIZED ECONOMIC ACTIVITY

What do local mobilizing structures and culturally available action repertoires have to do with economic production? We argue that episodic collective action rooted in the social networks of local players and taking the characteristic forms given in the local repertoire describes much contemporary economic activity as practiced in, for instance, Silicon Valley. 'Industrial district' was Alfred Marshall's term for the spatially clustered networks of (mostly small) firms that concentrated on a specific industry or set of related industries. Sheffield had steel, Lyon had silk, and Santa Clara County, California has microelectronics. Industrial districts are distinguished by the fact that geographic boundaries supercede organizational ones in analytical importance. Piore & Sabel (1984: 32) describe the system in Lyon:

> The variability of demand meant that patterns of subcontracting were constantly rearranged. Firms that had underestimated a year's demand would subcontract the overflow to less well situated competitors scrambling to adapt to the market. But the next year the situation might be reversed, with winners in the previous round forced to sell off equipment to last year's losers. Under these circumstances, every employee could become a subcontractor, every subcontractor a manufacturer, every manufacturer an employee.

The ability to size up the character of potential partners was regarded as critical to an individual's (or firm's) success. But perhaps more importantly, the district relied on a set of rules of fair behavior that constrained participants from taking short-term advantage of each other and favored the long-term vitality of the district. Such rules are not laws, and thus are not literally a property of a municipality. But nor are they properties of firms. Rather, they are more like an institution that provides mutual benefits to participants.

Silicon Valley has many characteristics of an industrial district, as described in AnnaLee Saxenian's (1994) book *Regional Advantage*. In the computer industry (broadly construed), rapid changes in technology and markets made it impractical for vertically-integrated firms to maintain a technical edge across all components. Specialist firms have little choice but to keep abreast of their area of specialization, both technically and in terms of price. According to Intel CEO Andy Grove, "Anything that can be done in the vertical way can be done more cheaply by collections of specialist companies organized horizontally" (Saxenian, 1994: 142). Thus, computer firms in the 1980s created collaborative relationships with their most important suppliers, all of which had a mutual interest in the success of the final product. Being located in the same geographical region facilitated frequent face-to-face contact and the development of trust. As in Lyon, the ability to size up potential partners effectively was critical for success. Again, shared understandings of the rules of the game (the local culture) made the construction of production networks feasible. The relatively short lifespan of any given project (e.g. a particular generation of a computer line) implied that partners were likely to meet again on the next round, further bolstering the incentives for consummate cooperation (cf. Axelrod, 1984). "The system's decentralization encourages the pursuit of multiple technical opportunities through spontaneous regroupings of skill, technology, and capital. Its production networks promote a process of collective technological learning that reduces the distinctions between large and small firms and between industries or sectors" and largely dissolves the boundaries between firms (Saxenian, 1994: 9). For instance, in creating Sun's workstations, ". . . it was difficult and somewhat pointless to determine where Sun ended and Weitek or Cypress [two of its suppliers] began. It was more meaningful to describe Sun's workstations as the product of a series of projects performed by a network of specialized firms" (Saxenian, 1994: 145). Nearly any new firm can claim the advantage of state-of-the-art manufacturing simply by 'buying' this function from a contractor, arguably creating a virtuous cycle of innovation.

This project-based dynamic extends even to manufacturing: to a surprising degree, high technology 'manufacturers' contract out much of the actual assembly of their products to firms specializing in manufacturing. Formerly known as 'board stuffers', firms such as Flextronics, SCI Systems, and Solectron do much of the assembly for 'original equipment manufacturers' (sic) such as Hewlett Packard and Sun Microsystems and enable start-ups to grow rapidly by providing a ready manufacturing base. Contractors routinely manufacture products for competing OEMs, but this is seen as having a collective benefit for the larger community as well as individual firms: "All of Solectron's customers benefited from learning that would formerly have been captured only by individual firms. Moreover, lessons learned in manufacturing for firms in one sector were spread to customers in other sectors, stimulating the diffusion of process innovation from industry to industry" (Saxenian, 1994: 154). Considering again Demsetz's question "when is a nexus-of-contracts *more firm like?*," some commentators are driven to ask whether all of Silicon Valley itself (rather than any of its constituent) is properly thought of as a 'firm' (Gilson & Roe, 1993). By Saxenian's account, it is this boundarylessness that is largely responsible for the economic success of Silicon Valley, whereas the bounded firm, mass production culture of Route 128 in Massachusetts is to blame for that region's waning performance in high technology.

The high technology production networks of Silicon Valley might have taken on any number of forms. In practice, however, these networks follow a relatively constrained set of repertoires. As Mark Suchman's work shows, local law firms, particularly Wilson Sonsini Goodrich & Rosati in Palo Alto, acted to compile "pre-processed infusions of relevant know-how." "Such information intermediaries act as interorganizational pollinators—monitoring various pools of constitutive information, determining which structures are 'appropriate' for whom, and compiling summary conclusions in the form of neat, cognitively coherent templates for action" (Suchman, 1998: 49). Law firms acted as veritable computer dating services, matching entrepreneurs, managers, techni-cal talent, and capital suppliers for new ventures from within the broader social network of the Valley. The governance structures of these projects (as indicated by venture capital financing contracts) became increasingly homogeneous over time, particularly within Silicon Valley compared to other locations (Suchman, 1995).

In short, the recurrent mobilization of episodic production through networks of economic 'activists', following locally familiar (and legitimate) repertoires, directly parallels the routine mobilization of sporadic protest events or campaigns by local activists. Like the production of local movement activity, the origins of routine economic initiative takes the form of routinized, episodic collective action.

CONCLUSION

The traditional focus in organization theory on corporations as bounded, sovereign, countable units of social structure (Scott's [1998] 'high modernism') is a poor fit with the emerging nature of the new economy. We identified two trends in particular as undermining the applicability of traditional organization theory: the increasingly 'boundaryless' nature of production processes, and the expanding scale and scope of financial markets and the resulting hegemony of their evaluative standards. Our critique of resource dependence theory and population ecology demonstrates the limits of describing the contemporary corporate sector in the United States using the vocabulary of organizations-as-units. Old constructs and mechanisms – such as organizational birth, death, structural inertia, and managing interdependence through mergers and interlocks – provide little explanatory leverage in a world of fluid production structures and hypertrophied financial markets. We also find the new (contractarian) theory of the firm in economics to be remarkably weak in characterizing changes in the American corporate sector. Although there can be little doubt that financial concerns are the North Star of corporate decision making, it is equally evident that the structure and evolution of the corporation result from political choices and social processes that the contractarian approach is ill-equipped to theorize. Making sense of the evolving structures of the new economy requires an approach that does not end with either organizations or markets alone.

We have argued that social movement theory provides an approach that is more fitting for the post-industrial economy. Like contemporary production structures, the boundaries around social movements are fluid, and impromptu productions follow regular processes of mobilization among participants choosing from among culturally familiar and legitimate forms of collective action. We compared the emerging media industry to the emergence of a national social movement, and everyday workings of the network economy of Silicon Valley to the routine mobilization of local movement activity. We found striking parallels. As anticipated by Zald & Berger (1978), forms of coordinated collective action, whether through 'organizations' or 'movements', are ultimately susceptible to the same forms of analysis. As collective economic action becomes increasingly episodic and network based, rather than rooted in, and dependent upon, the traditional practices of the integrated organization, the explanatory balance tilts in favor of social movement theory. Our argument, however, is ultimately to be judged on the fruitfulness of the work it stimulates. That is, will adopting the theoretical vocabulary of social movement theory lead researchers to ask more insightful questions than a vocabulary that begins with organizations? We think it will, but to this point we have offered only two very broad phenomena – movement and industry emergence and the routine mobilization of local movement/economic activity – for analogous theorizing. We want to close this chapter on a more modest note, by identifying specific research topics that might demonstrate parallels (and differences) between social movement and contemporary economic activity.

The first centers on recruitment to emergent economic and/or movement activity. If much contemporary economic activity really is more ephemeral and network driven than traditional theories of organizations suggest, then the processes by which these 'transitory teams' (McCarthy & Zald, 1973) are assembled should resemble the network-based recruitment dynamics that have been the subject of so much social movement research (Diani, 1995; Fernandez & McAdam, 1988; Gould, 1993, 1995; Kim & Bearman, 1997; McAdam, 1986; McAdam & Paulsen, 1993; Mische, 1998; Rosenthal et al., 1985; Snow, Zurcher & Ekland-Olson, 1980). To our knowledge, Roberto Fernandez (Fernandez & McAdam, 1988; Fernandez & Weinberg, 1997) is the only scholar who has analyzed network based recruitment dynamics for both emergent movement and economic activity. Certainly we think there might be much to gain from approaching the study of participation in emergent economic projects using the conceptual frameworks and methodological tools movement researchers have developed in the study of movement recruitment.

A second phenomenon that lends itself to a search for dynamic analogies between contemporary movement and economic activity would be the strategic framing and other 'representational' practices of both movement and economic entrepreneurs. In a post-industrial service economy, what is 'produced' is often not material products per se but perceptions and identities. Earlier we described Sara Lee Corporation's decision to drop its manufacturing capacity in order to focus on managing its brands, which involves promoting perceptions of product quality and the social status of their purchasers. The 'value added', in short, is perceptual, flowing from the creation of distinctive and desirable identities. The management of perceptions is aimed not simply at consumers of products, of course, but also at other participant groups necessary to make a venture work, including (actual and potential) employees and (actual and potential) investors, often using rather different messages. Because the nature of the product is perceptual, 'external' evaluations in such contexts are based largely on social rather than technical criteria (cf. Thompson, 1967). (Internet-based startup firms are only the most extravagant example, in which employees are recruited on the basis of the venture's likely appeal to IPO investors, and investors are recruited based on the venture's likely appeal to consumers.) Social movements are similarly in the business of producing perceptions and identities. Contenders making claims on incumbents engage in performances to demonstrate that, for instance, they are willing and able to disrupt political decorum to get what they want. In a recent article, Charles Tilly (1998: 15) argues that one of the central challenges confronting movement actors, and, by extension, motivating much everyday movement activity, is the need to demonstrate WUNC; that a movement's constituents are *worthy*, *united*, *numerous*, and *committed*. Comparative ethnographic work on the framing and representational practices of movement and economic actors would help to tease out the similarities and differences in these two forms of action.

A third prospective area for comparative research, following from the previous one, concerns the recent parallel ascendance of 'associations without members' and 'hollow corporations'. We have described how virtually any functional aspect of a business can be contracted out to a specialist firm, allowing the spread of 'manufacturers' who neither design, build, or distribute their products and employ few people. An analogous development has happened with the rise of issue-oriented interest groups and social movements. As Skocpol (1999) describes it, civic involvement for many citizens in the United States once entailed membership in associations that held face-to-face meetings, elected leadership, and debated issues before coming to positions. "Leaders who desired to speak on behalf of masses of Americans found it natural to proceed by recruiting self-renewing mass memberships and spreading a network of interactive groups." Now, in contrast, "When a new cause (or tactic) arises, activists envisage opening a national office and managing association-building as well as national projects from a center. Even a group aiming to speak for large numbers of Americans does not absolutely need members; and if mass adherents are recruited through the mail, why hold meetings? From a managerial point of view, interactions with groups of members may be downright inefficient" (Skocpol, 1999: 71). Potential members – at least those with more money than time – find benefits to this 'hollow' form as well: "Why should highly trained and economically well-off elites spend years working their way up the leadership ladders of traditional membership federations when they can take leading staff roles at the top, or express their preferences by writing a check?" We anticipate that research on the dynamics of both hollow movements and hollow organizations will benefit from cross-fertilization.

Our final candidate for the comparative study of movements and organizations involves research on the diffusion of innovative ideas, practices, and organizational forms. Recognizing the emergent nature of movement activity, movement researchers have focused considerable attention on the diffusion of the various innovations produced by the 'early risers' in a given 'protest cycle' (Tarrow, 1998). Some have studied the spread of new protest tactics (Soule, 1995, 1997; McAdam, 1983; Meyer & Whittier, 1994; Tilly, 1995b); others the diffusion of ideological frameworks (McAdam, 1995; McAdam & Rucht, 1993; Snow & Benford, 1992); still others the adoption of new organizational forms (Clemens, 1993). The diffusion of specific practices and structures has also been studied in the context of formal economic organizations (e.g., Davis

& Greve, 1997), but we believe movement research provides a more nuanced approach for studying the spread of ideological frameworks.

We have focused on the parallels between economic organization and social movements, but we must also note the fertile ground for traditional social movements provided by contemporary economic transitions under the broad rubric of 'globalization'. As financial markets globalize and the demands they make on business organizations become more exacting, corporate governance – the set of institutions that determine the balance of power among owners, managers, and other constituencies of corporations – becomes a pressing issue of political economy. As we argued above, these issues require political choices; for instance, the choice of whether to sell shares in a state-owned business, or whether to allow hostile takeovers, are made at the state level and therefore susceptible to popular influence. Both local and national movements have mobilized around issues of corporate governance raised by changes in ownership and control. In Germany, demonstrators pelted the CEO of steelmaker Krupp-Hoesch Group with eggs and tomatoes after Krupp announced a hostile takeover bid for rival Thyssen in March 1997. Shortly thereafter, 25,000 workers converged on Deutsche Bank headquarters in Frankfurt to protest Deutsche's part in helping to finance the bid, and German politicians successfully urged Krupp to abandon its foray into 'cowboy capitalism' (Davis & Useem, 1999).

Almost 100 years to the day after the 1898 US invasion of Puerto Rico, government workers led the biggest labor protest in the island's history, in which upwards of 500,000 workers joined in a two-day general strike that included demonstrations and a blockade of the highway to the international airport. The cause was the Governor's imminent sale of a controlling stake in the state telephone company to private investors led by GTE (*Wall Street Journal*, July 8, 1998). Similar mass protests have accompanied the attempts of South Korean chaebols to restructure through layoffs. The International Monetary Fund had required the institution of labor market 'flexibility' as a condition for its bailout of the Korean economy, and the new president sought restructuring of the chaebols in order to attract necessary foreign investment. As the imperatives of global political economy and corporate governance become increasingly merged, national and international social movements will have an increasing influence on the social structure of economic life.

So much for our all too brief survey of potential topics for comparative movement/ organizations research. We do not claim that these topics exhaust those that might reveal the increasing relevance of social movement theory and research to an understanding of economic action. At the same time, we are not certain what systematic comparative research of the sort we are proposing here will show. We have been deliberately provocative in this chapter, not so much because we know for certain how far various social movement theories can be applied to formal economic organizations, but to force organizational scholars to confront the theoretical challenges posed by the third industrial revolution. It now seems beyond dispute that a sea change is taking place in the locus, structure, and practices of large economic organizations. It seems just as certain that these changes are rendering traditional organizational theories less applicable to the realities of modern economic life. What theories will replace the older frameworks is not entirely clear. We predict a lively debate over the merits of various alternative perspectives, with social movement theory being one of the most viable.

ACKNOWLEDGMENTS

This chapter was written while the authors were Fellows at the Center for Advanced Study in the Behavioral Sciences, Stanford, California. The first author is grateful for financial support provided by the National Science Foundation Grant No. SBR-9601236 and by the Graduate School of Business at Columbia University. We thank Barry Staw for his generous and helpful comments and Bob Sutton for his superhuman patience.

NOTES

1. As Dahrendorf wrote in 1958: "Never has the imputation of a profit motive been further from the real motives of men than it is for modern bureaucratic managers."

2. This leads to some interesting peculiarities, particularly when pension funds are involved. Hostile takeovers were regarded as a direct cause of many plant closings and layoffs that decimated communities in the 1980s. Those who ran large corporations adopted several innovations (such as the 'poison pill') meant to make unwanted takeovers more difficult, often cloaking their actions in a rhetoric of concern for labor and other 'stakeholders'. Remarkably, the most vociferous critics of these protective measures were pension funds such as the College Retirement Equities Fund (CREF), which sought to have companies rescind their poison pills as an unacceptable violation of the funds' property rights. The Teamsters pension fund has been most active on this issue recently, charging that managers seeking to protect their firms are thereby violating the Teamsters' rights as investors.

REFERENCES

Auletta, K. (1998). *The Highwaymen: Warriors of the Information Superhighway*. San Diego: Harcourt Brace.

Axelrod, Robert, M. (1984). *The Evolution of Cooperation*. New York: Basic Books.

Baron, J. N. (1984). Organizational perspectives on stratification. *Annual Review of Sociology 10*, 37–69.

Baum, J. A. C., & Mezias, S. J. (1992). Localized competition and organizational failure in the
    Manhattan hotel industry, 1898–1990. *Administrative Science Quarterly, 37*, 580–604.
Black, Bernard S., & Gilson, R. J. (1997). Venture capital and the structure of capital markets:
    banks versus stock markets. Unpublished, Stanford Law School.
Burt, R. S. (1983). *Corporate Profits and Cooptation : Networks of Market Constraints and
    Directorate Ties in the American Economy.* New York: Academic.
Clemens, E. S. (1993). Organizational repertoires and institutional change: women's groups and
    the transformation of U.S. politics, 1890–1920. *American Journal of Sociology, 98,*
    755–798.
Costain, A. W. (1992). *Inviting Women's Rebellion: A Political Process Interpretation of the
    Women's Movement.* Baltimore: Johns Hopkins Press.
Dahrendorf, Ralf. (1959). *Class and Class Conflict in Industrial Society.* Stanford, CA: Stanford
    University Press.
Davis, G. F. (1994). The corporate elite and the politics of corporate control. In: C. Prendergast,
    & J. D. Knottnerus (Eds.), *Current Perspectives in Social Theory,* Supplement 1, (pp.
    245–268). Greenwich, Conn: JAI Press.
Davis, G. F. (1996). The significance of board interlocks for corporate governance. *Corporate
    Governance, 4,* 154–159.
Davis, G. F., Diekmann, K. A., & Tinsley, C. H. (1994). The decline and fall of the conglomerate
    firm in the 1980s: the de-institutionalization of an organizational form. *American
    Sociological Review, 59,* 547–570.
Davis, G. F., & Greve, H. R. (1997). Corporate elite networks and governance changes in the
    1980s. *American Journal of Sociology, 103,* 1–37.
Davis, G. F., & Mizruchi, M. S. (1999). The money center cannot hold: commercial banks in the
    U.S. system of corporate governance. *Administrative Science Quarterly, 44,* 215–239.
Davis, G. F., & Powell, W. W. (1992). Organization-environment relations. In: M. D. Dunnette, &
    L. M. Hough, (Eds.), *Handbook of Industrial and Organizational Psychology,* (2nd ed.), *3,*
    (pp. 315–375). Palo Alto, Cal.: Consulting Psychologists Press.
Davis, G. F., & Robbins, G. E. (1999). The Fate of the Conglomerate Firm in the United States.
    In: W. W. Powell, & D. L. Jones (Eds.), *How Institutions Change.* (Forthcoming, University
    of Chicago Press).
Davis, G. F., & Thompson, T. A. (1994). A Social Movement Perspective on Corporate Control.
    Administrative Science Quarterly, 39, 141–173.
Davis, G. F., & M. Useem. (1999). Top management, company directors, and corporate control.
    In: A. Pettigrew, H. Thomas, & R. Whittington (Eds.), *Handbook of Strategy and
    Management* (forthcoming, Sage).
Demsetz, H. (1991). The Theory of the Firm Revisited. In: O. E. Williamson, & S. G. Winter
    (Eds), *The Nature of the Firm: Origins, Evolution, and Development* (pp. 159–78). New
    York: Oxford University.
Diani, M. (1995). *Green Networks: A Structural Analysis of the Italian Environmental Movement.*
    Edinburgh: Edinburgh University Press.
Fernandez, R., & McAdam, D. (1988). Social Networks and Social Movements: Multi-
    organizational Fields and Recruitment to Mississippi Freedom Summer. *Sociological
    Forum, 3,* 357–82.
Easterbrook, F. H., & Fischel, D. R. (1991). *The Economic Structure of Corporate Law.*
    Cambridge, MA: Harvard University Press.
Emirbayer, M. (1997). Manifesto for a relational sociology. *American Journal of Sociology, 103,*
    281–317.

Fama, E. (1980). Agency Problems and The Theory of the Firm. *Journal of Political Economy, 88*, 288–307.

Fligstein, N. (1990). *The Transformation of Corporate Control.* Cambridge, Mass: Harvard University Press.

Galvin, T. (1994). Social influences on restructuring activity. Unpublished, Northwestern University.

Gilson, R. J., & Roe, M. J. (1993). Understanding the Japanese keiretsu: overlaps between corporate governance and industrial organization. *Yale Law Journal, 102*, 871–906.

Goldstone, J. (1991). *Revolution and Rebellion in the Early Modern World*, Berkeley: University of California Press.

Gould, R. (1993). Collective Action and Network Structure. *American Sociological Review, 58*, 182–96.

Gould, R. (1995). *Insurgent Identities: Class, Community, and Protest in Paris from 1848 to the Commune.* Chicago: University of Chicago Press.

Guthey, E. (1997). Ted Turner's media legend and the transformation of corporate liberalism. *Business and Economic History, 26*, 184–199.

Hannan, M. T., & Carroll, G. R. (1992). *Dynamics of Organizational Populations: Density, Legitimation, and Competition.* New York: Oxford University Press.

Hannan, M. T., & Freeman, J. (1984). Structural inertia and organizational change. *American Sociological Review, 49*, 149–164.

Hannan, M. T., & Freeman, J. (1989). *Organizational Ecology.* Cambridge, MA: Harvard University Press.

Harrison, B. (1994). *Lean and Mean: The Changing Landscape of Corporate Power in the Age of Flexibility.* New York: Basic Books.

Helper, S., MacDuffie, J. P., & Sabel. C. (1997). The Boundaries of the Firm as a Design Problem. Unpublished, National Bureau of Economic Research, Cambridge, Mass.

Jensen, M. C. (1988). The takeover controversy: Analysis and evidence. In: J. C. Coffee, Jr., L. Lowenstein, & S. Rose-Ackerman (Eds.), *Knights, Raiders, and Targets: The Impact of the Hostile Takeover* (pp. 314–354). New York: Oxford University Press.

Jensen, M. C. (1993). The modern industrial revolution, exit, and the failure of internal control systems. *Journal of Finance, 48*, 831–880.

Jensen, M. C., & Meckling, W. H. (1976). Theory of the firm: Managerial behavior, agency cost and ownership structure. *Journal of Financial Economics, 3*, 305–360.

Kim, H., & Bearman, P. S. (1997). The Structure and Dynamics of Social Movement Participation. *American Sociological Review, 62*, 70–93.

Koput, K. W., Powell, W. W., & Smith-Doerr, L. (1997). Interorganizational relations and elite sponsorship: mobilizing resources in biotechnology. Unpublished, University of Arizona.

Laumann, E. O., & Knoke, D. (1987). *The Organizational State: Social Choice in National Policy Domains*, Madison, WI: University of Wisconsin Press.

Manne, H. G. (1965). Mergers and the Market for Corporate Control. *Journal of Political Economy, 73*, 110–120.

March, J. G., & Simon, H. A. (1958). *Organizations.* New York: Wiley.

McAdam, D. (1982). *Political Process and the Development of Black Insurgency 1930–1970.* Chicago: University of Chicago Press.

McAdam, (1983). Tactical Innovation and the Pace of Insurgency. *American Sociological Review, 48*, 735–54.

McAdam, D. (1986). Recruitment to High-Risk Activism: The Case of Freedom Summer. *American Journal of Sociology, 92*, 64–90.

McAdam, D. (1995). 'Initiator' and 'Spinoff' Movements: Diffusion Processes in Protest Cycles'. In: M. Traugott (Ed.), *Repertoires and Cycles of Collective Action*, (pp. 217–39) Durham, N.C.: Duke University Press.

McAdam, D. (1999). *Political Process and the Development of Black Insurgency, 1930–1970, second edition*. Chicago: University of Chicago Press.

McAdam, D. & Paulsen, R. (1993). Specifying the Relationship Between Social Ties and Activism. *American Journal of Sociology, 99*, 640–67

McAdam, D., & Rucht, D. (1993). The Cross-national Diffusion of Movement Ideas. *Annals of the American Academy of Political and Social Science, 528*, 56–87.

McCarthy, J. D., & Zald, M. N. (1973). *The Trend of Social Movements in America: Professionalization and Resource Mobilization*. Morristown, N.J.: General Learning Press.

McMichael, P. (1996). *Development and Social Change: A Global Perspective*, Thousand Oaks, CA: Pine Forge Press

Meyer, D., & Whittier, N. (1994). Social Movement Spillover. *Social Problems, 41*, 277–98.

Meyer, J. W., & Rowan, B. (1977). Institutionalized organizations: formal structure as myth and ceremony. *American Journal of Sociology, 83*, 340–363.

Minkoff, D. C. (1997). The sequencing of social movements. *American Sociological Review, 62*, 779–799.

Mische, A. (1998). *Projecting Democracy: Dynamics of Youth Actions in the Brazilian Impeachment Movement*. Ph.D. Dissertation, Sociology Department, New School for Social Research.

Perrow, C. (1991). A society of organizations. *Theory and Society, 20*, 725–762.

Pfeffer, J., & Salancik, G. R. (1978). *The External Control of Organizations: A Resource Dependence Perspective* New York: Harper & Row.

Piore, M. J., & Sabel, C. F. (1984). *The Second Industrial Divide: Possibilities for Prosperity*, New York: Basic Books.

Reich, R. (1992). *The Work of Nations: Preparing Ourselves for 21st Century Capitalism*. New York: Vintage.

Roe, M. J. (1994). *Strong Managers, Weak Owners: The Political Roots of American Corporate Finance*. Princeton: Princeton University Press.

Rose, F. (1998). There's no business like show business. *Fortune* (June 22): 87–104.

Rosenthal, N., Fingrutd, M., Ethier, M., Karant, R., & McDonald, D. (1985). Social Movements and Network Analysis: A Case Study of Nineteenth-Century Women's Reform in New York State. *American Journal of Sociology, 90*, 1022–55.

Sabel, C. F. (1991). Moebius-Strip Organizations and Open Labor Markets: Some Consequences of the Reintegration of Conception and Execution in a Volatile Economy. In: P. Bourdieu, & J. S. Coleman, (Eds), *Social Theory for a Changing Society*, (pp. 23–54). Boulder, CO: Westview.

Sabel, C. F., & Zeitlin, J. (1996). Stories, strategies, structures: rethinking historical alternatives to mass production. In: C. F. Sabel, & J. Zeitlin (Eds.), *Worlds of Possibility: Flexibility and Mass Production in Western Industrialization*. Cambridge: Cambridge University Press.

Saxenian, A. (1994). *Regional Advantage: Culture and Competition in Silicon Valley and Route 128*. Cambridge, MA: Harvard University Press.

Scott, J. C. (1997). *Seeing Like a state: How Certain Schemes to Improve the Human Condition have Failed*. New Haven: Yale University Press.

Shiller, R. J. (1990). Speculative prices and popular models. *Journal of Economic Perspectives, 4*, 55–65.

Skocpol, T. (1979). *States and Social Revolutions*. Cambridge: Cambridge University Press.
Skocpol, T. (1999). Associations without members. *The American Prospect, 45*, 66–73.
Snow, D. A., & Benford, R. D. (1988). Ideology, Frame Resonance, and Participant Mobilization. In: B. Klandermans, H. Kriesi, & S. Tarrow (Eds.), *From Structure to Action: Social Movement Participation Across Cultures*, 197–217. Greenwich, CT: JAI Press.
Snow, D. A., & R. D. Benford. (1992). Master Frames and Cycles of Protest. In: A. Morris, & C. M. Mueller (Eds.), *Frontiers in Social Movement Theory* (pp. 133–55). New Haven, CT: Yale University Press.
Snow, D. A., Rochford, E. B. Jr., Worden, S. K., & Benford, R. D. (1986). Frame Alignment Processes, Micromobilization, and Movement Participation. *American Sociological Review, 51*, 464–81.
Snow, D. A., Zurcher, L. A. Jr., & Ekland-Olson, S. (1980). Social Networks and Social Movements: A Microstructural Approach to Differential Recruitment. *American Sociological Review, 45*, 787–801.
Soule, S. A. (1995). *The Student Anti-Apartheid Movement in the United States: The Diffusion of Protest Tactics and Policy Reform*. Ph.D. Dissertation, Sociology Department, Cornell University.
Soule, S. A. (1997). The Student Divestment Movement in the United States and Tactical Diffusion: The Shantytown Protest. *Social Forces*.
Suchman, M. C. (1995). Localism and Globalism in Institutional Analysis: The Emergence of Contractual Norms in Venture Finance. In: W. R. Scott, & S. Christensen (Eds.), *The Institutional Construction of Organizations* (pp. 39–63). Thousand Oaks, CA: Sage.
Suchman, M. C. (1998). *On advice of counsel: The role of law firms in the institutional ecology of Silicon Valley*. Unpublished, University of Wisconsin.
Thompson, J. D. (1967). *Organizations in Action*. New York: McGraw-Hill.
Tarrow, S. (1989). *Democracy and Disorder: Protest and Politics in Italy, (1965–1975)*. Oxford: Oxford University Press.
Tarrow, S. (1998). *Power in Movement*, (2nd ed.). Cambridge: Cambridge University Press.
Tilly, C. (1978). *From Mobilization to Revolution*. New York: Random House.
Tilly, C. (1995a). *Popular Contention in Great Britain, 1758–1834*. Cambridge, MA: Harvard University Press.
Tilly, C. (1995b). Cycles of Collective Action: Between Moments of Madness and the Repertoire of Contention. In: M. Traugott (Ed.), *Repertoires and Cycles of Collective Action* (pp. 89–116). Durham, N.C.: Duke University Press.
Tilly, C. (1998). Actors, Actions, and Identities. In: D. McAdam, S. Tarrow, & C. Tilly. (Eds), *Dynamics of Contention* Unpublished, Center for Advanced Study in the Behavioral Sciences.
Useem, M. (1984). *The Inner Circle*. New York: Oxford University Press.
Useem, M. (1996). *Investor Capitalism: How Money Managers are Changing the Face of Corporate America*. New York: Basic Books.
Useem, M. (1998). Corporate Leadership in a Globalizing Equity Market. *Academy of Management Executive, 12* (4), 43–59.
Uzzi, B. (1997). Social Structure and Competition in Interfirm Networks: The Paradox of Embeddedness. *Administrative Science Quarterly, 42*, 35–67.
Weick, K. E. (1979). *The Social Psychology of Organizing*, (2nd ed.). New York: McGraw-Hill.
Westphal, J. D., & Zajac, E. J. (1998). The Symbolic Management of Stockholders: Corporate Governance Reforms and Shareholder Reactions. *Administrative Science Quarterly, 43*, 127–153.

White, H. (1992). *Identity and Control: A Structural Theory of Social Action*. Princeton: Princeton University Press.

Zald, M. N., & Berger, M. A. (1978). Social Movements in Organizations: Coup d'etat, Insurgency, and Mass Movements. *American Journal of Sociology, 83*, 823–861

Zeitlin, M. (1974). Corporate Ownership and Control: The Large Corporation and the Capitalist Class. *American Journal of Sociology, 79*, 1073–1119.

Zuckerman, E. W. (1999). The Categorical Imperative: Securities Analysts and the Illegitimacy Discount. *American Journal of Sociology, 104*, 1398–1438.

POWER PLAYS: HOW SOCIAL MOVEMENTS AND COLLECTIVE ACTION CREATE NEW ORGANIZATIONAL FORMS

Hayagreeva Rao, Calvin Morrill and Mayer N. Zald

ABSTRACT

Organizational theory emphasizes how new organizational forms are produced by technological innovation but has glossed over the role of cultural innovation. This chapter suggests that social movements are important sources of cultural innovation and identifies the scope conditions under which social movements create new organizational forms. By doing so, it lends substance to the notion of institutional entrepreneurship and enlarges the theoretical reach of neo-institutionalism.

Research in Organizational Behaviour, Volume 22, pages 237–281.
ISBN: 0–7623–0641–6

INTRODUCTION

Consider the creation of consumer leagues – organizations concerned about fair prices and the standard of living that appeared at the dawn of the 20th century. Although rising prices were long acknowledged to damage the standard of living in America, the consumers were not a category of actors and there were no organizations dedicated to the cause of consumers. During the decade which lasted from 1880 until 1890, state governments created bureaus of labor statistics in the late 1880s to conduct cost of living inquiries. Activists used these studies to construct the consumer as a category, and exploited rising food and meat prices to establish clubs consisting of housewives to provide advice on spending and disciplining unscrupulous merchants with the threat of a boycott. Boycotts in one city mobilized interest in other cities, and led to the diffusion of consumer leagues in a social movement like process. So much so, that by 1912, the National Association of Housewives Leagues was established to coordinate activities.

As this vignette indicates, collective action and contention underlie the construction of new organizational forms. Yet, they have received little attention in organizational ecology and neo-institutionalism – two of the most vibrant traditions in organization theory. Although organizational ecologists note the importance of institutional processes (Hannan & Freeman, 1989: 56), they have yet to incorporate agency into their account of legitimation. Neo-institutionalists have noted the need for more attention to be devoted to the role of de-institutionalization (Oliver, 1992), the use of multiple logics by actors (DiMaggio & Powell, 1991: 30), and political competition among coalitions (Fligstein, 1996) in the study of new organizational forms.

In the preceding chapter, Davis & McAdam (2000) argued that a challenge facing organizational theorists is to "show more comprehensively the value of applying the constructs and mechanisms developed in social movement theory to economic action." We respond to their call by studying the *construction of new organizational forms as a political project involving collective action.* Our approach is situated in recent theoretical efforts to bridge between social movement theory and cultural-frame institutionalism, at the same time harkening back to Zald & Berger's (1978) application of social movement theory to intra-organizational change. We conceptualize the construction of new organizational forms as a political process in which social movements play a double-edged role: They de-institutionalize existing beliefs, norms, and values embodied in extant forms, and establish new forms that instantiate new beliefs, norms and values. Crucial in these processes are institutional entrepreneurs who lead efforts to identify political opportunities, frame issues and problems, and mobilize constituencies. By so doing, they spearhead collective attempts to infuse new beliefs, norms, and values into social structures, thus creating discontinuities in the world of organizations. We view our efforts as primarily sensitizing and, toward this goal, we focus our attention on identifying key concepts and mechanisms through the use of extended cases.

In the pages that follow, we first provide a working definition of organizational form, and discuss the relationships between new forms and legitimacy. We then turn to a theoretical discussion of four types of organizational and market failures from which social movements can arise. The next section of the paper investigates how organizational fields both constrain and enable social movements, as well as the organizational forms they produce, by comparing three cases under different field conditions: the establishment of alternative dispute resolution at the 'interstices' between fields, the spread of quality management in U.S. corporations within a 'fragmented' field, and the emergence of specialty breweries in a 'hierarchical' field. Finally, we draw on the creation of health maintenance organizations and the rise of consumer 'watchdogs' to examine the reactive politics of constructing new forms. Specifically, we explore how initiator movements generate spin-off and counter-movements, as well as how the boundaries of organizational forms operate as truces between competing forms. The chapter concludes with a number of directions for further research that link politics, social movements, and organizational change at the macro and micro levels. By making political opportunity a variable rather than an assumption, our analysis of social movements and new organizational forms complements other treatments (e.g. Swaminathan and Wade, forthcoming) which take political opportunity for new organizational forms as a given.

ORGANIZATIONAL FORMS AND LEGITIMACY

A useful starting point for understanding discontinuities between organizational forms is the distinction between core and peripheral properties of organizational forms. Core features include goals, authority relations, technologies, and marketing strategy, and vary in the ease with which they can be changed (Scott, 1995). At one extreme, goals are the innermost feature of organizational forms and are the most difficult to modify. At the other extreme, marketing strategy is relatively easier to change because organizations can introduce new products, reposition existing products or withdraw existing products. Other core characteristics occupy a middle ground between these two extremes.

Organizational forms constitute polythetic groupings, in that members of the form share common core characteristics but may differ with respect to peripheral features. Hence, one form or species differs from another primarily according to core characteristics of the form. The core features listed by Scott comprise a four-dimensional space in which new organizational forms appear or disappear over time. An advantage of focusing on core features is that they provide a parsimonious list of the dimensions on which an organizational form can differ from incumbent forms. The four features can also demonstrate how an organizational form links to ancestral forms.

Not all new organizational forms are equivalent. Arguably, a new form dramatically differs from pre-existing forms when it is different in all four core features – goals, authority relations, technology, and served markets. Such new forms illustrate *strong speciation*. Early American automobile manufacturers, for example, constituted new organizational forms that marked a strong departure from their precursors in the horse carriage industry in terms of: goals (slow vs. fast transportation), technology (traveling compartments moved by horses vs. traveling compartments moved by internal combustion engines), authority (cottage and decentralized vs. assembly-based), and served markets (mass vs. physicians and enthusiasts). Naturally, distinctions between new and old forms weaken when differences exist only in terms of markets or technologies, for example. *Weak speciation* occurs when the new form differs from existing ones only on one or two dimensions (Rao & Singh, 1999). For example, in the hotel industry, luxury hotels differ from budget hotels on the dimensions of customer base (market served) and the technology of service.

Institutional Entrepreneurs and Legitimacy

Stinchcombe (1965, 1968: 194) asserts that the creation of new organizational forms "is pre-eminently a political phenomenon" to the extent that a new form differs from pre-existing organizations. Thus, when a new form is an instance of strong speciation, the goals, authority structure, technology, and clients embodied in the new form must be validated if the new form is to garner resources. In some cases, unfilled resource spaces may exist in the environment but potential entrepreneurs still have to lay claim to 'free-floating' resources and justify their claims. In other cases, unfilled resource spaces may not exist, and entrepreneurs have to construct these spaces by justifying the need for new organizational forms, and pry resources away from existing uses.

In all cases, socio-political and constitutive legitimacy are required for the new form to attract resources and become viable (Meyer & Rowan, 1977; DiMaggio, 1988; Fligstein, 1996b, Powell, 1998). Socio-political legitimacy accrues when a new organizational form conforms to legal rules and gains endorsement from other powerful actors. Constitutive legitimacy is obtained when the new form becomes legitimized and ultimately, taken-for-granted as a social fact (Hannan & Carroll, 1992; Aldrich & Fiol, 1994; Baum & Powell, 1995).

Empirical research on new organizational forms, conducted principally by organizational ecologists, depicts socio-political and cognitive legitimacy as positive spill-overs flowing from individual instances of an organizational form (Delacroix & Rao, 1994). Density-dependence theorists propose that new forms become taken-for-granted as the number of organizations (density) embodying the form increase. Initial increases in density produce economies of scale in collective action, and collective learning in turn, boosting organizational founding rates and diminishing death rates. Beyond a point, however, growing density unleashes competition, depresses founding rates, and increases death rates (Hannan & Freeman, 1989). Numerous studies reveal an inverted U-shaped relationship between density and foundings, and a U-shaped relationship between density and deaths (see Hannan & Carroll, 1992). A parallel body of research suggests that inter-organizational linkages established by individual firms confer socio-political legitimacy on the form. Baum & Oliver (1993) demonstrated that relational density (links between existing firms with governmental organizations) initially increased birth rates and diminished death rates. In a similar vein, Hybels, Ryan & Barley (1994) demonstrated that strategic alliances between firms in a population increased founding rates.

The density-dependence and relational density perspectives imply that there is little collective action necessary to construct new organizational forms. In the density-dependence model, action consists of the existence of instances of an organizational form. In the relational density approach, action resides in the endorsement of individual firms by other prominent actors. Both perspectives portray legitimacy as a positive spill-over that obtains when there are enough instances of the form, or enough endorsements of individual firms by powerful actors.

However, recent versions of cultural frame-institutionalism suggest that the creation of new organizational forms entails an institutionalization project, wherein institutional entrepreneurs actively define, justify, and push the theory and values underpinning a new form (DiMaggio, 1988: 18; Clemens, 1993). In this line of argument, activists construct boundaries around activities and validate these boundaries such that a new category of organizations emerges. Because such activities often exhibit purposive goals and structured roles, some researchers liken such institutional projects to social movements (Fligstein,

1996a; Haveman & Rao, 1997; Rao, 1998; Davis & McAdam, forthcoming; Swaminathan & Wade, forthcoming; Lounsbury, Hirsch & Ventresca, 1999). However, social movements are likely to arise as a form of collective action only under certain conditions. Below, we elaborate these conditions.

ORGANIZATIONAL AND MARKET FAILURES AS SOURCES OF SOCIAL MOVEMENTS

Since the work of Robert Park and his associates, collective action and social movements have been recognized as extra-institutional sources of social change. In contrast to panics, riots, fads, and fashions that are evanescent forms of collective behavior with few structured roles, collective action refers to a broad range of purposive collective behavior, the most organized of which are social movements that occur over longer time stretches, are driven by long-term goals, and develop formal organizations.

Social movements may be defined as organized collective endeavors to solve social problems. The emerging consensus in the social movement literature is that the ability of institutional entrepreneurs/activists to bring about change depends upon framing processes, mobilizing structures, and political opportunities (McAdam, McCarthy & Zald, 1996). Institutional entrepreneurs can mobilize legitimacy, finances, and personnel only when they are able to frame the grievances and interests of aggrieved constituencies, diagnose causes, assign blame, provide solutions, and enable collective attribution processes to operate (Snow & Benford, 1992: 150). Collective vehicles through which people mobilize and engage in collective action are also essential for social movements; such structures include formal social movement organizations (McCarthy & Zald, 1977), work and neighborhood organizations, and informal friendship networks (Tilly, 1978). Finally, several studies suggest that organized attempts to establish new structures require political opportunity on which to thrive. In practical terms, this means that entrepreneurs can minimize or escape state repression, possess access to the political system, and have allies in elite groups (Tarrow, 1989). Political opportunity, mobilization structures, and framing processes are reciprocally intertwined such that skillful framing of an issue can create an opportunity and reduce mobilization costs, just as strong mobilization structures can broaden opportunity and reduce the need to broaden a frame. The background of such opportunities often consists of a priori organizational and market failures that create new possibilities for the rise of social movements. Below, we discuss a number of these failures.

The Failure of Trade Associations

When a new organizational form represents a case of strong speciation, it is novel, rare and can jeopardize vested interests. It must acquire endorsements from powerful collective actors, such as the state, and must be transformed from a novel artifact into a social fact. A commonplace presumption in organization theory is that new organizational forms in economic spheres can garner legitimacy by banding together through trade associations to secure governmental support and gain standing in consumer and financial markets.

However, trade associations can be crippled by influence costs (Milgrom and Roberts, 1992). When organizational decisions affect the distribution of wealth or benefits among constituents of trade associations and elite coalitions, the affected individuals can attempt to influence the decision to their benefit. As a result, agreements may be hard to negotiate, thus blocking sustained coordination among producers. When producers are unable to coordinate action, social movements powered by activists can play vital roles in establishing a field-wide environment around a new form. Thus:

> New organizational forms are legitimated through social movement processes when collective action by instances of the new form fails because of influence costs.

The early American automobile industry provides a striking example (Rao, 1999). As a novel product, the automobile was unfamiliar, and consumers were confused because the source of power, the number of cylinders, systems of steering and control, and the mode of stopping were topics of considerable controversy (Thomas, 1977: 19).

Initially, vigilante anti-speed organizations sought to restrict the use of the automobile by forcing municipal governments to impose speed ordinances. For example, the New York Committee of Fifty, a prominent anti-speed organization, obtained data on speeds using stopwatches, and convincingly showed that cars were driven at high speeds. The Long Island Highway Protective Society, described speeders as 'scorchers' and resorted to illegal tactics such as puncturing tires of speeding cars, and in some cases, even riddling tires with bullets. Sporadic opposition to the motor car was prevalent in rural areas during the touring season when speeding automobilists threatened livestock and horse-drawn traffic, and raised dust that damaged crops.

In the first four years of its existence, there were no trade associations to advance the cause of the automobile. The National Association of Automobile Manufacturers was established in 1900 in a bid to assure product quality, but was superseded by the Association of Licensed Automobile Manufacturers (ALAM), which was formed in 1903. ALAM was a trade association formed to liccnse the Selden patent, but the Selden patent was widely disregarded and, due to internal divisions, ALAM was unable to secure quality by enforcing its threat of litigation. A rival body, the American Motor Car Manufacturer's Association (AMCMA) was established in 1905, and also proved to be an ineffective mechanism of collective action. Both trade associations disintegrated during the period 1909–1911, as a result of legal battles. Professional societies did little to legitimate the new industry. The Society of Automobile Engineers (SAE) began in 1905 with a small group of journalists and automobile engineers, and established a standards committee by 1910.

It was in this context that automobile fans banded together into automobile clubs and promoted the 'automobiling' movement. Flink (1970:144) notes that the "automobile club became the most important institution championing the diffusion of the automobile in the United States. Voluntary associations of motorists propagandized to encourage a favorable image of the automobile and automobilists."

The American Motor League, set up in 1895, was the first attempt to organize a club, and it foundered. But by 1901, 22 local clubs had mushroomed in different cities such as Boston, Newark, and Chicago. In 1910, there were 225 local clubs affiliated with the AAA. Local clubs promoted the image of the automobile in two ways. First, they supported state ordinances requiring tags and mandating speed limits to prevent a maze of city-specific regulations and to defuse opposition to the car. More importantly, auto clubs codified rules for reliability and speed races, and provided the personnel for scheduling and supervising these contests.

Local automobile clubs also played a crucial role in establishing a legal environment for the automobile. When municipal governments promulgated ordinances to regulate speeding, automobile clubs initially challenged these city ordinances, but quickly realized that a maze of municipal regulations could only be checked if there were state-wide rules for registering and licensing automobiles. Although the National Association of Automobile Manufacturers, the abortive trade association, sought to have Federal legislation provide a national license, it made little headway because Congress and the Federal government were apathetic to the automobile until 1909. In these circumstances, governments in individual states conferred socio-political recognition on the automobile. If local automobile clubs prodded early adopters (such as New York) to introduce legislation on car tags and speed limits, other states emulated these laws. New York took the lead in 1901, and required that all cars have numbered tags and mandated a 20-mph speed limit. By 1903, eight other states had followed, and by 1915 all the states had motor vehicle registration, wherein, automobiles had to possess a numbered tag. By then, as a consequence of legislation, a motor vehicles department had become an integral part of each state's administrative apparatus.

The Inadequacy of 'Normal' Incentives

A problem for actors seeking to legitimate a new form is that it creates positive externalities. An externality ensues due to an inequality between private costs and benefits on the one hand and collective costs and benefits on the other. Positive externalities exist when those who incur the costs of an action are not the sole beneficiaries of that action, and those who benefit have not necessarily shared in the costs of undertaking this action. Standard economic theory holds that early entrants or pioneers of an industry incur the cost of legitimating the new form. Early entrants incur the costs of establishing a trade association, formulating technical standards and establishing supply and distribution networks. Pioneers play a key role in familiarizing financial and personnel markets with the new form, as well as habituating governmental bureaucrats to the new organizational form. However, the benefits of these activities also extend to later entrants to the industry and not just pioneers. In principle, pioneers should balk at incurring the costs of legitimating a new organizational form, but as standard economic theory points out, they bear these costs because they have an opportunity to gain a large share of the market (Schmalensee, 1983).

However, normal incentives can be inadequate to legitimate organizational forms that produce collective goods such as technical standards. In such cases, actors have incentives to free-ride. Olson (1965) observed that collective action is possible only when free-riders are excluded from the benefits of joining the group, and when selective incentives are made available to members. Social movements become viable when movement activists commit time because they overstate the costs of their not doing anything, and are able to exclude others from the psychological benefit of contributing to a cause. Thus:

> New organizational forms are produced by social movement processes when 'normal' incentives are inadequate to create public goods.

For example, standard-setting organizations emerged in the United States because of the standards movement initiated by activists concerned about inefficiency and waste. In 1894, an association of insurance underwriters (Underwriters Laboratory) received a charter to certify wires and light fixtures as fire-resistant in order to build insurable real estate, thus becoming the first standard setting organizations. However, this initiative did not stimulate further instances of the form because free-rider problems paralyzed action by producers and consumers. Only when the National Bureau of Standards (set up in 1901) instituted annual national conferences on weights and measures did interested activists gather to exchange ideas and plan initiatives about reducing waste and inefficiency in industrial production. Activists such as James Chase and Frederick Schlink (who were employees of the Bureau) wrote pamphlets that railed against the evils of wasteful variety, preached the virtues of standards, and recruited converts from the ranks of private corporations. As a result, large private corporations such as General Motors, General Electric, Westinghouse, and American Telephone and Telegraph set up special-purpose departments to establish standards for devices. AT&T was reputed to have saved a million dollars because of the use of a standardized repeater in long distance lines (Chase & Schlink, 1927: 235). The success of activists in recruiting converts in large private enterprises also enabled them to appeal to professional societies of automotive, materials testing, and electrical engineers to assume responsibilities for standards setting. In 1908, the National Bureau of Standards also founded the *Journal of Weights and Measures* for the 'benefit of Dealers, Sealers and the Purchasing Public'. The standards movement reached its zenith during World War I, when activists located in the War Industries Board pushed producers to standardize products and conserve resources. As a result, the colors of typewriter ribbons were reduced from 150 to 6, automobile tires from 287 types to 9, and buggy wheels from 232 sizes to 4 (Cochrane, 1966). After the war, the American Standards Association was formed in 1919, and persuaded hundreds of firms to adopt common standards with the active support of the Bureau of Standards and the then Commerce Secretary, Herbert Hoover, in a bid to improve efficiency.

The Failure of Market Mechanisms to Reduce Social Costs

Social costs or negative externalities obtain when some parties draw all the benefits and others are stuck with the costs. For example, steam locomotives, as Coase (1960) observed in a famous example, can emit sparks that set fire to fields, or deceptive advertising can harm the image of advertising agencies and defraud consumers. In principle, one could claim that social costs can be reduced wholly through market mechanisms; for example, farmers can sell rights to emit sparks on their fields or purveyors of deceptive advertisements can be eliminated because they acquire a bad reputation. However, market mechanisms may not work when transactions span large distances, or when victims are uninformed and lack recognized legal rights. Steel firms, for instance, can pollute air in another country. Consumers may not be able to discern honest from dishonest advertisers, and may even lack the right of legal redress. In such cases, social movements can arise to establish new firms to reduce social costs. Thus:

> New organizational forms are produced by social movements when market mechanisms are inadequate to reduce negative externalities.

For example, at the turn of the 20th century, deceptive advertising may have benefited some firms, but harmed the standing of advertising, therefore imposing costs on advertising agencies and their clients. In the abstract, one might have expected the purveyors of dishonest advertisements to disappear and the suppliers of honest advertisements to thrive because the former would acquire bad reputations. However, consumers were uninformed, and free-rider problems prevented advertising agencies from engaging in collective action. Widespread concerns about deceptive advertising, however, induced owners of advertising agencies to become activists and initiate the truth-in-advertising movement in a bid to professionalize advertising at the turn of the 20th century. Stung by the widespread criticism that advertising was misleading and dishonest, some advertisers formed clubs during the period 1896–1903. In 1904, several clubs merged to form the Associated Advertising Clubs of America (AACA), and by 1909, the AACA had established an educational committee to systematize training and to promote honest advertising. In the 1911 convention of the AACA, a proposal initiated by John Romer, the publisher of *Printers Ink,* was introduced making it illegal for an advertisement to contain deceptions or misleading facts. Romer also urged advertising clubs to establish vigilance committees to ascertain the truthfulness of advertisements issued by members, to discipline errant members, or even to take them to court. A National Vigilance Committee formed in 1912, and by 1914, twenty-four cities had also founded vigilance committees in a bid to signal the advertising community's commitment to probity and professional conduct. In 1916, vigilance committees were renamed as Better Business Bureaus and by 1930, more than 10,000 businesses supported these bureaus in numerous cities (Samson, 1980: 343).

The Exclusion of Actors from Conventional Channels

Actors may be excluded from access to legal recourse because of laws that favor vested interests, be denied access to media exposure, be deprived of support from agencies of the state, or various combinations of these exclusions. In such cases, new organizational forms can explicitly be created by activists to discredit existing arrangements, and can provide a vehicle for those who feel excluded from access to the existing system.

New organizational forms are produced by social movements when actors seeking to
challenge existing arrangements are excluded from conventional channels of access.

For example, investor rights watchdogs emerged from the shareholder rights
movement that arose when corporate managers exploited the existing legal
framework to enhance their interests. A growing wave of takeovers in the 1980s
also aggravated the conflict between managers of firms and their investors.
During the 1980s, 29% of the *Fortune* 500 industrial firms were targets of
takeover attempts by outsiders. Takeovers tended to benefit shareholders by
increasing stock prices, but jeopardized the interests of managers. Managers
sought to defend themselves through 'poison pills', 'shark repellents'
(mechanisms that depressed share prices and reduced shareholder discretion),
'golden parachutes' (handsome pay packages to executives fired in takeovers),
and 'greenmail' (buying back raiders' shares at a high premium while leaving
other shareholders disadvantaged; on all of these processes, see Hirsch, 1986).
The takeover controversies spawned innumerable Congressional hearings, and
60 bills to regulate takeovers were introduced between 1984 and 1987.
However, new legislation was not enacted due to the Reagan government's
opposition and the attitudes of the Securities and Exchange Commission
(Romano, 1993). Private pension funds, banks, and mutual funds were
beholden to the managers of business firms, and had little incentive to
discipline them. In contrast, public pension funds were not captives of
managers, and were compelled by the ERISA law to discharge their fiduciary
responsibilities to their constituents. Public pension fund managers realized
that the takeovers market could not discipline managers, and turned to political
oversight and activism to check errant managers (Romano, 1993). Public
pension funds, such as CalPERS (the largest) and the California State Teachers
Retirement Fund, founded the Council of Institutional Investors (CII) in
January, 1985. Soon, other watchdogs, such as the Investor Research and
Responsibility Center, were established to construct 'blacklists' of firms that
jeopardized shareholder interests because of poor performance, self-dealing, or
both. Investor-rights watchdogs began to articulate shareholders' grievances
and presented the exercise of voting rights as the solution to curtail the power
of errant corporate managers. Investor-rights activists also urged public pension
funds to bring governance-related resolutions challenging the management of
errant companies. Typically, such resolutions offered a rival slate of directors or
asked shareholders to disapprove management proposals deemed inimical to
shareholders' interests. Anti-management resolutions were attempts by investor-rights activists to browbeat managers into recognizing shareholders' rights
to receive information, influence fundamental business decisions, and set
acceptable levels of performance.

The preceding discussion suggests some of the conditions under which social movements thrive as vehicles of collective action. Although we portray organizational and market failures as antecedents of social movements, we also recognize the importance of cultural processes that can reconstitute existing fields and reframe benefits as costs. In the next section, we discuss the larger contexts in which such failures can occur, drawing attention to various cultural and structural mechanisms by which social movements construct new organizational forms.

ORGANIZATIONAL FIELDS AND SOCIAL MOVEMENTS

As we noted at the outset, we consider the construction of new organizational forms as pre-eminently a political process. Friedland & Alford (1991: 240–242) argue that the unfolding of new forms consists of:

> ... [I]individuals competing and negotiating, organizations in conflict and coordination, and institutions in contradiction and interdependency ... We conceive of these levels of analysis as 'nested,' where organization and institution specify higher levels of constraint and opportunity for individual action.

Organizational fields operate at a meso-level of analysis that mediates between organizations and institutions, and consist of regulatory agencies, professional societies, consumers, suppliers, and organizations that produce similar goods and services (DiMaggio & Powell, 1983). More than a mere aggregate of organizational players, however, fields exhibit distinctive 'rules of the game', relational networks, and resource distributions that differentiate multiple levels of actors and models for action. Fields also contain potential and realized forms of social control that can select or repress new organizational forms. As a result, fields set many of the political constraints and opportunities that social movements and new organizational forms face as they emerge and attempt to sustain themselves. We identify three field conditions – the 'interstices' or gaps between fields, 'hierarchical' fields, and 'fragmented' fields – that powerfully influence the activities and patterns of social movements and new forms.

Social Movements and New Forms at the Interstices of Multiple Fields

The project of constructing a field-wide environment for a new form becomes more challenging at the intersection of multiple organizational fields, due to diverse interests, multiple (often competing) frames, and entrenched sources of resistance in established fields. Mann (1986) points out that actors create 'tunnels' around existing institutions, up through the 'pores' of society, and suggests that 'interstitial emergence' is an important pathway of social change. But he does not shed theoretical light on the dynamics of such processes. Further complicating his usage of the concept is that it is simultaneously a gap in social space (an *interstice*), a process (of emergence), and an effect (resulting in change). Below, we draw on Morrill (forthcoming) to describe how social movements at the interstices of multiple organizational fields bundle together particular sets of practices into new organizational forms. We frame our discussion around the proposition that:

New organizational forms are produced at the intersections of multiple organizational fields through social movement processes.

An *interstice* is a gap between multiple industries or professions and arises when problems or issues persistently spill over from one organizational field to another. For example, the problem of 'wellness' spans practitioners located in numerous fields of medicine and alternative therapies. It is in this interstice that the authority of orthodox medicine has weakened and alternative practices of healing have developed as a way to treat complex, chronic illnesses (Kleinman, 1996). Initially, many interstices experience a lack of social visibility as they form vis-à-vis a majority of players in relevant organizational fields. Because most social attention and authority tends to concentrate on conventional practices, many people in a given organizational field will tend to be unaware of initial work in the gaps between fields.

Accompanying the development of alternative practices are critiques of conventional practices. Such critiques can take competing forms of broad attacks on institutional underpinnings or as criticisms of particular practices within organizational fields. During this stage, early innovators begin to label critiques and alternative practices, thus increasing their rhetorical portability. However, these innovations take hold only when innovators develop 'resonant' frames for alternative practices and mobilize mass support (e.g. Snow & Benford, 1992). It is only then that alternative practitioners are able to carve out legitimated social spaces for their practices through the establishment of professional organizations and various symbolic, cultural, and normative boundaries. Such structuration can ultimately modify the institutionalized narratives used to account for orthodox practices and reconfigure the institutional context by creating new organizational forms that compete with and modify existing forms.

A Case Example: The ADR Industry

The development of alternative dispute resolution (ADR) during 1965–1995 provides a vivid example of how new forms are realized at the interstices of multiple fields through social movement processes (Morrill, forthcoming).

During the late 1950s and 1960s, critiques of American courts frequently prophesied their 'doom'. Critics found one source of the law's failure in mismanagement and poorly-designed procedures. Another source resided in so-called 'minor disputes' – commercial conflicts over small amounts of money, domestic disputes (including divorce and child custody), and neighborhood squabbles – which placed intractable and complex demands on the courts. Yet a third source erupted during the 1970s and was dubbed the 'litigation explosion'. Here the problem focused on the excessive use of adjudication to solve all manner of problems from complex civil cases to minor disputes (Lieberman, 1983).

In the 1960s, lawyers, social workers, community organization therapists, and judges working for the courts, social work agencies, mental health agencies and community organizations (including churches) began to use a variety of so-called 'informal' methods for handling minor disputes that circumvented 'formal' adjudication. The nature of minor disputes meant that disputants often circulated through a variety of organizations searching for resolution, justice, or therapy to deal with their problems. As a result, personnel from organizations in different fields often interacted with one another to process minor disputes through multiple referrals. Many of these referrals crossed the border between the socio-legal and social services fields, thus suggesting a cross-fertilization of knowledge and sometimes frustration about minor dispute handling among incumbents in diverse occupations.

The techniques used to resolve minor disputes came from many sources. Some techniques traced back to informal methods used by clergy and town officials in communities throughout the U.S., some derived from the domestic relations courts, others approximated labor arbitration in the 1930s, and still others could be traced to informal methods used in tightly-knit ethnic enclaves. Community activists drew from 'anti-authoritarian' modes of political discourse, while social workers used therapeutic techniques and strategies for preserving and strengthening the social bonds of community through open discussions of conflict. Judges and other magistrates used mediation and negotiation in small-claims court settings and in conciliatory (divorce) courts to settle cases quickly and manage the emotional side of such cases. Some lower-court judges regarded informal negotiation and mediation in civil cases as akin to pretrial criminal diversion programs that attempted to route defendants away from the courts to externalize processing costs. Lawyers used informal negotiation in their offices far more than they went to court, although there was little formal education in such techniques and practitioners generally learned them on the fly through experience (Ray, 1982a, b). For those few people who called themselves mediators – a diverse aggregate of social workers, therapists, and educators – mediation was often ancillary to institutionalized practices of conflict resolution drawn from their professions (Tomasic, 1982).

Two critical masses of supporters arose in the 1970s from the diverse network of individuals and organizations that had experimented in fragmented ways with alternatives to adjudication. Social workers, community activists, legal service lawyers, law professors, and anthropologists formed the first critical mass that framed ADR as 'community mediation'. These individuals had worked and studied in the courts, in social service agencies, in Ford Foundation-funded community centers, and in non-Western settings that used informal dispute resolution. They criticized the courts for being unable to handle minor disputes in a satisfactory way and for limited access for less privileged disputants (i.e. poor people, ethnic and religious minorities, women, and the disabled). Judges, lawyers, and law professors formed a second critical mass that characterized ADR as a 'multi-door courthouse'. This group criticized the inefficiency of the courts, also linking their critiques to the litigation explosion and the influx of minor disputes. They wished to save adjudication for the most 'serious' cases (e.g. civil rights, Constitutional issues, large commercial disputes), leaving ADR to deal with the majority of minor disputes. Their idea was to transplant non-Western community 'moots' to urban U.S. settings as a means of handling minor disputes (Fisher, 1975). Anthropologists had studied indigenous moots in which small groups of community members gathered to facilitate discussion among disputants, to provide therapy via group discussion between victims and offenders, and to reintegrate the principals back into the local community (Lowy, 1973). Legal service lawyers interested in access to law had been interested in how poor disputants could solve their conflicts. The two groups formed something of an uneasy and unconventional alliance, meeting under the auspices of newly-formed interdisciplinary academic organizations (e.g. the Law & Society Association and the Society for the Study of Social Problems) and in small groups in older organizations (e.g. the American Anthropological Association). Out of these interdisciplinary encounters, the community mediation model received its most widely circulated treatment in a 1974 *Stanford Law Review* article by Richard Danzig.

In contrast to the community mediation frame, the multi-door courthouse emerged out of an alliance between high-powered elites: the American Bar Association (ABA) and the U.S. Justice Department. For the ABA, ADR appeared to be a means to judicial control and a way to clean up the 'nightmare' of minor disputes in the courts. Various ABA planning committees provided the Justice Department's Law Enforcement Assistance Administration (LEAA) with early plans for developing linkages between the LEAA's crime control and civil justice programs that would address minor dispute processing (Harrington, 1985: 74). In turn, the LEAA funded some of the earliest court-based ADR programs, which typically involved streamlined adjudication (e.g. the Boston Urban Court) or prosecutorial, pre-trial diversion (e.g. the Columbus Night Prosecutor). In 1976, the ABA sponsored the 'Popular Dissatisfaction with the Administration of Justice' Conference (referred to as the 'Pound Conference'), bringing together judges, attorneys, social scientists, and mediators to discuss the possibilities of ADR in the U.S. That same year Frank Sander, a Harvard professor of family law and clinical practice, wrote what was to become the most influential, early statement on the multi-door courthouse. In so doing, he, like Danzig through his influential *Stanford Law Review* article, became an important issue entrepreneur for the ADR movement. The multi-door courthouse converged with the community mediation model in its condemnation of the 'over-adjudicated' nature of the legal system and in the idea that not all disputes belonged in the courts.

The multi-door courthouse's goals were primarily bureaucratic: the efficient disposition of cases. Although the community mediation model claimed it too could unburden the court of minor disputes, the ultimate gains from that model derived more from preventing future conflict than from the quick disposition of cases. The models also diverged in their legitimating ideologies. Whereas the community mediation model was grounded in the obligation to preserve social relationships as a basis for community, the multi-door courthouse was based on the idea that an expanded dispute processing repertoire would ultimately save the courts for cases at the heart of liberal political order, namely, constitutional disputes (Sander, 1976: 133). Divergent legitimating ideologies also led to different uses of coercion in the two models. Danzig argued that moots could refer disputants back to the courts for adjudication (as an incentive to settle in the moot), but he implied that these measures should be held in reserve for recalcitrant cases. Community moots are primarily 'private [and] noncoercive' (Danzig, 1974: 53). The multi-door courthouse would have the power to mandate the 'best' forum for disputes. As such, the multi-door courthouse presented disputants with the paradox of mandating participation in dispute settlement processes, which is portrayed as consensual and voluntary, while also requiring settlement.

Professionals (judges, lawyers, case workers) would staff the multi-door courthouse, financed by municipal and state budgets. By contrast, the community mediation centers would rely on private grants, federal funding, and some local governmental funds in return for handling court referrals. The multi-door courthouse fit well with the decentralized state federalism building in the late 1970s, which took full shape during the Reagan and Bush

Administrations in the 1980s. Community mediation articulated with a fading 'Great Society' vision of grass roots activism and federally-funded social programs.

Although widespread evaluation was sparse, the critical masses pushing for community mediation and the multi-door courthouse claimed efficacy for their models, citing the scientific evaluations and technical performance of early demonstration projects. But without comprehensive sponsorship, ADR diffusion moved unevenly through the U.S. But divorce and child custody mediation provided a major fillip to ADR. Divorce represented a most difficult type of minor dispute: relationally complex, emotionally charged, and with high stakes for each party, but not, typically, for the court. Popular perception held that adversarial legal processes were inadequate to handle divorce cases. No-fault divorce statutes sought to "eliminate the adversarial nature of divorce and thereby reduce the hostility, acrimony, and trauma characteristic of fault-oriented divorce" (Weitzman, 1985: 15). No-fault divorce officially changed part of the rules of the game for marriage and family, enabling either spouse to declare that irreconcilable differences made their marriage untenable. During the 1970s, lawyers and therapists working inside the ABA developed the Uniform Marriage and Divorce Code (UMDC), which articulated well with the multidoor courthouse frame. Supporters intended the UMDC to help find the proper forum for divorce and custody disputes within the courts by creating a series of rationales for mediation and other forms of non-adversarial dispute resolution. No-fault divorce spread like 'prairie fire' across the U.S., articulating with several social trends, including the increasing economic independence of women, changing normative conceptions of the family, the women's moment, and the civil rights movement. By 1981 only South Dakota and Illinois lacked no-fault divorce laws on the books, and by 1985, thirty states had joint child custody statutes (Weitzman, 1985: 438, 430–435).

The divorce/custody arena provided a legitimate pulpit for ADR practitioners to preach the benefits of ADR, and reinforced the increasing dominance of the multi-door courthouse. Unlike the ambiguous arena of 'minor disputes', domestic relations courts increasingly defined ADR practitioners as 'family mediators' and embedded them firmly in the courts. In those states with joint custody statutes, mediators played even more prominent roles in the divorce process because of the opportunities for on-going disputes among parents with joint custody arrangements (Milne & Folger, 1988).

If no-fault divorce spurred on ADR's interstitial emergence, it also brought mediators directly into conflict with the legal profession over who would control the disputing process. Lawyers and judges, associated with the adversarial process, now faced professional jurisdictional competition from an emergent group with practices that corresponded with the non-adversarial intentions of no-fault divorce law. ADR practitioners thus rode the wave of the divorce revolution toward organized professionalization and the creation of a protofield for mediation with distinctive technical and normative boundaries. During the late 1970s and early 1980s, family mediators joined with mediators handling other types of minor disputes to begin professionalization activities along four key dimensions: (1) the development of a common body of knowledge, (2) the founding of professional organizations, (3) the codification of normative standards, and (4) the development of university-based training (Wilensky, 1964; DiMaggio, 1991).

O. J. Coogler, a family lawyer and marriage counselor, published *Structured Mediation in Divorce Settlement* in 1978, which became a central source of knowledge about divorce mediation. Academic and practitioner journals also appeared and carried the 'good word' about divorce mediation specifically, and mediation and ADR, more generally (e.g. *Family Advocate, Mediation Quarterly, Journal of Conflict Resolution, Negotiation Journal*). These venues also touted other forms of ADR as well, such as arbitration, judicial settlement, and the mini-court. Family mediators also began founding organizational vehicles to push their collective interests. They formed committees and interest groups for themselves in established organizations, such as the ABA, and the Association of Family and Conciliation Courts. As they became more organizationally invested, family mediators codified a body of normative standards about mediation: the ABA's 'Standards of Practice for Lawyer Mediators in Family Disputes' and the Association of Family and Conciliation Courts' 'Model Standards of Practice for Family and Divorce Mediation'. These standards in turn fed into more general mediation standards promulgated by NIDR and the Society of Professionals in Dispute Resolution (SPDR) for a wide range of disputing contexts.

These developments enabled NIDR and SPDR to take the lead in uniform training curricula for family mediators and mediators working in other areas of the law and the community. In turn, these curricula laid the groundwork for the first attempts to produce university-trained ADR experts. George Mason University began the Center for Conflict Analysis and Resolution in 1980, and in 1988 admitted its first class of doctoral students in conflict analysis and resolution (Avruch, 1991) By the mid-1990s over thirty degree granting programs existed in colleges and universities across the U.S.

Following on the heels of these professionalization efforts by family mediators, ADR became increasingly organized on several key dimensions that fostered its diffusion (DiMaggio & Powell, 1983). One, NIDR, SPDR, and other national ADR professional organizations increased the flow of information between ADR practitioners, legal officials and other interested parties through newsletters, ADR case studies, and instructional videos. Two, involvement in conference presentations and presentations to state bar committees, as well as small demonstration grants made by NIDR increased the density of interorganizational contacts between local courts and ADR professional organizations and programs. Finally, these activities reinforced an emergent collective definition of ADR (which was and continues to be split between mediation and other forms of ADR mentioned above) and its increasingly taken-for-granted place in the American socio-legal field.

As mediators became more legitimized and organized vis-à-vis the courts, judges increased their de facto practice of ADR in the lower courts, particularly in small-claims cases (McEwen, Mather & Maimen, 1984). When they engaged in ADR, judges most commonly engaged in 'judicial settlement', in which the judge, rather than simply presiding over litigation, became actively involved in fashioning an agreement between disputants. In 1983, amendments to Rule 16 of the Federal Rules of Civil Procedure gave federal judges the explicit authority to 'facilitate settlements'. Within eighteen months of the amendment's passage, 16 states passed statutes that increased the authority of judges to mandate ADR across several types of cases.

During the late 1980s and 1990s, the implementation of ADR at the state level has been spearheaded by various 'advisory boards' attached to state supreme courts. On these boards sit a wide range of interested players, among them judges, professional mediators, lawyers, social workers, therapists, and lay persons. Advisory boards typically pursue multiple goals, including awarding county courts state funds for ADR pilot programs, expanding existing court-based ADR programs, educating the public on the benefits of ADR, setting standards for the delivery of mediation and other ADR practices, and ultimately regulating court-based ADR programs. In Arizona, California, and Oklahoma, for example, the ADR advisory board facilitated legislation (introduced by like-minded legislators) that would establish state-mandated fees for court-based mediation and would require certification for practitioners participating in these programs. In effect, these developments are creating a market for ADR services legitimated and required by the court.

All of these processes provide sites for jurisdictional conflicts over ADR. The diversity of interests on advisory boards (typically commissioned by Supreme Court justices working in conjunction with legislators) in some ways replicates the diversity of specialties and professions that first experimented with ADR in the 1970s. As a result, advisory boards are as much about political contestation over the fate and direction of ADR as they are about creating a professional jurisdiction and further widening the legitimate niche for ADR in the socio-legal field. State certification efforts, in particular, appear to be headed toward pitched jurisdictional battles between mediators who increasingly are defining ADR as mediation and lawyers who view mediation and arbitration as additional, legitimate strategies in their out-of-court settlement repertoires.

In sum, the professionalization of mediation and the ubiquitous appearance of ADR statutes and court-based programs in the U.S. capped off three decades of interstitial emergence during which ADR was transformed from a set of little-noticed techniques used by practitioners operating in the interstices between the socio-legal and other organizational fields to an increasingly conventional set of practices that have altered the core technology of dispute resolution (adjudication) and have modified the legitimating ideologies of the courts. If court-mandated, fee-based mediation becomes pervasive in the U.S., the ADR movement will have expanded the primary markets for dispute resolution services from lawyers alone (and to a lesser degree, arbitrators), to mediators, and other ADR providers. In this sense, ADR will have created an emergent field-wide environment that may eventually challenge existing fields.

Social Movements and New Forms in Fragmented Fields

In contrast to the resistance and competition that social movements experience as they emerge out of interstitial locations to construct new forms, social movements within fragmented fields are typically consensual in that they find widespread support for a cause and encounter minimal opposition (McCarthy & Wolfson, 1992). Organizational fields can be fragmented because multiple state agencies at different levels have conflicting goals and overlapping jurisdictions (Meyer & Scott, 1983). Fragmentation is also exacerbated when professions have weak jurisdictions (Abbott, 1989), when producers are unable to band together into trade associations, and when consumers and suppliers exercise little influence and are disorganized (Powell, 1991). Thus

> Consensus movements are likely to arise in fragmented organizational fields to establish new organizational forms.

When organizational fields are fragmented and lack a clear center of power, elites are disorganized and possess little influence to change the system. Additionally, elites are also unlikely to have the incentives to be pioneers and join a collective enterprise on the 'ground floor'. Instead, elites are more likely to act as fast followers. Even when there is consensus about the need for structural innovation, there may not be an infrastructure to propagate and diffuse the innovation in question. Hence, mass mobilization is necessary if existing structures are to be replaced by new structures.

A Case Example: The TQM Movement

A striking illustration is the social movement that spawned organizational arrangements in America premised on the 'the new quality paradigm' chronicled by Cole (1999). While the 'old control paradigm' defined quality as 'conformance to requirements' and was concretized in a special department consisting of specialists, the 'new empowerment paradigm' focuses on customer preferences, presumes that quality is a corporate strategy, involves all employees in cross-functional teams, deploys a well-defined problem-solving methodology, and presupposes training.

During the early 1980s, a major quality gap between U.S. and Japanese companies was identified by engineering experts and market surveys. Quality, a low ranked criterion in consumer auto purchase decisions in the mid-1970s, became one of the highest-ranking criteria in the early 1980s. Despite customer dissatisfaction, few firms responded with innovative solutions, or even imitated Japanese advances. Managers in many U.S. firms ignored quality as a competitive factor and attributed the superior performance of Japanese firms to Japanese access to cheap capital, government support, and the manipulation of currency rates. Managers also believed that high quality and low cost were contradictory goals, and that diminishing returns would come from additional increments of quality (Cole, 1999). Many American managers perceived the model of continuous quality improvement as impractical. Although Japanese firms were willing to share their quality management initiatives, norms legitimating such sharing did not exist among American firms. A few firms (e.g. Fuji-Xerox, Ford-Mazda) with Japanese joint-venture partners, used these opportunities to learn about quality management.

In Japan, the Japanese Union of Scientists and Engineers (JUSE), a central organization collated field experiences of companies and developed a standard model of quality management. By contrast, the United States had a fragmented national infrastructure that was ill-suited to impose order on managerial understanding. The American Society for Quality Control (later rechristened as the American Society for Quality) was perceived as a group of low-status 'techies' who were associated with failed old methods of quality control, and did not have the stature of JUSE. Consequently, the new quality paradigm and its component social structures took root only after a social movement dedicated to total quality management emerged in the United States.

Issue entrepreneurs, such as W. Edwards Deming, Joseph Juran and Philip Crosby, critiqued the 'control' paradigm of quality and exhorted firms to implement the new quality paradigm through seminars, books, and pamphlets. But it was only after a community of activist organizations emerged that the model of total quality management began to diffuse. The quality movement was powered by seven groups of activists: GOAL/QPC, the Conference Board's Quality Councils, the American Supplier Institute, the American Society for Quality, the Malcolm Baldridge National Quality Award, the ISO 9000 series, and the emergent consultant industry. These activists created standards, identified bottlenecks, introduced new methodologies, publicized success stories, focused efforts, evolved forums for networking, and provided overall infrastructural support to users (Cole, 1999).

GOAL/QPC was originally a local community-based group seeking to revive industry in the Lawrence/Lowell, Massachusetts area, and after being inspired by Deming, began to focus on quality management and transforming themselves from a local to a national non-profit research corporation. In 1987, they set about creating an intercorporate research group that would identify best quality practices in Japan, translate key documents, and help interpret them. The organization was particularly prominent in assuming the early leadership to adapt and apply 'policy management' (*hoshin kanri*) in the United States. By 1992, GOAL/QPC had thirty-six sustaining prominent members drawn from firms, such as General Electric, Hewlett-Packard, Procter and Gamble, IBM, Ford Motor Co., Xerox, and Intel. GOAL/QPC conducted a great number of public seminars and conferences on quality subjects. By the early 1990s, its annual conference, begun in 1984, attracted between 1,000–1,500 participants (Cole, 1999). As a consortium of leading companies that experimented with new quality improvement methods, GOAL/QPC reduced the costs of learning from the Japanese and facilitated information-sharing across firms.

While GOAL/QPC's participants were middle-ranking executives closely involved with quality, the Conference Board's Quality Council catered to top corporate executives with quality responsibilities. The first U.S. Quality Council, begun in 1985, existed as a forum for information sharing and included firms from diverse industries. A major theme of initial council meetings was the comparison of strategies for increasing Chief Executive involvement in quality improvement efforts. The first council also involved itself in formulating national policy via the establishment of the Malcolm Baldridge National Quality Award. The Conference went on to establish 13 councils, and by 1997, some 150 organizations with a total of some 200 executives were participating in the councils. At the end of 1995, the Conference Board set up a Total Quality Management Center composed of the 147 participating companies, mostly in the private sector (Cole, 1999).

Industry-based organizations like the American Supplier Institute (ASI) were prominent in bringing the new quality approaches to auto industry suppliers. Founded in 1981, as the Ford Supplier Institute, the ASI separated from Ford in 1984, and became a non-profit educational institute. Its new Board of Directors included representatives of the major automotive supplier companies, as well as Ford, GM, and Chrysler. ASI came to play a major role in the diffusion of Taguchi methods, quality function deployment (QFD), and design of applications to product development among auto industry suppliers. ASI staff 'Americanized' Japanese methods, much as GOAL/QPC did, and by the late 1980s, ASI seminars and workshops had trained more than 25,000 engineers and executives from more than 150 major companies (Cole, 1999).

The creation of the Malcolm Baldridge National Quality Award was the single most important event that provided a fillip to the quality movement and widened its appeal. Until the Baldridge formulated a roadmap for achieving sustained quality improvement, the 1980s had been characterized by an era of competing gurus (Juran vs. Crosby vs. Deming vs. Armand Feigenbaum vs. Kaoru Ishikawa). Unlike the Deming Prize, the Baldridge Award emphasized rewards and outcomes, and was transparent. The Baldridge protocol – an audit framework for telling companies where and in what ways they must demonstrate proficiency to attain superior quality performance – codified best practices for quality improvement over a range of critical areas. By the mid-1990s, over one million copies of the Baldridge protocol were distributed to potential users (the peak number distributed was 240,000 in 1991). Many firms used it solely to conduct diagnostic activities and companies routinely sent their key quality personnel to be trained as Baldridge examiners. They returned to their firms with added expertise, and each year's Baldridge examiner class created important networks for the diffusion of best practice ideas. The Baldridge also spawned state and local awards, and by 1997, more than 40 states offered quality awards (Cole, 1999).

Social Movements and New Forms in Hierarchical Fields

Some organizational fields are characterized by a distinct dominance order in which a few groups of actors operate at the apex while others survive on the bottom. In such instances, groups of influential actors have vested interests in preserving the social order. Consequently, structural innovations seldom emerge out of the center of a hierarchically-organized field, but instead, originate in the periphery, and may conflict with the interests of central players. Since actors at the periphery of a field – similar to those in the interstices between fields – possess little influence and lack resources, social movements are the vehicles of collective action by which new forms become established. Such social movements typically assume a 'conflict-oriented' character in the sense that conflict arises when organized attempts to modify the prevalent institutional order encounter opposition from interest groups opposed to the change. Hence, "a range of definitions of the situation" can exist (Zald & McCarthy, 1980: 6), and rival coalitions of issue entrepreneurs can champion incompatible frames. Thus:

> Conflict-oriented movements are likely to emerge in hierarchically structured organizational fields to establish new organizational forms.

A Case Example: Craft-Brewing

The growth of the craft-brewing movement offers a striking example of a conflict-oriented movement producing a new organizational form in the U.S. hierarchical brewery field (Carroll & Swaminathan, 1998). Micro-breweries and brewpubs were outcroppings of a craft movement that arose in reaction to the 'industrial beer' produced by the dominant firms in the beer industry – especially Anheuser Busch, Miller, and Coors. In 1980, the U.S. beer industry was divided into domestic beers, which were light and inexpensive, and imports, which came in green bottles and had more flavor. The large domestic beer producers controlled virtually all of the beer market due to enormous economies of scale of their production, distribution, and marketing.

Beer aficionados were discontented due to the lack of choice, and the dearth of fresh and tasteful beer sold onsite at bars, restaurants, and other gathering places. 'Pro-choice' aficionados, such as Fritz Maytag, the owner of Anchor Brewing (producers of 'Anchor Steam' beer), exploited this discontent and began to produce small quantities of tasteful beer using traditional methods, and targeted consumers searching for such options. Soon, other micro-brewers and brewpubs commenced production of small quantities of beer using craft methods. The Great American Beer Festival, established in 1982, drew about 40 brewers and 700 beer enthusiasts. These first shots sparked a revolt against the 'beer establishment' and other enthusiasts started brewing in small quantities using traditional methods. By 1994, there were close to 500 establishments that are part of the $400 million craft beer movement in the United States and micro-brewers crafted more than 2 million barrels of beer, which produced revenues much less than the total sales of Michelob Light.

As a craft movement, then, the micro-breweries were by definition, less about scale and more an expression of a new identity. The identity of micro-brewers was premised on small scale, authentic and traditional methods of production, and fresh beer with a myriad of tastes. As aficionados armed with small kettles, fresh ingredients, and unique recipes began to produce a stunning variety of beers, other beer lovers sought to solidify the identity of craft brewing by establishing an infrastructure to support the craft-brewing movement (Carroll & Swaminathan, 1998).

A mainstay of the craft-brewing movement was the Institute for Brewing Studies (IBS). An association dedicated to craft brewing, it was founded in 1983 to provide technical data, the most recent statistics, updates on both local and federal regulations, and to distribute a magazine, *New Brewing*, to members. Craft-brewing aficionados also sought to educate the consumer. Festivals, such as the Great American Beer Festival or the Texas Brewing Festival, started to educate consumers about the choices available in the market and provided a platform for aficionados to assess how their beer fared vis-à-vis other specialty beers. The Great American Beer Festival initiated a consumer poll designed to choose the best five beers in 1983, and continued this poll until 1989. The poll was replaced by the Professional Blind Taste Test that chose winners and grew to become the most prestigious contest in the U.S.

The growth of the craft-brewing movement did not go unnoticed by the dominant industrial beer producers, who responded by establishing 'specialty beer' divisions. 'Contract brewers', who sub-contracted the production of beer, also grew. However, craft-brewing enthusiasts policed pretenders to their identity by quickly ridiculing them as impostors. Arguably, the policing of inauthentic incursions by craft-brewing enthusiasts sustained the identity of craft-brewing and spurred the growth of the movement. By 1998, the craft-brewing movement consisted of more than 1306 micro-brewers and brewpubs.

An important consequence of the craft-brewing movement's emphasis on choice, taste, and freshness also marked the birth of the homebrewing movement. The American Home Brewers Association was established by homebrewing aficionados to 'democratize' the production of beer, and fostered the growth of home-brewing clubs. It also created a 'Beertown University' for aspiring home-brewers, and by 1998, there were more than 600 home-brewing clubs, and a full-fledged contest to evaluate the quality of home-brewed beer.

This section has demonstrated how field conditions powerfully influence the political processes by which new forms are constructed. Movements that arise out of the interstices between fields face problems of internal solidarity and entrenched resistance in existing fields. Social movements in hierarchical fields face similar problems in terms of resistance when powerful actors first try to quash them and then infiltrate or imitate them to defuse challenges to their authority. By contrast, social movements in fragmented fields, such as the quality movement, often become consensus-oriented and face little entrenched resistance to their aims. Field conditions also affect the forms constructed by social movements. Movements that emerge between fields, if they are to succeed, must construct a new field-wide environment. Hence, the ADR movement has worked to create new production and consumer markets in which court-based ADR providers, private providers, and other ADR organizations would operate. To nourish new forms in hierarchical fields, social movements must create subfields (or subcultures) *within* an extant field, which in turn can lead to marginalization, that ironically, can feed into the preferred identities of supporters. In our discussion of changes in the production and consumption of beer, we demonstrated how the microbrewing and home-brewing movements created subfields in the shadows of industrial brewing, that by most accounts, fits the preferred identity of craft brewers and consumers. In fragmented fields, movements ultimately convert the field to the new form, thereby transforming the field-wide environment to suit the form. Our exploration of quality management amply illustrates this outcome. There are few venues within corporate or other large American organizations that do not at least pay lip service to the ways their organization achieves quality management. In the next section, we turn to other dimensions of the political processes by which new forms are constructed in response to social movements.

REACTIVE POLITICS, SOCIAL MOVEMENTS AND NEW FORMS

Until now, we have concentrated on movements that make initial thrusts to construct new forms between or within existing fields. Such movements, as we noted earlier, often occur in response to various types of organizational and market failures. However, movements themselves generate reactions to their own activities that can modify their development and impacts. We turn now to a discussion of three types of reactive politics and their implications for the construction of new forms: 'spin-off movements', 'counter movements', and 'boundary truces'.

Spin-off Movements and the Rise of New Forms

The preceding account of how the craft-brewing movement led to the home-brewing movement directs attention to how a movement can spawn spin-off movements. More formally, McAdam (1995) distinguishes between rare, but exceedingly important, initiator movements "that signal or otherwise set in motion an identifiable protest cycle" and more populous spin-off movements "that, in varying degrees, draw their impetus and inspiration from the original initiator movement". Spin-off movements represent the diffusion of the master logic animating an initiator movement, and entail the customization of the initiator movement's master logic. Thus:

> New organizational forms are likely to emerge when spin-off movements customize the master logic driving an initiator movement to a new locale.

A Case Example: HMOs

A striking example of this process – *initiator movement* → *spin-off movement* → *new organizational form* – occurred when the U.S. consumer movement led to the movement for health care reform in the 1970's that in turn spawned health maintenance organizations (HMOs). Medical professionals, through the American Medical Association (AMA) dominated the American health care field from 1940 until 1965 by framing and deciding key issues according to the professional models and norms. At the core of the AMA model was a concern for 'quality' and the standards of 'sound' medical practice. A turning point occurred in 1965 as the Johnson Administration accepted responsibility for caring for the elderly and the poor through the Medicare and Medicaid programs. As the federal government (regulators, funding agencies, and congressional committees) became the apex player in the health care field, its decisional locus shifted from quality to emphasize 'equity'.

In the early 1960s, a movement dedicated to consumer interests had already begun to gather fervor chiefly under the leadership of Ralph Nader. In contrast to the consumer movement of the early 1930s that constructed the consumer as a rational decision-maker and resulted in the growth of special-purpose ratings agencies, the consumer movement in the 1970s articulated the rights of consumers to affordable, safe and well-made products. Nader and other consumer activists critiqued automobile manufacturers and other industrial producers for making unsafe products and exploiting the consumer. They also persuaded the Kennedy Administration to recognize the consumer's interests by promulgating a Bill of Rights for the consumer, and launched a campaign to enforce these rights through legal activism.

The consumer movement led to a spin-off-movement within the health care field, and culminated in the production of health maintenance organizations in the 1970s, chiefly due to the efforts of Paul Ellwood. As the executive director of the American Rehabilitation Institute, Ellwood assailed the existing fee-for-service system because it rewarded physicians for treating illness and withdrew care when health was restored. He critiqued the system for shortchanging consumers and not providing them preventive and rehabilitative health care, and sought to create a system that promoted the interests of consumers.

Ellwood seized on the idea of pre-paid group practices, pioneered early in the 20th century in the American Northwest by two doctors who contracted with mills and lumber companies to deliver health care to enrolled employees for a pre-set fee every month. County medical service bureaus in Tacoma, Washington – the predecessors of local medical societies – resisted this scheme. After the Depression in 1929, pre-paid medicine received a shot in the arm when Michael Shadid sold shares for a community hospital in Oklahoma in return for medical care. The county medical society expelled Shadid and a few other physicians who emulated him. Both Shadid and his emulators fought back through lawsuits and won. Nonetheless, in 1932 the AMA opposed pre-paid medical care. While urban pre-paid practices sporadically cropped up in Washington and New York, industry interest in pre-paid practice did not whole heartedly begin until Henry Kaiser asked Dr. Sidney Garfield to establish a pre-paid scheme for workers in his shipyards in 1942. After World War II, the Permanente Health Plan opened to the public for enrollment, and unions began to establish pre-paid group health plans in the auto and mining industries. However, by 1970, there were only 39 pre-paid group practices in the United States (Mayer & Mayer, 1985).

The term 'health maintenance organization' did not enter the lexicon until Paul Ellwood, a Minnesota physician and big thinker, coined it in his push to get the government to support pre-paid health care. Ellwood recruited allies from the non-profit arena and sought to make health care affordable for consumers; he also emphasized preventive health and advanced the interests of consumers. Ellwood and other activists were able to persuade the federal government to endorse HMOs because the Nixon Administration did not have a health care policy plank. Rising public concerns about mounting health care costs and the Nixon Administration's concerns about the costs and ideology associated with Medicare and Medicaid also made health care a focal issue in the early 1970s.

The Nixon Administration sought to appoint Dr. John Knowles as the Assistant Secretary for Health and Scientific Affairs, then the highest health position in the government. They were thwarted by the AMA lobbyists who lobbied Congress against Knowles' appointment. Eventually, Dr. Roger Egberg was appointed as an alternative after a six month tussle between the AMA and the Nixon Administration. This delay proved propitious for Ellwood because non-physicians with a background in law and management rose to power in the leaderless department of Health and Scientific Affairs. Since senior Nixon Administration aides believed that they were behind, rather than ahead of, a rising popular concern with health care and health costs, they found Ellwood's proposal attractive. The Nixon aides entrusted with health care policy were non-physicians from California who were familiar with Kaiser Permanente and accepted the premise of pre-paid health care. Ellwood and his activist network lobbied the Nixon Administration to establish the HMO Act of 1973, which in part extended government grants to start-up HMOs. Moreover, the AMA could not strongly oppose the Act because it had just emerged from a bitter, losing political battle over Egberg's appointment, and an even larger conflict over the founding of Medicare and Medicaid. In order to further defuse opposition from the AMA, Ellwood and his allies replaced the label of 'pre-paid practice' with the more nebulous 'HMO' appellation.

An outcome of Ellwood and his network's lobbying efforts was the rapid growth of HMOs. Many of the early HMOs were founded along non-profit lines and were imbued with a sense of social mission. They belonged to the 'group' format, wherein the HMO employs medical staff and cares for patients for a pre-set fee, or contracts with one or more multi-specialty physicians' groups to do so. The number of group HMOs increased from 39 in 1970 to 200 in 1977, and by 1991, there were nearly 400 group HMOs in the U.S.

Counter Movements and New Forms

Another reaction to a social movement can be a counter-movement that defends interests unrepresented by the social movement and undermines those calling for institutional change (Useem & Zald, 1982). The conflict between 'pro-life' and 'pro-choice' movements exemplifies the tussle between a movement and a counter-movement. When a social movement dedicated to a cause establishes a new organizational form to embody and advance the cause, a counter-movement can respond by using its existing organizational infrastructure to mobilize support from the media, governmental organizations, and the professions. These tasks can become easier for a counter-movement because it incorporates important facets of the cause originally championed by its opponents. The counter-movement, for example, can establish organizations that emulate organizations founded by its opponents. The object in such instances can be outright 'identity theft', as in the case of lumber firms who founded organizations with names identical to environmentalist organizations in the American Northwest. 'Astroturf' organizations are a more subtle aspect of this in which environmental 'grass-roots' organizations are funded by corporations as a strategy to inject more moderate environmental 'concerns' into a political process, thereby drawing support and attention away from radical environmental groups. In other cases, the purpose of such strategies may be to yoke the organizational arrangements favored by opponents to the interests of the counter-movement. Thus:

New organizational forms are produced by counter-movements seeking to incorporate the identity of their opponents.

A striking illustration of this proposition was the effort by physicians to counter the 'group' HMO with HMOs organized on the model of an independent practice association (IPA). Since the birth of the first pre-paid group practice schemes, physicians have perceived it as a threat to their independence and way of life. As we noted previously, the pioneers of the Tacoma pre-paid group practice plan, and later, Michael Shadid, were expelled by their local county medical bureau and medical society. However, these expulsions were later overturned by court orders. After a while, the AMA lobbied against pre-paid health care, but supported what they considered a lesser evil, health insurance, that paved the way for the birth of the Blue Cross in 1932.

In the 1950s, the growth of the group HMO coupled with the legal victories won by group HMO pioneers induced physicians committed to the fee-for-service model to preserve free enterprise through a system of foundations for medical care. These organizations consisted of pre-paid service plans in which fee-for-service physicians were loosely bound together in an agreement to accept fixed-fee schedules, peer reviews, and the risks of financial loss. The first such effort, the San Joaquin Foundation for Medical Care, was created in 1954 as a response to the attempt by labor organizations to establish a branch of Kaiser Permanente (a group HMO). The San Joaquin Foundation became the forerunner of HMOs organized on the IPA format.

After Paul Ellwood and his activist allies helped the Nixon Administration push through the HMO Act of 1973, physicians committed to traditional medical practice arrangements began a full-fledged movement to establish HMOs premised on the IPA format. Physicians in IPAs are less dependent on the HMO than physicians in group HMOs; the former secure a maximum of 30% of their patients from the HMO, and the latter draw up to 70% of their patients from the group HMO. Local medical associations, in turn, sponsored IPA formation as a defensive, competitive response to group HMO formation (Brown, 1983), and provided an infrastructure for the IPA movement. In 1977, there were nearly 200 group HMOs but less than 50 HMOs based on the IPA format, but by 1988, HMOs on the IPA format reached more than 550, whereas, group HMOs had crested at 400 (Wholey, Christianson & Sanchez, 1993).

Boundaries of New Forms as Truces

When an unfilled resource space "calls forth and permits a range of definitions of the situation" (Zald & McCarthy, 1980: 6), rival coalitions of issue entrepreneurs can champion incompatible frames. The choice between frames and organizational embodiments becomes a political question (DiMaggio, 1994; Tarrow, 1989). The competition between the 'community mediation' and 'multidoor courthouse' frames in the ADR case illustrates such questions, as does the rivalry between group and IPA HMOs.

The success of collective action efforts, and the endorsement of powerful actors, shape the selection of frames and the concomitant choice of organizational boundaries. Collective action and the endorsement of powerful actors become even more important when technical differences amongst rival frames and structural proposals are minimal. In cases where the criteria for a good technical solution are contested, political and institutional processes shape not only what organizations can do, but which organizations can exist (Powell, 1991: 186–187).

The coalition that garners the greatest political support will find that its frame will be privileged (Brint & Karabel, 1991: 355; McAdam, 1994). Whether a coalition wins or not hinges on its size, the existence of political opportunity, the attitude of state actors, its support from professionals, and its ability to build a political coalition around an identity (Fligstein, 1996: 664). Hence, the scope of the form, that is, the goals, authority structure, technology and clients subsumed by the form, are outcomes of contending attempts at control and competing quests to impose a preferred definition of the identity of the constituencies that benefit from the form (White, 1992). In organizations, new routines also trigger conflict between members of the organization, and only become operative when there is a comprehensive truce, or when there is a cessation of conflict among members of an organization (Nelson & Winter 1982: 109–111). Analogously:

> The boundaries of a new organizational form become established only when there is a truce amongst the constituents of the organizational field about which frame will be used to organize activities.

Like truces among nations, truces among rival institutional entrepreneurs can be unequal, with some winning a larger slice of the cake and as a result, achieving a privileged position for their frame. March & Olsen (1989) suggest that conflict resolution can occur through the logic of aggregation and give and take, or the logic of integration wherein one of the parties learns from the other and even converts to the other's point of view. Those who lose can exit the arena, concentrate on a different niche, or even embrace the ascendant frame as a loyal supporter. When the proponents of a losing frame abandon deviant ideas and capitulate by adopting the ascendant frame, they can 'normalize' themselves and become integrated into the social system.

Truces increase the capacity for collective action by reducing comprehensiveness; some points of view are ignored or suppressed. The terms of a truce among rival institutional entrepreneurs can never be completely explicit; thus, the maintenance of truces depends upon the disincentives for actors to engage in provocative actions and the defensive alertness of parties keen on preserving the status quo. As a result, just like intra-organizational routines, organizational forms are "confined to extremely narrow channels by the dikes of vested interest. Adaptations that appear 'obvious' and 'easy' to an external observer may be foreclosed because they involve a perceived threat to the political equilibrium" (Nelson & Winter, 1982: 111).

A Case Example: Consumer Watchdogs
Below, we draw on Rao's (1998) account of non-profit consumer watchdog organizations for a compelling example of how the boundaries of new organizations spawned by social movements embody truces. Consumer watchdogs arose in the 1930s when growing durable goods expenditures, complex product choice, deceptive advertising, and the lack of product liability rules put the consumer in a perilous position vis-à-vis producers. In this context, two issue entrepreneurs, Stuart Chase and Frederick Schlink, diagnosed the problems facing consumers, and framed a new social control mechanism as the solution – the consumer watchdog organization. In a series of books, Chase and Schlink portrayed the consumer as an Alice-in-Wonderland created by advertising and product differentiation. They blamed manufacturers for failing to *serve* the consumer and instead, creating wasteful variety. They also urged consumers to imitate Schlink's consumer's club set up with the help of a church in White Plains, New York. This neighborhood club prepared two 'confidential lists' – one carrying products considered to be of good value in relation to their price; the second, products one might well avoid, whether on account of inferior quality, unreasonable price, or false and misleading advertising. The book sparked hundreds of inquiries, and Schlink transformed the neighborhood club into Consumers Research Inc. – an organization that sought to serve as an 'economist, scientist, accountant'. The list was renamed as the 'Consumers Research Bulletin' that would "investigate, test, and report reliably on hundreds of commodities . . .".

As a new form of social control, Consumers Research (CR) encountered very little opposition. Its founders deftly framed their critiques of business and advertising around the ideas of service to the customer and truth-in-advertising – concepts that businessmen and advertisers had begun to implement in a bid to professionalize their trades. CR's founders also borrowed elements of their solution – standards, testing, and science – from the work of industrial standard-setting bodies and the home economics profession. CR grew quickly.

In 1927, it had 656 subscribers and by 1933, there were 42,000 subscribers (Silber, 1983).

In 1932, budgetary disagreements within CR about how much money should be spent on testing vs. advocating reform of labor conditions flared into the open. Some employees and members of the board believed that CR should lobby for the reform of labor conditions. By contrast, Schlink and others thought that social questions concerning wages and working conditions were beyond their scope. Thus, CR was beset with a debate about whether it would be an impartial provider of information for consumers or a journal of radical political economy dedicated to the improvement of workers and labor conditions.

These tensions flared during a union recognition drive by CR's employees in August 1935. When 20 or more employees formed a Chapter of the Technical, Editorial and Office Assistants Union and asked for recognition, John Heasty, a chemist and union president, and two other union activists were fired. In the ensuing strike, Schlink and his allies believed the strikers were 'dupes of business' and 'Communists'. As a result, thirty workers led by Arthur Kallet established a new organization called Consumers Union Inc. (CU) that sought to unite the cause of consumers and workers. Its publication was to be called *Consumers Union Reports*.

CU was more than a breakaway faction of CR and was premised on a strikingly different diagnosis of the problems facing the consumer. The organization's founders believed a watchdog guarding consumers could not merely provide scientific, impartial, and objective information to them to make rational purchasing decisions. Instead, the CU's founders defined the consumer as a worker concerned with the standard of living and not just a rational actor seeking to get the best value for his or her money. The problem facing consumers was not one of variety and deceptive advertising, it was also one of wages and income.

Like its rival CR, CU also valued the norms of scientific analysis and rational purchasing and was committed to impartial testing. In contrast to CR, however, CU saw buying as a socially responsible act, urged members to picket anti-union stores, and pleaded with them to use labor conditions as a criterion in the purchase process. CU also committed itself to the norm of equity in incomes and viewed itself as a critic of companies exploiting their workers. Its founders were careful to signal their commitment to impartial testing by not only having a non-profit organization, but also by decoupling product ratings from evaluations of labor conditions. If CR focused its scope of operations on testing and concentrated on one constituency – consumers, CU diversified its operational scope and pursued two constituencies – consumers and workers, or ultimately joined the two in a single identity, consumers-*as*-workers.

As CU pursued its political path, CR's model of the consumer-as-rational-decision-maker diffused through governmental agencies and professional societies. In its wake, the Consumers Advisory Board was established in the National Recovery Administration in 1933, which in turn sponsored a report by Robert Lynd, the sociologist, that called for the creation of common standards and the allocation of funds for testing. A Consumer's Counsel was established in the Department of Agriculture in 1933 that issued a bi-monthly publication called *Consumer Guide,* which enjoyed a circulation of over 150,000. The concepts of rational decision-making, standardization, and scientific testing also spread in professional circles. The American Home Economics Association set up a Standing Committee on the Standardization of Consumer Goods in 1927, became a member of the American Standards Association in 1928, and organized cooperative standardization projects between women and merchants in several cities (Sorensen, 1941: 66). Later, other long-established national organizations, such as the National Education Association, the American Federation of Teachers, the American Marketing Association, the Mid-Western Economics Association, and others began to devote time to consumer education issues during their annual conferences.

By contrast, small newly-founded consumer groups such as the Consumer Conference in Cincinnati (1934), the League of Women Shoppers (1935), the High Cost of Living Conferences (1935), and the Milk Consumers Protective Committee (1939) endorsed CU. Increasing circulation of CU's *Consumers Union Reports* became crucially important to CU's founders for several reasons. First, they realized that their bulletin was not reaching low-income workers, and felt that boosting circulation could help them sustain inexpensive editions. Second, CU was wary about creating local groups because it did not want to be legally responsible for their conduct. Third, increasing circulation represented a way for CU's founders to jump-start the consumer movement and push for radical reform. Finally, resources from increased circulation were essential to fund an expansion of the product testing program and reward technical talent.

CU's attempt to increase circulation evoked resistance from diverse institutional actors. CU sought to advertise itself through mass media but faced a media boycott. Sixty-two newspapers, including the *New York Times*, refused to sell it advertising space. Other magazines and newspapers, especially those in the Hearst system, attacked CU. In its second issue, CU asked its readers to support a strike against Hearst's Wisconsin News, and from 1936 to 1939 issued articles that exposed the Good Housekeeping Institute – so much so, that the Federal Trade Commission investigated the Good Housekeeping Institute. As a result, William Hearst himself became a bitter enemy and charged that CU was a Communist front organization. The *Women's Home Journal* also ran editorials and essays accusing CU of undermining the American way of life.

The attacks reached their zenith in 1938 when a House Committee on subversive activities chaired by Congressman Dies sought to investigate if CU was in fact engaging in un-American activities harmful to the national interest. J. B. Matthews, an associate of Schlink's at CR, served as counsel for the Dies Committee, and suggested that Kallet's writings and the fact that a CU ex-employee, Susan Jenkins, had admitted to being an employee of a Communist newspaper, the *Daily Worker,* were proof that the organization was indeed a Communist front. Matthews went so far as to label CU a 'red transmission belt', which was then printed in several Hearst newspapers and a high-circulation Hearst magazine, *Good Housekeeping.* The pressure exerted by hostile activists (such as Matthews), elements of the media (Hearst news-papers), and politicians (such as Dies, and others on the House Committee on un-American Activities), impelled CU's founders to disengage from radical advocacy.

CU's adaptation to this new orientation was a gradual process of disengaging from the labor agenda. During the second annual meeting in 1938, three resolutions urging a focus on ratings and a disavowal of interest in labor and the threat of fascism or other 'ideologies' were introduced but not approved. In a turnabout in 1939, CU began to assert that "just the ordinary products bought each day can save members $50 to $300 a year" (*Consumer Reports*, April, 1939: 14). In 1939, Kallet and Colston Warne, the president, sought to derive support from the scientific community, and arranged a meeting with the Cambridge-Boston chapter of the American Association of Scientific Workers (AASW), a fledgling organization that was created in 1938 by a group of biologists at Woods Hole, Massachusetts. At this meeting, CU members confessed to the inadequacy of their testing and the AASW agreed to provide expert advice and testing for certain products. In 1940, the CU Board rejected an attempt by the editor of *Consumer Union Reports* to recruit union members as subscribers. In the same year, a National Advisory Committee comprised of academics was also created to establish linkages with colleges and uni-versities.

Over time, CU slowly ceased to be an engine of political, social, or moral reconstruction and reinvented itself as an impartial testing agency. CU began to recognize products as conditionally acceptable and expanded its testing. This ensured that testing was done in-house, instead of being subcontracted out as it was at CR. Its evaluations appeared in the form of tables and charts with numerical results of tests. Annual surveys of its members enabled it respond to its subscribers' needs. Even after introducing a segment on Health and Medicine in 1945 and providing careful summaries of medical research on smoking, *Consumer Reports* provided information on how to 'roll your own' cigarettes during the cigarette famine of 1945.

By emphasizing testing and science and by disavowing radical labor advocacy, Kallet and his colleagues not only shielded CU from external attack but transformed it into a scientific conservative to fit with the prevailing beliefs about science, rigor, and objectivity. The price of viability for the organization was unilateral abstinence from advocacy. CR may have won the tussle over what a non-profit watchdog ought to be, but it was outdistanced in the battle for circulation. By joining the media and politicians in critiquing CU, CR may have sown the seeds for its own decline because the embrace of scientific conservatism proved advantageous to CU. By 1949, with 500,000 subscribers, CU rated 1,793 brands spanning 116 products, and its technical division was divided into electronics, textiles, automobiles, special projects, chemistry, and foods. By contrast, CR had made little progress and refused to publicize its circulation details.

The case study of the origins of non-profit consumer watchdog organizations shows how the boundaries of organizational forms are defined by institutional processes rather than by transaction cost considerations. CU and CR represented two potential ways of bundling the activities of the non-profit consumer watchdog form. Neither model enjoyed a decisive technical advantage – if CR's focus reduced its coordination costs, then CU's diversified emphasis led to economies of scope in lobbying. Each model was premised on a different notion of the identity of the consumer. Chase and Schlink defined a consumer as a decision-maker keen on getting the best value for the money, promoted norms of efficiency, rationality and scientific analysis, and extolled watchdogs as impartial testers. Chalet and his allies viewed the consumer as a worker keen to better his standard of living, promoted norms of socially responsible buying and equity, and portrayed watchdogs as engines of radical change. CR and CU, therefore, represented alternative models for the social control of industry, premised on different ideals of identity.

Thus, a contest over the identity of the consumer delineated the boundaries of each form. When CU's founders bowed to pressure by embracing the model of an impartial tester and disavowing socio-political advocacy, there was a cessation of hostilities and a moratorium on the debate about the identity of consumers and non-profit consumer watchdogs. This truce on the contours of the non-profit consumer watchdog form persisted because CU's founders were keen to avoid the risks of political pressure from Congress, and the defensive alertness of actors opposed to socio-political advocacy. The absence of debate about the role of non-profit consumer watchdogs made it possible for them to rationalize consumption and to become influential monitors of big business.

CONCLUSIONS AND IMPLICATIONS

Our goal in this chapter has been to sensitize readers to the construction of new organizational forms as a political process in which various forms of collective action, especially social movements, play prominent roles. A political perspective directs attention beyond technological or transaction cost analyses of organizational change to consider how entrenched, field-wide authority is collectively challenged and restructured; how new norms, values, and ideologies are infused into social structures via political contestation; and how institutional entrepreneurs and activists play key roles in framing new practices, mobilizing resources (including constituencies), and garnering legitimacy for new forms. Along the way, we have considered how larger cultural and social contexts – organizational fields – influence social movements and have explored the reactive politics that social movements generate. Our approach thus paints a more conflictive portrait of the construction of new organizational forms than is usually offered in the economic, organizational ecological, or cultural-frame institutional literatures, and it is one we believe better captures the political realities of organizational change. This approach also raises several questions for future research on the politics of organizational change.

The first of these questions concerns the conditions that spawn social movements. Our approach presumed that organizational and market failures were givens and glossed over how they needed to be socially constructed and validated. Social movements draw on cultural stock for images and definitions of what constitutes a problem or an injustice, which in turn point toward particular policy and institutional changes. Similarly, social movements draw upon cultural repertoires for mobilizing, organizing, and protest strategies (Zald, 1996). Both of these observations suggest that future research must examine how organizational and market failures are collectively defined and linked to cultural repertoires. Moreover, future research also needs to consider the conditions under which the framing of failures become contested themselves. Central in these investigations should be the embedding of cultural stocks and repertoires in organizational fields. For it is at the field level that institutional entrepreneurs and individual organizations most acutely draw upon and are influenced by cultural elements. For example, ADR activists drew upon wider images of legal access to the courts (through 'multiple doors') and community clinics to construct their community mediation and multi-door courthouse frames. At the same time, we need to know the conditions under which activists 'jump' organizational fields to borrow repertoires of collective action from different fields. How did HMO activists, for instance, appropriate consumer quality movement rhetoric in their pursuit of new health care delivery forms?

The cultural turn in social movement research also provides a bridge to a second question regarding the outcomes of social movements, especially their failure to produce new forms. The social movement literature has concentrated more scholarship on the emergence of social movements, even though movement failure commonly occurs in the empirical world (Gamson, 1990). Moreover, the same factors that movement theorists point to as crucial for emergence – political opportunities, mobilizing structures, and framing – also play key roles in the demise and failure of movements (Voss, 1996). Structural sources of repression (e.g. policing and regulation) also are important for constraining movements and the production of new forms. Perhaps most difficult for movements to overcome are entrenched cognitive categories, or what Voss (1996: 256) calls, 'cognitive encumbrances'. Such encumbrances often emanate from a movement's early, successful attempts to develop resonant frames that then subsequently make it difficult for the movement to adapt to new cultural circumstances.

Inquiry about movement failure raises questions about the types of new forms produced by social movements. Based on our earlier analyses and descriptions, we argue that conflict movements that occur between fields or within hierarchical fields will likely produce forms that are posed against and sharply distinguished from existing forms. For example, ADR rhetoric often contrasts dispute resolution technologies (e.g. mediation, facilitation, negotiation) with those of conventional courtrooms in which various types of adjudication prevail. An even more extreme example occurs in the medical field where HMO proponents early on drew sharp distinctions between themselves and conventional health care decision making, delivery, and organization among medical professionals. By contrast, consensus movements in fragmented fields will likely produce forms that permeate an entire field and graft on to existing forms, thus moderately altering their core characteristics. The quality management movement provides an example of such an outcome. Quality management has pervasively altered the American corporate form along the dimensions of managerial technology and authority, but has not radically altered the basic contours of the corporation itself.

A third area of inquiry that our perspective invites is at the micro-level of analysis. Organizational sociology over the past two decades has largely deserted analyses of the internal workings of organizations, leaving such investigations to organizational psychologists, organizational behavior specialists, and assorted other disciplines. The action for organizational sociologists is on the macro side of things, in and between organizational fields, or at least at the level of interorganizational relations. With some exceptions (e.g. Katzenstein, 1998; Kurzman, 1998), current work that links social movements, organizational change, and institutional analysis also emphasizes macro investigations and ignores the emergence and impact of social movements and new forms as they are experienced on the front lines of organizations. We believe this to be a shortcoming that can be addressed in a number of ways. One strategy would be comparative case studies on the impact of social movements and new forms in particular organizations. Such studies could capture individual- and group-level adaptations and resistances to such processes. Another strategy would involve studies that link social movement repertoires within organizations to repertoires and other cultural resources in organizational fields. Yet another strategy would be investigations of the full range of politics – whether collective or not, organized or dispersed – that unfold in organizations. The goal of this strategy would be to link political repertoires in organizations to those that exist in relevant organizational fields and in wider societies. Both of these later strategies could begin to join the macro and micro analysis of the politics of organizational change as a single endeavor with multiple layers and integrated levels of analysis.

In conclusion, approaching the construction of new forms as a political process provides a wide-angle lens on organizational politics and change, and also deepens and extends political sociology and the study of social conflict. Davis & McAdam (2000) show how a social movement and collective action approach could amplify our analysis of organizational change. Our chapter underscores political processes – especially social movements and other types of collective action – as core mechanisms of organizational change, rather than a phenomena relegated either theoretically or empirically to the margins. A broad conception of the politics, social movements and collective action in and surrounding organizations, could very well redirect and reshape the future of organization theory itself.

ACKNOWLEDGMENTS

Barry Staw and Robert Sutton provided helpful suggestions and encouragement. We thank Galaye Debebe and Julia Welch of the University of Michigan, and students in the Politics of Organizations graduate seminar at the University of Arizona (led by Calvin Morrill and Mayer Zald) for providing feedback on some of the background ideas used in this chapter. We are grateful to our respective universities for their support. Additionally, Hayagreeva Rao thanks University of Michigan's Business School for their generous support in the form of a visiting professorship.

REFERENCES

Abbot, A. (1988). *The Systems of the Professions: An Essay on the Division of Expert Labor.* Chicago: University of Chicago Press.

Aldrich, H. E. (1999). *Organizations Evolving.* San Francisco: Sage.

Avruch, K. (1991). Introduction: Culture and Conflict Resolution. In: K. Avruch, P. W. Black & J. A. Scimecca (Eds), *Conflict Resolution: Cross-Cultural Perspectives* (pp. 1–18). NY: Greenwood Press.

Baum, J. A. C., & Oliver, C. (1992). Institutional Embeddedness and the Dynamics of Organizational Populations, *American Sociological Review, 57,* 540–549.

Baum, J. A. C., & Powell, W. W. (1995). Cultivating an Institutional Ecology: Comment on Hannan, Carroll, Dundas and Torres, *American Sociological Review, 50,* 529–538.

Baum, J. A. C. (1996). Organizational Ecology. In: S. Clegg & C. Hardy (Eds), *Handbook of Organization Studies,* New York: Oxford.

Brint, S., & Karabell, J. (1991). Institutional Origins and Transformations: The Case of American Community Colleges. In: W. W. Powell & P. DiMaggio, *The New Institutionalism in Organizational Analysis* (pp. 337–360). Chicago: University of Chicago Press.

Carroll & Swaminathan, (1998). Why the Micro-Brewery Movement: The Organizational Dynamics of Resource Partitioning in the American Brewing Industry After Prohibition, University of California at Berkeley.

Chase, S., & Schlink, F. (1927). *Your Money's Worth,* New York.

Clemens, E. (1993). Organizational Repertoires and Institutional Change: Women's Groups and the Transformation of American Politics, 1890–1920. *American Journal of Sociology, 98,* 755–798.

Coase, R. (1960). The Problem of Social Cost, *3, Journal of Law and Economics,* 1–44.

Cochrane, R. C. (1966). *Measures for Progress: A History of the National Bureau of Standards,* Washington, DC: Department of Commerce.

Cole, R. (1999). *Managing Quality Fads: How American Business Learned to Play the Quality Game,* Oxford University Press.

Coogler, O. J. (1978). *Structured Mediation in Divorce Settlement: A Handbook for Marital Mediators.* Lexington, MA: Lexington Books.

Danzig, Richard. (1974). Towards the Creation of a Complimentary, Decentralized System of Criminal Justice. *Stanford Law Review, 26,* 1–54.

Davis, G. F., & McAdam, D. Corporations, Classes, and Social Movements after Managerialism. *Research in Organizational Behavior,* Forthcoming.

Delacroix, J., & Rao, H. (1994). Externalities and Ecological Theory: Unbundling Density Dependence. In: J. A. C. Baum & J. V. Singh, (Eds), *Evolutionary Dynamics of Organizations,* (pp. 255–268). New York, N.Y.: Oxford University Press.

DiMaggio, P. J. (1988). Interest and Agency in Institutional Theory. In: L. G. Zucker (Eds), *Institutional Patterns and Organizations: Culture and Environment,* (pp. 3–21). Cambridge, MA: Ballinger.

DiMaggio, P. J. (1991). Constructing an Organizational Field as a Professional Project. In: W. W.
    Powell & Paul J. DiMaggio (Eds), *The New Institutionalism in Organizational Analysis*,
    (pp. 267–292). Chicago: University of Chicago Press.
DiMaggio, P. J. (1994). Culture and Economy. In: N. J. Smelser & R. Swedberg (Eds), *The
    Handbook of Economic Sociology*, (pp. 27–57). New York: Russell Sage.
DiMaggio, P. J., & W. W. Powell (1983). The Iron Cage Revisited: Institutional Isomorphism and
    Collective Rationality in Organizational Fields. *American Sociological Review, 48*,
    147–160.
DiMaggio, P. J., & W. W. Powell (1991). Introduction. In: W. W. Powell. & P. J. DiMaggio (Eds),
    The New Institutionalism in Organizational Analysis, (pp. 1–38). Chicago: University of
    Chicago Press.
Fisher, E. A. (1975). Community Courts: An Alternative to Conventional Adjudication. *American
    University Law Review, 24*, 1253–1291.
Fligstein, N. (1996a). How to Make a Market: Reflections on the Attempt to Create a Single
    Market in the European Union. *American Journal of Sociology, 102*, 1–33.
Fligstein, N. (1996b). Markets as Politics: A Political Cultural Approach to Market Institutions.
    American Sociological Review, 61, 656–673.
Flink, J. J. (1970) *America Adopts the Automobile*, 1895–1910, Cambridge: MIT Press.
Friedland, R., & Alford, R. R. (1991). Bringing Society Back In: Symbols, Practices, and
    Institutional Contradictions. In: W. W. Powell & P. J. DiMaggio. *The New Institutionalism
    in Organizational Analysis*, (pp. 232–262). Chicago: University of Chicago Press.
Gamson, W. (1990). *The Strategy of Social Protest*. Belmont, CA: Wadsworth. (First published in
    1975 Dorsey Press, Homewood, IL.)
Hannan, M. T., & Carroll, G. R. (1992). *Dynamics of Organizational Populations*. New York:
    Oxford University Press.
Hannan, M. T., & Freeman, J. (1989). *Organizational Ecology*. Cambridge, MA: Belknap Press.
Harrington, C. B. (1985). *Shadow Justice: The Ideology and Institutionalization of Alternatives to
    Court*. Westport, CT: Greenwood Press.
Haveman, H., & Rao, H. (1997). Structuring a Theory of Moral Sentiments: Institutional-
    Organization Co-Evolution in the Early Thrift Industry, *American Journal of Sociology, 6*,,
    1606–1651.
Hirsch, P. M. (1986). From Ambushes to Golden Parachutes: Corporate Takeovers as an Instance
    of Cultural Framing and Institutional Reintegration. *American Journal of Sociology, 91*,
    801–937.
Hybels, R. C, Ryan, A., & Barley, S. (1994) Alliances, Legitimation and Founding Rates in the
    U.S. Biotechnology Field, 1971–1989, Academy of Management Conference, Dallas, TX.
Katzenstein, M. F. (1998). Stepsisters: Feminist Movement Activism in Different Institutional
    Spaces. In: D. S. Meyer & S. Tarrow (Eds), *The Social Movement Society: Contentious
    Politics for a New Century*, (pp. 195–216). Totowa, NJ: Rowman and Littlefield.
Kleinman, S. (1996). *Opposing Ambitions: Gender and Identity in an Alternative Organization*.
    Chicago: University of Chicago Press.
Kurzman, C. (1998). Organizational Opportunity and Social Movement Mobilization: A
    Comparative Analysis of Four Religious Movements. *Mobilization, 3*, 23–49.
Lieberman, J. K. (1981). *The Litigious Society*. NY: Basic Books.
Lounsbury, M., Hirsch, P. M., & Ventresca, M. (1999). Social Movement Formalization and the
    Political Structuring of Discourse and Practice: The Co-Evolution of Recycling and the
    Solid Waste Management Field. Unpublished Manuscript, School of Industrial and Labor
    Relations, Cornell University.

Lowy, M. J. (1973). Modernizing the American Legal System: An Example of the Peaceful Use of Anthropology. *Human Organization, 32,* 205–209.

Mann, Michael. (1986). *The Sources of Social Power, Volume 1: A History of Power from the Beginning to A. D.1760.* Cambridge, England: Cambridge University of Press.

March, J. G., & Olsen, J. (1989). *Rediscovering Institutions.* NY: Free Press.

Mayer, T., & Mayer, G. (1985). HMO's Origins and Development, *New England Journal of Medicine, 32* (9), 590–595.

McAdam, D. (1994). Culture and Social Movements. In: E. Larana, H. Johnston & J. R. Gusfield (Eds), *New Social Movements,* (pp. 36–57).

McAdam, D. (1995). 'Initiator' and 'Spin-off' Movements: Diffusion Processes in Protest Cycles'. In: Mark Traugott (Ed.), *Repertoires and Cycles of Collective Action,* (pp. 217–239). Durham, NC: Duke University Press.

McAdam, D., McCarthy, J. D., & Zald, M. N. (1996). Introduction: Opportunities, Mobilizing Structures, and Framing Processes – Toward a Synthetic, Comparative Perspective on Social Movements. In: D. McAdam, J. D. McCarthy & M. N. Zald. *Comparative Perspectives on Social Movements: Political Opportunities, Mobilizing Structures and Cultural Framings* (pp. 1–20). Cambridge, England: Cambridge University Press.

McCarthy, J. D., & Wolfson, M. (1992). Consensus Movements, Conflict Movements and the Cooptation of Civic and State Infrastructures. In: A. D. Morris & C. McClurg Mueller (Eds), *Frontiers in Social Movement Theory,* (pp. 273–298). New Haven, CT: Yale University Press.

McCarthy, J. D., & Zald, M. N. (1977). Resource Mobilization and Social Movements: A Partial Theory. *American Journal of Sociology, 82,* 1212–1241.

McEwen, C. A., Mather, L., & Maiman, R. J. (1984). Lawyers, Mediation, and The Management of Divorce Practice. *Law & Society Review, 28,* 149–187.

Meyer, Meyer, J. W., & Rowan, B. (1977). Institutionalized Organizations: Formal Structure as Myth and Ceremony. *American Journal of Sociology, 83,* 340–363.

Milgrom, P., & Roberts, J. (1982) Predation, Reputation and Entry Deterrence, *Journal of Economic Theory, 27,* 280–312.

Milne, A., & Folberg, J. (1988). The Theory and Practice of Divorce Mediation: An Overview. In: J. Folberg & A. Milne (Ed.), *Divorce Mediation: Theory and Practice,* (pp. 3–26). NY: Guilford Press.

Morrill, C. Forthcoming. Institutional Change and Interstitial Emergence: The Growth of Alternative Dispute Resolution in American Law, 1965–1995. In: W. W. Powell & D. L. Jones, *Bending the Bars of the Iron Cage: Institutional Dynamics and Processes.* Chicago: University of Chicago Press.

Nelson, R. R., & Winter, S. G. (1982). *An Evolutionary Theory of Economic Change.* Cambridge, MA: Belknap Press.

Oliver, C. (1992) The Antecedents of Deinstitutionalization. *Organization Studies, 13,* 563–588.

Olson, M. (1965) *The Logic of Collective Action,* Cambridge, MA: Harvard University Press.

Powell, W. W. (1991). Expanding the Scope of Institutional Analysis. In: W. W. Powell & P. J. DiMaggio (Ed.), *The New Institutionalism in Organizational Analysis* (pp. 183–203). Chicago: University of Chicago Press.

Ray, L. (1982a). *Alternative Dispute Resolution: Bane or Boon to Attorneys?* Washington D.C.: American Bar Association.

Ray, L. (1982b). *Alternative Dispute Resolution: Mediation and the Law: Will Reason Prevail?* Washington D.C.: American Bar Association.

Romano, R. (1993), Public Pension Fund Activism, *Columbia Law Review, 93,* 795–953.

Rao, H. (1998). Caveat Emptor: The Construction of Nonprofit Consumer Watchdog Organizations. *American Journal of Sociology, 103*, 912–961.

Rao, H. (1998). Tests Tell: Reliability Contests and the Legitimation of the Automobile in America. Emory University.

Rao, H., & Singh, J. (1999). Types of Variation in Organizational Populations: The Speciation of New Organizational Forms. (Forthcoming). In: J. A. C. Baum & B. McKelvey (Eds), *Variations in Organization Science: In Honor of Donald T. Campbell*, (pp. 63–78). Sage Publications.

Samson, P. (1980) *The Emergence of a Consumer Interest in America*, University of Chicago Ph.D. thesis.

Sander, F. E. A. (1976). Varieties of Dispute Processing. *Federal Rules Decisions, 70*, 111-134.

Schmalensee, R. (1983). Product Differentiation Advantages of Pioneering Brands. *American Economic Review*, Vol. 72, 349–365.

Scott, W. R. (1995). *Institutions and Organizations*. Newbury Park, CA: Sage.

Snow, D. A., & Benford, R. D. (1992). Master Frames and Cycles of Protest. In: A. D. Morris & C. McClung Mueller (Eds), *Frontiers in Social Movement Theory*, (pp. 133-155). New Haven, CT: Yale University Press.

Starr, Paul. (1982). *The Social Transformation of American Medicine: The Rise of a Sovereign Profession and the Making of a Vast Industry*. NY: Basic Books.

Stinchcombe, A. L. (1965). Social Structure and Organizations. In: J. G. March (Ed.),*Handbook of Organizations*, (pp. 142–193). NY: Rand McNally.

Stinchcombe, A. L. (1997). On the virtues of the old institutionalism. *Annual Review of Sociology, 23*, 1–18.

Swaminathan, A., & Wade, J. B. (Forthcoming). Social Movement Theory and the Evolution of New Organizational Forms. In: C. B. Schoonhoven & E. Romanelli. *The Entrepreneurship Dynamic in Industrial Evolution*, Stanford, CA: Stanford University Press.

Tarrow, S. (1989). *Democracy and Disorder: Protest and Politics in Italy, 1965–1975*. Oxford, England: Oxford University Press.

Thomas, R. P. (1977). *An Analysis of the Patterns of Growth of the Automobile Industry, 1895–1929*, New York: Arno Press.

Tilly, C. (1978). *From Mobilization to Revolution*. Reading, MA: Addison-Wesley.

Tomasic, R. (1982). Mediation as an Alternative to Adjudication: Rhetoric and Reality in the Neighborhood Justice Movement. In: R. Tomasic & M. M. Feeley (Eds), *Neighborhood Justice: Assessment of an Emerging Idea*, (pp. 215–248). NY: Longman.

Useem, B. & Zald, M. (1982). From pressure group to social movement: organizational dilemmas of the effort to promote nuclear power, *Social Problems*, December. 144–156.

Voss, K. (1996). The Collapse of a Social Movement: The Interplay of Mobilizing Structures, Framing and Political Opportunities in the Knights of Labor. In: D. McAdam, J. D. McCarthy & M. N. Zald (Eds), *Comparative Perspectives on Social Movements: Political Opportunities, Mobilizing Structures, and Cultural Framings*, (pp. 227–258). Cambridge, England: Cambridge University Press.

Weitzman, L. (1985). *The Divorce Revolution: The Unexpected Social and Economic Consequences for Women and Children in America*. NY: Free Press.

Wholey, D., Christianson, J., & Sanchez, S., (1993). The Effect of Physician and Corporate Interests on the Formation of Health Maintenance Organizations, *American Journal of Sociology, 99*, 164–200.

Wilensky, H. (1964). The Professionalization of Everyone. *American Journal of Sociology, 70*, 137–158.

Zald, M. N. (1996). Culture, Ideology, and Strategic Framing. In: Do. McAdam, J. D. McCarthy & M. N. Zald (Eds), *Comparative Perspectives on Social Movements: Political Opportunities, Mobilizing Structures, and Cultural Framings*, (pp. 261–274). Cambridge, England: Cambridge University Press.

Zald, M, N., & Berger, M. A. (1978). Social Movements in Organizations: Coup d'Etat, Insurgency and Mass Movements. *American Journal of Sociology, 83*, 823–861.

Zald, M. N., & McCarthy, J. D. (1980). Social Movement Industries: Competition and Conflict Among Movement Organizations. In: L. Kriesberg (Ed.), *Research in Social Movements: Conflicts and Change*, Volume 3, (pp. 1–20). Greenwich, CT: JAI Press Inc.

THE KIBBUTZ FOR ORGANIZATIONAL BEHAVIOR

Tal Simons and Paul Ingram

ABSTRACT

The kibbutz is the equivalent of a laboratory for organization science. Its scope of activities, which includes agricultural and industrial production, the socialization and education of children, management of communal consumption, and national defense, is broader than any other organization. It therefore demonstrates the potential to extend organization to areas of life traditionally governed by other institutions. The kibbutz has also experimented with a number of practices aimed at balancing equality with progress. The success of the kibbutz by paying all participants the same, regularly rotating managers out of their posts, and eschewing hierarchy challenges widely held beliefs about motivation, control and coordination in organizations. Some efforts at equality failed, notably those regarding gender, but even the kibbutz's failures are informative about organizations. We analyze and integrate research on kibbutz structure, practices and external relationships in order to distill lessons for organization behavior.

The authors' contributions were equal and the order of authorship was randomly determined.

Research in Organizational Behaviour, Volume 22, pages 283–343.
ISBN: 0–7623–0641–6

Of the successful communes that are not cemented by loyalty to a ruling God, the Israeli kibbutz is perhaps the most influential and long-lived. (Tiger & Shepher, 1975, preface).

INTRODUCTION

As much as any twentieth-century organizational form, the kibbutz has captured the imagination and attention of the public and the research community. Countless books, papers and theses in fields such as psychology, sociology, economics, anthropology, political science, and education have focused on the kibbutz. Volunteering on a kibbutz has been a rite of passage for tens of thousands of young people, Jews and Gentiles, from around the globe. The political, military, and economic history of Israel has, at least until recently, given a starring role to the kibbutz. Even today, when a common perception is that the kibbutz has been marginalized, the organizational form still receives significant coverage from the world's major newspapers (see, for example, the front-page article in the *New York Times*, April 18, 1998).

Given all of the analysis of this organizational form, the question we address in this chapter is natural: What can be learned from the kibbutz about organizations and behavior within them? Yet, most kibbutz researchers have not only failed to answer this question, but have acted as though it were illegitimate. These researchers, who were often also kibbutz members, have emphasized the idiosyncrasy of kibbutz experience instead of the possibility of generalizing from the kibbutz to other organizational forms. They have characterized the kibbutz as a unique social artifact to be analyzed on its own terms, rather than as a type of organization. In contrast, we take the position that there can be real gains to organization science by thinking about kibbutzim (plural) as 'normal', at least in the sense of demonstrating the operation of some structures, processes and practices, which in different degrees and combinations, are relevant to other organizations.[1]

At the same time we try to generalize from the kibbutz to other organizations, we give full recognition to the ways that kibbutzim are different from other organizations. Indeed, it is these differences that account for the public and scholarly interest in kibbutzim, and which create the unusual conditions that make kibbutz experience so valuable as a laboratory for organization science. The fundamental differences between kibbutzim and many other organizations, particularly the American organizations that are the focus of so much organizational research, flow from the utopian-socialist ideology of the kibbutzim. Utopianism fascinates the Western world as a response to the fundamental tension of modernity, that between merit and equality (Ben-Rafael, 1997). Reference to utopia is fed by the common criticism that Western society sacrifices too much equality in the interest of progress. The kibbutz may be the finest example for those who claim a better balance can be struck between equality and progress. Against what is perceived as the natural tendency of communes and collectives towards oligarchy, kibbutzim have maintained a very-high level of direct democracy for decades. The case for the kibbutz is also strong on the criteria of progress. The feasible comparisons show that kibbutzim are more productive than the organizational forms they compete with. The record of kibbutzim for both innovation and adaptation to technological change is good. The evidence for human development is similarly impressive, with kibbutz members being over-represented in parliament and the elite units of the army, and (in some research) scoring better than the non-kibbutz population of Israel in tests of intellectual ability.

For scholars of organization, society's general interest in utopianism should be magnified, because that ideology gives the most prominent role to organizations. In capitalism the primary mechanism of control is the market and in scientific socialism it is the state, but in utopianism, organizations serve this role. New utopians such as Jones (1982) echo the old anarchist model of an institutional structure absent a central government, with cooperative organizations as the bedrock of social order. The kibbutz illustrates this fundamental role of organization: the kibbutz life, from cradle to grave, is the organized life. The influence of kibbutzim on their members has traditionally been 'total' in that the scope of the organization encompasses all aspects of life. The extensiveness of organizational influence on the kibbutz represents part of the unique contribution of kibbutz experience to organizational behavior. We are aware of no other context where there has been so much systematic experimentation with the extension of organization into areas of life traditionally governed by other institutions. Cooking and eating, leisure, child-rearing, and even power relations between the sexes have at times been within the scope of these organizations. The scope of organizational influence on the kibbutz shows organizational behavior applied to new tasks, and provides an unusual manipulation of some of the things that affect commitment and identification to the organization. It also provides a fresh look at, for example, work groups. A work group on the kibbutz may consist of members who have known each other all their lives, and who have extensive opportunities for interaction outside of work.

Ideology also conditioned the relationships between kibbutzim and their environment. Throughout their history, kibbutzim have operated in a mixed economy, which contained powerful organizational forms representing capitalist and utopian ideologies. As a result, there were competing ideological influences on the participants and potential participants of kibbutzim, and kibbutzim therefore made significant efforts at individual socialization. Their efforts in this regard are informative of the potential of organizations to affect individual ideology. Similarly, ideology was salient in kibbutzim interorganizational relations, with organizations representing rival ideologies often operating to discourage or change kibbutzim, while organizations sympathetic to utopianism operated to help them. These processes had implication for the internal operations of kibbutzim, but also for the dynamics of ideological belief and practice in the wider society. Kibbutz research therefore provides a rare opportunity to see the role of formal organizations in the rise and fall of ideologies.

In sum, the public and researchers have found kibbutzim interesting because of their utopian ideology, which has three implications that make kibbutzim fertile ground for discovering certain things about organizations. First, the ideology recommends a set of practices designed to achieve participant equality. These practices demonstrate the organizational effect of extreme levels of features, like job rotation and equal pay, that exist to some extent in many other organizations. Second, the ideology makes organization the preeminent mechanism of social control, extending the scope of organization to new domains and creating organizations that approach completeness in their influence on their members. Third, the ideology was in conflict with others in the relevant environment, creating the variance necessary to identify the role of ideology in organization-environment relationships.

The rest of this chapter describes research on the kibbutz and draws conclusions about what that research says about organizations broadly. Reflecting our assertion that there are gains from treating the kibbutz as a 'normal' organization, we structure our review of kibbutz research using an open systems model of the type that will be familiar to all organizational researchers. We begin inside the organization, addressing first the research on kibbutz structure, and then research on kibbutz work. Then we consider the community maintenance issues of kibbutz organization. Finally we move outside the organization to consider kibbutz-environment relationships and then we consider the interdependence of the internal organization and the environment by analyzing the kibbutz experience of organizational change. Before tackling the organizational research on kibbutzim, however, we briefly describe the organizational form and its history.

KIBBUTZ DESCRIPTION AND HISTORY

The first kibbutz, Degania on the shores of Lake Galilee, was established in 1910 by immigrants from Germany, Poland, Galitzia and Russia. It was among a number of organizational forms that contended to address the challenges faced by Jewish immigrants to Palestine, namely the needs to develop the capacity to perform manual work, to find work, and to make some meaningful claim on the land. Degania was unique among the alternative organizational forms because it combined these characteristics: communal production and consumption, a system of communal child-care, and permanence in population and in location on land owned by the Jewish National Fund. Its emergence as an archetype for settlement is attributable to practical and ideological factors. Degania was an initial economic success, turning a small profit in its earliest years, in contrast with the typical experience of Jewish agricultural settlements in Palestine. It did so while reflecting basic ideological tenets of the 'conquest of labor', which had come to be shared by much of the Jewish population of Palestine. The first component of the conquest of labor was the 'Religion of Work' philosophy promoted by A. D. Gordon, which held that physical labor was a form of art and that moral elevation through work required the full attention of a worker who was free from hierarchical supervision. The second component was the belief that only by working the land themselves could Jews develop a moral claim on the land of Palestine. These tenets constrained the Jew to be "neither the exploited nor the exploiter" (Gordon, 1938: 63).

After Degania took root, the population of kibbutzim grew in fits and starts, often as a function of immigration, war, and other major events in Palestine. Figure 1 displays the number of kibbutzim, and the total population of the kibbutz movement over time. The figure indicates that the growth of the kibbutz movement is disjointed, with growth much steeper before 1950 than after. We have argued that this pattern of growth reflects the role of kibbutzim for the generation of public order. Before 1948, kibbutzim played key roles in the absorption of immigrants and the defense of the Jewish population of Palestine. After 1950, the new Israeli State assumed these roles, undermining part of the motivation for the existence and growth of the kibbutz movement (Simons & Ingram, 1999). Still, it is notable that there is growth in both number and population of kibbutzim in the fifty years of the Israeli State. In the context of recent discourse that the kibbutz movement is declining it is important to recognize that even in the last fifteen years, the number and population of kibbutzim have been stable. The figure may, however, mask a decline in the *relative* significance of the kibbutz to Israeli society and economy. At the founding of the State in May 1948, kibbutzim accounted for about 8% of the

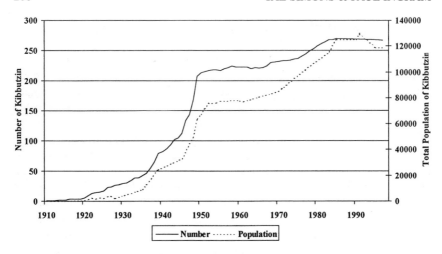

Fig. 1. Number and Population of Kibbutzim

Jewish population of Israel; in 1997 they accounted for only 2% (Near, 1997, Appendix 2).

A set of organizing practices, derived from ideology, delineate the boundaries of the kibbutz as an organizational form. Kibbutzim differ from other cooperative enterprises in Israel by their permanence of place and population, and from other rural settlements by their degree of communalism. All kibbutzim are permanent settlements, existing on land leased from the Jewish National Fund. Traditionally they all had common ownership and democratic management of financial affairs, communal consumption and child care, and a centralized labor allocation system, which emphasized job-rotation and the reliance on member (as opposed to hired) labor. Over time some of these practices have been relaxed. Starting in the 1950s many kibbutzim began to rely increasingly on hired labor, and the practice is now seldom questioned. In the 1970s there was a rapid move away from communal child-care to conventional family units on the kibbutz. As the economic activities of kibbutzim have diversified, particularly over the last three decades, there has been a transition from job-rotation to specialization of labor. Currently, some kibbutzim are altering their communality by giving families budgets to spend at their discretion on items such as food, clothing and entertainment.

With the exception of the most current changes in communality, which are still unfolding, the moves away from the traditional kibbutz can be seen as an evolution in the legitimated idea of what a kibbutz is, rather than fundamental disagreements which create different classes of kibbutzim. On other important ideological issues there were persistent splits among kibbutzim, and positions on these issues formed the basis for the grouping of kibbutzim into a number of political federations. The major questions had to do with the optimal size of a kibbutz, the appropriate economic activities, how tradeoffs between Zionism and socialism should be made, and to a lesser extent, what role Judaism should have on the kibbutz. Based on their positions on these questions, kibbutzim organized into four major federations which are described in Table 1.

ORGANIZATIONAL STRUCTURE

Kibbutz rationality as far as the management of its economy is concerned, applies only within the framework set by other, higher values. Etzioni (1980: 74).

We take two general lessons of organizational structure from research on the kibbutz. The first is that ideology creates a blueprint for organizing, such that ideological principles manifest themselves in organizational structures. The kibbutz serves to illustrate this general claim because its ideology is different from that of the capitalist organizations whose structures are most often studied. This difference highlights the ideological underpinnings of kibbutz structure, and provides the necessary variance to consider the more general effect of ideology on structure. The second lesson is on the necessity and interdependence of what Etzioni (1980) called the instrumental and expressive components of organization. Again, it is kibbutz ideology that facilitates studying this idea, but here it is not the uniqueness of kibbutz ideology, but a particular feature, its emphasis on expressive organizational components, that creates opportunities for scholarship. The interdependence of instrumental and expressive components of an organization affects the available options for organizational control, and thereby performance.

Ideology as an Influence on Structure

Our definition of ideology is not atypical, but now is the time to make it explicit. Ideology is ". . . a set of beliefs about the social world and how it operates, containing statements about the rightness of certain social arrangements and what actions would be undertaken in the light of those statements" (Wilson, 1973: 91–92). Ideology then, is both a cognitive map of sets of expectations and a scale of values in which standards and imperatives are proclaimed. It serves both as a clue to understanding and as a guide to action, developing in the minds of its adherents an image of the process by which desired changes can best be achieved.

The definition of ideology suggests that actors will pursue the ends their ideology values using means derived from their ideology. In this way, ideologies provide a set of first-order principles for organizational design.

Table 1.   Major Kibbutz Federations

Full name of federation	Ichud Hakvutzot Vehakibbutzim	Ha-Kibbutz Ha-Meuchad	Ha-Kibbutz Ha-Artzi	Ha-Kibbutz Ha-Dati
Referred to as	Ichud	Meuchad	Artzi	Dati
Federation development	Founded in 1929, merged with Meuchad to form Takam in 1980	Founded in 1927, merged with Ichud to form Takam in 1980	Founded in 1927	Founded in 1935
Archetypal kibbutz	Degania	Ein Herod	Beit Alpha	Tirat Zvi
Ideology	Moderate, non-marxist socialism, emphasizing Zionist goals	Doctrine of 'constructive socialsim', to expand the federation as the basis of a socialist society	Marxist, favoring a proletarian revolution after a constructive phase of Zionism	Socialism and Zionism combined with a commitment to Orthodox Judaism
Elements of kibbutz organization	Small kibbutzim (referred to as 'kvutzot'), based on agriculture	Large kibbutzim, with explicit reliance on both agriculture and industry	Heavy emphasis on member-socialization in youth movements, which created constraints on growth, employed a mixed economy	Employed technical and organizational 'innovations' to perform defense and agriculture within the constraints of Jewish law
Elements of association	Federative	Centralized, but with each kibbutz having economic autonomy	Strong central enforcement of democratically determined principles	Kibbutzim located in blocs to promote mutual assistance
% of kibbutzim in 1958	36	26	33	5
% of kibbutzim in 1993	62		31	7

Ideologies held by the designers of organizations are the primary source of the goals those designers have for their organizations. Ideologies also suggest which organizational configurations will be effective in attaining these goals. So, before other influences and considerations, ideology provides a blueprint for organization. We developed and illustrated this argument with reference to the kibbutz practice of reliance only on the labor of members (Simons & Ingram, 1997). Self-labor may be economically efficient in industries, such as transportation, where the supervision of hired labor is difficult (Russell, 1985). However, theoretical analysis (Izraeli & Groll, 1981), and empirical analysis at the level of the kibbutz population (Barkai, 1977) and the individual kibbutz (Ingram & Simons, 1999) all indicate that this practice was inefficient on the kibbutz. Self-labor on the kibbutz cannot be justified in objective efficiency terms, and indeed, this was never an argument for the practice. Rather, the practice was justified as a mechanism for achieving kibbutz members' ideological goals of self-actualization through work and avoiding the exploitation of others.

Etzioni (1980), in the classic study of kibbutz organizational structure, also identifies ideology as a fundamental influence on structure: "The very extensive commitment of the kibbutz to an elaborate set of values is a source of many organizational activities" (p. 60). He begins by analyzing the effect of the ideological value of equality of consumption to create the need for centralized organizational activity, and standardization. In a market society, individuals manage their own consumption, and money acts as the control. In the traditional kibbutz members had almost no money, with the kibbutz fulfilling their needs for consumption. This necessitates a set of centralized organizational activities to coordinate supply and demand of consumables, and manage their physical distribution. Kibbutzim also introduced the bureaucratic device of standardization to simplify the allocation of consumer goods, for example a rule that every male member will receive two work shirts each year. In evidence of the dynamic relationship between ideology and structure, Etzioni observed during his multi-year research a relaxation of kibbutzim's ideological commitment to equality of consumption and a corresponding simplification of the elements of organizational structure that managed consumption and distribution.

A variant on the claim that ideology provides a blueprint for organization is that rather than always leading action, ideology sometimes follows it, arising as a justification for previous behaviors (Perrow, 1986). The experience of kibbutzim is again suggestive in this regard. For example, hired labor has gradually increased and is now used by most kibbutzim, often extensively. Still, even though hired labor has been common for decades, kibbutz ideology has not shifted sufficiently that the practice is legitimate in the same way it is for capitalist organizations. Kibbutzim may express their ideological unease with the practices they adopt by modifying them to be less ideologically offensive. For hired labor, this typically means making concessions to employees with a goal of moderating what is seen as the exploitive nature of the employment relationship. Etzioni (1980) describes a kibbutz that needed hired labor to harvest an overproduction of peanuts, and divided all of the resultant profits among the employees, paying them two-and-a-half times the market rate for their labor. Our own interviews on a kibbutz which is viewed as being on the frontier of the trend to capitalist organizing principles revealed that even there, workers were paid more than the market rate, and given generous benefits.[2] The self-conscious employment of labor supports Saltman's (1983: 126) claim that on the kibbutz, "the pragmatic needs of the time have been constantly measured against the yardstick of ideological positions, and the latter have tended to adapt to the requirements of the former without radically changing its basic premise."

Instrumental and Expressive Components of Organization

Etzioni's (1980) analysis of kibbutz structure was based on a functional model he adapted from Parsons. Like Parsons, Etzioni identifies four functions that successful social systems must perform. The functions are performed by two categories of organizational sub-systems, the instrumental and the expressive. The instrumental category consists of the adaptive sub-system, which consists of activities such as production that relate the organization to its environment, and the managerial sub-system, including activities that allocate scarce resources for the attainment of goals. The expressive category consists of the integrative sub-system, which induces members to see each other as one social system, and the normative sub-system, which regulates the behavior of members. Etzioni (p. 49) provides this scintillating account of the interdependence of the systems:

> The four sub-systems are complementary to each other in the sense that action in each of them creates problems to be solved by the others. Adaptive activities create means which must be related to goals in order to acquire meaning. This 'meaning' is created and reinforced by the normative sub-system. The supply of means by adaptive activities is insufficient for meeting the demands of various goals internalized and institutionalized by the socializing activities of the normative sub-system. This creates the type of problems solved by the managerial sub-system, e.g. allocation. But every distribution of means and rewards creates frustrations as well as satisfactions. These tensions are disruptive to the social system and pose the type of problems handled by the integrative sub-system.

Etzioni's model is the basis of two compelling substantive arguments. The first relates organizational structure to a temporally driven cycle. Etzioni proposes that the 'differentiation of elites', by which he means the tendency of office-holders (organizational leaders) to limit their organizational participation to either instrumental or expressive functions, increases as organizations age. The causal logic behind this claim will resonate with anyone who has ever participated in or observed an organization from conception to maturity – as this evolution proceeds, the organization becomes more of a complete system in the sense of performing all of the necessary functions itself. As the achievement of the functions becomes an everyday expectation of the organization, a process of institutionalization occurs such that they become embedded in specific social roles and institutions. Kibbutzim, like high-tech startups, begin as charismatic movements, where participants do what it takes, across functions, to perpetuate and develop the organization. Eventually, if the organization is to survive, the systems that achieve its critical functions must congeal and become business as usual. Etzioni's evidence for this argument is interesting, although limited. He compares two kibbutzim, one young and one old, in terms of the likelihood that their officers who hold more than one-office span the boundary between the instrumental and expressive functions. In the older kibbutz, this almost never happens – a member of the Economic Committee may also be a member of the Security Committee, but is unlikely to sit on the Educational-Pedagogy Committee. In the young kibbutz, multiple-office holders span functional boundaries more often than not.

The second substantive argument that emerges from the expressive emphasis of the kibbutz concerns the creation of social control, and its role in organizational performance. Nee & Ingram (1998) propose a new institutional model of economic performance that puts the social control of work-groups in a primary position. In their model, economic performance is obtained if institutional structures are implemented that align the incentives faced by individuals with the demands of the environment. Organizations structure individual incentives with formal rules and informal norms. Formal organizational rules, such as a piece-rate or bonus system of pay, form the incentive environment faced by work groups, but it is the norms of work groups that exert the most immediate influence over individuals.

On the kibbutz, the emphasis on expressive functions, the activities that allow the individual member to perceive of herself "only as a portion of the entire community, and not as a self-sustaining entity" (Arian, 1968: 104), form the basis of powerful social control through norms. This is demonstrated in Warhurst's (1996) ethnography, aptly titled "high society in a workers' society." Warhurst describes a high-performing work group in a kibbutz plastic factory. The group represents an instance not explicitly foreseen by Nee and Ingram, in that there are no formal organizational rules to mediate between them and the market. The pace of work for the group was dictated "straight from the market," with members claiming that they "could feel" the pressures of the market. The group's experience indicates the problems that arise when the buffer of formal organizational rules is removed, as their informal decision-making processes were often overwhelmed. But Warhurst's point is to show the strength of social control for directing individual efforts to collective purposes. Formal control was completely absent, as indicated by the production manager of the kibbutz factory that was the group's home: "It's not my job to impose discipline on the line. If I'm working with other members there's no difference between us ... Discipline should come from the members themselves – self discipline" (p. 6). That the group members received social rewards for their performance was clearly evident as in the statements of group members that "you feel as if you're shining when you work in this place" (p. 10), and "loads of people on the kibbutz know how to appreciate this [group]" (p. 11). And the work group did not merely apply the social rewards and punishments that presented themselves from the close interaction of kibbutz life, but rather created their own sub-community, where the social bonds, and the capacity for social control, were even greater. The members would spend after-work hours in each other's homes, and would hold parties and barbecues, attended by group members and their families, that served to create a highly interdependent and cohesive group. The power of these social ties for motivating performance is clear in the statement of a member that "the reason I get up every morning is because of the people that I work with" (p. 13).

Moving beyond the kibbutz observed by Warhurst, Barkai (1987: 252) saw social control as part of the foundation of the high performance of kibbutzim. Social control operates on kibbutzim such that "absence from work, even for a legitimate reason, engenders feelings of discomfort and a sense of guilt; an individual who shirks his work responsibilities is severely criticized" (Talmon-Garber, 1972: 168). Work reputation on the kibbutz has been found to affect social esteem, prestige and the level of personal influence within the community (Macarov, 1975). Jobs that contribute most highly to the income of kibbutzim have been found to have the highest status (Vallier, 1983; Rosner, 1966; Ben-Rafael, 1988).

Finally, the grip of social control, and the resultant improvements to member motivation, can be linked to the processes of differentiation of the expressive and instrumental components identified by Etzioni (1980). The interdependence of functions in the young kibbutz, created by cross-office holding, and more generally, by the full participation of all members in the achievement of all functions, promotes social control. After all, social control of the type documented by Warhurst is really exchange between the expressive and instrumental domains, and is only possible if its subjects span those domains. In an older kibbutz, where individuals are more specialized in their functional contributions, social control is necessarily weakened. In response, "formal devices of control are developed to support, and to some degree to replace the informal mechanisms. The development of an organizational structure with a clear division of tasks and authority, as well as a center of decisions . . ." arises as a functional substitute for informal control (Etzioni, 1980: 164). Others see more potential for intense social control to persist into organizational maturity (Warhurst, 1998), but Etzioni's account has face-validity among some current kibbutz members. When we asked if shirkers on an older kibbutz received social punishments, we were told "it used to work that way in the old days, but not now."

WORK

"Work will heal us. In the center of all our hopes we must place work; our entire structure must be founded on labor." (Gordon, 1938: 56).

In kibbutzim ideological tenets determined the manner in which work was structured and managed. From socialism the ideas of equality and self-governance by the workers were most influential in shaping the way work was planned and performed. The motivation of members in the absence of differential material rewards was based on the acceptance of work as an end in its own right. Social status was associated with work, devoted workers received the community's respect and admiration. Job rotation and democratic decision-making processes in the workplace were pivotal in maintaining equality among members.

According to Rosner (1998), the organization of work in the kibbutz raises three key questions, each of which presents a dilemma between ideology and efficiency. In the absence of monetary remuneration, and given that the kibbutz members' needs are provided for regardless of work performance, what motivates them to work hard? Second, since a market mechanism can not be relied upon to determine supply and demand of labor, and since coercion is not an option either, what is the mechanism that ensures both an efficient (for the kibbutz) and a satisfying (for the member) allocation of the available work force? Lastly, given the democratic nature of the organization of work in the kibbutz, can it be managed efficiently ensuring economic and professional performance?

Motivation

One form of incentives typical of capitalist organizations, differential financial rewards, are not acceptable on the kibbutz.[3] Another motivational tool employed in capitalist organizations, hierarchical authority to enforce a variety of sanctions, is similarly taboo. Reflecting principles of equality among members and self-management, managers cannot discipline workers who are kibbutz members (Warhurst, 1996b). Thus, maintenance of high levels of human effort must be obtained by means other than those employed in the familiar organizations of Western capitalism. What, then, motivates kibbutz members' decision whether and how much effort to exert on the job or alternatively, to free-ride on the effort invested by others?

The complete severance of the connection between job performance and income, between work and organizational rewards and penalties seems, according to some analysts, to remove all motivation for individual perform-ance, and thereby doom the kibbutz to a speedy failure (Helman, 1994; Putterman, 1983). The evidence shows the contrary. A number of studies indicate that kibbutzim achieve high levels of profit per worker and high labor productivity when compared with the private sector in Israel (Kanovsky, 1966; Tannenbaum, Kavcic, Rosner, Vianello & Wieser, 1977; Barkai, 1977; Don, 1988; Near, 1997). Barkai's (1977) analysis of fifteen years of audited annual financial reports supported the conclusion that "the 6.2% annual average gain given by the varying-weights index for the kibbutz production sector is significantly higher than that for the economy as a whole (4.6%)" (p. 136). In 1977 the average productivity per kibbutz worker was 14% higher than in Israeli industry as a whole (Near, 1997: 241). Additional studies, mostly by economists interested in the 'incentive conundrum', find higher productivity of kibbutz workers relative to workers in the economy at large (Sadan, 1976; Barkai, 1978; 1987; Don, 1988).

Research on the relationship between workers' motivation and performance was conducted in kibbutz industry and agriculture, and investigated various theoretical issues similar to those studied in 'conventional' organizations. Leviatan and Eden (1980) report on a survey of more than 600 workers and managers in kibbutz plants (p. 27) and agricultural branches (p. 33). They test an elaborate theoretical model that includes seven major groups of variables, which follow one another in a causal flow towards the final outcome – organizational effectiveness. Of particular interest here are the individual attitudinal variables, which were based on both self-reporting and mangers' evaluations. These variables captured attitudes that reflect participants' internalization of organizational goals, indicated for example by "expressions of motivations to achieve the objectives of the organization." These attitudes were found to affect organizational effectiveness, measured by the rate of capital return and income per workday.

The general conclusion from the series of studies reported in *Work and Organization in Kibbutz Industry* emphasized the matching between organizational features and participant attitudes: "the more effective plants are those in which the organizational patterns and the expectations of kibbutz members are more congruent" (Rosner & Palgi, 1980: 29). For example, plants were more effective when they displayed a level of participative decision making that matched participants' expectation. So, the emergent position is consistent with influential arguments on the necessity of congruence of organizational components for effectiveness (Nadler & Tushman, 1997). However, the kibbutz research contributes to those familiar ideas by expanding the known set of effective organizational configurations, making concrete the open-system concept of equifinality. The kibbutz experience also shows that there is no inherent contradiction between organizing according to an ideology of no financial incentives and organizational performance.

Support for the congruence concept is found at the micro level in studies that examine the relationship between workers' values, their attitudes and work outcomes (Eden, 1975; Ronen, 1978). Ronen's (1978: 85) thesis is that "the main components of an individual's motivational set and job attitude depend largely on the system of social values with which he approaches the work environment, and the organizational reward system." Values are aggregated in two categories, one consisting of material wealth, prestige and power (labeled 'aggrandizement') and the second consisting of equalitarian, humanitarian, aesthetic, and intellectual values (labeled 'self-realization'). He hypothesizes that kibbutz workers and private sector workers will exhibit different values, different sources of job satisfaction (intrinsic vs. extrinsic) and a difference in the contribution of the contrasting values to overall job satisfaction and workers' evaluation of the reward system. Of the 500 questionnaires sent to kibbutz and private industrial organizations, those returned usable included 135 from kibbutz workers and 187 from employees of private firms. Measures included the Human Value Index, the Job Description Index (JDI), and the Brayfield-Rothe questionnaire for overall job satisfaction. Kibbutz workers scored significantly higher on self-realization values than the private sector workers, who in turn scored significantly higher on aggrandizement values. Both results held when samples were sub-divided by job level, seniority, age, education and birthplace, providing even stronger support to the hypothesis. Similarly, kibbutz workers demonstrated significantly higher satisfaction with the intrinsic aspects of their job and the private sector workers demonstrated significantly higher satisfaction with the extrinsic aspects of their job, again strengthened by controlling for demographic and job characteristics. The two groups also differed on the importance attributed to different job facets in forming overall job satisfaction. Kibbutz workers placed higher importance on intrinsic job facets while private sector workers placed higher importance on extrinsic job facets.

Ronen's (1978) conclusions from this study are that basic personal values of the individual affect their reaction to the work environment, and that overall job satisfaction and satisfaction with intrinsic or extrinsic aspects of the job are evaluated partially by the values the individuals hold. These conclusions are supported by another study in a kibbutz setting which showed that the effect of an incentive on motivation is more positive when the incentive is of a type (e.g. intrinsic or extrinsic) that is commensurate with a worker's expectations (Eden, 1975). Combined, these studies help to explain the effectiveness of the kibbutz worker in the face of the kibbutz ideological framework by demonstrating the efficacy of a match between the intrinsic rewards offered by the kibbutz, and the values of kibbutz workers.

While kibbutz members demonstrate a greater emphasis on intrinsic rewards than do other workers, there is evidence that the basic inputs to job satisfaction are similar for kibbutz members and others. Ronen (1977) administered the JDI to kibbutz and non-kibbutz workers in organizations that were matched on industry, size, industrialization level and organizational structure. The order of importance of the different job satisfaction facets was determined by correlating each facet with two overall job satisfaction indices for each group. The results for the two groups were almost identical: satisfaction with the work itself followed by satisfaction with supervision, promotion and co-workers for kibbutz workers; for the non- kibbutz workers the only difference was that satisfaction with promotion preceded supervision. Features of the similarity of the inputs to job satisfaction, particularly the unimportance of pay for all subjects, indicate an opportunity to apply features of the kibbutz motivational model to other organizations.

Another contribution to understanding of kibbutz motivation using mainstream models comes from Macarov (1972, 1975). He applied Hertzberg's two-factor model and found evidence of motivators and hygiene factors among kibbutz workers. Macarov (1972) surveyed 219 kibbutz members from both service (e.g. education, child-care, food preparation) and production (agriculture and industry) branches. After eliminating those factors that were mentioned by less than 10% of the respondents, four which resulted in more satisfaction than dissatisfaction were the work itself, achievement, interpersonal relations and responsibility. One factor resulting in more dissatisfaction than satisfaction was that of working conditions. Interpersonal relations that in Hertzberg's model belong to the hygiene factor were for the kibbutz workers a motivator. This reflects the centrality of social rewards in the kibbutz working environment. Macarov's (1972: 492) provocative conclusion is that "salary itself may often be overrated as a work motivator."

The question of what motivates kibbutz members to work as hard and efficiently as they do, without material rewards, still begs an answer. The statement, "I don't think that our economic intuition is our secret charm; it's our social spirit which preserved us" (Lieblich, 1981: 193), provides a hint to the answer. This position is expanded towards a more full explanation when Barkai (1987: 252) argues "the work norm and work discipline, informal social control over quality of performance, and a mechanism of self-selection can explain the high degree of motivation pushing kibbutz members to the frontier of feasible performance." Selection of members involves self-selection of individuals believing that material benefits are of minor importance. Over time this builds a population with a bias toward non-pecuniary stimuli and work discipline. As Eden (1975: 357) concluded, "workers self-select themselves into jobs that offer incentives which they are motivated to seek." This tendency is reinforced by socialization of kibbutz-born members and the voluntary aspect of the community that allows anyone who cannot adjust or tolerate the formal and informal rules of the kibbutz to leave. Commitment to the work norm and the discipline to put in 'an honest day's work' are instated in kibbutz members in the socialization process. Lastly, informal social control serves as an efficient and powerful mechanism, relying on individuals' need for respect and approval from the community. The mechanism of social control is demonstrated in a comparative study of managerial practices in five countries (US, Austria, Italy, Yugoslavia and Israel). Kibbutz workers favored the high opinion of co-workers more frequently than any other optional reward (e.g. high opinion of superior, praise from superior) for good work. It was also the highest favored item in comparison to other countries (Tannenbaum et al., 1977). Combined, the processes of selection, socialization, and social control yield a community of individuals strongly bonded by common values that are maintained by social rewards and sanctions.

The replication of this interrelated set of processes is vulnerable in at least two points. One involves kibbutz-born individuals who, unlike their parents, did not choose to live on a kibbutz. Self-selection does not apply to them and although continuous socialization is supposed to overcome this, they are nonetheless likely to "be more passively committed to the kibbutz ideal than those who deliberately chose this way of life by abandoning the non-kibbutz environment" (Barkai, 1987: 253). Of course, voluntary membership in the kibbutz applies to kibbutz-born persons as it does to their parents, and indeed many do leave, implying self-selection by those who stay. However, the founding generation both chose to establish or join a kibbutz and had the option to leave. Organizational growth of kibbutzim represents a second threat, as informal social control is more efficient in small communities. No one knows exactly at what size the strength of informal social control is no longer enough to maintain its influence over community members. Early on it was believed that a hundred members was the upper limit in which social control could be effective, but most kibbutzim have passed that mark while informal social control remained effective. Still, size remains an issue because it is clear that mechanisms of social control cannot function without close personal contact in a tightly knit community.

Rosner (1998) presents a chronological answer to the motivation question. He argues that at different times in the kibbutz history, different processes or mechanisms of motivation were in operation. At first, during the pioneering period, the sole motivation was commitment to kibbutz values and identification with the community. Later, in the 1950s and 1960s the focus turned to the social cohesion of the work groups and the resulting social control. In the 1970s and 1980s, Rosner argues, opportunities for self-realization through work becomes the chief sources of motivation. Of course, it is possible and reasonable that all along all of these motivators coexisted and it was only the specific perspective of observers or researchers at any given time that caused them to focus on one or the other.

Two additional points pertaining to the motivation of kibbutz workers are necessary. A crucial explanatory factor for motivation of kibbutz members as (industrial) workers is their high level of education (Tanenbaum et al., 1977; Don, 1988). Barkai (1977: 97) presents data showing that kibbutz men and women have higher median years of schooling then the Jewish population of Israel (2.5 and 3.5 years more respectively). The difference is somewhat smaller but remains when the comparison is between the kibbutz and other rural settlements. Since the increase in the economic value of education is more than the increase in the number of school years, Barkai concluded that the average economic potential of kibbutz men was about twice that of men in the economy as a whole. For women it was more than 3.5 times as much as that of women in the economy as a whole. Human capital theory attributes real returns to education for individuals in the workplace, in kibbutzim we see that the education level of the labor force is related to superior performance of the organization.

The second point is that kibbutz members are the owners, the managers and the employees of their economic enterprises. In that sense they can be compared to self-employed individuals whose motivations are different from those of employees. Kibbutz members have a vested interest in the success of their organization. Both more immediate and long range satisfaction of the community's and its members' needs is dependent on each member's performance. So in a way, material incentives are not completely absent from the relationship between motivation and performance. For example, it was only after the improvement in kibbutzim's economic situation that members could enjoy benefits such as travelling abroad, enlarging their living quarters and generally raising the standard of living. Of course, there is a free-rider problem associated with this collective material incentive. In the face of a free-rider problem, material gain for the collective will normally be insufficient to evoke effort from individuals. Other motivators are necessary, which demonstrates that we cannot be satisfied with one mechanism for motivation or control of a complex social system like the kibbutz. A myriad of interdependent processes account for its functioning and sustain it.

Job Placement, Management Philosophy and Job Rotation

The ideological premise of equality dictates that the community ensure an egalitarian redistribution of the common resources. "From each according to her ability, to each according to her needs" specifies both the expected contributions from members and the allocative principle of resources. Derived from these is the multifunctional role structure in which each member is expected to perform various types of roles that are within her abilities. That applies both to the content of work (e.g. milking cows, working in the field, caring for children, doing the accounting) as well as to the responsibilities involved (e.g. a managerial vs. a non-managerial function). Thus, practices involving kibbutz members' allocation to roles and the management of work are directed and constrained by equality considerations.

Staffing of jobs is based on the premise that the "kibbutz manpower is at the disposal of the community. Although individual desires are taken into account in job selection and choice of occupation, the allocation of members' time – between work, training and study, and leisure – is ultimately determined by the community" (Barkai, 1977: 7). Another important ideological premise is total intra-kibbutz (and inter-kibbutz) mutual guarantee. In the work sphere, that translates to providing employment for every kibbutz member. The obligation to find employment for every member created the necessity to place members without highly required skills, and those who are physically or mentally handicapped. Reflecting this, some researchers (e.g. Don, 1988) attribute kibbutz industrialization partly to the aging of the first generation,[4] which made them unable to perform the physically demanding agricultural work. Since work is a central value in the kibbutz, and because these members rejected the idea of complete 'retirement' (Talmon-Garber, 1972; Leviatan, 1980a), a workplace with easier, more comfortable working conditions was needed. From a managerial perspective, guaranteed employment presents a problem. Market mechanisms or purely rational considerations do not govern allocation of members to work, thus managers are sometime pressured to 'accept' workers who are not suitable. The outcome of such placement may be a negative balance between the member's contribution and the shadow wage charged to their employing group (Helman, 1994).

The philosophy towards management is derived primarily from the premise of equality which dictates a coordination and integration role rather than an authoritative one, as well as the rotation of managerial jobs (e.g. secretariat, branch manager) among members (Tannenbaum et al., 1977; Leviatan, 1978; Rosner, 1980b; 1998). The following statement provides a clear illustration: "To call a man a manger is a kind of blasphemy. Indeed the Hebrew term for manager is avoided in the [kibbutz]. Instead a softer, more culturally accepted term, coordinator, has been adopted" (Diamond, 1957: 84). Rotation reinforces the egalitarian structure and ensures that no one person or group acquires disproportional power and influence. More specifically the norm of managerial rotation addresses four distinct issues: First, preventing the monopolization of rewards by high-ranking officers and keeping a certain social equality among the members. Second, preserving the principle of the integration of mental and manual work. Third, because the kibbutz is a total organization and its members interact in and out of the workplace, permanency in office may hinder relationships among members as whole individuals rather than office- or role-holders. Lastly, equality also means a fair distribution of the managerial burden among more individuals (Leviatan, 1978). Rotation was to take place regardless of the individual's performance or the performance of the branch she manages. After serving in a managerial position the member goes back to the 'rank and file' for at least a year before they are assigned to a new managerial role, be it in the social or work sphere (Leviatan, 1980b). Although the rules for rotation were not uniform (e.g. the length of a managerial term), the federations had formal regulations and the practice was common to all kibbutzim. The most common duration in a managerial role is between three and five years (Leviatan, 1978).

A number of studies that examined kibbutz members' attitudes toward managerial rotation found a relatively high and enduring support for the practice, although there are some differences by federation (e.g. Rosner, Shur, Chizik & Avnat, 1989). These findings are complemented by apparent mixed attitudes towards managerial posts (primarily plant managers). On one hand there was an objection on ideological grounds and a wish to preserve equality and prevent the creation of a ruling strata; on the other it was recognized as an important role. Expectations were that office-holders are supposed to coordinate others' work and not control it, and that they balance being 'equal' and being 'more'. In practice these expectations were manifested by including the managers in night shifts, cleaning, and other 'low level' jobs (Palgi, 1998). More recently, Einat (1997) examined rotation practices (duration in post, external-hired managers vs. kibbutz mangers) and outcomes in 169 kibbutz plants. He found that until 1994 rotation was an existing norm and that the average term of a CEO varied between 3 and 4.6 years. In the past five years however, managerial rotation is being replaced by professional management (Getz, 1994).

The explanation for the relative persistence of managerial rotation given the rapid industrialization and sophistication of kibbutz production is twofold. The normative and value system that gave rise to the practice remained strong, thus creating powerful social expectations that it continue. Additionally, office-holders are usually happy to be replaced. A study that focused on the relation of reward distribution to role attractiveness was based on data from the poultry branch in 26 kibbutzim that employed 26 managers and 104 workers (Yuchtman, 1972). Measured rewards included intrinsic job satisfaction, power, and socio-emotional rewards. Two distinct aspects of role attractiveness were 'comparison level' (the subjective gap between actual and expected outcome) and 'comparison level for alternative' (the subjective gap between actual and the expected outcome from the best available alternative job). So, a person's preference to stay or leave a job is based on her evaluation of the satisfaction derived from her role and the potential of her alternatives. The results show that the managers' position is associated with more positive outcomes on intrinsic job satisfaction and power rewards. Workers and managers enjoyed similar levels of socio-emotional rewards. A much higher percentage of managers expressed an interest in leaving the branch (42) than workers (16) even though managers' own evaluation of the rewards were overall high. Yuchtman's (1972: 592) explanation, based on equity theory, is that the managers want out of the job because of a negative balance of rewards that they experience. "This group [of managers] consists mainly of professionals who are aware of their higher input levels and expect, accordingly, adequate outcomes from their office. The lower degree of role attractiveness for them may be attributed, therefore, to the apparent disproportion of outcomes versus inputs." We do not have enough information to determine whether the community consciously contributes to the negative balance of rewards. There is anecdotal information one can hear in almost every kibbutz about the negative inter-personal relations that managers are prone to have because of their role. In a total social system such as the kibbutz such an outcome carries a heavy weight.

Given that the managerial-rotation practice persisted for so long, it is of interest to understand its effects on the community, work organization and the individual. Studies have identified positive organizational effects of management rotation in the form of informed, motivated workers (Leviatan, 1978) and positive individual effects for current and past office-holders in the form of a number of measures of psychological well being (Leviatan, 1980b).

Some research on the kibbutz is a response to the claim that managerial rotation inhibits organizational effectiveness by wasting experience. Accumulated knowledge and experience in solving problems allow a manger to function effectively and utilize learning based on past mistakes, so an organization that loses an experienced manager due to rotation could suffer negative consequences. Don (1988) showed that management rotation on the kibbutz had resulted in frequent changes in management style as well as loss of managerial experience and know-how.

Evidence contradicting this argument comes from Einat (1997), who finds that there is no effect of CEO rotation (or succession) on performance in kibbutz industrial plants. The mechanisms behind this result are made more clear by Ingram and Simons' (1999) finding that, in a learning curve analysis, kibbutzim exhibited no decay over time of the positive effects of experience. Decay of experience benefits is usually attributed to organizational forgetting, so kibbutzim appear to have better 'memories' than other organizations. Likely, this is because former-managers stay within the organization after leaving their roles, and overall turnover (exits from the organization) is low. These results appear to repudiate the claim that managerial rotation necessarily implies the loss of knowledge and experience.

In the kibbutz rotation is sometimes internal, i.e. a former top officer is rotated out of office but remains in the same branch at a lower level role. If this transition can be made without causing frustration and negative behavior on the part of the 'demoted' manager, the quality of work as a whole should be improved through the development and circulation of ex-managers. The outcome of internal rotation is a more experienced and higher quality workforce composed of many workers with previous managerial experience. Less overseeing, guiding and training are likely to be required by managers of such a workforce. Additionally, practicing internal rotation increases feeling of equality among workers, which in turn raises their participation in contributing to the achievement of organizational goals. Lastly, the probability that workers will advance is higher when internal rotation is practiced, thus satisfying the need for achievement which should result in a higher level of satisfaction (Leviatan, 1978).

These ideas were explored in a study by Leviatan (1978), conducted in kibbutz industrial plants (27) and agricultural branches (33). Six-hundred questionnaires were analyzed, interviews were conducted with managers and economic performance data were collected. Thirteen variables were included in the study, such as: length of time in office, economic effectiveness, success of manager in office, communication effectiveness, proportion of past and present office holders, and motivation. Consistent with the practice of rotation, the mean time in office was only 3.3 years, but there was substantial variance in this measure, with 10% of managers serving for eight or more years. The findings showed a weak curvilinear relationship between a manager's length of time in office and the economic performance of the organization. This is a rejection of the assertion that accumulated experience of the manager has a positive monotonic effect on organizational performance, undermining claims of the preeminence of managerial experience. That tenure ultimately comes to harm performance supports the idea that veteran managers can become entrenched in the known ways for doing things in a manner that makes adaptation to changing conditions slow and difficult.

The study also found that organizations with higher proportions of present and ex-office-holders were more effective in their economic performance and managers in these organizations were able to devote less time to training and overseeing. Higher levels of motivation and commitment were found in organizations with higher proportions of present and ex-office-holders. The author's conservative conclusion regarding the general effect of manager's tenure on organizational performance is "that managerial turnover does not cause any harm to the organization" (Leviatan, 1978: 1015). As to the larger question of the effects of internal rotation on organizational performance, the conclusion is stronger. It is supported by other findings showing that in organizations where "strong legitimization for periodic managerial turnover existed and where the membership participated in picking a replacement for the manager, the relationships between the new management and the workers were less conflict-ridden and more harmonious." Thus, evidence from the kibbutz compliments arguments that turnover can have some positive effects for organizations (Staw, 1980; Mowday, Porter & Steers, 1982), and goes beyond those arguments to show that, at least in the kibbutz context, the positives outweigh the negatives.

While managerial rotation may have desirable or neutral outcomes at the organizational level, it seems logical that the individual manager will pay a psychological price as a result of rotation out of office. In a complimentary study to the one described above, Leviatan (1980b) presents the theoretical implications of managerial rotation on managers, and then tests them in the kibbutz context. The theorized effects appearing in the literature on demotion are all negative, entailing deterioration in well being, lowered self-esteem and resentment. Demotion is taken as a sign of failure and it involves loss of face, loss of prestige, loss of material rewards, and fear of never being able to advance again. Trying to resolve these negative outcomes of demotion, Leviatan explains the utility of establishing the rotation principle as norm. Once rotation becomes a norm demotion is not an indication of failure. Change is expected and can be planned for. Further, an organization in which hierarchical differentiation and the rewards related to it are small, will also mitigate some of the negative effects of demotion. In such circumstance the demoted manager may even enjoy continuing high esteem by fellow workers and his well being may be more positive as compared to another worker at the same rank because of 'residuals' from her past experience. Kibbutzim combine a norm of rotation with limited differential rewards to managers.

To empirically test this idea, Leviatan (1980b) compares the well being of three groups of workers: current office holders, past office holders-current rank and file, never held office-current rank and file. The empirical setting is identical to the one described above (Leviatan, 1978). A number of measures of self-esteem, depression, resentment, physical symptoms and alienation were used. Descriptive statistics show that rotation occurs in all the studied organizations though in different degrees. The findings show that current office holders exhibit higher scores on well-being measures than the others, confirming other results showing a positive relation between one's position in the organizational hierarchy and her well being. The more interesting hypothesis examines the well being of ex-office-holders, finding that in organizations where the rotation norm is accepted they show equal or better scores of well-being as their peers. In all ten measures of well-being ex-office holders scored more positively than their peers, and in five the difference is significant. So, under the norm of rotation not only does the well-being of 'demoted' managers not adversely affected, but they report better well-being than their rank peers.

Sociologists are very interested in the ability of a social system to persist without the emergence of social differentiation. As presented at the beginning of this section, a primary ideological reason for managerial rotation is to prevent the creation of a powerful managerial elite in the kibbutz. Has it been successful in achieving this goal? The answer according to some researchers is that although the practice itself persisted (longer than other ideologically derived practices such as communal children's quarters), it failed in accomplishing its ultimate goal (Rosenfeld, 1983; Ben-Rafael, 1988; Shapira, 1988; 1990). One claim is that with the advancement of technology, professionalization of the kibbutz economic enterprise led to a concentration of power in the hands of a few. The unwanted outcome is the appearance of a powerful elite group in control of the major decisions and functions. One cause of this is horizontal rotation, where kibbutzim employ the principle of rotation but rotate managers to parallel managerial posts rather than sending them back to the rank-and-file. A justification that is often mentioned for this phenomenon is a complementary need of the manager's skill and experience by the kibbutz and the manager's preference for a managerial position (Helman, 1994: 28). Helman blames these "permanent professional managers" for the economic crisis of the kibbutz because they created a source of inertia, failing to adjust to the dynamic developments and changes that took place around them.

Shapira (1988; 1990) offers the seemingly contradictory claim that managerial rotation breeds conservative managerial thought. In a case study conducted in a large (1000 members), industrialized and veteran kibbutz, he finds evidence for managerial conservatism. The process he identifies is complex. An elite composed of a few founding members established its position in the kibbutz. These people possessed power and influence both inside and outside the kibbutz. As time passed, their status was jeopardized because it was based less on actual contribution to the community and more on political control. At the same time they attempted to prevent any new ideas from materializing and individuals with those ideas from advancing and succeeding. The situation was aggravated by automatic rotation that did not allow new managers to establish themselves in their role and to gain enough experience, influence and power to implement their ideas over the established elite's active objections. A few radicals who exhibited leadership potential and had innovative ideas for change were neutralized and were never able to reach real leadership positions within the kibbutz. The most radical withdrew from activity or left the kibbutz altogether. Shapira gives detailed accounts of the history of each member of the elite and a few accounts of 'young Turks' trying to change things in the kibbutz. Shapira does not think that rotation should be eliminated, rather he suggests that it should be pragmatically practiced. Successful managers should be allowed to continue in their roles longer than the time prescribed by automatic rotation. They should be subject to a periodic vote by the community and as their number of terms rises, a larger majority will be needed to approve an additional term.

Teams

Working in teams coincides well with the egalitarian premise, and the associated workplace democracy, of the kibbutz. In other organizations, teams are common because they are believed to perform better than employees working alone. However, research findings indicate that teams do not always outperform individuals, and that the relative success of teams depends on factors such as the task, the nature of incentives, and the relationships between members. One of the arguments applied to understand circumstances where teams perform poorly is 'social loafing', which describes the idea that individuals exert less effort when their efforts are combined than when their efforts are individual. Some specific conditions have been argued to eliminate social loafing: the group consisting of close friends; group members thinking that others will not take advantage of them; a culture that supports contribution to the group; clear performance goals; and ease of monitoring individual output (Erez & Somech, 1996).

Internal relations of friendship and trust within the group, as well as the culture, or ideology of contribution to the group are both especially relevant to the kibbutz context. We should expect that with the extensive and comprehensive relations among kibbutz members, trust and friendship would characterize work-group relations. Further, their common goals based on a shared ideology of collectivist principles should create a work environment that is conducive to a group rather than an individual focus. The outcome should be expressed in better performance as compared to other non-kibbutz teams.

A study that looked at the effect of collectivist versus individualist values on group performance supports the claim that collectivist values contribute to performance (Erez & Somech, 1996). It utilized an experimental design and compared managers from cities and kibbutzim. Collectivist values differ from individualist values in the way people perceive themselves vis-à-vis the group. People in collectivist cultures (or organizations) put the group's interest ahead of their own, they place a higher valence on belonging to their group and their self-definition is extended beyond the individual to include a particular group of others. Thus social loafing is much lower or does not occur in a work group with collectivist values.

The effect that collectivist versus individualistic values will have on performance loss from social loafing was a central question of the study. Kibbutz ($N = 63$) and urban ($N = 59$) midlevel managers who had known each other for at least six months and matched on gender, age and education participated in the study. At the outset the participants filled out the Twenty-

Statement Test, a known measure of collectivist and individualist values. The results showed a distinct difference between urban and kibbutz managers, the former scoring higher on individualist values and lower on collectivist values than the latter. Results support the hypothesis that performance loss will be less when tasks are performed by groups with collectivistic values versus indvidualistic values. Results also indicated interactions between collectivistic values and two other influences on group performance, communication and incentives. Generally, intragroup communication increases awareness of the presence of others as potential evaluators (social facilitation), resulting in increased group performance. In the case of the kibbutz managers that was not the case. Erez & Somech's (1996) explanation is that kibbutz members are used-to the presence of others and thus are less sensitive to the change from no-communication to intragroup communication. Also, they took the opportunity to discuss issues unrelated to the task such that they were not fully focused on performing. And while group incentives typically lead to social-loafing, the performance of the kibbutz managers was highest when they faced a group goal with incentives for goal attainment. It is likely "that group incentives increase the valence of contribution to group goals, which is highly valued by the interdependent self" (Erez & Somech, 1996: 1533; the authors use 'interde-pendent self' to describe an individual for whom collectivist values are more important than individualist values).

Broadening the argument that team performance depends on values, the effectiveness of managerial practices can be seen as dependent on norms and values that are prevalent in organizations and the broader society. When there is congruence between the norms and practices, performance should be better than when they are incongruent. Erez (1986) tested the effect of using participative and non-participative goal-setting strategies in three settings, a kibbutz, a trade union and a private sector organization. These organizations span a continuum from highly participative to non-participative. The results showed that the greatest effectiveness was achieved when there was equivalency between the type of organization and the type of strategy used. So for example, in the private sector organization the most effective was the non-participative strategy. At a societal-culture level, Erez & Early (1987) compared the effect of nonparticipative and participative goal-setting strategies on three groups of students (American, Israeli-urban, and Israeli-kibbutz) that differed in collectivism. Participative goal-setting led to greater goal acceptance for all three groups, but performance toward the goal depended on the combination of culture and strategy. Israelis performed better in the participative than in the non-participative conditions, while the Americans did not.

Group solidarity, cohesiveness and homogeneity are interrelated and influence work groups' effectiveness. If groups become highly heterogeneous and group solidarity and cohesiveness break down, group performance on certain tasks likely to be adversely affected.[5] One of the most prominent features of kibbutz work groups is the distribution of their members in terms of ownership status: kibbutz members and hired employees (Rosner & Tannenbaum, 1987a). The difference between these two categories is substantial. Kibbutz members are the owners of their industrial and agricultural enterprises, they share values, more often than not they have a common background, and they have close relationship with one another as a result of the comprehensiveness of life in the kibbutz. A number of studies examined the effect of employing hired workers, particularly on performance (e.g. Abramovich, 1997). Unfortunately most studies were conducted at the plant level so we only have an indirect test of the presumed negative effects of heterogeneity on work groups. Among these undesirable consequences are the weakening of the group's cohesiveness thus impeding its performance, or generating higher alienation levels (Rosner & Tannenbaum, 1987a), or reduced democratic practices (Rosner & Palgi, 1980). Leviatan (1980c) cites a number of studies that found that plants without hired workers performed better than plants with hired workers. In his own study he compared ten plants selected as five matched pairs, matched on the basis of technology and federation but differentiated on whether they employed hired workers. Significantly more conflicts between workers and supervisors occurred in plants with hired workers, while outcomes such as motivation and commitment to the plant's goals were lower in the plants with hired workers. In a similar argument to the one made by Erez (1986), Leviatan concludes that "an organization can function well and its members feel well only if congruence exists between the organization's structure and way of conduct on one hand, and its members' values and expectations, on the other hand" (p. 73). Another cost of heterogeneity is demonstrated by Ophir, Ingram & Argote (1998) who argue that membership heterogeneity will reduce organizational learning by inhibiting communication and helping behavior. Their learning-curve study of kibbutz agriculture supports this claim.

Decision Making

Participative, democratic decision making is replicated in the kibbutz at all levels, starting from the highest governing body, the general assembly, through the economic and service organizations, to the various subsystems. It is derived from the combination of communal ownership and equality tenets. The ultimate decision making power resides with the total membership, i.e. the general assembly that meets on a regular basis (Tannenbaum et al., 1977). Also important is that the general assembly as the governing body makes decisions about all aspects of work and plant management. Lastly, a general trend from direct participatory democracy toward a more representative decision making by elected committees has occurred in all kibbutzim (Vallier, 1983; Rosner & Cohen, 1983; Ben-Rafael, 1997). Here we will focus on decision making at the kibbutz workplace, primarily the industrial plants. The case of the evolution of decision making processes and structures in industry are particularly interesting because they allow the contrast between the technological imperative and the ideological imperative (Rosner & Tannenbaum, 1987b).

A participative system is one where "all members determine in some degree the decisions of the organization" (Tannenbaum et al., 1977: 50). Formal participation involves the existence of explicit rules regarding decision-making structures through which all members contribute to the decisions. Formal participation can be done directly, with all organizational members participating in the process or indirectly through representatives. Also, decision domains determine where a participative mode is used, and where other decision making modes are practiced (e.g. hierarchical). Participation can also be informal when managers and supervisors are receptive to the ideas and suggestions of subordinates, and sensitive to their needs (Tannenbaum et al., 1977). The kibbutz workplace combines all of the above variants.

Another typology contrasts between political and motivational approaches to participation. The political approach is based on representative participation of workers in decision making. Motivational participation is based on workers' direct partaking in decision making, and particularly decisions pertaining to their work. In the kibbutz workplace an effort was made to combine both by creating formal structures for direct (general assembly of the plant workers) and indirect (representatives in committees) participation. These structures are augmented by group coordinators allowing informal participation of workers in decisions (Rosner, 1998).

Tannenbaum et al. (1977) found the kibbutz to be the most participative work environment in a five-country comparison that included the U.S., Austria, Italy, Yugoslavia and Israel. In a measurement of the discrepancy between 'ideal' and 'actual' participation, the American and the kibbutz plants had the smallest gap although they had low and high participation levels respectively. In other words, in those two samples, managerial practices and workers' expectations were congruent. Managerial style and manager-employee relations were the

TAL SIMONS & PAUL INGRAM

most participative in the kibbutz plants. Don (1988) also found that relationship and communication between office holders and rank and file members is direct and informal in kibbutz plants indicating that informal participation was practiced.

Studies examined the outcomes of participative decision making in kibbutz plants by comparing participation forms (e.g. formal/informal) and their effect on outcomes (e.g. Rosner & Palgi, 1980; Rosner & Tannenbaum, 1987b). In both these examples, like in many other studies, the authors examine the dialectic relationship between 'the logic of industrialization' and kibbutz ideology or between the technological imperative and the ideological imperative. Once again, they focus attention to the inherent tension between technology, efficiency and rationality on one hand, and values and ideology on the other. Data from fifty-three plants of the Artzi federation were collected, including structural features (size, automation level, etc.) and ideological conformity measures. One of the indicators of ideological conformity was internal democracy, which was measured by the influence of the workers' assembly in four areas, participation in the workers' assembly and degree of managerial rotation. The findings showed that older and larger plants had less internal democracy. There was no other evidence that an emphasis on functions involved in industrialization, such as an increase in the ratio of professionals, has an adverse effect on internal democracy (Rosner & Palgi, 1980).

An investigation into the relation between internal democracy and organizational effectiveness found mixed results. Formal participation in the workers' assembly had a negative effect on economic performance but a positive effect on organizational climate (trust in management and communication frequency). Informal participation at the group level had a positive relation to the kibbutz workers' motivation and commitment (Rosner, 1980c; Leviatan & Eden, 1980). These results, combined with those of other studies, lead to the conclusion that the primary effect of participation in the workers' assembly is on the organization, while the primary effect of participation in work groups is on the participating individuals (Rosner, 1998: 37). The decision-making structures in the kibbutz plant are different from those in the kibbutz as a whole in that they combine a democratic and a hierarchical structure. The assembly is the authority and selects the management that must carry out its decisions. When those decisions are acted on, in daily work, most of the assembly participants are subordinates of the management they elected. This ambiguous state of affairs may explain the mixed findings and provide another insight into the complexity involved in combining managerial practices and organizational structures that emanate from different value systems.

COMMUNITY MAINTENANCE

"The kibbutz . . . is excellent; it is men who are not worthy." Diamond (1957: 98).

"Ideology is not an infectious phenomenon that one gets by sheer exposure to it." (Leviatan, Quarter & Oliver, 1998: xiii).

A discussion of the community maintenance of the kibbutz, the processes that equate outputs and inputs to allow the organization to survive, must begin with the record. Of the 300 kibbutzim founded before 1984, only 38 have failed (Parag, 1999). And despite the casual claims by some that the population is now failing en masse as kibbutzim change into other organizational forms, Israel's Registrar of Cooperatives says only 5 to 7% of kibbutzim have "failed through change," even by the strict definition of kibbutz that he applies. This robustness is remarkable among organizations – compare it, for example, to that of Israeli workers' cooperatives, which shared kibbutzim's ideology and economic environment, yet experienced a failure rate of 90% (Ingram & Simons, 2000). Of course, kibbutz robustness must be partly attributed to the fact that they are residential communities as well as organizations, giving them the status of 'facts on the ground' which cannot easily be dismantled. Yet, their survival rate seems high even for rural villages, particularly in an environment as hostile as twentieth-century Palestine/Israel. Further, it must be remembered that a kibbutz failure does not require that a community be dismantled. Kibbutzim can change into other organizational forms by relaxing their policies of cooperation and communalism, which has happened occasionally in the past, and is happening somewhat more frequently now.

The key to community maintenance of the kibbutz was satisfying its members. Here, we consider the socialization processes that molded member expectations; the changing view of gender equality which fundamentally determines who gets what on the kibbutz; and the approach to consumption which directly satisfied member needs.

Socialization

Socialization is particularly necessary on the kibbutz, because of the differences between kibbutz ideology and that of the wider community from which it draws members, and with which it interacts. A capitalist organization in a capitalist society can rely on the forces of ideological hegemony – public schools, the media, art, etc. – to produce participants with the required values (Miliband, 1969). For the kibbutz, this was never a possibility. So, kibbutzim were forced to rely even more on their own mechanisms of socialization than most organizations. Kibbutzim's socialization mechanisms differ from those of capitalist economic organizations in that they operate on potential members from birth, but even in capitalist societies, there is no shortage of organizations that socialize children (schools, churches, clubs, etc.). The design and outcomes of kibbutz socialization mechanisms are informative for such organizations. For example, parallels can be drawn between the structure and product of the kibbutz education system and English public schools (Kahane, 1975). The kibbutz experience with socialization is also useful for understanding the processes by which the assumptions of an economic system come to be taken for granted.

A core element of the kibbutz socialization process is the education and child-rearing system. Until the 1970s, kibbutz children lived not with their parents, but in 'children's houses' with a cohort of age-mates, and a dedicated care-giver, called a metapelet. Despite the presence of the metapelet, the children operated with significant self-governance in what is referred to as a 'children's society', essentially a microcosm of the kibbutz with committees and a 'general assembly' operated by the children themselves. As for education, "rather than emphasizing conventional academic achievement and the encouragement of mobility aspirations among the learners, kibbutz education was to be focused on fostering such values as cooperation, responsibility, devotion to work . . . and the need for selfless dedication to the goals of the collective" (Devereux et al., 1974: 270). Education and socialization of the child was also seen as the responsibility of all kibbutz members, and the child's peer group.

Devereux et al. (1974) document some of the outcomes of this system in a survey of 287 sixth-grade children from Tel Aviv and 314 from kibbutzim with children's houses. The children rated teachers, parents, peers, and for the kibbutz children, the metapelet, in terms of a number of forms of support and discipline. The differences between city and kibbutz children indicate that the kibbutz child-rearing system was achieving its espoused goals. First, kibbutz teachers appeared to have more significant influence over the children than city teachers. They provided more support, discipline, and encouragement of children's independence. There was a corresponding difference in the role of parents, with kibbutz parents providing less discipline, and more instrumental companionship (e.g. help with homework) than their counterparts in the city. Combined, these differences reflect the traditional de-emphasis on the family, and the emphasis on the organization and its functionaries (the teacher) for socialization on the kibbutz. There were also telling differences in peer socialization. Peers on the kibbutz were more likely to exercise a number of forms of discipline, indicating the roots in childhood socialization of the social control that we have argued to be a key determinant of performance on the kibbutz. Kibbutz children were more likely to threaten social isolation, the withdrawal of affection, and physical punishment as mechanisms of disciplining their peers.

Shapira & Madsen (1974) present evidence that is particularly informative of the effect of this socialization system to create the behavioral capacities and tendencies that appear to be at the heart of the economic system of the kibbutz (Erez, 1996). In a series of experiments, they compared the behavior of 9–11 year olds from 17 kibbutzim with that of children from the city of Haifa in a game which required cooperation for success. Kibbutz children were more likely to cooperate than their counterparts from the city, and achieved three times as many successful outcomes. Post-trial interviews indicated that the city children's cooperative intentions were frustrated by a lack of organization and trust. They "often said that they would have [cooperated] but that the other children would not have reciprocated" (p. 142). In contrast, kibbutz children appeared to organize spontaneously, often utilizing an emergent, informal leader. In other experiments, kibbutz children appeared more ready to rally around their own group when it came into conflict with others.

The human capital produced by the education and socialization system of the kibbutz is one of the organizational form's most impressive outputs. One-third of kibbutz youth volunteer to spend a year on public service (Avrahami and Dar, 1993). An average of 15% of parliament seats have been held by kibbutz members and at times, they constituted a third of cabinet ministers (while about 4% of the population; Katz & Golomb, 1983). Three of Israel's ten prime ministers have been at some point in their lives kibbutz members, or were raised on a kibbutz. Kibbutz members have a reputation for heroism and over-representation in the elite units of the Israeli Defense Forces. In recent years, two successive army Chiefs of Staff were kibbutz 'products'. Kibbutz youngsters comprise more than 25% of voluntary combat units and in many of the airforce squadrons, kibbutz members comprise more than 60% of combat pilots (Katz & Golomb, 1983). Kibbutz casualty rates during the 6-day and Yom Kippur wars were four-times their proportion of the population (Near, 1997: 229).

Kahane (1975) attempted to explain the high commitment to universalistic values (with the willingness to act on those values), adaptive capacity and achievement orientation of the products of the kibbutz system of child-rearing and education by analyzing its specific features. He attributed value commitment to the non-hierarchical relations of the children's society, which forced its members to engage in a pattern of mutual adjustment, fostering commitment to the norm of reciprocity. The structural equality of the children was reinforced by the status structure that emerged from participation in a multi-dimensional pattern of activity which allowed children to exhibit capabilities other than the usually emphasized intellectual ones, such as artistic skills or athletic abilities. This pattern of activity enabled a multi-dimensional (informal) scale of evaluation, which produced quasi-equality of status. The adaptive capacity of individuals raised on the kibbutz, by which Kahane means flexibility and entrepreneurship, resulted partly from the early insertion of kibbutz youth into the roles of decision-makers that had to solve practical problems within the constraints of a strong ideology. Adaptive capacity also comes from the socialization system which puts parents, teachers, metaplot, and other adults in differentiated, yet overlapping roles. This causes regular conflict between the socializers, encouraging the socialized to develop flexibility to maneuver between constraints and conflicting demands. Finally, achievement orientation was produced by a sense of noblesse oblige which emerged from the elite consciousness of the kibbutz; by a norm of dissatisfaction and corresponding aspiration to perfection that derived from the image of the kibbutz as an example to the world; and by the extreme competitiveness of an education system which keeps children in constant contact.

Commitment to the kibbutz is another key output of the socialization system. Rosner et al. (1990) and Leviatan (1998) describe the results of studies, in 1969, 1971 and 1976, on member attachment to and retention by the kibbutz. Attachment was found to result from social and work satisfaction, which derive from political centrality and professional level of the work. Three times more important than satisfaction for predicting attachment, however, was adherence to utopian ideology. This adherence was found to result from the ideological emphasis in the members' education. At the same time that socialization may generate attachment, there is also an important effect of selection, as founders of a kibbutz have higher attachment than the 'second-generation', those born and raised on the kibbutz.

Attachment is behaviorally meaningful as it is negatively related to the likelihood of leaving the kibbutz, which was actually lower than for other rural settlements in Israel (or abroad). Twenty-percent of members who expressed a low attachment to the kibbutz in 1969 had left by mid-1971; only 4.6% of those with high attachment left over the same period. Women were more likely to leave than men. Controlling for age and skills, members who had been more active on the kibbutz (e.g. held important offices) were more likely to stay, while those who placed more value on standard-of-living were more likely to leave. The relevance of socialization for retention was strongly indicated by the complete failure of permanent characteristics of the kibbutz, such as age, location, and ethnic origin of founders, to predict retention rates.

Gender equality

For contemporary organizations, one of the most interesting features of the kibbutz experiment is its attempt to achieve the goal of full equality between the sexes in terms of the amount and type of work, and influence in the organization. As women's participation in the labor force is continuously growing, and as employers realize that the household and family domain does affect organizations and the labor market, the subject of gender equality in both spheres becomes crucial. Does the division of labor to 'female-type' and 'male-type' jobs and occupations in the household determine the division of labor in organizations and the labor market or vice versa? If the kibbutz is successful in eliminating the 'traditional' division of labor in one domain will this outcome spillover and affect the other? Various explanations for the origin of the observed division of labor have been offered: early socialization of girls and boys, differential skills, tendencies, and attributes of women and men, rational calculations based on who generates more income, or discrimination by employers. The comprehensiveness of kibbutz living and the fact that it is a system devoid of material rewards make it a remarkable setting for examining the effectiveness of education and attempts for equal allocation of women and men to jobs, in creating gender equality.

The fullness of the effort to promote gender equality is apparent in Spiro's (1958) account of life in the preschool children's houses of one kibbutz in 1951. Boys and girls played, slept, ate, showered and sat on their training toilets together. They shared the same toys, and played the same, sexually integrated and undifferentiated games. They were inculcated with the same values concerning agriculture and labor, working together in the 'children's farm'. Their responsibilities in the children's houses were undifferentiated and non-segregated. Except for differences in dress and in personal names, Spiro observed no promotion of sexual differences by the staff of the children's houses, whether by instruction or social reinforcement. Parents, in their two-hour daily visits to their children, presented a similarly gender-neutral example, displaying one parental role rather than differentiated 'paternal' and 'maternal' roles.

What resulted from the grand effort? The most complete picture of the lives of kibbutz women raised in the environment Spiro (1958) described comes from Tiger & Shepher (1975). Their findings are from analyses of the censi of two kibbutz federations in the early 1970s, and from a number of case studies and surveys. Their conclusions (pp. 262–263) are devastating for the ideal of gender equality on the kibbutz. Only in the earliest history of the kibbutz movement did most women work in production. By 1975 the sexual division of labor had reached 80% of maximum, with women concentrated in education and consumption services (laundry and food preparation) and men in production. Women are less active participants in the General Assembly, over-represented in committees dealing with social, educational and cultural problems and seriously under-represented in committees dealing with econ-omy, work, general policy and security. Years of education are roughly equal between men and women, but women receive more non-university higher-education leading to jobs such as teaching and nursing, while men receive more university higher-education leading to jobs such as agriculture, engineering and management. From the ninth grade on, women consistently fall below men in scholarly achievement, and this discrepancy is greater on the kibbutz than in comparable societies. Against original ideology, the family has become the basic unit of kibbutz social structure, as indicated by the move to children sleeping in their parents' apartments, higher and growing (in the 1960s and 1970s) rates of birth and marriage, and decreasing rates of divorce. Women were the main instigators of familiazation. For example, they opposed collective housing of children more than men. Women also express lower attachment to the kibbutz, and are more likely to leave (Rosner, Ben-David, Avnat, Cohen & Leviatan, 1990; Leviatan, 1998).

Why did the kibbutz fail so miserably to achieve the goal of gender equality? There are two classes of explanations. The first, 'cultural' or 'external' class is based on the view that sex-role differentiation is a cultural artifact too robust for the kibbutzim to abolish. Spiro (1979) details some promising cultural explanations. First is that "although the male pioneers were intellectually committed to female liberation, it might be argued that they were not sufficiently emancipated from their European sexist attitudes to provide the male support necessary for the feminist revolution to succeed" (pp. 65–66). In support of this explanation Spiro cites kibbutz males' unwillingness to share traditionally defined 'women's work' and their occasional expressions of sexist attitudes. Second is that women may have led familiazation as a mechanism to achieve status that was denied them due to their participation in service occupations, or because those occupations were often monotonous or difficult. While acceding that cultural influences probably had some influence in the 'counterrevolution' to re-establish traditional sex-roles, Spiro concludes that "it is doubtful . . . that they were the primary determinants." He does so because return to tradition was not the only possible response to persisting sexism, because women worked in services rather than production not due to social restrictions, but rather self-selection, and because men who worked in the services did not similarly support familiazation.

The second, 'sociobiological' or 'internal' class of explanations is based on the view that sex-role differentiation is an institutional consequence of basic human motives and sentiments. The concession to this approach of Spiro (1978:106), a cultural anthropologist, is notable: "I set out to observe the influence of culture on human nature . . . and found . . . I was observing the influence of human nature on culture." The most forceful statement of the sociobiological explanation comes from Shepher & Tiger (1981), who apply sociobiology's foundational causal factor, parental investment, to suggest the inevitability of gender-inequality on the kibbutz and in organizations broadly. Simply summarized, the dictates of mammalian biology are that females, as the limiting resource on reproduction, have a greater stake in, and therefore make a greater investment to bring to maturity, each child. The extra-effort required to make this investment causes females to favor work that does not take them far from the child. This is the basis of the sexual division of labor on the kibbutz, with women gravitating to the centrally located services, and particularly those directed at children. Indeed, even in the early days when women did participate in kibbutz agriculture, they favored vegetable gardens, orchards and poultry, which were close in proximity to the children's houses, rather than the far-flung fields (Blumberg, 1983). The theory of inclusive fitness suggests that allomothering, as occurred in the children's houses, is only sustainable under extreme situations, in which all energy is needed to provide the basic needs of life. So, when the kibbutz developed beyond its initial stage of intense poverty, pressure against the children's houses, particularly from women, also developed. The resistance to allomothering was apparent with the first two children born on the very first kibbutz. The mother of the first suggested to the mother of the second that they share childcare duties to allow each to do some other work, but the second mother preferred to care only for her child (Baratz, 1954). Finally, sociobiologists interpret kibbutz women's support for stable marriage as an effort to extract greater parental investment from the fathers of their children.

It is probably unnecessary to say that the sociobiological explanation of gender-inequality on the kibbutz sparked a heated debate. Culturalists have responded by refining their arguments and improving their evidence. Hertz & Baker (1983), for example, conclude from their fieldwork on one kibbutz that women are forced, often against their will, into differentiated jobs by an opportunity structure that develops from job-practice placements in high school. Young women are initially placed in child-care, young men in production, and later placements depend on the first through experience.

Large-scale surveys of kibbutz women reveal, however, that rather than begrudging the gender-differentiation of kibbutz work, they overwhelmingly accept it as proper and legitimate (Rosner, 1966). Other evidence against the opportunity structure argument is that women who work in a 'men's job' for their first job, and therefore have the production experience that creates opportunity, are still likely to make the transition to services with subsequent jobs (Tiger & Shepher, 1975).

Evidence for another cultural argument comes from Leviatan's (1985) finding that the accuracy of children's perceptions of the sex-composition of kibbutz jobs improves between the ages of three and ten. This is argued to show that socialization to gender roles takes place despite efforts to avoid it. However, that evidence was accumulated in the 1980s, and Spiro's original account of gender-neutral socialization comes from 1951. Even if kibbutz children now learn gender roles through observation, there was a generation that observed undifferentiated gender roles, but implemented differentiated ones.

Another approach has been to recast the implications of gender differentiation and familiazation. Rosner & Palgi (1982), while recognizing the objective facts of job specialization and familiazation, assert that the kibbutz has not recreated the roles of 'breadwinner' and 'housewife', allowing women more freedom to work outside the home. They also claim that women's jobs on the kibbutz do not entail lower status or other rewards. The first of these arguments may have been true before children moved into their parents' apartments, but now kibbutz women seem to be as burdened or as free as other working women. Kibbutz mothers' 'outside' working hours were even cut by 12.5% to 37.5% in recognition of the increased effort they would have to expend to care for their children in a family home. There was no corresponding reduction for kibbutz fathers. The second argument is questionable against the evidence. Ben Rafael (1988) asked 140 respondents from seven kibbutzim to rank ten 'branches' (the kibbutz term for a job location-type, e.g. factory or kitchen) in terms of status. Production branches dominated service branches in status. He also evaluated the status of 217 members of 15 kibbutzim, with a coding, verified by kibbutz 'judges' that was based on job-type and public activity. Men were found to be far more common in the highest of the four status-categories, making up 75% of the category. Men were also far more likely than women to be identified as a 'notable person' by respondents, although they were also more likely to be identified as 'isolated persons'. In a survey of 50 Artzi kibbutzim in the late 1950s, 35% of women thought that increasing the participation of men in consumer services was a route to make the work more satisfying (Viteles, 1967). Studies on various kibbutz samples indicate that work is less central for kibbutz women as opposed to men, although the differences appear to be smaller on the kibbutz than in other societies (Leviatan, 1985). A study of 569 adolescents indicated that kibbutz females had lower self-esteem than kibbutz-males, and than urban adolescents of either gender (Orr & Dinur, 1995).

Consumption

Production and consumption are basic processes in any society. In the kibbutz the two come together in Marx's aphorism "from each according to his ability, to each according to his needs," in which there is no stated conditional linkage between the two. The kibbutz federations have altered Marx's clause in some informative ways and have reinterpreted it over the years. In its 1958 conference, the Artzi federation restated the principle: " . . . Only if the member gives to the kibbutz to his fullest capacity can the ability of the kibbutz to care for the member is guaranteed." (cited in Saltman, 1983: 131). More than one federation has added a qualification, stating that "to each according to his needs" as long as it is "within the means of the community" (Barkai, 1977: 11). Underlying these changes is a salient characteristic of the kibbutz's existence and evolution, that of pragmatism.

Two principles guided consumption in the kibbutz. One is that the kibbutz provides for each member's needs and the other is the value of asceticism (Diamond, 1957; Talmon-Garber, 1972). So in effect, consumption in the kibbutz, ideally allows for individual differences in needs and tastes. After some experiments the system that emerged in the early kibbutzim included a combination of three consumption systems: the free-goods, the rationing, and the points systems (Barkai, 1977). Each was applied to a different set of goods. The free-goods system was to satisfy equality, individual tastes, and (communal) scarcity. So, goods included in this system were free at the individual level but within a budgetary constraint. An example is the communal eating in the dining-hall, where food was free and individuals could choose (from what was available) what they want to eat and how much of it. Medical-care, education and utilities such as electricity have all traditionally been free-goods. Direct rationing was practiced as a means to transfer the community budget constraints to the individual level, so for each member a set quantity (and later monetary equivalence) of clothes, cigarettes, and footwear was allocated. For some durable consumer goods the rationing system is not applicable. An obvious example is housing, since houses can not be strictly equal – even if their size would be the same, housing quality varies by time of construction and location. The solution for consuming relatively expensive, durable goods, based on the principle of potential equality was the point system. Seniority in the kibbutz and age were the major criteria for assigning points, representing the individual's contribution to production. An individual's point endowment was then used for determining what she is entitled to and when (Barkai, 1977).

Much research has examined asceticism associated with religion, however secular asceticism has not been studied. Asceticism, whether Protestant or kibbutz, implied a rejection of self-indulgence and accumulation of material goods for the purpose of raising the standard of living. Instead it emphasized a very modest lifestyle, cutting down on consumption expenditure and reinvesting in production. Based on a long and insightful analysis of asceticism as a dynamic part of kibbutz ideology, Talmon-Garber (1972) argued the following. The extreme compliance of the early kibbutzim with socialist ideas of equality and cooperation was the main incentive for asceticism, consumption was not to serve as a main source of motivation, and instead extreme normative control was required. "The pattern for regulating and balancing needs was laid down by the community. Most needs were met in kind in such quantity, rate, quality, and manner as was determined by the community, so that the individual had little scope for exchange and manipulation. Consumption practically ceased to be a legitimate personal outlet" (Talmon-Garber, 1972: 207). Asceticism is also rooted in the individual's value system, allowing total devotion to ideals (Rosenfeld, 1957). As a differentiating symbol, a life of destitution served as "a badge of distinction for the select group of those who were actively involved in the realization of the goal." Thus, kibbutzim life style did not only corresponded to their ideology, it signaled an elite status and served as a tangible evidence of the community's moral strength and influence.

Consumption related values and the resulting structures changed dramatically over time with the constant rise in kibbutzim's income levels (Rosenfeld, 1957; Talmon-Garber, 1972; Barkai, 1977; Rayman, 1981a; Saltman, 1983; Ben-Rafael, 1997; Gluck, 1998). The details of the various changes[6] are less interesting than the explanations for the changes. Talmon-Garber (1972) sees the change in ascetic values as a mirror of other changes in the kibbutz. She claims that internal inconsistencies in the original ideology created weak points where the erosion started. For example, the kibbutz asceticism was primarily goal-oriented thus combining materialism and idealism, a fusion that is bound to create strain. Achieving national independence, one of the foremost goals of kibbutzim, legitimized a gradual relaxation of the ascetic ideal: Now it was time for satisfaction of individual needs. Kibbutz members' attitudes reflect the on-going change, showing a move away from ideologically-based asceticism.

The outcome of the change from ascetic ideal to a greater emphasis on consumption is that "the rigid pattern of curbing expenditures breaks down, giving rise to ever growing demands. The growing desire for immediate satisfaction makes it more difficult for members to adjust to restrictions and delays in the supply of acknowledged needs. The sense of inequality becomes acute; kibbutz institutions are subjected to pressure and can no longer perform their function properly" (Talmon-Garber, 1972: 208).

KIBBUTZ-ENVIRONMENT RELATIONS

". . . [t]he kibbutz is a cultural island in its physical separation, in its relatively high degree of autonomy, and in its own norms and practices, but it is an island with many bridges to nearby islands and to the mainland" (Katz & Golomb, 1983: 67).

Like any other organization, the kibbutz is embedded in an environment containing other organizations and institutions. The kibbutz ideology, unlike that of many other utopian societies, never dictated a separatist stance (Kanter, 1972). On the contrary, the kibbutz movement always proclaimed openness to its surroundings, partly because it wanted to affect the society and spread its utopian-socialist way of life (Barkin & Bennet, 1983). The basis for the relationship between the kibbutzim and the Israeli society is a social exchange where kibbutzim received autonomy and resources, and contributed to the economy, the political and defense systems, and to the culture (Katz & Golomb, 1983). This social exchange is governed and managed by a set of interorganizational relationships. These relationships are complex and problematic exactly because of the relative openness of the kibbutz (Saltman, 1983).

Kibbutzim have had relationships with each other to form the federations, and regional enterprises to provide various centralized services such as cotton gins (Bijaoui, 1994; Niv & Bar-On, 1992). They have also had mutualistic and competitive relationships with other organizations. Mutualistic relations characterize organizations that share a goal such as promoting an ideology of socialism. Organizations that either disagree on ideological matters or compete for resources will have competitive relations (Ingram & Simons, 2000). Before detailing the kibbutzim's mutualistic and competitive relationships, we first consider their most prominent and complicated relationship, that with the State.

State-Kibbutz Relations

The kibbutzim offer a natural laboratory for investigating organization-state relations because their history spans the weak-state of the British Mandate in Palestine, and the strong Israeli State. Britain occupied Palestine in 1917, and in 1922 was granted a mandate to rule there by the League of Nations. From the beginning, however, British rule struggled. The frustrations of the persistent Arab-Jewish conflict combined with poor prospects for economic gain by the British, resulted in a de facto abdication of many responsibilities of governance (Migdal, 1988; Shalev, 1992). Organizations, notably the comprehensive labor federation, the Histadrut, expanded their role to fill the institutional vacuum that resulted (Ingram & Simons, 2000). The kibbutzim, as the vanguard members of the Histadrut, played a major role in this corporatist system. The contribution of the kibbutzim to the governance of Palestine's Jewish society was multifold, encompassing defense, settlement of immigrants, and the conquest of unproductive or contested land. We have claimed that the kibbutz population expanded to satisfy the 'demand for order', with supporting evidence that kibbutz founding was stimulated by political violence and Jewish immigration during the British Mandate (Simons & Ingram, 1999).

The establishment of the Israeli State in 1948 brought a marked change in the political role of kibbutzim by bringing into existence an actor with the interest and capacity to provide order in Israel. This created a fascinating form of competition, between the state and corporatist organizations. Qualitiative evidence of this competition comes from the rhetorical attacks on the kibbutzim by state officials. David Ben Gurion, Israel's first prime minister was vocal and persistent in criticism of the kibbutzim for failing to respond to state mandates, such as the demand that they absorb more immigrants (Near, 1997). The kibbutzim and their federative organizations were perceived as a threat to Ben-Gurion's view that the state alone should handle national objectives such as security and agricultural settlement. This attitude is succinctly summarized in a kibbutz member's recollection that [Ben-Gurion] "feared our strength, so he had to break us up. He didn't want any strong autonomous organizations, because he considered them a threat to the new State" (Lieblich, 1984: 119). The quantitative evidence of State-kibbutz competition is that after the formation of the Israeli state in 1948, political violence and Jewish immigration no longer stimulated kibbutz founding. Instead, organizations associated with the state arose in response to those needs (Simons & Ingram, 1999).

It would be easy to dismiss the relationships between kibbutzim and the state as idiosyncratic – few other organizational forms seem so central for the generation of order, and so much in conflict with the state. Our position, instead, is that the unusual experience of the kibbutzim serves to illustrate the underlying, but seldom observed, reality of state-organization relations. The state, despite some unique capabilities is really just an organizational actor, pursuing its interest of maintaining power by providing order. At the same time, other organizations can generate order, which can bring them into conflict with the state. The resulting view is of organizations and the state interacting in relations that are mutualistic or competitive, depending on state and organizational strength. This view is more useful for explaining state actions towards particular organizations, and gives a fuller account of the sources of order.

Mutualistic Relations

Kibbutz Federations

In recent years there has been a growing interest in the role of associations (organized interests) of organizations in the social-economic sphere. Business groups, as Granovetter (1994) refers to them, serve as an important intermediate level of analysis between atomized firms and macro-economic activity, but are understudied. The kibbutz federations perform many of the roles and activities that business groups do. The relations among kibbutzim in a federation facilitate interorganizational learning, and have operating implications for members (Ingram & Simons, 1999). Individual kibbutzim gave the right to regulate to the federation, thus relinquishing some of their autonomy. The federation establishes rules and norms of behavior and reduces transaction costs for member organizations by coordinating production (Ingram & Simons, 2000). The kibbutz federations were also active in the cultural, educational, political and ideological spheres.

The federations provided various services to the kibbutzim such as training in specific agricultural methods or new educational ideas (Ingram & Simons, 1999). They also carried out recruiting and initial screening of potential new members for the kibbutzim. Another important role was that of generating a sense of mutual responsibility and support among the kibbutzim. An example of such mutual support is getting people from older kibbutzim to go to newer ones where their experience and maturity are needed. Federations also channeled aid from wealthier kibbutzim to others in need within the federation as well as allocating resources obtained from the government or banks (Rosolio, 1994, 1998). Political representation and protection of kibbutz economical interests in the distribution of the national resources were other prominent roles. Generally, the efforts of the federations can be seen as attempts to do things that individual kibbutzim are too small to do themselves (Granovetter, 1994).

Federations also served as ideological centers and brokers. Each developed and shaped kibbutz ideology and translated it to strategic plans and daily operations. In doing that they had to balance between the ideological tenets and pragmatic considerations. A case in point is the issue of hired labor – many conventions and discussions were devoted to the ideological ramifications of this practice. All the federations had resolutions and plans for reducing the number of hired employees used by their member kibbutzim (Simons & Ingram, 1997). Thus, the federations were actively involved in monitoring the implementation of ideology and served as ideological supervisors. Ideological education is also achieved through institutions that the federations established, such as the youth movements and educational centers.

While each federation developed a different pattern of relations with their individual units, trends of centralization and decentralization of the Israeli state have led to parallel processes at the federations (Rosolio, 1998). This supports the idea that the state exerts isomorphic pressures on its subject organizations (Meyer, Scott & Strang, 1987). The Israeli State was initially centralized, reflecting the need to mobilize resources to meet early crises. As the need for the mission-oriented society gradually diminished so did the need for a centralized governmental system, and a shift of power from the center to the periphery occurred. This shift was accompanied by an increase in the number and power of various kibbutz regional associations (e.g. regional municipal councils, regional schools, and economic organizations) at the expense of the federations. In the face of the severe economic crisis of the 1980s the relationships between the federations and the individual kibbutzim became more strained, creating sentiment among the kibbutzim to further loosen ties to the federations (Ben-Rafael, 1997).

Other cooperative organizations
Kibbutzim have ties with ideologically similar groups both within Israel, such as the various urban cooperatives, and internationally (Daniel, 1976). Organizations sharing an ideology can support each other by sharing experience and information, patronage, money encouragement, and legitimacy, and by cooperating in efforts at political influence. That rationale explains the finding that the growth of two separate socialist populations – credit cooperatives and kibbutzim, decreased the failure rate of Israeli workers' cooperatives (Ingram & Simons, 2000).

More distant relations with utopian communities outside the borders of Israel exist and prosper. Cooperation between the kibbutzim and other organizations has often been in the form of knowledge sharing. Since the kibbutz has become world renowned for its success in fulfilling the utopian-socialist ideal, it has attracted attention and interest of those who were interested in implementing similar models. Representatives from Asia and Africa have visited kibbutzim training centers to gain an understanding of the kibbutz success (Katz & Golomb, 1983). Likewise, kibbutz members have always been drawn to organizations elsewhere that shared their ideology. A case in point is the relationship that has developed over the years between the Bruderhof communal movement and the kibbutz movement and is described in Oved's (1993) monograph titled 'Distant Brothers'. Even currently, when the kibbutz's status in the Israeli society is on the decline, interest from around the world persists (*Yediot Aharonot*, January 3, 1997).

Competitive Relations

The Moshav

A moshav is a cooperative smallholders agricultural settlement. Moshavim (plural) differ from kibbutzim primarily in the private ownership of homes and a lower degree of communalism and collectivism in the organization of production (Ben-David, 1983). Basic principles of all moshavim include cooperative marketing and purchasing, water supply, use of agricultural machinery and communal services. One type of moshav (moshav shitufi) has all-inclusive cooperative joint production and is thus close in ideology and structure to the kibbutz. However, the moshav-shitufi is a small minority among moshavim, so moshavim on the whole are less communal than kibbutzim (Viteles, 1966). A moshav, as an agricultural settlement, requires the same resources of land, water and people, as a kibbutz.

Kibbutzim and moshavim competed for resources and for the status of pioneering leaders in the Zionist struggle. Until 1948 kibbutzim had a great deal more manpower, prestige and public influence than moshavim and they performed better on a number of dimensions such as productivity and education. Kibbutzim had an advantage in recruiting because of their established ties with the youth movements and because, according to Near (1997), they were more attractive to young people. The influx of immigrants after 1948, however, lacked a youth movement background and any affinity to socialist ideas. Between 1948 and 1954, 180 moshavim were founded by immigrants, and 43 by the second generation from veteran moshavim. One hundred kibbutzim were founded in the same period. Ninety-seven of these new moshavim were located in vital and dangerous border areas as defined by military authorities (as were 64 of the new kibbutzim; Near, 1997). So, the moshavim, especially the new immigrant ones, were impinging on defense, traditionally one of the kibbutzim's primary functions. Another crucial function of the kibbutzim prior to the establishment of the state was the absorption of immigration (Ben-David, 1983). After 1948 the majority of immigrants that went to rural settlements went to moshavim. The competition between kibbutzim and moshavim is also borne out in Parag's (1999) analysis of the failure rates of kibbutzim. Those rates were found to increase as a function on the density of moshavim in a kibbutz's geographic region.

The competition between kibbutzim and moshavim is particularly notable in light of our earlier argument that organizations with similar ideologies (such as the kibbutzim and urban cooperatives) will have mutualistic relationships. Moshavim are less communal than kibbutzim, but their ideologies are clearly similar when considered relative to the set of ideologies that influenced other organizations in their environment. Certainly, both kibbutzim and moshavim are variants of rural cooperatives. Why then do they exhibit competitive rather than mutualistic relations? The answer is that there is an interaction between their similarity of ideology and similarity of required resources, such that the combination brings them into close competition. Unlike urban cooperatives, moshavim pursue a set of resources similar to those pursued by kibbutzim. Indeed, kibbutzim and moshavim may be seen as functional substitutes in terms of the exchange they sought with Israeli society. This indicates an important scope condition to the prediction of mutualism between organizations of similar ideology, that it will only occur if the organizations pursue substantially different sets of resources.

Development towns

These towns were established in the 1950s as massive waves of immigration arrived to the young state and many new immigrants, primarily from North Africa, were settled in them. Many development towns were located in the periphery, often close to Israel's borders with its adversary Arab neighbors. By 1957, thirteen development towns were founded in such localities. This created a substantive infringement on the status of kibbutzim as border posts. It also meant the kibbutzim now had new neighbors in their close vicinity, people who had a dramatically different background and as things evolved, very different socio-economic futures.

The development towns did not enjoy the same level of education, availability of work and amenities as their neighbor kibbutzim, and were excluded from the kibbutzim regional high schools and libraries (Rayman, 1981b). Development town residents were often employees in kibbutzim, and labor disputes were not uncommon. This situation was the basis for high levels of alienation and resentment of the development towns' residents toward the kibbutzim (Bijaoui Fogiel, 1988). This state of affairs is portrayed by a development town resident: "I do not care that they [the kibbutzniks] have a high standard of living, that they exploit workers from town, that they live in a closed society which forbids entrance to people of other classes ... What I care is that these fattened hens dress up like peacocks, that they live like rich farmers, but call themselves progressive, the best of the youth, socialists" (Ben Chorin, 1983: 84 in Ben-Rafael, 1997). The most dramatic manifestation of these sentiments was the 1977 election's campaign and results. Menachem Begin, the Likud (right wing) party leader, led a successful campaign that focused on the development towns' inferior circumstances as compared to the kibbutzim. For the development towns' residents the kibbutzim were equated with the establishment, which they perceived as discriminatory.

Some kibbutz members expressed their reservations about the hostile relations they had with the development towns (Ben-Rafael, 1997). Further, the kibbutz federations allocated money and personnel to help immigrant towns (Rosolio, 1994), focusing primarily on education related activities to youth after school hours and illiterate adults. Starting in 1965 many young kibbutz members spent a year of community service in development towns before going into the army. But those activities were often interpreted in the towns as attempts by the establishment to increase its control (Ben-Rafael, 1997; Near, 1997). So, although kibbutzim did not subscribe to isolationism, over the years, some segments in Israeli society consolidated a perception of the kibbutzim as an exploitative, affluent, elitist group. A slow but persistent process of erosion of the kibbutz movement's legitimacy and standing in Israeli society was the result.

Capitalist Organizations
There is a competitive analog to the tendency of ideologically similar organizations (excepting those that compete for the same resources) to help each other. Since ideology defines the propriety of social arrangements, organizations infused with one ideology can be expected to act to restrict, change or eliminate other organizations that subscribe to a different ideology. We generated evidence of this in the form of a finding that kibbutzim were more likely to forego their socialist organizing principles when they were indebted to capitalist banks and therefore subject to ideological coercion from the banks (Simons & Ingram, 1997). At the level of populations, we have shown that the growth of capitalist banks in Israel increased the failure rate of urban cooperatives (Ingram & Simons, 2000). As the Israeli society moves

away from socialism and embraces capitalism, the struggle between organizations representing those ideologies is probably at its climax. The current conditions are such that kibbutzim are considering dramatic departures from their ideologies and practices.

The rise of capitalist organizations, and of functional substitutes to the kibbutz such as moshavim and development towns, has been apparent in public attitudes. These indicate a gradual decline in the legitimacy of the kibbutz as a central organizational form in Israel. Until the mid–1980s appreciation of the kibbutzim's contribution to society and support for them were high. At about that time, it became apparent that the kibbutzim faced an economic crisis. The loss of political influence since the Likud victory in 1977, lagging agricultural markets, skyrocketing interest rates, and poor decisions on industrial investments and spending on consumption combined to create the crisis (Ben-Rafael, 1997). Total debt of kibbutzim more than doubled between 1984 and 1988, and ultimately, a bailout supported by major banks and the government was required. These events affected internal and external perceptions of the kibbutz. Results of a public opinions survey from 1996 show that 50% of the Israeli public still has a positive attitude toward kibbutzim (60% a decade earlier) but 25% expressed a negative attitude (8% a decade earlier). Another survey carried out in 1995 showed that only 54% (70% in previous years) thought that the kibbutzim contributed to the achievement of social and national goals (Leviatan, Quarter & Oliver, 1998).

CHANGE

We are losing our identity. The kibbutz movement nowadays is very heterogeneous; it is hard to say what the kibbutz movement consists of, what a kibbutz is. (Aharon Dagan, a Takam leader, in Ben-Rafael, 1997: 139).

Kibbutz, change, and crisis are three words that in the past 15 years seem inseparable, be it in research or popular writing (Ben-Rafael, 1997; Leviatan, Oliver & Quarter, 1998). Since the unveiling of the kibbutz financial crisis in the mid–1980s, there is a widespread sentiment that the old kibbutz is 'dead', and active speculation on the new form that the kibbutz will take. Consultants, academics and kibbutz leaders talk of mass privatization, separation of community and business, differential wages, and staffing committees with experts instead of kibbutz members (Getz, 1994, 1998). The Registrar of Cooperatives, who is the government official in charge of all cooperatives, including kibbutzim, gives facts that shed a different light on changes in kibbutzim. A kibbutz is a legal entity and as such there is a clear articulation of the parameters a community must exhibit in order for it to 'qualify' as a kibbutz. Kibbutzim that wish to incorporate changes that potentially contradict the legal parameters of a kibbutz have to submit the proposed change(s) to the Registrar for approval. If the proposed change is within the legal definition of the kibbutz and the process of its approval within the kibbutz was according to the law, then it will be approved. However, if it diverges from the letter of the law, the Registrar has the authority to refuse the change, and if a kibbutz tries to implement a change without approval, to prosecute the kibbutz. The Registrar is firm, for example, that kibbutzim that implement differential wages will lose their kibbutz status. According to the Registrar, as of June 1999, only 5 to 7% of kibbutzim have implemented or are in the process of trying to implement changes that will result in a change in their legal status. Thus, it seems that many accounts of the rapidly changing kibbutz are overstated. The debate on change is passionate and infused with rhetoric because of the ideological ramifications and because of the practical implications for kibbutz members' life now and in the future, the kibbutz movement, and the Israeli society and economy.

Ideology/Practicality 'Battle' as a Trigger to Change

All organizations and social systems either adapt to new circumstances by changing, or ultimately fail (Katz & Kahn, 1978). It is also reasonable to assume that, because all organizations are infused with ideology, many confront an ideological-practical conflict like that of the kibbutz (Rosner et al., 1990). This can occur even for organizations that employ an ideology that leads to favorable material outcomes, as did kibbutz ideology. Other organizations supporting rival ideologies may challenge an ideology's practicality with little regard for objective evidence. This happens, for example, when capitalists argue that cooperative organizations are inefficient, despite evidence to the contrary. And organizational participants may question the practicality of specific ideological practices apart from the overall effect of a set of practices. Ideology may also include a conception of organizational change, as on the kibbutz where there is a newer conception that the kibbutz has to adapt to the member instead of the other way around.

In the current change 'craze', the assumed contradiction between ideology and efficiency, between the ideological imperative and the technological imperative, are more salient than ever. The kibbutz ideology combined with its striving to exist as a viable economic community and remain open to its environment, render the dilemma inevitable. But kibbutzim always modified their structure and practices to address changing circumstances and needs. Examples abound: the abolishment of the communal sleeping arrangement because parents wanted their children in the family home; accepting the use of hired labor because of chronic manpower shortage; allowing the university matriculation exams in kibbutz high schools; and changing the form of personal budgets to allow greater autonomy and individual choice for members (Helman, 1994). So, is the current change debate different?

Most researchers seem to think that it is. While the fundamental issue is still the ideology/pragmatism conflict, two areas of difference appear. One is the kibbutzim's baseline situation as they enter the change debate. Kibbutzim were never in such economical dire straits accompanied by relatively weak public and political standing. This negative combination results in calls to strengthen the market approach both in the production and consumption spheres and to prevent intervention of 'irrelevant' social and ideological constraints in the management of economic enterprises. The second component has to do with the pace of changes and their origins (Ben-Rafael, 1997). In the past changes were diffused, and developed in an 'evolutionary process'. The changes were slow, communities could treat each change independently and in many cases grassroots initiators started the change. Now kibbutzim are facing clusters of changes and the pace is revolutionary rather than evolutionary. Kibbutzim may consider a number of simultaneous changes, such as charging for domestic electricity, allowing meals to be eaten in the home, implementing food budgets for families, establishing boards of directors for factories, broadcasting general assembly meetings via internal television, encouraging members to work outside the kibbutz, and opening the kibbutz swimming pool to the public (Ben-Rafael, 1997). The breadth of change makes careful consideration and evaluation less feasible. An 'ideology of change' is developing, potentially leading to a wholesale acceptance of anything that is different and new (Rosner & Getz, 1994).

Sources of Inertia

Change is always in the face of inertial forces that maintain an organization's existing structures and practices. The kibbutz experience illustrates that ideology is one such force. Ideology serves as a yardstick for evaluating change and thus any change that deviates from the ideological dictates is likely to be rejected. In practice, kibbutzim have been pragmatic in their evaluation of suggested changes. Nevertheless, the role of ideology as an inertial force should not be under-emphasized. The inertial properties of ideology are reflected in individuals' attitudes toward changes that are counter to their ideology.

Individuals vary in their interpretations of reality and their preferences for action to address it. Thus, responding to kibbutz members' interests isn't easy because there are multiple preferences and ideas for action. This is particularly relevant when discussing change in kibbutzim and analyzing the 'force field' of the opposing and supporting camps of the changes. In kibbutzim some of the most stable and consistent realities are tied to the process of change. One, mentioned above, is the ideology-practical conflict as a trigger for change. Another is the intergenerational difference in attitudes toward change and particularly change that involves a departure from the kibbutz ideological tenets (Rosner et al., 1990). As Ben-Rafael (1997: 155) stated more generally "we expect that in the kibbutz, aspirations and commitments to change, or, on the contrary, to the retention of existing social arrangements, might be accounted for not only by a variety of specific social interests, but also by tensions or dilemmas embedded in, or at least relating to, the structure of the collective identity." It is a widely accepted assumption that the younger generation is more supportive of changes than the older generation. In the context of kibbutzim the gap between the second generation and the founding generation should be even larger because of the latter's special character and their huge personal investments in establishing the kibbutzim (Rosner and Getz, 1994). Both Rosner et al. (1990) and Ben-Rafael (1997) find in their studies evidence supporting the more conservative attitudes among the first generation or older kibbutz members.

The kibbutz federations performed a dual role of linking between the kibbutzim and the environment but also as buffers for the kibbutzim. Their size, status and credibility enabled the federations access to resources that were then transferred to the individual kibbutzim. Any buffer that isolates, or protects an organization is also an inertial mechanism because of its shielding effect. The kibbutz federations did not view the 1977 overthrow of the Labor government as a political cultural change that requires adaptation by the kibbutz movement; they treated it only as a political accident. The changes in the economic policy were perceived merely as political moves. The federations' rigid interpretation of the occurrences in the social economic environment resulted in the continuation of their policies and economics as though nothing had changed. In their capacity as buffers the federations were in charge of interpreting the environment, thus the same attitude was passed on to the individual kibbutzim. In the face of a fundamental change in the government's attitude toward the state's role in the economy, the kibbutzim were not directed to change their economic plans and assumptions, nor did the federations change (Rosolio, 1994).

Last, is the inertia that results from the kibbutz's legal definition. The earliest legislation concerning cooperative societies is from the British Mandate period and it has remained, with some changes and additions, over the years. A number of elements of the kibbutz definition create an inertial force that reduces the likelihood for substantial changes. Maron (1994: 7–8) describes a kibbutz "that decided to end collective responsibility by the kibbutz as a whole and to shift that responsibility to the individual members. . . . At that point the government Registrar of Cooperatives stepped in and reminded the members that kibbutz principles, including that of a shared purse, are grounded in law and not subject to alteration only on the basis of internal decision-making within a particular kibbutz. Changes [required] transforming the particular settlement from 'kibbutz' to a different legal definition." Notably, when a kibbutz changes its legal form, it loses its beneficial status for tax and social security payments.

CONCLUSION

Recent interpretations of economic history, and the related evaluations of organizational forms, celebrate the triumph of capitalism. The alternative of state socialism seems destined for the junk-heap of failed social experiments. Many commentators seem to have doomed the kibbutz by association. In truth, the kibbutz is in much better condition than contemporary observers admit, but was never as glorious as observers of the past have boasted. The reality is an organizational form that has exhibited notable robustness and adaptiveness in an environment that was turbulent and often hostile. It can claim successes that will evoke envy from the stakeholders of many capitalist-hierarchical organizations. It has generated economic performance better than its alternatives, while achieving difficult political objectives, and maintaining a level of workplace democracy that appears to flaunt the 'iron law' of oligarchy. At the same time it has incurred failures that would appear to its founders to be devastating. Once sacred organizing principles have been sacrificed, principally those of self-labor and gender equality. The socialist society that all of the kibbutz federations pursued has not materialized.

To begin to summarize the implications of the kibbutz for organizational behavior, it is useful to think about how the kibbutz model would be received if it was introduced into the contemporary landscape of dominant under-standings about organization. What if a consultant proposed to senior management that hierarchical authority be abolished, and that social relations between employees be cultivated as the basis for emergent, normative control? If the founder of a dot-com enterprise explained to a venture capitalist that the organization would pay every participant in the organization the same, that it would give jobs to them as long as they and the organization both lived, and that she herself would soon become the mail clerk thanks to mandatory job-rotation? Or if an MBA student recommended to classmates that the subject-organization of a case study undertake not only to manage its production process according to a set of values that reflect economic and non-economic goals, but also to directly provide policing for its headquarter city? No doubt these proposals would be met with ridicule. Their advocates would probably be told that it is simply impossible for organizations to do these things while satisfying the material desires of their participants. Yet, the kibbutz has done all of these things and has a good record of providing for participants.

What should organizational behavior make of a model which is almost antithetical to our most accepted ideas about how to succeed as an organization, yet succeeds anyway? Our position is that the kibbutz experience should be interpreted for organizational behavior as an expansion of the possible. Yes, the kibbutz demonstrates the feasibility of a novel organizational configuration. But that configuration is not so novel as to be unrelated to other organizations. Instead, the kibbutz shows us what to expect when we push at the edges of familiar organizations – more integration between social and economic interests of participants; more democracy; more emphasis on the intrinsic value of work; more reliance on the collective good as a an internalized value and as a basis for social sanctions. In closer detail, we divide the lessons from the kibbutz into three sets. The first two mirror our common categorozation of influences on organizational behavior and performance as intra-organizational configurations or inter-organizational relations. The third points to ideology as a previously under-emphasized influence on organizations.

As to internal organization, the kibbutz demonstrates the feasibility of a control system that is decentralized and reliant on social control. This is in stark contrast to the pervasive hierarchical model. Whether social control is more or less satisfying to its subjects is an open question, but there can be no doubt that social control is very powerful. Often, we are more influenced by the approval of our peers than by the coercion of organizations (Nee & Ingram, 1998). Some capitalist organizations have stumbled across the benefits of social control, but there is little in the way of systematic advice to managers about how to use social control effectively. (Ineffective use of social control is fairly common, for example, at Levi Strauss, where group incentives resulted in the brutalization of under-performing group members [King, 1998].)

Beyond demonstrating the power of social control, the kibbutz illustrates the complete system of components necessary for it to fluorish. To begin with, there is a close coupling between the work and non-work spheres on the kibbutz. This creates cohesion which gives social sanctions their teeth. A worker that shirks in the field must face her coworkers over the dinner table. Social control on the kibbutz also relies on a socialization system that promotes collective values. These values go a long way to promoting cooperation, as indicated by the superior performance of kibbutz children in games that reward collective action. The socialization mechanisms used to produce these collective values are also notable. These mechansims are sufficiently powerful as to produce behavior that would be called 'irrational' by those who expect individuals to maximize individual utility.[7] The final component of the internal configuration of the kibbutz is workplace democracy. Again, the processes by which the kibbutz produces and maintains democracy are interesting in the face of pressures to oligarchy. Workplace democracy produces commmitment to the organization. Associated practices such as job rotation produce more expert and satisfied workers.

At the interorganizational level, the kibbutz storey is again one of collective action, as federations achieve ends that no lone organization could. The federations illustrate a broad pattern of interorganizational mutualism, with help and sharing of resources occurring across most aspects of economic, political and social life. This mutualism produces results, such as inter-organizational learning, that are ellusive goals for many organizations in Western economies. The success of the federations indicates something about the glue that secures interorganizational relations. The thick ties between kibbutzim in a federation produce a level of interdependence which is used to encourage individual kibbutzim to contribute to collective efforts of the federation (just as social relations within the kibbutz are used to encourage members to adhere to group norms). The performance of this system has been remarkable, as the federations, and other superorganizations such as the Histadrut, provided corporatist governance to Jewish society under the British Mandate. Through their collective efforts, the kibbutzim conquered land, settled immigrants, and helped win Israel's War of Independence. They absorbed many responsibilities that we normally associate with states, and their example prompts the recognition that organizations provide political order as well as rely on it.

Kibbutzim also demonstrated an interesting array of competitive inter-organizational relations. Their experience alerts us that organizations compete on multiple dimensions. Kibbutz rivalries with other organizational forms were based on competition for resources (with moshavim), the defense of ideological organizing principles (with capitalist banks) and even influence over new immigrants (with development towns). And their most significant competitive relationship is of a type that is almost unrecognized in organizational theory. Since the inception of the state of Israel, there has been intense competition between that organizational constellation and the kibbutzim. This competition has involved rhetoric and resources, and has been costly to kibbutzim. It is perhaps most significant for explaining the decline of the kibbutz in public perception, and the more recent economic difficulties they have experienced.

The final lesson is about the role of ideology for understanding organizational behavior. By now it is clear that kibbutzim's internal organization and external relations can only be understood in the context of their utopian ideology. There is no other way to understand why, for example, they chose not to employ outside labor when it was profitable, or why capitalist organizations coerced them to reverse that policy. Despite the obvious relevance of ideology to kibbutzim, however, our position is not that they are 'ideological organizations'. We believe that ideology affects all organizations, that General Motors is no less ideological than Kibbutz Degania. The salience of ideologies is lower in countries like the United States where organizations that make products and provide services are relatively homogenous in their commitment to capitalism's ideology. The difference for the kibbutzim is not that they are more ideological, but rather that their ideology differs from that of many organizations in their economic system. So, when looking at the kibbutz, we can see an ideological contrast from the organizations with which they interact. This contrast produces variance in the organizational practices employed by kibbutzim and other organizations. It also produces interorganizational conflict. These results of ideological contrast alert us that ideology operates to influence organizations, but we must realize that it is operating even in economies where there is less contrast in the ideologies that organizations pursue. We advocate recognition of and attention to the ideological character of all organizations as a means to a clearer understanding of why they do what they do.

NOTES

1. Etzioni (1980: 45) motivates his classic study of the kibbutz with a similar point, that despite some unique characteristics, analysis of the kibbutz is of generic interest. Rosner (1980a: 286) describes a general failure, even in Israel, to learn from the kibbutz, and gives a fuller account of the assumptions that cause kibbutz experience to be categorized as unique and idiosyncratic.

2. The justification on this kibbutz for generosity to hired labor is indicative of the ideological conflict present even in kibbutzim that have moved quickly to adopt capitalist organizing principles in the interest of efficiency. Our informant explained the overpayment of hired laborers by saying "we're fucked up. We have these crazy socialist ideas."

3. Today, a heated debate on the issue of incentives and motivation is taking place within the kibbutzim, with frequent proposals to modify the equal non-monetary rewards that characterized the kibbutz for almost 90 years.

4. From the Resolutions of the 41st Council of the Kibbutz Ha'Artzi: Industry in the Kibbutz (February, 1976 Kibbutz Gan-Shmuel): "Employing the elderly in industry; The council calls for the establishment of a staff of experts to study the problems of the employment of the elderly in industry and to classify the various industrial occupations that can fulfill the occupational needs and potential abilities of elderly male and female members" (Leviatan & Rosner, 1980:182).

5. See Williams & O'Reilly (1998) for a comprehensive discussion of the relationship between group heterogeneity and performance. Homogeneity and solidarity are most important for tasks which require group cohesion and individual sacrifice (e.g. Stouffer, 1949). For tasks requiring creativity, however, homogeneity may harm group performance (Williams & O'Reilly, 1998).

6. For example, from an inclusive budget that allocates the monetary worth of a strictly defined line of products directly to members while supplementing it with another group of products supplied by the kibbutz, to a comprehensive budget allocates the maximum directly to the member's personal budget.

7. Some might contend that the 'dovish' (in game-theory terms) products of kibbutz socialization are indeed irrational, and the the folly of their behavior would be obvious if they were exposed to a few 'hawks'. But remember that kibbutz members also thrive outside of the collective, in conflict-likely roles as Chief of Staff of the Israeli Defense Forces.

REFERENCES

Abramovich, A. (1997). The Factors Affecting the Proportion and Economic Efficiency of Hired Labor in Kibbutz Industrial Plants. MA thesis, Department of Labor Studies, Tel Aviv University (Hebrew).

Arian, A. (1968). *Ideological Change in Israel*. Cleveland: Cleveland University Press.

Avrahami, A., & Darm, Y. (1993). Collectivistic and individualistic motives among kibbutz youth volunteering for community service. *Journal of Youth and Adolescence*, 22, 697–714.

Baratz, J. A. (1954). *A village by the Jordan: Story of Dagania*. London: Hawill.

Barkai, H. (1977). *Growth Patterns of the Kibbutz Economy*. Amsterdam: North Holland.

Barkai, H. (1987). Kibbutz efficiency and the incentive conundrum. Research paper no. 196, The Maurice Falk Institute for Economic Reserch in Israel. The Hebrew University, Jerusalem.

Barkin, D., & Bennet, J. W. (1983). Kibbutz and colony: Collective economies and the outside world. In: E, Krause (Ed.), *The Sociology of the Kibbutz*. (pp. 343–370). New Brunswick: Transaction Books.

Ben-David, J. (1983). The kibbutz and the moshav. In: E, Krause (Ed.), *The Sociology of the Kibbutz*. (pp.37–49), New Brunswick: Transaction Books.

Ben-Rafael, E. (1988). *Status, Power and Conflict in the Kibbutz*. Aldershot, UK: Aubury.

Ben-Rafael, E. (1997). *Crisis and Transformation: The Kibbutz at Centurys End*. Albany, NY: State University of New York Press.

Bijaoui Fogiel, S. (1988). Regional Integration, Cooperation or Alienation. Ramat Efal: Yad Tabenkin (Hebrew).

Bijaoui Fogiel, S. (1994). The Emergence of Regionalism in the Kibbutz Movement: The Kibbutz at the Turn of the Century. Report No. 13. Ramat Efal: Yad Tabenkin (Hebrew).

Blumberg, R. L. (1983). Kibbutz women: From the fields of revolution to the laundries of discontent. In: M. Palgi, J. R. Blasi, M. Rosner, & M. Safir (Eds), *Sexual equality: The Israeli kibbutz tests the theories* (pp. 130–150). Norwood, PA: Norwood Editions.

Daniel, A. (1975). The kibbutz movement and hired labor. *Journal of Rural Cooperation, 3,* 31–41.

Daniel, A. (1976). *Labor Enterprises in Israel Vol. 1.* New Brunswick, NJ: Transaction Books.

Devereux, E. C., Shouval, R., Bronfenbrenner, U., Rodgers, R. R., Kav-Venaki, S., Kiely, E., & Karson, E. (1974). Socialization practices of parents, teachers, and peers in Israel: The kibbutz versus the city. *Child Development, 45,* 269–281.

Diamond, S. (1957). Kibbutz and shtetl: The history of an idea. *Social Problems, 5,* 71–99.

Don, Y. (1988). *Industrialization of a Rural Collective.* England: Avebury.

Eden, D. (1975). Intrinsic and extrinsic rewards and motives: Replication and extension with kibbutz workers. *Journal of Applied Social Psychology, 5,* 348–361.

Einat, J. (1997). Normative Rotation in Kibbutz Factories: The Effects of Executive Succession, Successor Type and Structural Changes on the Organizational Performance. MA thesis, Department of Labor Studies, Tel Aviv University (Hebrew).

Erez, M. (1986). The congruence of goal-setting strategies with socio-cultural values, and its effect on performance. *Journal of Management, 12,* 585–592.

Erez, M., & Early, C. P. (1987). Comparative analysis of goal-setting strategies across cultures. *Journal of Applied Psychology, 72,* 658–665.

Erez, M., & Somech, A. (1996). Is group productivity loss the rule or the exception? Effects of culture and group-based motivation. *Academy of Management Journal, 39,* 1513–1537.

Etzioni, A. (1980). *The Organizational Structure of the Kibbutz.* New York: Arno Press.

Getz, S. (1994). Implementation of changes in the kibbutz. *Journal of Rural Cooperation, 22,* 79–92.

Getz, S. (1998). Winds of Change. In: U. Leviatan, H. Oliver, & J. Quarter (Eds), *Crisis in the Israeli Kibbutz* (pp. 13–26). London: Praeger.

Gluck, Y. (1998). Individual needs and public distribution in the kibbutz. In: U. Leviatan, H. Oliver, & J. Quarter (Eds). *Crisis in the Israeli Kibbutz* (pp. 119–130). Westport, CT: Praeger.

Gordon, A. D. (1938). *Selected Essays.* New York: League for Labor in Palestine.

Granovetter, M. (1994). *Business Groups.* In: J. N. Smelser, & R. Swedberg (Eds), *Handbook of Economic Sociology* (pp. 453–475). Princeton, NJ: Princeton University Press.

Grinberg, L. L. (1991). *Split Corporatism in Israel.* Albany, NY: State University of New York Press.

Helman, A. (1994). Privatization and the Israeli kibbutz experience. *Journal of Rural Cooperation, 22,* 19–30.

Hertz, R., & Baker, W. (1983). Women and men's work in an Israeli kibbutz: Gender and allocation of labor. In: M. Palgi, J. R. Blasi, M. Rosner, & M. Safir (Eds), *Sexual equality: The Israeli kibbutz tests the theories* (pp. 154–173). Norwood, PA: Norwood Editions.

Ingram, P., & Simons, T. (1999). The exchange of experience in a moral economy: Embedded ties and vicarious learning in kibbutz agriculture learning. In: *Best Papers Proceedings,* Academy of Management.

Ingram, P., & Simons, T. (2000). State Formation, Ideological Competition, and the Ecology of Israeli Workers Cooperatives, 1920–1992. *Administrative Science Quarterly, 45,* 25–53.

Izraeli, O., & Groll, S. (1981). Implications of an ideological constraint: The case of hired labor in the kibbutz. *Economic Development and Cultural Change, 29*, 341–351.

Jones, B. (1982). *Sleepers wake!* Melbourne: Oxford University Press.

Kahane, R. (1975). The committed: Preliminary reflections on the impact of the kibbutz socialization pattern on adolescents. *British Journal of Sociology, 26*, 343–353.

Kanovsky, E. (1966). *The Economy of the Israeli Kibbutz.* Cambridge: Harvard University Press.

Kanter, R. M. (1972). *Commitment and Community.* Cambridge: Harvard University Press.

Katz, D., & Golomb, N. (1983). Integration, effectiveness and adaptation in social systems: A comparative analysis of kibbutzim communities. In: E. Krause (Ed.), *The Sociology of the Kibbutz* (pp. 51–74). New Brunswick: Transaction Books.

Katz, D., & Kahn, R. L. (1978). *The Social Psychology of Organizations.* 2nd Edition, New York: John Wiley and Sons.

King, R. T. (1998). Infighting rises, productivity falls, employees miss piecework system. *Wall Street Journal*, May 20, 1998: A1.

Leviatan, U. (1978). Organizational effects of managerial turnover in kibbutz production branches. *Human Relations, 31*, 1001–1018.

Leviatan, U. (1980a). Work and age: centrality of work in the life space of older kibbutz members. In: U. Leviatan, & M. Rosner (Eds), *Work and Organization in Kibbutz Industry* (pp. 43–52). Norwood, PA: Norwood Editions.

Leviatan, U. (1980b). Individual effects of managerial rotation: The case of the demoted office holder. In: U. Leviatan, & M. Rosner (Eds), *Work and Organization in Kibbutz Industry* (pp. 153–169). Norwood, PA: Norwood Editions.

Leviatan, U. (1980c). Hired labor in the kibbutz: Ideology, history and social psychological effects. In: U. Leviatan, & M. Rosner (Eds), *Work and Organization in Kibbutz Industry* (pp. 53–63). Norwood, PA: Norwood Editions.

Leviatan, U. (1985). Interpretations of sex differences in work centrality among kibbutz members. *Sex Roles, 13*, 287–310.

Leviatan, U. (1998). Second and third generations in kibbutzim – is the survival of the kibbutz society threatened? In: U. Leviatan, H. Oliver & J. Quarter (Eds), *Crisis in the Israeli Kibbutz* (pp. 81–96). London: Praeger.

Leviatan, U., & Eden, D. (1980). Structure, climate, members reactions and effectiveness in kibbutz production organizations. In: U. Leviatan & M. Rosner (Eds), *Work and Organization in Kibbutz Industry* (pp. 82–101). Norwood, PA: Norwood Editions.

Leviatan, U., Quarter, J., & Oliver, H. (1998). Summary and conclusions. In: U. Leviatan, Oliver, H., & Quarter, J. (Eds), *Crisis in the Israeli Kibbutz* (pp. 159–164). London: Praeger.

Leviatan, U., & Rosner, M. (Eds) (1980). *Work and Organization in Kibbutz Industry.* Norwood, PA: Norwood Editions.

Lieblich, A. (1981). *Kibbutz Makom.* New York: Pantheon Books.

Macarov, D. (1972). Work patterns and satisfaction in an Israeli kibbutz: A test of the Herzberg hypothesis. *Personnel Psychology, 25*, 483–493.

Macarov, D. (1975). Work without pay: Work incentives and patterns in a salaryless environment. *International Journal of Social Economics, 2*, 106–114.

Maron, S. (1994). Recent developments in the kibbutz: An overview. *Journal of Rural Cooperation, 22*, 5–17.

Meyer, J., Scott, W. R., & Strang, D. (1987). Centralization, fragmentation, and school district complexity. *Administrative Science Quarterly, 32*, 186–201.

Miliband, R. (1969). *The State in Capitalist Society.* New York: Basic Books.

Mowday, R. L., Porter, L. W., & Steers, R. M. (1982). *Employee-Organization Linkages.* New York: Academic Press.

Nadler, D. A. and Tushman, M. L. (1997). *Competing by Design.* New York: Oxford University Press.

Near, H. (1997). *The Kibbutz Movement Volume 2.* London: Littman.

Nee, V., & Ingram, P. (1998). Embeddedness and beyond: Institutions, exchange and social structure. In: M. C. Brinton, & V. Nee (Eds), *The New Institutionalism in Sociology.* (pp. 19–45). New York: Russell Sage Foundation.

Niv, A., & Bar-On, D. (1992). *The Dilemma of Size from a System Learning Perspective: The Case of the Kibbutz.* Greenwich, CT: JAI Press.

Orr, E., & Dinur, B. (1995). Social setting effects on gender differences in self-esteem: Kibbutz and urban adolescents. *Journal of Youth and Adolescence, 24,* 3–27.

Oved, Y. (1993). *Distant Brothers: History of the Relations between the Bruderhof and the Kibbutz.* Ramat Efal: Yad Tabenkin.

Palgi, M. (1994). Attitudes toward suggested changes in the kibbutz as predicted by perceived economic and ideological crises. *Journal of Rural Cooperation, 22,* 114–130.

Palgi, M. (1998). Organization in kibbutz industry. In: U. Leviatan, H. Oliver, & J. Quarter (Eds), *Crisis in the Israeli Kibbutz* (pp. 41–56). London: Praeger.

Parag, Y. (1999). Organizational Death? The Failure of Kibbutzim. MA thesis, Department of Labor Studies, Tel Aviv University (Hebrew).

Perrow, C. (1986). *Complex Organizations.* Third edition. New York: Random House.

Putterman, L. (1983). Incentives and the kibbutz: Toward as economics of communal work motivation. *Journal of Economics, 43,* 157–188.

Rayman, P. (1981a). *The Kibbutz Community and Nation Building.* Princeton, NJ: Princeton University Press.

Rayman, P. (1981b). Co-operative movement confronts centralization: Israeli kibbutz regional organizations. *Economic and Industrial Democracy, 2,* 483–520.

Ronen, S. (1977). A comparison of job facet satisfaction between paid and unpaid industrial workers. *Journal of Applied Psychology, 62,* 582–588.

Ronen, S. (1978). Personal values: A basis for work motivational set and work attitudes. *Organizational Behavior and Human Decision Processes, 21,* 80–107.

Rosenfeld, E. (1957). Institutional change in the kibbutz. *Social Problems, 5,* 110–136.

Rosenfeld, E. (1983). Social stratification in a classless society. In: E. Krause (Ed.), *The Sociology of the Kibbutz* (pp. 157–166). New Brunswick: Transaction Books.

Rosner, M. (1966). *Research Summaries on Woman-Members.* Givat Chaviva: The Research Institute of Kibbutz Society (Hebrew).

Rosner, M. (1980a). Assessment. In: Albert Cherns (Ed.), *Quality of Working Life and the Kibbutz Experience* (pp. 286–287). Norwood, PA: Norwood Editions.

Rosner, M. (1980b). Hierarchy and democracy in kibbutz industry. In: U. Leviatan, & M. Rosner (Eds). *Work and Organization in Kibbutz Industry* (pp. 128–138). Norwood, PA: Norwood Editions.

Rosner, M. (1980c). Self management in kibbutz industry: Organizational patterns as determinants of psychological effects. In: U. Leviatan, & M. Rosner (Eds). *Work and Organization in Kibbutz Industry* (pp. 102–116). Norwood, PA: Norwood Editions.

Rosner, M. (1993). Organizations between community and market: The case of the kibbutz. *Economic and Industrial Democracy, 14,* 369–397.

Rosner, M. (1998). Work in the kibbutz. In: U. Leviatan, H. Oliver, & J. Quarter (Eds), *Crisis in the Israeli Kibbutz* (pp. 27–40). London: Praeger.

Rosner, M., David, I. B., Avnat, A.,Cohen, N., & Leviatan, U. (1990). *The Second Generation: Continuity and Change in the Kibbutz*. New York: Greenwood Press.

Rosner, M., & Cohen, N. (1983). Is direct democracy feasible in modern society? The lessons of the kibbutz experience. In: E. Krause (ed.), *The Sociology of the Kibbutz* (pp.209–235). New Brunswick: Transaction Books.

Rosner, M., & Getz, S. (1994). Towards a theory of changes in the kibbutz. *Journal of Rural Cooperation*, *22*, 41–61.

Rosner, M., & Palgi, M. (1980). Ideology and organizational solutions: The case of the kibbutz industrialization. In: U. Leviatan, & M. Rosner (Eds), *Work and Organization in Kibbutz Industry* (pp. 17–33). Norwood, PA: Norwood Editions.

Rosner, M., & Palgi, M. (1982). Equality between the sexes: Retreat or new significance. In: M. Rosner (Ed.), *Democracy, equality and change: The kibbutz and social theory* (pp. 22–37). Norwood, PA: Norwood Editions.

Rosner, M., Shur, S. Chizik, M., & Avnat, A. (1989). *Trends in Kibbutz Socialism: Similarities and Differences between the Kibbutz Movements*. Tel Aviv: Sifriat Poalim. (Hebrew).

Rosner, M., & Tannenbaum, A. (1987a). Ownership and alienation in kibbutz factories. *Work and Occupations*, *14*, 165–189.

Rosner, M., & Tannenbaum, A. (1987b). Organizational efficiency and egalitarian democracy in an intentional communal society: The kibbutz. *The British Journal of Sociology*, *38*, 521–545.

Rosolio, D. (1994). The kibbutz movement and the way it functions as a cause of the kibbutz crisis: A study of political economy. *Journal of Rural Cooperation*, *22*, 63–78.

Rosolio, D. (1998). Inter-kibbutz organizations and cooperatives. In: U. Leviatan, H. Oliver & J. Quarter (Eds), *Crisis in the Israeli Kibbutz* (pp. 147–158). London: Praeger.

Russell, R. (1985). Employee ownership and internal governance. *Journal of Economic Behavior and Organization*, *6*, 217–241.

Sadan, E. (1976). Financial indicators and economic performance in the kibbutz sector. In: N. Halevi, & Y. Kop (Eds), *Israel Economic Papers* (pp. 242–52). Jerusalem: Israel economic Association and Falk Institute (Hebrew).

Saltman, M. (1983). Legality and ideology in the kibbutz movement. In: E. Krause (Ed.), *The Sociology of the Kibbutz*. (pp.125–148). New Brunswick: Transaction Books.

Satt, E., & Ginzberg, H. (1992). On the dynamic effects of using hired labor in the kibbutz – theory and case studies. *Journal of Comparative Economics*, *16*, 688–700.

Satt, E., & Schaefer, Z. (1994). The anatomy of using hired labor in the kibbutz: Interdisciplinary approach and new data. *Journal of Rural Cooperation*, *22*, 131–147.

Shalem, E. (1998). The Financing of Collective Organizations: Between External Control, Dependence on Public Capital and Economic Independence. MA thesis, Department of Labor Studies, Tel Aviv University (Hebrew).

Shapira, A., & Madsen, M. C. (1974). Between- and within- group cooperation and competition among kibbutz and nonkibbutz children. *Developmental Psychology*, *10*, 140–145.

Shapira, R. (1988). Rotation, management and leadership in kibbutz. Discussion paper No. 42. The Golda Meir Institute, Tel Aviv University, Tel Aviv (Hebrew).

Shapira, Reuven. (1990). Automatic rotation and organizational conservatism in the kibbutz. *Megamot*, *32*, 522–536 (Hebrew).

Shepher, J., & Tiger, L. (1981). Kibbutz and parental investment. In: P. A. Hare, H. H. Blumberg, V. Kent, & M. Davies (Eds), *Small groups: Social-psychological processes, social action and living together*. London: Wiley.

Simons, T., & Ingram, P. (1997). Organization and ideology: Kibbutzim and hired labor, 1951–1965. *Administrative Science Quarterly, 42*, 784–813.

Simons, T., & Ingram, P. (1999). Competition in the supply of political order: State power and kibbutz founding, 1910–1996. Paper presented at the Academy of Management meetings, Chicago.

Spiro, M. E. (1958). *Children of the Kibbutz*. Cambridge: Harvard University Press.

Spiro, M. E. (1979). *Gender and culture: Kibbutz women revisited*. Durham, NC: Duke University Press.

Staw, B. M. (1980). The consequences of turnover. *Journal of Occupational Psychology, 1*, 253–273.

Stouffer, S. A. (1949). *The American Soldier*. New York: Wiley.

Talmon-Garber, Y. (1972). *Family and Community in the Kibbutz*. Cambridge: Harvard University Press.

Tanenbaum A. S., Kavcic, B., Rosner, M., Vianello, M., & Wieser, G. (1977). *Hierarchy in Organizations*, San Francisco: Jossey-Bass Publishers.

Tiger, L., & Shepher, J. (1975). *Women in the Kibbutz*. New York: Harcourt Brace Jovanovich.

Vallier, I. (1983). Structural differentiation, production imperatives, and communal norms: The kibbutz in crisis. In: E. Krause (Ed.), *The Sociology of the Kibbutz* (pp. 333–342), New Brunswick: Transaction Books.

Viteles, H. (1966). *A History of the Co-operative Movement in Israel. Book 1: The Evolution of the Cooperative Movement*. London: Vallentine Mitchell.

Viteles, H. (1967). *A History of the Co-operative Movement in Israel. Book 2: The Evolution of the Kibbutz Movement*. London: Vallentine Mitchell.

Warhurst, C. (1996a). High society in a workers society: Work, community and kibbutz. *Sociology, 30*, 1–19.

Warhurst, C. (1996b). The management of production and the changing character of the kibbutz as a mode of production. *Economic and Industrial Democracy, 17*, 419–445.

Warhurst, C. (1998). Recognizing the possible: The organization and control of a socialist labor process. *Administrative Science Quarterly, 43*, 470–497.

Williams, K. Y., & C. O'Reilly. (1998). Demography and diversity in organizations: A review of 40 years of reseach. In: B. M. Staw & L. Cummings (Eds), *Research in Organizational Behavior* (Vol. 20, pp. 77–140). Greenwich, CT: JAI Press.

Wilson, J. (1973). *Introduction to Social Movements*. New York: Basic Books.

Yuchtman, E. (1972). Reward distribution and work-role attractiveness in the kibbutz – reflections on equity theory. *American Sociological Review, 37*, 581–595.

THE NETWORK STRUCTURE OF SOCIAL CAPITAL

Ronald S. Burt

ABSTRACT

This is a review of argument and evidence on the connection between social networks and social capital. My summary points are three: (1) Research and theory will better cumulate across studies if we focus on the network mechanisms responsible for social capital effects rather than trying to integrate across metaphors of social capital loosely tied to distant empirical indicators. (2) There is an impressive diversity of empirical evidence showing that social capital is more a function of brokerage across structural holes than closure within a network, but there are contingency factors. (3) The two leading network mechanisms can be brought together in a productive way within a more general model of social capital. Structural holes are the source of value added, but network closure can be essential to realizing the value buried in the holes.

Research in Organizational Behaviour, Volume 22, pages 345–423.
ISBN: 0–7623–0641–6

INTRODUCTION

Social capital is fast becoming a core concept in business, political science, and sociology. An increasing number of research articles and chapters on social capital are appearing (look at the recent publication dates for the references to this chapter), literature reviews have begun to appear (e.g. Nahapiet & Ghoshal, 1998; Portes, 1998; Sandefur & Laumann, 1998; Woolcock, 1998; Foley & Edwards, 1999; Lin, 1999; Adler & Kwon, 2000), books are dedicated to it (e.g. Leenders & Gabbay, 1999; Baker, 2000; Lesser, 2000; Lin, Cook, & Burt, 2001; Lin, forthcoming), and the term in its many uses can be found scattered across the internet (as a business competence, a goal for non-profit organizations, a legal category, and the inevitable subject of university conferences). Portions of the work are little more than loosely-formed opinion about social capital as a metaphor, as is to be expected when such a concept is in the bandwagon stage of diffusion. But what struck me in preparing this review is the variety of research questions on which useful results are being obtained with the concept, and the degree to which more compelling results could be obtained and integrated across studies if attention were focused beneath the social capital metaphor on the specific network mechanisms responsible for social capital. For, as it is developing, social capital is at its core two things: a potent technology and a critical issue. The technology is network analysis. The issue is performance. Social capital promises to yield new insights, and more rigorous and stable models, describing why certain people and organizations perform better than others. In the process, new light is shed on related concerns such as coordination, creativity, discrimination, entrepreneurship, leadership, learning, teamwork, and the like – all topics that will come up in the following pages. I cover diverse sources of evidence, but focus on senior managers and organizations because that is where I have found the highest quality data on the networks that provide social capital.[1] The goal is to determine the network structures that are social capital.

SOCIAL CAPITAL METAPHOR

Figure 1 is an overview of social capital in metaphor and network structure. The figure is a road map through the next few pages, and a reminder that beneath the general agreement about social capital as a metaphor lie a variety of network mechanisms that make contradictory predictions about social capital.

Cast in diverse styles of argument (e.g. Coleman, 1990; Bourdieu & Wacquant, 1992; Burt 1992; Putnam, 1993), social capital is a metaphor about

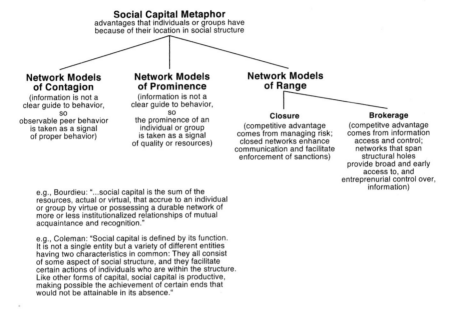

Fig. 1. Social Capital, in Metaphor and Network Structure.

advantage. Society can be viewed as a market in which people exchange all variety of goods and ideas in pursuit of their interests. Certain people, or certain groups of people, do better in the sense of receiving higher returns to their efforts. Some enjoy higher incomes. Some more quickly become prominent. Some lead more important projects. The interests of some are better served than the interests of others. The human capital explanation of the inequality is that the people who do better are more able individuals; they are more intelligent, more attractive, more articulate, more skilled.

Social capital is the contextual complement to human capital. The social capital metaphor is that the people who do better are somehow better connected. Certain people or certain groups are connected to certain others, trusting certain others, obligated to support certain others, dependent on exchange with certain others. Holding a certain position in the structure of these exchanges can be an asset in its own right. That asset is social capital, in essence, a concept of location effects in differentiated markets. For example, Bourdieu is often quoted as in Fig. 1 in defining social capital as the resources that result from social structure (Bourdieu & Wacquant, 1992, p. 119, expanded from Bourdieu, 1980). Coleman, another often-cited source as quoted in Fig. 1, defines social capital as a function of social structure producing advantage (Coleman, 1990, p. 302; from Coleman 1988, S98). Putnam (1993, p. 167) grounds his influential work in Coleman's argument, preserving the focus on action facilitated by social structure: "Social capital here refers to features of social organization, such as trust, norms, and networks, that can improve the efficiency of society by facilitating coordinated action." I echo the above with a social capital metaphor to begin my argument about the competitive advantage of structural holes (Burt, 1992, pp. 8, 45).

So there is a point of general agreement from which to begin a discussion of social capital. The cited perspectives on social capital are diverse in origin and style of accompanying evidence, but they agree on a social capital metaphor in which social structure is a kind of capital that can create for certain individuals or groups a competitive advantage in pursuing their ends. Better connected people enjoy higher returns.

NETWORK MECHANISMS

Disagreements begin when the metaphor is made concrete in terms of network mechanisms that define what it means to be 'better connected'. Connections are grounded in the history of a market. Certain people have met frequently. Certain people have sought out specific others. Certain people have completed exchanges with one another. There is at any moment a network, as illustrated in Fig. 2, in which individuals are variably connected to one another as a function of prior contact, exchange, and attendant emotions. Figure 2 is a generic sociogram and density table description of a network. People are dots. Relations are lines. Solid (dashed) lines connect pairs of people who have a strong (weak) relationship.

In theory, the network residue from yesterday should be irrelevant to market behavior tomorrow. I buy from the seller with the most attractive offer. That seller may or may not be the seller I often see at the market, or the seller from whom I bought yesterday. So viewed, the network in Fig. 2 would recur tomorrow only if buyers and sellers come together as they have in the past. The recurrence of the network would have nothing to do with the prior network as a casual factor. Continuity would be a by-product of buyers and sellers seeking one another out as a function of supply and demand.

Networks Affect and Replace Information

Selecting the best exchange, however, requires that I have information on available goods, sellers, buyers, and prices. This is the point at which network mechanisms enter the analysis. The structure of prior relations among people and organizations in a market can affect, or replace, information.

Replacement happens when market information is so ambiguous that people use network structure as the best available information. Such assumption underlies the network contagion and prominence mechanisms to the left in Fig. 1. For example, transactions could be so complex that available information cannot be used to make a clear choice between sellers, or available information could be ambiguous such that no amount of it can be used to pick the best exchange. White (1981) argues that information is so ambiguous for producers that competition is more accurately modeled as imitation. A market is modeled

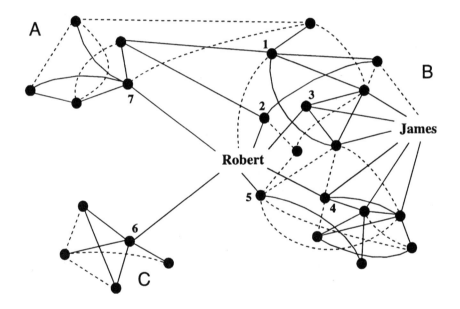

Density Table of Relations Within and Between Groups

.65			Group A (5 people and 8 ties; 5 strong, 3 weak)
.05	.25		Group B (17 people and 41 ties; 27 strong, 14 weak)
.00	.01	.65	Group C (5 people and 8 ties; 5 strong, 3 weak)

Fig. 2. Social Organization.

as a network clique (in other words, a small, cohesive group distinct from an external environment). Price within the clique is determined by producers taking positions relative to other producers on the market schedule. Information quality is also the problem addressed in Podolny's concept of status as market signal (Podolny, 1993; Podolny, Stuart & Hannan, 1997; Benjamin & Podolny, 1999). In his initial paper, Podolny (1993) described how investors not able to get an accurate read on the quality of an investment opportunity look to an investment bank's standing in the social network of other investment banks as a signal of bank quality, with the result that banks higher in status are able to borrow funds at lower cost. More generally, presumptions about the inherent ambiguity of market information underlie social contagion explanations of firms adopting policies in imitation of other firms (e.g. Greve, 1995; Davis & Greve, 1997; see Strang & Soule, 1998, for review; Burt, 1987, on the cohesion and equivalence mechanisms that drive contagion). Zuckerman's (1999) market model is an important new development in that the model goes beyond producer conformity to describe penalties that producers pay for deviating from accepted product categories, and the audience (mediators) that enforce the penalties.

The network contagion and prominence mechanisms describe social capital. Contagion can be an advantage in that social structure ensures the transmission of beliefs and practices more readily between certain people and organizations (a theme in Bourdieu's discussion of cultural capital), and of course, network prominence has long been studied as an advantage for people (e.g. Brass, 1992) and organizations (e.g. Podolny, 1993).

Although contagion and prominence mechanisms can be discussed as social capital, they are more often discussed as other concepts – for example, imitation in institutional theory, or reputation and status in economics and sociology – so I put them aside for this turn-of-the-century review. Future reviewers will not be so lucky. The contagion and prominence mechanisms are not ideas around which current social capital research has accumulated, but they certainly could be, and so are likely to be in future if the social capital metaphor continues to be so popular.

The other two mechanisms in Fig. 1, closure and brokerage, have been the foundation for work on social capital. These two mechanisms do not assume that networks replace information so much as affect the flow of information and what people can do with it.

Both mechanisms begin with the assumption that communication takes time, so prior relationships affect who knows what early. Information can be expected to spread across the people in a market, but it will circulate within groups before it circulates between groups. A generic research finding is that information circulates more within than between groups – within a work group more than between groups, within a division more than between divisions, within an industry more than between industries. For example, the sociogram in Fig. 2 and the density table at the bottom of the figure show three groups (A, B, C), and the generic pattern of in-group relations stronger than relations between groups (diagonal elements of the density table are higher than the off-diagonals, each cell of the density table is the average of relations between individuals in the row and individuals in the column). The result is that people are not simultaneously aware of opportunities in all groups. Even if information is of high quality, and eventually reaches everyone, the fact that diffusion occurs over an interval of time means that individuals informed early or more broadly have an advantage.

Network Closure as Social Capital

Coleman's (1988, 1990) view of social capital focuses on the risks associated with incomplete information. I will refer to Coleman's view as a closure argument. Networks with closure – that is to say networks in which everyone is connected such that no one can escape the notice of others, which in operational terms usually means a dense network – are argued to be the source of social capital.

Specifically, closure is argued to do two things for people in the closed network. First, it affects access to information (Coleman,1990, p. 310; cf. 1988, p. S104): "An important form of social capital is the potential for information the inheres in social relations . . . . a person who is not greatly interested in current events but who is interested in being informed about important developments can save the time required to read a newspaper if he can get the information he wants from a friend who pays attention to such matters." For example, noting that information quality deteriorates as it moves from one person to the next in a chain of intermediaries, Baker (1984; Baker & Iyer, 1992) argues that markets with networks of more direct connections improve communication between producers, which stabilizes prices, the central finding in Baker's (1984) analysis of a securities exchange.

Second, and this is the benefit more emphasized by Coleman, network closure facilitates sanctions that make it less risky for people in the network to trust one another. Illustrating the trust advantage with rotating-credit associations, Coleman (1988, p. S103; 1990, pp. 306–307; see Biggart, 2000, for a closer look at how such associations operate) notes; "But without a high degree of trustworthiness among the members of the group, the institution could not exist – for a person who receives a payout early in the sequence of meetings could abscond and leave the others with a loss. For example, one could not imagine a rotating-credit association operating successfully in urban areas marked by a high degree of social disorganization – or, in other words, by a lack of social capital." With respect to norms and effective sanctions, Coleman (1990, pp. 310–311; cf. 1988, p. S104) says; "When an effective norm does exist, it constitutes a powerful, but sometimes fragile, form of social capital . . . . Norms in a community that support and provide effective rewards for high achievement in school greatly facilitate the school's task." Coleman (1988, pp. S107-S108) summarizes; "The consequence of this closure is, as in the case of the wholesale diamond market or in other similar communities, a set of effective sanctions that can monitor and guide behavior. Reputation cannot arise in an open structure, and collective sanctions that would ensure trustworthiness cannot be applied." He continues (Coleman, 1990, p. 318); "The effect of closure can be seen especially well by considering a system involving parents and children. In a community where there is an extensive set of expectations and obligations connecting the adults, each adult can use his drawing account with other adults to help supervise and control his children."

Coleman's closure argument is prominent with respect to social capital, but it is not alone in predicting that dense networks facilitate trust and norms by facilitating effective sanctions. In sociology, Granovetter (1985, 1992, p. 44) argues that the threat of sanctions makes trust more likely between people who have mutual friends (mutual friends being a condition of structural embeddedness): "My mortification at cheating a friend of long standing may be substantial even when undiscovered. It may increase when the friend becomes aware of it. But it may become even more unbearable when our mutual friends uncover the deceit and tell one another." There is an analogous argument in economics (the threat of sanctions creating a reputation effect, e.g. Tullock, 1985; Greif, 1989): Mutual acquaintances observing two people: (a) make behavior between the two people public, which (b) increases the salience of reputation for entry to future relations with the mutual acquaintances, (c) making the two people more careful about the cooperative image they display, which (d) increases the confidence with which each can trust the other to cooperate. This chapter is about social capital, so I focus on Coleman's prediction that network closure creates social capital. I have elsewhere discussed the network structures that facilitate trust, showing that closure's association with distrust and character assassination is as strong as its association with trust (Burt, 1999a; 2001).

The closure prediction, in sum, is that in comparisons between otherwise similar people like James and Robert in Fig. 2, it is James who has more social capital. Strong relations among his contacts are argued to give James more reliable communication channels, and protect him from exploitation because he and his contacts are more able to act in concert against someone who violates their norms of conduct.

Structural Holes as Social Capital

Participation in, and control of, information diffusion underlies the social capital of structural holes (Burt, 1992). The argument describes social capital as a function of brokerage opportunities, and draws on network concepts that emerged in sociology during the 1970s; most notably Granovetter (1973) on the strength of weak ties, Freeman (1977) on betweenness centrality, Cook & Emerson (1978) on the benefits of having exclusive exchange partners, and Burt (1980) on the structural autonomy created by complex networks. More generally, sociological ideas elaborated by Simmel (1955 [1922]) and Merton (1968 [1957]) on the autonomy generated by conflicting affiliations are mixed in the hole argument with traditional economic ideas of monopoly power and oligopoly to produce network models of competitive advantage.

The weaker connections between groups in Fig. 2 are holes in the social structure of the market. These holes in social structure – or more simply, structural holes – create a competitive advantage for an individual whose relationships span the holes. The structural hole between two groups does not mean that people in the groups are unaware of one another. It only means that the people are focused on their own activities such that they do not attend to the activities of people in the other group. Holes are buffers, like an insulator in an electric circuit. People on either side of a structural hole circulate in different flows of information. Structural holes are thus an opportunity to broker the flow of *information* between people, and *control* the projects that bring together people from opposite sides of the hole.

Structural holes separate nonredundant sources of information, sources that are more additive than overlapping. There are two network indicators of redundancy: cohesion and equivalence. Cohesive contacts (contacts strongly connected to each other) are likely to have similar information and therefore provide redundant information benefits. Structurally equivalent contacts (contacts who link a manager to the same third parties) have the same sources of information and therefore provide redundant information benefits.

Robert and James in Fig. 2 have the same volume of connections, six strong ties and one weak tie, but Robert has something more. James is connected to people within group B, and through them to friends of friends all within group B. James can be expected to be well informed about cluster B activities. Robert is also tied through friends of friends to everyone within group B, but in addition, his strong relationship with contact 7 is a conduit for information on group A, and his strong relationship with 6 is a conduit for information on group C. His relationship with 7 is for Robert a network bridge in that the relationship is his only direct connection with group A. His relationship with contact 6 meets the graph-theoretic definition of a network bridge. Break that relationship and there is no connection between groups B and C. More generally, Robert is a broker in the network. Network constraint is an index that measures the extent to which a person's contacts are redundant (Burt, 1992). James has a constraint score twice Robert's (30.9 vs. 14.8) and Robert is the least constrained of the people in Fig. 1 (− 1.4 z-score). Network betweenness, proposed by Freeman (1977), is an index that measures the extent to which a person brokers indirect connections between all other people in a network. Robert's betweenness score of 47.0 shows that almost half of indirect connections run through him. His score is the highest score in Fig. 1, well-above average (47.0 is a 4.0 z-score), and much higher than James' 5.2 score, which is below average.

Robert's bridge connections to other groups give him an advantage with respect to information access. He reaches a higher volume of information because he reaches more people indirectly. Further, the diversity of his contacts across the three separate groups means that his higher volume of information contains fewer redundant bits of information. Further still, Robert is positioned at the cross-roads of social organization so he is early to learn about activities in the three groups. He corresponds to the opinion leaders proposed in the early diffusion literature as the individuals responsible for the spread of new ideas and behaviors (Burt, 1999b). More, Robert's more diverse contacts mean that he is more likely to be a candidate discussed for inclusion in new opportunities. These benefits are compounded by the fact that having a network that yields such benefits makes Robert more attractive to other people as a contact in their own networks.

There is also a control advantage. Robert is in a position to bring together otherwise disconnected contacts, which gives him disproportionate say in whose interests are served when the contacts come together. More, the holes between his contacts mean that he can broker communication while displaying different beliefs and identities to each contact (robust action in Padgett & Ansell, 1993; see Brieger, 1995, on the connection with structural holes). Simmel and Merton introduced the sociology of people who derive control benefits from structural holes: The ideal type is the *tertius gaudens* (literally, "the third who benefits," see Burt, 1992, pp. 30–32, for review). More generally, Robert in Fig. 2 is an entrepreneur in the literal sense of the word – a person who adds value by brokering connections between others (Burt, 1992, pp. 34–36; see also Aldrich, 1999, Chap. 4; Thornton, 1999). There is a tension here, but not the hostility of combatants. It is merely uncertainty. In the swirling mix of preferences characteristic of social networks, where no demands have absolute authority, the *tertius* negotiates for favorable terms. Structural holes are the setting for *tertius* strategies, and information is the substance. Accurate, ambiguous, or distorted information is strategically moved between contacts by the *tertius*. The information and control benefits reinforce one another at any moment in time and cumulate together over time.

Thus, individuals with contact networks rich in structural holes are the individuals who know about, have a hand in, and exercise control over, more rewarding opportunities. The behaviors by which they develop the opportunities are many and varied, but the opportunity itself is at all times defined by a hole in social structure. In terms of the argument, networks rich in the entrepreneurial opportunities of structural holes are entrepreneurial networks, and entrepreneurs are people skilled in building the interpersonal bridges that span structural holes. They monitor information more effectively than bureaucratic control. They move information faster, and to more people, than memos. They are more responsive than a bureaucracy, easily shifting network time and energy from one solution to another (vividly illustrated in networks of drug traffic, Williams, 1998, or health insurance fraud, Tillman & Indergaard, 1999). More in control of their surroundings, brokers individuals like Robert in Fig. 2 can tailor solutions to the specific individuals being coordinated, replacing the boiler-plate solutions of formal bureaucracy. To these benefits of faster, better solutions, add cost reductions; entrepreneurial managers offer inexpensive coordination relative to the bureaucratic alternative. Speeding the process toward equilibrium, individuals with networks rich in structural holes operate somewhere between the force of corporate authority and the dexterity of markets, building bridges between disconnected parts of a market where it is valuable to do so.

In sum, the hole prediction is that in comparisons between otherwise similar people like James and Robert in Fig. 2, it is Robert who has more social capital. His network across structural holes is argued to give him broad, early access to, and entrepreneurial control over, information.

The Social Order of Disequilibrium

The difference between brokerage and closure continues into implying different roles for social capital in broader theories of markets and societies. Exaggerating the difference to clarify the point, closure is about stasis while brokerage is about change. Closure is about advantages that go to people in a cohesive group. Strategy guided by the closure argument involves locating a group, and closing ranks with like-minded people. In contrast, the hole argument is about advantages that go to people who build bridges across cohesive groups. Strategy guided by brokerage involves locating a position at the edge of two groups, and building relations between dissimilar people. Brokerage must be the more difficult strategy, but the further difference is that brokerage is explicitly about action that cuts across structural holes in the current social structure.

The greater cost of brokerage must be off-set by greater gains. There is abundant evidence of the gains associated with brokerage, some discussed in the next few pages, but the gains can be expected to disappear as more and more people build bridges across the same structural hole. When the first entrepreneurs benefit from synthesizing information across a structural hole, others join them, and the advantage of bridging the hole disappears. If Fig. 2 were an academic market, for example, and Robert produced a useful idea because of Group A technology he discovered from Contact 7, other academics in Robert's line of work can be expected to develop relationships with contacts in Group A (Contacts 1 and 2 in Group B), eventually eliminating the structural hole between Groups A and B.

The rate of decline in value is a question for future research, but the functional form of the decline is probably nonlinear. Imagine X-Y coordinates where Y is the value of building a strong relationship across a structural hole and X is the number of such relations that exist. The value of Y at X equal one would be the value of the first bridge across the hole, the value at X equal two would be the value of the second bridge, and so on. No one knows how Y decreases across increasing X, but it seems likely that the decrease is steeper for the first few bridges than for the last few. Value is certainly eliminated long before everyone eligible to span the hole has done so. Holes are closed by individuals, not populations. To cite a line of academic work familiar to people reading this chapter, the acclaim that Hannan and Freeman (1977) received for synthesizing organization theory from sociology and population biology was much higher than the acclaim accorded subsequent elaborations within the population ecology of organizations.[2]

Value declines with subsequent entrants down to some equilibrium level at which value is marginally higher than the cost of bridging the hole. Regardless of the rate of decline in value, there is no competitive advantage at system equilibrium to a network that spans structural holes because sufficient people have networks across the structural holes so as to eliminate the value of additional people spanning them. Network entrepreneurs have moved the market to equilibrium by eliminating holes in the market where it was valuable to do so. So viewed, the social capital of structural holes is about a short-run advantage on the path to equilibrium. At equilibrium, the advantage is gone.

That is, unless the system is forever on its way to equilibrium. The short-run advantage of brokerage can become a long-run advantage if social structure is held constant as by culture (e.g. Siamwall, 1978, on Chinese middlemen in the Thai economy; Light & Karageorgis, 1994, on socially excluded ethnicities for whom entrepreneurial activities are the route into society), or technology (e.g. Burt, 1988, 1992, on industry structure-performance differences in the American economy; Burt, 1992, Chap. 6; Bothner, 2000, on structural holes and White's network model of markets as cliques). Or, the short-run advantage of brokerage can be a long-run advantage if information grows quickly out-of-date, as seems to be the case for senior managers (see Mintzberg, 1973; Stinchcombe, 1990, on the short half-life of information in organizations). Such a situation could arise as follows: An industry of managers and organizations moves toward equilibrium. Managers with more social capital have an advantage in identifying and developing the more rewarding opportunities. Technological change and events create new priorities, so the industry begins moving toward a new equilibrium. Again, managers with more social capital have an advantage in identifying and developing the more rewarding opportunities. If the industry is subject to continuing change so that information continues to quickly grow out-of-date, managers with more social capital have a continuous competitive advantage, leaving a residue of association between social capital and performance illustrated by the cross-sectional results discussed in the next few pages.

In short, the hole argument stands apart from closure both in its empirical predictions and in describing a world of change – a world of discovering and developing opportunities to add value by changing social structure with bridges across holes in the structure. The argument, describing competitive advantage on the path to equilibrium, is a story about the social order of disequilibrium.

EVIDENCE

Three kinds of empirical evidence support the argument that social capital is a function of brokerage across structural holes. Lab experiments with small-group exchange networks show that resources accumulate in brokers, people with exclusive exchange relations to otherwise disconnected partners (e.g. Cook & Emerson, 1978; Cook et al., 1983; Markovsky, Willer & Patton, 1988; see Willer, 1999, for review).

Census data on economic transactions have been used to describe how producer profit margins increase with structural holes in networks of transactions with suppliers and customers. Burt (1983) described the association in 1967 with profits in American manufacturing markets defined at broad and detailed levels of aggregation, and extended the results to include nonmanufacturing through the 1960s and 1970s (Burt, 1988, 1992). Burt, Guilarte, Raider & Yasuda (1999) refined the nonlinear form of the model to more accurately describe the association between performance and market network, and extended the results through the early 1990s. Using profit and network data on markets in other countries, similar results have been found in Germany during the 1970s and 1980s (Ziegler, 1982), Israel in the 1970s (Talmud, 1994), Japan in the 1980s (Yasuda, 1996), and Korea in the 1980s (Jang, 1997).

Third, archival and survey data on interpersonal relations have been used to describe the career advantages of having a contact network rich in structural holes. An early, widely known, study is Granovetter's (1995 [1974]) demonstration that white-collar workers find better jobs faster through weak ties that bridge otherwise disconnected social groups (see Burt, 1992, pp. 25–30, on weak ties across structural holes). Lin worked with several colleagues to present evidence of the importance of ties to distant contacts for obtaining more desirable jobs (e.g. Lin, Ensel & Vaughn, 1981; Lin & Dumin, 1986; Lin, 2001, Forthcoming). Similar empirical results appear in Campbell, Marsden & Hurlbert (1986), Marsden & Hurlbert (1988), Flap & De Graaf (1989), Boxman et al. (1991), Lin & Bian (1991), Wegener (1991), Bian (1994, Chap. 5), and in more recent empirical studies (Leenders & Gabbay, 1999; Lin, Cook & Burt, 2001). Lin (1999, Forthcoming) provides an integrative review of such research through a focus on networks as a resource for status attainment.

Individual and Group

Managers in particular have been a fruitful site for network studies of social capital. I can be brief here pending detailed discussion below ('Evidence from Five Study Populations'). Burt (1992, 1995, 1997a) and Podolny & Baron (1997) present survey evidence from probability samples of managers in two high-technology electronics firms showing that senior managers with networks richer in structural holes are more likely to get promoted early. Mizruchi & Sterns (2000), studying loan officers in a large commercial bank, show that the officers whose networks span structural holes in the firm (in the sense of being less dense and less hierarchical) are more likely to be successful in bringing a deal to closure. Burt, Hogarth & Michaud (2000) present evidence from a French chemical firm of salary increasing with the structural holes in a manager's network, and Burt (1997a, 2000b) presents evidence of more positive peer evaluations and higher bonus compensation to investment officers with networks richer in structural holes. Mehra, Kilduff & Brass (2000) find that supervisors in a small high-technology company give higher performance evaluations to employees whose networks bridge otherwise disconnected parts of their organization. Working with more limited data, Sparrowe & Popielarz (1995) innovatively reconstruct past networks around managers to estimate the effects of holes in yesterday's network on promotion today (cf. Hansen, 1999, p. 93), Gabbay (1997) shows that promotions occur more quickly for sales people with strong-tie access to structural holes (cf. Meyerson, 1994, on manager income as a function of strong ties), and Gabbay & Zuckerman (1998) show that expectations of promotion are higher for research and development scientists whose networks are richer in spanning structural holes.

Information and control benefits to individuals aggregate to the management teams on which they serve. For example, Rosenthal (1996) studied the performance of quality management teams in several Midwest manufacturing plants as a function of individual team-member networks within and beyond the team. As discussed below, Rosenthal's data show a dramatic association between team performance and the average social capital of individuals on the team. Teams composed of employees with more entrepreneurial networks were more likely to be recognized for their success in improving the quality of plant operations. Hansen (1999) studied new-product teams in one of America's leading electronics and computer firms, a firm segmented by geography and product lines into 41 divisions. The network data are aggregate in that Hansen asked the R&D manager in each division to describe the extent to which people in his or her division had frequent and close working relationships with other divisions. Team performance is measured by the relative speed with which a team moves from initiation (first employee dedicated to the project) to completion (product released to shipment). Faster solutions are to be expected from teams with the social capital of bridge relationships that span the structural holes between divisions, and Hansen found that teams reached completion more quickly when they were in divisions with frequent and close relations to other divisions.[3] Hansen, Podolny & Pfeffer (2000) study the interpersonal networks around the teams. Each team member was asked to name intra-division contacts from whom he or she had regularly sought information and advice, then asked about relations between the contacts. Teams more quickly completing their assigned task contained people with more non-redundant contacts beyond the team (measured by 'advice size' and 'sparseness').

Related results are reported by Krackhardt & Stern (1988) on higher performance in student groups with cross-group friendships, and in numerous studies of inter-organization networks (also see Leana & Van Buren, 1999, on corporate social capital): Fernandez & Gould (1994) on organizations in broker positions within the national health policy arena being perceived as more influential, Provan & Milward (1995) on higher performing mental health systems that have a hierarchical, rather than a dense, network structure, Geletkanycz & Hambrick (1997) on higher company performance when top managers have boundary-spanning relationships beyond their firm and beyond their industry, Ahuja (1998) on the higher patent output of organizations that hold broker positions in the network of joint ventures or alliances at the top of their industry, Pennings, Lee & Witteloostuijn (1998) on the survival of accounting firms as a function of strong partner ties to client sectors, Stuart & Podolny (1999) on the higher probability of innovation from semiconductor firms that establish alliances with firms outside their own technological area, McEvily & Zaheer (1999) on the greater access to competitive ideas enjoyed by small job manufacturers with more non-redundant sources of advice beyond the firm (and see McEvily & Marcus, 2000, on the lower absorptive capacity of these organizations when their sales network is concentrated in a single customer), Sørensen (1999) on the negative effect on firm growth of redundant networks beyond the firm, Llobrera, Meyer & Nammacher (2000) on the importance of non-redundant networks to the development of Philadelphia's biotechnology district, Koput & Powell (2000) on the higher earnings and survival chances of biotechnology firms with more kinds of activities in alliances with more kinds of partner firms, and Podolny (2000) on the higher probability of early-stage investments surviving to IPO for venture-capital firms with joint-investment networks of otherwise disconnected partners.

Suggestive results come from research in which networks beyond the team are inferred from the demography of the people within the team. Ancona & Caldwell (1992a) provide a study of this type describing 409 individuals from 45 new-product teams in five high-technology companies. Teams were distinguished by managerial ratings of innovation, member reports on the volume of communication outside the team (Ancona & Caldwell, 1992b, distinguish types of communication), functional diversity (members from multiple functions) and tenure diversity (members vary in their length of time with the firm). Structural holes are implicit in the boundaries between corporate divisions and the boundaries between cohorts of employees in that each division or cohort is presumed to have its own unique perspectives, skills, or resources. A team composed of people from diverse corporate functions spans more structural holes in the firm, and so has faster access to more diverse information and more control over the meaning of the information, than a team composed of people from a single function. For tenure diversity, replace the timing and control advantages of access to more functionally diverse information with the same advantages stemming from access to information that differs between employees long with the firm who are familiar with how things have worked before and newer employees more familiar with procedures and techniques outside the firm.

More innovative solutions are to be expected from teams with the social capital of bridge relationships that span the structural holes between divisions (see 'Creativity and Learning' below for detailed discussion), and Ancona and Caldwell report higher managerial ratings of innovation for teams with more external communication, and more external communication by teams drawn from diverse functions.

Tenure diversity has the opposite effect. Ancona and Caldwell report some benefits of tenure diversity associated with higher evaluations of team performance, but the aggregate direct effect of tenure diversity is lower performance. Presumably, people drawn from widely separate employee cohorts have more difficulty with communication and coordination within the team.

The conflicting results are brought together in a productive way by Reagans & Zuckerman (1999) in their study of performance in 223 corporate R&D units within 29 major American firms in eight industries. They report higher levels of output from units in which scientists were drawn from widely separate employee cohorts (implying that their networks reached diverse perspectives, skills and resources outside the team) *and* there is a dense communication network within the unit. In other words, the negative association between performance and tenure diversity reported by Ancona and Caldwell could have been positive if the density of communication within the team had been held constant. Tenure diversity (or other kinds of diversity, see Williams & O'Reilly, 1998) can be disruptive because of the difficulties associated with communicating and coordinating across different perspectives, but when communication is successful (as implied by a dense communication network within the team), team performance is enhanced by the timing and control advantages of the team having access to more diverse information (as Ancona and Caldwell initially predict, and as predicted by the hole argument).

This is a productive observation because it is consistent with the performance effects of structural holes in market networks. The aggregate profit margin for a market increases with the organization of producers in the market and the disorganization of suppliers and customers (Burt, 1992, pp. 91–97). The market model applied to team performance predicts that high performance teams will be those in which member networks beyond the team span structural holes (giving the team access to diverse perspectives, skills and resources), and strong relations within the team provide communication and coordination (so the team can take advantage of its access to diverse perspectives, skills and resources; see Fig. 5 below on the joint benefits of network closure and structural holes).

At the same time that group performance is enhanced by the social capital of its members, organization social capital can enhance employee performance. For example, Bielby & Bielby (1999) describe a decade of data on the careers of almost nine thousand film and television writers. Social capital in their study is held by the talent agency that represents a writer. About half of the writers had no representation (52% in 1987, down to 38% in 1992; Bielby & Bielby, 1999, p. 73). A quarter had the traditional representation of an agency that "finds work . . . and in exchange it receives a 10-percent commission from the client's earnings." (Bielby & Bielby, 1999, p. 66). The remaining quarter of the writers were advantaged by having what Bielby & Bielby (1999, pp. 66–67) describe as 'core' representation; representation by an agency that brokers connections between functional areas to propose whole projects in which the writer is a component: "Instead of seeking out projects for their clients, they initiate projects on their own. They negotiate unique arrangements with the talent guilds and cultivate long-term relationships with those who finance, produce, and distribute new projects." Bielby and Bielby (1999, pp. 70, 72) do not have network data, so they reduce social capital to binary distinctions between those who have it and those who do not; nevertheless, they obtain strong evidence of more likely employment and higher compensation for writers affiliated with the agencies that have it (cf. Yair & Maman, 1996, on the social capital of songwriters attributable to their country's network position among other countries; Jacob, Lys & Neale, 1999, on the more accurate company earnings predictions from analysts employed in brokerage houses providing the information advantages of many other analysts and specialists in the company's industry).[4]

Creativity and Learning

The advantages of bridging structural holes emerge from an individual generating constituency for new ideas synthesized from the diverse information clusters to which a network entrepreneur has access. Creativity and learning are thus central to the competitive advantage of structural holes, and so should be observed more often where relationships bridge structural holes.

Anecdotal evidence can be found in the remarks of prominent creatives. In an often-cited lecture on the influence of commerce on manners, Adam Smith (1766, p. 539) noted that; "When the mind is employed about a variety of objects it is some how expanded and enlarged." Swedberg (1990, p. 3) begins his book of interviews with leading academics working across the boundary between economics and sociology with John Stuart Mills' (1848, p. 581) opinion: "It is hardly possible to overrate the value . . . of placing human beings in contact with persons dissimilar to themselves, and with modes of thought and action unlike those with which they are familiar . . . . Such communication has always been, and is peculiarly in the present age, one of the primary sources of progress." Moving to more contemporary and practical creatives, Jean-René Fourtou, as CEO of the $17-billion-in-sales French chemical and pharmaceutical company Rhne-Poulenc, observed that top scientists were stimulated to their best ideas by people outside their own discipline. Fourtou emphasized *le vide* – literally, the emptiness; conceptually, what I have discussed as structural holes – as essential to creative work (Stewart, 1996, p. 165): "*Le vide* has a huge function in organizations . . . . Shock comes when different things meet. It's the interface that's interesting . . . . If you don't leave *le vide*, you have no unexpected things, no creation. There are two types of management. You can try to design for everything, or you can leave le vide and say, 'I don't know either; what do you think?'" (cf. Hatch, 1999, on the importance of empty places to the integrated improvisation among jazz musicians playing together, and by analogy to the integrated improvisation of managers working together).

A more explicit network perspective underlies Yair & Maman's (1996) conclusion that certain songwriters had a better chance of winning the Eurovision Song Contest because of their country's network position among other countries. Erickson (1996) innovatively measured network diversity for a cross-section of people in the security industry (guards, not financial analysts) by asking whether they have friends and acquaintances in 19 disparate occupations. The more diverse their non-kin contacts (i.e. the more occupations in which they have friends and acquaintances), the broader their knowledge of diverse cultural genres; sports, art, books, restaurants, and business magazines (see Erickson, 2001, for the method applied to an informal local economy showing that participants with more diverse contact networks enjoy higher earnings). In his panoramic analysis of the history of philosophy, Collins (1998) presents sociograms of the intergenerational social networks among philosophers to illustrate his argument that the philosophers of greatest repute tend to be personal rivals representing conflicting schools of thought for their generation (Collins, 1998, p. 76); "The famous names, and the semi-famous ones as well who hold the stage less long, are those persons situated at just those points where the networks heat up the emotional energy to the highest pitch. Creativity is the friction of the attention space at the moments when the structural blocks are grinding against one another the hardest."

Detailed network data underlie Giuffe's (1999) analysis of the 159 fine art photographers who received National Endowment for the Arts photography grants (1986–88) or had solo shows in a New York City gallery (1988). Studying the network of gallery affiliations among the photographers from 1981 through 1992, she finds three structurally distinct careers; peripheral careers of photographers who drop in and out of the gallery world, 'long unbroken careers' in a 'tight knit clique' of densely interconnected photographers, and 'long unbroken careers' in 'loose knit networks' of sparsely interconnected photographers. In terms of structural holes, the peripheral photographers had the least social capital, those with a clique career had little, and those with a career in loose knit networks had the most (cf. Sediatis, 1998, esp. pp. 373–374, on the greater flexibility, adaptability, and volume of business in Russian commodity markets created by organizers who had little previous contact with one another). Relative social capital has a statistically significant association with relative success measured by critical attention to a photographer's work. Giuffe counted the number of reviews each of the photographers received over the study decade in the two major trade magazines, *Art News* and *Art in America*. The peripheral photographers received the least attention (one review for every four photographers), photographers with a clique career received slightly more (p. 84 per photographer), and those with a career in a loose-knit network received the most (3.23 per photographer).

Experience seems to be the answer to questions about where, when, or how people learn about brokering connections across structural holes. Evidence comes from experiments with people learning social structures. Using DeSoto's (1960) experimental design for measuring the difficulty of learning a social structure, Freeman (1992, pp. 123–124) asked college students to learn the relations in a small network that contained a structural hole. Errors occurred when students failed to recall a relationship that existed, but the most frequent error was to fill in the structural hole by saying that the two disconnected people were connected. Janicik (1998) used DeSoto's design with older (M.B.A.) students and added a control for the network around each student in his or her most recent or current job. Students in a job where they were exposed to structural holes learned the network significantly faster, in particular because they quickly recognized the structural hole in the network. If Freeman's undergraduates lived in dense friendship networks as is typical of college students, then they would be disadvantaged in learning the hole-containing network that Freeman presented to them. A conclusion from Freeman's and

Janicik's experiments is that experience matters: People experienced with networks that contain structural holes more easily recognize the holes in new networks.

There is related evidence from fieldwork. Gargiulo & Benassi (2000) describe managers in the research consulting unit of a large Italian firm. They measure 'coordination failure' as the extent to which a manager consults with people not relevant to his assigned projects. They show that coordination failures are significantly more likely for managers with small, dense networks (cf. Barker, 1993). Lofstrom (2000) asked 262 key individuals (scientists, physicians, and engineers) how much they learned from their firm's participation in an alliance intended to develop or extend a medical device technology. Individuals with more non-redundant contacts, especially contacts within their own firm, were more likely to report that they had 'learned a great deal' in the alliance. Burt (2000b) describes change in the colleague networks of 345 bankers over a four-year period, focusing on the decay of the relationships, bridges, that span structural holes. The rate of decay is high (nine out of ten disappear from one year to the next), but significantly lower for bankers who have more experience with such relationships. Inasmuch as the bridges are social capital associated with bonus compensation, and bridge relationships are less subject to decay when they involve people more experienced with bridges, the conclusion is that social capital accrues to those who already have it.

There is also indirect evidence at the level of organizations. Granting that technological change can affect social structure (e.g. Barley, 1990, pp. 92–95, provides a clear illustration with network data), social structure has its own effects on an organization's ability to productively manage technological change. Electronics and biotechnology have been favored research sites for studying such network effects, with Walter Powell (e.g. Powell & Brantley, 1992; Powell, Koput & Smith-Doerr, 1996; Powell et al., 1999; Koput & Powell, 2000) and Toby Stuart (Stuart, 1998; Stuart, Hoang & Hybels, 1999; Stuart & Podolny, 1999; Stuart & Robinson, 2000) prominent ports of entry into the work. More generally, Kogut (2000) builds on a series of studies (e.g. Shan, Walker & Kogut, 1994; Kogut & Zander, 1996; Walker, Kogut & Shan, 1997) to propose a network theory of the firm in which value is derived from a firm's ability to create and lay claim to knowledge derived from its membership and participation in networks (cf. Nahapiet & Ghoshal, 1998, on social capital and knowledge; Powell & Smith-Doerr, 1994, on information in the economic sociology of networks, especially with respect to inter-organization networks).

More specifically, accumulating empirical research shows that structural holes are a correlate of organizational learning, often discussed in terms of an organization's ability to learn – what Cohen & Levinthal (1990, p. 128) describe as an organization's absorptive capacity: "the ability of a firm to recognize the value of new, external information, assimilate it, and apply it to commercial ends." which can be studied in terms of industry factors that facilitate absorption (e.g. Cohen & Levinthal, 1990) and external networks that enhance an organization's absorptive capacity (e.g. Cockburn & Henderson, 1998).

To the extent that the information and control benefits of bridging structural holes enhance organizational learning, the following hypothesis should be true: Organizations with management and collaboration networks that more often bridge structural holes in their surrounding market of technology and practice will learn faster and be more productively creative. This is the hypothesis that Lofstrom (2000) uses to interpret her observation that people in medical-device alliances report more learning when they have a broader network of non-redundant contacts. The hypothesis is related to Ancona & Caldwell's (1992a) report that teams judged more innovative had more external communication with contacts in diverse corporate functions (and see the evidence on group brainstorming in the next section). The hypothesis is explicit in several organization-performance studies cited in the previous section: Ahuja (1998) reports higher patent output for organizations that hold broker positions in the network of joint ventures or alliances at the top of their industry. McEvily & Zaheer (1999) report greater access to competitive ideas for small job manufacturers with more non-redundant sources of advice beyond the firm (and McEvily & Marcus, 2000, show lower absorptive capacity for these organizations when their sales network is concentrated in a single customer). Stuart & Podolny (1999) report a higher probability of innovation from semiconductor firms that establish alliances with firms outside their own technological area. Comparing the biotechnology districts in Minneapolis and Philadelphia, Llobrera, Meyer & Nammacher (2000) attribute the growth and adaptation of Philadelphia's district to its many overlapping but non-redundant networks around organizations in the district. Koput & Powell (2000) report higher earnings and survival chances of biotechnology firms with more kinds of activities in alliances with more kinds of partner firms. Podolny (2000) argues that the information and control advantages of structural holes should be a competitive advantage for venture-capital firms detecting and developing ventures at an early stage of development. He studies panel data on investments from 1981 through 1996 to distinguish venture-capital firms that span structural holes in the sense that they bring together as co-investors other firms that are not investing together. Under attractively stringent controls for autocorrelation, Podolny (2000, p. 22) finds that: "As a venture capital firm acquires a 'deal-flow' network that is rich in structural holes, the firm makes a greater proportion of its investments in the earlier stages." This, in addition to the earlier cited finding of more early-stage investments surviving to IPO for the venture-capital firms whose co-investment network span structural holes.

Whatever the explanation for these results – bridging structural holes enhances an individual's ability to learn, or more intelligent people learn faster and so better report holes in the social structure around them – there is an association between structural holes and learning. The implication, untested in empirical research, is that the social capital of structural holes cumulates over a career so it is critical to encounter holes early in the career (cf. Sørensen, 2000, on the cumulative effects of social heterogeneity on mobility). Managers with experience of structural holes are more likely to see the holes in a new situation, and so enjoy the enhanced performance associated with spanning the holes, and so be promoted to more senior positions, which broadens their opportunities to add value by brokering connections across structural holes.

Process of Brokering

Complementing the above evidence on brokerage's correlates and consequences, there is evidence on the processes by which people create value as they bridge structural holes.

Historical accounts describe processes by which certain brokers became successful. Caro (1982, Chap. 15) provides an often-cited account of Lyndon Johnson's creation of a Washington power base in 1933 from the 'Little Congress', through which he brokered connections between journalists and prominent people in government. Dalzell (1987, Part I) describes brokerage in the creation of an industry. Cotton production in the late 1700s was concentrated in England and consisted of a process in which product moved between separate establishments as it was transformed from raw cotton, to thread, to cloth. The separate establishments reflected the way the industry developed in England. Francis Lowell, looking for a commercial venture, saw during a visit to England the gains to be had if production were integrated across the separate establishments. He drew up plans and assembled what became known a century later as the Boston Associates, a group of investors recruited from family and close friends. With a shared vision of their role in society and reputation keeping their money in the venture over time, the Boston Associates created a thriving American industry with a production process integrated from raw cotton to cloth. DiMaggio (1992, pp. 129–130) describes

Paul Sachs role as broker in establishing the Museum of Modern Art in New York; "Sachs could employ his talents precisely because his strong ties to sectors that had previously been only weakly connected – museums, universities, and finance – placed him at the center of structural holes that were critical to the art world of his time." Padgett & Ansell (1993) describe Cosimo de Medici's use of his contacts with opposing elite family factions to establish his Medicean political party in Renaissance Florence. McGuire & Granovetter (2000) describe Samuel Insull's use of his network of contacts in finance, politics, and technology to shape the electric utility industry at the turn of the century.

Direct observation of brokers offers richer detail. Kotter's (1982) cases illustrate the information and control advantages of an entrepreneurial network in performing the two tasks of successful general managers: reading the organization for needed business policy and knowing what people to bring together to implement the policy. Mintzberg (1973) is similarly rich in case material on the central importance to managers of getting their information live through personal discussions rather than official channels. Adding scope to Macaulay's (1963) intuitions from preliminary interviews with local business-men, Uzzi (1996, 1997) offers selections from fieldwork with producers in the apparel industry illustrating the importance they put in having personal, trusting relationships (termed embedded ties) with key buyers and suppliers rather than having impersonal transactions (termed arm's-length ties, see Appendix; cf. Douthit, 2000, on bridge vs. embedded supervision).

Brainstorming groups are another source of leads into understanding the process of brokerage, specifically as brokerage is associated with creativity. Laboratory and field studies of brainstorming groups show two things: (a) Groups generate fewer, and fewer high-quality, ideas than the same number of people working separately, but (b) people in these studies nevertheless report that groups generate more ideas and as individuals report higher personal performance within groups (e.g. Diehl & Stroebe, 1987; Mullen, Johnson & Salas, 1991, for review; Paulus, Larey & Ortega, 1995, for field illustration in an organization). The connection to social capital is that performance is significantly improved if individuals come to the brainstorming group from heterogeneous backgrounds (Stroebe & Diehl, 1994, pp. 293–297). In other words, the value of group brainstorming is a function of the group facilitating the exchange of ideas across structural holes that separate members in the absence of the group. This is a useful analogy because: (a) it fits with the story emerging about the social capital of groups increasing as a function of network density inside the group combined with bridge relationships spanning structural holes outside the group (see 'Individual and Group' above), and (b) it means that the brainstorming studies which analyze group process can be used to better understand the process of brokerage. For example, Sutton & Hargadon (1996) and Hargadon & Sutton (1997) describe processes by which a firm, IDEO, uses brainstorming to create product designs, creating a status auction within the firm. The firm's employees work for clients in diverse industries. In the brainstorming sessions, technological solutions from one industry are used to solve client issues in other industries where the solutions are rare or unknown. The firm profits, in other words, from employee bridge relationships through which they broker the flow of technology between industries (cf. Allen & Cohen, 1969, on gatekeepers; Lazega & Pattison, 2001, on network management of the status auction).

Finlay & Coverdill (1999a, 1999b) provide selections from their fieldwork with executive headhunters and managers on brokering connections across the structural holes between organizations and market segments. In contrast to research on the consequences of social capital, Finlay & Coverdill (1999b, p. 1) are interested in the "exercise of social capital – on the actual brokering itself." Headhunters offer advantages to a hiring manager in the form of faster search (headhunter has up-to-date data on suitable candidates; "What people are paying me for is somebody with experience to step in to do something right away."), broader search (headhunter knows attractive candidates happy where they are who wouldn't apply for an advertised job, and can recruit from customer or supplier organizations from which recruitment by the hiring manager could threaten his organization's relationship with the raided customer or supplier), and more successful search (headhunter puts time into selecting candidates suited to the job because their compensation depends on their candidate accepting the job). The complication is that the hiring manager's organization has a human resources staff (HR) responsible for recruiting, so brokerage for the headhunter involves matching candidate with the hiring manager while buffering the manager from HR. The tension is indicated by the headhunter phrase for HR staff, 'weenies', and their characterization by one industry trainer, as people who "didn't have the personality to become morticians" (Finlay & Coverdill, 1999a, p. 20). In other words, bridging structural holes in this case involves a simultaneous process of creating holes. As Finlay & Coverdill (1999a, p. 27) conclude: "When headhunters buffer hiring managers from HR or when they shield a client from a competitor, they open gaps in these relationships that the headhunters themselves then bridge. The success of headhunters, and their attractiveness to employers, rests on this dual function of creating and filing holes."

Entrepreneurship

Conspicuous in its absence is evidence on entrepreneurs, in the colloquial sense of entrepreneurs being people who start a business. Such people are inherently network entrepreneurs in the sense of building bridges across structural holes. As Nohria (1992, p. 243) quotes one of his Route 128 entrepreneurs; "A high-technology venture is like a jig-saw puzzle. Each of the pieces is unique and must fit together perfectly if you want the venture to be a success. So the chase in which everybody is involved – be it the entrepreneur, the venture capitalist, the management candidate or whoever else is in the game – is the search for those perfect 'matches' that will help put the puzzle together." Bringing together separate pieces is the essence of entrepreneurship, whether the venture is one of the high-technology ventures so often analyzed by professors in business schools, or the less capital-intensive ethnic ventures so often analyzed by sociologists. There is no value to the venture if it only connects people already connected. As Stewart (1990, p. 149, deleting quotation marks and citations from original) reports from economic anthropology, entrepreneurs focus on: "those points in an economic system where the discrepancies of evaluation are the greatest, and . . . attempt to construct bridging transactions. Bridging roles are based on the recognition of discrepancies of evaluation, which requires an edge in information about both sides of the bridge. Because this requires an information network, bridgers will commit time, energy, travel, and sociability to develop their personal networks. For many entrepreneurs, their most significant resource is a ramifying personal network."

It is a quick step to hypotheses. Here are three: (1) In a cross-section of individuals, those richer in the social capital of strong ties bridging structural holes are more likely to launch entrepreneurial ventures, and the ventures they launch are more likely to succeed. Early access to a broad diversity of perspectives, skills, and resources: (a) is associated with faster learning to identify the holes in new situations, (b) provides a broad base of referrals to customers, suppliers, alliances and employees, (c) helps the entrepreneur identify promising opportunities with respect to customers, suppliers, alliances, employees, financing, and alternative business models, and (d) increases the probability that the entrepreneur knows which of alternative ways to pitch the venture will most appeal to specific potential customers, suppliers, or other sources of revenue. (2) For the same reasons, entrepreneurs with more social capital are more likely to be able to recover ventures that get into trouble. They are aware of trouble sooner, more flexible in re-shaping the venture to adapt to change, and more able to control the interpretation others give to information about the venture. (3) Entrepreneurs richer in the social capital of strong ties to exploitable – exploitable meaning that the contacts have no alternatives to working with the entrepreneur – labor (usually relatives, especially children) or emotional support (usually relatives, especially the spouse or life-partner) are more likely to be successful in their venture.

Although entrepreneurship is a promising site for work on the network forms of social capital, empirical research on the role of networks in entrepreneurship has been limited to the most rudimentary of network data (with rare exceptions such as Stuart, Hoang & Hybels', 1999, analysis of prominent affiliations speeding a venture's time to IPO in biotechnology). See Aldrich (1999, Chap. 4) and Thornton (1999) for broad review, Aldrich in particular for intuitions about the changing role of networks over the course of an entrepreneurial venture (Steier and Greenwood, 2000, provide case-study description with respect to structural holes). As Nohria (1992, p. 249) observed in his study of Route 128 entrepreneurs: "search consists of a matching process in which participants first use categories, typifications or classificatory criteria to identify a set of potential participants; second, they use relational criteria (the index of the other's relations) to establish the trustworthiness of the participant; and third, they use emotional criteria (generated in fact-to-face interaction) to decide whether they should pursue the interaction further."

Two examples are sufficient to illustrate the point: Birley (1985) is a pioneering study in the genre. Focusing on businesses created between 1977 and 1982 in the county surrounding the city of South Bend in Indiana, Birley (1985, pp. 107–108) showed that: "the main sources of help in assembling the resources of raw materials, supplies, equipment, space, employees, and orders were the informal contacts of family, friends, and colleagues. The only institution that was mentioned with any regularity was the bank, which was approached towards the end of the process when many of the resources were assembled and the elements of the business set in the entrepreneur's mind." Network data here are ratings of kinds of contacts (Birley, 1985, p. 113): "Available sources of help were listed and respondents were asked to rank the value of that source in assembling the resources of the firm. No rating for a category indicated that as far as the entrepreneur was concerned, no help was received." Similar network data were used in what could be the most authoritative study of networks in entrepreneurship. Brüderl & Preisendörfer (1998) interviewed in 1990 a random sample of 1,700 entrepreneurs who had started five years earlier a business in Upper Bavaria, Germany. The network data were ratings of kinds of contacts (Brüderl & Preisendörfer, 1998, p. 217): "To get an impression about the role of social contacts in the start-up period of new businesses, participants of our study were asked on a scale ranging from 1 (no support) to 5 (full support) whether they received any support from different kinds of people." With separate measures of active and emotional support from the entrepreneur's spouse, the network data were analyzed as levels of support from two broad categories of people; weak ties (defined as business partners, acquaintances, former employers, or former coworkers), and strong ties (spouse/life-partner, parents, friends, or relatives). Brüderl and Preisendörfer report that entrepreneurs whose business had survived the five years to the survey were more likely than nonsurvivors to give credit to their spouse and strong ties for support.

These two studies are exemplars of the interesting and productive work that has been done on networks and entrepreneurship, but they reveal nothing about the association between network structure and entrepreneurship. The studies do not include data on the variable strengths of an entrepreneur's relations with individual contacts, and the variable strengths of connections between pairs of contacts. Ratings of support from, or acquaintance with, broad categories of contacts leave unknown the network structure variables that measure an entrepreneur's social capital.[5]

So, although entrepreneurship is inherently an exercise in the social capital of structural holes, the topic remains virtually untouched by theory and empirical research on the network forms of social capital. This is an area ripe for study with advances in network theory and analysis. Burt & Raider (2000) provide suggestive evidence. In a representative sample of alumnae from the University of Chicago's Graduate School of Business, they find that the women who became entrepreneurs cited significantly more contacts beyond family and work, and connections with key client contacts in particular were bridge relationships beyond the entrepreneur's immediate circle of contacts.

NETWORK DIMENSIONS OF SOCIAL CAPITAL

My summary conclusion from the preceding section is that the social capital of structural holes can be found in research on diverse substantive questions. The studies reviewed, however, vary dramatically in the depth and precision of their measurement strategies. Broad conclusions are possible – networks across structural holes are clearly a form of social capital – but it is difficult to make exact comparisons across the studies (a problem made worse by population differences correlated with the value of social capital, see 'Contingency Factors' below). So, to draw more precise conclusions, my next step in the review is to present empirical results with comparable network measures in multiple study populations.

I have performance and network data on people in five study populations. Each population was drawn from a medium to large organization, and each has been the subject of detailed analysis elsewhere. The study populations together contain 841 observations, individual managers in four populations, teams in the fifth population. The network measures to be discussed were computed in all five study populations from survey network data. Managers in four of the populations completed network questionnaires in which they were asked to name (see Fig. 4 below on kinds of relations): (a) people with whom they most often discussed important personal matters, (b) the people with whom they most often spent free time, (c) the person to whom they report in the firm, (d) their most promising subordinate, (e) their most valued contacts in the firm, (f) essential sources of buy-in (g) the contact most important for their continued success in the firm, (h) their most difficult contact, and (i) the people with whom they would discuss moving to a new job in another firm. After naming contacts, respondents were asked about their relationship with each contact, and the strength of relations between contacts (see Burt, 1992, pp. 121–125; 1997b; Burt, Hogarth & Michaud, 2000, for item wording and scaling to measure strength of relations with and between contacts).

Network Constraint

There are many ways to measure social capital. Even a simple count of bridge relationships seems to work; people with more bridges do better (Burt, 2000b). As a summary measure of social capital, I use a network constraint index, C, defined in the Appendix (along with details on some alternative measures). Constraint describes the extent to which a person's network is concentrated in redundant contacts (Burt, 1992, Chap. 2). Constraint is high if contacts are directly connected to one another (dense network) or indirectly connected via a central contact (hierarchical network). As a frame of reference, network constraint scores multiplied by 100 have a mean of 27.9 across the 841 observations in the five study populations, with a 10.5 standard deviation. The network around Robert in Fig. 2 is less constrained than the average (C = 15). The network around James is slightly more constrained than average (C = 31).

Association between performance and network constraint is a summary test between the two leading network mechanisms argued to provide social capital. More constrained networks span fewer structural holes, which means less social capital according to the hole argument. *If networks that span structural holes are the source of social capital, then performance should have a negative association with network constraint.* More constraint means more network closure, and so more social capital according to the closure argument. *If network closure is the source of social capital, then performance should have a positive association with constraint.*

Network Size

More specifically, network constraint varies with three dimensions of a network: size, density, and hierarchy. Network size, N, is the number of contacts in a network. For example, Robert and James in Fig. 2 have 7 contacts each, versus an average size of 14.7 in the five study populations). Other things equal, more contacts mean that a manager is more likely to receive diverse bits of information from contacts and is more able to play their individual demands against one another. With respect to measurement, constraint is lower in larger networks because the proportion of a manager's network time and energy allocated to any one contact on average decreases as the number of contacts increases (− 0.66 correlation between network constraint and size across managers in the five study populations). *If networks that span structural holes are social capital, there should be a positive association between performance and network size.* Numbers of contacts are not a variable in the closure argument, but it seems reasonable to expect that more contacts would be advantageous as long as they do not weaken closure. So, association between performance and network size is not a powerful evidential criterion for testing between the closure and hole arguments.

Network Density

Network density, D, is the average strength of connection between contacts. Density is sometimes discussed as a proportion because in studies limited to dichotomous data (two people are connected or not), the average strength of connection between contacts is also the proportion of contact pairs who are connected. With strong ties in Fig. 2 set to a strength of 100, weak ties to 50, and no tie set to zero, density equals 0.0 for Robert in Fig. 2 since none of his contacts have relations with one another. Density is for 35.7 for James. Applying the same scale to relationships in the five study populations, network density is 36.7 on average.

Density is only one form of network closure, but it is a form often discussed as closure. Contacts in a dense network are in close communication so they can readily enforce sanctions against individuals who violate shared beliefs or norms of behavior. *If network closure is the source of social capital, performance should have a positive association with network density.* At the same time, strong connections between contacts increase the probability that the contacts know the same information, and the direct connections eliminate opportunities to broker information between contacts. Dense networks offer less of the information and control advantage associated with spanning structural holes. *If networks that span structural holes are the source of social capital, performance should have a negative association with network density.*

Network Hierarchy

Density is a form of closure in which contacts are equally connected. Hierarchy is an alternative form of closure in which a minority of contacts, typically one or two, stand apart as the source of closure. In the extreme case, a network is hierarchical to the extent that it is organized around one contact. For people in job transition, such as M. B. A. students, that one contact is often the spouse. In the organization, hierarchical networks are often built around the boss. Where network constraint measures the extent to which contacts are redundant, network hierarchy, H, measures the extent to which the redundancy can be traced to a single contact in the network. Network constraint increases with density or hierarchy, but density and hierarchy are empirically distinct measures, and fundamentally distinct with respect to social capital (a central point below in 'The Social Capital of Outsiders'). In the five study populations to be described, for example, network constraint has a strong correlation with density (0.71) and with hierarchy (0.56), but the correlation between density and hierarchy is low (0.18, see Burt, 1992, p. 143, for illustrative graph). *As a form of network closure, hierarchy should have a positive association with performance if closure provides social capital.* In contrast, the central contact in a hierarchical network gets the same information available to the manager and cannot be avoided in manager negotiations with each other contact. More, the central contact can be played against the manager by third parties because information available from the manager is equally available from the central contact since manager and central contact reach the same people. In short, the manager whose network is built around a central contact runs a risk of playing Tonto to the central contact's Lone Ranger. *If networks that span structural holes are the source of social capital, performance should have a negative association with network hierarchy.*

Evidence from Five Study Populations

Component effects are separated in Table 1 for aggregate effects in Fig. 3. The vertical axes in Fig. 3 measure performance (explained below for each study population). The horizontal axes are the summary network constraint index C. Robert, with his 15 points of constraint would appear to the far left of each graph. These are the managers expected to do well because they have networks rich in structural holes – and all six graphs in Fig. 3 show the hole prediction of a negative association between performance and network constraint.

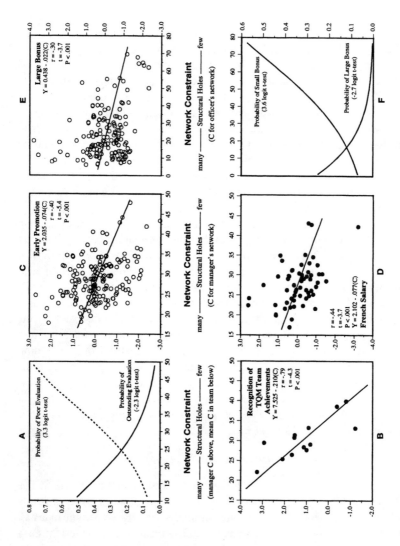

Fig. 3. Social Capital Matters. (More contraint means fewer structural holes, less social capital, and so lower performance [*z*-score performance except in A and F]).

Performance Evaluations

Graphs A and B describe performance evaluations. Fig. 3A is based on a representative sample of staff officers within the several divisions of a large financial organization in 1996 (Burt, Jannotta & Mahoney, 1998). The dependent variable is job performance evaluation, taken from company personnel records. Employees are evaluated at the end of each year on an A, B, C scale of outstanding to poor with plus and minus used to distinguish higher from lower performances within categories. The evaluations stay with an employee over time to affect future compensation and promotion. Women are the majority of the several hundred employees in the staff function (76% of all officers within the function). Of 160 staff officers who returned network questionnaires, the majority are women (69%). The results in Fig. 3 and Table 1 are for the women. I turn to the men in Table 2. Graph A in Fig. 3 shows how the probability of an 'outstanding' and a 'poor' evaluation changes with network constraint. The graph is based on a logit regression predicting the two extremes with the middle category a reference point.[6] Officers with less constrained networks, like Robert, have a significantly higher probability of receiving an outstanding performance evaluation. The stronger effect is the tendency for officers living in the closeted world of a constrained network to receive an evaluation of 'poor'. The results in the first panel of Table 1 come from predicting the evaluations (A = 3, B = 2, C = 1) holding job rank constant.[7] The aggregate negative association between evaluation and network constraint (− 3.8 t-test in Table 1) is primarily a function of network density. Evaluations have a weak positive correlation with network size, and a weak negative correlation with network hierarchy. The significant effect in the regression equation is the tendency for people with dense networks to receive lower evaluations.

Figure 3B is taken from Rosenthal's (1996) dissertation research on the social capital of teams. I do not have the component measures of size, density, and hierarchy, so there are no corresponding results in Table 1. Troubled by the variable success of total quality management (TQM) teams, and inspired by Ancona & Caldwell's (1992a, 1992b) demonstration that networks beyond the team are associated with team performance, Rosenthal wanted to see whether the structure of external relationships had the effect predicted by the hole argument. She gained access to a midwest manufacturing firm in 1994 that was in the process of using TQM teams to improve quality in all of its functions in its several plants (a total of 165 teams). She observed operations in two plants, then asked the senior manager responsible for quality in each plant to evaluate the performance of each TQM team in his or her plant. Evaluations were standardized within plants, then compared across plants to identify functions in which team performance most varied. The study population was teams assigned to a function with high success in some plants and low success in other plants. Selecting two functions for study, Rosenthal sent to each employee on the selected teams a network questionnaire and the survey data were used to compute constraint in each person's network within and beyond the team.

The vertical axis in Fig. 3B is the standardized team evaluation, and the horizontal axis is average constraint on people in the team (average was more predictive than minimum C score in team, maximum C score in team, or

Table 1. Social Capital Effect Disaggregated to Component Size, Density, and Hierarchy Effects

	Multile Correlation	Size	Density	Hierarchy
Performance Evaluation				
Job performance evaluations, staff function within financial company (− 0.34 correlation with constraint across 111 senior women in Figure 3A, − 3.8 t-test)		0.13	− 0.34	− 0.23
	0.39	0.12	− 0.33	− 0.10
		(1.0)	(− 3.4)	(− 0.8)
Promotions				
Early promotion, electronics manufacturer (− 0.40 correlation with constraint across 170 senior men in Figure 3C, − 5.4 t-test)		0.27	− 0.33	− 0.13
	0.49	0.27	− 0.43	− 0.23
		(3.8)	(− 5.7)	(− 3.0)
Compensation				
Relative salary, chemical and drug manufacturer (− 0.44 correlation with constraint across 60 senior managers in Figure 3D, − 3.7 t-test)		0.42	− 0.41	0.02
	0.51	0.30	− 0.33	0.21
		(2.2)	(− 2.3)	(1.7)
Relative bonus, investment officers within financial company (− 0.30 correlation with constraint across 147 senior men in Figure 3E, − 3.7 t-test)		0.33	− 0.38	− 0.34
	0.43	0.08	− 0.26	− 0.18
		(1.0)	(− 3.8)	(− 2.5)

Note: Pearson correlations are given in the first row of each panel, standardized regression coefficients in the second (with routine t-tests in parentheses).

variance within team). The association is as predicted by the hole argument, and quite striking (-0.79 correlation). Teams composed of people whose networks extend beyond the team to span structural holes in the company are significantly more likely to be recognized as successful.[8]

Promotions
Figure 3C describes promotion. The data are taken from a probability sample of senior managers in a large electronics manufacturer in 1989. Performance and network data on these managers have been discussed in detail elsewhere (Burt, 1992, 1995, 1997a, b, 1998). Survey network data were obtained on diverse relationships using the questions described above. Performance and background data on each manager were taken from company personnel records. Company personnel records provided each manager's rank (four levels defined by the firm), date promoted to current rank, date entered the firm, functional area of responsibility (defined by the firm as sales, service, manufacturing, information systems, engineering, marketing, finance, and human resources),and the usual personnel-file variables such as gender, family, income, and so on.

Income in the study population was too closely tied to job rank to measure the relative success of individual managers. Time to rank was a better performance variable (Burt, 1992, pp. 196–197). Whether promoted internally or hired from the outside, people promoted to senior rank in large organizations have several years of experience preceding their promotion. A period of time is expected to pass before people are ready for promotion to senior rank (see Merton, 1984, on socially expected durations). How much time is an empirical question, the answer to which differs between individual managers. Some managers are promoted early. Early promotion is the difference between when a manager was promoted to his current rank and a human capital baseline model predicting the age at which similar managers are promoted to the same rank to do the same work: E(age) minus age. Expected age at promotion E(age), is the average age at which managers with specific personal backgrounds (education, race, gender, and seniority) have been promoted to a specific rank within a specific function (rank, function, and plant location). Expected age at promotion is 12% of the population variance in promotion age, and residuals are distributed in a bell curve around expected promotion age (Burt, 1992, pp. 126–131; 1995). The criterion variable in Fig. 3C and Table 1 is the early promotion variable standardized across all 284 respondents to zero mean and unit variance.

The predicted social capital effect is evident from the negative association in Fig. 3C between early promotion and network constraint. The results are for the

170 most senior men responding to the survey. Women are a minority (12% of the study population, slightly higher 18% of the 284 survey respondents to ensure that there women appear in all sampling categories). I return to the women below in discussing the social capital of outsiders. In Fig. 3C, men promoted early to their current senior rank tend to have low-constraint networks (left side of the graph), while those promoted late tend to have high-constraint networks (right side of the graph). The regression results in the second panel of Table 1 show that significant contributions from each of the component network variables. Men with large networks were promoted early to their senior rank. Men with dense or hierarchical networks were promoted late.[9]

Compensation

The other graphs describe compensation. Figure 3D contains a representative sample of senior managers across functions in one division of a large French chemical and pharmaceuticals company in 1997 (Burt, Hogarth & Michaud, 2000). All 60 respondent managers are included in Fig. 3D and Table 1. Again, survey network data were obtained on diverse relationships using the questions described above. Performance and background data on managers in the study population were taken from company personnel records. Seventy-two% of the study-population variance in annual salaries can be predicted from a manager's job rank and age (salary slightly more associated with age than seniority). The residual 28% of salary variance defines the performance variable in Fig. 3D and Table 1. Relative salary is based on the difference between a manager's salary and the salary expected of someone in his rank at her age: salary minus E(salary). Associations with other background factors are negligible with rank and age held constant (Burt, Hogarth & Michaud, 2000). Relative salary is standardized across all 85 managers in the study population to zero mean and unit variance (a score of 1.5, for example, means that the manager's salary is one and a half standard deviations higher than the salary typically paid to people in his rank at his age).

Relative salary has a negative association with network constraint in Fig. 3D. The managers who enjoy salaries higher than expected from their rank and age tend to be managers with networks that span structural holes in the firm. The component results in the third panel of Table 1 show that the aggregate effect is primarily due to network size and density; relative salary increasing with the number of manager's contacts, and decreasing with the density of relations between the contacts. Building a network around a central contact is not as dangerous here as it is in the American firms. The association with network hierarchy is not significantly positive, but it is clearly not significantly negative as predicted by the hole argument. The component effects in Table 1 are virtually unchanged if I delete the three sample managers who are minorities in the sense that they are not white, married, French men.

Figure 3E contains investment officers in a financial organization in 1993 (Burt, 1997a). The study population includes bankers responsible for client relations, but also includes a large number of administrative and support people who participate in the bonus pool. Performance, background, and network data on the study population are taken from company records. Seventy-three percent of the variance in annual bonus compensation, which varies from zero to millions of dollars, can be predicted from job rank (dummy variables distinguishing ranks defined by the organization), and seniority with the firm (years with the firm, and years in current job). Salary is almost completely predictable from the same variables (95% of salary variance). With rank and seniority held constant, there are no significant bonus differences by officer gender, race, or other background factors on which the firm has data. The residual 27% of bonus variance defines the performance variable in Fig. 3E and Table 1. Relative bonus is based on the difference between the bonus an officer was paid and the bonus typical for someone in his rank, at her age, with his years of seniority at the firm: bonus minus E(bonus). I standardized relative bonus across all officers in the study population to zero mean and unit variance (a score of 1.5, for example, means that an officer's bonus is one and a half standard deviations higher that the bonus typically paid to people at his rank or her rank, age, and seniority). A random sample of officers analyzed for social capital include 147 men in Fig. 3E, and 39 women below in the discussion of outsiders.

The work of this population requires flexible cooperation between colleagues. It is impossible to monitor their cooperation through bureaucratic chains of command because much of their interpersonal behavior is unknown to their immediate supervisor. The firm is typical of the industry in using peer evaluations to monitor employee cooperation. Each year, officers are asked to identify the people with whom they had substantial or frequent business dealings during the year and to indicate how productive it was to work with each person. The firm uses the average of these peer evaluations in bonus and promotion deliberations. The firm does not look beyond the average evaluations. However, there is a network structure in the evaluations that, according to structural hole theory, has implications for an officer's perform-ance, which in turn should affect his bonus (see Eccles & Crane, 1988, Chap. 8). From peer evaluations by the investment officers and colleagues in other divisions of the firm, I identified the people cited as productive contacts by each of the officers, then looked at the evaluations by each contact to see how contacts evaluated one another. I then computed network constraint, size, density, and hierarchy from the network around each officer.

What makes the study population analytically valuable is the time order between the network and performance data. The hole argument gives a causal role to social structure. Consistent with the argument, I assume the primacy of social structure for theoretical and heuristic purposes. I am limited to assuming the primacy of social structure because the data collected in the four study populations discussed above are cross-sectional and so offer no evidence of causation (see Burt, 1992, pp. 173–180, for discussion). It is difficult to gather survey network data, wait for the relative success of managers to emerge over time, then gather performance data. The network data on the investment officers were obtained in the routine of gathering peer evaluations to affect bonus compensation five months later.

There is a negative association in Fig. 3E between bonus compensation and network constraint (–3.7 t-test). The managers who received bonuses higher than expected from their rank and seniority tend to have networks that span structural holes in the firm (and the effect continues over the next three years, Burt, 2000b). The component results in the fourth panel of Table 1 show that the aggregate effect in Fig. 3E is due primarily to network density and hierarchy. Bonus compensation increases with the number of an officer's contacts, but the association disappears when density and hierarchy are held constant. The significant contributions are the tendency for low bonuses to go to officers with networks of densely connected contacts and to officers who have built their network around a central person.

The logit results in Fig. 3F show that the social capital effect is even stronger than implied by the results in Fig. 3E. There is a triangular pattern to the data in Fig. 3E. On the right side of the graph, officers with the most constrained networks receive low bonuses. On the left, officers receiving larger bonuses than their peers tend to have low-constraint networks, but many officers with equally unconstrained networks receive small bonuses. I attribute this to annual data. The low-constraint networks that span structural holes provide better access to rewarding opportunities, but that is no guarantee of exceptional gains every year. There is a 0.47 partial correlation between bonus in the current year and bonus in the previous year (after rank and seniority are held constant). Even the most productive officers can see a lucrative year followed by a year of routine business. So, the logit results in Fig. 3F more accurately describe the social capital effect for the investment officers. I divided the officers into three bonus categories: large (bonus more than a standard deviation larger than expected from rank and seniority) medium, and small (bonus more than a standard deviation larger than expected from rank and seniority). Network constraint this year significantly decreases the probability of receiving a large bonus next year, but the stronger effect is the increased probability of receiving a low bonus next year.

Across the Five Study Populations
The illustrative evidence supports two conclusions: First, the social capital of networks that span structural holes matters for manager performance; improving evaluations of the manager's work, the probability of early promotion, and the manager's compensation relative to peers. Second, performance associations with the three component variables vary across the populations, but strongly support structural holes over closure as the source of social capital. Performance is higher for managers with large networks, but the positive association with size is only significant in two of the Table 1 populations. Performance is weaker for managers whose network is built around a central person, but the negative association with hierarchy is only significant in two Table 1 populations, and almost positive in another population. The one consistent association is between dense networks and substandard performance. Network density has a significantly negative association with performance in all of the study populations.

CONTINGENCY FACTORS

The case is not as simple as implied by the evidence thus far. My final step in the review is to describe the contingent value of social capital. A contingency factor is a variable that affects the strength of association between social capital and performance. I review five contingency factors: personality and culture, kinds of relationships, peers and task uncertainty, network closure, and the distinction between insiders versus outsiders. These factors are productive to review because, as I explain, debate over network mechanisms responsible for social capital can be resolved in large part by understanding contingency.

Motivation: Personality and Culture

Brokerage opportunities do not by themselves turn into success, and people are not equally comfortable as brokers between groups. Is the connection between performance and brokerage contingent on being a person who is comfortable working with structural holes?

One response is to assume the motivation issue away. For example, if individuals are rationally self-interested in a micro-economic sense, personal preference about brokering connections is not a contingency factor. To know who succeeds, you only need to know who has the opportunity to succeed.

Or, motivation can be dismissed as a correlate of network structure, and so not necessary to measure once one has a measure of network structure (Burt, 1992, pp. 34–36). For reasons of a clear path to success (a person is more likely to see brokerage opportunities in a large, sparse network), or the personality of the individual who constructed the network (people inclined toward brokering connections between others build large, sparse networks), or the nature of exogenous factors responsible for the structure of the network (persons forced to live in large, sparse networks are more likely to learn about brokering connections between others) – large, sparse networks are more likely to surround a person motivated to be entrepreneurial in the sense of building networks that span structural holes.

Or, the motivation issue can be addressed directly by adding personality or culture to the equation predicting performance. For example, McClelland (1961) argues that the childhood formation of a need to achieve is a personality factor critical to later entrepreneurial behavior, and Weber (1905) makes the culture argument that Protestant beliefs encouraged capitalism by making entrepreneurial behavior righteous.

The little empirical research available on this issue expands, more than revises, the hole argument. Burt, Jannotta & Mahoney (1998) identify personality characteristics associated with structural holes, and the character-istics are consistent with the hole argument. People in networks that span structural holes, like Robert in Fig. 2, claim the personality of an entrepreneurial outsider (vs. conforming and obedient insider), in search of authority (vs. security), thriving on advocacy and change (vs. stability). The association with personality, however, only exists for people in technical and clerical jobs, where contact networks are shaped by personal taste rather than performance. At higher job ranks, where the social capital of structural holes more strongly affects performance, there is no association between personality and structural holes. Regardless of their personal tastes, middle and senior managers seem to adapt to the demands of building networks that span structural holes (see Mehra, Kilduff & Brass, 2000, for an analysis in which the performance effects of network and personality are additive). Burt, Hogarth & Michaud (2000) discuss national culture as a contingency factor in their comparative study of senior managers in a French firm and a similar American firm. The French managers build their networks in ways distinct from the Americans, ways consistent with research documenting the more bureaucratic nature of French business. Where the French are emotionally uncomfortable with bridge relationships to colleagues not close to one another, the Americans are comfortable. Where the French build from long standing personal friendships that rarely span the boundary of the firm, the Americans build from long-standing work relationships that often span the boundary of the firm. These differences in the etiology of network connections notwithstanding, manager performance in both firms is associated with personal networks that span structural holes (Fig. 3D plots the French managers). The French and American managers build their networks differently, but as predicted by the hole argument, performance is enhanced for both when they build to span structural holes.

Network Content

The four network variables reviewed (constraint, size, density, hierarchy) are measures of network form in that they describe the strength of relations. Network content is about the substance of relationships, qualities defined by distinctions such as friendship versus business vs. authority.

Content as a contingency factor asks how the value of social capital varies with the kinds of relationships on which it is based. Is brokering connections in a friendship network, for example, viewed as rude or adding value? Is brokering in an authority network adding value or disrupting the chain of command?

Content in General

It is all too easy for distinctions between kinds of relations to be no more than a semantic distinction in the mind of the observer – what is friendship distinct from business in one study population can be two sides of the same relationships in other study populations – so it makes sense to check that the content distinctions being tested for contingency are meaningful to the population under study.

This is a generic issue in network analysis, for which there are generic solutions (e.g. Romney & D'Andrade, 1964; Burt & Schøtt, 1985; Carley, 1986; Burt, 1990; Krackhardt, 1990). The presumption is that behavioral distinctions precede cognitive distinctions. Two kinds of relations distinguished in a study are in fact the same kind of relationship to the extent that everyone with whom I have the first kind of relationship, I also have the second. The spatial displays, or cognitive maps, in Fig. 4 describe how the American managers from Fig. 3C and the French managers from Fig. 3D distinguish kinds of relationships (see Burt, Hogarth & Michaud, 2000, for discussion of the maps). Each map is a multidimensional scaling of joint probabilities. Kinds of relations are close together to the extent that they tend to reach the same people.[10] For example, the 60 French managers cited a total of 275 colleagues as most valued, 227 as essential sources of buy-in, and 115 as both, defining a

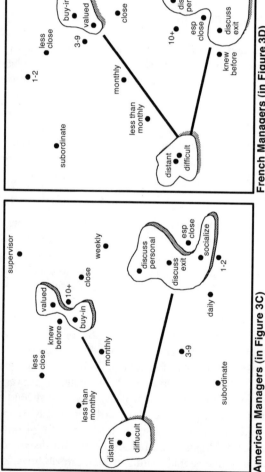

American Managers (in Figure 3C)

French Managers (in Figure 3D)

Key to Kinds of Relationships: "1-2" known for less than three years, "10+" known for ten or more years, "buy-in" contact is an essential source of political support for manager, "close" 2 on a 4-point scale of emotional closeness to manager, "daily" speaks with contact at least once a day, "difficult" contact is manager's most difficult colleague, "discuss exit" manager would discuss moving to another firm with this contact, "discuss personal" manager has disscussed personal matters with contact, "distant" 1 on a 4-point scale of emotional closeness to manager, "esp close" 4 on a 4-point scale of emotional closeness to manager, "knew before" before joining the firm, manager knew this contact, "less close" 3 on a 4-point scale of emotional closeness to manager, "less than monthly" speaks with contact less than once a month, "monthly" speaks with contact at least once a month, "socialize" gets together for informal socializing, "subordinate" most promising of the people supervised by manager, "supervisor" manager's boss, "valued" contact is one of manager's most valued work contacts, "weekly" speaks with contact at least once a week.

Fig. 4. Manager Distinctions Between Kinds of Relationships. (Relations close together reach the same contacts).

joint probability of 0.297 between valued and buy-in. 'Valued' and 'buy-in' are close together in Fig. 4 because the 0.297 joint probability of a contact being cited for buy-in and valued is higher than most other joint probabilities.

The most obvious feature of the maps is their similarity. The three kinds of relations distinct in each map were circled (personal, work, and negative). Personal relations (in the southeast of each map) are to people with whom the manager socializes and discusses personal matters such as leaving for a job with another firm. These are people to whom the manager feels especially close and with whom he speaks daily. Work relations (in the northeast of each map) are to people the manager cites as his most valued contacts at work and essential sources of buy-in for initiatives coming out of his office. These are people to whom the manager feels close, but not especially close, and with whom he speaks once a week or so. Negative relations (to the west of each map) are with people to whom the managers feels emotionally distant, or people cited for having most made it difficult for the manager to carry out his job responsibilities.

The two broad content distinctions illustrated in Fig. 4 are evaluative distinctions between good and bad (east-west in each map), and work distinguished from personal (north-south in each map). These broad distinctions also occur in survey network data on national probability samples, so they are probably reliable content distinctions for social capital research. The evaluative distinction occurs in network data on probability samples of Americans (Marsden & Campbell, 1985; Burt, 1990), as does the distinction between work and personal relationships (Burt, 1990).

The distinction between positive and negative seems an obvious distinction between network contents, but it has not entered social capital research. Virtually all social capital research has been on networks of variably positive relations (exceptions include Labianca, Brass & Gray, 1998; Burt 1999a, 2001; and Labianca & Brass, 2000, on the strategic importance of negative relationships for integrating the concepts of trust and brokerage).

Authority in Particular
Among positive relations, there is mixed evidence of a contingency distinction between personal discussion relationships versus the relations through which corporate authority flows. Podolny & Baron (1997) argue that the value of brokering structural holes is concentrated in networks of personal relationships, such as confiding and socializing in the southeast of the maps in Fig. 4. These are discretionary connections through which managers derive early access to information and shape its distribution within an organization. In contrast, Podolny and Baron argue, performance can suffer from structural holes in the

authority network, as defined by relation such as buy-in and work advice in the northeast of the maps in Fig. 4. These are the channels through which a manager receives normative information about what is proper, and instrumental information on priorities to be pursed. Structural holes in the authority network increases the chances of a manager receiving contradictory information on properties and priorities, which might confuse the manager and so erode performance. With network data on a representative sample of managers in a high-technology engineering and manufacturing company, Podolny and Baron show that large, sparse networks of contacts cited for task advice and strategic information increase the odds of manager promotion. They also show, as predicted by their content distinction, that large, sparse networks of buy-in relations lower the odds of manager promotion.

Similar results exists on the managers in Fig. 3C (Burt, 1997b). Network constraint scores computed from the network of contacts cited as personal ties (socialize, discuss personal matters, discuss exit) have the strong negative association with early promotion predicted by the hole argument and displayed in Fig. 3C (–4.7 t-test). In contrast, constraint scores computed from the network of corporate ties (supervisor and essential sources of buy-in), have no association with early promotion (0.3 t-test). The difference is consistent with Podolny and Baron's argument, though holes in the corporate network do not have a negative association with performance so much as they are independent of performance.

Still, evidence is mixed on the destructive nature of structural holes in the corporate bureaucracy. One issue is that many contacts are cited for both work and personal reasons, which creates an extended network in which managers develop personal relationships with key sources of buy-in. Though replicating the Podolny and Baron content distinction, Burt (1997b) reports the strongest social capital effects with network constraint measured from the combined network of work and personal relationships. Similarly, though Flap, Völker & Bulder (2000) report for their study of two government agencies that material job satisfaction increased with instrumental work ties while satisfaction with the social aspects of a job increased with other contents, 'networks that branch out' enhance satisfaction with both the material and social aspects of a job.

Douthit's (2000) analysis of direct reports raises a second issue. If structural holes are a problem in the buy-in network around manager, they must be a particularly difficult problem when they separate manager and boss. With network data on samples of staff officers from two financial organizations, one of which includes the senior people in Fig. 3A, Douthit compares supervision in a segregated context of manager and boss sharing no key contacts, to supervision embedded in an integrated context of manager and boss sharing mutual key contacts. Supervision in the segregated context is a bridge that spans the structural hole between manager and boss. She discusses bridge supervision as the exercise of authority across a structural hole, and argues that bridge supervision should be less productive than embedded supervision. There are two empirical results. In an analogy to segregated networks in Bott's (1957) analysis of conjugal roles, Douthit describes the tendency for bridge supervision to accompany social disintegration between manager and boss in the form of less joint decision-making, less informal discussion of office politics, less personal compatibility. Nevertheless, the disintegration associated with bridge supervision does not affect the association between network constraint and performance evaluations. Interaction between network constraint and bridge supervision is negligible in predicting performance evaluations. Officers with networks that span structural holes are more likely to receive high performance evaluations, whether or not they are working under bridge supervision. In sum, network content can be, but need not be, a contingency factor in the value of brokering structural holes.

Peers and Task Uncertainty

For any individual, there is some number of people – call them peers – who do the same work. A manager could have many peers, a few, or none if no one else is doing the same work.

Contingency Function

The value of social capital varies with the number of peers. More peers, less value. For example, the -0.4 correlation in Fig. 3C between early promotion and network constraint varies between categories of managers; from correlations close to zero for lower-rank managers in engineering (many peers), up to correlations stronger than -0.8 for high-rank managers in sales and service (few peers). More specifically, there is a contingency function in which the magnitude of the correlation between early promotion and network constraint, which indicates the value of social capital, decreases as a power of the number of a manager's peers (Burt, 1997a, p. 385; see Fig. 6 below).

The competition and legitimacy associated with peers can be used to make sense of the negative association between value and peers (Burt, 1997a). Having many peers affects a manager's freedom to define his job, and the firm's response to the manager's definition. First, many peers are a competitive frame of reference. Their aggregate behavior indicates how the manager should perform, and peer competition keeps the manager tuned to peers' job performance (see Burt, 1987, on network conditions for competition and imitation among peers). Beyond informal pressures to conform, the firm is likely to provide guidelines for jobs held by a large number of employees. Second, legitimacy is established by many people doing the same work. The way in which the job is performed is legitimate not because of content or quality, but because many people perform it that way (e.g. economists in a business school).

The two conditions are reversed for a manager who has few peers: First, there is no competitive frame of reference. There are no peers for informal guidance, and it would be inefficient for the firm to define how a job specific to a few employees should be performed. The manager has to figure out for herself how best to perform the job (see Kohn & Schooler, 1983, on occupational self-direction). Second, legitimacy does not come with the job; it has to be established. With few people doing the work, establishing the legitimacy of a manager's job performance depends on getting others to accept her definition of the job (e.g. sociologists in a business school).

Social capital can be expected to be more valuable to the manager with few peers as described by the contingency function. The information and control benefits of structural holes put a manager in a position to better read the diverse interests in their organization to define needed policy and to know better who can be brought together productively to implement policy. The ability to identify and develop opportunities is essential to the manager evaluating how best to fulfill his or her job responsibilities in a way valued by the firm and the market. Such ability has little value to the manager whose work is defined by corporate convention or the boss.

Task Uncertainty

Peers and task uncertainty are related contingency factors. More peers working on a task means that the task will be less uncertain for the two reasons just discussed: many peers provide a competitive frame of reference for how to do the task, and there are more likely to be established guidelines for a task on which many people work. In other words, managers assigned to more unique tasks face more uncertainty in how to do the tasks. The information and control benefits of social capital can be expected to be more valuable to people working on uncertain tasks for the same reasons that they are more valuable to people whose tasks involve few peers.

Corroborating evidence can be drawn from several research areas, but direct evidence is rare at this time. Gabbay & Zuckerman (1998) describe the greater importance of social capital for anticipated promotions in research groups where individual distinctions are more valued, and Belliveau, O'Reilly & Wade (1996) describe the significance of relative social capital. There is a related contingency effect in research on the use of social capital by employers to evaluate prospective employees. Employers should check via social capital on candidates for jobs in which performance can be expected to vary with social capital. Marsden & Gorman (2000) show with a national probability sample that informal, social capital, search strategies are more likely to be used to fill vacancies for jobs that require autonomous decision-making. Flap & Boxman (2001) show a similar result even for employers evaluating college graduates applying for their first full-time job. On the other hand, social capital can be a productive criterion for recruitment even where it is irrelevant to job performance. Fernandez, Castilla & Moore (2000) show that personal referrals are a cost-effective strategy to locate employees to answer telephones at a credit-card processing center. Social capital has no value in the job, but the people most likely to survive in such a regulated, wearing job, a job characterized by high turnover, are people with little social capital in their personal lives. Who better to locate people without social capital (prospective employees) than other people without social capital (current employees)?

Moving up to the level of teams, Hansen, Podolny & Pfeffer (2000) report task contingency for new-product teams in a leading electronics and computer firm (also see Hansen, 1999, in note 3). They find that teams composed of people with more non-redundant contacts beyond the team complete their assigned task more quickly – for teams working on a new product for an unfamiliar market or a new product involving unfamiliar technology (termed 'exploration' work following March's, 1991, distinction between exploration versus exploitation). If the team was working on a new product based on a familiar technology for a familiar market, however, the network effect is negligible. In other words, the external network spanning structural holes is more valuable to the teams working on more uncertain tasks. Hansen, Podolny and Pfeffer's task contingency is related to peer contingency to the extent that engineers in routine jobs for which there are many peers and low returns to social capital were more likely to be assigned to the new-product teams working with familiar technologies for familiar markets.

At a still more aggregate level, Podolny (2000, Table 6) describes the contingent value to venture-capital firms of a co-investment network that spans structural holes. Firms with a network rich in structural holes do a large proportion of their investments in ventures at an early stage of development (which is where uncertainty is highest about the market potential of a venture) and the ventures in which they invest are significantly more likely to survive to IPO (4.4 test statistic). However, the association with IPO only exists for their investments in early-stage ventures. Their second-stage investments are no more likely to survive to IPO than the investments of other venture-capital firms (0.5 test statistic), and their investments in more mature ventures have a still weaker tendency to survive to IPO (–0.9 test statistic). The social capital of bridging structural holes is more of an advantage in more uncertain ventures.

Network Closure

The contingency argument regarding peers and task uncertainty is both structural and ecological. Structural holes among peers allow outsiders to play the peers against one another, which erodes the value of whatever social capital the peers hold (Burt, 1992, pp. 44–45). A manager's ability to develop broker connections across holes is constrained by the presence of one or more peers in a position to undercut or denigrate the manager's proposals. The contingency argument is analogous to ecological arguments describing the competition and legitimacy consequences of an increasing number of organizations in a market (Hannan & Freeman, 1989, pp. 131–141; Burt, 1992, pp. 215ff.; Han, 1993, 1994). I focus on the implications of peer numbers, but the competition and legitimacy mechanisms are familiar from research in organization demography (e.g. Pfeffer, 1983; Haveman & Cohen, 1994). The contingency prediction is that peers erode the value of social capital to the extent that disorganization among peers intensifies competition between the peers and elicits behavioral guidelines from higher authority.

It is a short step from disorganization among peers to disorganization within a group, but it is a step that brings together the closure and hole arguments in a productive way.

Internal and External Networks
Begin with the table in Fig. 5. Rows distinguish groups by external network. Groups can be distinguished on many criteria. I have in mind the two network criteria that define information redundancy (cohesion and structural equivalence) but it is just as well to have in mind more colloquial definitions of group; family, team, neighborhood, ethnicity, or industry. Whatever the definition, some groups have social capital in the sense that its members have many non-redundant contacts beyond the group – as illustrated by the three-person sociograms at the top of the table in Fig. 5. People in each of the two groups have a total of six non-redundant contacts beyond the group.

With respect to network measurement, non-redundant contacts mean a lack of external constraint on the group. The horizontal axis in Fig. 3B, for example, measures the average network constraint on individuals in TQM teams. Low-constraint teams, to the left in the graph, were composed of employees with many non-redundant contacts beyond their team. In spanning structural holes beyond the team, their networks reached a diverse set of perspectives, skills, or resources. They were the high-performance teams. At the other extreme, to the right in Fig. 3B, low-performance teams were composed of individuals with redundant contacts beyond the team. The sociogram at the bottom of Fig. 5 is an illustration. The group's four contacts beyond the team are interconnected, and so redundant by cohesion. Such a team has access to a single set of perspectives, skills, or resources, and is expected not to see or successfully implement new solutions, as illustrated in Fig. 3B by their poor performance with respect to TQM.

Columns in Fig. 5 distinguish groups in terms of network closure within the group. Structural holes within a group weakens in-group communication and coordination, which weakens group ability to take advantage of brokerage opportunities beyond the group. Closure eliminates structural holes within the team, and so improves communication and coordination within the team. The sociogram to the left of the table in Fig. 5 shows a group with disconnected elements in the group. The two sociograms to the right of the table show groups with all three elements connected. Density or hierarchy can provide network closure, though hierarchy seems to be the more potent form of closure (e.g. Crane, 1972, on the center-periphery structure of invisible colleges; Greif's, 1989, pp. 862–863, observation that the Maghribi traders sanctioned not through their dense network with one another but through "a public appeal to the Jewish communities" in which they were embedded; Provan & Milward, 1995, on higher performing mental health systems that have a hierarchical, rather than a dense, network structure; or Koza & Lewin, 1999, pp. 648–649, on coordination problems that arise if there is only density without hierarchy). A leader with strong relations to all members of the team improves communication and coordination despite coalitions or factions separated by holes within the team.

Performance Surface
The graph at the top of Fig. 5 shows group performance across the cells of the table. Performance here is an undefined mixture of innovation, positive evaluation, early promotion, compensation, and profit. Points A, B, C, and D at the corners of the table in Fig. 5 correspond to the same points in the graph.

Performance is highest at the back of the graph (quadrant A), where network closure within the group is high (one clear leader or a dense network connecting people in the group) and many non-redundant contacts beyond the group (member networks into the surrounding organization are rich in disconnected perspectives, skills, and resources). Performance is lowest at the front of the graph (quadrant C), where in-group closure is low (members spend their time bickering with one another about what to do and how to proceed) and completely redundant contacts beyond the group (members are limited to similar perspectives, skills, and resources).

Figure 5 is my inference from three bits of evidence in the preceding review. In fact, the Fig. 5 interaction between brokerage and closure is the concept of structural autonomy from which the hole argument emerged (Burt, 1980; 1982; 1992, pp. 38–45).

First, the functional form of the graph comes from research with census data describing the association between industry profits and market structure. The left graph in Fig. 6 plots industry profit margins by network structure within and beyond the industry (Burt et al., 1999, Fig. 3; cf. Burt 1992, p. 95). Industry profit margins decrease with network constraint within an industry (where internal constraint is measured by the extent to which industry output is spread across many independent producers, t-tests for the beta coefficient in Fig. 5 estimated from the market data vary from -9.9 to -4.8; Burt et al., 1999, Table 4) and network constraint beyond the industry (where external constraint is measured by the extent to which producers have few independent suppliers and customers, t-tests for the gamma coefficient in Fig. 5 vary from -9.3 to -4.1; Burt et al., 1999, Table 4).

Analogy with the market structure research is productive in two ways. First, the market results are based on a census of market conditions, so they include data on the performance-network association at extremes not present in most samples of managers. Second, the market results across a broader range of network conditions show a nonlinear form of returns to network structure. The strongest network effects occur with deviations from minimum network constraint. With respect to network structure within a group, in other words, performance should be weakened more by the first significant disconnection in the group than by one more disconnection within an already disorganized group. With respect to external structure, performance should be weakened more by the entry of one strong perspective, or skill, or resource in the surrounding organization than it is by the entry of another external pressure on a group already frozen by external pressures.

A second bit of evidence for the integration is Reagans & Zuckerman's (1999) study of performance in corporate R&D units. As discussed earlier ('Individual and group'), they report higher levels of output from units in which scientists were drawn from diverse employee cohorts (implying that their networks reached diverse perspectives, skills and resources outside the team) and there is a dense communication network within the unit. Tenure diversity (or other kinds of diversity, see Williams & O'Reilly, 1998) can be disruptive

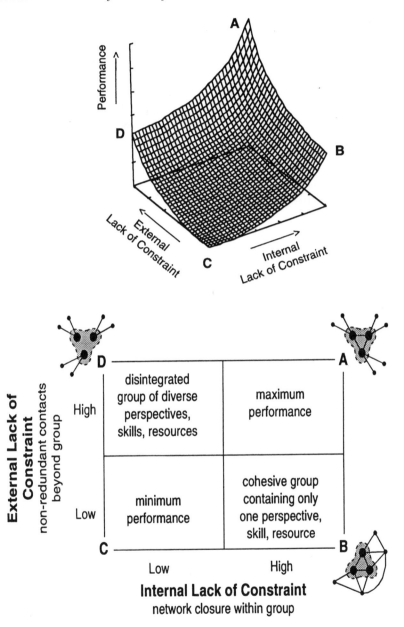

Fig. 5. Group Performance Surface, across Structural Holes and Network Closure.

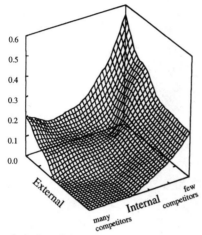

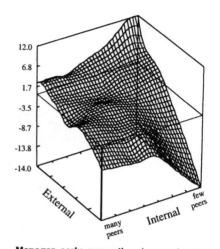

Industry price-cost margins as a function of internal constraint (one minus concentration ratio within industry) and external constraint (measured by lack of structural holes among the industry suppliers and customers; 509 observations of American markets from 1963 to 1992, Burt et al., 1999: Figure 3).

Manager early promotion (years ahead of peers at promotion to current rank) as a function of internal constraint (number of peers) and external constraint (measured by lack of structural holes in the manager contact network; 170 senior male managers in electronics firm, see Figure 4B; Burt, 1997a:Figure 6).

Fig. 6. Performance Surface in Figure 5 Specific to Markets and Managers.

because of the difficulties associated with communicating and coordinating across different perspectives, but when communication is successful (as implied by a dense communication network within the team), team performance is enhanced by the brokerage advantages of the team having access to more diverse information. Reagans and Zuckerman's data are distributed along a segment somewhere between points A and C on the performance surface at the top of Fig. 5.

A third bit of evidence for the integration comes from the peer contingency just discussed. The value of social capital declines in proportion to the number of managers – peers – doing the same work. Data for the contingency function are plotted in the graph to the right in Fig. 6 so as to make more clear the analogy with the market data. The vertical axis is manager performance measured as early promotion relative to peers so there is no performance variance along the internal constraint axis. The line around the middle of the graph box shows the zero point for early promotion at each level of internal constraint. There is a steep slope to the surface at the back of the graph box (for managers who have few peers and so are unconstrained by peers). The steep slope is highest for managers with many non-redundant contacts (far corner of the graph box, low external constraint), and lowest for managers with primarily redundant contacts. This corresponds to the line between point A and point B on the team performance surface at the top of Fig. 5. As the number of peers increases, the performance surface becomes more flat – there is less of a difference between managers who are low versus high in external constraint.[11] This corresponds to the line between point D and C on the team performance surface at the top of Fig. 5.

Assume that network closure among peers decreases with their number; closure among many people being more difficult to sustain than closure among a few people. Then the negative association between peers and the value of social capital is a negative association between closure and the value of social capital. The social capital of brokerage across structural holes is more valuable to a group where there is network closure within the group (point A at the back of the graph in Fig. 5). Low closure means poor communication and coordination within a group and such a group can be expected to perform poorly, benefiting least from hole-spanning external networks (point C to D in the graph).

Integrating Research Results
The synthesis of closure and holes as complementary forms of social capital in Fig. 5 is interesting in its own right, but beyond interesting it is powerful as a frame of reference for integrating research results across studies. A study can show exclusive evidence of social capital from network closure or structural holes without calling either argument into question.

For example, Greif (1989) argues that network closure was critical to the success of the medieval Maghribi traders in North Africa. Each trader ran a local business in his own city that depended on sales to distant cities. Network closure among the traders allowed them to coordinate so as to trust one another, and so profitably trade the products of their disparate business activities. The traders individually had networks rich in brokerage opportunities, but they needed closure with one another to take advantage of the opportunities. More generally, in an environment rich in diverse perspectives, skills, and resources, group performance depends on people overcoming their differences to operate as a group. Group performance will vary with in-group closure, not brokerage, because brokerage opportunities beyond the group are high for all groups (this is the Fig. 5 surface from point A to point D).

Rosenthal's (1996) study of TQM teams illustrates the other extreme. People on the teams had been trained to act as a team and there was enthusiasm for quality management in the firm – so the teams did not differ greatly in their closure. Closure was high in all of them. Therefore, team performance varied as illustrated in Fig. 3B with a team's external network. If a cohesive team can see a good idea, it can act on it. With all teams cohesive, those with numerous non-redundant contacts beyond the team had the advantage of access to a broader diversity of perspectives, skills, and resources. I earlier discussed several recent studies that report high performance from groups with external networks that span structural holes (see 'Individuals and Groups'). With Fig. 5 in mind, these studies tell me not that the closure argument is in error so much as they tell me that closure within business groups is less often problematic than brokerage beyond the group. More generally, the relative performance of cohesive groups will vary with the extent to which a group is composed of people with networks rich in structural holes, not network closure, because closure is high for all of the groups (this is the Fig. 5 surface from point A to point B, illustrated in Fig. 3B).

In short, structural holes and network closure can be brought together in a productive way. The synthesis is only with respect to empirical evidence. The mechanisms remain distinct. Closure describes how dense or hierarchical networks lower the risk associated with transaction and trust, which can be associated with performance. The hole argument describes how structural holes are opportunities to add value with brokerage across the holes, which is associated with performance. The empirical evidence clearly supports the hole argument over closure. The point illustrated in Fig. 5 is that while brokerage across structural holes seems to be the source of added value, closure can be critical to realizing the value buried in the structural holes.

The Social Capital of Outsiders

There is one step further to go with closure as a contingency factor. Closure is essential to the social capital of outsiders, but it is network closure of a specific kind, a kind that indicates borrowed access to structural holes.

Insiders, Outsiders, and Sponsors

There is a delightfully descriptive Yiddish word, *mishpokhe*, that refers to people who are 'one for us'. The word is specifically about extended family, but it is popularly used to refer to people who are one of us. Rosten (1989, p. 338) illustrates with Chase Manhattan Bank's advertising campaign built around the slogan "You have a friend at Chase Manhattan," In a window of the bank next to a Chase Manhattan branch there appeared a sign; "– BUT HERE YOU HAVE MISHPOKHE!"

We are each *mishpokhe* in some settings, outsiders in others. Example outsiders are an economist arguing the merits of his model to an audience of sociologists, an American pitching a deal to a Japanese investor, a woman arguing the merits of a business policy to a sexist male, a baby-faced youngster proposing new theory to a senior scholar, a manager representing her group's interests on a team composed of more senior managers from another group. The list is as infinite as the differences among us.

In the interpersonal politics of competition, *mishpokhe* are twice advantaged as legitimate members of a population. Investors are more likely to believe they understand the motives and probable actions of someone like themselves, which means they feel more confident in predicting the future behavior of *mishpokhe*. Second, it is easier for investors to trust *mishpokhe* because his or her reputation among us will be tarnished if investors are treated poorly. These reasons for preferring insiders are grounds for excluding outsiders, which in American business are disproportionately women.

The well-known solution is for the outsider to speak through an inside sponsor (e.g. Giacalone & Rosenfeld, 1989, on impression management). Every manager needs a sponsor at one time or another. Company leaders don't have time to check into the credibility of everyone making a bid for broader responsibilities. They are looking for fast, reliable cues about managers on whom they do not already have information. A manager deemed suspect for any reason – a new hire, someone just transferred from another country, a new addition to a cohesive group – needs an established insider to provide the cues, sponsoring the manager as a legitimate player to open the mind of a contact not ready to listen seriously to the manager's proposal. The phenomenon is succinctly illustrated by an anecdote that Kilduff & Krackhardt (1994, p. 87) quote from an unattributed source in one of Cialdini's (1989, p. 45) papers on impression management. The financier Baron de Rothschild is asked by an acquaintance for a loan, to which the great man is reputed to have replied: "I won't give you the loan myself; but I will walk arm-in-arm with you across the floor of the Stock Exchange, and you soon shall have willing lenders to spare."

The solution is especially obvious when relations cross corporate or cultural boundaries. It is official in Japan. There are industry-specific directories of people available to help outsiders develop relations with Japanese firms.[12] The people in these directories are usually retired corporate executives who prefer the active life of consulting to life in a window seat. These people do not bring technical skills, they bring connections. Without the proper personal connections, outsiders don't do business in Japan. Corning Glass is a concrete illustration. Corning has a history of joint ventures that give Corning access to a market where the partner firm is established. Nanda & Bartlett (1990) offer illustrative examples in the United States and Europe, but I particularly enjoy their quote from a Corning executive commenting on the result of Corning's alliance with the Japanese firm Asahi (Nanda & Bartlett, 1990, p. 14): "When our salespeople began calling on the Japanese TV set manufacturers, we felt as if a veil came over them when they dealt with us. Their relationships with their Japanese suppliers ran very deep, while they were very distant with us. Last week, Asahi people escorted me to meeting with the worldwide TV tube manager of a large Japanese company and introduced me properly to him. We had extremely fruitful conversation. I wouldn't have even been able to meet him and discuss issues between us if it were not for the Asahi connection." Japan is merely an extreme case. Stuart, Hoang & Hybels (1999), for example, study the growth of young American biotechnology companies to IPO. Cost, profit, and uncertainty are high in the industry. Prominent investors, or alliances with prominent companies in the industry, can be a competitive advantage in signaling the value of a young company. As expected, companies with prominent associates move more quickly to IPO and earn greater valuations at IPO (see Stuart, 1999, for similar effects on company growth in the semiconductor industry; Gulati, 1998, for broad review).

Hierarchical Networks Indicate Borrowed Social Capital
Sponsorship as a network phenomenon is illustrated in Fig. 7 with two women, Karen and Jane (pseudonyms). To make their network differences more obvious, neither woman is included in the Fig. 7 sociogram of her network. Only the network among each woman's contacts is presented.

Karen and Jane were among the sample senior managers from the electronics manufacturing firm displayed in Fig. 3C. The performance variable was early promotion, on which Jane was doing much better than Karen. The two women held the same rank in the company, but Jane was promoted nine years earlier than other women in her line of work with the same background. Karen was promoted seven years late.

Scores on the network constraint index and component network variables are displayed in the figure. The two women are similarly about average in network constraint, so constraint cannot explain their performance difference. Neither is network size the explanation. Jane's eight contacts are similar to Karen's nine. Network density is also similar for the two women: the average strength of relation between contacts is 36 in both networks.

The difference is hierarchy. Jane's network is more hierarchical than Karen's. Jane's network is more hierarchical because so many of her contacts are connected through Sam (a pseudonym). Sam has especially close ties with all but two of Jane's contacts, and close ties with the remaining two. More, there would be few relations between contacts if Sam were removed from the network. In contrast, Karen's contacts are connected directly. With respect to

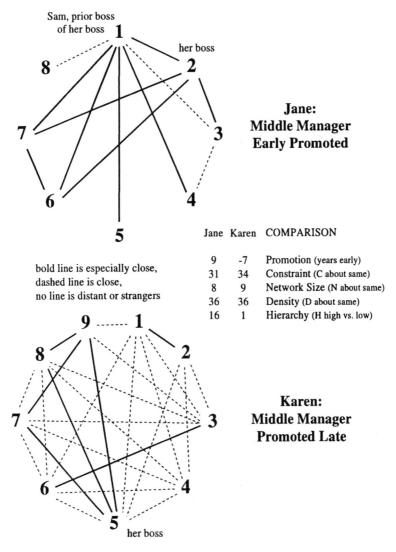

Sam, prior boss
of her boss 1

her boss 2

**Jane:
Middle Manager
Early Promoted**

bold line is especially close,
dashed line is close,
no line is distant or strangers

Jane	Karen	COMPARISON
9	-7	Promotion (years early)
31	34	Constraint (C about same)
8	9	Network Size (N about same)
36	36	Density (D about same)
16	1	Hierarchy (H high vs. low)

**Karen:
Middle Manager
Promoted Late**

her boss

Fig. 7. Illustrative Hierarchy Effect.

hierarchy in the networks of the other sample managers in this study population, Jane's network is two standard deviations above average. Karen's is three standard deviations below average.

I know something about the contacts in each network. From Karen's questionnaire I know that her network is concentrated in her immediate work group. Her boss, contact 5, is the most central contact in her network. He had especially close relations with three of the four other contacts, and close relations with another four. Contacts 3, 4, 6, 7, 8, and 9 are all other people who worked with Karen under her boss.

Relative to Karen, Jane's contacts were more disconnected from one another. Only two of her eight contacts were from her work group; contact 3, and her boss, contact 2. Jane's other contacts were essential sources of buy-in beyond her group (contacts 1, 4, 5, and 6), and people further removed who Jane cited as valuable sources of support and advice. The key to this network is understanding Sam's role in it. Sam was Jane's sponsor in the organization.[13] Jane's boss maintained a strong relation with his prior boss, Sam. On her boss's recommendation, Jane represented her group in a project under Sam's direction. Sam was impressed with Jane and took her under his wing, brokering introductions to other senior managers. Senior managers dealing with Jane felt that they were dealing indirectly with Sam, which greatly simplified Jane's work with them. Jane's situation is a familiar story of sponsorship. The point here is to illustrate the association between performance, sponsorship, and hierarchical networks.

Table 2 contains systematic evidence of the performance-hierarchy association illustrated in Fig. 7. The evidence presented in Fig. 3 and Table 1 was only for insiders. Evidence on other employees, the outsiders, is given in Table 2. For the moment, let me postpone to below the method used to distinguish insiders from outsiders ('Detecting People Deemed Outsiders'). The fourth panel in Table 2 is empty because there were no outsiders in the French study population (all but five managers in the 85 person study population were white, married, French men).

The second panel in Table 2 describes women and entry-rank men in the electronics manufacturer where Karen and Jane worked. Performance, measured by early promotion, is independent of network size and density, but has a strong positive association with network hierarchy (3.2 t-test). Prediction for the 50 senior women alone also yields no performance association with size or density (−1.4 and 1.6 t-tests), but a significant positive association with network hierarchy (2.6 t-test, see Burt, 1998, p. 26, for details).

Women were outsiders in the study population of investment officers. Bonus compensation has the predicted negative association with network constraint

Table 2. Component Social Capital Effects for Outsiders

	Multile Correlation	Size	Density	Hierarchy
Performance Evaluation				
Job performance evaluations, staff function within financial company (0.20 correlation with constraint across 49 senior men, 1.1 t-test 3A, − 3.8 t-test)		0.02	0.22	0.39
	0.45	0.01	0.22	0.39
		(0.0)	(1.6)	(2.9)
Promotions				
Early promotion, electronics manufacturer (0.22 correlation with constraint across 114 women and entry-rank men, 2.3 t-test)		− 0.06	0.13	0.30
	0.55	− 0.14	0.17	0.30
		(− 1.5)	(1.8)	(3.2)
Compensation				
Relative salary, chemical and drug manufacturer (no outsiders)	—	—	—	—
Relative bonus, investment officers within financial company (0.24 correlation with constraint across 39 senior women, 1.5 t-test)		− 0.16	− 0.03	0.49
	0.55	0.06	− 0.24	0.16
		(0.4)	(− 1.8)	(4.6)

Note: Pearson correlations are given in the first row of each panel, standardized regression coefficients in the second (with routine t-tests in parentheses).

for men (Fig. 3E), and the panel at the bottom of Table 1 showed that density and hierarchy are both significant components in the effect. Men who built dense networks of interconnected colleagues, or who built their network around a sponsor, received a smaller bonus than the average bonus to their peers. Women, in contrast, had to build around a sponsor. The statistically significant association in the panel at the bottom of Table 2 is the strong positive association between bonus and network hierarchy (4.6 t-test).

Men were outsiders in the staff-officer population. Most of the officers were women, for whom performance evaluations have the negative association with network constraint predicted by the hole argument (Fig. 3A), and the first panel in Table 1 showed that the primary component is poor evaluations of women in dense networks. Men, in contrast, have to build around a sponsor. The first panel in Table 2 shows that performance evaluations for the men are independent of network size and density, but increase significantly with network hierarchy (2.9 t-test).

I interpret the results in Table 2 as evidence of social capital borrowed from a sponsor, a strategic partner, whose network spans structural holes. Beyond the value of having a sponsor, the results in Table 2 show that value depends on the kind of network a sponsor has. Hierarchical, not dense, networks are associated with performance. Think back to Robert and James in Fig. 2 and imagine that each were to sponsor a person newly hired into their group. James introduces the new hire to his contacts, who form the core of the new person's network. The result is a dense network around the new hire. When Robert introduces his new hire around, the result is a hierarchical network. The contacts, previously connected indirectly through their relations with Robert, are now also interconnected through the new hire. From the new hire's perspective, he is sharing his network with one other person also at the center of the network, Robert. More precisely, since the network was Robert's initially, the new hire is working within a network that he borrowed from Robert. Borrowed networks are not all hierarchical. A borrowed network could be either dense (James sponsors the new hire), or hierarchical (Robert sponsors the new hire). Hierarchy results from borrowing a network that spans structural holes (Robert sponsors the new hire; and the higher the hierarchy score, the broader the borrowed network because the hierarchy increases, as I have measured it, with the number of contacts reached through the central contact, see Fig. A1 in the Appendix). Karen and Jane in Fig. 7 illustrate a systematic pattern in their firm of women getting ahead by borrowing the social capital of an insider's network that spans structural holes.

Detecting People Deemed Outsiders
It is one thing to borrow social capital occasionally to succeed in a new venture. It is another to have to borrow social capital if any of your ventures are to succeed. If borrowing social capital is a strategy by which outsiders get access to the benefits of social capital, then a category of people for whom success depends on borrowing social capital is a category of people who have a legitimacy problem (as described with respect to number of peers). *The fact that women fall behind in Karen and Jane's company when they build their own social capital* (indicated by the positive association between performance and network constraint), *and move ahead when they borrow social capital* (indicated by the positive association between performance and network hierarchy independent of density), *implies that women have a legitimacy problem in the company.* There is a two-step rule to distinguishing employees

who are being treated as outsiders in a population (see Burt, 1998, pp. 28–30, for illustrative analysis):

First, Table 2 contains all categories of employees for whom network constraint has a positive association with performance (rather than the negative association predicted by the hole argument). Across the 615 observations in Table 1 on insiders within the five study populations, there is a strong negative association between network constraint and relative performance within each population measured by the z-scores in Fig. 3 (-0.31 correlation, -8.1 t-test). The association is strongly positive for the 226 observations in Table 2 on outsiders within the populations (0.23 correlation, 3.6 t-test).

Second, confirmation of outsider status comes from positive performance associations with network hierarchy in Table 2 independent of network density. In fact, a network rich in direct access to brokerage across structural holes, like Robert's in Fig. 2, is the worst choice for outsiders. Sort the observations from the five study populations into three broad categories of networks (see Fig. 8 below): entrepreneurial networks (C below average within a population, H below average), cliques (C above average, H below average), and hierarchical networks (H above average). For the 615 insiders, performance is significantly above average with entrepreneurial networks, low with cliques and hierarchical networks (mean Fig. 3 performance z-scores of 0.29, -0.17, and -0.22 respectively; 5.9 t-test for the higher performance associated with entrepreneurial networks). Across the 226 outsiders, performance is lowest with entrepreneurial networks, average with a clique, and significantly above average with a hierarchical network (mean performance z-scores of -0.23, -0.06, and 0.29; -2.3 t-test for the low performance associated with entrepreneurial networks). It is clumsy, rude, and ultimately unproductive for outsiders to try without a sponsor to broker connections between insiders.

Sponsor Legitimacy

Here are two bits of evidence that corroborate an interpretation of hierarchical networks as borrowed social capital:[14] The first is the source of borrowed social capital. Consider the familiar academic job market. Graduate students who have just completed the requirements for a Ph.D. enter the job market via the networks of their Ph.D. advisor. Murray, Rankin & Magill (1981) show that strong ties more than weak ties lead to better jobs. Legitimacy is an obvious issue here. The valuable strong ties are to sponsoring professors who loan to the student the professor's external network of colleagues. The student whose advisor is limited to strong ties within a clique of interconnected colleagues has less access to the market than the student whose advisor has a network of strong ties to colleagues in diverse institutions and areas (cf. Granovetter's,

1983, p. 211, interpretation of Murray et al.'s, 1981 results). Advisors cannot play the same role in the later promotion to tenure. One expects to see an individual's Ph.D. advisor sponsor the individual for tenure; indeed, the lack of sponsorship is a problem that has to be explained. Letters that make the case come from referees who can appear to be more neutral in evaluating the individual.

The same is true in business promotions in the sense that supervisors are expected to sponsor their subordinates. What the boss says reflects on his or her own work, and competent people usually say positive things about their subordinates. If legitimacy is the issue resolved with a hierarchical network for the women in Karen and Jane's company, then a network anchored on the boss will not resolve the issue as well as a network anchored on a more distant contact. Consistent with this argument, the boss was a poor sponsor: Early promotions were significantly more likely to go to women with hierarchical networks anchored on people outside their immediate work group (Burt, 1992, Chap. 4). Having a sponsor outside the work group adds a corroborating external voice to the boss's sponsorship (as illustrated by Karen in Fig. 7). Effective hierarchical networks were built around a contact sufficiently distant to speak with an authoritative voice of ostensible objectivity.

Illegitimate Men

Second, certain men in Karen and Jane's company rise by borrowing social capital and they have a more obvious legitimacy problem as senior managers. The men are new arrivals to the senior manager population. These entry-rank men are senior managers in the firm, but recent arrivals to senior management so they were outsiders when promoted into their current rank, with their legitimacy suspect as new members of senior management (akin to assistant professors just hired from graduate school). Early promotion to the entry-rank of senior management is associated with having a hierarchical network, indicating borrowed social capital (Burt, 1998, pp. 28–30). The hierarchy effect on early promotion for women, which could indicate a legitimacy problem, also occurs for a kind of man for whom legitimacy is more obviously a problem.

It is important, and probably therapeutic, to emphasize that the insider-outsider distinction is not a gender distinction. It is easy to confuse the two in studies of organizations because women are so often the outsiders (which makes them a substantively rich study population for social capital research). Among the investment officers, it was women who were the outsiders. In the electronics company, it was primarily women who were the outsiders. Seeing these results in my management classes, women often conclude that they always need a sponsor, and men conclude that they never need a sponsor. Not so. You need a sponsor whenever you try to broker a connection into a group not likely to accept you as a legitimate member of the group. In the electronics company, entry-rank men faced a legitimacy issue along with their female colleagues. Among the predominantly female staff officers, it was the men who faced a legitimacy issue. More generally, we are each insiders, *mishpokhe*, in some settings, outsiders in others. The practical point is that individuals have to decide whether they are insider or outsider in a role, then select a network for the function it serves, rather than selecting a network for the kind of people who have selected it in the past (Burt, 1992, pp. 159–163, 1998, pp. 33–35, on optimum networks).

CONCLUSIONS

In conclusion, the network structure of social capital boils down to the three kinds of networks in Fig. 8. The natural evolution of networks left untended is toward a clique of people known to, and supporting, one another as friends of friends. *Clique networks* are small, dense, non-hierarchical networks associated with leisure activities, the lack of social capital, and poor manager performance. The most consistent empirical finding in this review has been that dense networks are associated with substandard performance. In Table 1, network size and hierarchy sometimes matter as predicted, but network density consistently has a strong negative association with performance as predicted by the hole argument. In Table 2, density has no statistically significant association with performance after network hierarchy, the predictor indicating borrowed access to structural holes, is held constant.

The information and control benefits of structural holes that constitute social capital lie in two directions away from a clique. One direction is to build social capital with a network that spans structural holes as at the top of Fig. 8 (and Robert in Fig. 2). In keeping with the image of a network entrepreneur in the hole argument, I have discussed such networks as *entrepreneurial networks*, though they could just as well be discussed simply as *broker networks*. At their best, these are large, sparse, non-hierarchical networks rich in opportunities to broker connections across structural holes. This is the network structure associated in research on diverse topics with more creativity and innovation, more positive job evaluations, early promotion, and higher earnings.

The alternative is to *borrow* social capital, which creates the hierarchical network in Fig. 8 (and Jane's network in Fig. 7). *Hierarchical networks* are large, sparse networks anchored on a central contact. This is the network structure associated with higher performance by outsiders, that is to say managers not yet accepted as legitimate members of a population (e.g. women in many populations of senior managers, men who are too young to be taken seriously as members of the population, or men in an organization that is primarily women). Entrepreneurial networks were their worst choice. It is

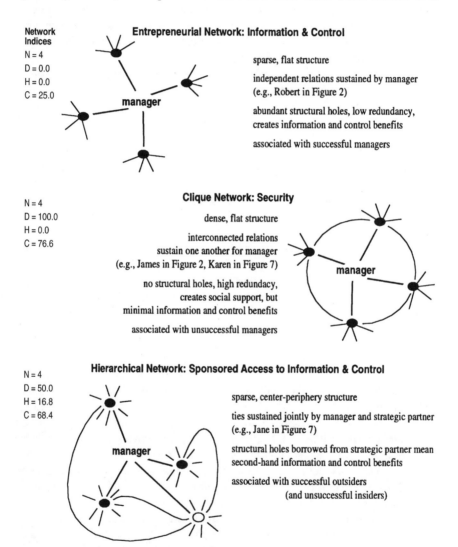

Network Indices

N = 4
D = 0.0
H = 0.0
C = 25.0

Entrepreneurial Network: Information & Control

sparse, flat structure

independent relations sustained by manager (e.g., Robert in Figure 2)

abundant structural holes, low redundancy, creates information and control benefits

associated with successful managers

N = 4
D = 100.0
H = 0.0
C = 76.6

Clique Network: Security

dense, flat structure

interconnected relations sustain one another for manager (e.g., James in Figure 2, Karen in Figure 7)

no structural holes, high redundacy, creates social support, but minimal information and control benefits

associated with unsuccessful managers

N = 4
D = 50.0
H = 16.8
C = 68.4

Hierarchical Network: Sponsored Access to Information & Control

sparse, center-periphery structure

ties sustained jointly by manager and strategic partner (e.g., Jane in Figure 7)

structural holes borrowed from strategic partner mean second-hand information and control benefits

associated with successful outsiders
                    (and unsuccessful insiders)

Fig. 8. Three Network Forms of Social Capital.

clumsy, rude, and ultimately unproductive for outsiders to try without a sponsor to broker connections between insiders. Outsiders with entrepreneurial networks received significantly less positive job evaluations, later promotions, and lower compensation. Nevertheless, brokerage is the source of social capital for outsiders as it is for insiders. The difference is that outsiders do not have direct access. They have to borrow from an insider the network through which they broker connections. The central contact in a hierarchical network is, for the manager at the center of the network, positioned to be a sponsor such that a hierarchical network indicates social capital borrowed from the sponsor. The positive association between performance and network hierarchy is a reduced-form coefficient; the result of a strong tie to a sponsor and the entrepreneurial network of the sponsor. The two combine to define a hierarchical network around the manager, and it is access to the sponsor's entrepreneurial network that has the positive effect on performance. Sponsors who had a dense network did not enhance performance. In the end, outsiders are exceptions that prove the rule: social capital is a function of direct or indirect access to brokerage across structural holes.

Two contingency factors stand out in the review for their capacity to integrate ostensibly contradictory research results. One is the distinction between insiders and outsiders. As just described, evidence of social capital can be reversed for insiders and outsiders. The negative association between performance and network constraint for insiders can be positive for outsiders because of the constraint inherent in a hierarchical network. It is only when performance is regressed across the component variables in network constraint – size, density, and hierarchy – that the direct association with hierarchy, and so borrowed social capital, is apparent.

The second contingency factor that stands out is network closure and its correlates, numbers of peers and task uncertainty. The information and control benefits of brokerage is more valuable to people working on more unique tasks, which means tasks on which they have few peers, and so tasks in which there is uncertainty about how to best proceed. This is the point illustrated by the performance surfaces in Fig. 5 and Fig. 6. Performance increases more steeply from point B to A at the back of the graphs (few peers, high task uncertainty) than it does from point C to point D at the front of the graphs (many peers, low task uncertainty). More, the two leading network mechanisms argued to provide social capital, structural holes and network closure, are brought together in a productive way in Fig. 5. Available empirical evidence supports the hole argument over closure, but the performance surface in Fig. 5 shows how differences between study populations can result in research showing exclusive evidence of social capital from network closure or structural holes without calling either argument into question. Although brokerage across structural holes is the source of added value, closure can be critical to realizing the value buried in the holes.

Having completed the review, I return to the summary conclusion with which I began: What struck me in preparing this review is the variety of research questions on which useful results are being obtained with the concept of social capital, and the degree to which more compelling results could be obtained and integrated across studies if attention were focused beneath the social capital metaphor on the specific network mechanisms responsible for social capital. We have only begun to see the advances possible with this powerful concept.

APPENDIX

The Appendix to this chapter, 'Implications for Research Design', contains four sections: One is about selecting a study population to get rich data on social capital and its effects (focus on places where competitive advantage would result from better access to, and control over, information). The second section is about network measures of social capital. The third is about positional measures (contacts are sorted into kinds, relations between contacts are typically unknown, and social capital is inferred from relations with kinds of contacts). The fourth is a caution about predicting change (social capital is more often a by-product than a goal). The review in this chapter should interest the broad audience of people interested in social capital, but the Appendix will only interest those few planning research on the topic so the Appendix is not included with this already-long chapter. Copies of the Appendix are available from my webpage (http://gsbwww.uchicago.edu/fac/ronald.burt/research).

NOTES

1. For two reasons, focusing on managers probably means more evidence of social capital. First, Carroll & Teo (1996) use survey network data on a probability sample of Americans to show that manager networks (relative to nonmanagers) involve more participation in voluntary associations, more core discussion contacts, a larger proportion of contacts who are colleagues or co-workers, and more contacts who are total strangers to one another. Second, managers have more work autonomy than nonmanagers (Kohn & Schooler, 1983), and social capital is more of an advantage for people who have more autonomy (Burt, 1997a). More evidence of social capital makes professionals and managers a productive research site for studying social capital, but warrants a caution against generalizing to other populations.

2. In fact, the nonlinear decline in value is probably nonmonotonic. There are disadvantages to being the first to propose an innovative product or idea. Subsequent entrants with the same product have an advantage because problems revealed by the first

entrant can be anticipated and eliminated. Whatever the value of bridging a structural hole for the first entrant, value is probably higher for the next few entrants, decreasing for subsequent entrants.

3. The social-capital prediction is only true, however, for teams coordinating poorly documented, personal knowledge across divisions. Where knowledge was unambiguous, teams reached completion more quickly if they didn't have to coordinate at all (in the sense that they were in a division that had infrequent and distant relations to other divisions, 'tie weakness' main effect, Hansen, 1999, p. 102).

4. The implication is that it would be productive to separate two levels of social capital. Distinguish the 'first-order' social capital of a person's personal network (see Barnes, 1969, on the first-order zone of a person's network), from the 'second-order' social capital of the organization, or contacts more generally, with which the person is affiliated (cf. Burt, 1992, pp. 38–44, on primary versus secondary structural holes; Podolny, 1993, on status-enhancing affiliations). The two levels are combined in Bielby & Bielby's (1999, pp. 74–79) analysis: A writer with a contact network that spans structural holes had a competitive advantage in securing and delivering on projects such that (a) his or her earnings would be correlated in adjacent years, and (b) he or she would be more attractive to the 'core' agencies. Therefore, core agencies had more social capital for the reasons given by Bielby & Bielby, and because they could attract writers with more social capital. The task for future research would be to separate the performance effects of an individual's (first-order) social capital from the (second-order) social capital of the organization(s) with which he or she is affiliated.

The task is more difficult than estimating social capital effects within organizations because performance has to be compared across organizations, and organizations differ in performance criteria. Consider professors at major and minor universities. The distinction can be difficult, but universities differ in quality such that a major-minor distinction can be drawn where a major university has more organizational social capital because of its central location in a great many extramural networks of high quality faculty and students (a 'core' university to use Bielby & Bielby's term). Given two professors of equal ability, one at a major, the other at a minor, university, the professor at the major university is more likely to be well compensated (major universities treat their faculty well to attract the most sought-after faculty) and be stimulated to produce important work (able people more often meet and exchange ideas at major universities). This is the performance effect of organizational social capital discussed in the text. However, minor universities can compete for able faculty by offering early promotion to tenure or other senior rank. This is the 'promotion paradox' that Phillips (2000) observes in lawyer promotions to partner (and Phillips & Sørensen, 1999, observe in promotions to manage television stations): The probability of promotion to senior rank is higher in young, small, low-status organizations.

5. Still, approximations can be made from the distribution of contacts across categories typically separate in social structure. This is the intuition behind Lin's (2001) positional measurement of social capital (see Appendix). Renzulli et al. (2000) is a recent illustration in entrepreneurship. They report on the discussion contacts of men and women in the Chapel Hill area of North Carolina who are thinking about starting a business. Renzulli et al. do not have data on relations between contacts, but they know the sector from which each contact was drawn (family, friends, business associates, etc.), so they compute a measure of the extent to which all of a person's contacts come from the same sector. Consistent with the hole argument, Renzulli et al. (2000, Table 4)

report that the people who actually do start a business were more likely to draw their contacts from multiple sectors.

6. Evaluations are adjusted for the four management job ranks defined by the firm because more senior officers are more likely to be evaluated as 'outstanding' (Burt, Jannotta & Mahoney, 1998, p. 84). In Fig. 3A, job rank is a predictor along with network constraint in the logit model. In the first panel of Table 1, the dependent variable is the residual of regressing at the population level the raw 1–2–3 job evaluation variable across job rank for all employees in the staff function (not just the 160 who returned a completed network questionnaire). Job rank describes 5% of the variance in the 1–2–3 evaluation variable. The regression models in Table 1 will be familiar to a wide audience. I get the same results with a logit model predicting from job rank and the network variables a binary variable distinguishing officers who received an 'outstanding' evaluation, or an ordered-logit model predicting the three evaluation categories.

7. See the preceding footnote.

8. The observations in fact fall along two parallel regression lines in the raw data. There is an upper line of teams in which evaluations decrease with increasing network constraint, and there is second line of lower evaluations which decreases with increasing network constraint. Teams on the lower line were significantly more likely to include a quality-control manager. The criterion variable on the vertical axis of Fig. 3B is the raw z-score evaluation adjusted for the presence of a quality-control manager (estimated by regressing raw z-score evaluations of all 67 teams across a dummy variable equal to 1 if a team included a quality-control manager). Rosenthal explains that teams encountering difficulty were assigned a quality-control manager. Difficulty must have resulted from many factors since teams assigned a quality-control manager could not be distinguished with plant variables, or function variables, or variables for the backgrounds of the people assigned to a team.

9. Luthans, Hodgetts & Rosenkrantz (1988) report the promotion-network connection for a sample of American managers in several firms, and Luthans, Welsh & Rosenkrantz (1993) report the connection for a sample of managers in a Russian textile factory. Manager success was measured by the ratio of a manager's rank to his or her years with the firm (which, presuming an internal labor market, measures the speed with which a manager has been promoted across ranks), and networks were measured with an observer's count of the frequency with which a manager was seen (Luthans et al., 1988, Chap.1; Luthans et al., 1993, p. 751): "interacting with outsiders and socializing/politicking during working hours." In both studies, managers were often observed performing the functions of planning, solving problems, monitoring performance, exchanging routine information and processing paperwork, but it was network activity that was most associated with the promotion measure. Figure 3C makes the same point with more precise measures of performance and network structure.

10. The multidimensional scalings are based on Kruskal's (1964) algorithm preserving monotonic distances between points, and the spatial displays are a good summary of the data (0.21 and 0.23 stress coefficients for the French and American maps respectively; 0.91 correlation between logs of the observed and predicted distances between elements in the French map, 0.90 for the American map).

11. Statistical tests show that only the slope of the surface is changing. Average promotion date and average intensity of network constraint are the same for managers with few or many peers. Early promotion and network constraint are equally varied for

managers with few or many peers. What is different across numbers of peers is the extent to which early promotion is correlated with network constraint – strong for managers with few peers, weak for managers with many peers.

12. I am grateful to James E. Schrager for calling my attention to these directories. Professor Schrager's knowledge of them comes from their importance in his work arranging partnerships between American and Japanese firms through his firm, Great Lakes Consulting Group.

13. Sponsor is my word, not Jane's. I telephoned Jane in 1993, four years after the original study, in the course of preparing the graphic in Fig. 7 for a course. I identified Jane and Karen from the sample data distribution because they nicely illustrated the hierarchy association with early promotion, but I wanted more information on Jane to bring her to life for the business students. I explained the nature of the call, and was graciously given a better understanding of Sam's role in her work at the time of the study.

14. There is a third, methodological, bit of corroborating evidence. Freeman's (1977) betweenness index measures the extent to which connections in a network all run through a central person. The measure is independent of network size. When computed for the three hierarchical networks in Fig. A1 in the Appendix, for example, the betweenness index is its maximum of 1.0 because all ties are through the central person. The Coleman-Theil index I use to measure hierarchy increases with network size as illustrated in Fig. A1 in the Appendix. In other words, the index measures the volume of social capital borrowed; hierarchy is lower for a person who borrows a small network rather than a large network. I re-estimated the association with early promotion in Table 2 using a betweenness index of hierarchy and obtained statistically significant, but substantially weaker, hierarchy effects (Burt, 1998, pp. 26–27). The stronger effect with a hierarchy measure that increases with network size corroborates the point that successful women are doing more than just borrowing a network, they are borrowing a network that contains many non-redundant contacts.

ACKNOWLEDGMENTS

Work on this chapter was supported by the Institute Européen d'Administration d'Affaires (INSEAD) and the University of Chicago Graduate School of Business. Portions of the material were presented in 1998 at a 'Social Networks and Social Capital' conference organized by Nan Lin and Karen Cook at Duke University, and a 'Economic and Organizational Sociology' conference organized by Mauro Guillén and Douglas Massey at the University of Pennsylvania, in 1999 at a 'Local Standards and Global Standards in the Age of Multiculturalism' conference organized by Noriyoshi Shiraishi and Yuki Yasuda at Rikkyo University, and in 2000 at the annual Organization Science Winter Conference, Michigan State University, and the annual Sunbelt Social Network Conference. The text has been improved in response to comments from Ranu Capron, Joseph Galaskiewicz, Bruce Kogut, Edward Laumann, Michael Moore, Joel Podolny, Holly Raider, William Starbuck, Robert Sutton, Brian Uzzi, and Yuki Yasuda.

REFERENCES

Adler, P., & Kwon, S. (2000). Social capital: the good, the bad, the ugly. In: E. L. Lesser (Ed.), *Knowledge and Social Capital* (pp. 89–115). Boston, MA: Butterworth-Heinemann.

Ahuja, G. (1998). Collaboration networks, structural holes, and innovation: a longitudinal study. Paper presented at the annual meetings of the Academy of Management.

Aldrich, H. E. (1999). *Organizations Evolving*. Thousand Oaks, CA: Sage.

Allen, T. J., & Cohen, S. (1969). Information flow in R&D labs. *Administrative Science Quarterly, 14*, 12–19.

Ancona, D. G., & Caldwell, D. F. (1992a). Demography and design: predictors of new product team performance. *Organization Science, 3*, 321–341.

Ancona, D. G., & Caldwell, D. F. (1992b). Bridging the boundary: external activity and performance in organizational teams. *Administrative Science Quarterly, 37*, 634–665.

Baker, W. E. (1984). The social structure of a national securities market. *American Journal of Sociology, 89*, 775–811.

Baker, W. E. (2000). *Social Capital*. Thousand Oaks, CA: Sage Publications.

Baker, W. E., & Iyer, A. (1992). Information networks and market behavior. *Journal of Mathematical Sociology, 16*, 305–332.

Barker, J. R. (1993). Tightening the iron cage: concertive control in self-managing teams. *Administrative Science Quarterly, 38*, 408–437.

Barley, S. R. (1990). The alignment of technology and structure through roles and networks. *Administrative Science Quarterly, 35*, 61–103.

Barnes, J. A. (1969). Networks and political processes. In: J. C. Mitchell (Ed.), *Social Networks in Urban Situations* (pp. 51–76). Manchester, England: Manchester University Press.

Belliveau, M. A., O'Reilly, C. A., & Wade, J. B. (1996). Social capital at the top: effects of social similarity and status on CEO compensation. *Academy of Management Journal, 39*, 1568–1593.

Benjamin, B. A., & Podolny, J. M. (1999). Status, quality, and social control in the California wine industry. *Administrative Science Quarterly, 44*, 563–589.

Bian, Yanjie (1994). *Work and Inequality in Urban China*. Albany, NY: State University of New York Press.

Bielby, W. T., & Bielby, D. D. (1999). Organizational mediation of project-based labor markets: talent agencies and the careers of screenwriters. *American Sociological Review, 64*, 64–85.

Biggart, N. W. (2000). Banking on each other: the situational logic of rotating savings and credit associations. Paper presented at the 2000 Organization Science Winter Conference.

Birley, S. (1985). The role of networks in the entrepreneurial process. *Journal of Business Venturing, 1*, 107–117.

Bothner, M. S. (2000). Network position and product performance: an analysis of price gaps and shipment growth in the U.S. personal computer industry. Department of Sociology, Columbia University.

Bott, E. (1957). *Family and Social Network*. New York: Free Press.

Bourdieu, P. (1980). Le capital social: notes provisoires. *Actes de la Recherche en Sciences Sociales, 3*, 2–3.

Bourdieu, P., & Wacquant, L. J. D. (1992). *An Invitation to Reflexive Sociology*. Chicago, IL: University of Chicago Press.

Boxman, E. A. W., De Graaf, P. M., & Flap, H. D. (1991). The impact of social and human capital on the income attainment of Dutch managers. *Social Networks, 13*, 51–73.

Brass, D. J. (1992). Power in organizations: a social network perspective. In: G. Moore, & J. A. Whitt (Eds), *Research in Politics and Society* (pp. 295–323). Greenwich, CT: JAI Press.

Brieger, R. L. (1995). Socioeconomic achievement and the phenomenology of achievement. *Annual Review of Sociology, 21*, 115–136.

Brüderl, J., & Preisendörfer, P. (1998). Network support and the success of newly founded businesses. *Small Business Economics, 10*, 213–225.

Burt, R. S. (1980). Autonomy in a social topology. *American Journal of Sociology, 85*, 892–925.

Burt, R. S. (1982). *Toward a Structural Theory of Action*. New York: Academic Press.

Burt, R. S. (1983). *Corporate Profits and Cooptation*. New York: Academic Press.

Burt, R. S. (1987). Social contagion and innovation, cohesion versus structural equivalence. *American Journal of Sociology, 92*, 1287–1335.

Burt, Ronald S. (1988). The stability of American markets. *American Journal of Sociology, 93*, 356–395.

Burt, R. S. (1990). Kinds of relations in American discussion networks. In: C. Calhoun, M. W. Meyer, & W. R. Scott. *Structures of Power and Constraint* (pp. 411–451). New York: Cambridge University Press.

Burt, R. S. (1992). *Structural Holes*. Cambridge, MA: Harvard University Press.

Burt, R. S. (1995). Le capital social, les trous structuraux, et l'entrepreneur (translated by Emmanuel Lazega). *Revue Française de Sociologie, 36*, 599–628.

Burt, R. S. (1997a). The contingent value of social capital. *Administrative Science Quarterly, 42*, 339–365.

Burt, R. S. (1997b). A note on social capital and network content. *Social Networks, 19*, 355–373.

Burt, R. S. (1998). The gender of social capital. *Rationality and Society, 10*, 5–46.

Burt, R. S. (1999a). Entrepreneurs, distrust, and third parties. In: L. L. Thompson, J. M. Levine, & D. M. Messick (Eds), *Shared Cognition in Organizations* (pp. 213–243). Hillsdale, NJ: Lawrence Erlbaum.

Burt, R. S. (1999b). The social capital of opinion leaders. *Annals, 566*, 37–54.

Burt, R. S. (2000a). The social construction of trust and reputation. *Graduate School of Business*, University of Chicago.

Burt, R. S. (2000). Bridge decay. *Graduate School of Business*, University of Chicago.

Burt, R. S. (2001). Bandwidth and echo: trust, information, and gossip in social networks. In: A. Casella & J. E. Rauch (Eds), *Integrating the Study of Networks and Markets*. New York: Russell Sage Foundation.

Burt, R. S., & Schøtt, T. (1985). Relation contents in multiple networks. *Social Science Research, 14*, 287–308.

Burt, R. S., Jannotta, J. E., & Mahoney, J. T. (1998). Personality correlates of structural holes. *Social Networks, 20*, 63–87.

Burt, R. S., Guilarte, M., Raider, H. J., & Yasuda, Y. (1999). Competition, contingency and the external structure of markets. *Graduate School of Business*, University of Chicago.

Burt, R. S., Hogarth, R. M., & Michaud, C. (2000). The social capital of French and American managers. *Organization Science, 11*, 123–147.

Burt, R. S., & Raider, H. J. (2000). Creating careers: women's paths through entrepreneurship. *Graduate School of Business*, University of Chicago.

Campbell, K. E., Marsden, P. V., & Hurlbert, J. (1986). Social resources and socioeconomic status. *Social Networks, 8*, 97–117.

Carley, K. M. (1986). An approach for relating social structure to cognitive structure. *Journal of Mathematical Sociology, 12*, 137–189.

Caro, R. A. (1982). *The Path to Power.* New York: A. A. Knopf.

Carroll, G. R., & Teo, A. C. (1996). On the social networks of managers. *Academy of Management Journal, 39*, 421–440.

Cialdini, R. (1989). Indirect tactics of image management: beyond basking. In: R. A. Giacalone, & P. Rosenfeld (Eds), *Impression Management in the Organization* (pp. 45–56). Hillsdale, NJ: Lawrence Erlbaum.

Cockburn, I. M., & Henderson, R. M. (1998). Absorptive capacity, coauthoring behavior, and the organization of research in drug discovery. *Journal of Industrial Economics, 64*, 157–182.

Cohen, W. M., & Levinthal, D. A. (1990). Absorptive capacity: a new perspective on learning and innovation. *Administrative Science Quarterly, 35*, 128–152.

Coleman, J. S. (1972). Systems of social exchange. *Journal of Mathematical Sociology, 2*, 145–163.

Coleman, J. S. (1988). Social capital in the creation of human capital. *American Journal of Sociology, 94*, S95-S120.

Coleman, J. S. (1990). *Foundations of Social Theory.* Cambridge, MA: Harvard University Press.

Collins, R. (1998). *The Sociology of Philosophies.* Cambridge, MA: Harvard University Press.

Cook, K. S., & Emerson, R. M. (1978). Power, equity and commitment in exchange networks. *American Sociological Review, 43*, 712–739.

Cook, K. S., Emerson, R. M., Gillmore, M. R., & Yamagishi, T. (1983). The distribution of power in exchange networks: theory and experimental results. *American Journal of Sociology, 89*, 275–305.

Crane, D. (1972). *Invisible Colleges.* Chicago, IL: University of Chicago Press.

Dalzell, R. F. (1987). *Enterprising Elite.* New York: W. W. Norton.

Davis, G. F., & Greve, H. R. (1997). Corporate elite networks and the governance changes in the 1980s. *American Journal of Sociology, 103*, 1–37.

Diehl, M., & Stroebe, W. (1987). Productivity loss in brainstorming groups: toward the solution of a riddle. *Journal of Personality and Social Psychology, 53*, 497–509.

DiMaggio, P. (1992). Nadel's paradox revisited: relational and cultural aspects of organizational structure. In: N. Nohria & R. G. Eccles (Eds), *Networks and Organizations* (pp. 118–142). Boston, MA: Harvard Business School Press.

Douthit, M. W. (2000). Supervision and social capital. *Graduate School of Business*, University of Chicago.

Eccles, R. G., & Crane, D. B. (1988). *Doing Deals.* Boston, MA: Harvard Business School Press.

Erickson, B. H. (1996). Culture, class, and connections. *American Journal of Sociology, 102*, 217–251.

Erickson, B. H. (2001). Good networks and good jobs: the value of social capital to employers and employees. In: W. Lin, K. S. Cook & R. S. Burt (Eds), *Social Capital.* New York: Aldine de Gruyter.

Fernandez, R. M., & Gould, R. V. (1994). A dilemma of state power: brokerage and influence in the national health policy domain. *American Journal of Sociology, 99*, 1455–1491.

Fernandez, R. M., Castilla, E., & Moore, P. (2000). Social capital at work: networks and hiring at a phone center. *American Journal of Sociology, 105*, 1288–1356.

Finlay, W., & Coverdill, J. E. (1999a). The search game: organizational conflicts and the use of headhunters. *Sociological Quarterly, 40*, 11–30.

Finlay, W, & Coverdill, J. E. (1999b). Risk, opportunism, and structural holes: how headhunters manage clients and earn fees. Department of Sociology, University of Georgia.

Flap, H. D., & Boxman. E. (2001). Getting started: the influence of social capital on the start of the occupational career. In: N. Lin, K. S. Cook, & R. S. Burt (Eds), *Social Capital*, New York: Aldine de Gruyter.

Flap, H. D., & De Graaf, N. D. (1989). Social capital and attained occupational status. *Netherlands Journal of Sociology, 22*, 145–161.

Flap, H. D., Völker, B., & Bulder, B. (2000). Social capital at the workplace and job satisfaction. In: W. Raub & J. Weesie (Eds). *Management of Durable Relationships*, Amsterdam: Thesis.

Foley, M. W., & Edwards, B. (1999). Is it time to disinvest in social capital? *Journal of Public Policy, 19*, 141–173.

Freeman, L. C. (1977). A set of measures of centrality based on betweenness. *Sociometry, 40*, 35–40.

Freeman, L. C. (1992). Filling in the blanks: a theory of cognitive categories and the structure of social affiliation. *Social Psychology Quarterly, 55*, 118–127.

Gabbay, S. M. (1997). *Social Capital in the Creation of Financial Capital*. Champaign, IL: Stipes.

Gabbay, S. M., & Zuckerman, E. W. (1998). Social capital and opportunity in corporate R & D: the contingent effect of contact density on mobility expectations. *Social Science Research, 27*, 189–217.

Gargiulo, M., & Benassi, M. (2000). Trapped in your own net: network cohesion, structural holes, and the adaptation of social capital. *Organization Science, 11*, In Press.

Geletkanycz, M. A., & Hambrick, D. C. (1997). The external ties of top executives: implications for strategic choice and performance. *Administrative Science Quarterly, 42*, 654–681.

Giacalone, R. A., & Rosenfeld, P. (Eds) (1989). *Impression Management in the Organization*. Hillsdale, NJ: Lawrence Erlbaum.

Giuffe, K. A. (1999). Sandpiles of opportunity: success in the art world. *Social Forces, 77*, 815–832.

Gorton, G. (1996). Reputation formation in early bank note markets. *Journal of Political Economy, 104*, 346–397.

Granovetter, M. S. (1973). The strength of weak ties. *American Journal of Sociology, 78*, 1360–1380.

Granovetter, M. S. ([1974] 1995). *Getting a Job*. Chicago, IL: University of Chicago Press.

Granovetter, M. S. (1983). The strength of weak ties: a network theory revisited. In: R. Collins (Ed.), *Sociological Theory 1983* (pp. 201–233). San Francisco, CA: Jossey-Bass.

Granovetter, M. S. (1985). Economic action, social structure, and embeddedness. *American Journal of Sociology, 91*, 481–510.

Granovetter, M. S. (1992). Problems of explanation in economic sociology. In: N. Nohria, & R. G. Eccles (Eds.), *Networks and Organization* (pp. 29–56). Boston: Harvard Business School Press.

Greif, A. (1989). Reputation and coalition in medieval trade: evidence on the Maghribi traders. *Journal of Economic History, 49*, 857–882.

Greve H. R. (1995). Jumping ship: the diffusion of strategy abandonment. *Administrative Science Quarterly, 40*, 444–473.

Gulati, R. (1998). Alliances and networks. *Strategic Management Journal, 19*, 293–317

Han, S.-K. (1993). Churning firms in stable markets. *Social Science Research, 21*, 406–418.

Han, S.-K. (1994). Mimetic isomorphism and its effect on the audit services market. *Social Forces*, *73*, 637–664.

Hannan, M. T., & Freeman, J. H. (1977). The population ecology of organizations. *America Journal of Sociology*, *82*, 929–964.

Hannan, M. T., & Freeman, J. H. (1989). *Organizational Ecology*. Cambridge, MA: Harvard University

Hansen, M. T. (1999). The search-transfer problem: the role of weak ties in sharing knowledge across organization subunits. *Administrative Science Quarterly*, *44*, 82–111.

Hansen, M. T., Podolny, J. M., & Pfeffer, J. (2000). So many ties, so little time: a task contingency perspective on the value of social capital in organizations. Paper presented at the 2000 Organization Science Winter Conference.

Hargadon, A. B., & Sutton, R. I. (1997). Technology brokering and innovation in a product development firm. *Administrative Science Quarterly*, *42*, 716–749.

Hatch, M. J. (1999). Exploring the empty spaces of organizing: how improvisational jazz helps redescribe organizational structure. *Organization Studies*, *20*, 75–100.

Haveman, H. A., & Cohen, L. E. (1994). The ecological dynamics of careers: the impact of organizational founding, dissolution, and merger on job mobility. *American Journal of Sociology*, *100*, 104–152.

Jacob, J., Lys, T. Z., & Neale, M. A. (1999). Expertise in forecasting performance of security analysts. *Journal of Accounting and Economics*, *28*, 51–82.

Jang, H. (1997). *Market Structure, Performance, and Putting-Out in the Korean Economy*. Ph.D. Dissertation, Department of Sociology, University of Chicago.

Janicik, G. A. (1998). *Social Expertise in Social Networks: Examining the Learning of Relations*. Ph.D. Dissertation, Graduate School of Business, University of Chicago.

Kilduff, M., & Krackhardt, D. (1994). Bringing the individual back in: a structural analysis of the internal market for reputation in organizations. *Academy of Management Journal*, *37*, 87–108.

Kogut, B. (2000). The network as knowledge: generative rules and the emergence of structure. *Strategic Management Journal*, *21*, 405–425.

Kogut, B., & Zander, U. (1996). What firms do? coordination, identity, and learning. *Organization Science*, *7*, 502–518.

Kohn, M. L., & Schooler, C. (1983). *Work and Personality*. Norwood, NJ: Ablex.

Koput, K., & Powell, W. W. (2000). Not your stepping stone: collaboration and the dynamics of industry evolution in biotechnology. Paper presented at the 2000 Organization Science Winter Conference.

Kotter, J. P. (1982). *The General Managers*. New York: Free Press.

Koza, M. P., & Lewin, A. Y. (1999). The coevolution of network alliances: a longitudinal analysis of an international professional service network. *Organization Science*, *10*, 638–653.

Krackhardt, D. (1990). Assessing the political landscape: structure, cognition, and power in organizations. *Administrative Science Quarterly*, *35*, 342–369.

Krackhardt, D. (1995). Entrepreneurial opportunities in an entrepreneurial firm: a structural approach. *Entrepreneurship Theory and Practice*, *19*, 53–69.

Krackhardt, D., & Stern, R. N. (1988). Informal networks and organizational crisis: an experimental simulation. *Social Psychology Quarterly*, *51*, 123–140.

Kruskal, J. B. (1964). Multidimensional scaling by optimizing goodness of fit to a nonmetric hypothesis. *Psychometrika*, *29*, 1–27.

Labianca, G., Brass, D. J., & Grey, B. (1998). Social networks and perceptions of intergroup conflict: the role of negative relationships and third parties. *Academy of Management Journal, 41*, 55–67.

Labianca, G., & Brass, D. J. (2000). Negative relationships in organizations: the case for negative asymmetry in social networks.

Lazega, E. (1994). Analyse de réseaux et sociologie des organizations. *Revue Française de Sociologie, 34*, 293–320.

Lazega, E. & Pattison, P. E. (2001). A social mechanism as a form of corporate social capital: status auctions among peers. In: N. Lin, K. S. Cook, & R. S. Burt (Eds), *Social Capital*, Chicago, IL: Aldine de Gruyter.

Leana, C. R., & Van Buren III, H. J. (1999). Organizational social capital and employment practices. *Academy of Management Review, 24*, 538–555.

Leenders, R. & Gabbay, S. M. (Eds), 1999). *Corporate Social Capital and Liability*. Amsterdam: Kluwer Academic Publishers.

Lesser, E. L. (Ed.) 2000). *Knowledge and Social Capital*. Boston, MA: Butterworth-Heinemann.

Light, I., & Karageorgis, S. (1994). The ethnic economy. In: N. J. Smelser, & R. Swedberg (Eds), *The Handbook of Economic Sociology*, (pp. 647–671). Princeton, NJ: Princeton University Press.

Lin, N. (1999). Social networks and status attainment. *Annual Review of Sociology, 25*, 467–487.

Lin, N. (Forthcoming). *Social Resources and Social Action*. New York: Cambridge University Press.

Lin, N. (2001). The position generator: a measurement for social capital'. In: N. Lin, K. S. Cook, & R. S. Burt (Eds), *Social Capital*, New York: Aldine de Gruyter.

Lin, N., Cook, K. S., & Burt, R. S. (eds., 2001). *Social Capital*. Chicago, IL: Aldine de Gruyter.

Lin, N., & Dumin, M. (1986). Access to occupations through social ties. *Social Networks, 8*, 365–385.

Lin, N., & Bian, Y. (1991). Getting ahead in urban China. *American Journal of Sociology, 97*, 657–688.

Lin, N., Ensel, W., & Vaughn, J. (1981). Social resources and strength of ties: structural factors in occupational status attainment. *American Sociological Review, 46*, 393–405.

Llobrera, J. T., Meyer, D. R., & Nammacher, G. (2000). Trajectories of industrial districts: impact of strategic intervention in medical districts. *Economic Geography, 76*, 68–98.

Lofstrom, S. M. (2000). Absorptive capacity in strategic alliances: investigating the effects of individuals' social and human capital on inter-firm learning. Paper presented at the 2000 Organization Science Winter Conference.

Luthans, F., Welsh, D. H. B., & Rosenkrantz, S. A. (1993). What do Russian managers really do? an observational study with comparisons to U.S. managers. *Journal of International Business Studies, 24*, 741–761.

Luthans, F., Hodgetts, R. M. & Rosenkrantz, S. A. (1988). *Real Managers*. Cambridge, MA: Ballinger.

Macaulay, S. (1963). Non-contractual relations in business: a preliminary study. *American Sociological Review, 28*, 55–67.

March, J. G. (1991). Exploration and exploitation in organization learning. *Organization Science, 2*, 71–87.

Markovsky, B., Willer. D., & Patton. T. (1988). Power relations in exchange networks. *American Sociological Review, 53*, 220–236.

Marsden, P. V. (1983). Restricted access in networks and models of power. *American Journal of Sociology, 88*, 686–717.

Marsden, P. V., & Gorman, E. H. (2000). Interpersonal ties and social capital in employer staffing practices. In: N. Lin, K. S. Cook, & R. S. Burt (Eds), *Social Capital*, New York: Aldine de Gruyter.

Marsden, P. V., & Hurlbert, J. (1988). Social resources and mobility outcomes: a replication and extension. *Social Forces, 66*, 1038–1059.

Marsden, P. V., & Campbell, K. E. (1985). Measuring tie strength. *Social Forces, 63*, 482–501.

McClelland, D. C. (1961). *The Achieving Society*. Princeton: Van Nostrand.

McEvily, B., & Zaheer, A. (1999). Bridging ties: a source of firm heterogeneity in competitive capabilities. *Strategic Management Journal, 20*, 1133–1156.

McEvily, B., & Marcus, A. (2000). The acquisition of competitive capabilities as social learning. Paper presented at the 2000 Organization Science Winter Conference.

McGuire, P., & Granovetter, M. (2000). The social construction of the electric utility industry, 1878–1919. In: J. Porac, & M. Ventresca (Eds), *Constructing Industries and Markets*, New York: Elsevier.

Mehra, A, Kilduff, M., & Brass, D. J. (2000). Combining personality and network theory: the effects of self-monitoring and structural position on workplace performance. *Department of Management*, University of Cincinnati.

Merton, R. K. ([1957] 1968). Continuities in the theory of reference group behavior. In: *Social Theory and Social Structure*, (pp. 335–440). New York: Free Press.

Merton, R. K. (1984). Socially expected durations: a case study of concept formation in sociology. In: W. W. Powell, & R. Robbins. *Conflict and Consensus*, (pp. 262–283). New York: Free Press.

Meyerson, E. M. (1994). Human capital, social capital and compensation: the relative contribution of social contacts to managers' incomes. *Acta Sociologica, 37*, 383–399.

Mills, J. S. ([1848] 1987). *Principles of Political Economy*. Fairchild, NJ: Augustus M. Kelley.

Mintzberg, H. (1973). *The Nature of Managerial Work*. New York: Harper and Row.

Mizruchi, M. S. & Brewster Sterns, L. (2000). Getting deals done: the use of social networks in bank decision making. Paper presented at the annual International Sunbelt Social Network Conference.

Mullen, B., Johnson. C., & Salas, E. (1991). Productivity loss in brainstorming groups: a meta-analytic integration. *Basic and Applied Social Psychology, 12*, 3–24.

Murray, S., Rankin, J., & Magill, D. (1981). Strong ties and job information. *Sociology of Work and Occupations, 8*, 199–136.

Nahapiet, J., & Ghoshal, S. (1998). Social capital, intellectual capital, and the organization advantage. *Academy of Management Review, 23*, 242–266.

Nanda, A., & Bartlett, C. A. (1990). Corning Incorporated: a network of alliances. Harvard Business School Case 9–391–102. Boston, MA: Harvard Business School Press.

Nohria, N. (1992). Information and search in the creation of new business ventures: the case of the 128 venture group. In: N. Nohria, & R. G. Eccles (Eds), Networks and Organizations, (pp. 240–261). Boston, MA: Harvard Business School Press.

Padgett, J. F., & Ansell, C. K. (1993). Robust action and the rise of the Medici, *American Journal of Sociology*, (pp. 1400–1434), *98*, 1259–1319.

Paulus, P. B., Larey, T. S., & Ortega, A. H. (1995). Performance and perceptions of brainstormers in an organizational setting. *Basic and Applied Social Psychology, 17*, 249–265.

Pennings, J. M., Lee, K., & van Witteloostuijn, A. (1998). Human capital, social capital, and firm dissolution. *Academy of Management Journal, 41*, 425–440.

Pfeffer, J. (1983). Organizational demography. In: L. L. Cummings & Barry M. Staw (Eds), *Research in Organizational Behavior*, (pp. 299–357). Greenwich, CT: JAI Press.

Phillips, D. J. (2000). The promotion paradox: the relationship between organizational mortality and employee promotion chances in Silicon Valley law firms, *1946–1996. American Journal of Sociology, 106*, In Press.

Phillips, D. J., & Sørensen, J. B. (1999). The power to deny: competitive position and promotion rates. *Graduate School of Business*, University of Chicago.

Podolny, J. M. (1993). A status-based model of market competition. *American Journal of Sociology, 98*, 829–872.

Podolny, J. M. (2000). Networks as the pipes and prisms of the market. Graduate School of Business, Stanford University.

Podolny, J. M., Stuart, T. E., & Hannan, M. T. (1997). Networks, knowledge, and niches: competition in the worldwide semiconductor industry, 1984–1991. *American Journal of Sociology, 102*, 659–689.

Podolny, J. M., & Baron, J. N. (1997). Relationships and resources: social networks and mobility in the workplace. *American Sociological Review, 62*, 673–693.

Portes, A. (1998). Social capital: its origins and applications in modern sociology. *Annual Review of Sociology, 24*, 1–24.

Portes, A., & Landolt, P. (1996). The downside of social capital. *American Prospect, 16*, 18–21.

Powell, W. W., & Brantley, P. (1992). Competitive cooperation in biotechnology: learning through networks? In: N. Nohria & R. G. Eccles (Eds), *Networks and Organizations*, (pp. 366–394). Boston, MA: Harvard Business School Press.

Powell, W. W., & Smith-Doerr, L. (1994). Networks and economic life. In: N. J. Smelser, & R. Swedberg. *Handbook of Economic Sociology*, (pp. 368–402). Princeton, NJ: Princeton University Press.

Powell, W. W., Koput, K. W., & Smith-Doerr, L. (1996). Interorganizational collaboration and the locus of innovation: networks of learning in biotechnology. *Administrative Science Quarterly, 41*, 116–145.

Powell, W. W., Koput, K. W., Smith-Doerr, L., & Owen-Smith, J. (1999). Network position and firm performance: organizational returns to collaboration. In: S. Andrews & D. Knoke (Eds), *Research in the Sociology of Organizations*, (pp. 129–159). Greenwich, CT: JAI Press.

Provan, K. G., & Milward, H. B. (1995). A preliminary theory of interorganizational network effectiveness: a comparative study of four community mental health systems. *Administrative Science Quarterly, 40*, 1–33.

Putnam, R. D (1993). *Making Democracy Work*. Princeton, NJ: Princeton University Press.

Raider, H. J., & Burt, R. S. (1996). Boundaryless careers and social capital. In: M. B. Arthur, & D. M. Rousseau (Eds), *The Boundaryless Career*, (pp. 187–200). New York: Oxford University Press.

Reagans, R., & Zuckerman, E. W. (1999). Networks, diversity, and performance: the social capital of corporate R&D units. Graduate School of Industrial Administration, Carnegie Mellon University.

Renzulli, L. A., Aldrich, H. E., & Moody, J. (2000). Family matters: gender, networks, and entrepreneurial outcomes. *Social Forces, 79*, In Press.

Romney, A. K., & D'Andrade, R. G. (1964). Cognitive aspects of English kin terms. *American Anthropologist, 566*, 146–170.

Rosenthal, E. A. (1996). *Social Networks and Team Performance*. Ph.D. Dissertation, Graduate School of Business, University of Chicago.

Rosten, L. (1989). *The Joys of Yinglish*. New York: McGraw-Hill.

Sandefur, R., & Laumann, E. O. (1998). A paradigm for social capital. *Rationality and Society, 10*, 481–501.

Sediatis, J. (1998). The alliances of spin-offs versus start-ups: social ties in the genesis of post-Soviet alliances. *Organization Science, 9*, 368–381.

Shan, W., Walker, G., & Kogut, B. (1994). Interfirm cooperation and startup innovation in the biotechnology industry. *Strategic Management Journal, 15*, 387–394.

Siamwalla, A. (1978). Farmers and middlemen: aspects of agriculture marketing in Thailand. *Economic Bulletin for Asia and the Pacific*, 29, 38–50.

Simmel, G. ([1922] 1955). *Conflict and the Web of Group Affiliations*, (translated by Kurt H. Wolff and Reinhard Bendix). New York: Free Press.

Smith, A. ([1766] 1982). *Lectures on Jurisprudence*. Indianapolis, In: Liberty Fund.

Sørensen, J. B. (1999). Executive migration and interorganizational competition. *Social Science Research*, 28, 289–315.

Sørensen, J. B. (2000). Changes in group composition and turnover: a longitudinal study. *American Sociological Review, 65*, 298–310.

Sparrowe, R. T., & Popielarz, P. A. (1995). Weak ties and structural holes: the effects of network structure on careers. Department of Management, University of Illinois-Chicago.

Steier, L., & Greenwood, R. (2000). Entrepreneurship and the evolution of angel finance networks. *Organization Studies, 21*, 163–192.

Stewart, A. (1990). The bigman metaphor for entrepreneurship: a 'library tale' with morals on alternatives for further research. *Organization Science, 1*, 143–159.

Stewart, T. A. (1996). The great conundrum: you vs. the team. *Fortune, 134* (November), 165–166.

Stinchcombe, A. L. (1990). *Information and Organizations*. Berkeley, CA: University of California Press.

Strang, D. & Soule, S. A. (1998). Diffusion in organizations and social movements. *Annual Review of Sociology, 24*, 265–290.

Stroebe, W., & Diehl, M. (1994). Why groups are less effective than their members: On productivity losses in idea-generating groups. In: W. Stroebe & M. Hewstone (Eds), *European Review of Social Psychology*, Volume 5, (pp. 271–303). London: Wiley.

Stuart, T. E. (1998). Producer network positions and propensities to collaborate: an investigation of strategic alliance formations in a high-technology industry. *Administrative Science Quarterly, 43*, 668–698.

Stuart, T. E. (1999). Interorganizational alliances and the performance of firms: a study of growth and innovation rates in a high-technology industry. *Graduate School of Business*, University of Chicago.

Stuart, T. E., Hoang, H., & Hybels, R. C. (1999). Interorganizational endorsements and the performance of entrepreneurial ventures. *Administrative Science Quarterly, 44*, 315–349.

Stuart, T. E., & Podolny, J. M. (1999). Positional causes and correlates of strategic alliances in the semiconductor industry. In: S. Andrews & D. Knoke. *Research in the Sociology of Organizations*, (pp. 161–182). Greenwich, CT: JAI Press.

Stuart, T. E. & Robinson, D. T. (2000). Network effects in the governance of strategic alliances in biotechnology. Paper presented at the 2000 Organization Science Winter Conference.

Sutton, R. I. & Hargadon, A. B. 1996. Brainstorming groups in context: effectiveness in a product design firm. *Administrative Science Quarterly, 41*, 685–718.

Swedberg, R. (1990). *Economics and Sociology*. Princeton, NJ: Princeton University Press.

Swedberg, R. (1994). Markets as networks. In: N. J. Smelser & R. Swedberg. *The Handbook of Economic Sociology*, (pp. 255–282). Princeton, NJ: Princeton University Press.

Talmud, I. (1994). Relations and profits: the social organizations of Israeli industiral competition. *Social Science Research, 23,* 109–135.

Thornton, P. H. (1999). The sociology of entrepreneurship. Annual Review of Sociology, *25,* 19–46.

Tillman, R., & Indergaard, M. (1999). Field of schemes: health insurance fraud in the small business sector. *Social Problems, 46,* 572–590.

Tullock, G. (1985). Adam Smith and the prisoners' dilemma. *Quarterly Journal of Economics, 100,* 1073–1081.

Uzzi, B. (1996). Embeddedness and economic performance: the network effect. *American Sociological Review, 61,* 674–698.

Uzzi, B. (1997). Social structure and competition in interfirm networks: the paradox of embeddedness. *Administrative Science Quarterly, 42,* 35–67.

Walker, G., Kogut, B., & Shan, W. (1997). Social capital, structural holes and the formation of an industry network. *Organization Science, 8,* 109–125.

Weber, M. ([1905] 1930). The Protestant Ethic and the Spirit of Capitalism, (translated by Talcott Parsons). New York: Charles Scribner's Sons.

Wegener, B. (1991). Job mobility and social ties: social resources, prior job, and status attainment. *American Sociological Review, 56,* 60–71.

White, H. C. (1981). Where do markets come from? *American Journal of Sociology, 87,* 517–547.

Willer, D. (ed., 1999). *Network Exchange Theory.* New York: Praeger.

Williams, K. Y.. & O'Reilly, C. A. III (1998). Demography and diversity in organizations: a review of 40 years of research. In: B. M. Staw & L. L. Cummings, *Research in Organizational Behavior,* (pp. 77–140). Greenwich, CT: JAI Press.

Williams, P. (1998). The nature of drug-trafficking networks. *Current History, 97,* 154–159.

Woolcock, M. (1998). Social capital and economic development: toward a theoretical synthesis and policy framework. *Theory and Society, 27,* 151–208.

Yair, G., & Maman, D. (1996). The persistent structure of hegemony in the Eurovision song contest. *Acta Sociologica, 39,* 309–325.

Yasuda, Y. (1996). *Network Analysis of Japanese and American Markets.* Tokyo: Bokutaku-sha.

Ziegler, R. (1982). Market structure and cooptation. Institut für Soziologie, Universität München.

Zuckerman, E. W. (1999). The categorical imperative: securities analysts and the legitimacy discount. *American Journal of Sociology, 104,* 1398–1438.